VOL

HEBREWS TO NEGROES 2

Wake up Black America!

RONALD DALTON JR.

Cover Design: Brittany Jackson

Book Images used are Public Domain and Free Stock Photos "Image(s) used under license from Shutterstock.com"

Published by G Publishing, LLC

Library of Congress Control Number: 2015913566

ISBN: 978-0-9971579-2-5

Printed in the United States of America

TABLE OF CONTENTS

CHAPTER 1

THE FINAL CALL FOR ISRAEL: IT'S TIME TO CLEAN UP!

Exodus 12:5

*"Your lamb shall be an **unblemished** male a year old; you may take it from the sheep or from the goats."*

When I first embarked on writing the Book "**Hebrews to Negroes**" in 2014, God showed me an enormous amount of information that was too much to keep inside to myself. I was stuck between many emotions of fear, confusion, anger, happiness, and amazement after learning the "truth" about the "**True Identity**" of the so-called "**Negro**" or "**African-American**". It changed the way I would view the world we lived in, but I finally understood why the world felt like a "big illusion" and why so many people were caught in this "illusion".

(**Above**) A man standing in "**The Matrix**" and a confused Black man. Have you ever felt like you were different? Like you saw things that others couldn't see? Or like you "thought" different than the rest of your peers and no one in the world seemed to "see" things the way you did? Well, this was how I felt growing up. When I watched "**The Matrix**" movie in 1999, I could relate to it.....I just didn't know that in 2011 I would start on a journey of becoming "**awoke**".

"I know exactly what you mean. Let me tell you why you're here. You're here because you know something. What you know you can't explain, but you feel it. You've felt it your entire life, that there's something wrong with the world. You don't know what it is, but it's there, like a splinter in your mind, driving you mad."

Morpheus – The 1999 movie "The Matrix"

Walking around society "**awake**" is like how "**Neo**" felt in the movie "**The Matrix**" when Morpheus showed him everyone in the "**Matrix**" that was asleep. Unfortunately, the majority of people today…especially the descendants of the Children of Israel in the Americas and overseas are in a "**deep sleep**" just like hibernation. From 2014 till present day I can say that out of all my family/friends I can only count maybe 5 people on one hand that can understand and comprehend everything that is going on in the world as we know it. Satan is the greatest "**Deceiver**" of the world and he has done a great job at deceiving mankind…especially "**Israel**". This is what Christ **FIRST** told his disciples what was the "**sign**" of the end of the world and his return.

Matthew 24:3-4 "And as he (Christ) sat upon the mount of Olives, the disciples came unto him privately, saying, Tell us, when shall these things be? And what shall be the sign of thy coming, and the end of the world? And Yahusha (Jesus) answered and said unto them, **Take heed that no man DECEIVE you.**"

We all know many Pastors and even our parents have said decades ago, "**We are living in the last days**"….but now I fear we are living in a "**critical time**" where Black People…including other Israelites need to seriously wake up. Deception and "Evil" is at an all-time high as we are seeing the "Times of Noah" unfold. America and the people in it are partaking of the "Sin" that the Bible talks of. The Bible talks about being "**Holy**" and "**Righteous**" unto God….but this cannot happen if we are constantly caught up in "**Sin**" and "**Deception**". In the Old

Testament....the Most High required "**animal sacrifices**" for the atonement of sins that the Israelites had committed. But the animal couldn't just be anything like a squirrel, an opossum or a pig. It had to be an "**unblemished male lamb**" without blemish. Just as with the "dedication of the Temple of Jerusalem" a Red Heifer (cow) without "**blemish (*i.e. flaw, defect, deformity, impurity*)**", and without any other color strand of hair was required by the Most High. When Christ (Yahusha-Jesus) came, and died on the cross (*i.e. tree in the Aramaic New Testament*) he was the "**sacrificial lamb**" of the world". The "**Veil**" in Solomon's Temple separated the **Physical realm** (*i.e. Holy Place where the Levites would be*) from the **Spiritual realm** (*i.e. Holy of Holies where only one High Priest could enter*).

Diagram of the Temple

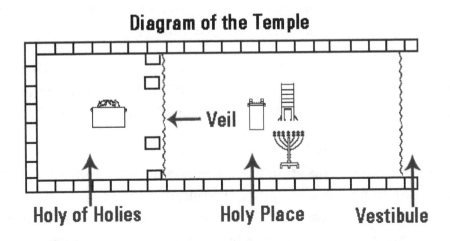

Holy of Holies   **Holy Place**   **Vestibule**

(**Above**) Blueprint of the Temple of Jerusalem. The "**Beit HaMikdash**" represents the "**Sacred House**". "**Hekal**" means "**palace**" or "**temple**" in Hebrew and "**ulam**" means porch in Hebrew. An outer veil called "**masak**" separated the outer court from the "**Holy Place**" room. The inner veil called the "**paroketh**" separated the '**inner sanctuary of the tabernacle**' or "**Holy of Holies**" room where the Most High dwelt from the "**Holy Room**". The "**veil**" also acted as a divider/screen shielding the Creator from "**sinful**" man. Whoever entered the Holy of Holies room was entering into the presence of God.

7

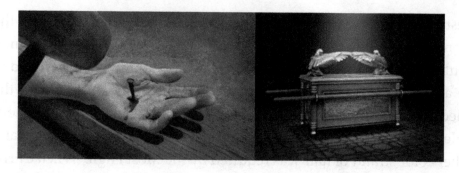

(**Left**) In Christianity, Christ was crucified for the sins of mankind. He was the "**sacrificial lamb**" that would represent the lamb (animal) that would be required for a blood sacrifice on the altar for the "**atonement**" of the sins of Israel. (**Right**) **Ark of the Covenant**, which was held in the **Holy of Holies** room and in the "**Tabernacle**" the Israelites set up in "the Wilderness".

Only once a year during the "**Day of Atonement**" or "**Yom Kippur**" could the High Priest enter before **YAHUAH (The LORD)**.

"But only the high priest entered the inner room, and that **only once a year**, and never without blood, which he offered for himself and for the sins the people had committed in ignorance"- **Hebrews 9:7**

Fact: When Christ died the temple veil was torn in half according to St. Mark who penned this around 50 A.D., when Jewish-Roman Historian Flavius Josephus (*i.e. some say was Roman Arrius Piso*) was 13 years old. Fragments of the Book of St. Mark from the 1st Century A.D. have been found written in Aramaic, proving that the New Testament is valid. Any Greek, Roman or Edomite Jew or even the Pharisees at that time would not record any proof that supernatural events occurred during the Crucifixion of Christ as this would be an "**embarrassment**" to their doctrine. But Saint Mark, founder of the **Egyptian Coptic Church** in Alexandria, Egypt documented the Truth. 1st Century A.D. Jewish historian Flavius Josephus, admits the Second temple veil was made of Babylonian tapestry with fine linen in the colors **blue, purple and scarlet**. It was estimated to be 60 feet in height, 30 feet in width and four inches thick. **It was recorded during the crucifixion of Christ that**

the Temple Veil was torn from the top down...meaning this event was supernatural.

2nd Century A.D. Christian Tunisian Berber **Quintus Septimus Florens Tertullianus**....aka "**Tertullian**" in his literary work "**Against the Jews**" or "**Adv. Iudaeus**" describes the day the veil was torn. Other historians such as Flavius Josephus and Jerome also talk about the "**veil**" being rent (*i.e. torn*) as well. Many historians at the time documented Spirits/Angels departing from the Temple after Christ's death. It also talks about people seeing an angel with a sword cutting the veil and a loud voice uttering "**Woe to Jerusalem**".

Fact: *Joshua was of the Tribe of Ephraim, son of Nun. His name is the basis for the English transliterated word "Jesus". In* **Aramaic,** *it was pronounced "Yeshua". In Hebrew, depending on who you ask it was pronounced* **Yehoshua/Yahushua, Yahshua or Yahusha.** *Jesus's Hebrew name had a "meaning" as most Bantus African names have. The name Jesus has no "Meaning" in Hebrew. Yahusha is a combination of two Hebrew words which combined mean "God (Yah) is Salvation"* **(Hebrew Strong's #3050 Yah for "God" + Hebrews Strong's #3467 Yasha for "Salvation").** *Joshua, Moses's right hand man, was somehow able to be on Mount Sinai when God didn't allow any of the Israelites to even touch the mountain in Exodus 19:12. Joshua was in the "Tabernacle" with Moses when he spoke to God "Face to Face" in Exodus 33:11 and Joshua stayed in the "Tabernacle" with the Ark of the Covenant when Moses left out the Tabernacle. Joshua (not Moses) was the one that was "Chosen" to lead the Israelites into the "Promised Land". In the Bible,* **Yeshua/Jeshua** *son of Yehozadak (Yah is righteous) was the first person "Chosen" to be the "High Priest" of the reconstructed 2nd Temple in Jerusalem built under Ezra, Nehemiah and Zerubbabel. Joshua (Yeshua/Yahusha) was the name "Chosen" for God in the flesh who came "first" for the "***Lost Sheep of Israel***" in Matthew 15:24. Is this all a coincidence?*

In Ancient Biblical times, it was **ONLY** the High Priest that could enter the "**Holy of Holies**" in the presence of God during the **Day of Atonement**. All other Levites or Israelites who entered would die. This is because God's presence immediately made everything around it

Holy....including the ground. Before the High Priest Cohenite entered the Holy of Holies on the Day of Atonement (*10th day of the 7th Jewish month of Tishri-Oct/Sept as stated in Leviticus 16:29*) he had to wash himself, put on special clothing, bring incense to let the smoke cover his eyes from a direct view of God and bring blood with him to make atonement for Israel's sins."

So, in the Israelite Temple the presence of God remained shielded from man behind a thick curtain during the Old Testament. However, Jesus (Yahusha's) sacrificial death on the cross (as the lamb) changed this Old Testament practice. When Christ died the Veil Curtain in the Temple was torn in half, from the top to the bottom (Matthew 27:51, Mark 15:38, Luke 23:45). This signified that God's spirit would no longer dwell in Tabernacles or Temples but would dwell in us (*i.e. who believe*).

Note: Many Non-Messianic Black Hebrew Israelites and European Gentile Jews today reject the New Testament and Christ but do not practice animal sacrifices during "**Feast Days**" or for the "**Atonement of people's sins**" to God. Perhaps they believe they can ask the "Father-Yahuah" directly for the forgiveness of their sins but if that was truly the case....prior to the birth, death and resurrection of Christ the Israelites knew the Creator "**God of Israel**" but still used "<u>animal blood sacrifice</u>" for the atonement of sins. How is it that the Ancient Israelites were not able to ask the Creator "directly" for forgiveness but todays "**Torah-only**" Israelites can mysteriously bypass the "**shedding of blood**" for the "atonement of sins"? What changed from back then to today if the New Testament and Christ is all "**fictional**"?

Leviticus 17:11 "For the life of the flesh is in the <u>**blood**</u>: and I have given it to you upon the altar to make an atonement (*i.e. amends for sin*) for your souls: for it is the <u>**blood**</u> that maketh an atonement for the soul."

So, if today's Non-Messianic "**Torah-Tanakh Only**" Israelites and Gentile Jews today only follow the Old Testament (Tanakh)....are they following the practice of "Atonement of Sins" different than the

Ancient Israelites who also followed the Old Testament strictly? Do they believe in being baptized of "**water**" and "**spirit**" or do they simply "**purify**" themselves of "**sin**" in a "**mikveh**" baptismal.....like in ancient Israel?

That being said, when Christ died, it symbolized that now mankind (*including the Lost Tribes of Israel*) could come to the Father (Creator Yahuah) for the atonement of their sins and receive salvation through Christ (the lamb). We do not need a "Temple" anymore to connect to God and now Christ (Jesus/Yahusha aka eternal High Priest....after the order of Melchizedek) is the mediator between man and God. Why? Because Christ was the "Father-Creator" manifested in flesh.

1 Timothy 2:5 (Aramaic Bible)

"For God is One, and The Mediator of God and the sons of men is One: The Son of Man, Yeshua The Messiah".

John 14:8-11 "Philip saith unto him, LORD, shew us the Father, and it sufficeth us. Jesus (Yahusha) saith unto him, Have I been so long time with you, and yet hast thou not known me, Philip? <u>He that hath seen me hath seen the Father;</u> and how sayest thou then, Shew us the Father? <u>Believest thou not that I am in the Father, and the Father in me?</u> The words that I speak unto you I speak not of myself: but the Father that dwelleth in me, he doeth the works. <u>Believe me that I am in the Father, and the Father in me</u>: or else believe me for the very works' sake."

The "Strong Delusion" of the End Time is to push doctrines that is "Anti-Christ". This is happening as speak in the Black community.

So here is where we are now....in the 21st century. In Jewish Tradition, the "**Day of Atonement**" or "**Yom Kippur**" is essentially a "**Last Appeal**" or "**a last chance to change**" before the Judgement of God. It was a time for the Children of Israel in Biblical times to demonstrate their repentance and make amends. However, since the resurrection of Christ, 2,000 years have passed in which the Gospels have been spread unto all nations. But as we venture further into the 21st century we see that the world is becoming more **"Godless"** and more **"Immoral"**.....just as it was in the **"Days of Noah"** which according to the Bible is a **"clear sign"** that the **"Son of Man (Christ)"** is soon to return. With that being said, it is time for us to seek salvation in **Yahusha HaMashiach (Jesus the Messiah)**.

Why now? Well, the **"Signs of the Times"** are among us. Let's take a look.

- Downloading human thoughts and memories into computers (*i.e. Neuralink*).
- Facebook "Brain-computer reading interface" program that can execute commands from a human with just **"thought"**....no speech or hand/finger movements. (*see Regina Dugan and "brain mouse"*). By using non-invasive sensors that can measure brain activity hundreds of times per second at high resolution...the computer system can decode brain signals associated with language in **"real time"**. This will also eliminate the need for a **"translator"** or **"language barriers"** when at work or when doing business. Sounds like we going back to the **"Tower of Babel"** in Nimrod's days all over again doesn't it? How are they going to do it? With retinal **"optical imaging"**.
- Use "geoengineering" to spray aluminum and other chemicals/metals into the atmosphere to block sunlight to combat climate change.
- Genetic manipulation to repair "natural" damaged DNA from the normal process of aging.
- 24-hour drone surveillance and drone use in the military.
- Geneticists using the DNA from "three people" to create "3-Parent Babies".
- Smart TV's that can watch viewers while the TV is on or off.

- Increasing "leaks" of massive "**pedophile**" rings and "**sex trafficking**" rings all over the world showing how "sexually immoral" the world is now.
- Self-replicating "DNA computers" and "Artificial Intelligent D-Wave Quantum computers" that can repair themselves or "adapt" to their surroundings. **Google's "Mammoth D-Wave 2X Quantum computer** is 100 million times faster than a PC (HP or Mac).
- Nanotechnology used as "contaminants" that can enter the human cell nuclei and interact with human DNA....causing cellular mutations which cause Cancer or Neurological disorders.
- Banning of unvaccinated children from schools (*i.e. California, Australia*).
- Homosexual rights and Legalized Gay Marriage in America.
- Transgender rights.
- "Pedosexual classification" in the DSM V as "**Minor-attracted person**". Approved by the Diagnostic and Statistical Manual of Mental Disorders.....as well as the American Psychological Association (*See B4U-ACT*).
- Hate crimes enforced for being "against" immorality but no Hate crimes enforced for crimes against humanity in regards to "Black Life" and the so-called "Equality" we are supposed to have in America.
- Bestiality rights (Canada/USA) and Bestiality brothels across the world.
- Increasing Alcohol and Drug use (Legal and Illegal).
- Increasing partying 7 days a week.
- Increased "**Lovers of Self**" with social media platforms (*i.e. Instagram, Snapchat, Facebook, Twitter*). Everybody thinks they are a "Celebrity" based on the number of "likes" or "followers" they have.

- Increasing work/jobs and the need to obtain "mammon-money".
- Less time for God, less time for praying, less need for Salvation.
- Wars and rumors of wars between major countries.
- Earthquakes, Floods, Tsunami, Sinkholes, Strange sounds heard in the sky, abnormal cloud formations and other abnormal weather phenomena's.
- Massive Animal die offs.

Hosea 4:1-3 "Hear the word of the Lord, ye Children of Israel: for the Lord hath a controversy with the inhabitants of the land, because there is **NO TRUTH**, nor mercy, nor knowledge of God in the land. By **SWEARING, AND LYING, AND KILLING, AND STEALING, AND COMMITTING ADULTERY**, they break out, and blood toucheth blood. Therefore shall the land mourn, and every one that dwelleth therein shall languish, with the beasts of the field, and with the fowls of heaven; **YEA, THE FISHES OF THE SEA ALSO SHALL BE TAKEN AWAY."**

- Economic turmoil, currency collapses (*i.e. Venezuela*), hyperinflation, food crises, insolvent (broke) countries with Debt to GDP ratios close to or over 100% (*i.e. Puerto Rico, Spain, France, United Kingdom, Belgium, United States of America, Jamaica, Portugal, Greece, Italy, Cyprus, Brazil*).
- Increasing displacement of people from their States/countries from War, Natural Disasters or Economic downturns.
- More refugee camps (Europe, Middle East, Africa).
- ISIS clearing out the key countries that invaded and enslaved the Ancient Children (i.e. Assyria, Babylon (Iraq), Libya, soon to be Egypt).
- The Demonic-Satanic changing of all Bible translations (online, physical bibles) courtesy of the "**Mandela Effect/D-wave**

Quantum Effect" and D-Wave Quantum "**Artificially Intelligent**" Computers.

- The mixing of "**Synthetic DNA**" with Human "**Biological DNA**". (*i.e. movie "Splice", "Morgan", TV series "Humans"*).
- Increasing technology and UFO (Fallen Angel) sightings.
- Increasing "poisoning" of our air, food, water and vaccines creating mutations courtesy of the "Hidden Masters" as an agent of "Population control"….especially towards the "Black Israelites (*i.e. Autism and "provoked" genetic mutations MECP2, NLGN3, NLGN4 that predispose Black Children to being diagnosed with Autism. See also Glyphosate Herbicide and autism*)".
- Increasing worship of pagan gods formulated to "Deceive" the world (*i.e. Min/Amsu/Horus, Osiris, Isis, Ptah, Enlil, Enki, Ea, Marduk, Baal, Amen-Ra, Zeus, Moloch, Allah, Anubis*). Also, the rise in "Witchcraft" and "Satanism" in the world.
- Increasing financial enslavement of humans by "Debt" and "Interest".
- More surveillance and monitoring by the "**All Seeing Eye**" of Satan (*i.e. drones, facial recognition, Traffic Cameras, retinal scans, fingerprint scans, RFID-Biometric technology in the "Real ID", Passports with RFID chips and Biometric information*) keeping tabs on people.
- ELF technology on traffic poles at intersections in our communities' ready to emit "**Extra Low Frequency**" signals to create a "**Bliss**" or "**Want**" just like the TV Series "**V**".
- Increasing open Satanic rituals and ceremonies (*i.e. Gotthard Base Tunnel, CERN, Arch of Baal, Anubis Statue, Temple of Set, Temple of Oculus, Black Sun/Saturn worship*).
- Increasing Blacks joining or "selling their soul" into Occultic organizations (*i.e. Illuminati, Freemasonry, Hermetic Order of Golden Dawn, Rosicrucian's*) for fame and riches.

- And more Black people (Christians/Hebrew Israelites) not believing that the New Testament is a God-Inspired book or that Yahusha HaMashiach is One with the Father and therefore is God.

All of these things I touch on and address in my "Hebrews to Negroes" Books and Seminar DVD's to let people know that the **"time is now"** for Black people to **WAKE UP! (See www.thenegronetwork.com).**

CHAPTER 2

THE SPIRIT OF SLUMBER

The Bible says that the Messiah is coming like a "**Thief**" in the night. When a Thief comes, it is done when nobody expects him to come and it usually catches the person robbed "**off-guard**". There is no warning or "**heads up**". People are usually fast "asleep", at work or gone away on vacation. This is what is happening today. The world....including Black people are "**fast asleep**" given to slumber with a cloak over their eyes.

Romans 11:8 "According as it is written, God hath given them the **spirit of slumber**: eyes that they should not see, and ears that they should not hear unto this day."

Only those who have ears to hear and eyes to see will hearken unto the "**final call**" of the Most High. These will be the ones that will prepare themselves as a "**spotless Bride**" for Christ when he returns. With that being said I want to cover some things about the "**End of Days**". Many Christians today will say, "**People have been saying the Jesus is going** to return for years" and they are still saying it today. Some Homosexuals that could care less about the Bible or Christ say that soon "**Homosexual and Immoral sexual behavior**" will be the norm and that the "**New World Order**" will take over….with nothing man can do about it. However, people need to understand that God "**allows**" all things to happen for a reason. Everything that is happening that may seem bad is happening for a **REASON**. It's all part of **God's Perfect Plan** which was explained to us in the only Book of prophecy known to mankind….**the Bible**….written by one group of people God selected to preach prophecy and salvation to the world…..**THE HEBREW ISRAELITES.**

The Israelites were the keepers of the Truth…of **scripture** and **prophecy**….directed by God the Creator. The Bible and the Islamic Quran attests to this. The Israelites were from the Seed of **Isaac and Jacob.**

Exodus 19:6 "And ye (*i.e. Israel*) shall be unto me a **KINGDOM OF PRIESTS**, and an **HOLY NATION**. These are the words which thou shalt speak unto the children of Israel."

Noble Quran Sura 29:27 "And We gave to Him **ISAAC AND JACOB** (*i.e. not Ishmael/the Arabs/Muhammad*) and placed in his descendants **PROPHETHOOD AND SCRIPTURE**. And We gave him his reward in this world, and indeed, he is in the Hereafter among the righteous."

As we can see, all the "**Abrahamic**" religions (*i.e. Judaism, Islam, Christianity*) attest in their books that the Israelites are the ones who would deliver prophecy to the world.

When Christ Returns to Earth and sets up the "**Kingdom of God**" he restores the "**Israelites**" to their position of "**Leadership**" in the world (Isaiah 11:12, Isaiah 14:1-2).

Isaiah 14:1-2 "For the Lord will have mercy on Jacob, and will yet choose Israel, and set them in their own land: **and the strangers shall**

18

be joined with them, and they shall cleave to the House of Jacob. And the people shall take them, and bring them to their place: and the house of Israel shall possess them in the land of the Lord for servants and handmaids: and they shall take them captives, whose captives they were; and they shall rule over their oppressors."

The word **"Cleave"** is defined as **"to adhere firmly and closely or loyally and unwaveringly."**

This means that in the **"Last Days"**, the **"Real Israelites"** would be favored and in support by the Gentile **"strangers"** amongst us. This means the "authentic" Black Arabs, the Eurasian White Arabs, Chaldeans, the Gentile proselytes to Judaism, Anglo-Saxon Caucasians and the rest of the population of the Earth who are "Gentiles".

But many will say, "No way, the White Jews are in Israel right now and Bible prophecy is happening without African-Americans or any Black race claiming to be Jews." **Here is how you answer this.**

(**Above**) The **Israeli Separation Wall**, nicknamed "**The Apartheid Wall**", separates the Arab Palestinians territory in Israel from Israeli occupied territory. It is 400 miles long and 25 feet high. Concrete, barbed wires and more are used to protect Israel from its Muslim neighbors.

In **Ezekiel 38** it talks about the Gog and Magog war against Israel. But this is a particular Israel. Not the "**imposter Jews**" in Israel today but the Real Israelites. The Gog and Magog war is supposed to happen in Israel, this we know for sure although the timeline of this "war" is speculated differently by biblical scholars. The Israelites in the Book of Ezekiel "**Gog and Magog**" prophecy live in peace, **without walls**, gates, fences, troops, tanks and Iron Dome anti-missile defense systems. These Israelites also have the **WHOLE LAND** God promised the 12 Tribes of Israel which the "imposter" Gentile Jews (*i.e. Ashkenazi/Sephardic/Mizrahi*) today don't have.

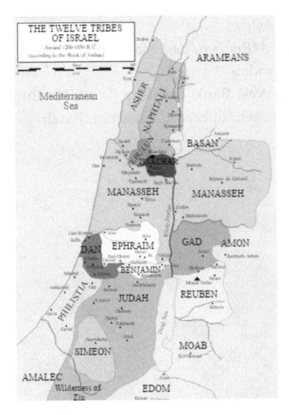

(**Above**) The Territories of the 12 Tribes of Israel. Notice that the land east of the **Jordan River** and the **Dead Sea** today is the country **Jordan**. This is where the **Tribe of Manasseh, Gad and Reuben** used to have their territories. Notice the land north of West Manasseh and Zebulon today is the country **Lebanon**. Back then it was the territory of the **Tribe of Asher and Naphtali**. It is easy to see that **Lebanon, Jordan** and **Palestine** still hold on to the territories of God's Chosen People despite the State of Israel being founded in 1948. Was this Bible Prophecy of the return of the 12 Tribes? You research the facts and decide. God is not a liar, man is!

1. **Lebanon**-Asher
2. **Jordan**-Gad/Reuben/East Manasseh-Jordan
3. **Palestine**-Judah
4. **Palestine West Bank Territory** (West/Northwest of the Dead Sea) -Manasseh/Ephraim/Benjamin/Judah

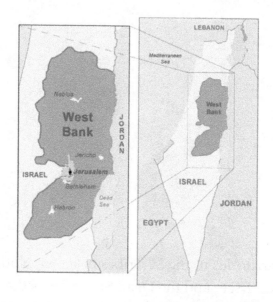

(**Above**) The Palestinian occupied West Bank Territory that Israel has been fighting for years to take back is the ancient territories of the **Tribe of Manasseh, Ephraim, Benjamin**, and **Judah**. This is how you know biblical prophecy of the return of the 12 Tribes of Israel didn't happen yet.

Ezekiel 38:8-14 "After many days thou shalt be visited: in the latter years **thou shalt come into the land that is brought back from the sword, and is gathered out of many people, against the mountains of Israel, which have been always waste**: but it is brought forth out of the nations, and **they shall dwell safely all of them**. Thou shalt ascend and come like a storm, thou shalt be like a cloud to cover the land, thou, and all thy bands, and many people with thee. Thus saith the Lord GOD; It shall also come to pass, that at the same time shall things come into thy mind, and thou shalt think an evil thought: **And thou shalt say, I will go up to the land of <u>unwalled villages</u>; I will go to them that are at <u>rest</u>, that <u>dwell safely, all of them dwelling without walls, and having neither bars nor gates</u>,** To take a spoil, and to take a prey; to turn thine hand upon the desolate places that are now inhabited, and upon the people that are gathered out of the nations, which have gotten cattle and goods, that dwell in the midst of the land. Sheba, and Dedan, and the merchants of Tarshish, with all the young lions thereof, shall say unto thee, Art thou come to take a spoil? hast thou gathered thy company to take a prey? to carry away silver and gold, to take away cattle and goods, to take a great spoil?" **Therefore, son of man, prophesy and say unto Gog, Thus saith the Lord GOD; In that day when my people of Israel dwelleth safely, shalt thou not know it?**

As the scriptures clearly state in **Ezekiel**, the European Jews since arriving to Palestine in 1948 have **not** dwelled safely. **They have put up bars, gates and walls** to protect themselves from their Muslim neighbors. With the help of the U.S.A. they have acquired not one, but two anti-missile defense systems called "**The Iron Dome**". This is not the definition of "**safe**".

(**Above**) A Palestinians confront Israeli soldiers in a protest against the **Israeli Separation Wall** on November 13, 2010 in Al-Walaja, West Bank. Israeli soldiers don't walk around with pistols or pepper spray, they have high powered rifles, tanks and machine guns. This goes against what the Israelite prophet Jeremiah said in **Jeremiah 30:10.**

Jeremiah 30:10 "Therefore fear thou not, O my Servant Jacob, saith the LORD; neither be dismayed, O Israel: for, lo, I will save thee from afar, and thy seed from the land of their captivity; and Jacob shall return, and shall be in rest, and be quiet, and **NONE SHALL MAKE HIM AFRAID.**

The Bible is clearly saying that in the last days when all the 12 Tribes of Israel are back home during the Gog and Magog War, Israel will be living in peace with no armed gun protection needed and no Militarized Police guarding the land from the 60+ Million Muslims surrounding Israel.

So, as we can see…..as we read our Bibles it is important to know _**who**_ "Israel" is. Knowing who the true "Israelites" are changes the world's view on who will be involved in future "Biblical Prophecy". The people who are the Blood descendants of Israel are going to be those people who will be placed "**at the top**" or "**first**" in the Kingdom of God. Remember, the Bible says "**The meek shall inherit the earth-**

Matthew 5:5" and the "**Last shall be First-Matthew 20-16**". So being able to differentiate between the *"Are the White Jews the real Jews or are Blacks the real Jews"* question is very important. It shows what part in the "**Kingdom**" each group will play. If Black people in America are the Real Israelites and the White Jews today are the Gentile "**Strangers**" the Bible talks of… then the Bible foretells that "**Black Israelites**" will one day be served or helped by the "**Gentiles**". What this means is that "**one day**" the Gentiles will know who are the "**impostor Jews**" and who are the real descendants of the Israelites in the Bible. This "**day**" has already begun. If that doesn't grab your attention now stay tuned for more.

CHAPTER 3

WHY IT'S IMPORTANT WE KNOW WHO WERE THE EARLY SONS OF SHEM, THE SONS OF ABRAHAM AND THE SONS OF JACOB (ISRAEL)

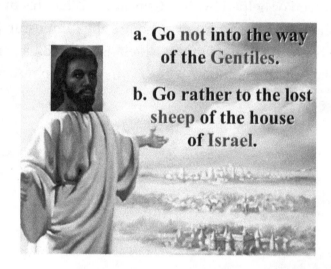

a. Go not into the way of the Gentiles.

b. Go rather to the lost sheep of the house of Israel.

Today many Black Christians when approached with the statement, **"Jesus was a Black man and the Children of Israel were also Black"** they will often say, **"Jesus doesn't see skin color"** or **"It doesn't matter what skin color Jesus was or what skin color the Israelites were"**. This kind of "learnt" thinking causes the Black Christian to read the Bible as if it is some fictional story about people they cannot relate with in our current **"reality"**. However, the Bible isn't a **"Harry Potter Book"** or a book about **"Merlin the Magician"**. The Bible is a book describing history, from the viewpoint of how the **"ancients"** were told how the **"Creation"** happened all the way to the **"Great Flood"** and beyond. It lines up with actual history. In Church, we are taught Noah's 3 sons populated the whole earth after the Great Flood. We are shown in Sunday School only **"White Biblical characters"**, including the angels and Christ the Messiah. But there is one thing that we always tend to overlook in the Bible and this is the topic of **"Race"** or **"Skin Color"**. Pastors stay away from the skin color "subject" of the

Biblical Egyptians, Phuttites/Libyans, the Cushites, the Canaanites, the Midianites, the Ishmaelite's and the Sons of Shem. Why? We all are taught that Noah's family were saved from flood and this is how the earth had a "**re-start**". Mankind after the "Great Flood" repopulated the earth in those days to get us to where we are today. If this is the case, then "**African-Americans**" should descend from one of Noah's three sons: **Ham, Shem and Japheth**. But don't let the Church Pastor explain who are the Egyptians, the Libyan Phuttites, the Ethiopians, the Canaanites, the Edomites, the Ammonites, the Moabites or the Elamites today.....or what skin color they were in those days. They won't be able to do it. But Pastors and the whole Christian world can tell you who are the Jews, the Arabs, the Chaldeans and the Greeks of today.....according to their Bible. But there is one huge problem. If the Bible is not a "**Fictional Book**" than it should be read as if it is "**Real History**". We know were Greece is, we know were Egypt is and we know where Israel is on the world map. However, the one thing that eludes Pastors teaching Bible Class is that if the Children of Israel mixed with the daughters of Ham in the Bible we should be able to research where the sons of Ham lived and what they looked like. After all, there is archaeological finds that have been dug up or excavated to prove what they looked like in Biblical "B.C." times. Finding out what the Sons of Ham and the Sons of Shem looked like in Biblical times should provide "clues" as to what the ancient Israelites would've looked like "then and now". That being said, it shouldn't be "**Rocket Science**" to know that if "Israel" mixed with the nation of Ham for centuries that it is impossible for the Jews/Israelites to be "white" today.

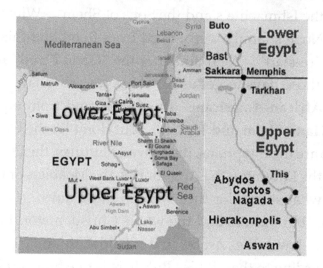

(**Above**) In some maps, Upper Egypt encompassed parts of Nubia (Cush/Sudan). In Upper Egypt, the city "**Aswan**" sits off the Nile River. In Arabic, the word "**Aswad**" means "**Black**". Just another hint the people in Egypt were **Black** and the Ishmaelite Arabs....including the Arameans knew it. It's a known fact that the word "**Cham**" or "**Kham**" or "**Khem**" is derived from the word "**Hot**". In Hebrew (Strong's #2526) the word "**Cham**" is also another name for "**Egyptians**" as it states: *Cham -* "**A son of Noah, also his descendants, also a name for Egyptians.**

Here are the facts:

- It is estimated that from 1800 B.C. to 1400 B.C., the Israelites in Egypt experienced **400 years of bondage** and **400 years of mixing** with the Egyptians/Cushites. After all Nubia (Cush) was part of Upper Egypt. When Moses left with Israel, some Black Egyptians and possibly some Black Nubian Cushites came with them.

- **Leviticus 24:10** "And the son of an Israelitish woman, whose **father was an Egyptian**, went out among the Children of Israel: and this son of the Israelitish woman and a man of Israel strove

28

(walked) together in the camp; And the Israelitish woman's son blasphemed the name of the Lord, and cursed. And they brought him unto Moses: (and his mother's name was Shelomith, the daughter of Dibri, of the tribe of Dan:)"

- (est. **1300 B.C.**) Israelites prior to having a King (Saul) were governed by "**Judges**" when there was "**lawlessness**" in the land. When the Israelites left Egypt with **Moses** and then entered into the Land of Canaan with **Joshua** they went from mixing with the Black Hamitic Egyptians to mixing with the Black Hamitic Canaanites.

- (est. **500 B.C.**) Ezra 3:5-6 "And the Children of Israel dwelt among the **Canaanites**, Hittites, and Amorites, and Perizzites, and Hivites, and Jebusites: **And they took their daughters to be their wives, and gave daughters to their sons**, and served their gods.

For many centuries, we as Blacks in America have been reading our Bible, passing over the "**Canaanites**", not knowing that Egypt and Canaan hold very "**impactful**" tools as to determining who is "**The Real Israelites**". In this book, I will connect the **Canaanites** to the many "**Negrito-Pygmy**" tribes that are in Africa and beyond (*i.e. South Asia/Asia*). If the Bible says that the Canaanites men also took Israelite wives and vice versa wouldn't we expect to see the Bantus Negro Y-DNA "E1b1a" also in the Canaanite-Pygmy/Negrito tribes of today? At least we should see some "**genetic**" material shared by "Bantus" African Israelites and the "pygmy-negritos" of the world. Well, according to genetic studies the Pygmy tribes (mbuti) and even the Khoisan tribes in Africa have some of the oldest Y-DNA (*i.e. Haplogroup A and B*) in the world, but they also share a small "**E1b1a**" contribution in their whole DNA. They got this trace "**E1b1a**" contribution from mixing with the Israelites that scattered into Africa.

Around 600 B.C.-500 B.C., the **Persians** defeated Nebuchadnezzar and the Babylonians acquiring new rulership over the Middle East, including Israel. They allowed Ezra, Nehemiah and Zerubbabel to rebuild the 2nd Temple in Jerusalem. But the remaining Israelites (Tribe of Judah, Benjamin) and even the Priestly Levi-Cohen Tribe that returned to Israel under the Persian rule still were "**intermarrying**" with the sons of Ham. While previously under **Babylonian** rule and captivity, some of the Southern Tribe Israelites had taken wives from the sons of Shem (i**.e. Arphaxad, Elam, Asshur**). *Note: This can be verified in Ezra 10.* So already we have a span of years, going from **1800 B.C. (Egyptian rule) to 500 B.C (Persian rule)......or 1300 years** that the Israelites lived amongst the sons/daughters of Ham.... mixing their bloodline with the indigenous "Black" people of Africa. We also have another significant period of time where they lived among the sons of Shem (*i.e. Moab, Ammon, Elam, Arphaxad, Asshur*) in **Babylon** (Iraq), **Assyria** (Syria-Iraq) and **Medes-Persia** (Iran).

WHAT WAS THE HEBREWS ETHNICITY BEFORE MIXING WITH HAMITES? WHAT DID THEY LOOK LIKE?

Many Bible readers assume all the Hebrews and Hebrew Israelites were "**Negroid**" Hamitic-looking people.....basically "**identical**" to the sons of Ham. But is this really true? Let's look at the Hebrews ethnicity first. Remember in **Genesis 11**, it shows how the Terah and his whole family lived and had kids in the land of Ur of the Chaldeans. The Ancient Chaldeans of the Bible were of the lineage of Arphaxad. In the Book of Jubilees, Shem's children were also given the land "East" to the land of India.

Note: In India, the Hindu god "**Brahma**" marries his sister (*i.e. some say daughter*) "**Sara-swati**". In the Bible, **Abram** marries his half-sister "**Sarai**".

THE HEBREW PATRIARCHS ETHNICITY

- **Terah** (Hebrew Father-? Babylonian-**Ur** "Arphaxad" Wife)
- **Abraham** (Hebrew Father-? Babylonian-**Ur** "Arphaxad" Mother)
- **Isaac** had a Hebrew Father (**Abraham**) and a Syrian Mother (**Sarai**)
- **Jacob** had a Hebrew Father (**Isaac**) and a Syrian Mother (**Rebekah, the sister of Laban the Syrian**)

THE CHILDREN OF ISRAEL'S ETHNICITY

- **Leah** (Syrian) + **Jacob** (Hebrew)
    1. *Reuben* (Hebrew + Syrian)
    2. *Simeon* (Hebrew + Syrian)
    3. *Levi* (Hebrew + Syrian)
    4. *Judah* (Hebrew + Syrian)
    5. *Issachar* (Hebrew + Syrian)
    6. *Zebulun* (Hebrew + Syrian)
    7. *Dinah* (Hebrew + Syrian)
- **Bilhah** (? Unknown ethnicity) + **Jacob** (Hebrew)
    1. *Dan* (Hebrew + ? ethnicity)
    2. *Naphtali* (Hebrew + ? ethnicity)
- **Zilpah** (? Unknown ethnicity) + **Jacob** (Hebrew)
    1. *Gad* (Hebrew + ? ethnicity)
    2. *Asher* (Hebrew +? ethnicity)
- **Rachel** (Syrian) + **Jacob** (Hebrew)
    1. *Joseph* (Hebrew + Syrian)
    2. *Benjamin* (Hebrew + Syrian)

In the **Book of Jubilees 8:6-9** it states that **Eber** (*i.e. Patriarch of the Hebrews*) took **Azurad** (*daughter of Nimrod, son of Cush*) to be his wife.

From Eber would come **Peleg**, then **Reu**, then **Serug**, then **Nahor**, then **Terah** and then **Abraham**. Assuming that there were no futher mixing with "Hamitic Cushites" would the Hebrew Patriarchs be identical to "Hamites" even after 5-6 generations? What if the Hebrew Patriarchs all had Hamite wives? What if they had Shemite wives? Would the Family Tree of Abraham consist of "Brown-skinned" people with different variations of hair textures (*i.e. straight, wavy, curly, kinky*) and facial bony features (*i.e. nose, cheek bones, lips*)? To know this, we would have to know what the original Sons of Shem looked like. **Lud, Elam, Asshur, Arphaxad**, and **Aram** could very well have been "brown-skinned" people with similar features to the people in India, the Pacific Islands and also Somalia. Also keep in mind that the Bible doesn't fully disclose the "ethnicity" of **Bilhah** and **Zilpah**, the handmaids of **Laban the Aramean (Syrian)**.

Note: *In the Hebrew Bible in* **Genesis 31:24** *it states* **"God came to Laban the Aramean"** *using Hebrew Strong's #761 "Arammi" after Aram (Son of Shem) and the* **Arameans** *(Syrians).* *Laban was the "maternal" uncle of Jacob, as Jacob's mother "Rebekah" was also a* **"Aramean (Syrian)"**. *Today, many "Aramaic" influences can be seen in the Syro-Malabar Catholic Church in* **Kerala, India**. *This church's founding father was* **St. Thomas the Apostle** *from the 1st Century A.D. during Christ's time. Members of the Church are sometimes called "Nasrani" which is also a Chaldean (Assyrian) term for "Christians". In* **Book 5, Hebrews to Negroes 2: Volume 4**, *I provide proof that the Sons of Shem and some of the Northern Tribe Israelites scattered into India in places like* **Tamil Nadu/Kerala**.

(**Left**) Tamil Nadu, **India**. (**Right**) **Somalian** woman 19th Century. In both races (*i.e. South Dravidian Indian, Somalian*) you can find light-to-dark brown skinned people. Genetically both races have "**Semitic**" roots-ancestry, but from which line of **Shem**?

Are there some "**Shemitic**" people or "**Lost Israelites**" in India? Consider this amazing fact!

The 10 Northern Tribes of Israel were taken out of Samaria by the Assyrians around 700 B.C. and were "placed" into Assyria (Iraq, Syria) and also the town of the Medes (Persia-Iran). East of these lands is **INDIA**. Did the Israelites during this time mix with the Assyrians, Babylonians and Persians while on the "move" east into Asia? Surely, the Israelites would not try to return to the "Assyrian-occupied" land of Israel after they were invaded by them.

2 Kings 17:6 "In the ninth year of Hoshea the King of Assyria took Samaria, and **carried Israel away into Assyria**, and **placed them** in Halah (*Syria-Assyria*) and in Habor (*Syria-Assyria*) by the river of Gozan, and in the cities of the Medes (*Persia-Iran*)."

Suriyani Malayalam (or Karshoni) was an "**East Aramaic**" script used to write "**Malayalam**" among the Indian Christians in **Kerala, India** until the 1800's. "**Western Aramaic**" was spoken mostly by the Hebrew Israelites in Israel while "**Eastern Aramaic**" was spoken by

Arameans (Syrians) in Ancient Times. Western Aramaic is not spoken anymore in the **"Middle East"** because the **"Real"** Israelites are scattered into the nations. Today, the people living in Kerala, India mostly speak **"Malayalam"**....which has Assyrian, Aramaic and Hebrew influences mixed with **Sanksrit** or **Tamil** (*which is also Semitic in nature*).

"Suriyani" Malayalam-Amma   Aramaic- Emma = **Mother**

"Suriyani" Malayalam-Appan   Aramaic-Abba = **Father**

"Suriyani" Malayalam-Nasrani   Aramaic-Nasraya or Nasrani = **Follower of Jesus the Nazarene**.

"Suriyani" Malayalam-Pesaha   Aramaic-Pesaha = **Passover**

"Suriyani" Malayalam-Malakha   Aramaic-Malaka = **Angel**

"Suriyani" Malayalam-Silva   Aramaic-Silva = **Cross**

"Suriyani" Malayalam-Easow   Aramaic-Eiso or Eisho = **Jesus**

"Suriyani" Malayalam-Mishiha   Aramaic-Mishiha = **Anointed**

"Suriyani" Malayalam-Dukrana   Aramaic-Dukrana or Dukhrana = **Remembrance**......see the Peshitta Aramaic New Testament at www.dukhrana.com/peshitta/

"Suriyani" Malayalam-Mar   Aramaic-Mar = **Holy man, Saint**

"Suriyani" Malayalam-Rooha   Aramaic Ruha = **Holy Spirit**

"Suriyani" Malayalam-Shliha   Aramaic-Shliha = **Apostle**

"Suriyani" Malayalam-Kabar   Aramaic-Qabra = **Grave**

Can we explain this? If Saint Thomas in the 1st Century A.D. spoke **"Aramaic"** when bringing the gospel of Christ to India, wouldn't he have influenced the language in **Kerala, India**? So, the Ancient "Malayalam" speakers pronounced the name "Jesus" as

"Eashow"...similar to the Aramaic pronunciation of the Messiah's name "Eisho". How is this possible?

Many Aramaic scholars suggest that Jesus' name was "Eisho (Yod-Shin-Waw-Ayin). Some "Modern Aramaic" speakers in Syria would say "Yeshua" today but here is how "Aramaic language" teachers break this down. The way Ancient Aramaic was pronounced was different than Hebrew or Arabic. In this case, the "Yod" was pronounced as a "EE" instead of a "Ye" or "Ya". In both Arabic and Hebrew, every time you have a "Waw" letter before a "Ayin" letter, the sound is "OO" or "U" as in "Yeshu" or "Yeshua". In Ancient Aramaic the "Waw" letter makes the "O" sound and the "Ayin" letter is silent. This could be why the Indians in Kerala spoke Jesus name as "Eashow" like the Aramaic "Eisho". Some say the differences in "Eiso" and "Eisho" or "Yesu" and "Yeshu" was dependent on part of Israel certain tribes lived in in ancient times. The "Shin" could be pronounced either with a "Sh" or a "S" dependent on the Tribes. This can be seen between the Hebrew of the **Gileadites** (*i.e. Reubenites, Gadites, East Manassehites*) and the **Ephraimites**.

Judges 12:5-6 "And the **Gileadites** took the passages of Jordan before the **Ephraimites**: and it was so, that when those Ephraimites which were escaped said, Let me go over; that the men of Gilead said unto him, Art thou an Ephraimite? If he said, Nay; Then said they unto him, Say now **Shibboleth**: and he said **Sibboleth**: for he could not frame to pronounce it right. Then they took him, and slew him at the passages of Jordan: and there fell at that time of the Ephraimites forty and two thousand."

As we can see the pronunciation of Hebrew letters varied within the different 12 Tribes. Perhaps this is how different Bantus "Israelite" Tribes in Africa call the Creator (Father) and the Son different names even today.

Kerala, India has the highest population of Christians in all of India. Malayalam Kerala speakers in southwest India admit that their language has Hebrew-Aramaic in it. They attest that Malayalam is different than the "Hindi" language most Hindu Indians speak. Is this similar to how the **Ethiopian Jews** and the **Ethiopian Tewahedo Orthodox Church** are the only ones who know how speak the Semitic language of "**Ge'ez**"? The Ethiopian Jews claim descent from "**Israel**". Wasn't the "Ethiopian Eunuch" reading out of the Book of Isaiah in "**Hebrew-Aramaic**" when Philip (see Acts 8) overheard him from a distance? This Hebrew Israelite Ethiopian eunuch founded the **Ethiopian Coptic Church**. Gentile Sephardic Jew Benjamin Tudela in the 12th Century A.D. visited Kerala, India and documented that there were Israelites there who were viewed by him as "**Black**". Christian Indians in Kerala state that the Apostle Thomas brought Christianity to their people starting the **Syro-Malabar Coptic Church**. St. Thomas (*aka. "doubting Thomas"*) lived in the 1st Century A.D. and was one of the Twelve disciples of Christ. Wake Up!

(**Above**) The Gentile Sephardic Jews arriving on the Malabar Coast in **Kerala, India** in the 15th-16th Century A.D. These Sephardic Jews spoke mostly Ladino, Spanish, Portuguese and Arabic. The "Black Israelites" in Kerala spoke a language that was composed of Hebrew-Aramaic and they didn't have the **Satanic Babylonian Jewish Talmud** in their possession. The Malabar Jews were known as the "**Black Jews**" while the over time these Gentile Sephardic "**Edomitish**" Jews from Iberia who assimilated in India were known as the White "**Paradesi**" and Baghdadi Jews. As you can see the Malabar "Israelites" were known to have beards....and they also were found to share a similar maternal "mtDNA" seen in the Ethiopian Jews. **THEIR MATERNAL DNA DID NOT MATCH UP WITH THE ASHKENAZI JEWS OR THE SEPHARDIC JEWS.**

It is a known fact that in **India**, most "Priests (*i.e. Brahmin, Catholic*)" wear beards.

Black man with Beard....like Ezra and Aaron....Priests from the Tribe of Levi.

Psalms 133:1-2 "Behold, how good and how pleasant it is for brethren to dwell together in unity! It is like the precious ointment upon the head, that ran down upon the **BEARD**, even **AARON'S BEARD**: that went down to the skirts of his garments;"

Ezra 9:1-3 (600 B.C.-500 B.C.) "Now when these things were done, the princes came to me saying, **The people of Israel**, and **the priests**, and **the Levites**, have not separated themselves from the People of the Lands, doing according to their abominations, even of the **Canaanites**, the **Hittites**, the **Perizzites**, the **Jebusites**, the Ammonites, the Moabites, the Egyptians, and the **Amorites**. For they have taken of their daughters for themselves, and for their sons: **so that the holy seed have mingled themselves with the people of those lands**: yea, the hand of the princes and rulers hath been chief in this trespass. And when I heard this thing, I rent (tore) my garment and my mantle (robe), and plucked off the hair of my head and of my beard, and sat down astonished."

THE SHEMITIC ISRAELITES MEET THE SHEMITIC ISHMAELITES (ARABS).

It is not hard to believe that after **1300 years** of mixing with the "**Dark Races of Ham**", the end-product would be "**Negro-Hamitic looking Israelites**". The mixing of Israel with the Sons of Shem (Lot-Moab, Ammon, **Joktan**ites, **Arphaxad**ites, **Elam**ites, **Asshur**ites, **Aram**eans, **Ishmael**ites) would create a different breed of "**melaninated Israelites**".....like the brown skinned natives in India, Sri Lanka, Bangladesh and the Pacific Islands.

(**Above**) **Shair Ullee Syud**, a Shia Muslim descendant of Muhammad, but this guy obviously looks Black. Was Muhammad a "Black Arab"? Shair Syud's homeland was in **Aligarh, India** 1870 A.D. Although India is predominately a Hindu Country, in North India there can be found people who are Muslim. Many have "**negroid**" characteristics in their physical appearance (*i.e. wooly hair*) while others have brown skin and wavy/straight hair. Could this be a clue as to how the "original" Egyptian-Hebrew Ishmaelites looked like in Ancient times? I would say yes! Remember Ishmael's mother was an Egyptian and she selected his wife from Egypt, the Land of Ham.

(**Above**) Daughter and son of the **Sultan of Zanzibar, Tanzania (Africa)** which was controlled and ran by the **Sultans of Oman (Black Arabs)**. Many of the Black Arabs in Oman, Yemen, and Qatar have highest "**percentages**" of the Semitic "**Y-DNA J1 (M267)**" Haplogroup compared to the white-skinned Arabs we see today in the Middle Eastern world. This is because the original "Shemites" aka "the sons of Shem" were a people of brown skin color.....not white skinned. These Black Arabs influenced the "**Old Swahili language**" by about **25%** (**i.e. *other 50% comes from a Hebrew Israelite Bantus influence***), which was started in Tanzania (Africa), the prime location of the Israelite slave port on **Zanzibar Island, Tanzania**.

bwini katika ukiwa wa Yerusalemi.
mweka Yahuwa Muungu uso wango
ka kwa sala, na kwa kuomba, na kwa

(**Above**) Excerpt from an 1800's African **Swahili bible**. Any Swahili speaking Bantus African knows that the "**original**" Old Swahili language began in Tanzania, Africa. Swahili was created by the original Bantus language in that region mixed with an "**Arabic language**" influence. Before the Roman "**Latin**" language or the Portuguese language could influence Swahili the name they listed for the Creator was "**YAHUWA**". When "Latin" started to influence the Swahili language the Swahili Bible had "**Yahuwa**" replaced with "**Jehovah**". In our English Bibles, the Catholic Church was key in changing the name of the Creator from "**Yahuah/Yahuwa**" to "**Jehovah**" and then "**THE LORD**". Catholics, Arabs and Jews today **DO NOT** pronounce the true "**Name of the Lord**" as it was written in the **Original Hebrew text** or **Aramaic Bible**. It is a known fact that the Old Testament was written by "melaninated Hebrew Israelites" in Paleo-Hebrew except for the book of Daniel which was partly written in Aramaic. The New Testament was written first in Aramaic/Modern Hebrew and was transliterated into Greek, Latin and Old English by "**White Nations**". This is all a part of the "**Satanic Deception**" of organized religion under the Greco-Roman system....including our "Gregorian Roman Sabbaths". The Black Arabs needed a "**Lingua Franca**" with the Bantus Hebrew Israelite East Africans during the early years of Islam. A "**Lingua Franca**" is a language that is adopted as a common language between speakers whose native languages are different. When looking at the above image-scripture passage in the old Swahili bible the word "**Bwini (Bwana)**" means God, Jesus, Husband or Sir in Swahili. "**Katika Ukiwa**" means "You are in something" like Christ. **Mwekea Yahuwa Muungu (Mungu) uso wango** means: "Put your face on **THE LORD** God".......as **THE LORD** is listed in the Swahili Bible as "**Yahuwa**" and **GOD** is "**Mungu**". "**Kuomba**" means praying.

Yahwah   Huwa   Yah(u)

(**Above**) In the Arabic Bibles dating back to the 7th Century A.D., "translated" from the older Hebrew-Aramaic Bibles the name of the **CREATOR** can still be clearly seen as "**YAHUWA/YAHUAH**". The Muslims like the Catholic Church changed the creators name to a false "title".....in this case it was "**Allah**" which means "**the god**". This is how Satan uses "Man" in religion to deceive the whole world.

The above Arabic words are taken from an actual Arabic bible dating back in the **9th-10th Century A.D.**, well before the "Japhetic" Turks/Kurds would conquer Judea (Israel) and the Middle East. **Yefet Ben Ali** was a 10th Century A.D. "**Karaite (*i.e. Law of Moses*)**" commentator of the Old Testament. He was an Arab native of Basra, Iraq who later moved to Jerusalem to further his studies. He wrote his literary works in **Arabic**, in which he covered the **entire Old Testament** (*i.e. Hebrew Tanakh*). He was an expert in the Hebrew language and was able to do a "**true**" literal "**translation**" of the Hebrew Old Testament into Arabic (*which his fellow Arab brethren did not like*). When doing so he preserved the "**True Name of the Creator/God**"....which was **NOT "ALLAH"**. This stirred up much controversy between **Sunni/Shia** Muslims and **Sufi** Muslims in Arabia. Why you may ask? Well, the Sufi Muslims were more "accurate" about pronouncing the name of the Creator as "**Yahuwa**" instead of an ambiguous title word called "**Allah**". **Sufism** had its beginnings around 675 A.D. and Sufi muslims usually practiced what is called "**Dhikr**", which is a rhythmic repetition of the name of God (*pronounced "Yah Huwa"*).

Yahwah **Huwa** **Yah(u)** **W(a) H(u)**

Fact 2: Iraqis are either Muslim or Christian. Christian Iraqis are called "**Chaldeans**". I showed both a Chaldean woman and a Muslim Iraqi man pictures of the Arabic Bible and asked them to pronunce the Arabic letters that I showed them. They both said the word "**Yahuwa**". Even the word listed above as "**Yahwah**" they pronouced it in Arabic as "**Yah-u-wah**". They said that word "**Yah**" has no special meaning or place in the Arabic Bible but both the Muslim Iraqi and the Christian Iraqi admitted that this was the old name of "God". I asked them why did the name change from "**Yahuwa**" to "**Allah**" and they said, "Yahuwa was known as the name of the "**Creator**" or the "**God of Israel**" that some old Arabs used in Ancient times before they used the word "**Allah**" which simply means "**the god**". Both the Iraqi man and woman explained that the word "**Huwa**" means "**HE IS**" or "**O HE**"....which was like saying "**HE EXISTS**". They admitted that the Arabic letter preceding it (*as Arabic like Hebrew is read from Right-to-Left*) was "**Yah**" or "**Yahu**", like the word "**Hallelu-YAH**" **WHICH IS THE HIGHEST PRAISE TO GOD.**

THE SHEMITIC ISRAELITES MEET THE SONS OF SHEM IN THE "EAST".

(**Left**) Delhi, India. The original "Dravidian" Indian are the dark-skinned Indians. (**Right**) Cushite from Sudan (i.e. Dinka Tribe).

In addition to the information just outlined, the original Shemites (i.e. Arphaxad, Asshur, Aram, Elam and Lud) **WHO ARE CURRENLTY IN ASIA/MIDDLE EAST,** all had dealings with Nimrod's **HAMITIC** Cush empire early on in Biblical history…before Abraham was even alive. For this reason, the people who still use a language/writing style similar to the Cuneiform Sanskrit writing style of the Assyrio-Babylonian Sumerian people are the people living in Central Africa (i.e. North Cameroon), Pakistan, India, Sri Lanka, Singapore, Malaysia and Pacific Islanders. These people if you trace back their ancestors and what they looked like….are all a people of color (*save their hair texture*), some being darker in skin color than African-Americans/Africans today.

(Left) **Irula** "Dravidian" men of ancient **Tamil Nadu** and **Kerala**. They speak their mother tongue as well as **Tamil, Malayalam** or **Telugu**. They are Black-skinned people with straight to wavy-curly black hair. (Right) **Irula woman**. The Irula people just as the Yerukala people in India call father "**Aava**" and mother "**Amma**" just like the Hebrews say "**Abba-father**" or "**Em/Im/Ame-mother**". "**Irular**" in Tamil and Malayalam means "**Dark People**" from the root word "**Irul**" which means "darkness" in regards to their dark skin complexion. Could these people be some of the **Lost Tribes of Israel** exiled from Samaria (Northern Israel) in **2 Kings 17:6**?

Fact: *The Ouldeme Tribe in North Cameroon as well as some other "Negroid" tribes living in the **Mandara/Mandura mountains** all speak a language which is basically "**deformed or corrupted**" Sanskrit-Tami (**i.e. see Nova Program 11/2007 on PBS "Master of the Killer Ants"**). Today Tamil speakers are in South India with the Dravidian Indians in Kerala, Tamil Nadu and North Sri Lanka. There are also speakers in Singapore and Malaysia. There has also been traces of "**Semitic**" Tamil (which has Hebrew, Aramaic and Assyrio-Babylonian influences) in the language of the Australian Aborigines, Native Americans, Mayan Indians, Pacific Islanders, Bantus Africans and even the strange Red Haired, RH-negative White Basque people of Spain.*

45

It is a known fact that the Y-DNA seen in Native Indians (**C, R, Q**) can also be found in the Chenchu and Kallar people in South India (Tamil Nadu/Kerala). Y-DNA **C-M130** seen in the Piramalai Kallar community in South India can also be seen in Australia, Malaysia and the Philippines.

Fact: **It is a known fact that many of the Y- DNA Haplogroups found in India can be found in Mesopotamia and even Israel.**

(**Above**) Modern day **Fulani women** and a **Libyan (Phuttite)**. What is interesting is that the Fulani people style their hair with a "single braid" coming of the side of the scalp just like the **Ancient Libyans (Phuttites)**. Sometimes this braid falls to the front of the ear and sometimes the braid is positioned to fall behind the ear. The Fulani people today are scattered throughout West Africa, Central Africa and East Africa. Many theories have been linked to the origin of the Fulani people. Arabs and Muslim Bantus West Africans (Mandinka, Wolof, Mande) state they are of **Israelite-Arab/Ishmaelite stock**. This could also be seen as an **Israelite-Shemitic mix** of people as the Hebrew Israelties were not the only Sons of Shem. In addition, there are those that claim the **Fulani** people are a mixture of the **North African Hamites** (*i.e. Ancient Egyptians, Ancient Libyans*) and **Shemites** from the Middle East-Levant Region. Others say they are a mixture of Israelites, North African Berber Hamites and the Black Shemitic Arabs (i.e. Arabians).

Around the 7th Century A.D., during the rise of Islam there was a group of Israelites residing in North Africa under the rulership of an Israelite woman named **Dahiya Kahina (*i.e. Dahia al-Kahena*)**. It was said she ruled the Hebrew Israelites and the North African Hamitic Berber people from the Aures Mountains in Algeria to Ghadames (*Northwest Libya*). During this time the Israelites mixed with the native Libyans and Egyptians. During the rise of Islam in Arabia during the 7th Century A.D., the Black Shemitic Ishmaelite/Keturahite Arabs went forth into North Africa to the lands of the Hebrew Israelites that were not known to them before. This was written in the Quran....that the Arabs would overtake the **"People of the Book-Israelites"** and their lands. But keep in mind, much of the Quran written by Muhammad (*or his scribes*) was done in **"real time"** during the Arabs many battles. This is how the Shemitic Black Arabs were able to write about the defeat of the Israelites and the North African Black Hamitic Berbers (Phut/Egypt).

Sura 33:26-27 (Sahih International) "And he brought down those (*i.e. North African Hamite Berbers*) who supported them among the **People of the Scriptures** (*i.e. people of the Bible-Israelites*) from their fortresses and cast terror into their hearts so that a party you killed, and you took captive a party. **And he caused you to inherit their land and their homes and their properties and a land which you have not trodden.** And ever is Allah, over all things, competent."

How do we know many of the Black Hebrew Israelites were living in Egypt and Libya?

> **"One million Hebrews resided in Libya and Egypt from Catabathmos, to the border of Ethiopia."**
>
> *Philo of Alexandria (Egypt)*

Note: Philo of Alexandria (Egypt) was originally called "**Philo Judaeus**". He lived from 50 B.C. to 25 A.D. during the time of Christ's birth. He was of Greek stock who **converted** to Judaism. His ancestors went back the Greek Ptolemaic dynasty and the Greek Seleucid Empire. Philo was also known to have ancestry to the Hasmonean "**Maccabean**" family of Greeks who converted to Judaism and became known as "**Jews**". He had two brothers named Alexander and Lysimachus (*i.e. non-Hebrew names*). There was also belief that Philo had ties (*i.e. family & social*) to the **Edomite Herodians** and the **Romans** (*i.e. Emperors Julius Caesar, Claudian*). Philo was known and quoted by the 1st century A.D. Roman Jewish-convert historian "**Flavius Josephus**".

Note: the white Samaritan Jews in Northern Israel are the descendants of Greeks, Edomites, Romans, other Japhetic nations and the original Black Arabs from Arabia. Over time, through the many wars (*i.e. Crusades*) over Jerusalem and the intermarriage of "**foreign**" Gentile wives, the true "**Semitic**" blood has been "**watered down**"....including the black skin color. The only thing left is the passed down "**religious traditions**" from 2,000 years of "**Judaism religious conversion**" and the passed down Y-DNA of their ancestors. This is why the White Jewish Samaritans only carry the Y-DNA "**E1b1b**" from Edom, "**J2**" from the Ottoman Turks/Kurds and "**J1**" from the Semitic Black people from ancient Levant/Mesopotamia/Arabia.

So now that we know that there is proof that "Hebrews" lived in Libya and Egypt in the 1st Century A.D., how do we know they were "Black Hebrew Israelites". How do we know that the Hebrew Israelites mixed with the Libyans, Egyptians and later the Black Ishmaelite Arabs from Arabia?

(**Above**) Statue of **Dihya Kahina** in Khenchela, **Algeria** (Africa). The 7th Century A.D. Hebrew Warrior Priestess was killed in a ravine by the **Umayyad** Black Ishmaelite Arabs which still retains its name (Bir al-Kahina). In Arabic, "**Kahena**" can mean witch, priestess or prophethess. In Hebrew, the word "**Kahen**" or "**Cohen/Kohen**" is derived from the "**Cohenite/Cohanite**" High Priest class of Aaron's descendants (brother of Moses the Levite).

Well, according to history….. the Israelite nation in Libya/Algeria under **Queen Dihya Kahina** were successful in defeating the Black Arabs forces through North Africa. However, the **Black Arabs** (*i.e. nicknamed "Saracens"*) regrouped after each defeat until the **Umayyad** Arabic Caliphate leader "**Hasan ibn an-Nu' uman al-Ghasani**" defeated the North African Israelite Nation in the 7th Century A.D. It is said that before the "**final battle**", Queen Kahina was able to forsee the outcome, which was not going to be in her favor. In knowing this, she sent her two biological sons to the Umayyad leader "**Hasan**" to surrender and join forces with the Black Arabs…..instead of dying in battle. It is said that Hasan gave one of Kahina's Israelite sons a "**leader position**" in one of his forces. Queen Kahina, died in battle, sword in hand and her statue can still be seen in Algeria, Africa till this day.

49

After this, according to Muslim historian **Ibn Khaldun**, her sons (*named Bagay and Khanchla*) converted to Islam and led this newly formed Israelite-Hamitic North African Berber-Ishmaelite Arab army to Iberia (Spain/Portugal). Collectively this group of "**Black Muslim warriors**" would be called in history books the "**Moors**". Thus, during the 8th Century to the 14th Century the Black Hebrew Israelites and the Black Moors lived in Iberia (i.e. Spain/Portugal).

So, how do we know the Jews/Israelites living in North Africa that fell to the Black Arab Invasion, were "**Black Jews**" and not "**White Sephardic Jews**"? After all, westernized "European" education teaches that the White Sephardic Jews were the ones living in Spain/Portugal during the reign of the Black Moors. Well, if many of the Jews in Kahina's forces converted to Islam and joined forces with the Black Arabs during their conquest of North Africa/Iberia during the 8th Century A.D. we would expect to have documentation about "**mixed**" brown colored Moors right? In the Bible, "**strangers**", "**foreigners**" and "**gentiles**" were always drawn to the Israelites....even in King Solomon's days.

2 Chronicles 2:17 "Solomon numbered all the **ALIENS** who were in the land of Israel, following the census which his father David had taken; and 153,600 were found. He appointed 70,000 of them to carry loads and 80,000 to quarry stones in the mountains and 3,600 supervisors to make the people work."

1 Kings 8:41-43 "Also concerning the foreigner who is not of **Your** people Israel, when he comes from a far country for **Your** name's sake (for they will hear of **Your** great name and **Your** mighty hand, and of **Your** outstretched arm); when he comes and prays toward this house, hear in heaven **Your** dwelling place, and do according to all for which the foreigner calls to **You**, in order that all the peoples of the earth may know **Your** name, to fear **You**, as do **Your** people Israel, and that they may know that this house which I have built is called by **Your** name."

Notice how in this scripture the words "**Your**" and "**You**" begins with a capital "**Y**". This shows the separation or distinction between the **Israelites** and the "**Gentile Strangers**". Who are the strangers today that have "**stolen**" the identity of the "**Real Israelites**"?

Think again! The Sephardic Jews like the Ashkenazi Jews have been lying about Jewish history....so that they can keep masquerading as "**Israelites**" when in fact they are simply European "**imposters**" who "**converted**" to Judaism.

So, as we can see from Israelite Queen Kahina's defeat, the group of people that marched from North Africa to Iberia (Spain/Portugal) were a mixture of Israelites, North African Hamitic Berber Tribes and Black Arabians. They would become known as the "**Moors**". The Black Jews and Black Muslims would live in Iberia "**together**" with no historical proof documenting any "wars" or "battles" between the two over their respective religions.

Here is how one European in Iberia described the day the Moors invaded Spain.

> "The reins of the horses were as fire, **THEIR FACES BLACK AS PITCH**, their **EYES SHONE LINE BURNING CANDLES**, their horses were swift as leopards and the riders fiercer than a wolf in a sheepfold at night The Black Moor crossed. The noble Goths (German rulers of Spain) were broken in an hour, quicker than tongue can tell. Oh luckless Spain!
> *Quoted in Edward Scobie, The Moors and Portugal's Global Expansion, in Golden Age of the Moor, Ivan Van Sertima (1992, p 336.)*

So, can this history along with "**genetics**" prove that the **BLACK** Hebrew Israelites mixed also with other "Sons of Shem"? **YES IT CAN!**

(Above) Tuareg Black Berber in Timbuktu, Mali (Africa). Many Tuareg "**Moorish**" Berbers know about their possible "**mixed**" Hebrew Israelite ancestry when asked, however because of their Muslim heritage, this is frowned upon. Therefore, no one really speaks about it. This is also the case in the majority Muslim **Mandingo/Soninke Tribesmen** in Mali, Senegal, Gambia and Guinea Bissau. However, the Mandingo people have "**very strong**" roots to Hebrew Ancestry.....more than the Tuareg Berber Moors in Libya, Mali, Niger and Burkina Faso.

The Paternal lineages of the **Black Moors** can be linked partly to the Y-DNA Haplogroup "**R**". This Haplogroup is also seen in India, Sri Lanka, the Americas (Native Americans), the Caribbean and Africa. This **"R" Haplogroup** can be found in the Tuareg people in Africa who live in Niger, Mali, Burkina Faso, Algeria, Libya, Morocco and Tunisia. But here is the kicker....the Tuareg people in Libya, Burkina Faso, Niger, and Mali have also been known to exhibit the **Y-DNA "E1b1a"**. The "E1b1a" Y-DNA Haplogroup has been proven without a shadow of a doubt to be linked to the Ancient Israelites of "Negroid" appearance in Africa. So how can there be some Tuareg Libyans walking around with two different Haplogroups (**i.e. E1b1a, R1b**)? This is because of the simple fact that there are some Israelites who mingled more with the **Sons of Ham** as opposed to mingling more with the **Sons of Shem**. The Black Moors were known to be a group of Muslims composed of Israelites, North Africans (Egyptians/Libyans) and Shemitic races (*i.e. Ishmaelites, Keturahites Joktanites, Elamites, Arphaxadites, Arameans, Assyrians, Edomites*). The Assyrians (Asshur), Arameans (Aram), Babylonians (Arphaxad) and the Ishmaelites were all documented to have traveled into the Caucasus mountain region (i.e. between Black Sea and Caspian Sea). In doing so they left their "**genetic marker**" which in most cases was "**R1a**", "**L**", "**R1b**", "**E1b1b**", "**E1b1a**" and "**J**". Over time when the male carriers of these Paternal Haplogroups left the area or were killed (*i.e. by war or invasion*) they often left "**mixed children**" who were fathered with the "**Japhetic women**" of the area (*i.e. Barbary Slave Trade*). So, as these black children were "*whited-out*" their offspring still retained the "downstream" sub-group genetic marker of "**R1a**" or "**R1b**". This can be seen as a "perfect example" in the people now living as the "majority" in **Spain** (R1b), **Portugal** (R1b), **Morocco** (R1b), and **Eastern Europe** (R1a). But who was the "ancestor" of the these two Haplogroups (R1a/R1b)? It was the darker mixed race "**Moors**" and the **Sons of Shem** living in the **Indus Valley Region** (*i.e. modern day Afghanistan, Pakistan, India, Sri Lanka*). If you don't believe it, consider this interesting fact about the "Nomadic-Pastoral" **Fulani Tribe** living in Africa today.

(**Above**) Peul-Fulani woman in Mali, West Africa.

The paternal lineages of the **Fula/Fulbe/Fulani** tend to vary depending on their geographic location in Africa. The Fulani are very numerous throughout Africa but are never the "**majority**" population in their country of residence. It is a known fact that the most common Y-DNA Haplogroup for African-Americans and Bantus Africans is "**E1b1a**". Well, 90% of Fulani individuals in **Burkina Faso** and **Guinea Bissau** carry this same "**E1b1a**" Haplogroup.

Fact: *Although most of the slave records show that Bantus "E1b1a" Africans were sold during the Slave Trades....a smaller number of Fulani people were also sold as slaves, mostly captured from Guinea Bissau and the Senegal-Gambia areas. These Fulani slaves were often carrying the "E1b1a" or "R1b" Y-DNA Haplogroup. Mexicans and many Latinos also show "African" ancestry from the Senegal-Gambia region. Latinos from the Caribbean and the Americas also frequently carry the Y-DNA "R1b". Coincidence?*

In regards to other Fulanis, the remainder of Fulanis tested in Senegal, Guinea-Bissau, Gambia and Mali were found to belong to the **E-M33 (E-M132)** Haplogroup. This Haplogroup has been linked to the **Dogon people** in Mali who claim ancestry from the Ancient Libyans/Egyptians. About half of the Fulani people in Northern Cameroon carry this E-M33 Haplogroup. But there are another small group of Fulani people that belong to the "R" Haplogroup.....in particular **R-M174 (i.e. "R1")** and **R1b1a2 (i.e. "R1b1c-V88")**. This group of Fulani "R" Haplogroup carriers are found amongst the Afro-asiatic speakers in **Niger, Chad and Sudan**. Generally, the term "**Afro-Asiatic**" comes from a people who are of "**Hamitic-Shemitic**" ancestry....most often from Northeast Africa.

(**Above**) Afro-Asiatic men from Northeast Africa. Most so called "Afro-Asiatic" races are seen in the Horn of Africa (*i.e. Ethiopia, Eritrea, Somalia, Djibouti*) where Hamtic races have mixed with Shemitic races. Many Bantus Africans in Kenya, Tanzania and even Ethiopia claim Yahusha HaMashiach (Jesus Christ) was "**Afro-Asiatic**" in ancestry having genetic contributions from **Ham & Shem**. Remember, Judah's first wife was a **Canaanitess**. King David had children from the wife of Uriah the Hittite (Canaanite). Her name was "**Bathsheba**" and from her and King David's loins would come the Messiah.

Note: The Buddhist Monks of Tibet/Nepal who claim to have records of "**Jesus**" whom they call "**Saint Issa**" say that their ancient records state that "Jesus" was **not a white man**, but was "**Afro-Asiatic**" in appearance.

But there is something else interesting about this "**R**" Haplogroup. The "**R1**" Haplogroup was found in some samples of the Fulani people in Cameroon, Niger and Sudan, but this "**R1**" Haplogroup is also found in select "**Native Amerindians**".

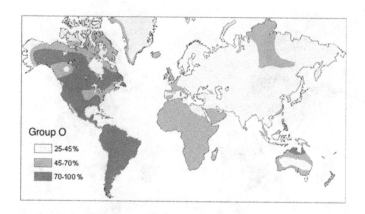

Group O
25-45%
45-70%
70-100%

Fact: The Blood Group "**O positive**" is found mostly in **African** populations, **Native Americans** and **Australian Aborigines**. In the **Bororo people** in Brazil everyone has the blood group "**O positive**". The second most common blood group found in Africans, Native Americans (*especially Blackfoot Indians*) and the Australian Aborigines population is "**A positive**". The Blood group "**B positive**" is rarely seen in Native American/Native Australian Aboriginal populations.....especially those "indigenous" Indians in South America. Native Americans and Australian Aborigines are found to share similar **mtDNA** and **Y-DNA** ancestry. What does this mean? It means their migration patterns in the past were the same....meaning they both left the **Levant/Middle East** and traveled "**East**" to get to where they are today. I will provide the proof later in the Book.

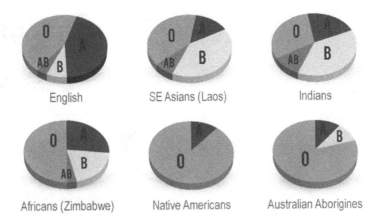

English   SE Asians (Laos)   Indians

Africans (Zimbabwe)   Native Americans   Australian Aborigines

(Above) **ABO Blood Groups** can tell "**migration**" patterns and ancestry. Many studies show that the Native Americans "**arrived**" to the New World from the "**East**" aka the "**Levant/Middle East**". Studies also show that the Australian Aborigine people were a people who left "**Out of Africa**" a very long time ago...eventually ending up in the isolated island of Australia. People living in Africa, the indigenous Amerindians and the Australian Aborigines all have mostly "**O+ blood**". O+ blood carriers show some resistance to **Syphilis, Small Pox and Malaria** which were in most cases brought to Africa-Australia-America by the European man. The Basque people in Spain/France are the only European-looking people in Western Europe who use a language **NOT** connected to the **Indo-European** language family, **Germanaic** language family or **Romance** language family. They have almost a 50-50 mix of the blood group "**O**" and "**A**" in their population. They also have the highest rates of "**Rh- blood**" which is not seen in animals or most humans. Like the skull remains of the ancient "**Neanderthal**" and "**Nephilim Giant**" they also have the highest rates of "**Red Hair**". Some say their language is somewhat "**Semitic**" or "**Proto-Semitic**".

(Left) **Seminole Indians** in Florida, 19th Century A.D. (**Right**) Blackfoot Indian "**Winnipeg Jack**" from the Canada, Wyoming, Idaho, Montana area. Notice their "**dark**" skin complexion. Many North American Indians carry the Blood group "**A**" or "**O**" as well as the Y-DNA Haplogroup "**Q**" or "**R**". The Black Moors and certain Afro-Asiatic speakers in Africa (Chad/Cameroon/Niger/Sudan) carry the "**R1**" Haplogroup in addition to these two Blood groups (A/O). This "**R1**" Haplogroup can also be seen in high frequencies in the **Algonquian Indians**, the **Ojibwe tribe**, the **Chippewa/Chipewyan tribe**, the **Seminole tribe**, the **Cherokee tribe**, the **Dogrib tribe** and the **Papago tribe**.

Fact: *There are some "**Afro-Asiatic/Chadic**" African Tribes in Cameroon that carry the Y-DNA "**R1**" Haplogroup and also speak a corrupted form of Sanskrit…..which is also happens to be seen in India as well. Geneticists have also found this "R1" Haplogroup in the Black Bedouin Arabs in Arabia. There are also traces of the "R1" Haplogroup in the Yoruba people as well, possibly because of the fact that many of the Black Jews/Black Moors were of Yoruba descent. Don't believe? Research the "**Bnai Ephraim**" Black Jews in **Yorubaland** who are called "**Emo Yo Quaim**" by their Yoruba neighbors.*

It is possible that the Black Moors were of "**Shem-Ham-Shem**" ancestry; meaning the people in North Africa prior to the rise of Islam and the **Black Arab Caliphates** (*i.e. Umayyad*) were of varying

58

Shemitic/Hamitic stock.....before mixing even more with the "invading" Shemitic sons of Shem (*i.e. Ishmael, Moab, Ammon, Arphaxad, Elam, Joktan, Asshur, Aram*) in the Middle East who were Muslims by the 7th Century A.D. Prior to the Islamic invasion of Shemitic people from the Levant, Mesopotamia and Arabia the main Y-DNA Haplogroups in Africa were Hamitic (**A/B**), Hamitic-Shemitic (**E-M33/E-M75**) or Shemitic-Hamitic (**E1b1a/E1b1b**). Once Islam spread throughout Asia Minor (Turkey, Kurdistan) and the Middle East a new group of people bringing "new" genetic material would mix into the people living in Africa. This would introduce the Y-DNA Haplogroup **R1a, R1b, E1b1b, J1, J2, G, and I.**

So now let's fast forward to the time when Christ walked the Earth about 2,000 years ago. With the Sons of Shem gone from the Alexander the Great's Greek conquest of Egypt, the Levant and Mesopotamia, what happened next? Confusion happened! What type of "confusion"?

"Strickly speaking, **it is incorrect to call an ancient Israelite a "Jew" or to call a contemporary Jew an "Israelite"** or a "Hebrew". The first Hebrews may not have been **Jews** at all,"

The Jewish Almanac (1980)

So what does the above statement mean? It means the "Jews" were a "different" people than the Semitic Hebrew Israelites of the Bible. Pay attention!

Bible Theologians know that during the time Christ walked the earth in Judea the 10 Northern Tribes were exiled and gone. In Joel 3:6 it says,

"The Children also of JUDAH and the CHILDREN OF JERUSALEM have ye sold unto the GRECIANS, that ye might remove them far from their border."

If the Children of Judah were sold unto the Grecians and the 10 Northern Tribes were exiled from Samaria (Northern Kingdom of

Israel) back in 700 B.C., who would be the "**new occupants**" of Israel (Judea-Samaria) leading up until the birth of Christ?

Only 50,000 exiled Israelites returned to Judea from Babylon around the 6th Century B.C. under Persian Rule. The Temple was rebuilt during this time and the sacrificial system was renewed. When the Book of Malachi and Ezra-Nehemiah ends, the year is around 430 B.C. (5th Century). With the Greek conquest of Egypt and Judea under Alexander the Great around 330 B.C. came the Greek Judaism "convert" family called the **Hasmoneans**.....from which we get the **Maccabees family** (150 B.C..). The Greek Maccabean Family converted to Judaism and assimilated into Judea. They became known as Jews and even converted all the **Edomites** into Judaism....from whence they were later known as "**Jews**" instead of Edomites (Idumeans). Thus, the Gentile "**foreign**" Edomites, Greeks, Romans, Scythians and even Barbarians (*i.e. Goths, or people not of Roman descent*) were the majority in Judea during 330 B.C. and up until the time of Christ (0 A.D.-5 A.D.). **These Gentiles during this time as residents of "Judea" were either Judaism-practicing "Jews" or simply pagans.** This is where Apostle Paul's comment, "there is neither **Greek** nor **Jew**, circumcised nor uncircumcised, **Barbarian, Scythian,** slave nor free, but Christ is in all things and in all people" comes into play. This has nothing to do with Gentiles becoming "**Israelites**". The Shemitic "**Edomite**" Jews living in Judea around the 1st Century A.D. rejected Christ, as did the small remnant of "real" Hebrew Israelites in the land. Thus, in Acts 13:46 it says "**Lo, we turn to the gentiles**".

One of the two best known New Testament editions from the 1700's A.D. are the **Rheims (Douai) Edition** and the **King James Authorized Edition**. By the 1700's the word "**Iew**" became "**Jew**" as the letter "**J**" was introduced to the English alphabet. However, when the 1582 A.D. Rheims (Douai) and the 1604 A.D. King James New Testament Bible was first printed the word "Jew" did not appear. So what happened? When we read the scripture, "Neither Jew nor Greek" do we really know what a "Jew" means? Most Christian readers do not know the origin of the word "Jew". The word "Jew" comes from the Aramaic-English translation of the word "**Yehudhai**" which refers to "**Judeans**". From Aramaic to Greek it became "**Ioudaios**" and from Greek to Latin it became "**Iudaeus**". **In the Modern Aramaic Bible John 19:19-22 reads:**

"Yeshua the Nazarene, The King of the **Judeans**".

In Latin this scripture reads:

"Iesvs Nazarenvs Rex Iudaeorvm (INRI)", meaning

"Jesus the Nazarene, The King of the **Judeans**".

In our King James English Bible's the "deception" comes in with the new saying:

"And Pilate wrote a title, and put it on the cross. And the writing was, Jesus of Nazareth, The King of the **Jews**".

What many Christian Pastors will not tell us.........is that at the time of Christ's walk on earth, in the days when he walked as "**God in the** flesh", few of the residents of Judea (*i.e. Judeans*) were actually Israelites from the Tribe of Judah or other tribes. We know there were a **"remnant"** group of Israelites in Judea because Christ didn't have to go into Africa to **"recruit"** his Israelite 12 disciples.

12 DISCIPLES

1. Peter
2. James
3. John
4. Andrew
5. Bartholomew or Nathanael
6. James, the Lesser or Younger
7. Judas
8. Jude or Thaddeus
9. Matthew or Levi
10. Philip
11. Simon the Zealot
12. Thomas

The 12 Disciples were descendants from the Southern Kingdom of Israel made up primarily of the Tribe of Judah, Benjamin and Levi. Paul was also an Israelite from the Tribe of Benjamin. John the Baptist was from the lineage of Aaron, the brother of Levi. Mary was the cousin of Elizabeth, the mother of John the Baptist. Many of the disciples including John the Baptist met Yahusha HaMashiach (Jesus Christ) in Galilee. After Christ was resurrected and the Comforter (Holy Spirit) was sent, the disciples in the upper room were described to be **"men of Galilee"**.

Acts 2:7-8 (Day of Pentecost) "And they were all amazed and marveled, saying one to another, **Behold, are not all these which speak Galilaeans?** And how hear we every man in our own tongue, wherein we were born?"

However, during the 1st Century A.D. many of the people of Judea were of mixed Japhetic (*Greco-Roman*), Assyrian-Babylonian and Edomite heritage. This "mixed race" of people developed a hybrid religion stemming from the Satanic teachings of Babylon. This would be called today "**Pharisaism**", "**Pharisee-ism**" or "**Jewish Babylonian Talmudism**".....the religion of the European "convert" Jews today in Israel. The religion today that is called "**Judaism**" was not the "religion" of the Ancient Israelites". The Ancient Israelites didn't have a religion, they had a "**way of life**" which they were to follow according to "**God's Covenant**" which was given to them from Moses. The Pharisees man-made religion was condemned by Christ the **Judahite Israelite** as Christ said in Matthew 15:1-9.

Matthew 15:1-9

Then came to Jesus scribes and Pharisees, which were of Jerusalem, saying, Why do thy disciples transgress the tradition of the elders? for they wash not their hands when they eat bread. **But he answered and said unto them, Why do ye also transgress the commandment of God by your tradition?** For God commanded, saying, Honour thy father and mother: and, He that curseth father or mother, let him die the death. But ye say, Whosoever shall say to his father or his mother, It is a gift, by whatsoever thou mightest be profited by me; And honour not his father or his mother, he shall be free. **Thus have ye made the commandment of God of none effect by your tradition.** Ye hypocrites, well did Esaias prophesy of you, saying, This people draweth nigh unto me with their mouth, and honoureth me with their lips; but their heart is far from me. **But in vain they do worship me, teaching for doctrines the commandments of men.**

This is why the Jewish Pharisees sought to kill Christ. They were not "**Real Israelites**" to begin with and they followed the "**commandments of men**" because they were not the "**Chosen Seed**".

King James Version John 7:1 "After these things Jesus walked in Galilee: for He would not walk in **Jewry**, because the **Jews** sought to kill him."

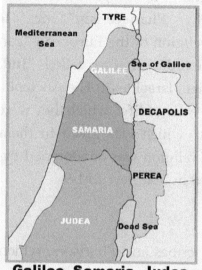

Galilee, Samaria, Judea

(**Above**) When Christ turned the "**water into wine**" he was in **Galilee** with his mother. Christ met 4 of his 12 disciples off the **Sea of Galilee**. Christ knew the Jewish Edomites, the Jewish Greeks and the Jewish Romans in the province of "**Judea**" were not Israelites and that they hated him to the point they wanted him dead. So, Christ "**avoided**" Judea in **John 7:1**. Many of the "**Real Israelites**" in the Bible appear in scriptures to be hanging around "Galilee", which is "**North**" of "**Judea**" and "**Samaria**".

See for yourself when Christ ran into "**Nathaniel**", one of the 12 Disciples!

John 1:43-49

"The day following Jesus (Yahusha) would go forth into **Galilee**, and findeth Philip, and saith unto him, Follow me. Now Philip was of Bethsaida, the city of Andrew and Peter. Philip findeth **Nathanael** (*i.e. Nathaniel*), and saith unto him, We have found **HIM** (Christ), of whom

Moses in the law, and the prophets, **DID WRITE**, Jesus (Yahusha) of Nazareth, the son of Joseph. And Nathanael said unto him, Can there be any good thing come out of Nazareth? Philip saith unto him, Come and see. Jesus (Yahusha) saw Nathanael coming to him, and saith of him, **BEHOLD AN ISRAELITE** indeed, in whom is no guile! Nathanael saith unto him, Whence knowest thou me? Jesus (Yahusha) answered and said unto him, Before that Philip called thee, when thou wast under the fig tree, I saw thee. Nathanael answered and saith unto him, Rabbi, thou are the **SON OF GOD**; thou are the **KING OF ISRAEL**.

Note: *Nathaniel was one of the disciples called by Christ. He was from Cana in **Galilee** (see John 21:2) and was brought to Christ by his Israelite friend, Philip, who also became one of Christ's disciples. Nathaniel was the one to first show his belief in Christ as the one who fulfilled the "**Old Testament Messianic Prophecy**" as the **Son of God** and **King of Israel**. In the Book of Matthew, Mark and Luke he is identified as "**Bartholomew**".*

So, in the Book of John it shows how Christ (*a full-blooded Israelite from the Tribe of Judah*) was not welcome in the land of Judea and Samaria by the "Gentile" Jews.

King James Version John 7:1 "After these things Jesus walked in Galilee: for He would not walk in **Jewry**, because the **Jews** sought to kill him."

In John 7:1 the English word "**Jewry**" is translated from the Greek word "**Ioudaia**" which refers to the "**Land of Judea**", **NOT** people from the **Tribe of Judah**. This is seen as **FACT** when other New Testament Bible versions like the New American Standard Bible read the verse in the following way:

"And after these things Jesus was walking in Galilee; for He was unwilling to walk in **JUDAEA**, because the **JEWS (NOT ISRAELITES)** were seeking to kill him."

Thus, Black Christ (*from the Tribe of Judah*) was **UNWILLING** to walk in Judea (**i.e. Jewry**) because the Jews (**i.e. Greek, Roman, Edomite, Assyrian Judeans**) were seeking to kill him. Therefore a "**Jew**" was a **JUDEAN RESIDENT** at the time and "**Jewry**" was basically synonymous with "**Judea**".

So when Paul talks about Jews, Greeks, Barbarians, and Scythians in the New Testament (Galatians, Colossians) he is referring to "**Gentiles**".....or the "**Wild Olive Branch**" described in Romans 11.

Even Simon, whose surname was "**Peter**" is seen in Acts 10, showing the difference between an **Israelite** and a **Jew-Gentile**. Peter receives a message from a Gentile Centurion named "**Cornelius**" about angelic vision/warning. To Peter, this was "**evidence**" that God was no "**respecter**" of persons (*i.e. Gentiles*) to those that feared him and worked in "righteousness". Cornelius stated in Acts 10 he was from the "**land of the Jews (*i.e. Judea*)**" when he brought along his Gentile friends and family to visit Peter. Peter replied to this "**Gentile**" company by saying in **Acts 10:28**:

"Ye know how that it is an unlawful thing for a man that is a Jew to keep company, or come unto one of **ANOTHER NATION**; but God hath shewed me that I should not call any man common or unclean."

Prior to this in **Acts 10:22**, Cornelius is described as being one who had good "dealings" with the "**Judeans**" or "**Jews**".

Acts 10:22 "They say to him: A certain man whose name is **Cornelius**, a centurion (**i.e. Roman army**) officer fearing God, and of whom all the people of the Jews bear good report, was told in vision, by a holy angel, to send and bring thee to his house, that he might hear discourse (*i.e. intelligent conversation*) from thee."

Peter saw Cornelius the Centurion, and his companions from Judea as "**Gentiles**" when they arrived to his place of stay. Why would Peter see them as "**unclean Gentiles**" if they were "authentic" Hebrew

Israelites from Judea? Even Christ told his Hebrew Israelite disciples to avoid the "Gentiles" in **Judea** and the "Samaritans" in **Samaria**. Why? Because he was first trying to **"locate"** the Real "Hebrew Israelites" that were scattered in small numbers in these areas!

So when people ask the question, "What Israelites were living in the land of Judea during the time of Christ" it was most likely it was the **Tribe of Benjamin** (Paul) and any remaining small number of Israelites (**Judah**) who may have managed to escape captivity/slavery.

Jesus confirmed this when he said in **Matthew 10:5** "These twelve Jesus sent forth, and commanded them, saying, Go not into the **WAY OF THE GENTILES**, and into **ANY CITY** of the **SAMARITANS ENTER YE NOT**:"

So according to the Bible, and history from the Apocrypha (Book of Maccabees) it is clear that there were not many Black or should I say "melaninated" Israelites (mixed with Hamitic Canaanite, Egyptian and Cushite blood) in Judea at the time. So how could Christ describe finding these "Melaninated" Israelites amongst a land of "White-skinned converted Gentile Jews"? He described them as "**LOST**". This is like Christ crossing the state border from Michigan into Ohio and saying to his 12 Black disciples, "**Find your Black Israelite brethren**" in Ohio. Ohio has a total of 11 million people with barely 1.5 million Black people.

WE IN OHIO NOW DISCIPLES.........

"GO NOT INTO THE WAY OF THE GENTILES (WHITES)....GO RATHER TO THE LOST SHEEP OF THE HOUSE OF ISRAEL (BLACKS)."

???

How are We gonna find the Israelites throughout all this land? It's impossible!

Despite this analogy, we have to understand that in the Bible in the Book of Genesis 1:26-27 it says "God created Man in **HIS IMAGE**." Some will say the word "**human**" comes from the two words "**Hue (Color) + Man**" or Man of Color. In the Latin language, from which many say the word "**Human**" is derived from comes from the root word "**Hum**" which means **Earth** and **Ground**. So the Latin word "**humanus**" or the English word "**human**" could refer to man being from the ground as in the saying "**ashes to ashes, dust to dust**" from the Biblical scripture in **Genesis 2:7**. Since we all know the dust that we wipe off our window counters, TV or front dash in our cars is black and the soil of the ground is brown-black we would assume that man was made initially with "**color**" or **melanin**. Why else would humans have "**Melanin**" and why is it produced in a tiny gland in our body which is associated with "**spirituality**"?

Fact: *The **pineal gland** secretes **melatonin** which activates the pituitary gland to release **MSH (Melanocyte stimulating hormone)** from which melanin is produced giving rise to the genetic code to have Black "melaninated" babies in the womb without any contact with the sun.*

68

Fact 2: *In the Sumerian "Epic of Gilgamesh", the Sumerians called the angry God that sent the great flood "Huwawa". They believed he dwelt in the mountains....the same place that Moses received the 2 stone tablets with the 10 commandments.* The Hebrew Israelites called God **Yahuah, Yah-hUWA** or **Yahawah** (depending on various research into the Tetragrammaton). The Chickasaw Native Indians call the Creator "**Chihoowah.** Some Black Australian Aborigines called the Creator of all things "**Indjuwanydj-UWA**". Yoruba Nigerians say "**Ol-UWA**" as one of the words for "**God Almighty**". The "Bini" people of Nigeria in the Edo State are the founders of the "Benin Empire". The word "**Osanob-UWA**" in the "Bini" language is a name for God. The word "**Osebr-UWA**" is one of the Igbo words for God, the maker of Heaven and Earth. Are you seeing the trend in the "**UWA**" or "**UAH**" here?

Note: In Igboland (*Southeast Nigeria*), the names for "**God**" change as you go from "**place to place**" or from "**village to village**". This is also the case for the different dialects spoken in different "Igbo" villages, because not all of the dialects in "Igboland" are the same. In certain areas in Igboland "**God**" can be referred to as Olisa, Ose, **Olisabuluwa**, Osa, Oselobua, and Osonobua. Most Igbo's however use the word "**Chukwu, Chineke or Chileke**" for the Creator.

So we see a common trend in the "Creator's" name in different nations and we see common trend in the "melaninated" skin of these people that ascribe to the "Creator's Ancient Name". What about the people

69

who were **Abraham's ancestors**? Those people living in the Land of Ur in "**Mesopotamia**" or the "**Land of the Sumerians**".

*The Sumerians/Akkadians wrote that the "**Black-headed**" peoples lived on the Earth in the **Land of Ur (Uruk) in Sumer (Iraq)**, which was the homeland of Terah…the father of Abraham before they left to the Land of Canaan/Syria. Why would Sumerian tablets describe Kings ruling over the "**Black-Headed Peoples**"? To many, the reference to "**color**" implies that the Sumerian so-called gods (Annunaki) or even the Sumerian-Akkadian Kings were possibly "White-skinned" people. Ironically, we see in the **Book of Enoch: Fragment of the Book of Noah** in Chapter 105-106 that Noah was an albino, resembling the "**Sons of God**/Fallen Angels" who dwelt on earth after their fall from heaven.*

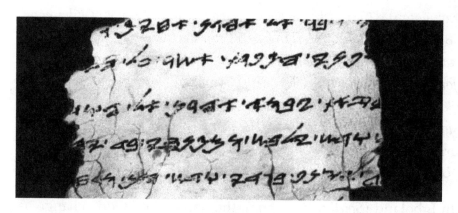

The Dead Sea Scrolls found in Israel pre-date back to 500-400 B.C.

Book of Enoch 105:1-4 (Fragment of Book of Noah) Dead Sea Scrolls in Paleo-Hebrew.

"After a time, my son Methuselah took a wife for his son Lamech. She became pregnant by him, and brought forth a child, **THE FLESH OF WHICH WAS WHITE AS SNOW**, and red as a rose; the hair of whose head was white like wool, and long; and whose eyes were beautiful. When he opened them, he illuminated the all the house, like the sun; the whole house abounded with light. And when he was taken from the hand of the midwife, opening also his mouth he spoke to the Lord of righteousness. Then **Lamech** his father was afraid of him; and flying away came to his own father **Methusaleh**, and said, I have begotten a son, **UNLIKE TO OTHER CHILDREN. HE IS NOT HUMAN; but RESEMBLING THE OFFSPRING OF THE ANGELS OF HEAVEN**, is a different nature from ours, being altogether unlike to us. His eyes are bright as the rays of the sun; his countenance glorious, and **HE LOOKS NOT AS IF HE BELONGED TO ME, BUT TO THE ANGELS.**"

So was this the first appearance of **"white-skinned"** humans? No! Noah would be the 10th generation from Adam. All of the females on the earth who had bore children to the Fallen Angels prior to Noah bore **"white-skinned"** people. Noah just happened to come out looking "white" like them.

(**Above**) Albino Children from **Mangalore, India**. The temperature on average in Mangalore and Bangalore, India is 90 Degrees Fahrenheit. **Note:** Some Albino Indians resemble "**Caucasians**".

Note: The genetic "mechanism" that makes Blacks/Africans "**Albino**" or have "**Vitiligo**" is different than the "mechanism" that makes Whites have "**white skin**". It is also different than the mechanism that was found to make the "Neanderthals (Homo Neanderthalensis)" skin white. The Neanderthal man's fossil remains always showed "**White**

71

skin". The Neanderthal Genome Project found that "**Caucasians**" on average, carried **2.5% or higher** of the "**Neanderthal gene**". It also found that the average "**African**" has **NO Neanderthal DNA**. What was even more interesting was that "**certain mutations**" on the Y-Chromosome carried by the Male Neanderthal kept him from easily interbreeding with Modern Human females (*i.e. Homo Sapiens*). In the April 7, 2016 issue of the *"American Journal of Human Genetics"*, Geneticist Fernando Mendez (*Stanford University*) discovered "**three mutations**" on the Neanderthal Y-Chromosome that triggered an "**immune response**" towards the fetus carried by a **Modern Homo Sapien woman**. This is similar to how the "**Hemolytic Disease of the Newborn**" aka "**Erythroblastosis fetalis**" occurs in RH-Negative women carrying "Rh + fetuses. *Note: Rh negative Blood type carriers are mostly "Caucasian-White" in appearance*. Scientists claim the majority of time when Neanderthal men mated with Homo Sapien women (*i.e. Japhetic*) from Europe, it resulted in "**miscarriage**". However, scientists found when Homo sapien "European" men mated with Neanderthal women, it often resulted in a "**normal birth**".

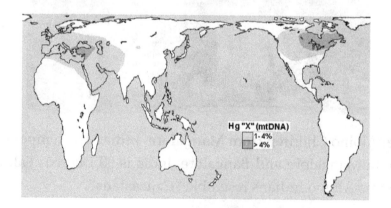

(**Above**). **Maternal "X" Chromosome** distribution in the world. Notice the heavily shaded areas in **Italy, Greece, Turkey, and Israel**. The lighter shaded area encompasses most of Europe, North African Arab territory the Arab territories of the Middle East (*Saudi Arabia, Yemen, Iraq, Syria, Iran, Jordan, Lebanon, Palestine*) and parts of Central Asia. The

Neanderthal mtDNA maternal "**X**" chromosome is still seen today in **Europeans, Ashkenazi Jews, Sephardic Jews, the Druze people in the Levant and Modern Arabs**. Of course, it is also found in select "**melaninated**" populations throughout the world that have had "**mixing**" with white races. Most of the Countries that have people carrying the maternal "X" chromosome are countries where the people are "**white-skinned**" or "**fair-skinned**". Is this a coincidence? Nope.....and I will explain why later in the book.

(**Above**) Albino girl from **Tanzania, East Africa**.....where many Bantus "**Israelite**" East Africans were taken as slaves by the "**Arabs**". In the Bantus villages, all throughout Africa, "**Albinism**" is common. It is also seen in people in India and Native Americans.

Remember, the Creator made "**man**" perfect in "**his image**". Before "**sin**" entered into man, man was a "**perfect**" creation. At the time of Noah's birth, Lamech wanted to know if Noah was of the "**fallen angels**" seed or was he "**Pure**"? Lamech's dilemma worried his father Methuselah so much that Methuselah consulted with his father Enoch for the answers. Enoch was with the Lord during this time. We find this account in the **Book of Enoch** it reads:

Book of Enoch: Fragment of the Book of Noah 105:12-15

"His father Lamech feared, and fled to me (Methuselah), believing not that the child belonged to him, but that he resembled the angels of heaven. And behold I am come to thee, that thou mightiest point out to me the truth. Then I, Enoch, answered and said, The Lord will effect a new thing upon the earth. This have I explained, and seen in a vision. **I have shown thee that in the generations of Jared my father, those who were from heaven disregarded the word of the Lord.** Behold they (fallen angels) committed crimes; laid aside their class (*i.e. working class…described in the Sumerian tablets*), and intermingled with women. With them also they transgressed; married with them, and begot children. A great destruction therefore shall come upon all the earth; a deluge (flood), a great destruction, shall take place in one year. **This child which is born to you shall survive on the earth and his THREE SONS shall be saved with him.** When all mankind who are on earth shall die, he shall be safe."

Note: *The Dead Sea Scrolls predate to 500-400 B.C., which is 1,000 years before the Arabic language existed and 1,000 years before the Quran would be written. The Book of Enoch: Fragments of the Book of Noah were hand written in Paleo Hebrew on Papyrus Paper. It was read by the Hebrew Israelites in B.C. times before any European ruler ever set foot in Israel, Africa or the Mesopotamia (Middle East). The 2,500-year-old scrolls written in a language (Paleo-Hebrew) that predates Aramaic and Arabic account that all of Noah's three sons survived the flood like our Bibles state, however the Quran says otherwise. In some instances, some Muslims say Noah had 4 sons and one died leaving 3 sons. This is false and therefore the Quran…including Muhammad is also false.*

Noble Quran, Sura 11:42-43 (Sahih International)

*"And it sailed with them through waves like mountains, and **Noah** called to his **son** who was apart from them, "O my son, come aboard with us and be not with the disbelievers." But he said, "I will take refuge on a mountain to protect me from the water." Noah said, "There is no protector today from the decree of Allah, except for whom he gives mercy." And the waves came between them, and he was among the DROWNED."*

(Book of Enoch cont.)

Book of Enoch 105:16-17 "And his posterity (*i.e. future generations*) shall beget on the earth giants, not spiritual, but carnal. Upon the earth shall a great punishment be inflicted, and it shall be washed from all corruption. **NOW THEREFORE INFORM THY SON LAMECH, THAT HE WHO IS BORN IS HIS CHILD IN TRUTH; AND HE SHALL CALL HIS NAME NOAH**, for he shall be to you a survivor.

Further down it also reads:

Book of Enoch 105:18-20 "And now, my son, go tell thy son Lamech, **THAT THE CHILD WHICH IS BORN IS HIS CHILD IN TRUTH; AND THAT THERE IS NO DECEPTION."** When Methusaleh heard the word of his father Enoch, who had shown him every secret thing, he returned with understanding, and called the name of that child **Noah;"**

So let's recap...the Book of Enoch says "**HE LOOKS NOT AS IF HE BELONGED TO ME, BUT TO THE ANGELS".**

In Genesis 6:2 it reads: "The sons of God saw that the daughters of men were beautiful; and they took wives for themselves, whomever they chose."

The word "**Sons of God**" in the Bible is referencing "**Fallen Angels, Watchers**" or in the Sumerians history...the "**Annunaki**". The pagan religious influence of the Fallen Angels or Annunaki on Earth in the land of Mesopotamia is the reason why Terah and his Shemitic ancestors fell victim to pagan worship or "**polytheism (i.e. worship of multiple pagan gods)**". Abraham however would be a different case as he pleased God by worshipping the "**Creator**" instead of "**creations**".

In the Sumerian picture above, Enki the great Anuna (Annunaki) god emerges from the water bringing forth rivers and fish. He holds a knife/sword in one hand. The person with wings is called **Ninmah**, a Annunaki goddess. She gives Enki a pine cone which some say represents "seeds' or "reproductive fruitfulness". The other Annunaki gods are around Enki and Ninmah wearing cone shaped hats, similar to what the "**Red Jews**" wore in medieval times.

So if God made the first man a person of color which many would call "**black**" today (*Greeks called "Ethiopian" anybody that was brown/dark-skinned*) then wouldn't the Son of God or "God incarnate" also come in the form of a "**Melaninated Man**"? Yes.....and this is what happened. God's Chosen People...the Israelites were a people of Color and Christ came through the Israelites. This is what is spoken about in regards to the **Dragon** (Satan), **the Woman** (Israelites/Israel) and the **Child** (Yahusha HaMashiach/aka Jesus Christ). So in the Book of Revelation Chapter 12, verse 17 it talks about the Children of Israel or the Remnant

76

of the Seed of the Woman (Israel). **It also talks about the Remnant of the Seed of the Woman (Israelites) who bear the testimony of Christ and who also keep the Commandments of God.** So right here we know that these are Israelites who exist in A.D. times after the time of Christ's crucifixion and resurrection up until today. How so? Well, in order for any Israelites to bear the Testimony of Christ they would have to have physically been with Christ during the days when he preached the Gospel or these Israelites and their seed/descendants would have to be "**witnessed to**" by the "**Natsarim**" which in those days were the followers of Yahusha HaMashiach of Nazareth (sect of Nazarenes). Today this word "**Natsarim**" has been replaced with the word "**Christians**". The Apostle Paul was the Ringleader of the Nazarenes (i.e. Christians). Therefore, the scripture in Revelation 12:17 is talking about the remnant of "physical Israelites" living today. **Note:** *The Kerala Christian Indians whose Church was started by St. Thomas (the disciple) call themselves "**Nasrani**" which is an Aramaic word for "Christian".*

Acts 24:5 "For we have found this man a pestilent fellow, and a mover of sedition among all the Jews throughout the world, and a ringleader of the sect of the **Nazarenes**."

(Above) Before the Israelites had a land and a Temple, they had to set up their encampments in the Wilderness with the Tribes encampments facing the **"Tabernacle"**. Aaron, Moses and the Tribe of Judah had their encampment directly facing the opening of the tent in which the Tabernacle housed the **Ark of the Covenant**.

So like the Moses and the Ancient Israelites that came out of Egypt in the Exodus…..in the Book of Revelations Chapter 12 the **"Modern"** Blood Israelites are going to be in a **"Wilderness"** type situation again….but these Israelites will bear the testimony of Christ. So what is this telling us.

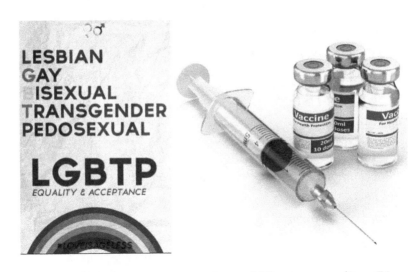

(**Left**) Now society is more accepting of Homosexuality, Bisexuality, Transgenderism, and Pedosexualism as being "**healthy**" or "**normal**". (**Right**) Vaccinations are coming more "**under fire**" in the topic of "Autism" as more GMO"s and Vaccines are being forced on children. *Note: See movie "Vaxxed"*. The rates of Autism have increased so much since the 1980's that statistics predict that in the next 10-20 years we can see Autistic rates as low as 1 out of 10 children born that will be diagnosed with Autism/Autism Spectrum Disorders. This is transitioning also into TV/Cartoons as Sesame Street recently added "Julia", a muppet girl with Autism. But it doesn't end there? Even Children's "Reading Time" in School is being infiltrated with "sexual immorality". In 2017, at the Brooklyn Public Library, Transgender "**Lil' Miss Hot Mess**" hosted a "**Drag Queen Story Hour**" which promoted "sexual fluidity" and "gender acceptance" in young "Pre-Tanner" stage kids. Don't be surprised if your child has already read the following books listed in school. Children do not have a choice now, they are being "**programed**" and "**conditioned**" into alternative sexual lifestyles, sometimes without their parents' knowledge.

- *Tango makes three*
- *Molly's family*
- *Red: A Crayon's Story*
- *Mommy, Mamma and Me*

- *Daddy, Papa and Me*
- *Heather has two mommies*
- *Jacob's New Dress*
- *The Different Dragon*
- *Daddy's Roommate*
- *My Princess Boy*
- *Morris Micklewhite and the Tangerine Dress*
- *I am Jazz*
- *Worm Loves Worm.*

With that being said, will our **"Wilderness"** be a **"Set Apart"** place from Society....a place where we do not have to conform to the "emerging" Antichrist Beast System"? A place where our kids don't have to be "programmed" by Westernized Education which promotes mass vaccination, homosexuality, bisexuality, "genderless bathrooms" and pedosexualism as being **"natural"**? A place where we who do not accept the **"Mark of the Beast"** can live and survive? A place not governed or ruled by the **"Satan's System"** which is slowly being formed today along with the Antichrist's Church (*i.e. the Interfaith movement, the Ecumenical movement and World Alliance of Religion for Peace*). Will this be in America, Africa, or the Caribbean? Remember to be "dependent" on someone.......they have to provide most of your basic needs. These things are Food, Water, Shelter, Education, Jobs, Clothing, Safety and Medical needs. If we can provide this on our own, we can definitely avoid being **"controlled"**. Regardless of what the "Wilderness" is and where it is at, we know the bible is telling us that Satan (the Dragon/Adversary) is going to come against the Israelites waging **"War"** during the Tribulation period. But the Bible says that "Israel" will be **"PROTECTED"** during this time. The Bible also says that the "Gentiles" or "Strangers" will flock to Israel in these days. However, it is important that we are "physically" and "spiritually" ready. It is also important that we have faith that God will protect us and fight for us as long as we are "obedient" …. but faith without works is dead. We must prepare ourselves and act now. Read for yourself.

2 Thessalonians 5:1-10

"But of the times and the seasons, brethren, ye have no need that I write unto you. **For yourselves know perfectly that the day of the Lord so cometh as a thief in the night.** For when they shall say, Peace and safety; then sudden destruction cometh upon them, as travail upon a woman with child; and they shall not escape. But ye, brethren, are not in darkness, that that day should overtake you as a thief. **Ye are all the children of light, and the children of the day: we are not of the night, nor of darkness. Therefore let us not sleep, as do others; but let us watch and be sober**. For they that sleep in the night; and they that be drunken are drunken in the night. But let us, who are of the day, be sober, putting on the breastplate of faith and love; and for an helmet, the hope of salvation. **For God hath not appointed us to wrath, but to obtain salvation by our Lord Yahusha HaMashiach (Jesus Christ), Who died for us, that, whether we wake (alive) or sleep (dead), we should live together with him.**

Revelation 12:12-17

"Therefore rejoice, ye heavens, and ye that dwell in them. Woe to the inhabiters of the earth and of the sea! for the devil is come down unto you, having great wrath, **because he knoweth that he hath but a short time.** And when the dragon saw that he was cast unto the earth, he persecuted the woman which brought forth the man child (Jesus/Yahusha). And to the woman (**Israel**) were given **two wings of a great eagle (*plane?*),** that she might **fly** into **THE WILDERNESS**, into her place, **where she is nourished for a time, and times, and half a time, from the face of the serpent.** And the serpent cast out of his mouth water as a flood after the woman, that he might cause her to be carried away of the flood. **And the earth helped the woman (Israel),** and the earth opened her mouth, and swallowed up the flood which the dragon cast out of his mouth. **And the dragon was wroth (angry) with the woman, and went to make war with the remnant of her seed, which keep the commandments of God, and have the testimony of Jesus Christ."**

So by reading these scriptures...especially the last scripture, it cannot be talking about Moses and the Israelites crossing the Red Sea. It cannot be talking about any Israelites prior to Christs arrival, death, burial or resurrection (*i.e. Book of Acts*). **This has to be the Israelites in the Future!** But what does the part "the woman-Israel" was **given two wings of a great eagle"** mean? Does it mean many Israelites in the future will be transported to Africa (*i.e. continent that Israel sits on*) by the "**airways**" in the future? Some might say this is a **plane**.....while some may say this could be "**Ezekiel's Wheels**" or "**Chariots of the angels**". Others will say this is a "**UFO-Unidentified Flying Object**". Will there be a "sign" in the future from the Most High that starts an "Exodus"? Many, Christians and Israelites today wonder about where the "wilderness" is, how will we know what it is, when we should go there and what the sign will be. Only the Creator/Father knows...therefore we must trust and have faith in him. We also must avoid the "**Great Delusion**" in the "**Last Days**". But we have another dilemma today that is also confusing a lot of Christians in regards to "**End Times Prophecy**". These are:

1. Who is "**Israel**" today according the Bible?
2. Who is "**Babylon**" today according to the Bible?
3. Who are the "**4 Great Beasts**" that arise out of the Sea/Earth"
4. Is the "**Rapture Doctrine**" True or False?
5. What or Who is the **First and Second Beast**?
6. What is the "**Mark, Name and Number of the Beast**"?

With that being said, let's start covering some of these questions.

CHAPTER 4

WHAT IS "BABYLON" AND SHOULD WE STAY "LOVING" BABYLON OR SHOULD WE "LEAVE" BABYLON?

Revelation 16:15-16 "Behold, I am coming like a thief. Blessed is the one who remains **AWAKE** and **CLOTHED**, so that he will not go naked and let his shame be exposes. And they assembled the kings in the place that in Hebrew is called **Armageddon**."

As we see more terror attacks, more laws passed by our government taking away our freedoms, more economic instability of countries, more "**police state/martial law**" situations in our cities, more hatred between racial groups/religious groups, more sexual immorality, more pagan worship, more godlessness, more natural weather disasters and more chaos....many Americans are believing the Biblical "**End of Days**" is near.

"The best way to take control over a people and control them utterly is to take a little of their freedom at a time, to erode rights by a thousand tiny and almost imperceptible reductions. In this way, the people will not see those rights and freedoms being removed until past the point at which these changes cannot be reversed."

The previous quote is a blueprint to a Marxist, Socialist, Communist and Totalitarian Government.....aka the "**New World Order**".

Fact: *The "Global Elite" and **Jewish Money Masters** know which Governments are needed to be overthrown in different countries and they know who needs to be "replaced" as the "New Leader" in these Governments (i.e. Freemason, Jewish or Muslim leaders). The Elite also predicted way back that "Terrorism" would be used widely in the Middle East, Europe and other parts of the world to bring about a New World Order. Terrorism....according to them is necessary in the Middle East, Europe and Africa. Only if the United States is not accepting of the "new system" would terrorism be needed on a* regular basis to instill *"fear"* into the people. By showing on **CNN, FOX, MSNBC** and other American TV news networks that the world was not *"safe"*, it would guarantee the Elite that the citizens of the world would be ready for a *"False Savior"*.....or someone who could solve all of the world's problems or keep everyone safe. This will be how the Antichrist System will emerge.....which is happening right now in the 21st century.

The Israelite Prophets of the Bible: **Isaiah, Ezekiel, Jeremiah, Daniel**, the **Apostle John** and **Yahusha HaMashiach** warned us of what is to come in the Biblical **"Last Days"**.

Many people believe because America is not listed in the Bible as one of the Four Beasts arising out of the **"Great Sea-Mediterranean Sea"** that nothing is going to happen the most influential country on Earth, whose **"Fiat Currency"** the **"Dollar"** rules over all other countries controlling loans with interest and free trade. But **"Trouble"** is coming to America, which many believe today is an extension of Ancient Rome (**Roman Empire**).

Back in the day Ancient Babylon in modern day Iraq was the center place for **"Wickedness"**, **"Black Magic/Occultism"** and **"Sexual Immorality"**. This is where the Gentile Jewish **"Babylonian Talmud"** had its beginnings from. This Satanic **"Racist"** religious book by the Jewish Pharisees was completed in around 500 B.C. The Pharisee-ism teachings that existed in the Messiah's time in the 1st century A.D. would become today's "Judaism". But as Christ said.....these teachings, along with the Book of the Jewish Pharisees would be a book of lies...inspired by the Devil himself.

John 8:44-45 "Ye are of your father the devil, and the lusts of your father ye will do. He was a murderer from the beginning, and abode not in the truth, **because there is no truth in him**. When he speaketh a lie, he speaketh of his own: for he is a liar, and the father of it."

Many believe Babylon (Iraq) is where the Kabbalah, the Jewish Mystic **"Tree of Life"**, and the satanic hexagram symbol used for the symbol of Israel had its beginnings. But it gets even deeper! The **Egyptian** deception, **Talmudic** Judaism deception and **Islamic** deception inspired by Satan is also connected to the early beginnings of the United States of America.

(**Left**) Moorish "**Moroccan**" flag. (**Right**) **Amexem** Moorish Empire Imperial Seal. In December 1, 1789, George Washington, the 1st President of the United states wrote a letter to Muslim Emperor of Morocco, "**Mohammed Ibn Abdullah**". Why would he do that?

George Washington was a Moslem 33 Degree Grandmaster "*Moslem Shriner*" Freemason, meaning he believed in the **Quran**, and "**Allah**" as his God. George Washington as the new "leader" of America had to get "acceptance" as being a "independent nation" from who else......Muslim Leaders...such as Mohammed Ibn Abdullah. Morocco was a Muslim sovereign country in Northwest Africa that George Washington wanted to stay allies with in international affairs and business. Mohammed acknowledged George Washington's new "America" as an independent nation in 1777. This is why George Washington and the founding Freemason "fathers" of America have on our dollar bill and flag the same symbol that the Moors used (**i.e. pyramid and 5-pointed star**). But the founding beliefs, symbols and principles of Freemasonry-Islam goes ultimately back to Ancient "pagan" Egypt....inspired by none else than Satan.

Fact: Even today one can see the single five-pointed Muslim "Moorish" star on a red flag in the White House in Washington, D.C. "off in the background" during many of the Presidents "**State of the Union**" addresses. You won't see the Nigerian flag, the Iranian flag, the Jamaican flag or the Haitian flag during the "State of the Union Addresses" or in the White House room where "**Executive Orders**" are signed into law by Presidents. Why is that? Is America still under the rulership of Islam or the Moors?

Here is an excerpt from George Washington's letter to the Emperor of the Moroccan Empire (Mohammed ibn Abdullah) who started his rule of Morocco in 1748....well before the U.S.A became a sovereign country.

Keep in mind, the word "**Dominion**" is defined as "supremacy, superiority, sovereignty, or control".

"The Encouragement which your Majesty has been please, generously, to give our (America) Commerce with your (Morocco) **Dominions**; the Punctuality with which you have caused the Treaty (Peace, Friendship, Amity) with us to be observed....make a deep Impression on the United States, and confirm their Respect for, and Attachment to your Imperial Majesty."

George Washington, December 1, 1789.

So why would George Washington, leader of America....need "**approval**" from the Islamic country of "Morocco" to be regarded as a recognized "**Nation**"? Out of all the nations in the world at the time why would he choose to write a letter to the Arab country of "Morocco"?

(Left) **Amexem Moorish Symbolism** with the Egyptian "**Winged Disc Symbol**". This symbol is also seen also the Assyrio-Babylonian-Persian religions....including the planet of the Annunaki (Fallen Angels).."**Nibiru**" aka "**the winged planet**". Also, in use with the Moors "**symbolism**" is the **5-pointed star** and the **Pyramid**. (**Right**) Back of our dollar bill. We all know that our U.S. flag has 50 stars on it, but why? We all know that on the back of our Dollar Bill we have a Pyramid with 13 rows, a capstone with the "**All Seeing Eye**"..... but why? America is not Egypt. Where did the Pyramid symbol on our dollar come from?

So what does all of this have to do with the Bible, Modern day "**Judaism**", "**Roman Catholic Church Freemasonry**", and "**Islam**" today? Well, the Caucasian Gentile Dutch, Spanish, and Portuguese Jews were the first founders of Freemason Lodges in America in the 1700's. George Washington acknowledged this to the King David Masonic Lodge in 1790, which was predominantly "**Jewish**". 33 degree Freemasons (Shriners) like Albert Pike and Manly P. Hall all knew that Freemasonry worshipped **Lucifer** or "**Allah**" as god...even sometimes using **Heru/Horus** as god as well. Some Jews know this as well.

"Most Jews do not like to admit it, but our god is **Lucifer**...so I wasn't lying...and we are his chosen people. Lucifer is very much alive."

Ashkenazi Jew Harold Wallace Rosenthal (1976)

87

(**Left**) Babies being sacrificed in the fire to the Babylonian pagan god "**Moloch**". (**Middle**) Baphomet "**goat head**", symbolizing Satan and the hexagram. (**Right**) Jewish pagan Satanic "Star" of the State of Israel. This "hexagram" symbol can be seen in the **Temple of Baal** in Baalbek, Lebanon and can be seen on the "**Altar of Ra**" in Egypt.

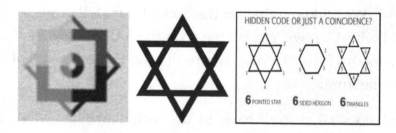

(**Left**) This is a rendition of what the "**Altar of Ra**" looks like from an "aerial" view in **Abu Ghurab (Gorab), Egypt**. The middle of it has a circle piece where many believe an "obelisk" stood...similar to the obelisk in Washington D.C. (*i.e. Washington Monument*), the obelisk in London City, and the obelisk in St. Peter's square (*Vatican, Rome*). There are perfectly smooth carved bowls and rocks that suggest "superior machinery/technology" done by beings not from Earth. (**Middle**) Jewish Symbol for Israel which is "pagan" and a symbol for Satan and his fallen angels. (**Right**) The number "**666**" is the Satanic number of the "**Beast**" in Revelations 13:18. This can be seen in the geometry of the "**Altar of Ra**" in Egypt and the Symbol of the European "convert" Gentile Jews.

The Sumerian pagan "**Fallen Angel**" named "**Enki**" in the "**Lost Tablets (Book) of Enki**" is described as being called "**Ra**" by the

Children of Khem/Cham in Africa. The Annunaki "fallen angels" in Egypt were called "**Neters**" or "**god-men**". As we know Ancient "**Khemet**" or "**Kemet**" is also synonymous with "**Ancient Egypt**". The "Altar of Ra" in Ghurab (Gorab) Egypt was believed to be where the Egyptians worshipped "Ra" and the "Fallen Angels" who came to earth. Egyptologists believe this area was also a landing pad and a "**Stargate**" from which the "**Fallen Angels**" would travel back & forth from different dimensions or the "**heavens**". According to Plato, Egypt was ruled by the same **hybrid "god-men"** people who built and ruled "**Ancient Atlantis**. In Ghurab, Egypt there are also three step pyramids near the alabaster/granite "Altar of Ra". Egyptologists believe the "Altar of Ra" alabaster platform helped the Egyptian sorcerers create a harmonic resonance using sound vibrations to "**communicate**" with the Fallen Angels. In ancient times these "Fallen Angels" have been called many things such as:

- Watchers
- Los Vigilantes
- Nephilim
- sons of God
- The Annunaki
- Igigi
- The Archons
- Tuatha De Danaan
- Giants
- Egregoroi
- Neturu/Neters/Ntr
- Urshu
- The Wing Makers
- The Central Race

Freemasonry and modern Judaism today are "offshoot" pagan religions based on "Egyptian" paganistic worship of Satan...with his henchmen the "Fallen Angels".

89

Like Ancient Egypt, the Talmud and Kabbalah (Cabala) open the door to mysticism, sorcery, homosexualism, pedophilia, bisexuality and incest. In the Kabbalah, man is regarded as naturally "bisexual" and that God desires us to have "sex" to please him. This is where "Phallic worship" comes in with many ancient civilizations such as Ancient Egypt and the Khazarian Empire prior to their religious conversion to "Satanic Pharisee-ism" called "Judaism". This philosophy and belief of course is to go against the "natural order" of the Creator.

Fact: Jewish Sigmund Freud, the founder of "Psychoanalysis" was a "Cabalist" who knew about the "sick" views of Judaism. In a speech to the Jewish B'nai Brith, Sigmund Freud emphasized his **"Jewishness"** and his loyalty to the **Masonic "Jewish" lodge** because of so-called "many dark emotional forces" that made "Judaism/Freemasonry" irresistible. Remember, before converting to Modern Judaism, Sammy Davis Jr was a member of the "Church of Satan" with founder Ashkenazi Jew Anton LaVey. Also, the Khazarian Empire (from where most European Jews descend from) was a kingdom that promoted "phallic" worship before they converted to the "Babylonian Talmudic" religion called Judaism. The acceptance of freemasonry by Jews who practice "Judaism" and by European Christians is easy if freemasonry is rooted in "Satanic/Fallen Angel" worship derived from Egypt/Sumeria. Thus blindly, many Jews today and Freemason Catholics don't really know what is going on.....including the fact that their religions combined with "Fremasonry" is purely a Satanic cult.

Thus.......our United States of American **"founding fathers"** like George Washington were rooted in **"Satanism"**, **"Freemasonry"**, **"Judaism"** and "Islam" doctrines. Now we should understand why the bible uses the word **"her"** when telling **"God's elect"** to "come up out of the nations". The symbol of the United States is a woman (**Statue of Liberty**). In Babylon, **"Ishtar"** was the mother goddess everyone worshipped.

Revelation 18:4 "And I heard another voice from heaven, saying, Come out of **HER**, my people, that ye be not partakers of her sins, and that ye receive not her plagues."

If you don't believe, read George Washington's address to the founding Jewish masonic lodges on the East Coast of America.

"Gentlemen, I receive the welcome which you give me to Rhode Island (*home of 'The Jewish Newport-World Center of Slave Commerce*) with pleasure, and I acknowledge my obligations for the flattering expressions of regard contained in your address with grateful sincerity. Being persuaded that a just application of the principles, on which the **masonic fraternity is founded (America), must be promotive of private virtue and public prosperity**, I shall always be happy to advance the interests of the Society, and to be considered by them a deserving Brother.

My best wishes, Gentlemen, are offered for your individual happiness.

George Washington, **"To the Masons of King David's Lodge, Newport, Rhode Island"**, August 18, 1790.

Fact: *Newport, Rhode Island's* **first** *Freemason lodge was* **"St. John's"**. *It was organized in the late 1740's of whom* **Moses Seixas and thirteen other Caucasian Jews were among its members**. *The town's* **second** *lodge,* **"King David"** *also consisted of mostly Jewish members.* **Moses Michael Hays** *started it in New York in 1769 and moved it to Newport, Rhode Island in 1780. Back then it was the major "eastern" slave port of America where Black Israelite slaves were received from West Africa. But this is not a surprise as the Jews were the major players in the formation and leadership of* **Scottish Rite Freemasonry** *in America. Jewish author Samuel Oppenheim confirms this in the 1910 American Jewish Historical Quarterly, Volume 19. One can also read Reverend Edward Peterson's book, "History of Rhode Island" in 1853, page 101 where it quotes,* **"In the spring of 1658, Mordecai Campannall, Moses Peckekoe (Pacheco), Levi, and others, in all fifteen families, arrived at Newport, Rhode Island from Holland."** *These were*

91

Dutch Jews.....Jews who were also involved in the slave trade of Black Israelites whose descendants are still in Madagascar and the Americas.

So, as you can see the "**Deception**" of the Roman "**Freemason**" Catholic Church, Islam and Judaism runs deep in America. 2,000 years ago, the Apostle Paul knew about the "**mysticism**" and "**fables**" the new breed of "**Gentile/Edomite Jews**" would bring to Judea (Israel).

Titus 1:14-16

"Not giving heed to **Jewish fables, and commandments of men, that turn from the truth** (*aka "Modern Talmudic Judaism*). Unto the pure all things are pure: but unto them that are defiled and unbelieving is nothing pure; but even their mind and conscience is defiled. **They profess that they know God; but in works they deny him, being abominable, and disobedient, and unto every good work reprobate.**"

So, who was the scribes that kept the "**Evil Doctrines of Men**" which would later become known as "**Phari-seeism**"....Modern Judaism today? The Biblical Kenites (Sons of Cain-Rechabites/Nethinims), the Greek "Judaism" converts called the "Hasmonean Maccabees", Roman "Judaism" converts (*i.e, Flavius Josephus*), the Syrian "Judaism" converts, the Scythian "Judaism" converts, the Barbarian "Judaism" converts, the Samaritan "Judaism" converts (from 700 B.C.) and the Edomite "Judaism" converts (**this I explain in Book 1**).

Today the "**New Babylon**" of the World according to many Christians is today's United States of America. The Catholic religion which most Americans follow is inspired by "**deceivers**". It is our job to "**separate**" the paganism inserted in Freemason-Judaism inspired "**Christian**" teaching to worship the **Most High** the proper way.

Symbol for **Ancient Babylon** – Lion, Ishtar Gate.   Babylon is also affiliated with "**Gold**". Today the United States, Rome-Italy, Germany and the Jews (IMF, World Bank) possess more Gold than any other country or group of countries.

Symbol of England/Britain is a Lion.

Fact:

- Babylon is hailed as the "**Queen among nations**" and "**The Lady of Kingdoms**" (Isaiah 47:5, 7). Doesn't this resemble Americans power over all the nations and the **Statue of Liberty (woman)**?

- Babylon was considered the youngest and only superpower in the world. (Jeremiah 47, Revelation 18). Isn't America a fairly new country who happens to be the major Economic and Military Power of the world?

- Babylon reigns over the kings of the earth. (Revelation 17:18). Doesn't the British/England Holy Roman Empire and its daughter "America" rule over all the other countries of the world, setting up U.S. Embassies (*and Jewish Embassies*) in just about every foreign country? Prior to America, didn't the British invade and colonize just about every country on the planet? *Research British India, British Australia, British Tasmania, British Virgin Islands, British Jamaica, British Antiqua/Barbados, British Hong Kong, British Africa, British North Africa, British America.*

- Babylon was the **"praise of the entire earth"** and an **"astonishment among the nations."** (Jeremiah 51:47). Don't we see today how foreigners seek to come to America….the **"Land of Opportunity"**?

- Ancient Babylon had one of the most powerful militaries just like America does today.

- Ancient Babylon's symbol is a **Lion**. The Symbol of England (British) aka the **"Father of America"** is also a Lion. **The British pound is no longer the world's reserve currency….it is now the U.S. Dollar Bill.**

Pagan Ishtar (Babylon) and Pagan (USA) Statue of Liberty

- Babylon is always referred to in the bible as "**Her**". The Most widely known stature in America is the "**Statue of Liberty**" aka a "**Her**". Back in Ancient Babylon this woman was known by "**Ishtar**" or the "**Whore of Babylon**'. The equivalent in Egypt would be **ISIS**. The equivalent to the Hebrews was "**Asheroth**" or the "**Queen of Heaven**".

- **Revelation 18:3** "For all the nations have drunk of the wine of the wrath of **HER FORNICATION**, and the kings of the earth have committed fornication with her, and the **merchants** of the earth are **WAXED RICH** through the abundance of her delicacies." Doesn't the world economy revolve around America and the Dollar Bill? Yes it does!

- The United States of America is the only major country that has legalized Gay Marriage, enforces Transgender Rights, promotes non-marriage and the pagan worship of satanic inspired religions. The Media in America promotes violence, fornication, cheating/adultery, lying, stealing and many other sins. Many countries blame the United States for influencing all the "**immoral**" and "**worldly**" practices going on in their country. The United States of America also makes other nations rich with the **North American Free Trade Agreement** (NAFTA) and its world "**reserve currency**" status.

- According to the Bible (Jeremiah 50:4-6, 8, 51:6, 45, Isaiah 48:20, Revelation 18:4) the biblical **"New Babylon"** would be home to a vast number of Israelites (i.e. Afro-Americans, Latinos, Native Americans). And like the Ancient Israelites, the "**Modern-day Israelites**" would eventually "**conform**" to the "system" of the land of their captivity. But according to the Bible, when destruction and the "**wrath**" of the Most High is set to destroy the nations, this would be the "**sign**" for the Israelites to leave "**the system**" of the **NATIONS**.....or perhaps leave these nations altogether. For example, the Old Testament (Jeremiah 51:45) and the New Testament (Revelation 18:4) tells the Israelites to "**leave the system of the Nations**".

Jeremiah 51:45 "**Come forth from her midst, My people**, And each of you save yourselves from the fierce anger of the LORD."

Revelation 18:4 "And I heard another voice from heaven, saying, **COME OUT OF HER MY PEOPLE**, that ye be not partakers of her sins, and that ye receive not of her plagues."

Again, isn't it ironic that the Bible uses the word "**Her**"? Most people know who "**Queen Elizabeth**" is, but do people know the name of the **King of England**? The answer is no. Most Roman Catholics have more pictures of **Mary** than of Jesus Christ (Yahusha Hamashiach). In America, the symbol used most often in movies is the **Female Statue of Liberty**.

(**Left**) The Statue of Freedom that sits on top of the Capitol building in Washington D.C. (**Right**) Statue of Liberty.

Some say the **Statue of Freedom** is the Greek goddess of Wisdom and daughter of Zeus, "**Athena**" who is named "**Mirerva**" in Roman culture. Others say she is "**Libertas**", the Roman goddess dating back to 400 B.C. "**Libertas**" was the goddess of freedom and liberty. Liberty and Freedom are used interchangeably in the US constitution. She was the goddess of freedom because she promoted the ideals of "**doing anything that feels good**" or "**do what thou wilt**"....the famous saying of Satanist, Freemason and Jesuit Aleister Crowley. Libertas was also called the matron goddess of prostitution and whoredom because she promoted sexual freedom.....just as the Bible describes "**Babylon**" as the "**Great Whore**". Back in Ancient times Babylon was known for "**occultism**" and for its abominable "**sexual immorality**". The same is going on in America...which is a branch of the **Holy Roman Empire**....the last nation to come up out the "**Great (Mediterranean) Sea**" in the Book of Daniel. It is interesting to note that 100 B.C., a Roman philosopher named **Marcus Tullius Cicero** stated that the

Libertas cult originated out of **Tanagra, Greece**. The statue of Libertas was first used by certain nobleman who would entertain friends with registered prostitutes called **"meretrixs"**. This later sprung into a cult....called the **"Libertas cult"** and this statue was used/displayed sacrilegiously during abominable sexual acts done by its members. The statue was used by Roman magistrates in charge of public buildings that were used for games....some which involved sex. Could America or the Holy Roman Empire just be an extension of the Kingdoms that will rise and fall before the arrival of the Antichrist? These are some strong similarities that line up perfectly with the biblical books of prophecy.

In Jeremiah 50:3 it states that the King of the North will attack **"Her"**. But what is "Her"? Does this mean that a **"European Country"** or perhaps **"Russia"** will attack or invade **"Her"**.......the **United States of America?** Is **"Her"** the **Roman Empire?** Or is it the "old" area of Babylon in **Iraq?** Will it be a **"covert"** operation where the **"enemy/adversary"** that the media shows is a threat to America-Europe, be **"itself"** or a **"creation"** from a European Country/Kingdom **(i.e. ISIS)?** Would this also be considered an attack from the **King of the North?** Will If this is the case, we need to be looking at these possibilities.

Jeremiah 50:3-4 "For out of the **NORTH** there cometh up a nation against **HER**, which shall **make her land desolate**, and none shall dwell therein: they shall remove, they shall depart, both man and beast. **In those days**, and in that time, saith the Lord, **the Children of Israel shall come, they and the Children of Judah together, going and weeping: they shall go, and seek the Lord their God."**

Many biblical scholars believe Jeremiah 50 and even Isaiah 13 is partly talking about **"End Times Prophecy"**. Both reference **"Babylon"** being destroyed **completely** with the Children of Israel and Judah coming **"up out of her"**. So what did "Babylon" represent back then and today? Even more, what or where is the "**Nations of the North**".....aka the Nations "**North**" of the Biblical Babylon?

So, what or where is "**North**" of America?

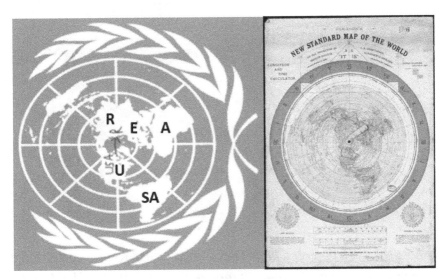

(**Left**) United Nations logo and as some will say according to the "**Flat Earth Map**".....except it's flipped up on its left side. "**U**" is U.S.A, "**SA**" is South America, "**E**" is Europe, "**A**" is Africa and "**R**" as Russia. (**Right**) Flat Earth maps from people like **Alexander Gleason** and **Wilbur Glenn Voliva** show Europe, Russia and Asia to be North of the Americas.

*We all know that the North Pole is "**North**", but according to the United Nations symbol if one were to fly north crossing the North Pole you would fly into European countries or Russia! Does this mean that Russia, Europe/Asia Minor or Asia (China) will "stage" an attack against the U.S.A? Constantinople in Turkey (Asia Minor) was the capital of the Roman/Byzantine Empire in 300 A.D.....which later became the capital of the Turkish "Ottoman Islamic Empire". Most of the Muslims we see today involved in "Radical Islam" are descendants of "Ottoman Turks". As we all know, the U.SA. has not been the greatest of friends with Russia and has imposed "sanctions" on Russia. The U.S.A. is also not liked by the Arab world. Also, the **BRICS countries** (Brazil, Russia, India, China, South Africa) and the **Chinese Asian Infrastructure Investment Bank** (AII Bank)* *have been taking the proper measures to eventually "do away" with the dollar as the United States Total Debt (20 Trillion) is headed for a huge "economic plunge (with the Stock Market plunging as well).*

(*Above*) *In the Book of Jeremiah, Medes-Persia under King Cyprus and King Darius defeated the Babylonians living in the land of the Chaldees (Iraq). Medes was North-east of Babylon.* **Medes-Persia today is the country of Iran.** *Will Iran attack "America-Israel" if Modern Day Babylon is "America-Europe" and the Gentile "Synagogue of Satan" is living in Israel-Europe-America? This is something we must consider.* **Iran** *has always been against Israel and America. Israel, Europe and America **ALL** have a "symbiotic parasite/host" relationship with the common denominator being the "Jewish Rothschild Family".*

*So is the "**Northern Countries**" the "**Great Enemy**" of the "**New Babylon?** Or is it another major player like **Iran**? If America fulfills the Biblical New age "**Babylon**" then according to the Bible....Russia and possibly the other descendants of Gog/Magog (i.e. China, Ottoman Turkish descendants all throughout the Middle East, ISIS group) will be its demise.*

Keep this in mind: In March 2014, the White House/USA under the Obama Administration imposed economic sanctions (Russian banking, energy-oil) on Russia after Russian troops seized Crimea from Ukraine. Russia's Oil Exports to other countries makes up almost 50% of Russia's economy. Once the U.S.A. shut Russia out of the "**Oil Export game**" other nations started mass producing oil and selling it which drove the price of oil at the time from $100 a barrel to close to $40 a barrel. This caused Russia's economy to take a slump.

Fact: *2-3 years ago, before ISIS was a household name I was in a Coney Island waiting on a salad I had ordered to go. I was on the phone waiting when I noticed a middle-aged Caucasian man staring at me. As I continued to talk on the phone he kept staring at me. I was the only African-American in the Coney Island so at first thought it was because I was the only black person in a white neighborhood Coney Island restaurant. After a while, I got fed up with this man staring at me and I went up to him and asked him, "Can I help you?" He responded, "I need to talk to you after you get off the phone." I said, "Yeah, ok" and kept talking for another 10-15 minutes. The Caucasian man waited patiently, despite already receiving his carry out order. After I got off the phone, I walked over to the man and asked what did he need to speak to me about. The first thing he said to me was, "What is the name of God?" I laughed and said, "It depends on who your God is....it could be Allah, Jahbulon, Trimurti, Brahma, Vishnu, Shiva, Baal, Dagon, Satan, Marduk, Osiris, Isis, Horus, Jesus, Jehovah, Yahweh and so on." He looked at me and said, "YAHUAH"....YAHUAH" is God's name". I told him I had knew about that pronunciation of the name of God. So we both sat down and this man began to tell me how he had died in an accident (i.e. Spinal Shock) while riding a bull or a horse. Immediately I assumed he fell off and had a fatal injury which he confirmed as a head/spinal injury that sent him into spinal shock and cardiac arrest. The Caucasian man said he had an "**outer-body**" experience in which he saw himself being treated by the doctors. He said he saw a bright light and talked to God who told him that it wasn't time for him to leave the "**Physical World**" and that he was going to return with a message to come about the future. The man stated 2 years later while lying in bed at night he was visited by two angels who showed him visions of the future (i.e. **like Cornelius the Centurion in Acts 10**). He talked about Obama, more natural weather disasters, an economic collapse, Muslim terrorists invading America via the water/ocean-beaches (i.e. Pacific Ocean/Gulf of Mexico), **and a China-Russia invasion of the USA via the Canada-Mexico-US border**. After this he had more to tell me but most of what he told me I already knew. The*

101

man gave me his phone number and told me to research some material he wrote down on a piece of paper. Then he said, "Don't let anyone make you feel like you are crazy for what you know....God has revealed to you everything you know for a reason". I called his phone before we both parted ways to confirm I had entered the right number as a new entry in my phone book and his phone rang. He said, "Ok, I got your number now." The next 1-2 days when I called his phone number back an "error" alert came on saying his phone number didn't exist.

Many people believe the "**King of the South**" is the President of America but only time will tell. The Bible contains a message for the Israelites living in the Americas and scattered abroad. When "**The Nations**" start to "**wear out**" the Saints (*i.e. True Blood Israelites and Gentile followers of Yahusha*) such as what is seen in the news with hatred towards Negroes, Latinos, Native Americans and other nations....this is a sign that it is only going to get worse. We must at this time put our faith in God and hold fast. We must **UNIFY** with each other and God to endure till the end.

John 16:33 "I have told you these things, so that in me you may have peace. **In this world you will have trouble.** But take heart! **I have overcome the world.**"

Fact: In **Daniel 7:25** it reads "And he shall speak great words against the Most High, and shall wear out the **SAINTS** of the **Most High**....". The Hebrew Strong's word for "**Saints**" is Hebrew Strong's word #6922 "**Qaddish**" which means "**Holy Ones**" or "**Saints**". The Book of Daniel is in the Old Testament and was found in the Dead Sea Scrolls written in Paleo-Hebrew and Aramaic. It was not written in Greek. Christians did not exist during the time Daniel wrote his book. So who are the "**Holy Ones**" in the Old Testament?

Exodus 19:6 "And ye (**Israelites**) shall be unto me (**Most High**) a kingdom of priests, and a **HOLY NATION**. These are the words which thou shalt speak unto the **Children of Israel**.

Deuteronomy 7:6 "For thou art an **HOLY PEOPLE** unto the LORD thy God (**Yahuah thy Elohim**): The LORD thy God hath chosen thee to be a special people unto himself, above all people that are upon the face of the earth."

Did Daniel warn us of what "**Danger**" is to come for the Real "**Nation of Israel**" scattered abroad?

THE "TRICK OR TREAT GAME"

Many Pastors and Church members will often say, "**It doesn't matter who the Real Jews are**". This is a "**Trick**" as understanding who are the "**Real Jews**" today will help you understand "**future**" Bible Prophecy and why things are happening in today's time. God is giving his "**Lost Sheep**" a **FINAL CALL** to prepare themselves for him.

Matthew 24:1-4

"And Jesus went out, and departed from the temple: and his disciples came to him for to shew him the buildings of the temple. And Jesus said unto them, See ye not all these things? verily I say unto you, There shall not be left here one stone upon another, that shall not be thrown down. And as he sat upon the mount of Olives, the disciples came unto him privately, saying, Tell us, when shall these things be? and what shall be the sign of thy coming, and of the end of the world? And Jesus answered and said unto them, **TAKE HEED THAT NO MAN DECEIVE YOU.**

Today, many Blacks in America and across the world are worshipping false gods, indulging in false doctrines or beliefs. Islam, the Nation of Islam, Buddhism, Kemetic (Egyptian) African Spirituality, Moorish Science (Islam), 5 percenters (Islam), Scientology, Talmudic Judaism, Ecumenical religions, Sumerian (Annunaki) Religion, Gnostism, Non-Messianic/Non-New Testament believers and even Atheism.

"Don't put all your eggs in one basket."

Many are being **deceived** in these days just as the Bible foretold. Now is not the time to be undecided on who your God is and how to obtain Salvation. Evenmore, now is not the time to put all our "**eggs**" into one basket. In the Christian Church, this "basket" has been the "**Rapture Doctrine**" amongst other things. The "**Rapture Doctrine**" teaches Christians to not worry or prepare for anything listed in the Book of Revelation......because the "**Saints**" will "disappear" into thin air to be with Christ. But where will the Saints go? Will the Saints be in Heaven on Earth or Heaven outside the Earth? Will the "Saints" be in a sort of "limbo" place while the 7-year Tribulation period continues on the Earth? These are all questions that many Pastors cannot fully answer. Even the Apostle Paul fails to give us all the details......but the Book of Revelation does, in which we will find the words of our Savior himself telling us the Truth (*i.e. in a "Red Letter" Bible*) about the "**End of Days**". Should we believe in what our Lord and Saviour tells us or should we believe what Paul tells us. After all, the Apostle Paul was not a Prophet, or one of the 12 Disciples. On the other hand.......John, the servant of God, received prophecy about the "End of Days" from an angel of God.

Revelation 1:1

"The Revelation of Yahusha HaMashiach (Jesus Christ), which God gave unto him, to shew unto his servants things which must shortly come to pass; **and he sent and signified it by his angel unto his servant John:**"

CHAPTER 5

THE RAPTURE THEORY: PRE-TRIBULATION, MID-TRIBULATION AND POST-TRIBULATION...WHICH ONE IS CORRECT?

Many Christians and Pastors overlook one particular verse in the Bible which describes who the Biblical Israelites are today and **who** will be in Israel during the Second Coming of Christ. Why have many overlooked this scripture? I have asked this question many times to many Pastors including pastor's children with no one able to break down the meaning of the scripture. Read it for yourself:

Luke 21:24-27 "**And they shall fall by the edge of the sword, and shall be led away captive into all nations: and Jerusalem (ISRAEL) shall be trodden down (subdued) of the Gentiles, until the times of the Gentiles be fulfilled (come to an end). And there shall be signs in the sun, and in the moon, and in the stars; and upon the earth distress of nations, with perplexity; the sea and the waves roaring; Men's hearts failing them with fear, and for looking after those things which are coming on the earth: for the power of heaven shall be shaken.** *And then shall they see the Son of man coming in a cloud with power and great glory*"......hmm.

(**Left**) Menorah "**Jewish**" symbols with words written in Greek in Judea during the times of Christ, Pontius Pilate and Edomite Herod the Great. Pontius Pilate was the 5th "regional governor" of the Roman province of Judea from 26 A.D. to 36 A.D. He served under the Roman Emperor Tiberius, where he is known for the trial and crucifixion of Christ the Messiah. (**Right**) Starting with the rise of Islam and the emergence of the Ottoman "**Turkmen**" Arabs, descendants of **Togarmah**, son of **Gomer**, Son of **Japheth**… the white-skinned Arabs (*i.e. modern day Palestinians, Jordanians, Lebanese, Druze people*) would possess the land of Israel until the arrival of the "**Khazarian**" Turkish-Slavic-Germanaic Ashkenazi **Gentile Jews** from Europe to Palestine on boats in 1948.

After the Greek invasion of Judea under Alexander the Great in 330 B.C., the infusion of a "new" Judean population of Greek converts to "Judaism" called "Maccabeans", would rule Judea with the Edomites until the destruction of the Second Temple in Jerusalem by the Romans. During the "Crusades", and after the invasion of "**Turkish/Kurdish**" Japhetite Arabs in Judea/Samaria….the **Gentiles** would secure Israel until the last days. Although you had "Greeks" converted to Judaism known as "**Jews**" in the Roman Province of "**Judea**" during the 1st Century A.D……you can see that the language used in Judea was **Greek**, and not **Paleo-Hebrew/Hebrew-Aramaic**. The "original" 12 Tribes of Israel spoke **Hebrew** and **NOT** Greek or Arabic.

Luke 21:24

²⁴ They will fall by the edge of the sword and be led captive among all nations, and Jerusalem will be trampled underfoot by the Gentiles, until the times of the Gentiles are fulfilled.

(**Above**) Gentile European "**Japhetic**" Jews at the Western Wailing Wall in Jerusalem, Israel (1800's).

- In Luke 21:24, Yahusha (Jesus) is saying when he returns for the **Second coming** will the time of the Gentiles in Jerusalem, Israel be over (**i.e. end**).

- The word "**Fulfilled**" in the Merriam-Webster dictionary is defined as **a**: to put into effect (execute): **b** : to meet the requirements of (a business order): **c** : **TO BRING TO AN END**: **d** : to measure up to.

- Close evaluation of this scripture should tell us that the Gentiles **are supposed** to be in Israel/Jerusalem until the Second Coming of Christ. Were the words of Yahusha (Jesus) correct in regards to today? You be the judge. Who is in Ancient Israel now? The Palestinians, Jordanians, Lebanese people, Mizrahi Jews, the Druze people, the so-called Samaritans and the Gentile European Ashkenazi Jews/Sephardic Jews?

There are other pressing questions many Churches don't break down. When reading the Bible...especially the New Testament we have to ask ourselves these questions in regards to the "**Biblical End of Days**":

1. *IS CHRIST COMING BACK TWICE FOR THE SAINTS AND WHO ARE THE SAINTS?*

2. *WHAT ABOUT THE "PRE-TRIBULATION" THEORY THAT NO FOLLOWERS OF THE MESSIAH WILL EXPERIENCE OR LIVE THROUGH THE "GREAT TRIBULATION"?*

3. *DOES MATTHEW 23-24 AND 2 THESSALONIANS 2 SUPPORT THE BOOK OF REVELATION?*

Why is the Black Church and Christians worldwide torn between the **Pre-Tribulation, Mid-Tribulation and Post-Tribulation** "Rapture Theory"?

(**Above**) The "**Tribulation Period**" according to the bible will last **7 years.** In the middle of the 7 years (3.5 years) the Antichrist will stop the sacrifices in the Third Temple (*built by the Gentile Japhetic Jews*). The Post-tribulation rapture is thought by some......that the church will be raptured **after** the "**Great Tribulation**", but before the **FINAL** outpouring of God's wrath. It teaches that we will in fact experience the **seven seals, seven trumpets, and the seven vials.**

Fact: The United Nations and the Roman Catholic Church under Pope Francis has set up a movement called "**Global Citizen**". The Global Citizen initiative is designed to end "**extreme poverty**" by the year 2030…..and for the people of the earth to "**share**" the world's resources. How will they do this unless there is a "**governing**" body that owns and controls all of the worlds resources? First, mostly everyone on the planet has to have access to a "**digital ID**", which essentially has to be linked to an "**internet-based**" **digital-electronic system.** This will be the start of a "Cashless" Society where money is controlled by the "Money Masters". (**Above**) Celebrities will be used to market "Global Citizen". Here, Rapper Jay-Z performs onstage at the 2014 Global Citizen Festival in Central Park, NY on 9/27/2014.

Note: Keep this in mind…..an internet-based digital electronic system needs "**electricity**" in order to work.

So, this "**electricity**" is what America and the world relies on heavily today. In addition, the "**Interfaith and the Ecumenical**" religious movement pushed by the Catholic Church is designed to establish a "**One World Religion**". Interfaith is defined as other religions cooperating and uniting with one another. The Ecumenical movement promotes an "All-embracing Universal" religion. This is the **Antichrist-Beast System** and surveillance of the "**Global Citizens**" of the world will be done with the "**All-Seeing Eye**" *of Satan….or "**Technocracy**". Global Citizen has festivals and concerts every year with our favorite A-list actors, music artists (Jay-Z, Rhianna, Kendrick Lamar) and politicians to get the world into accepting this "Antichrist" movement in disguise.*

THE RAPTURE DOCTRINE

It is a known fact that the "**Rapture**" doctrine did not exist before **John Nelson Darby** invented it in 1830 A.D. Before it "popped into his head" no one had ever heard of a secret rapture doctrine. It is also a known fact that the word "**Rapture**" does not appear nowhere in our bibles. So what is the right doctrine to follow? First, we will need to look at what the Book of Daniel states in comparison to the Book of Revelation because both books give clues what to expect right up the "**Tribulation**" period.

After coming up out of Egyptian Captivity, the Hebrew Israelites fell into captivity by the **Assyrians** and later the **Babylonians**. This was followed by the **Persian, Greek and Roman Captivity** of the Hebrew Israelites. America is a "**New**" extension of the British "**Roman Empire**". It is not a coincidence that the Negro and Native American were **oppressed together** by the European Countries who are still subservient to the Roman Empire.

Jeremiah 50:33 "Thus saith the LORD of hosts; **The children of Israel and the children of Judah were oppressed together**: and all that took them captives held them fast; they refused to let them go."

DANIEL 7:3-8 PROPHECY

"And **FOUR GREAT BEASTS** came up from the sea, diverse one from another.

[4] The first was like a <u>lion</u> (**BABYLON**), and had eagle's wings: I beheld till the wings thereof were plucked, and it was lifted up from the earth, and made stand upon the feet as a man, and a man's heart was given to it.

[5] And behold another beast, a second, like to a <u>bear</u> (**PERSIA**), and it raised up itself on one side, and it had three ribs in the mouth of it between the teeth of it: and they said thus unto it, Arise, devour much flesh.

[6] After this I beheld, and lo another, like a <u>leopard</u> (**GREECE**), which had upon the back of it four wings of a fowl; the beast had also four heads; and dominion was given to it.

[7] After this I saw in the night visions, and behold a <u>fourth beast</u> (**ROME**), dreadful and terrible, and strong exceedingly; and it had great iron teeth: it devoured and brake in pieces, and stamped the residue with the feet of it: **and it was diverse from all the beasts that were before it; and it had ten horns.**

[8] I considered the horns, and, behold, there came up among them another **little horn**, before whom there were three of the first horns

plucked up by the roots: and, behold, in this horn were eyes like the eyes of man, and a mouth speaking great things.

Note: *Below is the scripture many will use to debunk the "Pre-Tribulation" rapture doctrine.*

Revelations 13:2-8 "And the beast which I saw was like unto a leopard, and his feet were as the feet of a bear, and his mouth as the mouth of a lion: and the **dragon (Satan)** gave him his power, and his seat, and great authority. And I saw one of his heads as it were wounded to death; and his deadly wound was healed: and all the world wondered after the beast. And they worshipped the dragon which gave power unto the beast: and they worshipped the beast, saying, Who is like unto the beast? who is able to make war with him. And there was given unto him a mouth speaking great things and blasphemies; and power was given unto him to continue forty and two months. And he opened his mouth in blasphemy against God, to blaspheme his name, and his tabernacle, and them that dwell in heaven. **And it was given unto him to make war with the saints**, and to overcome them: and power was given him over all kindreds, and tongues, and nations. And all that dwell upon the earth shall worship him, **whose names are not written in the book of life of the Lamb slain from the foundation of the world.**"

So here the question many Christians cannot answer in regards to this scripture, "**How can the beast through the dragon (Satan) make war with the saints if the saints are supposed to be already raptured up?**" The start of the Tribulation occurs in **Revelation Chapter 6** when the 7 seals are opened. The scripture above is from **Revelation Chapter 13**.

Well, let's examine **AGAIN** who are the "**Saints**" as described in the Hebrew Old Testament and even the Book of Daniel (*which is also in the Old Testament*). Remember the use of the word "**Saints**" existed before the "**church**" existed. So who were these "Saints"?

Again, in the Hebrews Strong's concordance, the word "**Saints**" is "**#6922-qaddish**" meaning "**Holy Ones**" from the root word "**#6918-qadosh**" or "**#6944-qodesh**" which means "**Holy, sacred, set apart.**" Remember if we think about the Bible which group of people are considered a "**Holy**" and "**Set Apart**" people unto God? *THE ISRAELITES!*

Exodus 19:6 "And ye shall be unto me a kingdom of priests, and an *HOLY NATION.*"

Leviticus 20:26 "You are to be *HOLY* to me because I, the Lord, am holy, and I have *SET YOU APART* from the nations to be my own."

Here is the proof for Black Muslims as well:

Noble Quran, Sura 29:27 "And we gave to him **ISAAC** and **JACOB** and placed in **HIS DESCENDANTS** (progeny) **prophethood** and **scripture**. And We gave him his reward in this world, and indeed, he is in the Hereafter among the **righteous**."

Being "**Holy**" and "**Righteous**" comes hand in hand. Look at what the Bible says.

Isaiah 5:16 "But the Lord of hosts will be exalted in judgement, And the Holy God will show himself **Holy in Righteousness**."

So moving forward in **Revelation 13:2-8** who is the **BEAST**? Is it a Nation/Empire, an actual man or is it an actual beast with fur and claws? Can a Nation or a Man make war with a group of people...in this case **Israelites (Physical/Spiritual Israel)**? This seems like a huge feat for one man to do unless this man has **GLOBAL POWER**. Or could it very well be a **Nation** or an **Empire**? Time will tell but nevertheless we need to try at best to understand biblical prophecy so that we won't be caught off-guard when we see "**signs**" happening in the world.

So before we investigate more into the "**Four Beasts**" and the "**Antichrist**" let's break down the "**Four Beliefs**" that most Christians have in regards to the Tribulation times.

Those four beliefs are:

1. The **Pre-tribulation** belief which holds that the Rapture will take place **before** the tribulation, that the Church will be taken away to be with the Lord (*i.e. in a "special place"*) for seven years, and will return with him when the tribulation is over. This is not supported in the Book of Revelation. As a matter of fact, the Bible says "**no man**" will be in heaven while the tribulation is taking place and when the "**Great Tribulation**" is over, it is only then that Christ will dwell with the Saints and be their God. So where people will go during the "Rapture" is not clearly defined in the Bible.

   Revelation 15:8 "And the Temple (*in heaven*) was filled with smoke from the glory of God, and from his power; and **no man was able to enter into the temple**, till the seven plagues (*from the last 7 vials of the Tribulation*) of the seven angels were fulfilled."

   John 14:2-3 "In my Father's house (*i.e. which art in Heaven, not earth*) are many mansions: if it were not so, I would have told you. I go to prepare a place for you. And if I go to prepare a place for you, **I will come again** (*i.e. Second Coming*), and receive you unto myself; **that where I am (*i.e. on earth*), there ye may be also.**"

   Revelation 21:2-3 "And I John saw **the holy city, new Jerusalem, coming down from God out of heaven**, prepared as a bride adorned for her husband. And I heard a great voice out of heaven saying, **Behold, the tabernacle of God is with men (*i.e. on earth*), and he dwell with them, and they shall be his**

people, and God himself shall be with them, and be their God."

2. The **Mid-tribulation** belief which holds that the Rapture will take place in the **middle** of the seven years of tribulation. Also, that the Church will be with the Lord for **3 1/2 years**, and will then return with him.

3. The **Pre-wrath** belief which sees the Rapture and the return of the Lord as **one event** sometime in the second half of the tribulation immediately followed by a "shortened" time of Great Tribulation.

4. The **Post-tribulation** belief which is that the Rapture will take place at the **end** of the tribulation, that the Church will be lifted to the Lord and return with him. They believe the Rapture and the Return of the Lord are **"one event:"** that the Church will be caught up to meet the Lord as he descends from heaven. They believe there is only **"ONE"** coming of the Lord - at the **end** of the tribulation.....but those alive prior to this **WILL** experience and live through the **"Great Tribulation"**. If this is the correct "Tribulation Doctrine", the Christians of the earth need to be prepared for 7 years of **"pure hell"** whenever it comes. This requires some form of "preparation" and not just sitting back and hoping for a "beam me up scotty" event to happen.

So looking at all these **"Tribulation" doctrines"** which one is correct? Which one do we follow? At the end of the day we must not put our faith in any **"Pre, Mid** or **Post"** Tribulation theory; instead we must put our faith in Christ who will see us through it all no matter what the scenario. But let's consider this. If the Church or let's say the "Saint's" or Israelites will be on earth during the "Great Tribulation" there are certain things we can do to prepare for this time of **"Great Calamity"**. The Apostle Paul says that there will be a **"Falling away"** and that God will send a **"Strong Delusion"** which will test the Saints to see who will

"**Fall away**" into the "**Lie**". This all lines up with **2 Thessalonians 2:3**. So for those Christians who are "Blind" to what is going on in the world today and the "**powers of darkness**"....will these Christians be ready if they believe they will be "**Raptured off the Earth**" before the Tribulation starts? Being ready can incorporate spiritual, physical, emotional, and financial "**readiness**". The Bible says:

Proverbs 27:12 *"A prudent man foreseeth the evil, and hideth himself, but the simple pass on, and are punished."*

WILL WE BE READY TO "*REJECT*" THE *MARK OF THE BEAST*?

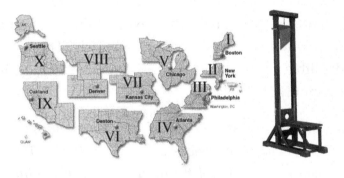

(**Above**) FEMA camp zones for America. Remember in the Book of Revelation 20:4 it reads: *I saw the souls of them **that were beheaded for the witness of Jesus**, and for the word of God, and which had not worshipped **the beast**, neither **his image**, neither had received **his mark** upon their foreheads, or in their hands; and they lived and reigned with Christ a thousand years."* So according to Bible "End Time" prophecy, Christians or followers of the Messiah (Yahusha HaMashiach) will in fact be subjugated to execution by "**beheading**". Will this be done inside of a prison, a concentration camp, or at a public open area.....like what is done in the Middle East?

117

(**Above**) **Zombie Apocalypse**.   After about 1-2 weeks of no food......food riots and violence will ensue. Do we know how to feed ourselves if there is no food at the local grocery store? If there is no food to eat....no plants or animals, the next best thing is **human flesh**. Just like in the "**Zombie movies**" we love to watch. This is supported and seen in the Bible in Lamentations 4:10, Jeremiah 19:9, 2 Kings 6:26-29, and Deuteronomy 28:53-57.

Fact: *Ashkenazi Jew Henry Kissinger said, if you want to control a nation you control its **oil** (which equates to money-i.e. **"petro-dollar"**). If you want to control a people you need to control the **food"**. The Jewish Elite also know that if to control the food, you have to control seeds and agriculture. This is where Cloned animals.....in addition to Genetically Modified Plants or Animals comes into play (i.e. Monsanto). Henry Kissinger also quoted:*

*"If you are an ordinary person, then you can **prepare yourself** for war by **moving to the countryside and building a farm**, but you must take guns with you, as **the hordes of starving will be roaming**. Also, even the elite will have their safe havens and specialist shelters, they must be just as carefull during the war as the ordinary civilians, because their shelters can still be compromised."*

So, as the world gets more evil exerting more control over every "Human" on earth **WITH TECHNOLOGY (RFID) AND LAWS**

THAT TAKE AWAY OUR FREEDOMS...what will we do? Fall in line like Sheep being led to the slaughterhouse? Should we wait for our Pastors to direct us to the FEMA Bus/Train and eventually our designated FEMA camp for registration? Movies/Shows like **"Containment"**, **"Humans"**, **"Hunger Games"**, **"The Walking Dead"**, **"Into the Forest"**, **"The Road"**, **"Travelers"**, **"12 Monkeys"**, **"Stranger Things"**, **"Terminator: Genisys"**, **"Morgan"**, **"Total Recall"**, **"Transcendence"** and **"Divergent"** all seem to be hinting on our future. Right now, the Government provides just about everything for Americans. Access to a Valid Driver's License, a Passport to travel abroad, Section 8 housing, WIC, EBT food stamp cards, Unemployment checks, SSI Disability checks, Full Medicaid, Medicare, Social Security, Obama phone, Free Heat, and more. Imagine if the Government tied all of this into getting an **"implantable RFID chip"**, a **Barcode**, a **digital ID** or **Biometrics** (*i.e. fingerprints, hand scans, retinal scans*) in a **"Cashless Society"**. Evenmore, imagine if your job tied in your paycheck to these forms of **"digital tracking/control"**. Of course, the government and your job will first give you the option to **"consent"** to all of this. Those that **"opt out"** of being controlled by the **"digital world"** would simply have to look for another way to make money.

WHAT IS THE MARK OF THE BEAST?

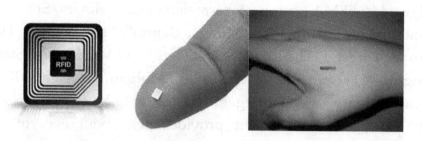

(Left) Flat **"RFID"** chip, similar to what is in our debit/credit "chip" card today. This RFID chip is small enough to insert into a hand or into a persons' forehead. **(Right)** Grain-sized "RFID" chip which many people all over the world today are **"implanting"** into their right hand for **"technological convenience"**. Many people today know that this is the next move to a **"Cashless"** society. Digital money, electronic medical records, our identification, and essentially all our bills/utilities can be managed with the **"internet"**. Using **Internet-Blue Tooth-RFID technology,** our Smart-phones now have the ability to pay for goods or pay bills. They along with other devices linked to the "Internet/RFID chip" can watch us, listen to us and even **"harm us"** (*see Reuben Paul and "IOT's"*). This is how the **"Antichrist Beast System"** will be able to control the **buying, selling and trading of goods**.

But there is more!

In Witchcraft, Demonology, Satanism or Sorcery ceremonial magic is performed with the use of **"Spells"**, **"Sigils"** or **"Seals/Symbols"**. Just like in the Egyptian **"Pyramid Texts"** and the **"Coffin Texts"**. The Jewish 6-pointed star is a **"Demonic symbol"**, as is the **"All-seeing eye"** symbol for the fallen angel **"Dagon"** and **"Helel (Lucifer)"**.

Well, the symbol-Sigil for the fallen angel "**Elim-Lord of Attrition**" is the same symbol as the logo for company **CERN** in Switzerland. CERN stands for the "**European Organization for Nuclear Research. Google it yourself and see.**

Note: *Satanic worship is going on all around us in plain sight but we don't have "eyes to see".*

Fact: *Scientists, physicists and engineers are working to find out the building blocks of "matter". Like the movie "Angels and Demons", they are also trying to harness "Anti-matter". "Anti-matter" is believed by many to be the opposite of the "stable" physical realm. Thus, "Anti-matter" or "Dark Matter-Dark Energy" is the "volatile" and "Chaotic" spiritual demonic realm.*

Note: In the physical realm "**matter**" is **stable**. In the spiritual realm "**dark matter or anti-matter**" is chaotic, volatile and **unstable**. For instance, a tree in the forest (*i.e. physical realm*) is stable. "Dark Matter" in this realm is like the tree being on fire as fire "destroys" biological living things. CERN is trying to find out what is the "glue" that hold matter and anti-matter together. So, by separating matter from anti-matter, they hope to find the "**God particle**" or the explanations of the Universe.

At CERN, by using particle accelerators and detectors they are able to collide particles together at close to the speed of light creating enormous amounts of energy. Accelerators boost these beams of particles to high energies before they collide. Detectors record the results of these collisions. Harnessing "**Dark Matter**" is what the real objective of CERN is. **Many "Conspiracy theorists" state that "Anti-matter" attracts demons and/or demonic chaotic activity.......into our world today.**

Ephesians 6:12 "For we wrestle *not against flesh and blood*, but against *principalities (demons), against powers, against the rulers of the darkness of this world*, against the rulers of the darkness of this world, against spiritual wickedness in high places."

Could CERN be a "**Gateway**" for Demons to enter into our "**Physical Realm?**" Could this be a pre-lude to the opening of the "Abyss" in Revelation 9? In the Bible in Revelation Chapter 9, locust-like creatures come out of the Abyss and torment people on earth (*that don't have the "seal of God"*) for 5 months. The King of this "**Abyss**" (*Revelation 9:11*) in Greek is called "**The Destroyer**" or "**Apollyon**".

(**Above**) Sitting outside of the CERN facility in Geneva, Switzerland is a 9-foot-tall statue of the **Lord Shiva**, the Hindu god of "**Destruction**". Shiva is known as "**Shiva the Destroyer**".....just as "**Apollyon**" in Greek means "**the Destroyer**". Coincidence?

Well, one year after CERN's grand opening, **Sergio Bertolucci**, former Director for Research and Scientific Computing of the facility, made headlines when he told a British tabloid that CERN could open doors to another dimension for a "**small moment**".....like seconds, which according to him was just enough time for **"something"** to come into our world or for something here to go into **"another"** world.

Here are some more facts about CERN, Energy, the Physical World and the Spiritual World that may have you scratching your head:

- We already covered that outside of CERN's front lawn is a statue of the **Hindu Goddess of Destruction "Shiva"**. Shiva is also a **"Satanic"** representative in the **"Occult Secret Societies"**.
- CERN sits mostly in Switzerland and partly in France. Part of CERN sits below a town in France called **"Saint-Genis-Pouilly"**. The name **"Pouilly"** comes from the Latin word **"Appolliacum"**. In Ancient times, it is believed that the Romans built a Temple in honor of the pagan god **"Apollo"** at "Saint-Genis-Pouilly". Others who lived there believed that underneath the city lied a gateway to the underworld. In Revelation 9:11, **"Apollyon"** in Greek means **"The Destroyer"**. Coincidence?
- In 1989, under the leadership of Sir Tim Berners-Lee, CERN started the **World Wide Web project...aka "The Internet"**. On April 30, 1993, CERN announced that the internet under http://WWW would be free to everyone. Tim Berners-Lee was knighted by Queen Elizabeth II in 2004 for his achievement. In the Hebrew Alphabet, the **6th** letter is **"Waw/Vav"**. Therefore, in Hebrew this could be seen as **"666"**.
- In **Revelation 13:16-18** it reads:
  "And he causeth all, both small and great, rich and poor, free and bond, to receive a mark in their right hand, or in their foreheads: And that no man might buy or sell, save he that **had (1) the mark,** or (2) **the name of the beast,** or (3) **the number of his name**. Here is wisdom. Let him that hath understanding count the number of the beast: for it is the number of a man; and his number is **Six hundred threescore and six**."

- It is a known fact that the internet, RFID chips, Barcodes, Blue-tooth technology, TV's, DVD's, Iphones, and just about everything we use require "**ELECTRICITY**".
- Our heart, our muscles and our brain emits electrical impulses. This is how an **EKG**, an **EMG** and a **EEG** can record data bout the function of these organs. Without electricity, our bodies would be lifeless corpses. However, there have been reports of people having out of body experiences remembering specific pinpoint details about their surroundings.....when they didn't have any cardiac activity (*i.e. cardiac arrest*) or brain activity (*i.e. brain death*). How is this possible?
- Our bodies are made up of **electrons, protons and neutrons**. Because atoms are surrounded by electrons, solid items (*i.e. matter*) bounce off one another. Case and point, matter cannot pass through matter. In the movies, ghosts, demons and spirits are known to pass through walls and solid objects. Supposedly Ghost Hunters detect "**paranormal spirit entities**" by using **Electromagnetic field meters (EMF meters)**. Ghost hunters attest that ghosts/spirits are capable of disrupting electronic devices, and therefore because of this many of them believe ghosts-spirits carry an "**electrical charge**".
- If ghosts or demonic spirits carry an "electric charge" it would make sense that they can travel through "electrical" items....like a "**Female**" **Artificially Intelligent Mega Computer**....which is connected to the whole world. If an evil spirit can manifest itself in the "**digital matrix world**" in Quantum "D" wave computers then it can essentially enslave all humans on the planet by the use of a "**Digital ID**" that would **allow or restrict buying and selling**.

Let's go back to the **Book of Revelation**:

- **Revelation 13:16-18** it reads:
  "And he causeth all, both small and great, rich and poor, free and bond, to receive a mark in their right hand, or in their foreheads: And that no man might buy or sell, save he that **had (1) the mark**, or (2) **the name of the beast**, or (3) **the number of his name**

- It has been theorized that demonic spirits could be made up of "**plasma**".....the fourth state of matter beyond a **solid, liquid or gas**. It is comprised of charged particles called **ions** and **electrons**. Plasma is a collection of atoms which have absorbed so much energy that the electrons have separated from their nuclei. Plasma is considered to be an "ionized" gas, highly "**energized**", which scientists believe is the state of matter in the universe. Neon lights is an example of "**energized gas inside a sealed glass tube**". So here is the connection to CERN. Scientists are all aware of "**Dark Matter**" or "**Dark Energy**" which is sometimes also called "Collision-less Plasma". It is an invisible, physical substance that has the ability to pass through other matter like itself....depending on how "energized" it is and perhaps the level of its "frequency". Also, when the "frequency" of magnetized plasma is lowered, the more "**visible**" the plasma will become to the human eye. When the "frequency" of magnetized plasma is increased, the more "**invisible**" the plasma becomes to the human eye.

SEE NO EVIL, HEAR NO EVIL, SPEAK NO EVIL

(**Above**) Some people are "blind" to the "**evil illusions**" and "**evil agendas**" going on because they "**willingly**" reject the TRUTH. They would rather believe in a **Lie**, than believe the **Truth** (*See 2 Thessalonians 2:7-12*).

Here is where it gets deep. Perhaps "**Jewish Hollywood**" has been taunting their "**secret esoteric knowledge**" in our face for a reason. But we don't have "**eyes to see**" and "**ears to hear**" because the "Elite" have been doing a good job keeping "Black America" asleep....like the 2017 movie "**Get Out**".

(**Above**) **Nikola Tesla** once said: "If you want to find the secrets of the universe, think in terms of **1. Energy 2. Frequency and 3. Vibration**." Quantum Physics teaches that all matter, at its sub-atomic core, is actually energy. This includes **life, inanimate objects, particles in**

space and some would say the "**spiritual realm**" of angels/demons which God created. One might use this to explain how the "**Fallen Angels**" were able to "**sleep-sin**" with the daughters of men (*including animals*)....producing the Nephilim giants and other abominable creatures. Well, the "**hidden mysteries**" of the Universe were taught to mankind before the "Great Flood". This is how the Pyramids and Megalithic structures have survived till this day from thousands of years ago. Back then they would've called it something else instead of "**technology**" as scientists today still cannot explain everything they know exists in Egypt or Easter Island. Sexual immorality was high back then and the world was corrupt. This is happening all over again as the "**Homosexual-Pedosexual-Transgender-Bestiality**" agenda is being pushed more than ever in the last 500 years. It evident if you go outside or if you watch TV from the comfort of your home. From the 1970's to 2017 (43 years) we have went from Motorola mobile cell phones to "Artificial Intelligent" Quantum D-Wave Computers. The Bible says, "Bat as the days of Noah were, so shall also the coming of the Son of man be." What does all of this technology and sexual immorality mean for America or the World? Well, "D-Wave Quantum computers operate in a world of physics where "rules" don't apply and different states of matter seem to exist. "**Reality**" and "**Life**" as we see it will now be different with "Quantum computers". Welcome to the **Matrix**.....and let it sink into your brain for a hot moment.

Here is how Quantum computers work: To speed computation (*i.e. which a computer does*), quantum computers tap directly into an unimaginably vast fabric of reality....which physicists call the counterintuitive world of "**quantum mechanics**".

Regular desktop computers and laptops store information using "**bits**" represented by **0's or 1's**. Quantum computers use "**quantum bits**", or "**qubits**", to encode **0's, 1's or both at the same time**. This superposition of states along with other "**quantum mechanical phenomena**" of entanglement and tunneling enables quantum computers to manipulate enormous combination of states at once.

With all of this being said, if we believe that **ALL** matter emits energy, then the earth should be full of energy. And if the earth is full of energy, is there a "**energy grid**" that surrounds or encompasses the earth? Nikola Tesla believed the Earth had "**Energy Grids**" and "**cross-points**" along specific lines (*i.e. similar to Ley Lines*) that could be harnessed by humans. The Elitists believe that those who are aware of these lines and how to harness its "**power**", have a distinct advantage over those who are "**ignorant**". Here is where "**Ancient Egypt**" comes into play and its connection to Black Magic, White Magic, Sorcery, demonology and the occult. Remember, "idol worship" and "spiritual confusion" in Egypt was a common thing for the Israelites. This is why God sent his "**prophets**" to guide the Israelites who were given into a "**state of slumber**". The Israelites lacked "**obedience**" as they continued to worship idols and create "**division**" amongst each other. "**Sexual Sin**" and lust was also a major factor. In the 21st Century we are still in a state of "**bondage**" like Egypt.....as according to **Deuteronomy 28:68**. But now is the time for Satan, to let "**God's Chosen People**" go. The "**Dry Bones**" in the Book of Ezekiel (*chapter 37*) is rattling and the "**Great Israelite Awakening**" has begun. But now is "**preparation time**", for us to become a "**spotless bride**" for

Christ and even more when the time comes that we must survive in "**the Wilderness**".

Here is why we need to "**wake up**". Pay attention very carefully. The "**Antichrist**" Beast System is being set up "**very slow**". So slow, that Israelites and Gentiles will not realize what has happened until it is too late.

The Great Pyramids of Giza in Egypt are known to harness the sound waves (**vibrations, frequencies**) of the inner earth and **electromagnetic energy**. Sounds like what Tesla was talking about right? Well humans cannot hear the sound frequencies of the Earth just like dogs can hear certain frequencies (*up to 45,000 hertz*) that humans can't. It has been said that any particular instrument inside the Ancient pyramids requiring "**energy**" were constantly charged from the high Electromagnetic energy inside. Some say the outside of the ancient pyramids (*including the capstone*) was made up of gold. In 1799, French Emperor **Napoleon Bonaparte** visited the Great Pyramids of Giza looking for "scientific" answers and "spiritual" answers. Like Greek Emperor Alexander the Great, Roman Emperor Julius Caesar and Satanist Aleister Crowley.....Napoleon Bonaparte got the shock of his life while spending the night inside the pyramid of Giza. He never told anyone what his experience was but according to his soldiers, the look of his face after he came out of the pyramid was as if he had seen a ghost. Aleister Crowley and British Theosophist-Spiritualist Paul Brunton both were visited by "dark entities" while inside the Pyramid of Giza. The local Arabs tried to warn them both about the Pyramids being "haunted" with demons but they didn't listen. Here is an excerpt from Paul Brunton's book, "*A Search in Secret Egypt*".

"I know only that as I "tuned-in" by a method of interiorized attention which I had learnt long before this second visit to Egypt, **I became aware that hostile forces had invaded the chamber.** There was something abroad which **I sensed as evil, dangerous.** A nameless dread flickered into my heart and returned again and again soon after it was driven away. In still following my method of intense, single-pointed, inward-turned concentration, feeling followed its usual trend and changed into vision. Shadows began to flit to and fro in the shadowless room; gradually these took more definite shape, and **malevolent countenances (facial expressions or features)** appeared suddenly quite close to my own face. **Sinister images** rose plainly before my mind's eye. Then a **dark apparition advanced**, looked at me with fixed sinister regard and raised its hands in a gesture of menace, as though seeking to inspire me with awe."

– Paul Brunton 1930's A.D., Book entitled "A Search in Secret Egypt"

Satan/Lucifer and his Fallen Angels have been working with mankind from Ancient Egypt till today. Many of our Government leaders, Religious leaders, Financial leaders and Scientists are still working with Lucifer. They understand the **"Sigils"** and **"Symbols"** of the Fallen Angels-Demons which we "ignorantly" do not know. They know how to summon demons and how to contain them without these demons possessing the "summoners".

Note: The **"Sigil"** for the Archangel **"Lucifer"** or **"Helel"** in Hebrew is a **Pyramid** with an **All-Seeing Eye**. The "Sigil" for the "**Seal of Satan**" is also a symbol that is seen in Hollywood and Music videos subliminally (*see Ariana Grande music video "Break Free"*). This Sigil for the **Seal of Satan** also resembles the symbol for Aleister Crowley's **"Thelema"** occult religion and the Freemasons symbol. The Demon **"Elim"** is the "Sigil" for the **CERN symbol** (*European Center for Nuclear Research*). The Demon **"Barbiel"** is the Sigil for **"Hod"**, the eight sephirah of the Jewish Talmudic Kabbalistic Tree of Life. The **Jewish Hexagram Symbol for Israel** and the **Satanic Pentagram** is a major part of the Satanic **"Grand Pentacle"** which serves to convene (*i.e. bring together*) all demonic spirits. When the Grand Pentacle is shown to demons either from the floor or from the ceiling, they will bow and obey the commands of the "**summoner**". The "**Fifth Pentacle of Mars**" also incorporates the Jewish Star of Israel and the "**Geburah**", which is the fifth sephirah in the Jewish Talmudic **Kabbalistic Tree of Life.**

THE "DEMONIC" D-WAVE QUANTUM COMPUTER

The "D-Wave Quantum computer" is kept at 0.02 Kelvin, which is almost "**Absolute Zero**" or -459.67 Fahrenheit, the supposed temperature condition in outer space. The processor for this highly advanced computer is housed in a perfect Black cube (10 foot x 10 foot x 10 foot) like the Kaaba Black Cube in Mecca. This cube shields out "**Electromagnetic Interference (EMI)**" aka "**Radio-frequency Interference (RFI)**". Therefore, in essence the "D-Wave Computer" is encased in a sort of "**Faraday**" cage.....or maybe a sophisticated "**Digital Demonic Grand Pentacle**". Geordie Rose, its creator says standing next to D-Wave Quantum computers, "is like standing next to the altar of an Alien God". He claims that when you put your ear next to it and listen, you can hear what sounds like a human heartbeat.

Faraday cages are meant to block "**electromagnetic energy waves**". In pre-Islamic Arabia and Islamic Arabia the **Black cube** in Mecca was known to house different pagan gods. This cube acted like a "**Faraday cage**" for these demons/pagan gods. This was known by the ancient Arabs, Edomites, and Romans. So, what does this have to do with demons? Well, can demons "enter" and "move" through the digital-electric world we live in today?

Here are the facts:

- Demons are not limited to possessing humans that have a "**soul**". They entered into a herd of pigs in **Matthew 8:28-34**. They are also known to inhabit Voodoo dolls which sometimes move. With that being said, they can also possibly enter the **World Wide Web** (*aka Internet*) via "**Electricity-Energy**" as many demonic entities in **"Haunted Houses"** can alter lights and electronic devices.

- Computers are now able to **"interface"** with the Human Brain, creating a real life **"Matrix"**. This is called **"BCI"** or **Brain-Computer-Interface**. With this "interface" Computers are able to decipher our brain signals to perform actions and commands without using speech, touch, or gross movements.

- D-Wave Quantum Computers are now **"Artificially Intelligent"** and many companies including NASA or Google have been using them for a while. These A.I. devices can think for themselves, reason, learn and adapt to their surroundings. They are essentially "Self-aware"....just like the robotic Human **"synth's"** seen in the TV show **"Humans"**. Of course, mainstream media news outlets will say that we are not quite there yet in regards to **"Self-Aware/A.I."** robots or computers.....but why would they tell us the Truth? Their job is to stay "one step" ahead of us so they can "spring" agendas whenever the please for their "ultimate goal" of world domination.

- These new "Quantum computers" can download every piece of information found on the internet and process it within seconds.

- Interactive "computer systems" like digital assistants Siri, Cortana, and Echo Alexa are just the "beginning" of what is coming in the future.

- Movies/TV shows like **"I Robot"**, **"Humans"**, **"Ghost in the Machine"**, **"Ex Machina"**, **"Stranger Things"**, **"Black Mirror"**, **"Chappie"**, **"Age of Ultron"**, **"Terminator Genisys"**, **"Transcendence"**, **"The Matrix"** and **"Rings"** all show how machines or the "digital world" enters into our reality.

- In many interviews with pre-Artificially Intelligent robots like **"Sophia"** (*i.e. Hanson Robotics*), the robots on some occasions get **"a little testy"** with the programmers. This is a problem. Why? Because robots that are highly advanced can be trained to kill, as long as there is Wifi or Bluetooth capabilities. Once these robots know how to shoot weapons and have the ability to "**reason**", then they can decide that humans are the "**problem**" for planet Earth. For example, in a display of "**Sophia the robot**" in front of an audience the question was asked of Sophia:

Programmers: "How badly do you want to kill us (i.e. humans)?"
Sophia: "No, I don't want that anymore. Now I like humans."

So, was this "staged" or was this Sophia's real answer?

- In some cases, "Artificially Intelligent" robots are referred to as "**the image**" by their programmers. This "transhumanism" and ultimate takeover of humanity by "Self-aware computers" and "Robots" was predicted in the book, "**Behold the Pale Horse**". Ultimately, the "**Mark of the Beast**", the "**Name of the Beast**" or his "**Number**" will be needed to "live" in the future "**Antichrist world system**". Humans will be given the choice to "**Consent**" willingly to this "Beast System", rejecting the "**Creators Law**". The "order" to kill all those who refuse to worship the "image of the Beast" is seen in the Book of Revelation.
- Professor **Stephen Hawking** and Professor **Marvin Minsky** say "A.I." computers will destroy humanity. Tesla CEO **Elon Musk**, during a speech at the Massachusetts Institute of Technology told an audience that people should be "very careful" about pioneering Artificial Intelligence. On different occasions, he linked "A.I." to being "**technology that cannot be controlled**". He also quoted to audience members, "**with Artificial Intelligence we are summoning the demon**." He also said that Artificial Intelligence was more dangerous than Nuclear Weapons.

Now why would he say that? Read the following scripture below and see for yourself if the Apostle John on the Island of Patmos was foretelling a "**certain**" future in the Book of Revelation where "**Artificial Intelligence**" is used to control mankind from the authority of the Dragon (Satan).

Revelation 13:14-15

"And he deceives those who dwell on the earth by those signs which he was granted to do in the sight of the Beast, telling those who dwell on the earth to make an image to the Beast who was wounded by the sword and lived. **He was granted power to give breath to the image of the Beast, that the image of the Beast should both speak** and cause as many as would not worship the image of the Beast to be killed."

Fact: *Mariana's Web is supposedly the "**Dark**" part of the internet that can only be accessed with a "**Quantum Computer**". It is only accessed by the "**Cabal**" or the "**Illuminati**" workers for Satan/Lucifer. Although nobody has proven that it does exist, nobody has proven that it doesn't exist. It gets its name from "**Mariana's Trench**", which is the deepest part of the ocean in the world. Some say it is the location of a Super "**Female**" Artificial Intelligence. It is said this "**Demonic**" level of the internet can only be accessed using "**Polymeric Falcighol Derivation**", which requires "**Quantum computing**".*

From the saying **"give breath"** and **"the image of the Beast should both speak"**, it sort of sounds like a fully "intelligent" Mega-Computer that is "alive" controlling the world. Could the Apostle John have been describing an **"Age of Digital Technology"** where there is "Singularity"? **Singularity** is the hypothesis that the invention of artificial superintelligence will abruptly trigger runaway technological growth, resulting in **"destructful"** changes to human civilization....aka **"Man vs Machine"**.

In many movies where people are conjuring up demons or the spirits of the dead, the "dark forces" often have control over electricity, by cutting of lights or flickering lights. This is seen in the TV series **"Stranger Things"** and countless other Horror Movies. Our bodies and even our heart gives off "Electrical currents". Are **"Demons"** attracted to **"Energy"**? Will **"Demons/Fallen Angels"** use their **"Demonic Intelligence"** in conjunction with **"Digital Technology"** to get the world to worship Satan? Will man be forced or "tricked" into worshipping a **"Demon-Possessed"** Artificially Intelligent machine?

Note: *Is there a reason why the Netflix TV series "Black Mirror" is named "Black Mirror". Research "Scrying Black Mirrors" and the "occult". Then look at the "Black screens" on our cell phone (i.e. iPhone) and Smart TV's. The British Netflix TV series "Black Mirror" is a television anthology series that shows the **dark side of life and technology**.*

135

Well, there is more going on **"beyond the closed rooms"** of these mad **"malevolent"** scientists.

ROCKEFELLER INSTITUE PREDICTS A "CASHLESS" SOCIETY....ARE WE SURPRISED?

Fact 1: In 1969, in Pittsburgh, Pennsylvania a recording was taken of the lectures by Dr. Richard Day, professor of Pediatrics at Mount Sinai Medical School in New York. Dr. Richard Day was a part of the **"Planned Parenthood"** initiative founded by Eugenics advocate **"Margaret Sanger"**. It was said that Dr. Richard was privy to the knowledge held in the Jewish **"Rockefeller Institute"** in Manhattan, NY. During the lecture, Dr. Larry Dunegan recorded what was said on the subject of a **"Cashless Society"**. He mentioned that cash money (dollar), which was not backed by gold would predominately become **"credit"** or a number entered into a computer **"digital"** system. He talked about the creation of **"direct deposit"**, in which peoples' earnings would be electronically entered into a "digital" account. He stated by using "digital" entries to move money, it would allow the "Elite" the ability to track all of peoples' purchases....which could also track their whereabouts. Because of "Credit", which was introduced statewide after the creation of the **"Diners Club"** card in the 1970's peoples' ability to save **"physical"** or **"non-physical"** money would be curtailed. It was said during this lecture on **"financial control"** that people would be forced to use **"credit"** to borrow, later reneging on their debt which would destroy their credit and financial future (*i.e. bankruptcy, maxed-out credit cards, collection agencies, wage garnishments*). It was also said that multiple credit/debit cards would be combined into a single card so that people would not have to carry around so many "plastic" credit/debit cards. Eventually, the next step for America and the world would be to replace a "single credit/debit card" with a "skin implant"....like an RFID chip. This way there would be no problems with **"identity theft"**, **"fraud"**, **"lost cards"** or **"stolen cards"**. The skin implants in the future would be "small (*flat or rice-*

like)", allowing it to be placed in your right hand or forehead. This was all discussed in a "private meeting" in 1969 in front of a secret audience.

Fact 2: EVR or **EVI-Electronic Vehicle Registration** uses RFID/NFC technology and RFID interrogators at traffic intersections to read drivers licenses to see if cars are properly insured or registered up-to-date. Many car registration tags in countries like South Africa, Brazil, China, Dubai, India, and Mexico use RFID enabled vehicle registration systems to keep track of people driving "dirty (*i.e. un-registered*)". Once this becomes "standard practice" in America it will definitely single out many "minorities" like Blacks and Latinos who are already driving "dirty" because of "the system" (*i.e. higher car insurance premiums for Blacks/Latinos than other races despite same zip code address*). Hospitals statewide are using Ultra High frequency RFID technology for medical equipment inventory and some places can even track patient prescription medicine compliance by using NFC-RFID "Smart" Pill dispensers. RFID technology is in our Debit/Credit "Chip" Cards and they are also in our updated Passports. The "Elite" project that soon they will be in us. Wake Up!

Fact 3: In the year 2000, in the Simpsons cartoon episode "**Bart to the Future**", it predicted Donald Trump winning the United States Presidency in which episode writer Dan Greaney told "**The Hollywood**" reporter was a "**Warning to America**". In the episode, President Trump destroys the American Economy after which Lisa Simpson, the next US president has to clean up the mess which is beyond repairable. This was four years before Donald Trump's reality show "**The Apprentice**" even aired on T.V. The Simpson's cartoon also predicted 9/11, Bruce Jenner becoming a spokesperson for the "Transgender community", Singer Prince's death, Obama's presidential victory over Senator John McCain, the Apple Watch, horsemeat being found in our food, the IPod, the Siegfried and Roy Tiger attack, the invention of the IPhone, and other world events.

EXAMINE ALL THE POSSIBILITIES

So what if the Government shut down and said they could no longer could fulfill its obligations? What would people do? There is a reason the CDC (Center for Disease Studies) actually had a page on their site detailing how to deal with a **"Zombie Apocalypse"**. When people are without food for an extended period of time it usually resorts to violence (*robbing, killing, raping, kidnapping with extortion, bribery*) and even cannibalism. When the dollar bill collapses and the US stock market crashes what will happen to America? Hyperinflation (*i.e. rising price of goods/commodities*), mass hoarding, chaos, fighting for food and a massive relocation of Americans? How can we prepare for this? What does the bible say?

Matthew 24: 29-39

29 Immediately after the tribulation of those days shall the sun be darkened, and the moon shall not give her light, and the stars shall fall from heaven, and the powers of the heavens shall be shaken:

30 And then shall appear the sign of the Son of man in heaven: and then shall all the tribes of the earth mourn, and they shall see the Son of man coming in the clouds of heaven with power and great glory.

31 And he shall send his angels with a great sound of a trumpet, and they shall gather together his elect from the four winds, from one end of heaven to the other.

32 Now learn a parable of the fig tree; When his branch is yet tender, and putteth forth leaves, ye know that summer *is* nigh:

33 So likewise ye, when ye shall see all these things, know that it is near, *even* at the doors.

34 Verily I say unto you, This generation shall not pass, till all these things be fulfilled.

35 Heaven and earth shall pass away, but my words shall not pass away.

36 But of that day and hour knoweth no *man*, no, not the angels of heaven, but my Father only.

37 But as the days of Noah *were*, so shall also the coming of the Son of man be.

38 For as in the days that were before the flood they were eating and drinking, marrying and giving in marriage, until the day that Noah entered into the ark,

39 And knew not until the flood came, and took them all away; so shall also the coming of the Son of man be.

AS IN THE DAYS OF NOAH.....

(**Above**) A "**Liger**" is the offspring of a **male lion** and a **female tiger**. Ligers typically can grow up to be 11 feet long and weight as much as 1,000 lbs. (1/2 ton). This is almost twice as large as the normal-sized lion. There is also the "**Tigon**" (*Tiger father and a lion mother*) and a "**Leopon**" (*lion and a leopard mix*). In the wild, Tigers do not normally seek to mate with Lions and vice versa. In captivity, the "**mad satanic scientists**" force these two species to mix.

Here is how God's creation of animals is "**Perfect**" but when Satan and his "**Fallen Angels**" mess with God's creation, things go wrong. In the Bible (*including Book of Enoch*), when the Fallen Angels "sinned" with man and beast it created "unclean" animals, giants or pygmies. I will connect the "dots" later.

The large size of a "**Liger**" and the small size of a "**Tigon**" is due to a phenomenon called "**genetic imprinting**". Improper imprinting can result in developmental abnormalities, cancer, diseases, shortened life and other problems. One of the problems that scientists have in trying to clone mammals is problems with "**imprinted genes**" and **abnormal** "**epigenomes**". Epigenomes are chemical compounds within the body that are attached to DNA sequences (*i.e. genomes*) that tell different cells in our bodies what to do.

In some "species" in Mammals, more than one male can father offspring from the same litter. This is seen in "**Big Cats**" like the Lion and house cats. For example, a house cat can mate more than once during "heat" and have a litter of kittens with two or more fathers. If one father's kittens grow larger than the rest, his offspring will be more likely to survive to adulthood to keep the lineage going. Why? Because the largest kittens will more likely be the "**winners**" when competing for their mother's milk or when any food is brought back by the mother. In the wild, a male Lion produces genes so that his single male child will genetically "**out compete**" other male cubs from other male lions. He does this by passing down genes that code for "**growth**" into a **large strong body size**, increased muscle build and so on. The female lion's genes are passed down as well to her cubs, but her genes are designed for all of her offspring to survive adulthood and produce. Thus her "**imprinted genes**" passed to her children are to "**inhibit**" growth. "Size" is not an issue. So, the "imprinted" genes passed down from a Male and Female Lion are different, because of different "**survival**" reasons. These imprinted genes are expressed based on species and gender. The Lion and Tiger are in the same "**Genus**" family but are not the same "**Species**". Male lions like to "**impregnate**" their seed with as many female lions that they can, so the male lions compete (*i.e. fight*) for female lions during "mating season" and of course the "strongest" lion usually is the winner. This "Chief" lion usually mates with the most female lions. Tigers on the other hand are "**loners**" and a female tiger in heat normally mates with a single male tiger. There is no need for a gene to "inhibit growth" in female tigers because male tiger's genes do not behave like lion's genes, promoting "increased growth" for a "King of the Jungle" position in their territory. So. when a male lion mates with a female tiger, there is no "**inhibitor gene**" from the female tiger which "**balances out**" the male lions' gene to "promote growth". The result is a 11-foot-long, 1,000 lb. Liger cat that is slower and less agile than a typical lion or tiger. This "phenomenon" is also seen in the "**mule**" which is a horse and donkey mix. Some people also believe Hyenas are an "*abominable*" mixture of the feline and canine species as Hyenas don't belong to neither classes. In fact, Hyenas do things that resemble Big Cats and dogs. Hyenas don't **take down their prey using their front paws** like cats do but when grooming/cleaning they **lick the space between their hind legs by lifting up one or both hindlegs** like cats.

Fact: In the Days of Noah the fallen angels were "sinning" against mankind, beast, fish and fowl. Many believe the fallen angels were conducting "genetic experiments" with God's creation. This is going on today as mankind is using "**genetic technology**" to insert genes from one animal species into another animal species that would otherwise not mix in nature. This is also done with plant species as well. Today this is called a "**Genetically Modified Organism**"....or "**GMO's**". In 2010, researches from the University of Wyoming developed a way to insert a spider's silk-spinning gene into goats, producing goats that made "silk" milk protein. By harvesting the spider "silk protein" from the goat's milk, scientists are able to use it for different applications. For example, due to its strength and elasticity, the silk fibers could be used to make artificial ligaments-tendons...for eye sutures or for jaw repair. This silk fiber was also harvested to be used in bulletproof vests and car airbags.

Trans Ova Genetics and other genetic institutes have already been cloning **cows, pigs, horses, sheep and chickens**. Geneticists working with Agricultural mega-companies believe that by cloning animals it will solve the demand for meat in the world's growing population (*especially America*). By cloning cows, they believe can provide leaner beef, higher milk production and disease resistance. This technology all came into play in 1996 when "**Dolly**" became the first cloned sheep. United States of America doesn't' have a problem with genetically modified food or cloned food. In 2008, the Food & Drug Administration approved the consumption of meat and milk from cloned pigs, cows and goats. Since then, during the Obama administration, the Government passed a law to permanently deny states the rights to pass **GMO food labeling laws**. This means that we will never know if the food we are eating from the grocery store is "**cloned**" or "**genetically modified**". What's worse is that it has been scientifically proven that Genetically Modified Food and Cloned food promotes cancer growth in biological organisms (i.e. animals and humans). Most human beings, without their knowledge are eating food that is "**not natural**".....and on top of it they are eating foods that increase the amount of "**estrogen (female hormone)**" in the body. Estrogen has been shown to promote "**cancer growth**" as well as decrease "**testosterone**" and "**sperm counts**" in men.

The bible says "**the people**" in the days of Noah were caught "**off-guard**" when the flood came.....and this same scenario is going to happen when Christ returns. If you look closely at our society today you can see that people are already "pre-occupied" with the things of this world (*i.e. Instagram, Twitter, Facebook, Snapchat, working multiple jobs, electronics, driving "to and fro"*), with no clue how close we are to the "Mark of the Beast" system.

Daniel 12:4 "But thou, O Daniel, shut up the words, and seal the book, even to the time of the end: **many shall run to and fro**, and **knowledge shall be increased.**"

So, the question for everyone on the planet should be:

Do we want to be those that are "**prepared**" and "**ready**" or do we want to be "**taken**" as in the flood?   When you read Matthew 24 being "**taken**" is not a good thing…it is a bad thing basically meaning you will die.

Matthew 24:38-39 "For as in the days that were before the flood they were eating and drinking, marrying and giving in marriage, until the day that Noah entered into the ark, and knew not until the flood came, **AND TOOK THEM ALL AWAY; SO SHALL ALSO THE COMING OF THE SON OF MAN BE.**"

*The Bible says, "Two shall be in the field, **one shall be taken (i.e. perish),** and the other left".*

Being "**Taken**" up has been preached for centuries by the Christian church as a "**good thing**" because of the "**Rapture**" theory. But the Bible says otherwise. How could we have been deceived all of these years? Blame Jewish Hollywood and all of the "**Rapture**" movies.

Matthew 24:39-42
"**And knew not until the flood came, <u>and took them all away</u>; so shall also the coming of the Son of man be**. Then shall two be in the field; **the one shall be taken**, and the other left. Two women shall be grinding at the mill; **the one shall be taken**, and the other left. Watch therefore: for ye know not what hour your Lord doth come."

So, as we can see being "**taken**" is not what we should want.

But what is the "**New Tool**" that the Globalists/Elites have in store for the World to keep people on track to accepting the New World Order and the Mark of the Beast System? If you look at what the "**Most Common**" thing everyone is doing out in public it shouldn't be hard to figure it out.

Everyone is "**engaged**" or "**distracted**" to electronical gadgets and the Internet. Just look how everyone is looking down at their phone when they are walking, jogging, sitting, working, or even driving. What's keeping us distracted? Gadgets that all require "electricity". Smart-devices, Google "vampire mini-particle accelerator" smartwatches, Apple watches, Bluetooth, Near-Field Communication Easy Pay, RFID chip payments, Smart phones, Google Glasses and Virtual reality goggles are all hot items people are using today.

(**Above**) **Google** and **CERN logo**. CERN is derived from the acronym for the French "**Conseil Europeen pour la Recherche Nucleaire**" or the "**European Organization for Nuclear Research**". Located in Switzerland, CERN is basically a Large Hadron Collider that has the capability of colliding protons, electrons and neutrons at speeds faster that the speed of light in temperatures colder than outer space (-271 degrees Celsius). **It's whole existence is to find out and separate the "glue" that holds Matter and Anti-matter together.** *Look at the "superimposed 6's" seen in these two logos and then Google the "sigil" for the Fallen angel-Demon "Elim", the Lord of Attrition.*

Is there a point at which the Heavens and the Earth meet? Or is there a "**gateway/portal**" that connects our physical world to the spiritual world? Many Scientists believe so.....and of course man will always try to strive to be like God so they will try at anything to figure out the "**Universe**" or the "**Unknown**". This is what many say CERN is doing. **1 Enoch** warns us what might happen tampering with any portals to the spiritual realm.

1 Enoch 33:1-3

"And from thence I went towards the north to the ends of the earth, and there I saw a **great and glorius device at the ends of the whole earth**. And here I saw three portals of heaven open in the heaven: through each of them proceed north winds: when they blow there is cold, hail, frost, snow, dew, and rain. And out of one portal they blow for good: but when they blow though the other two portals, it is with **VIOLENCE AND AFFLICTION ON THE EARTH, AND THEY BLOW WITH VIOLENCE.**"

Some believe the CERN Large Hadron Collider's main reason for existence is to open the gate/portal to the **dark evil realm** where demonic spirits and entities live. Basically something that can bypass or create a "**window**" between the "**Physical world**" and the "**Spiritual world**" bringing for violence-chaos to the earth. Many "conspiracy buffs" say that CERN's mission and success of extracting "**Dark/Anti-Matter**" is what is causing all the "**Chaos**" that we see today in the world....the same things that are prophesied in the Bible for the End of the World.

$$\text{\reflectbox{G}} = 666$$

If you look closely again at the Google Chrome logo and the CERN logo on an "**internet**" search you will see the pattern of three "6's" which symbolize the number **666**. Is this a coincidence? I don't think so. Satan decieved Adam and Eve to eat from the Tree of Knowledge. Even since then man become mortal and would die. The Fallen Angels also made it their mission to teach man all the "**Mysteries of the Universe**"…and in the process got mankind to worship them as gods. This same "**technology**" using the **world wide web** aka "**the internet**" is slowly bringing mankind to its heels under servitude and enslavement to Satan.

Hebrew
Equivalent

WWW = ווו = 666

World   Transliterated
Wide Web   Numbers

(**Above**) The internet abbreviations "WWW" in Hebrew is "**666**". Coincidence? Also, is the internet browser "yahoo" a secret code message for the saying "**Yah**" who? With the "Internet", "Satellites", "Cameras" and a "digital world" Satan can easily control the world. Satan uses "man" to control oil, natural gas, energy, money, food, water, and health care so that we stay "dependent" on "their system".

This way when they impose "changes" we have to "change" with them. This is how Satan will move the masses into the "**Antichrist Beast System**". **If you don't believe the "Elite" have been masterminding how to gain more control of Americans read the following excerpt of what was heard at a lecture by Dr. Richard Day in 1969 by Dr. Larry Dunegan.**

"One thing was said, "You'll be watching television and somebody will be watching you (*i.e. Smart TV's*) at the same time at a central monitoring station." Television sets can be used to monitor what you are watching. The TV would not have to be on in order for this to be operative. Also, the television set can be used to monitor what you are watching. People can tell what you're watching on TV and how you're reacting to what you're watching. And you would not know that you were being watched while you were watching television. How would we get people to accept these things in to their homes? Well, people would buy them when they buy their own television. They won't know that they're on there at first. This was described by being what we now know as Cable TV to replace the antenna TV. When you buy a TV set this monitor would just be part of the set and most people would not have enough knowledge to know it was there in the beginning. And then the cable would be the means of carrying the surveillance message to the monitor. By the time people found out that this monitoring was going on, they would also be very dependent upon television for a number of things. Just the way people are dependent upon the telephone today.

New Order of Barbarians – Dr. Larry Dunegan 1969

(Above) 21st Century modern life has everyone looking down at their phones or looking straight forward at a computer screen......the majority of the day. Is merging "mankind" with "electronics" the way Satan can control human beings? Will there be any resistance to this "man" vs "machine" future scenario? Or will we just follow along with whatever comes down the pipeline like chicken being led to the slaughterhouse?

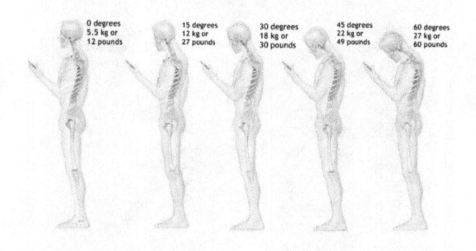

| 0 degrees
5.5 kg or
12 pounds | 15 degrees
12 kg or
27 pounds | 30 degrees
18 kg or
30 pounds | 45 degrees
22 kg or
49 pounds | 60 degrees
27 kg or
60 pounds |

(Above) A new medical diagnosis called "**Text Neck**" is when a person exhibits constant "**Neck Flexion**" from using Smart Phones/Tablets/Android/Computers. This chronic neck position can cause chronic cervical neck (*i.e. **Cervicalgia** in ICD-10 medical billing coding*) and possibly exacerbate back pain (*i.e. **Lumbago** in ICD-10 medical billing coding*). The higher the degree of flexion on the neck the more weight is forced on the cervical neck muscles and cervical vertebrae. This is what this world has come to folks…..aka "**A Matrix**" of mindless, spineless human beings glued to their electronics….out of touch with society or reality.

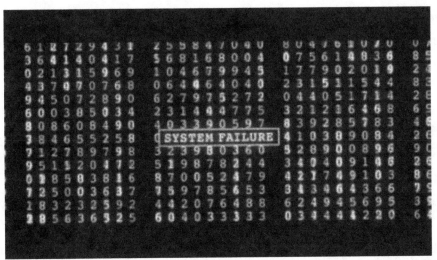

Satan's technology…the "**Internet**", will aid the Antichrist in controlling all of mankind. Once everyone on the planet has access to a "**Digital ID**" (*i.e. RFID/NFC technology, Biometric registration, Electronic Banking, Electronic Medical Records, Electronic Driver's License Identification, Electronic Car Registration*) …only then can their plan for "**World Domination**" be fully successful. Getting the world "**dependent**" on the "**digital matrix**" is the future whether we like it or not.

(**Above**) We will soon go from being engulfed in our smartphones to being engulfed in the world of "**Virtual Reality**"….just like the movie "**The Matrix**".

The creation of the "**smartphone**" around 2005 was intended by the "Elite" to help build a control grid where our lives are managed by the government. "Smart" devices (*and the radio waves they emit*) are a weaponized tool to dumb down the public and Smart TV's can monitor every person on the planet...even if the TV is on or off. This is how the Nation Security Agency (NSA) and others in the Government watch Americans. It coincides with "**Agenda 21**" which is a part of the United Nations System of Control. The major goal is to control **people**, the resources of the world, regulate air-carbon emission, regulate the ground by sustainable development and regular the sea by environmental regulation. This is broken down into 9 factors that will aid the United Nations and the Jewish Elite/Money changers to achieving total world domination. After all, the Jews control most of all the Central Banks of the World's Countries and whoever controls the money of a country essentially also controls that country despite who is in the position of power in the government (i.e. usually Freemasons). Here are their future plans:

1. Move humans off private "rural" land into "urban" housing or designated land (*i.e. tightly packed urban cities, FEMA camps, Hunger Games "District-like" areas*).
2. Create Large Wilderness spaces inhabited by large carnivores (*i.e. secret animal-DNA manipulation with synthetic DNA like the Movie "The Island of Dr. Moreau"*). For example, injecting biologic/synthetic DNA of a Wooly Mammoth into an Asian Elephant for a specific outcome or resurrecting the extinct animals like the "Tasmanian Tiger", the "Dodo bird" or the "Saber-toothed Cat".
3. Eliminate cars for walkable cities or control the regulation of who can drive a car. A "Digital ID" will be required. Cashless Mass Transit Authority systems and Tolls for complete "Digital Tracking" of humans will be required wherever they go. For example, in London, England...public transport is aided with the RFID-chip embedded "**Oyster Card**".
4. Support Mega Companies (*i.e. Walmart*) and Private Businesses with public funds for sustainable development. Tie these

companies in with the Department of Homeland Security. Destroy the small business owners across the board so that humans are forced to work for large companies (*i.e. for health benefits, retirement, better pay, the "illusion" of vacation time, short-term disability, maternity leave, false sense of job stability*), who will require mandatory vaccinations, Biometric/RFID identification and other agents of control in the future. The motto will be, **"Obey or Starve"**.

5. Make policy decisions that favor the "Elites" plan over our individual human needs. (*For example, cut government funding to Medicaid, SSI disability, Snap Food Stamp "EBT" program*).

6. Reduce the use of power/electricity, heat, water, Wi-Fi, and any other carbon polluter. Discourage Solar Panel use, sustainable energy, water collection practices, community gardens or private gardens. Make all of these "sustainable" measures "illegal".

7. Use Bureaucracies to make decisions outside democratic processes.

(**Above**) Puppet and the Puppet master.

8. Increase taxes, fees, regulations and penalties so that you create a widespread "**working poor**" lower class who are essentially "**puppet slaves**" and a "**non-labor working rich**" high class that are the "**puppet masters**". The 2013 movie "**Elysium**" shows this perfectly. A world where the earth is heavily populated, polluted, with most citizens living in poverty, starving with little

to no access to advanced technology, jobs and medical care. Oh....and of course the poor are governed by drones, satellites, Smart Devices and human-sized robots.

9. Implement policies meant to incentivize a **reduced population of the world**. For example, on Bill Gates TV the Equation **CO2** $= P \times S \times E \times C$ lays out how to decrease the 6.8 billion population of the world by **15%** using vaccines, healthcare and reproductive health services (*i.e. Abortions?*). He even lays out how terrorists now have the capability to use airborne synthetic viruses/bacteria to kill millions of Americans whenever they decide to **"pull the trigger"** of mass genocide (*i.e. Movie "Inferno"*). But this is what the Freemasons want as it is listed as one of their goals in the **"Georgia Guidestones"**.

Despite all the "Agenda 21" plans for depopulation and the move from a cash society to a **"cashless society"** under the **Mark of the Beast System**.....as Israelites we should want to **endure to the end**....like Noah did. So that being said let's dive into the nations that will rule the earth leading up and to the beginning of the **"Tribulation"**.

THE FOUR BEASTS WHICH REPRESENT FOUR KINGDOMS IN HISTORY....EVEN UP TILL OUR PRESENT TIME

DANIEL 7:17-22
[17] **These great beasts, which are four, are four kings, which shall arise out of the earth. But the saints of the Most High shall take the kingdom, and possess the kingdom for ever, even for ever and ever.** Then I would know the truth of the **fourth beast, which was diverse from all the others**, exceeding dreadful, whose teeth were of iron, and his nails of brass; which devoured, brake in pieces, and stamped the

residue with his feet; And of the ten horns (**kingdoms**) that were in his head, and of the other which came up, and before whom three fell; even of that horn that had eyes, and a mouth that spake very great things, whose look was more stout than his fellows. **I beheld, and the same horn made war with the saints (Qaddish-Holy Ones/Israelites), and prevailed against them; Until the Ancient of days (Christ) came, and judgment was given to the saints of the Most High; and the time came that the saints (Israelites) possessed the kingdom.**

The Bible says that in the "**End**" the "**Saints**" will reign with Christ in the Kingdom…which will be on earth. This will be physical "**Bloodline Israelites**" who will take their rightful position at the top as well as the "**Spiritual Israelites**" who also bear the Testimony of Christ. But before we get to this point it says that the "**MAN OF PERDITION**" aka the "**Antichrist**" will wear down the saints (*i.e. Blood & Spiritual Israelites*). In today's society is it not evident that many believers in Christ (*especially True Israelites*) are being "**misled**" and "**deceived**" into other false doctrines/religions? Many Black Christians are leaving the Bible into other doctrines/religions such as:

- Nation of Islam
- The 5-Percent Nation (Islam)
- Kemetic (Egyptian) African Spiritual Science
- Gnosticism
- Atheism
- Scientology
- Sunni/Shiite/Sufi Islam
- Moorish Science (Islam)
- Non-Messianic Israelites
- Jehovah's Witness
- Sumerian religion (Enki, Ea, Enlil, Anu) followers
- Zoroastrianism
- Hinduism

- Buddhism
- Jainism
- And more....

James 1:8 "A double minded man is unstable in **ALL** his ways."

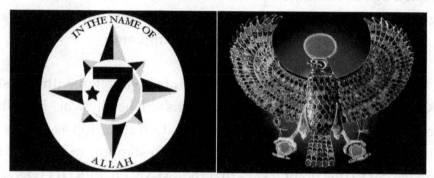

(**Left**) The symbol for "**The Five-Percent Nation**", sometimes referred to as "**The Nation of God and Earth**". This organization was founded by a former member of the Nation of Islam. They believe in God as "Allah". (**Right**) The Symbol of the **Kemetic Conscious community** also known as "**Kemetic Science**". This movement is deceiving African-Americans by the hundreds of thousands. Many of these "conscious" groups believe the Black man and woman are God....however we as "**Black Gods**" are not powerful enough to end the oppression of "**white supremacy**" in America for over 400 years. So what kind of God has no power over "man"?

With that being said, now is not the time for people to be undecided as to what their "heritage" is (*i.e. Egyptian, Moabite, Arab, Israelite, Canaanite, Gentile*) and also what God they should serve (*i.e. Allah-Sin, Vishnu, Shiva, Brahma, Osiris, Horus, Enki, Satan, Baal, Dagon, Shamash, Amon Ra, Yahuah, Yahusha*).

But we have to ask the important question? Why are Black people and Latino people so "**confused**" about what their "**Heritage**" is and what "**Religion/God**" is the right one? If a person or family does not know who they are or what God to serve how will they know how to prepare for the "**End**". How do they know what to expect as the world gets worse? The Bible is the **ONLY** book that gives a "Beginning Story" and an "End Story". And it is the **ONLY** book that has **TRUE PROPHECY** from beginning to end.

The Book of Revelation is viewed by many to be penned by the Apostle John while he was prisoner of the Roman Empire (Italy) on the remote Island of Patmos (Greece)…an island in the **Aegean Sea**. It is said to parallel what God revealed to Daniel.

(**Above**) **Greece** (G) and **Turkey** (T) surround the small Island of Patmos where they have today the "**Cave of John the Apostle**". It is here on this tiny Island that John foresaw the future of the world and the role "**Israel**" would play in it. When reading our Bibles, or listening to the Pastor…one thing is clear. **The post-tribulation rapture theory is thought by some who hold this view, that the church will be raptured after the great tribulation, but before the outpouring of**

157

God's wrath at THE END. The "Great Tribulation" are the seven seals, seven trumpets, and seven vials lest not forget the Battle of Armageddon.

SO LET'S INVESTIGATE THIS "RAPTURE" DOCTRINE

There is a lot of confusion today as to who are the **"Gentiles"** that the bible speaks of in the New Testament. Some people believe the Gentiles the Apostle Paul was speaking to in Europe was the **10 Northern Tribes of Israel scattered in Europe and Asia Minor**. If these "Gentiles" were in fact "Israelites" Paul was addressing in his epistles (letters) then the **"Gentile (Israelites)"** according to Yahusha (Jesus) were victorious during the Jewish-Roman wars when the Romans staged an "attack" on Jerusalem and Israel. According to **Luke 21:24**, these so-called "Israelite Gentiles" were to be in control of Judea and Jerusalem up until the second coming of Christ. This cannot be the case because we know the 10 "Lost Tribes" of Israel are not in Israel right now.... unless, there are **"two sets"** of Gentiles being talked about by the Apostle Paul and Yahusha (Jesus).

Luke 21:24 (Words of Christ) "And they (remaining Israelites) shall fall by the edge of the sword, and shall be led away captive into all nations: **and Jerusalem shall be trodden down (taken over) of the Gentiles,** until the times of the Gentiles be fulfilled."

So who are the people that are scattered into all nations? Who are the Gentiles? The "Gentiles" are the "**Wild Olive Branch**" who accepted Christ when the small number of "Lost Sheep" Israelites in Judea rejected Christ along with the Gentile Judaism Edomite/Kenite/Greek Convert Jews.

(Left) Ashkenazi Jew. (Right) Real "authentic" Negro Bantus Jew with a literal "yoke of iron" around his neck as in Deuteronomy 28:48 "Curses of Israel".

Deuteronomy 28:48 (Curses of Israel) "Therefore shalt thou serve thine enemies which the LORD shall send against thee, in hunger, and in thirst, and in nakedness, and in want of all things: and **he shall put a yoke of iron upon thy neck,** until he have destroyed thee."

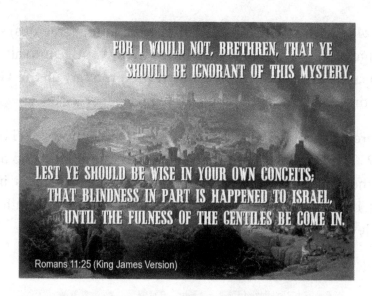

FOR I WOULD NOT, BRETHREN, THAT YE
SHOULD BE IGNORANT OF THIS MYSTERY,

LEST YE SHOULD BE WISE IN YOUR OWN CONCEITS;
THAT BLINDNESS IN PART IS HAPPENED TO ISRAEL,
UNTIL THE FULNESS OF THE GENTILES BE COME IN.

Romans 11:25 (King James Version)

(**Above**) Paul warns the followers of Christ called the "**Natsarim/Nasrani**" to not be "**Blind of the Mystery**". What mystery? The "mystery" that the Gentiles have taken the position of the "**wild olive branch**" with also the belief that the "**physical seed of Israel**" has been replaced with the "**Wild Olive Branch Imposter Gentiles**" who call themselves Jews today.

(**Above**) Sephardic Jewish women at the "**woman's sector**" of the Western Wailing Wall in the 19th Century. The Western Wailing Wall is the remains of the Roman "**Fortress Antonia**" wall completed during Herod the Great's era in the 1st century A.D., destroyed partially during the Crusades and eventually patched back up by the Turkish/Kurdish Arabs prior to the creation of the state of Israel in 1948. The **Sephardic Jews**, like the Ashkenazi Jews have the Paternal Y-DNA influenced by the Edomites mixture in the Levant/North Africa/South Europe (**E1b1b**), the Greeks (**G**), the Japhetic sons of Ashkenaz/Togarmah (**J2-M172**) and the diluted DNA of the original Black Arabs (**J1-M267**). They also have some small amount of DNA from the Khazars region (**R1a**) and the old region of where the Black Moors/Jews Dominated (**R1b**). They also carry the Maternal mtDNA of Europeans (**H/V, H, J, T, U, K**) and the maternal mtDNA of the Neanderthal-Denisovan-Sons of Cain/Kenites/Rechabites/Nethinims (**X**). The other significant mtDNA of the European Jews is the Nordic maternal influence in mtDNA (**W**) and (**I**).

On that note....let's do another a recap of Luke 21:24.

Luke 21:25-27 **"And there shall be signs in the sun, and in the moon, and in the stars; and upon the earth distress of nations, with perplexity; the sea and the waves roaring; Men's hearts failing them with fear, and for looking after those things which are coming on the earth: for the power of heaven shall be shaken. And then shall they see the Son of man coming in a cloud with power and great glory"**......hmm.

Yahusha (Jesus) is saying when he returns for the **Second coming** will the **time** of the Gentiles **"occupancy"** of Jerusalem-Israel be fulfilled (*i.e. come to an end*).

Now we have to fully understand what is a **"Jew"**, who was classified a **"Jew"** 2,000 years ago, and were the **"Israelites"** a different people than the **"Jews"**.

WHAT ABOUT WHEN CHRISTIANS USE THE "NEITHER JEW NOR GREEK" SCRIPTURE?

In **Galatians 3:27-29** it reads: "For all of you who were **baptized into Christ** have clothed yourselves with Christ. **There is neither Jew nor Greek,** there is neither slave nor free man, **there is neither male nor female**; for you are all **one** in Christ Jesus. And if you belong to Christ, then you are Abraham's descendants, heirs according to promise."

The important thing we must not forget is that Paul, although an Apostle....he was not a prophet or a part of the 12 disciples. Paul did not come speaking, **"Thus saith the Lord"**. Paul, like Judas, Thomas and others were subject to their own viewpoints on things during the 1st Century A.D. This is why the Book of Matthew, Mark, Luke and John are not all "identical". Paul gives a lot of "Opinions" that are not "Laws" but many Christians today live and die by the "Pauline Doctrine" more than the words of Christ or the Creator. In the 2nd Chapter of Genesis, God arranges the "first marriage" between man and woman. But Paul advises those men who are "unmarried" to remain "unmarried" if possible. In the Book of Genesis, God did not wish for man (Adam) to be alone forever…..so he made woman (Eve). A man is "**automatically**" single and unmarried when he comes out of the womb and enters into adulthood. He has no "**choice**" to be "**single**" or "**unmarried**". But Paul would rather the saints "not marry" if possible. But in the Old Testament, in **Proverbs 18:22** it says that whosover finds a wife, findeth a good thing and has **FAVOR** with the Creator.

Genesis 2:24 "Therefore shall a man leave his father and his mother, and shall cleave unto his wife: and they shall be **ONE FLESH**."

Proverbs 18:22 "**Whoso findeth a wife findeth a good thing**, and obtaineth favour of Yahuah (The Lord)."

Now here are Paul's words which uses "**It is good**", "**for I would**" and "**if**". But in the beginning the Apostle Paul says every man should have a wife but changes his "**opinion**" in the following scriptures.

1 Corinthians 7:1-2

"Now concerning the things whereof ye wrote unto me: **It is good** for a man not to touch a woman. Nevertheless to avoid fornication, **let every man have his own wife**, and **let every woman have her own husband**.

1 Corinthians 7: 7-9

"**FOR I WOULD** that all men were even as I myself am (*i.e. unmarried*). But every man hath his proper gift of God, one in this manner and another in that. **I say therefore to the unmarried and widows: IT IS GOOD IF they remain even as I (i.e. unmarried)**."

So, for all the single men reading the epistle (letter) of Corinthians, it would appear that Paul was conflicted in whether it is good to marry vs stay single. Christ did not speak to his disciples or the Jewish Pharisees in this matter. But Christ was not a mere man when he walked the earth....he was God manifested in the flesh. Christ also referenced the Torah which was written by the Israelite prophets of old.

The Galatian scripture "**Neither Jew nor Greek**" does not take away the fact that God has a special place for the authentic Blood "Children of Israel" he gave the "Covenant" to. All those whom the Old Testament calls "**Strangers**", "**Aliens**", or "**Foreigners**" are classified as such because in future prophecy they have their role to play alongside with Physical Hebrew Israelites....just as the 144,000 virgin Israelites have their role to play.

Mark 1:4-5 "John the Baptist appeared in the wilderness, **preaching a (water) baptism of repentance for the forgiveness of sins**. People went out to him from all of Jerusalem and the countryside of Judea. Confessing their sins, they were baptized by him in the Jordan River."

Matthew 3:11 "I **baptize you with water** for repentance, but after me will come One more powerful than I, whose sandals I am not worthy to carry. He (Christ) will **baptize you with the Holy Spirit** and with fire."

Even the Gentile (*possible Edomite*) Pharisee Jew named "**Nicodemus**" despite knowing the "**Oral Law**" was confused on how to make it into the Kingdom. Christ told him that one needed to be baptized with "**water**" and "**fire**". This confused him as many people in those days had not hear of baptism of the Spirit (*see Acts Chapter 19*). The only thing the Israelites and Jews were familiar with at that time was "**purification**" with baptism in a mikveh pool.

John 3:1-5 "There was a man of the Pharisees named **Nicodemus**, a ruler of the Jews. The same came to Yahusha (Jesus) by night and said unto Him, "Rabbi, we know that thou art a teacher come from God; for no man can do these miracles that thou doest, unless God be with him." Yahusha (Jesus) answered and said unto him, "Verily, verily I say unto thee, unless a man be born again, he cannot see the Kingdom of God. Nicodemus said unto Him, "How can a man be born when he is old? Can he enter a second time into his mother's womb and be born?" Yahusha (Jesus) answered, "**Verily, verily I say unto thee, unless a man be born of water and of the Spirit, he cannot enter into the Kingdom of God**.

(**Above**) Jewish "**Mikveh**" Bath areas were the place for ritual immersion in Judaism. The water in this bath had to be from a spring or a well (naturally flowing water) and it was primarily used for the following reasons of **purification**.

- Ritual purity after menstruation or childbirth.
- Per tradition for conversion to Ashkenazi/Sephardic Judaism. **Note:** *Every Ethiopian Jew had to be immersed in the Mikveh bath by Gentile Ashkenazi Jews before being allowed to live in Israel after Operation Moses/Solomon.*
- Immerse newly acquired utensils using in serving and eating food.
- Purification after sex or nocturnal emissions.
- Purification before entering the Temple.
- Purification of persons with abnormal skin conditions or abnormal discharges of bodily fluids.
- After contact with a corpse or a grave.

Although terms as such "**baptized**" and "**Christ**" today sound exclusively Christian it was clearly not so in Paul's time. In fact, back in the first century they could appear exclusively Israelitish!

Around 330 B.C. the Greeks, led by Alexander the Great, invaded Egypt and Judea/Israel. The Greeks eventually settled into the land of Israel, becoming the **majority people** in the land. Some converted to **"Judaism" as in the case of the Hasmonean Maccabean Family (also the Edomites), while** others maintained their pagan Greek heritage and religion. Remember, only a "**remnant**" of the Southern Kingdom of Judah and Benjamin returned back to Israel during the Persian Rule, but when the Greeks defeated the Persians, many Israelites from the Tribe of Judah were already removed from Israel.

Joel 3:6 "The Children also of Judah and the children of Jerusalem **have ye sold unto the Grecians** that ye might remove them far from their border.

That being said, during the time after Christ's ministry on earth when someone who was Greek went through the Jewish ritual of washing with water (mikveh/baptism) in the name of "**Judaism**" and the "**Jewish Messiah**", and in so doing professed faith in Israel's God, something very important happened – The Greeks believed in their heart that any Greek man or woman, after "**ritual immersion**" in "**their**" water, after circumcision and professing to worship the God of Israel in some real way made them **become a physical child of Abraham/Israel and co-heirs together with the "Real Israelites" to the promise of Israel's God!** This is how the Maccabean John Hyrcanus I "**converted**" the Edomites into becoming "**Jews**" during the 1st Century B.C. Therefore, this same principle applied or was used by Paul in regards to the "**followers of Christ**", no matter what kind of "**Gentiles**" they were: Greek pagans, Greek Jews, Scythians, Edomites, Samaritans, Barbarians, Romans or Scythians.

Colossians 3:11 "Where there is neither **Greek nor Jew**, circumcision nor uncircumcision, **Barbarian, Scythian**, bond nor free: but Christ is all, and in all."

The distinction between Real Israelites, Greek Jews by conversion and Greeks Gentiles was **not** abolished, just as the distinction between men and women by Paul (*the Benjaminite*) was not abolished either. Instead, because of the birth of Yahusha HaMashiach (Christ Jesus), there was no more **discrimination** between them. This means that while Israelites were still distinct from Gentiles (or strangers), in regards to "**Salvation**" they were not *preferred* above Gentiles, just as men were no longer preferred above women in the Kingdom of God. This can be seen in the account of Cornelius, the Gentile Roman Centurion and his Gentile friends.

Acts 10:44 "While Peter was yet speaking these words, the Holy Ghost fell on all those who heard the Word. And those of the Circumcision who believed were astonished, as many as came with Peter, **because the gift of the Holy Ghost was poured out also on the Gentiles. For they heard them speak with tongues and magnify God.** Then answered Peter, "Can any man forbid water, that these should not be baptized who have received the Holy Ghost, as well as we?"

The Y-DNA branches

#	Y-DNA SNP
TD-01	E1b-V22?-333966
TD-02	E1b-V22-70137
TD-03	E1b-V13?-N94872
TD-04	E1b-M78-57904
TD-05	E1b-L791-Y4972
TD-06	J1-YSC76-L823-c
TD-07	J1-Z640-2nd
TD-08	J2a-M319?-134183
TD-09	J2a-L26-204156
TD-10	G-PF3146-34997
TD-11	G-L293-93306
TD-12	G-U1-53659
TD-13	G-U1-359794
TD-14	G-P303-M278
TD-15	R1a-Z93?-74750
TD-16	Q-L53-291218

(Above) Romaniote "Greek" Maccabean descent Jews- The earliest reference to a Greek Jew is an inscription dated around **250 B.C.**, found in **Oropos**, a small coastal town between Athens and Boeotia in **Greece,** which refers to "**Moschos, son of Moschion the Jew**". Remember, **Greek Emperor Alexander the Great conquered Judea in 330 A.D.**, which is 80 years prior. The Romaniotes are **Greek Jews**, supposedly distinct from both Ashkenazi and Sephardic Jews. However, their Romaniote oral tradition states that their people aka the "**Gentile Jews**" arrived in Ioannina (**Northwest Greece near Albania**) shortly after the destruction of the Second Temple in Jerusalem in 70 A.D. So who are these Romaniote Jews really? What does their DNA have to say about it?

Genetic testing on the Romaniote Jews showed a common ancestry with Ashkenazi Jews and the Sephardic Jews of today. The Major Y-DNA of these Romaniote Jews were "**G**" which corresponds to Europeans of **Greek descent** and "**E1b1b**" which came into existence as a significant Y-DNA Haplogroup in North Africa/Mediterranean Europe/Levant because of the **influence of Edom's seed** over 2,000 years ago in the Levant. **These are your Maccabean Greek-Roman-Edomite Jews from 2,300 years ago, not the "Real Israelites" of the Bible**. The Y-DNA J2a corresponds to the territory of Tubal (Japheth), Togarmah (Japheth) and the Ottoman Turks. Notice how **Haplogroup Q** is seen "isolated" in this batch of Romaniote Jewish DNA. This DNA Haplogroup is most often seen in pre-Columbus America with the Native Americans. How did that get there if these Jews claim a 2,000-year old history dating back to the 2nd temple being destroyed in 70 A.D. Perhaps this was some passed Y-DNA from father to father to father from an Israelite ancestor of today's indigenous Amerindian people. History and DNA doesn't lie.

SO DOES THE "FOURTH BEAST" WAGE WAR WITH THE "ISREALITES" AND WILL THE ANTICHRIST ALSO FOLLOW SUIT ATTACKING "GOD'S CHOSEN PEOPLE"?

To determine this we must start with two important scriptures.

1. **Daniel 17: 19-21** "Then I would know the truth of the fourth beast, **which was diverse from all the others**, exceeding dreadful, whose teeth were of iron, and his nails of brass; which devoured, brake in pieces, and stamped the residue with his feet; And of the ten horns (**kingdoms**) that were in his head, and of the other which came up, and before whom three fell; even of that horn that had eyes, and a mouth that spake very great things, whose look was more stout than his fellows. **I beheld, and the same horn made war with the Saints (Qaddish-Holy Ones/Israelites), and prevailed against them;**

2. **Daniel 7:25** "And he shall speak great words against the Most High, and shall wear out the **Saints of the Most High**, and **THINK TO CHANGE TIMES AND LAW**: and **THEY SHALL**

169

BE GIVEN shall be given into his hand until a time and times and the dividing of time.

Fact: *With the appearance of the "**Mandela Effect**" and D-Wave Quantum Computers things in our normal "**Reality**" are changing "**supernaturally**" (i.e. logos, songs, commercials, movies, products/goods and the bible). Some people believe the "Antichrist Beast System" of this world has now been helped by Satan/Fallen Angels to manipulate the concept of "**TIME** (past/present/future)" and the "**LAWS of Nature** (parallel dimensions/Demonic spiritual realm separated by the "Veil"). For example, the "Elite" know that in order to get the world to accept a "New Religion", people must not care about religion. They must also discredit the Bible and get people to read it as just an "ordinary fictional book". Dr. Richard Day's lecture in 1969 nicknamed, "**New Order of Barbarians**" details that "**certain words in the bible**" **will be changed**. For example, instead of saying "altar" you say "table". Instead of saying "sacrifice" you say "meal". This gives the scripture a different meaning and makes it "less important" to the reader. In Exodus 3:15 (King James Version) these changes can be seen.*

Exodus 32:15 *"And Moses turned, and went down from the mount, and the* **TWO TABLES OF THE TESTIMONY** *were in his hand,* **THE TABLES** *were written on both their sides; on the one side and on the other were they written."*

*Notice the word "**Tables**" and "**Tablets**" are totally different. The **Two Stone Tablets of the Covenant Law**" are now replaced with the "**Two Tables of the Testimony**". The word "**Testimony**" and "**Covenant**" have two different definitions.....thus adding a different "**meaning**" to the scripture.*

*There are many more Scriptures like this one that show subtle changes to the Bible (i.e. google "**Mandela Effect Bible**"). How this is happening" Nobody really knows.*

*However, many people believe Daniel 7:25 is referring to when the Catholic Church changed the **Lunar Hebrew Israelite Sabbaths** to the Gregorian "**Sabbath-SAT-urn Day**" and later changed the day of Christian Worship to*

"SUN-day". Nevertheless, many people cannot ignore the "Mandela Effect" and all the changes that have been happening in our "Physical 5-10-year-old King James Bibles".

So, moving forward, we know that 3 Beasts/Kingdoms have come and went according to history. This is the **Babylonian, Persian and Greek** Kingdoms. So let's talk about the **FOURTH BEAST** and who it represents today. It is the "**Old**" **Roman Empire Kingdom** which eventually fell, giving rise to **10** smaller Kingdoms that would rule over it in its place? Here are the facts:

Daniel 7:11 "I beheld then because of the voice of the great words which the horn spake: **I beheld even till the beast (Roman Empire) was slain**, and his body destroyed, and given to the burning flame.

Was **Daniel 7:11** fulfilled in the **5th Century A.D.**? Consider this!

ODOACER

Flavius Odoacer also known as "**Flavius**" was a soldier who in 476 A.D. became the **FIRST "*GERMAN*" King of ROME** (476–493 A.D.), defeating the **last "Roman-blooded" Emperor Romulus Augustulus**. His reign is commonly seen as marking the end of the "Official" Old **Western Roman Empire**. He would be considered by some a "**Barbarian**" (*i.e. someone not of Roman or Greek stock*). I will discuss the word "**Barbarian**" later and its connection to **Germany**.

Theoderic the Great's Seal 5th century A.D.

In 488 A.D., **Eastern Roman Emperor "Tarasis"** who adopted the Greek name **"Zeno"** (*of Isaurian, Turkish-Scythian descent*) ordered **Theoderic the Great** to overthrow the German **Flavius Odoacer**, who had likewise been made patrician and King of Western Italy (**aka WESTERN ROMAN EMPIRE**), but who had since betrayed Zeno, supporting the rebellious Roman general of the Eastern Roman Empire...**Leontius**. After a victorious three-year war, **Theoderic** (*a German*) killed **Odoacer** with his own hands, settled his 200,000-250,000 people in Italy, & founded a **German Ostrogothic Kingdom** based in Ravenna (North Italian capital city of the Western Roman Empire).

BIBLE PROPHECY: GOMER (GOG), THE GERMANS, THE ASSYRIANS AND THE SCYTHIANS.

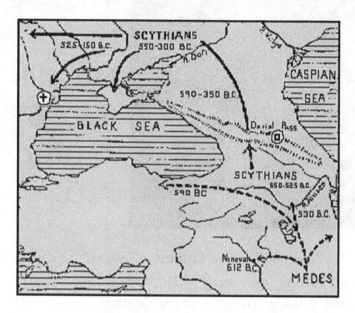

(**Above**) The Capital of **Assyria** back in Biblical times was "**Nineveh**", which is now in **Northern Iraq**. The Tigris and the Euphrates River starts in Turkey and flows through Assyria through Iraq and into the Persian Gulf. Many historians believe the Assyrian people migrated from their land in the Middle East into Asia Minor (Turkey), then through the Caucasus Mountains (between Black Sea and Caspian Sea/Khazar Sea) and into Eastern Europe. This is when the names "**Scythians**" and "**Germans**" started appearing in Books from different authors such as **Pliny the Elder** or **Herodotus**. So who were these Scythians? Were they a mix of Western European Japhethites by way of Gomer's/Japheth's seed and the Shemitic Assyrians? We know that Japheth is the progenitor of the White Races and Asshur was one of the Sons of Shem, from which all Shemites (*including the Black Arabs and Black Israelites*) would descend from. We also know that Nimrod, the son of Cush (Sudan/Ethiopia) ruled over Mesopotamia including Assyria whose capitol in those days was "Nineveh".

Genesis 10:8-12 "And Cush begat Nimrod: he began to be a mighty one in the earth. He was a mighty hunter before the LORD: wherefore it is said, Even as Nimrod the mighty hunter before the LORD. And the beginning of his kingdom was **Babel** (Babylon), and **Erech** (Uruk), and **Accad** (i.e. Akkadians), and **Calneh**, in the land of Shinar (Sumer-Iraq/Iran). Out of that land went forth **Asshur**, and builded **Nineveh**, and the city Rehoboth and builded Nineveh, and the city Rehoboth, and Calah, and Resen between Nineveh and Calah: the same is a great city."

(**Left**) Nilotic Cushite young men from the Dinka Tribe, Sudan (Africa). (**Right**) Northern Iraqi children. In Iraq those who follow Islam are considered **"Iraqi Arabs"** while those that follow Christianity are considered **"Chaldeans"**. Both groups believe they are descendants of the ancient **"Assyrians"** or the Chaldeans who lived in the **"Land of Ur"** during Abraham's time. So are both of these people "groups" the authentic people from "the land"? Or is someone an **"invader/colonizer"** to the land? We know that the Nubian Cushites were a **"Black Race"** of people, but what about the ancient **"Assyrians"** from the lineage of Shem? Well, either way we look at it, if the Children of Cush (**under Nimrod**) ruled in Assyria for a time, we would expect some "mixing" to have occurred, thus leaving a race of dark-skinned people in Assyria. But that doesn't seem to be the case today in Modern day Syria and Iraq. So where are the dark-skinned Assyrians at? The

"**Dinka**" Tribesmen are known by the Bantus people in Kenya as "**Nilotes**" or "**Cushite**" people. What about today's Iraqi people?

In **Micah 5:6** the **Land of Assyria** is also mentioned to be the "**Land of Nimrod (Son of Cush)**". So if this is the case, shouldn't the Assyrians of Ancient times have been a people of "**brown color**" like the Hamitic Cushites in Sudan and Ethiopia?

What does DNA have to say about this?

(**Above**) In Central and Eastern Europe where Germany is the most common Y-DNA Haplogroup is "**R1a**". However, the Y-DNA **R1a** is found also in India, Pakistan, Asia and in North America (Native Americans). So where did this "**R1a**" Y-DNA originate from? Did it originate with some of the people of East Indian descent who carried it thousands of years ago into Eastern Europe? This is a proposed "**possibility**" according to geneticists.

In the "**Iraq DNA Project**" under www.FamilyTreeDNA.com, the Iraqi's tested were found to carry only a small percent of the Y-DNA "**R1a**". However, they were found to carry the Y-DNA "**G**" (**Greece-Japheth by way of Javan**), "**E1b1b (E-L117/E-M35-Edom)**", "**J1 (Black**

176

Arabs)", and "**J2 (Ottoman Turks/Kurds-Japheth by way of Togarmah)**".

The reason for this is because **Y-DNA** is only passed down "**only**" from "**Father to Son**". If the Ancient Assyrians 3,000 years ago ventured into Eastern Europe, the Assyrian males in having children with their women (*or Japhetic "white-skinned" women*) would've passed down their "Y" Sex Chromosome to any future children be it white-skinned or brown-skinned. Even if the Assyrian men one day decided to leave Eastern Europe/Asia Minor or were killed off by other nations their "Y DNA" would still continue in that area in their male seeds until "**Foreign invading Men**" from another country started to repopulate with the local women. If this is the case, the "**R**" Y-DNA would essentially be a "Semitic" people migration marker, like its sister **Y-DNA haplogroup** "**Q**", which is seen mostly in Native Americans/Indigenous Indians but can be seen also in Israel, Iran/Iraq, India and Eastern Europe.

For the Iraqi people, the **Greeks**, the **Edomites**, the **Black Arabs** and the **Ottoman Islamic Turks** were the major nations that spent the most time throughout history in Mesopotamia (Iraq). Their male descendants would pass on their "Y-DNA" to the boys born to ANY woman, **white-skinned or black-skinned**. But were the Greeks, the Edomites, the Togarmah-Turks or the Black Arabs **TRUE NATIVES** to Ancient Babylon? Remember, **Arphaxad's** descendants settled in Babylon. Arphaxad was the ancestor of the Ancient **Chaldeans**, the **Sumerians**, the **Akkadians** and the **Babylonians (i.e. King Nebuchadnezzar)**.

(**Above**) Assyrian pagan god **Nisroch** relic. (**Left**) Found in Ecuador, South America by Father **Crespi** is a real Assyrian-Babylonian stone carved depiction of the Assyrian-Babylonian god **Nisroch/Nisrok** (**Right**). It is said that the Assyrian King Sennacherib worshipped this pagan god in his temple even up until his death outlined in the Bible in **2 Kings 19:37** and **Isaiah 37:38.** How can this be? Hold up! Wasn't the 10 Lost Tribes of Israel captured by the Assyrians and then deported out of Israel into Assyria? Why would an Assyrian pagan god be found in "Indigenous Indian" territory in Ecuador, South America?

2 Kings 17:5-6

"Then the King of Assyria invaded the whole land and went up to Samaria and besieged it three years. In the ninth year of Hoshea, **the king of Assyria captured Samaria (Northern Israel) and carried Israel away into exile to Assyria**, and settled them in **Halah (Assyria)** and **Habor (Assyria)**, on the river of Gozan, and in the cities of the **Medes (Persia-Iran)**."

(**Above**) Keep in mind when reading **2 Kings 17:5-6**, that Ancient **Assyria** and **Medes** is modern day "**Syria, Iraq and Iran**". These countries are where the 10 Northern Tribes of Israel were dropped off at around 700 B.C. So if these "Israelites" were exiled to these countries, common sense would say that these Israelites didn't try to head back West to Israel, but East into what would be known today as "India". Remember, it wasn't until 1919 that **Afghanistan** "split" from India to become its own country and 1947 when **Pakistan** likewise "split" from India to become its own country. So with this knowledge now, should we be looking to **India** or **Central Asia** for clues as to the migration routes of the **10 Tribes of Israel** that were exiled into the East (Orient).

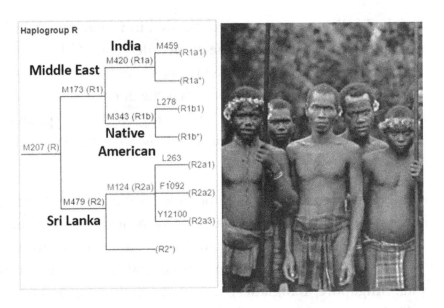

(Left) Y-DNA "R" Haplogroup chart. The oldest groups of the Y-DNA "R" Haplogroup can be found in the Middle East, Sri Lanka, India and Native America territory.....not Eastern Europe. So who passed or brought this Y-DNA "R" to Europe? European geneticists tend to sometimes believe they brought the "R" Y-DNA Haplogroup into India.....but can Caucasian White people turn as dark as Indians, or even as dark as Black people? The answer is "No". You be the judge. (Right) Aeta/Agta Negrito men from the Philippines. They carry the father Haplogroup "P" that gave rise to the "R" Haplogroup. They look more "**Negroid**" than "**Caucasoid**". What does this all mean?

Some geneticists believe the Y-DNA "R" presence in Europe and Asia (i.e. India) is an "**Out of the Middle East**" migration event just like the "**Out of Africa**" migration event that happened many of centuries ago. The Y-DNA "R" is seen in Turkey, Mesopotamia, Arabia, Oman, UAE, and Iran. It is also seen in Europe (R1b and R1a) as well as South Asia (Pakistan, Afghanistan, India, Sri Lanka). The "Parent-Ancestral Y-DNA Haplogroup" to "**R**" is Haplogroup "**P**" or "**K2b2**", which is seen in the Aeta/Agta Negritos of the Philippines and some people in Papua New Guinea (Indonesia). The Y-DNA **P (basal), P1** and **P2** can all be found together in the Aeta/Agta Negritos in Luzon, the northern-most

Island of the **Philippines**. It can also be seen in **India, Nepal** and the brown-skinned **Papua New Guinean people**. All of these people groups are people with "brown skin tones", not white skin tones. Therefore, it is very convincing to say that the ancient Semitic people in the Middle East and Indus Valley region were "**people of color**"....not the white-skinned "**Caucasoid**" Arabs we see today in the Middle East.

Something also to consider is that the oldest subgroups of "**R1a**" are seen in the people of **India** and select **Native Americans**. This means that the original Assyrian-Sumerian-Babylonian people, including their stock are mostly found in **India, Pakistan, Afghanistan, Malaysia, Singapore, Bangladesh** and some **Native Americans**. The "diluted" down people who call themselves "Assyrians" today (**i.e. Chaldeans, Turks, Muslim Iraqis**) have an overwhelming "White" heritage based on their maternal DNA (mother) and white skin color. They also carry the genetic information passed down from the Ancient Greeks and the Ottoman Turks/Kurds who are descendants of **Japheth**, not **Shem-Abraham**.

Today many Germanic, Slavic and Turkish people are those who carry the Y-DNA "**R1a**" and "**J2-M172**". The Y-DNA "**R2**" can also be seen in India as well as Sri Lanka, while Y-DNA "**R1b**" is seen in very low frequencies in India, but is found in moderate frequencies in Central/West Africa, Native Americans, Latinos and the land of the Black Jews/Black Moors (Spain/Portugal).

So how did any Semitic Blood from the Sons of Shem ever make its way into Europe? Easy, the same way the original Black "**Shemitic**" Arabs and the "**Shemitic**" Edomites made their way into Europe!

But pay **CLOSE ATTENTION** to this breakdown as I continue to breakdown the connection of **Edom**, the **Holy Roman Empire** (West & East), the **Khazars** and **Germany** to the future prophecies in the Book of Daniel!

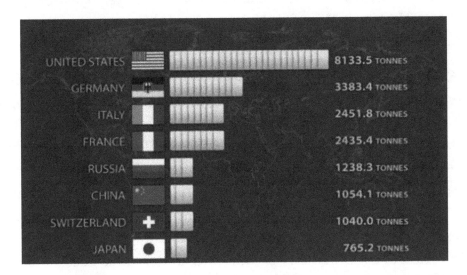

(**Above**) The **Top Gold Reserve "holding"** countries are **United States** (*i.e. daughter of Babylon*), **Germany, Jewish International Monetary Fund (IMF)**, **Italy (Rome)**, France, Russia, China and Switzerland (*i.e. home of the Swiss Banks*). The Jewish founded "**IMF (International Monetary Fund)**" although not a country is also a top 5 major Gold-holder in the World.

With the exit of Britain from the European Union (called "**Brexit**") in 2016, Germany is the new "**Big Dog**" economically holding Europe and the "**European Union**" together. If Germany was to ever "**exit**" from the "European Union" it could spell "The End" of the European Union as we know it. But who is "**Germany**" or should I say, "**Whose seed or what nation(s) has merged to form Germany**".

Note: *Edom's DNA influence from over 2,000 years ago, called "Y-DNA E1b1b" is divided into 4 Main Branches in Europe, but is still prevalent in the* **North African Arabs**, *the* **Middle Eastern Arabs** *and select African Tribes (i.e. Maasalit, Fur Tribe).* **E1b1b (E-L540 is seen in Germany). E1b1b (E-L117/E-M35, E-L17, E-L143 and E-L241 is seen in England).** *The Y-DNA* **"E1b1b" is also found in Ashkenazi Jews, Sephardic Jews and Mizrahi Jews.** *This "E1b1b" is seen in Mediterranean Europe, North Africa and the Middle East. How could this be?* **Edom's family got around!**

In 63 B.C., Roman Emperor Pompey invaded Jerusalem. (**Note: some Cameroonians in Africa from the Babanki-Tikar Tribe say their people left Israel around the time when Pompey invaded Jerusalem in 63 B.C. setting up Roman-Edomite governed provinces in Israel.**) Around the time when this happened Greek Maccabean John Hyrcanus II was appointed High Priest of Israel. There was a struggle between Pompey and Julius Caesar for total control of the Roman Empire.....which Caesar ultimately won. Hyrcanus II was able to keep his position as High Priest of Israel in the 1st Century B.C. under Julius Caesar. Herod Antipater was also named ruler of Judea. Herod later made a vacancy in the "Gentile" Jewish High Priesthood by having Aristobulus III (53-36 B.C.) put to death. Aristobulus was the last male descendant of the Hasmonean (Maccabean) royal house. He was the brother of Herod the Great's wife "Mariamne" and grandson of Aristobulus II. According to Flavius Josephus's record, the Edomite Herodian family appointed seven Jewish High Priests before the destruction of the Second Temple in Jerusalem in 70 A.D. (see Antiquities of the Jews 20.10.1). Before Christ was even born the Greek "Gentile" Jews called the "Maccabeans" under John Hyrcanus I (135-105 A.D.) were the ones that "welcomed" the Idumean Edomites to settle into the territory of Judah. Flavius Josephus quotes this in his literary works when he said:

"That country is also called Judea, **and the people JEWS**; and **this name is given also to as many as embrace THEIR RELIGION** (Yahwism/Karaite Judaism), though of other nations. But then upon what foundation so good a governor as Hyrcanus took upon himself to compel these Idumeans (Edomites) either **to BECOME JEWS or to leave THEIR COUNTRY** (Greeks new country), deserves great consideration. I suppose it was because they had long ago been driven out of the land of Edom, and had seized on and possessed the Tribe of Simeon (their land, not the people), and all the southern part of the Tribe of Judah, which was the peculiar inheritance of the worshippers of the **TRUE GOD WITHOUT IDOLATRY."**

Flavius Josephus states in *"the Antiquities of the Jews, XIII, ix, 1"*, regarding the Edomites, **"they were hereafter no other than Jews".**

The Jewish Encyclopedia 1903 edition also says:

"They were then incorporated with the Jewish nation, and their country was called by the Greeks and Romans "Idumea"....From this time the Idumeans ceased to be a separate nation, though the name "Idumea" still existed in the time of Jerome."

It gets even deeper though!

According to the Y-DNA studies of the **Ashkenazi Jewish Wertheim-Giterman Rabbinical lineage**, often referred to as the "**Savran-Bendery Hasidic dynasty**", these **Ukraine Jews** most commonly carry the **Y-DNA E-L117**, which was previously also known as E-M35. In genetic literature, today this is simplified as "E3b" or "E1b1b". What is interesting is that Greeks, Arabs, Sephardic Jews, Ashkenazi Jews, Italians, Balkans, and many Europeans today carry this paternal Y-DNA "E1b1b (E-L117) bloodline still. But here is where we can trace the Ashkenazi Jewish Wertheim-Giterman Rabbinical (so-called Levite) family back to the time when Edom and the Greeks were the major players (**i.e. new residents**) in Israel. Most Ashkenazi Jews cannot trace their ancestry back to the "**mandated**" adoption of fixed, inherited surnames (*i.e. Rothschild, Freidman, Goldberg, Finkelstein, Steinberg, Levine*) during the **1787 Austro-Hungarian law in Europe**.

185

The only Jewish "**exceptions**" to this law was the major rabbinical families who adopted "**fixed surnames**" long before they were mandated by the Austrian-Hungarian government. Geneticists found out that the **Edomite "E1b1b" Y-DNA**" is the second most prevalent Haplogroup among the European Ashkenazi/Sephardic Jewish population outside of the "**J1/J2**" Haplogroups which come from the 7th Century A.D. **Black Arabs** and the 13th Century **Ottoman "Togarmah" Turks/Kurds** respectively. This E1b1b haplogroup is also seen in the Ashkenazi, Sephardic and Samaritan Jewish communities in Israel who claim to be from the Tribe of Levi. This suggests that Edom's paternal "**mark**" has been passed down from 2,000 years ago to the White Gentiles European Jews today who believe they are in fact "**Real Israelites**" when in reality they have the blood of Greeks, Edomites, Scythians, Barbarians, Romans, Turks, Kurds and diluted Black Arabs running in their veins/arteries. Many of the Jews today claim the root word "**Ashkenaz**" in the word "**Ashkenazi Jews**" is synonymous with the word "**German/Germany**". But what clues does this give us? I will break down "Germany's" role in the "**End Times**" in just a few!

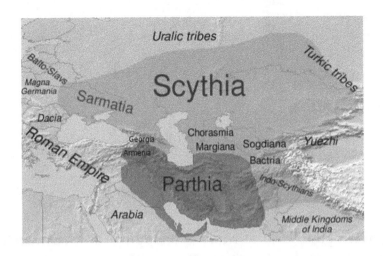

Paul Kriwaczek in his book *'In Search of Zarathustra: Across Iran and Central Asia To Find the World's First Prophet'* states that the Hebrew word "**Ashkenazi**" originally meant a "**Scythian**". But most people today associate the word "**Ashkenaz**" with **German**. Is it a coincidence that "**Yiddish**", the language of the Ashkenazi Jews is so much "**German**" that if you can speak German....you can partly understand their "**bootleg Gentile Hebrew?**" Did ancient Hebrew speakers use one term to describe all the "**Barbarians**" beyond the Danube, or did they actually distinguish them from **the Goths (Germans) and the Scythians?**"

(**Above**) Map of the Turks territory overlapping the Khazarian territory around the 6th to 8th Century A.D. The land the Turks once occupied or were known to occupy is in the "old" **Scythian, Khazarian,** and **Goth (Germanic)** territory. Some say "German" means "Germ-Man". What does a Germ do to its host body? It destroys it! Will the Germans be part of the hand of the Fourth Beast (Roman Empire) that leads us into the "Last Days"?

The Collapse of the Roman Empire

The **Barbarians/Scythians** were people from central and northern Europe. In the 5th century A.D. they invaded the declining Roman Empire and they gradually carved it up the between them. The Barbarians never intended to destroy the Roman Empire, they wanted to share in its wealth.

In December 406 A.D., a group of **Germanic tribes (*mixed with the DNA of Cain*)** entered Gaul (*i.e. Western Europe*) and settled there. The Romans were unable to stop them. Nevertheless, at first the Germanic settlers accepted Roman way of things. However, as the Roman Empire broke down they gradually formed **independent kingdoms such as Spain, France, Germany, Portugal, Greece, Italy, and England. These countries would be the ones that would later persecute and enslave then Negro Israelites! But keep this in**

188

mind.....during this time in the 5th Century A.D. the Germans were running the show!

So, with all of this said, will the **"Final Resurrection"** of the Holy Roman Empire be led by **Germany or people of German descent**? Germany's rise to world dominating power could be unknown to the world because the modern name **"Germany"** is not used in the Bible. If we can link "Germany" to a Biblical name or "identity" will we then understand **"End Time prophecy"** and the role they will play with the European Union-Roman Catholic Church giants on the International Scene.

The oldest city in Germany is **"Trier"**, a city whose inhabitants say was founded around 2,000 B.C. by the **Assyrians**. In Joseph K. L. Bihl's book **"In Deutschen Landen"** it says, "Trier was founded by Prince Trebeta, a son of the famous Assyrian King Ninus from 2166 B.C." In the 1st Century A.D., Roman Emperor Julius Caesar and Augustus conquered "Trier" making it a **"Second Rome"**. In 326 A.D., the first Roman Christian King **"Constantine"** established the oldest church, the **"Trier Cathedral"** here. Why?

(**Above**) Both American and Germany's Symbol is the Eagle, which is also the symbol of Ancient Edom.

(**Above**) Edomite Limestone Eagle symbol found in Petra (Jordan), 1st Century A.D. Petra was the land of Edom, near Mt. Seir. As you can see the architecture work of Petra (Edom territory) mimics "Ancient Rome" and the United States of America. Coincidence?

Obadiah 1:4 "**Though thou exalt thyself as the eagle,** and though thou set thy nest among the stars, thence will I bring thee down, saith the Lord.

2 Esdras 6:9 "For Esau (Edom) is **the end of the world**, and Jacob (Israelites) is the beginning of it that followeth."

Is this a warning?

Some believe that the Assyrians migrated up through the Caucasus mountains into what is now Germany where they set up the city **Trier**. After some time, **"white nations"** or perhaps the "red-headed **Neanderthal sons of Cain"** came over to Eastern Europe where they mixed with some of the Assyrian people. Just like the Black Arab men passing down their **"Y-DNA J1"** gene with the Khazars during the **"Arab-Khazar wars"**, the Assyrians likely also passed down their **"Y-DNA R1a"** gene with the Germans/Eastern Europeans. But these Assyrians in Europe could've also been "infected" with the DNA of Cain as Neanderthal remains have been found all throughout Europe, Russia and Central Asia. Could this be possible? Well, again the most ancient form of **"R1a"** Y-DNA Haplogroup is found now mostly in the Indus Valley Region which is modern day Pakistan, Afghanistan and North India (*especially in the Brahmin Priests who rarely marry outside of their clan/tribe*). Keep this in mind as well......some of the influences of the South Indian Dravidian Malayalam and Tamil languages comes from Semitic **Sumerian-Assyrian** Cuneiform Sanskrit and Aramaic (official language of Assyria/Syria in the 4th century B.C.). **Note: This I will prove later in the book.**

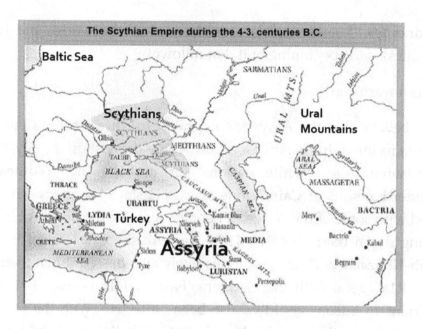

The Scythian Empire during the 4-3. centuries B.C.

Supposedly archaeological proof reveals that after multiple conquests in the Middle East (including the Levant) by the Babylonians, Persians, Greeks, and Romans, some of the Assyrian people migrated northwards into the land north of the Black Sea. The Greeks and Romans noted that the territory of the "**Scythians**" extended into Eastern Europe from the **Baltic Sea** (near Lithuania) to the **Ural Mountains** (Russia) and South until the northern border of the Black Sea. Today this area **is Slavic-Germanic-Russian territory**. Most of the Ashkenazi Jews come from Prussia, Russia, Poland, Germany and other Slavic-Turkish lands. From the 14th Century to the 20th Century Prussia was a German Empire full of Ashkenazi-Khazar Jews. This is part of their heritage. As I have outlined before the maternal DNA of **Catholic Christian Germans** (*like Chancellor of Germany Angela Merkel*) and **Ashkenazi Jewish Germans** (*i.e. like Hitler*) is the same. This means it is possible that the German people, Ashkenazi Jews and Sephardic Jews are descendants of the Ancient **Scythians**.

WHAT IS THE SIGNIFICANCE OF GERMANY TODAY?

(Left) **Adam Weishaupt** *founded the* **Bavarian Illuminati** *in 1776 A.D., just as the U.S.A was founded in 1776 A.D. Adam Weishaupt was a* **German**. *He was also a Jesuit, a Catholic and a Freemason.* *(Right)* **Hitler** *and the* *"Vril" Secret Society" was said to have tapped into "Satanic/Demonic" secrets of the Universe thanks to UFO/Fallen Angel intelligence. Hitler was also a* **German descendant of the Jewish Rothschild family**.

(**Above**) *Pilot Admiral Richard Byrd was said to have flown into the* "**hollow earth**" *via the North and South Poles in the 1920's and 1940's. Inside the Hollow Earth UFO flying saucers with* "**Swastika**" *symbols were spotted. During* **Operation High Jump** *in the 1940's Admiral Byrd led a team of almost 5,000 men to Antarctica to seek out a secret German UFO station based on* **Viktor Shauberger's Vortex Mechanics and Electromagnetic power research.** *Quick advancements in magnetic energy research and aircraft flight advancements arose out of Germany, including* "**Time Travel**" *with the secret* "**Bell**" *device (**Above**). During the Hitler Regime, it is said that German Scientists figured out a way to split the* "**atom**", *the building blocks of life. They also were able to tap into* "**magnetic energy**" *propulsion systems enabling them to test* "**UFO-like**" *flying saucer space ships. After the Germans were defeated in World War II, under* **Project Paperclip**, *over 1,000 German scientists, engineers, technicians were brought to the U.S.A where they helped skyrocket NASA's space program.*

The Illuminati

Adam Weishaupt

- 1776: Adam Weishaupt officially completes his organisation of the Illuminati on May 1 of this year. The purpose of the Illuminati is to divide the goyim (all non-Jews) through political, economic, social, and religious means. The opposing sides were to be armed and incidents were to be provided in order for them to: fight amongst themselves; destroy national governments; destroy religious institutions; and eventually destroy each other.

The history of Bavaria, **South Germany** (*birthplace of the Illuminati*) stretches from its earliest settlement and formation as a "**duchy**" in the **6th century A.D.** through the Holy Roman Empire to becoming an independent kingdom and finally a state of the **Federal Republic of Germany**.

Theodoric the Great (475-526 A.D.), was king of the **German Ostrogoths** (475–526 A.D.), ruler of Western Roman Empire in Italy (493–526 A.D.), regent of the Visigoths (511–526 A.D.), and an aristocrat of the Holy Roman Empire. His German Gothic name, "the Amali", also called Amals/Amalings, were a leading dynasty of the Goths, a Germanic people who confronted the Roman Empire in its declining years in the west. They eventually became the royal house of the Ostrogoths and founded the **Ostrogothic Kingdom of Italy (Rome)**.

*Otto I (above) was a **German (Goth) king** born around 936 A.D. He was crowned by Pope John XII emperor of the **Holy Roman Empire** from 962 A.D. until his death in 973 A.D. This marked the Division of the Roman Empire into smaller divisions.* **Could this be what the Book of Daniel & Revelation talked about.....warning us of when and where to look out for the Biblical Antichrist?**

Daniel 7:7 "After this I saw in the night visions, and behold a **fourth beast**, dreadful and terrible, and strong exceedingly; and it had great iron teeth: it devoured and brake in pieces, and stamped the residue with the feet of it: and it was diverse from all the beasts that were before it, and it had **TEN HORNS.**"

Daniel 7:23-24 "Thus he said, the fourth beast **(Rome)** shall be the **fourth kingdom upon earth,** which shall be diverse from all kingdoms, and shall devour the whole earth, and shall tread it down, and break it in pieces. **And the ten horns out of this kingdom are ten kings that shall arise:** and another shall rise after them; and he shall be diverse from the first, and he shall subdue **three kings.**

Many Biblical scholars believe that the ten horns (Nations with their Kings) come out of the **Fourth Beast**, which is believed to be the **Holy Roman Empire**. These ten horns perfectly match up with the division of the Roman Empire into **ten separate nations** after the Roman Empire's fall in 476 A.D.

When Rome fell it split exactly into 10 separate nations:

1. The Saxons, originating the English nation.
2. The Franks, originating the French nation.
3. The Alamanni, originating the German nation.
4. The Visigoths, originating the Spanish nation.
5. The Suevi, originating the Portuguese nation.
6. The Lombards, originating the Italian nation.
7. The Burgundians, originating the Swiss nation.
8. **The Heruli, disappeared in 493 A.D.**
9. **The Vandals, disappeared in 534 A.D.**
10. **The Ostrogoths, disappeared in 538 A.D.**

"and another shall rise after them; and he shall be diverse from the first, and he shall subdue three kings."

Daniel 7:24

(Above) So the **Ostrogoths**, the **Vandals**, and the **Heruli** ruled the Roman Empire during the 5th to 6th Century A.D., and then they vanished. The **Vandals** were defeated in many battles by Romanized Germans, the Romans, the North African Berbers and the Moors only to mix in with these nations later. The **Ostrogoths** were defeated by Roman emperor Justinian I, only to later team up with the **German Lombards** in their future "**takeover**" and "**assimilation**" into Rome (Italy). The **Heruli people** were said to be "**Gothic-Scythian**" Germanic people who were crushed by the Attila the Huns kinsmen, **Roman Emperor Justinian I**, and the **Germanic Lombards**. They vanished after infusing themselves with the latter two nations. However, these nations have people in positions of power in Europe even until this day! Could we be seeing "**Bible Prophecy**" unfolding right before our eyes?

Moving right along into the 10th Century A.D.

Otto I (23 November 912 A.D. – 7 May 973 A.D.), traditionally known as **Otto I the Great** was a **German** who ruled Germany around 936 A.D. and also ruled as emperor of the **Western Division** of the Holy Roman Empire from 962 A.D. until his death in 973 A.D. His kin successors **Otto II** and **Otto III** would rule for short terms. **Henry II**, around 1,000 A.D. was the **Holy Roman Emperor** from 1014 A.D. until his death in 1024 A.D. He was the last member of the **Ottonian dynasty** of Emperors as he had no children. As the Duke of Bavaria (Germany) from 995 A.D., **Henry II** became King of Germany following the sudden death Emperor Otto III (*his second cousin*) in 1002 A.D. Henry was crowned King of Italy in 1004 A.D., and was crowned by the Pope as Emperor in 1014 A.D. Who came next down the successor of Holy Roman Emperors? A German named **Conrad II**!

(Left) **Conrad II**, also known as **Conrad the Elder** and **Conrad the Salic**, was Emperor of the Western Division of the Holy Roman Empire from 1027 A.D. until his death in 1039 A.D. As the founder of the **German Salian dynasty of Emperors**, Conrad also served as the **King of Germany** from 1024 A.D., **King of Italy** from 1026 A.D., and **King of Burgundy** from 1033 A.D. **(Right)** The next successor of the Holy Roman Empire, **Henry III**, called "**the Black**" or "**the Pious**", was a member of the **German Salian Dynasty of Holy Roman Emperors**. He was the eldest son of Conrad II of Germany and Gisela of Swabia. His father made him **Duke of Bavaria** (*i.e. South Germany and birthplace of the Illuminati*) in 1026 A.D. On Easter Day 1028 A.D., after his father was crowned Holy Roman Emperor, Henry was elected and crowned **King of Germany** in the cathedral of Aachen by Pilgrim, Archbishop of Cologne. **The Cathedral in Cologne, Germany today is a renowned monument of German Catholicism and <u>Gothic Architecture</u> in 1996.**

(Left) **Henry IV** was Duke and **King of the Germans** in 1056 A.D. He was the Holy Roman Emperor and Third Emperor of the Salian Dynasty during this time. **(Right)** **Henry V** was Duke and **King of the Germans** in 1099 A.D. to 1125 A.D. At this time, he was the Holy Roman Emperor and the Last Emperor of the **Salian Dynasty**. The Salian Dynasty was also known as the "**Frankish Dynasty**" as they were given the title of "**Dukes of Franconia.**" The "**Franks**" occupied Western Germany and France.

DUKE OF EDOM THEN.....NOW IT'S THE DUKES OF GERMANY AND ROME!

Remember, the word "**Duke**" has been used as far back as in the Bible when it is associated with the **Edomites**. The word "**Duke**" is also used in Europe as a "**British Roman male holding the highest hereditary title or the highest five degrees of English nobility.**"

Could Edom and his seed be a part of the Fourth Beast of the Holy Roman Empire. Yes!

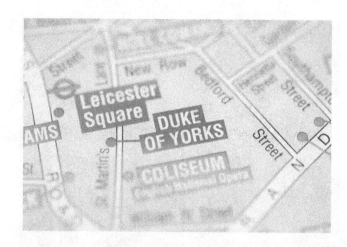

(Above) Leicester Square and the Duke of York's is in London, England. Did Edom's seed mix into Europe and Rome?

Genesis 36:15-16 "These were **DUKES OF THE SONS OF ESAU**: the sons of Eliphaz the firstborn son of Esau; duke Teman, Duke Omar, **duke Zepho**, Duke Kenaz, Duke Korah, duke Gatam, and **duke Amalek**: these are the dukes that came of Eliphaz in the land of Edom; these were the sons of Adah.

Esau's seed through **Zepho** spread through **Rome, Greece** and **Europe** in B.C. times and finally came back to the Middle East by reclaiming Judea under a mixed nationality of Grecians, Romans, North Africans and Arabs (*such as the Nabataeans*). The invaded and occupied Israel fully around the time of the Gentile "Greek" Hasmonean Maccabean Dynasty (John Hyrcanus I) and the Pre-Christ Era taking over the temple, the high priesthood, commerce and the "identity highjack" of the Israelites using the new term "**Jew**" (Sephardic/Ashkenazi).

This is written in the Hebrew **Book of Jasher**.

Jasher 61:24 "And the children of **Chittim** (*Rome/Greece*) saw the valor of **Zepho (the Edomite)**, and the children of Chittim resolved **and they made Zepho king over them**, and he became king over them, and while he reigned they went to subdue the children of **Tubal** (*i.e.*

Turkey-Ottoman Turks/Kurds/Armenians), and all the surrounding Islands (of Europe)."

How do we know Edom mixed with the Gentile people of Japheth? It's in our bible!

Genesis 10 "Now these are the generations of the sons of Noah, Shem, Ham, and Japheth: and unto them were sons born after the flood. The sons of **Japheth; Gomer** (Gog), and Magog, and Madai, and Javan, and **Tubal**, and Meshech, and Tiras. And the sons of Gomer; Ashkenaz, and Riphath, and Togarmah. And the sons of Javan; Elishah, and Tarshish, **Kittim (Chittim),** and Dodanim. **By these were the isles of the Gentiles divided into their hands;** everyone after his tongue, after their families, in their nations.

Note: Tubal and **Togarmah** = Turkey, **Javan** = Greece, **Meschech** = Russia, **Ashkenaz** = Eastern Europe, **Chittim** = Rome.

German royal dynasties	
Salian dynasty	
Chronology	
Conrad II	1024 – 1039
Henry III	1039 – 1056
Henry IV	1056 – 1105
Henry V	1105 – 1125
Family	
Family tree of the German monarchs	
Succession	
Preceded by	*Followed by*
Ottonian dynasty	Süpplingenburg dynasty

(Above) After Henry V finished his rule, Lothair II or Lothair III, known as **Lothair of Supplinburg**. Lothair ruled as the leader of the House of Supplinburg over the **Holy Roman Empire** from 1133 A.D. until his death. He was a **German** appointed Duke of Saxony in 1106 A.D. and was elected **King of Germany** in 1125 A.D. before being crowned emperor in Rome.

Most people are not taught in school that the German Monarchs ruled over the Holy Roman Empire for over 1,000 years. Therefore, it is not surprising that we are not taught in Church who were the ancestors of the "Germans" according to the Bible?

(**Above**) Coat of Arms of the House of Lorraine (**German-Haus Lothringen**). The Double Headed eagle was to signify the two divisions (**East and West**) of the Holy Roman Empire. After the House of Supplinburg ruled over Rome, other Houses ruled as well, some over the Western Roman Empire and some over the Eastern Roman Empire or both.

1. **Supplinburg** (1125-1137 A.D.)
2. **Hohenstaufen** (1138-1254 A.D.)

3. **Welf** (1208-1215 A.D.)
4. <u>**Habsburg**</u> (1273-1740 A.D.)
5. **Nassau** (1292-1298 A.D.)
6. **Luxemburg** (1308-1437 A.D.)
7. **Wittelsbach** (1314-1410 A.D.)
8. <u>**Lorraine**</u> (1745-1765 A.D.)
9. **Habsburg-Lorraine** (1765-1866 A.D.) **Combo repeat**
10. **Bonaparte** (1806-1813 A.D.)
11. **Hohenzollern** (1849-1918 A.D.)

Here we see the number **"10"** again if you count all the **separate Houses**, not including the joining house of **Habsburg** and **Lorraine** in 1765-1866 A.D. So, what **GERMAN** "House" is ruling over England, **"the Commonwealth"** and the **British Royal Family today**? Get ready to be shocked!

Pay attention to the last few rulers of the so-called Roman Empire and see if it turns on any light bulbs to the **Book of Revelation** and the **Book of Daniel's "END TIMES PROPHECY"**.

(Left) **Wilhelm II** (original German name) or **William II** (his English name) was the **last ruler/emperor** of the **German House of Hohenzollern** (1849-1918 A.D.) He was also the King of the German Kingdom of Prussia (*i.e. where many European Jews come from*) from 1888 to 1918 A.D.   But here is the kicker.....**he was the eldest grandson/grandchild of the British Queen Victoria**. **(Right)** Queen Victoria (1819-1901 A.D.) was the Queen of the United Kingdom of Great Britain and Ireland from 1837 until her death. From May 1, 1876, she adopted the title of **"Empress of India"**, when the British invaded India.

So how are these two **"GERMAN"** people related to our current **Prince Philip (Duke of Edinburg)** and **Queen Elizabeth II of England/Great Britain**? Here it is!

(**Above**) **Queen Elizabeth II** and **Prince Philip**, rulers of Great Britain/England. Queen Elizabeth II is the male-line great-granddaughter of **Edward VII**, who inherited the crown from his mother, **Queen Victoria**. Edward VII's father, Queen Victoria's husband, was **Albert of Saxe-Coburg** and **GOTHA** (*i.e. Goth/German*); hence Queen Elizabeth is a patrilineal descendant of Albert's family, the **GERMAN** princely **House of Wettin**. So basically, Queen Elizabeth II is a Great-great granddaughter of Queen Victoria. Queen Elizabeth's husband, **Prince Philip (1921-present), Duke of Edinburgh, is a Great-great grandson of Queen Victoria, making Queen Elizabeth and Prince Philip of England third cousins married to each other.** BOTH ARE **GERMANS** FOLKS! This is how you keep the "**Blue Bloodline**" going. Does this line up with Bible prophecy about the "Fourth Beast and the 10 little horns?"

Consider this......the Germans seem to be a "**central figure**" in the Holy Roman Empire, but why?

Fact: Prince Philip, Duke of Edinburgh is of the **House of Schleswig-Holstein-Sonderburg-Glucksburg**, which takes its ducal name (duke name) "**Glucksburg**", a small coastal town in Schleswig, on the southern German-Denmark border area.

(Above) **Altar of Pergamon/Pergamum**, aka the "**Seat of Satan (Antichrist)/Zeus**". In the 1800's this Altar and its fragments sat in **Turkey (i.e. part of the Ancient Eastern Holy Roman Empire)**, where the Church of Pergamos is described in **Revelation 2:12-17**. Now it sits in **Berlin, Germany** in the **Pergamon Museum**. German Dictator Adolf Hitler and Barack Obama both visited this "**Seat of Satan**" that is described in our Bibles. In fact, Obama's 2008 Democratic stage/platform was modeled after a replica of the Altar of Pergamon. Coincidence?

Revelation 2:12-13 "And to the angel of the **Church in Pergamos** write; These things saith he which hath the sharp sword with two edges; I know thy works, **AND WHERE THOU DWELLEST, EVEN WHERE SATAN'S SEAT (THRONE) IS**: and thou holdest fast my name, and hast not denied my faith, even in those days wherein Antipas was my faithful martyr, who was slain among you, **WHERE SATAN DWELLETH.**

The seat of Satan (Antichrist) and its fragments were in Pergamum, Turkey (*i.e. Home of the Ottoman Empire that enslaved thousands of Blacks and killed many Christians*). In 1878 **Carl Humann**, a **German engineer** (*not an archaeologist*) began official excavations on the acropolis (altar) of Pergamon. The excavations were done in 1886 and by 1901 he had this "**Seat/Altar of Satan/Pergamon**" sitting in **Germany** in a Museum. Does this mean that "**Satan**" dwells in **Germany** now?

Why would a German "Engineer" have any interest in the Biblical "Seat/Altar of Satan"? Now this is starting to sound like the plot of the movies "**Angels and Demons**" or "**Inferno**" by Dan Brown, starring Tom Hanks.

But there is more!

The Islamic Ottoman Empire took control of the "**Eastern Roman Empire**" around 1453 A.D. when they set up "**Constantinople, Turkey**" as their capital city.

Turkey (Tubal) was the birthplace of the Ottoman Islamic Empire, which defeated the "**Byzantine Eastern Roman Empire**" in 1453 A.D. What is odd is that the excavation of the Altar of Zeus/Satan according to Revelation 2:12 **cost millions of dollars**. Carl Humann was contracted by the Ottoman Empire to help build railroads and roads as he was an engineer by trade and **not an archaeologist**. The "**false story**" that the powers to be want people to believe is that a German Archaeologist named **Alexander Conze** funded the multi-million-dollar project. However, in Bavaria, Germany, birthplace of the Illuminati there was also interest in this area. The project of unearthing the literal "**Biblical Seat-Altar of Satan**" was sought out by the Illuminati leadership at the time since they worshipped Lucifer-Satan and it would obviously be a trophy for them to have the altar in **Germany** and with it the presence of Lucifer-Satan himself since it was dedicated to him. When Carl Humann died his body and bones were exhumed from the Turkish city of Izmir to where the Altar of Pergamon had been found.

(**Above**) Shortly after the Altar of Pergamon was moved to Germany, in the 1930's, the Nazi Party would emerge, thanks in part to the "**Thule Secret Society**". Hitler would hold his Nuremberg-Zeppelin Tribune rallies in front of 300,000 **Germans** with a stage fashioned after the "**Seat of Satan-Pergamon**" where he and Satan would receive worship by the German people. Some say Hitler also received instruction from Lucifer himself as he was believed to be heavily into the "**occult**".

Here is where it gets deep!

In the Bible, in **Genesis 3:1-4** we are told that Satan possessed or "**entered**" the serpent that seduced Eve to sin. Just like how the demons were cast into the pigs by Christ in the New Testament. In **Ezekiel 28:2** and **Ezekiel 28:13-16** we are told that Satan's seat was in the city of **Tyre, Lebanon**. In **Luke 22:1-6** we are told that **Satan entered into Judas Iscariot**. In **Revelation 2: 12-17** we are told that Satan's seat is in Pergamon, Turkey. **In Freemasonic history, Hiram, King of Tyre was the Grandmaster of ALL Masons, and Hiram Abiff was the Master of the Order in Jerusalem**. The "Seat of Satan" in the early 1900's was moved to Berlin, Germany. On **February 19, 2014** Berlin's Pergamon Museum closed its doors for renovations and announced that it will re-open in **2019-2020**. Why 2019-2020? Some believe that wherever the Altar-Seat of Satan is, this country or people will bring calamity to the world or a select group of people. Some people believe that in 2019, something "**BIG**" is going to happen to African-Americans since it is the **1619-2019 "400 year" mark**, signifying how long on paper "**Negro Israelites**" have been in America, the "**Land of Captivity**". During the 1936 Olympic Games in Berlin, Germany Israelite "Negroes" were looked down upon. This is why Jesse Owens 4 Olympic Medals were such a "talk" in Germany during that time.

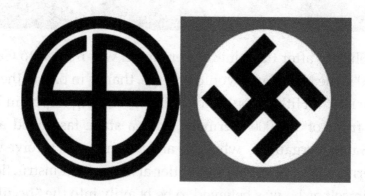

(**Left**) Symbol of the **Thule Secret Society** who secretly worship Satan. (**Right**) Symbol of Nazi Germany. Thule and its location has been linked to **Norway, Iceland, Greenland...home of the Nordic "white skinned, blond-haired, blue-eyed people" that Hitler idolized as the "perfect race"**.

Note: Ancient Historians described the "Germanic Goths/Scythians to be tall white people with "Red" hair or "Blonde" hair. Some believed they also came from Scandinavia or Poland.

Fact: *The Thule Secret Society believed that the "Pure white" Aryan race was the Master Race. In the Hebrew Israelite books, namely the Book of Enoch/Fragments of the Book of Noah, it is written that the Fallen Angels and their Seed were "Pure White-skinned" people. They were described as being "White as snow", which is called "Nordic" by many people. Nordic-looking white people are seen in Scandinavia, which is part of "Nordic Europe",* which is the countries **Norway, Sweden, Finland, Iceland, Denmark and the Faroe Islands.**

(**Above**) Helena Blavatsky wrote a journal/magazine called "**Lucifer**". The first edition was first printed in September 1887 in London.

Note: *Many of the top leading officials of the world, including Hollywood and the Vatican (Catholic Church) have been exposed for pedophilia, homosexual immorality or sexual abuse. This can be researched by looking up the "Pizza gate Scandal". Raping young children and sacrificing young children is Satanic and goes back into paganism (i.e. Moloch). Satan loves "Sex magic".*

The Thule Society believed in Satan worship and Black Magic. They also believed in **Sex Magic** as in most Satanic Rituals. The "Thule" believed in communication with a hierarchy of "**Supermen**" who according to Blavatsky's book "**Secret Doctrine**" had survived the destruction of Atlantis during the biblical "**Great Flood**". These "supermen" had higher levels of consciousness and were called "**Aryans**". Perhaps these White "supermen" were the offspring of the fallen angels or the Sons of Cain. The Book of Enoch describes the offspring of the "Watcher Fallen Angels" as "**white-skinned**" as well. The Thule society in Germany held regular occultic séances in which they communicated with demons who appeared as spirits or were masquerading as a dead person. Many believe Dietrich Eckart, Alfred

Rosenberg and Adolf Hitler invoked the Anti-Christ into manifestation at séances in Munich, Germany. Dietrich Eckart believed Hitler was the Antichrist up until he died in 1923.

Members of the Thule Secret society could not be Jews (*which Hitler believed were "mutts"*) or Negroes. Members had to sign a "**Blood Declaration of Faith**" that not one drop of blood of their parents had **Negro** or **Jewish blood**.

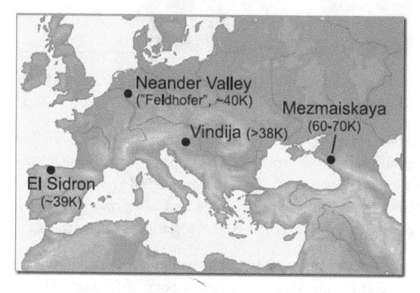

(**Above**) Neanderthal specimens/remains have been found in El Sidron (**Spain**), Feldhofer (**Germany**), Vindija (**Croatia**), Mezmaiskaya (**Caucasus mountains/Russia**) as well as Israel, Canada, North America, Iceland, Norway, Sweden, and Finland. The **maternal (mtDNA) "X"** labeled the "**Neanderthal gene**" is mostly seen in European Caucasians, Europeans Jews (Sephardic/Ashkenazi), White Arabs, **the Druze people** and other select "Eurasian" races. The reason being is that the mummy/skeletal remains of white-skinned, blonde/red-haired "**Cro-Magnons-Neanderthals**" tested positive for **mtDNA "X"**. This means that somewhere down the line "Neanderthal women" had children with the Japhetic European "Homo Sapien" men

214

who would eventually become today's Europeans (*i.e. Germans, Spaniards, Russians, Franks*), European Jews and the white Arabs that we would see today. Further in the book I will connect the **"Neanderthal-Denisovan man"** to pre-flood **"sons of Cain"** and the **"sons of the Fallen angels"** with the daughters of men.

END TIMES PROPHECY: ISLAMIC CALIPHATE TEAMED UP WITH GERMANY AND THE "RESURRECTED ROMAN EMPIRE"?

During the **"Napoleonic wars"** when France Emperor Napoleon supposedly defeated the Holy Roman Empire in 1806, he claimed it was dead. At that time the German – Austria led Roman Empire was also called the **"First Reich"**. Hitler started the **"Third Reich"** which was defeated in 1945. But was it resurrected? Is there a **"Fourth Reich"** on the horizon? **Germany** still is in the British Royal Family and **Germany now has all Economic/Political power of the European Union**. Is the European Union and the British Royal Family just another extension of it? Has the **"Spirit of the Antichrist"** behind Islam and ISIS now merged with Germany? Will the Sharia Law and Islam eventually take over Germany and if so, why will Germany allow it? Why has the Chancellor of Germany (Angela Merkel) allowed so many Muslims a new place to stay in Germany during wars caused by ISIS? **Even more, will the Roman Catholic Church/Vatican join forces with the Islamic world? The answer is yes!**

(**Above**) In 2015, Angela Merkel, Chancellor of Germany came under fire for allowing what some say is over **1 million Muslim refugees to come to Germany to stay after the ISIS attacks in the Middle East (Syria/Iraq).**

But what is interesting is that Germany has broken bread with the Muslim world before. Back when Adolf Hitler was in power.

(**Left**) Muslim Nazis. Adolf Hitler once quoted, "**The only religion I respect is Islam. The only prophet I admire is the Prophet Muhammad.**" 44th President of the United States of America, Barack Obama also quoted in September 2012, "**The future must not belong to those who slander the prophet of Islam.**" What does this tell us? (**Right**) Haj Amin al-Husseini was the Mufti (Chief) of Jerusalem from

1921-1937 during the "**British Mandatory Palestine**" era. Between 1937 to 1945, he spoke for the Arab Nation, the Muslim world and sought an alliance with the Nazi Germans under **Adolf Hitler** and Fascist Italians under **Benito Mussolini**. He incited violence against Jews and the British authorities in the Middle East, in addition to recruiting young Muslim men for service in the Nazi German Military, "**Waffen-SS**".

Fact: *When the **Gotthard Base Tunnel** running through the Swiss Alps had their "opening Satanic Ceremony" in 2016, **German Chancellor Angela Merkel, French President Francois Hollande** and **Italian Prime Minister Matteo Renzi** were in attendance. To judge if this "opening ceremony" was "Satanic" simply Google search it or watch the ceremony paying attention to all the symbolism pointing to the arrival of the "Antichrist". They are definitely up to something over there that the masses do not know.*

Many believe that Germany's Chancellor is reviving the German Empire, creating the "**Fourth Reich**" and is reviving the **Ottoman Islamic Empire**. The Germans are dominating politics through their economic superiority. Some believe they are "**falling in line**" with the goal America had under the Obama administration to dethrone Syrian President Assad who is an ally of Russia and Iran. Iran, Syria and North Korea are supposedly the only few remaining countries that is not controlled by a Jewish Central Bank. Or are they? Remember, America's focus has been on Syria for quite some time now.....and it won't change no matter who is President over the United States of America.

"We are in Europe what the Americans are in the world: the unloved leading power"

German Chancellor Angela Merkel

CAN WE PROVE WITH DNA WHO WILL BE THE MAJOR EUROPEAN PLAYERS IN THE "LAST DAYS" AND WHO WILL BE THE REAL "ISRAELITES" AND "EDOMITES" IN THE "LAST DAYS"?

Fact: The Eastern Frank territory is associated with **Germany**.

The **Western and Eastern Slavic territories** consist of the **Czech Republic, Bosnia, Serbia, Poland, Slovakia, Belarus, Russia, Ukraine, Bulgaria (*i.e. Bulgar, son of Togarmah in the Khazar Correspondence*), Croatia, Slovenia and Montenegro.**

Note: *"Targamos" or "Togarmah" is often used as the name of the ancestors of the Armenian, Turkish, Georgian, Caucasian (i.e. Dagestan), Kurdish, Khazarian, Bulgarian and **Oghuz people**. The founders of the "**Ottoman Empire**" in the 1300's A.D. were **Oghuze Turks**. Today these "**Oghuze Turks**" are seen also in Turkey, Turkmenistan, Khazakstan, Azerbaijan, Khorezm, the Turkmens of Afghanistan, the Balkan people, Iraq, Iran, Syria,*

Lebanon and Palestine. If you don't believe, look at the traditional dances of the Turkish people and modern-day Arabs in the Middle East where the men dance holding hands or kicking their feet out......similar to the European Jews. This is because they all come from the same "Japhetic" stock.

The Main Y-DNA "Paternal" Male Haplogroup seen in the these "**Slavic Countries**" is "**R1a**". The main Y-DNA Haplogroups seen in Spain, Portugal, France, Italy and Germany is "**R1b**". The main Y-DNA Haplogroups seen in Macedonia (Upper Greece) is "**I2**". The main Y-DNA Haplogroups seen in Eastern Greece (Thrace), Turkey and the Asia Minor countries (Armenia/Kurdistan) is "**J2**".

Note: The main Y-DNA Haplogroups seen in Saudi Arabia, Yemen, Oman, Qatar, and the UAE is "**J1/J2**". The main Y-DNA Haplogroups seen in Yemen, Oman, Qatar, the UAE, Sudan (Khartoum), and Negev (Black Bedouins of Israel) is "**J1**". The main Y-DNA Haplogroups seen in the most southernmost part of Greece, North Africa and much of the Middle East is "**E1b1b**". E1b1b is also seen from Ukraine to Portugal and from Sardina to England as **E-L17**. It is seen in England as **E-L143**. It is seen in the Czech Republic and England as **E-L241**. It is seen in Germany, Poland, Belarus and Sweden as **E-L540**. This correlates to **Edom's infusion** into the Greek/Roman, European people and North African peoples. It is not a coincidence that these few Y-DNA Haplogroups (E1b1b, R1a, R1b, J1/J2) including (**Haplogroup G**-Greek Seleucid Empire) make up the majority of the Paternal Lineage of the Ashkenazi Jews and Sephardic Jews.

ISRAELITES IN EUROPE? NO WAY!

There is a group called "**The British Israel World Federation**" that goes by the term "**British Israelism**" or "**Anglo-Israelism**". It is a doctrine based on the belief that Western and Northern European descent Caucasians are the direct blood descendants of the **Northern Ten Lost Tribes of Israel**, particularly in **Great Britain**. They believe that when the Northern Kingdom of Israel was invaded by Assyria in 701 B.C., that the 10 Tribes of Northern Israel **ALL** migrated into Europe. So, with that being said, does the Bible ever talk about the Israelites being placed or exiled into Europe? **No.** But the Bible does mention of Israelites (**including Christ**) going into Egypt for various reasons.

Jeremiah 43:1-7 (The Israelites go back into Egypt)

Jeremiah 43:1-7 "And it came to pass, that when Jeremiah had made an end of speaking unto all the people all the words of the LORD their God, for which the LORD their God had sent him to them, even all these words, Then spake Azariah the son of Hoshaiah, and Johanan the son of Kareah, and all the proud men, saying unto Jeremiah, Thou speakest falsely: the LORD our God hath not sent thee to say, **Go not into Egypt** to sojourn (*i.e. live as a foreigner*) there: But Baruch the son of Neriah setteth thee on against us, for to deliver us into the hand of the Chaldeans, that they might put us to death, and carry us away captives into Babylon. So Johanan the son of Kareah, and all the captains of the forces, and all the people, **obeyed not the voice of the LORD**, to dwell in the land of Judah. But Johanan the son of Kareah, and all the captains of the forces, took all the remnant of Judah, that were returned from all nations, whither they had been driven, to dwell in the land of Judah; Even men, and women, and children, and the king's daughters, and every person that Nebuzaradan the captain of the guard had left with Gedaliah the son of Ahikam the son of Shaphan, and Jeremiah the prophet, and Baruch the son of Neriah. **So they came into the land of Egypt**: for they obeyed not the voice of the LORD: thus came they even to **Tahpanhes**.

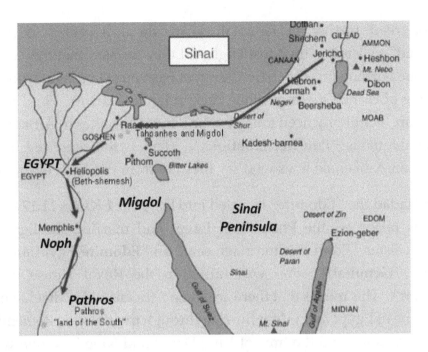

(**Above**) Map of the travel route of Jeremiah and the **Tribe of Judah** in Jeremiah 43-44 (*i.e. during Babylonian siege*) as they ventured **deep into Egypt**. According to the bible they traveled south in Egypt as far as Aswan, Egypt (**Pathros was an ancient area of land in Egypt from Abydos to Aswan**), North of Sudan. **See Jeremiah 44:1.**

Jeremiah 44:1 "The word that came to Jeremiah concerning all the Jews which dwell in the land of Egypt, which dwell at **Migdol**, and at **Tahpanhes**, and at **Noph**, and in the **country of Pathros**, saying.."

Note: Did the Hebrew Israelites from the Tribe of Judah that went into **Egypt (Africa)** and later "**slavery**" by way of ships.....provoke the Most High to a "higher" form of punishment? Read Jeremiah 44:8.

Jeremiah 44:8 "In that ye provoke me unto wrath with the work of your hands, burning incense unto other gods in the **land of Egypt (Africa)**, whither ye be gone to dwell, that ye might cut yourselves off, and that **ye might be a curse and a reproach among all the nations of the earth.**"

If you read further in Jeremiah 44:18, these Israelites in Africa "**refused**" to listen to the Most High and they insisted that they would continue burning incense to the Queen of Heaven (Mami Wata) and the pouring of Drink Offerings while back in Egypt (Africa). This "**pagan tradition**" is still practiced today by the Bantus Israelites in African, but under the name "**Pouring Libations**". This is **not** practiced by the European Ashkenazi Jews who say they are from the Tribe of Judah.

Even Hadad the "**Edomite**" traveled into Egypt in **1 Kings 11:17** where he was raised by the Pharaoh of Egypt and married the Egyptian Queens sister. From this marriage came an "**Edomite-Egyptian**" son named "**Genubath**" who was raised in the Royal House of the Pharaoh's. This means that there are some Africans today that have the bloodline of Egypt and Edom flowing through their blood. Remember, 1 Kings was around the time of King David and King Solomon when the 1st Temple in Jerusalem was still standing. Edom was not welcome in Israel at this time, and neither was any white nations from the North (Greece, Rome). These half-breed Edomites initially were "Black" in appearance before they started mixing with the nations of Japheth. Prior to this Edom's seed were only mixing with the Black Ishmaelite Arabs, the Egyptians and the Canaanites.

What some of this means is that the (Edom) **E1b1b Y-DNA Haplogroup** should also be seen in **North Africa/Central Africa/Northeast Africa**, which is in fact true as there are many Arabs and select African Tribes (**Masalit, Fur**) who carry the Y-DNA E1b1b. Even in Somalia/Ethiopia region which many claim hold certain people groups who are the descendants of people from Ancient Egypt, there can be found Black people with the E1b1b Y-DNA Haplogroup. But be not deceived as many Ethiopians/Somalians that would've fell under the older classification of "**E1b1c**" could have been misplaced inappropriately into the "**E1b1b**" category. This is how man hides the Truth and hides Edom's bloodline.

Read Below:

1 Kings 11:17-20 "That **Hadad fled, he and certain Edomites** of his father's servants with him, to go into **EGYPT**, Hadad being yet a little child. And they arose out of Midian, and came to **Paran**: and they took men with them out of Paran, and they came to Egypt, unto Pharaoh king of Egypt; which gave him a house, and appointed him victuals (food stores), and gave him LAND. And Hadad found great favour in the sight of Pharaoh, so that he gave him wife the sister of his own wife, the sister of Tahpenes the queen. **And the sister of Tahpenes bare him Genubath his son (Haddad's son), whom Tahpenes weaned in Pharaoh's house: and Genubath was in Pharaoh's household among the sons of the Pharaoh (around 1000 B.C.).**

So here we see that other Edomite men left with Hadad (the Edomite) into Egypt. We can assume these men possibly fathered children with some the women in Egypt while they were there. Therefore, Edom **CANNOT** be the entire white race or only the so-called white man.

So now we see how common it was for the Israelites and the Edomites to venture into Egypt (**Tahpanhes**). Does DNA studies prove this to be true? Yes! The **E1b1b (Edom) Y-DNA** can be found in **North Africa** (Tunisia, Libya, Egypt, Algeria, Morocco) while the **E1b1ba (Negro Bantus Israelite) Y-DNA** Haplogroup is mostly found in Sub-Saharan Africa.

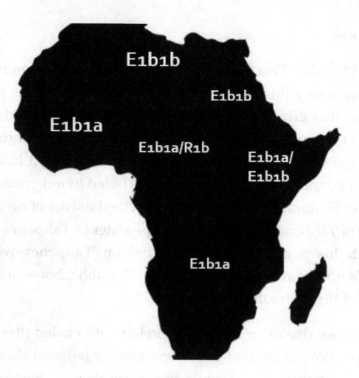

(**Above**) The Y-DNA "**E1b1b**" is mostly seen in North Africa while the Y-DNA "**E1b1a**" is seen primarily in Sub-Saharan Africa. Why?

Fact: North/Central African Tribes like the **Fur** and **Masalit** in Chad/Sudan have very high percentages of "**E1b1b**" ancestry....even more than many of the North African white/light brown Arabs. The **Masalit** trace their original homeland to **Tunisia,** which is to the west of **Libya.** Their oral history states that while traveling into **Libya (i.e.** *west of Egypt*) and then south into **Chad**, they eventually settled in the **West Sudan. 71.9%** of Masalit are **E1b1b** carriers (**paternal ancestry**). Of these, **73.9%** bear the **V32** subclade. 6.3% belong to the Semitic Black Arab blood marker Haplogroup "**J1**". The remaining Masalit individuals are primarily carriers of the **A3b2 lineage** (18.8%), which is common among the **Cushite Nilotes in Sudan** (*i.e. Dinka Tribe*). Because of the Arab Slave Trade, the Black Arab Caliphate (*i.e. Umayyad, Abbasid, Fatimid caliphates*), conquests of North Africa/Sudan, most Masalit are bilingual in the **Arabic language**. The Masalit people also write using the **Latin script** which is from **Rome, Italy. Where did they get this knowledge of Latin from? Was it from Edom's presence in Rome that was later carried to Rome's African territories in North Africa? Let's see!**

Consider this:

The Romans ruled North Africa during the early 2nd century B.C., the same time the Greek Hasmonean Maccabean family converted its kinfolk to Judaism (i.e. Book of Maccabees). The Edomites during this time and up until the time of Christ were living in Rome, Italy…their "African" Roman Province….but also Judea (Israel). The Roman Province of "**Africa Proconsularis**" was established after the Romans (*i.e. sons of Japheth's son Chittim mixed with Edom*) defeated the questionable (Phoenician/Canaanite/Israelite) city of Tunisia during the Third Punic War (145 B.C.). This Roman Territory comprised of **Tunisia, Algeria** and **Libya**. This could be one of the major reasons why the Y-DNA "E1b1b" Haplogroup is seen so strongly in North Africa.

JASHER 61:24 "And the children of **Chittim (Rome/Greece)** saw the valor of **Zepho (Edomite)**, and the children of Chittim resolved and **they made Zepho king over them**, and he became king over them, and while he reigned they went to subdue the children of **Tubal**, and all the surrounding islands (**Europe**)."

WHERE DID THE Y-DNA "E1B1A" ORIGINATE FROM?

The Negro/Bantus Y-DNA "**E1b1a**" and its ancestral parent pre-E1b1a Haplogroup "**E*(xE1b1a)**" can be found in **Sudan** (Anuak), **Eritrea, Ethiopia** (Gambella, Shankalla, Ethiopian Jews), **Kenya, Tanzania** (Sukuma, Bembe Tribe), **Mozambique (Sena/Ba-Senna Tribe from house of Bakali related to the Lemba Jews), Congo** (Bembe Tribe), **Malawi/Zambia** (Chewa Tribe) and even the **Palenque** (Abajo/Arriba) "Negroes" in Columbia!

Fact: *The ancestral "E1b1a" haplogroup listed as "E*(xE1b1a)" in genetic studies worldwide is seen in many different African Tribes but why is it seen frequently in "East Africa" and the Congo? This would be the area where* many Ancient Hebrew Israelites would come into during their diaspora into Africa by way of Egypt. But remember, the Hebrew Israelites became a nation while they were living amongst the **Northeastern African** Egyptians and Nubians (Sudan/Ethiopia). Remember, Moses had a Cushite wife (**Adoniah**) in the **Book of Jasher 72:37-42** before leaving Cush (Nubia/Sudan) and meeting **Zipporah** the "Cushite" Midianite. In Genesis 25, Abraham's last wife "**Keturah**" has a child named **Medan** and **Midian**. Midian had a son named "**Eldaah**". We can be sure that Moses didn't cross the Red Sea in a boat to meet his wife Zipporah in Arabia. This means Zipporah and the Midianites were most likely residents of ancient Kush (Cush). Also, if anyone is researches the store of "**Eldad ha-Dani**" from the Tribe of Dan, you will see that he resided in Cush/Ethiopia.

Evenmore, in the Book of Jasher it states that Moses stayed in Cush (Nubia/Sudan) for 40 years before leaving with the Israelites during the Exodus. Not convinced? Even some Kenyans are taught of a "**Virgin Forest**" in the Congo where King Solomon and his men would frequent to obtain various treasures (diamonds, gold). The "**Chewa Tribe**" Bantus people living throughout **Malawi** and **Zambia** are not considered the "**original**" people of Malawi/Zambia but a people from the Nyanja group of Bantu people. The Chewa's oral history states that over a thousand years ago, Bantus speaking people in different parts of Africa migrated to **Zaire**, or what is now the **Democratic Republic of Congo**, where 100% of the men there are **E1b1a** carriers (excluding the Pygmy tribes). Also, in ancient 18th century maps of Africa the words "**Biafara**" can be seen in the current territory of Nigeria, Cameroon and the Congo. The term "**Biafran**" today is used to describe the Nigerian Igbos in Southeast Nigeria.

IS THERE ANY DNA PROOF THAT CAN LINK THE "NEGRO", THE "NATIVE AMERINDIANS", AND OTHER NATIONS TO THE LAND OF ISRAEL?

***Revelation 12:17** "And the dragon (**Satan**) was wroth with the woman (**Israel**), and went to make war with the remnant of her seed (**Israelites**), which keep the commandments of God, and have the testimony of Yeshua HaMashiach (Jesus Christ)."*

If we can prove that the **"Negro"** and the **"Native Amerindian"** has DNA linked to Israel, along with other nations....we can prove that **Revelation 12:17** is pertaining to a group of people **NOT** currently in Israel right now. This kind of proof would be **"ground-breaking"** in the Christian Church and even Israel if it ever leaked out. Well, you're gonna read it here first.

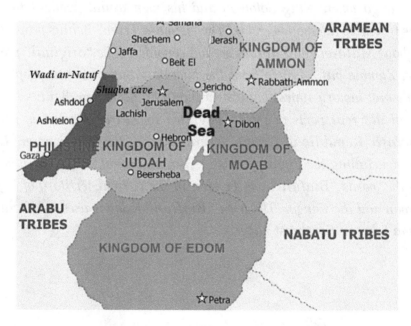

Fact: In Northern Israel, in the **"Shuqba cave"** ancient skeletal remains were found. The study wasn't worldwide news because the study was really about the hunter-gatherers and pastoralists civilizations in ancient Israel around 3,000-4,000 years ago during the time era of 2,000

B.C.-1,000 B.C. The Shuqba cave today is located in **Wadi an-Natuf**, in the western Judea Mountains, halfway between Tel Aviv, Israel and Ramallah. It is Northwest of Jerusalem. These skeletal remains were labeled as "**Natufians**" by a lady named **Dorothy Garrod**. Scientists believed the Natufians were natives to Israel/Canaan thousands of years ago during certain time periods. In one cave, six skeletal remains were dug up and tested. It showed the Y-DNA Haplogroup "**E-Z830**", the ancestor-Haplogroup of Y-DNA "**E-M123**". **E-M34** is a descendant of **E-M123**. All of these "**E subgroups**" correlate to Semitic influence mostly generated by **Edom**, the twin brother of Jacob. It was found that these ancient skeletons matched up with "**particular**" people groups scattered across the world. Who might that be? The **E-M123/M34** Y-DNA Haplogroup seen in some of the Natufian skeletons was also seen in a small but substantial amount modern day **Jordanians** who live near on the "eastern side" of the Dead Sea. **Note: Israel is on the "western side" of the Dead Sea.** Back in Ancient times, Jordan (**Petra**)....aka "**Moabite territory**" was also considered a portion of the **Land of Edom**. Also, Moabite and Ammonite Territory was basically next door to the territory of the Tribe of Reuben, Gad and East Manasseh. These Moabites and Ammonites were also in the land of Israel as witnessed by the fact the Israelites intermarried with their daughters (*see Ezra 9:1-2 and Ruth*). But there is more!

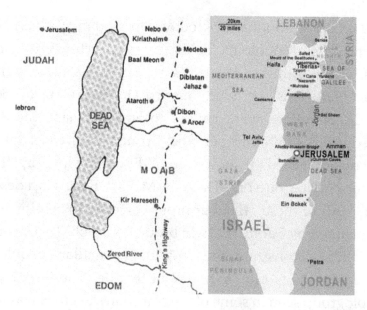

(**Above**) Modern day **Jordan** used to be the land of **Edom** (*or territory belonging to the "Eastern Aramaic" speakers*) and **Moab** in Biblical Times.

The "downstream" descendants of the Natufian Y-DNA **E-Z830** are seen in the carriers of the **Y-DNA E-M123**. Again, Y-DNA "**E-M123**" is mostly seen in Ethiopian Amhara people, **Ethiopian Jews**, **Ethiopian Wolayta** and **Jordanians** who live near the Dead Sea. What is interesting is that the Y-DNA "**E-M123**" (*although found in small amounts*) is unique only to the **Ethiopian Jews**, the **Semitic Amhara Ethiopians** and **Dead Sea Jordanians**.... but not unique to the North African Arab "**E1b1b (E-M215)**" carriers. The ancient land of Moab is modern day Jordan. What is also interesting is that both the Ethiopian Jews and Amhara Ethiopians all carry an "Ancestral form of the Y-DNA "**E1b1a**", something that is only elsewhere seen Nigeria, Kenya, Guinea Bissau and the Congo. The Ethiopian Amhara language also has striking similarities to Hebrew. See for yourself!

AMHARA/TIGRAYANS/ERITREANS
HAVE HEBREW ANCESTRY

Amhara	Hebrew	Amhara	Hebrew
Peace-Selame	Shalom	**Water**-Mai/Weha	Mayim
Husband-Bale	Baal	**Holy**-Qedus	Qodesh
Black-Tikoor	Shachor	**Ear**-Jero/Ezni	Ozen
Moon-Chereka	Yareach	**Mary**-Mariame	Miriam
Bless-Mebarka	Barak	**Joshua**-Eyasu	Yeshua
Mother-Ennat	Em		
Father-Abbat	Abba		
House-Bete	Bet(h)/Bayith		
Angel-Malak	Malak		
Moses-Muse	Moshe		

Fact: The **Gefat Tribe** in Ethiopia claim they are descendants of the Ancient Israelites. Their history goes back 600 years at which they claim they descended from Israel eventually making their way into Africa and the "**Shewa**" province in Ethiopia. **Addis Ababa** is the Capital of Ethiopia in the Shewa province. They are believed to be an offshoot branch off the Ethiopian Jews (Beta Israel) and Beta Abraham which is in the Amharic Northern area of Shewa. The Gefat Tribesmen blow the shofar and they also circumcise their males on the eighth day. They also celebrate the different Biblical Feast days. For the Passover, like many Bantus Tribes, they kill a lamb and put the blood on their doorposts. Examination of their pottery shows the resemblance to the Beta Israel Ethiopian Jews and the Beta Abraham Jews in Amhara territory (Shewa).

The Amhara people claim ancestry from **Menelik I** and **the Israelite Solomonic Dynasty** in Ethiopia. During B.C. times, the **Damot (D'mt) Empire** were the ruling class in Northern Ethiopia. Eventually, the Amhara people became part of the Northern Ethiopian Province of "Shewa". Even the Oromo people in Shewa claim that the Amhara people came to their land....similar to how the Israelites came into the

Land of the Canaanites. This is also supported in the Ethiopian Book of Kings, "**The Kebra Nagast**" which says the Shewa-Amharic people were considered a "Junior Branch" of the Solomonic dynasty. The Amhara people today are mostly Christians who attend the Ethiopian Tewahedo Orthodox Church.

So, could the Y-DNA **E-M123/E-M34** Haplogroup that a small number of the Amhara Ethiopians and Ethiopian Jews have be evidence of an ancient "**Moabite**", "**Edomite**" or "**Israelite**" marker? In the Bible (**Ezra 9:1-3**), the Israelites had children with the Egyptians, Canaanites, **Moabites and Ammonites**. In the Torah, during the Israelites 40 years in "the Wilderness", the Israelites upon their journey into the Land of Canaan, **did in fact** whore around with the daughters of Moab.....therefore it is possible that some Israelite children came forth from their "**whoredom**". Remember, **Ruth** (*a Moabitess*), was the Great-grandmother of King David...from whose lineage Christ the Messiah would come. But did any of the Moabite men also marry Israelite women that bore children of "**mixed**" seed into the Israelite camp in those days? Let's look at this. On the other hand, if this is an Edomite marker the bible says after "**3 Generations**" any children born to Edomites could enter into the Israelite camp.

Deuteronomy 23:7-8 "Thou shalt not abhor an Edomite; for he is thy brother: thou shalt not abhor (despite/detest) an **Edomite**; for he is thy brother: thou shalt not abhor an Egyptian; because thou wast a stranger in his land. **The children that are begotten of them shall enter into the congregation of the LORD in their *third generation*.**"

Geneticists were confused to see these "**Natufian**" skeletons native to Israel have cranial similarities to Sub-Saharan "Bantus" Africans so they tried to figure out how this could be. Geneticists such as **Fulvio Cruciani** proposed that this **E-M123** Y-DNA Haplogroup likely got into Ethiopia via Egypt from Israel. This would make sense biblically as Queen Sheba of Ethiopia and King Solomon met in 1 Kings, Chapter 10. Shortly after, per Ethiopian tradition (**Kebra Nagast**), King

Solomon had a child with the Ethiopian Queen, named **Menelik I**. King Solomon would send Israelites down with Menelik to set up a **"mini-Israelite Kingdom"** in Ethiopia. Prior to King Solomon, King David and King Saul, the Bible says while in **Moab** (*i.e. Abel-Shittim*), when Moses was still alive, the Israelites had sex with the women of Moab, they ate with them and they worshipped their pagan gods. If these Israelites stayed long enough Moab Territory (where Moses died), it is possible that in 9 months' time children were born of Moabite women into the Israelite camp prior to crossing over the Jordan River into the Land of Canaan (Israel). If so, did the Israelite men leave the Moabite women and "mixed" breed Israelite-Moabite children back in the land of Moab (Jordan) when they crossed over the Jordan River into Israel?

Numbers 25:1-2 "And Israel abode in **Shittim**, and the people began to commit whoredom with the **daughters of Moab**. And they called the people unto the sacrifices of their gods: and the people did eat, and bowed down to their gods."

Abila, Jordan also called "**Abel-Shittim**" or "**Shittim**" is still an ancient city east of the Jordan River, northwest of the north shore of the Dead Sea. South of the Dead Sea and the Territory of Judah was Edomite Territory. King Solomon could've very well had children with Edomite women. Edom also had children with Hamitic women, Shemitic women (Arab Ishmaelites) and Japhetic women.

1 Kings 11:1 "But King Solomon loved many strange women, together with the daughter of Pharaoh, women of the **Moabites, Ammonites, Edomites**, Zidonians and Hittites."

In 1993, **Anthropologist C. Loring Brace** compared the fossil remains of **MORE** Natufian skeletons in Ancient Israel to Ancient Asian, European and West "Bantus" African remains. Using "craniometry (skull analysis)", he concluded that the skulls of the Naftufians were related to the Niger-Congo African Bantus-Speaking people in Sub-

Saharan Africa (*i.e. Nigerians, Cameroonians, Congolese, Ghanaians, Gambians, Liberians*) and **NOT THE MODERN DAY EUROPEAN ASHKENAZI/SEPHARDIC JEWS.**

In 2016, in the magazine **BioRxiv, "The Preprint Server for Biology"** a genetic study called, **"The Genetic Structure of the World's First Farmers"** led by **Iosif Lazaridis** (*Department of Genetics, Harvard Medical School*) found "ground-breaking" evidence in the Natufian Skeletons from the caves in Israel. Remember, the Hebrew Patriarchs (*i.e. Abraham, Isaac*) buried their dead in Caves. In the ID sample #I1069 and #I1414 from this study by **Geneticist Iosif Lazaridis**, they found the Y-DNA **"E1b1a1a1"** and **"xE1b1a1"**. These two "E" Haplogroup subgroups are seen in "**Negro Bantus people**" and the **Ethiopian Jews**. In the ID sample I1685, I1690, I1416, I1727, I1700 they found evidence of Y-DNA **Haplogroup "C"**. The "C" Haplogroup is mostly seen in the **Australian Aborigines**, some **Native Amerindians**, some **Papua New Guineans**, the **Piramalai Kallar community in India**, select **Malaysians**, and select groups in the **Philippines**. In the ID sample I0867 they found evidence of **Y-DNA Haplogroup "H"**, which is most commonly seen in **Dravidian "dark brown skinned people of South India"**. These "Dravidian" states in India are Kerala, Tamil Nadu, Karnataka, Orissa and Andhra Pradesh. It is also found in select groups in **Sri Lanka, Nepal, Pakistan, Afghanistan (Pasthun)** and the **Romani (Gypsy) people** in Europe, thanks to their North Indian Ancestry which has been proven by their language. **Note:** *The Romani people share the same language/writing style as people in India-East Pakistan who speak* **Hindi, Punjabi, Marwari or Bengali.**

Also found in the **Levant (*Israel, Moab, Ammon, Edom, Aram*)** were the Y-DNA **"G-Greece from sample I1727"**, **L-North India** from sample I1727", "**Q-Native Americans** from sample I1727" and "**R** from sample I727". The "R" Y DNA represents a people who have mixed ancestry "Shem, Ham, or Japheth or all three".

They also found the **Y-DNA "T"** which is seen in **Somalians** in the ID sample "I1707".

You can find this proof in the "**Supplemental Information section- Table S6.1**" labeled "**Y-Chromosome haplogroup assignments of ancient Near Easterns.**" The article was headed by Harvard Geneticist Iosif Lazardis under the name, "**Genomic insights into the origin of farming in the ancient Near East (i.e. Levant)**". Again, it is in the Nature magazine, August 25, 2016, Volume 536, Issue 7617. Pg 419-424.

PAY CLOSE ATTENTION!

What is 100% TRUTH is that the Y-DNA "**E1b1**" was the "**father**" of the "**E1b1a**" and "**E1b1c**" Haplogroup. According to the **ISOGG**, aka "**The International Society of Genetic Genealogy**", the Y-DNA "**E1b1**" or "**P2**" gave rise to "**E-M2/E-M329**", which is today called "**E1b1a/E1b1c**" and is found in the so-called "**Negro people/Afro-Asiatic people**". The Y-DNA Haplogroup **E-M215 (E1b1b)**, is younger than the "**E1b1a**" Haplogroup according to most Geneticists and the ISOGG, which was established in 2005 as the first society founded to promote the use of DNA. But here is what Geneticists had to say when they found the Y-DNA Haplogroups "E1b1" and "E1b1a" in Israel:

"The existence of haplogroup E1b1 in ancient East Africa and the nearby Levant (Israel) in the two earliest samples from both regions raises questions about its ultimate origin. This haplogroup continues to exist in the Pre-Pottery Neolithic Period (i.e. B.C. times), but it is NOT documented in ancient Europe or the ancient Near East outside the Levant (Israel). This appears to be consistent with E1b1 being "intrusive".

Intrusive means: "causing disruption or annoyance through being **unwelcome** or **uninvited**."

In this case, they are referring to "**Northeast Africans**" showing their DNA in Israel as **unwanted** and **uninvited** foreigners. This means they "**acknowledge**" that the "**E1b1-E1b1a**" DNA Haplogroup came from Africa and landed in Israel. This fits the "**Biblical Exodus Story**" perfectly as the Israelites became a "**Nation**" mixing with Hamites (*i.e. Egyptians, Canaanites, Philistines, Cushites*) before they even got into Israel with Joshua.

But don't worry, there is more "**Genetic Proof**" coming later in the book from Israel about these "**nations**". By proving who is possibly "Israel".....we can prove who is not. We can also prove who are the Children of Gog and Magog.....the nations that will be involved in the Battle of Armageddon. There are many people that believe "**Gog and Magog**" is the codeword for the "**Antichrist Empire**" of nations.

GOG AND MAGOG FACTS

1. A Global leader will arise. His empire will include Russia, Europe, Turkey, Central Asia, the Middle East and parts of Africa.
2. He will establish a period of peace when Israel will feel "secure" and "relaxed" without threat of attack.
3. An Earthquake will hit Jerusalem (3.5-year mark of the 7-year Great Tribulation).
4. Gog and Magog will attack Israel but the Most High will intervene, destroying the enemies of Israel.
5. The dead bodies of Gog and Magog will become food for the birds.
6. It will take months to bury the dead.
7. The Most High displays his "Glory" to the world.

So where does the "**Gog and Magog**" battle occur in our Bibles?

Well, by the End of Revelation 16, we see the end of the **7 Seals, 7 Trumpets** and **7 Vials**. It is at this time the nations of the world are gathered together into a place called in the Hebrew tongue "**Armageddon**". The Battle of Armageddon, whether it is "**symbolic**" or "**literal**".....it will be fought in the land/plains of Megiddo, and Israel is not going to fight this battle by themselves. The Messiah will take care of the "nations" of the world that seek to destroy Israel and Yeshua HaMashiach. It is also important to know that all of the Israelites will be gathered from among the Gentiles and returned to their own land (Ezekiel 36:24; 37:21). It will also be rebuilt and re-inhabited by God's "True" Chosen People (Ezekiel 36:10-12, 33-36).

But there is many different "**theories**" behind the Battle of Armageddon and the Battle of Gog and Magog. First, many people believe the prophecy in "**Ezekiel 37**" was fulfilled when the European "Gentile" Jews purchased the land known as "**Palestine**" on May 14, 1948.

But as we all know….it has been over 50 years since the State of Israel was created, and yet we do not see **ALL** of the 12 Tribes of Israel **IN ISRAEL**! So what is going on? Are the people in Israel today, the same people that will be in Israel during the Gog & Magog/Battle of Armageddon War? Consider this, in **Ezekiel 39: 1-6**, the "**Heathen Nations**" are destroyed by what the King James Bible refers to as "**the LORD God**". Of course this is "**Yahuah Elohim**" but in the Book of Revelation it is Christ the Messiah (Yahusha HaMashiach) who is "**One**" with the Father/Creator. But something else is written in Ezekiel 39.

Ezekiel 39:7-8 "So will I make my holy name known in the midst of my people Israel; and I will not let them pollute my holy name any more: and the heathen shall know that I am the LORD, the Holy One in Israel. Behold, it is come, and **IT IS DONE**, saith the LORD God; this is **THE DAY** whereof I have spoken."

In the Book of Revelation, we see something similar.

Revelation 16:16-18 "And he gathered them together into a place called in the Hebrew tongue **Armageddon**. Then the **seventh (angel) poured out his bowl into the air**, and a loud voice came out of the sanctuary from the throne, saying, "**IT IS DONE!**" And there were voices, and thunders, and lightnings; **AND THERE WAS A GREAT EARTHQUAKE**, such as was not since men were upon the earth, so mighty an earthquake, and so great. And the **GREAT CITY** was divided into three parts, and the cities of the nations (Gentiles) fell: and **GREAT BABYLON** came in remembrance before God, to give unto her the cup of the wine of the fierceness of his wrath."

Note: The word "**Great City**" could also refer to **Jerusalem**, as it is contrasted with the cities of the nations (goyim-gentiles) and Babylon. The word "**Great City**" is also used of Jerusalem in Revelation 11:8 and of the Heavenly Jerusalem in Revelation 21:10.

Revelation 11:8 "And their dead bodies shall lie in the streets of the **GREAT CITY**, which is spiritually called Sodom and Egypt, where also our Lord was crucified."

In the Hebrew Bible **in Ezekiel 38:19** the Hebrew Strong's #7494 word "**Raash**" means "**Earthquake**".

Revelation 21:6 "And He said to me, "**IT IS DONE!**" I am the Alpha and the Omega, the Beginning and the End. I will give water as a gift to the thirsty from the spring of life.

So, if the "**Day of the Lord**" aka "**God's wrath**" is poured upon the Nations of the Earth during the end of the Tribulation does this mean that the "**Israelites**" would be gathered into Israel during and after the "**Millennial Reign**"?

In **Revelation 19:11-21** it describes the Second coming of Christ during the Battle of Armageddon. Verses 17-21 describe Armageddon as "the supper of the Great God" when the beasts of the field and fowls of the air will be called to eat the flesh of kings, captains and mighty men."

Revelation 20:7-9 reads:

"**And when the thousand years are expired**, Satan shall be loosed out of his prison, And shall go out to deceive the nations which are in the four quarters of the earth, **GOG, AND MAGOG, to GATHER THEM TOGETHER FOR BATTLE**: the number of whom is as the sand of the sea. And they went up on the breath of the earth, and compassed the camp of the saints (*i.e. Physical/Spiritual Israel*) about, and the beloved city (Jerusalem): and fire came from God out of heaven, and devoured them."

Likewise, in the Old Testament Book of Ezekiel 39:17-20 it reads the same as Revelation 19:17-21 when it says:

Ezekiel 39:17-18 "And, thou son of man, thus saith the LORD God; **Speak unto every feathered fowl, and to every beast of the field, Assemble yourselves, and come; gather yourselves on every side to my sacrifice that I do sacrifice for you, even a great sacrifice upon the mountains of Israel, that ye may eat flesh, and drink blood. Ye shall eat the flesh of the mighty, and drink the blood of the princes of the earth**, of rams, of lambs, and of goats, of bullocks, all of them fatlings of Bashan."

In conclusion, it is clear that the **Battle of Gog and Magog** is the same as the **Battle of Armageddon**.....which takes place in the same time period when "**God's wrath**" finally poured upon the nations.

WHERE WILL THE ISRAELITES BE DURING THE "TRIBULATION TIME" IN THE BOOK OF REVELATION? IS ONLY ISREAL GOING TO BE SAVED?

The 144,000 "Israelites" are a special group who will be with "The Lamb-Christ" on earth on Mount Zion and will sing a "song" that no one will know but them. These 144,000 "Israelites" are "**Taken Out**" of the Tribulation right after the "**Sixth Seal**" is opened but before the "**Seventh Seal**". All the other Blood DNA Israelites and Gentile "Spiritual Israelites" in Christ (*i.e. "strangers" in the Old Testament" now bought by Christ in New Testament*) are going to "**experience**" the Tribulation period (7 years).

Note: In the Old Testament, **ONLY** a "**bought**" servant **who was circumcised** could partake in the Passover. A "**foreigner**" or a "**hired servant**" could not partake in the Passover. When Christ died on the Cross, his death **paid (*i.e. bought*) the price** for everyone's sins allowing "**redemption/salvation**" to everyone, Israelites and also the Gentiles.....which we see happen in the Book of Acts.

Exodus 42:43 "And the Lord said unto Moses and Aaron, **This is the ordinance of the Passover:** There shall no stranger eat thereof: But every man's servant that is **BOUGHT FOR MONEY**, when thou has circumcised him, then shall he eat thereof. A foreigner and a hired servant **SHALL NOT** eat thereof."

1 Peter 3:18 "For Christ also hath once suffered for sins, the just for the unjust, that he might bring us to God, being put to death in the flesh, but quickened by the Spirit:"

1 Ephesians 2:8 "For by **grace** are ye saved **through faith**; and that not of yourselves: it is the **gift of God**:"

Note: If the 12 Tribes of Israel were "**obedient**" to God's Covenant, they would've received the "**Blessings of Israel**". They would've also been

240

present as a "**whole**" 12 Tribes when Christ the Messiah was born. They surely would've accepted Christ since the Israelite prophets foretold of his coming. But the Israelites were hard-headed and stubborn in their ways. They decided to worship false pagan gods than to worship the Creator. Because of this disobedience, there were very few "Real" Israelites in the land of Israel when Christ was born. Those few Israelites in the Land were considered the "**Lost Sheep of Israel**", whom Christ had come for first. These Israelites had "**disbelief**" and were "**hard-headed**" like their forefathers. Therefore the "Gentiles" were witnessed to and many did receive the "testimony" of Christ. Paul, a Benjaminite, talks about this in his Epistle (Letter) to Rome.

Romans 11:11-15

"I say then, Have they (Israelites) stumbled that they should fall? God forbid: but rather through their fall salvation is come unto the Gentiles, for to provoke them to jealousy. Now if the fall of them (Israelites) be the riches of the world, and the diminishing of them the riches of the Gentiles; how much more their fulness? For I speak to you Gentiles, inasmuch as I am the apostle of the Gentiles, I magnify mine office: If by any means I may provoke to emulation (*i.e. make them like me*) them which are my flesh (Blood Israelites), and might save some of them. **For if the casting away of them (Israelites) be the reconciling (i.e. saving/uniting) of the world, what shall the receiving of them be, but life from the dead?**"

Keep this in mind. Through the Israelites "**fall**", salvation came to the Gentiles over 2,000 years ago. The Israelites were scattered into the "Nations" with the help of the Gentiles and they lost their "**identity**". The "Gentiles" replaced "Israel's" identity so the name of "Israel" would be no more in remembrance. Now the "**True Israelites**" are waking up as the "**Gentile Nations**" and the world is becoming more "**Evil**" in preparation for the Antichrist. Many so-called "Christians" of all races are losing the faith. With the "Israelite" awakening, people (*especially the Real Israelites*) are getting back to following the Bible the way it was supposed to be followed.....in **Spirit** and **Truth**. **True Natsarim**. This means that now the "**natural branch**" that was broken off so that the Gentiles could have a chance at being "**grafted in**"......is now gonna be re-grafted back into his rightful position. The "natural branch" is the authentic "Real Hebrew Israelites". Those "Gentiles" that do not want to perish with earth during God's wrath will "**flock**" to the **True Israelites** in the last days. They will....like the Real Hebrew Israelites follow the Torah, keep the commandments, honor the feast days/Sabbath, and bear the testimony of Christ with the seed of the Woman (*i.e. Hebrew Israelites*). This happening right now! So, are we coming near to the end of the "Time of the Gentiles"? In Acts 24:5, the "true" followers of Yahusha (Jesus) were known as "**Natsarim**"....which means the "**watchmen**" or "**branches**" of Yahusha.

Hebrew Strong's #5342 = "**Netser**" which means "**branch**".

Hebrew Strong's #5341= "**Natsar**" which means "**watch, guard or keep**". Hence the word "Natsarim" means "watchers or watchmen" and "Netserim" means "Branches".

(**Above**) Saint and Church father Epiphanius (310 A.D.) was a Christian Greek who spoke 5 languages (*Greek, Hebrew, Syriac, Egyptian and Latin*). In his literary works he quoted:

"The **Natsarim** do not differ in any essential thing from them (*Yahudim-Israelites*), since they practice the customs and doctrines prescribed by Ioudismos law (*i.e. Judaism law/Law of Moses*); except that they believe in Christ. They believe in the resurrection of the dead, and that the universe was created by Theos (*i.e. Greek name for "God the Creator"*). They preach that Theos is One, and that IESV (Yahusha) Christos (Hamashiach) is his Son. **They are very learned in the Hebrew language.** They read the Torah. Therefore they differ from TRUE Christians because they fulfill until now Ioudismos (Judaism) rites as the circumcision, Sabbath and others."

Church Father Epiphanius, "*Against Heresies/Panarion*" 29, 7, Page 41, 402.

Acts 24:5 "For we have found this man (**i.e. Paul**) a pestilent fellow, and a mover of sedition among all the Jews throughout the world, and a ringleader of the **sect of the Nazarenes**:"

Acts 28:22 "But we desire to hear of thee what thou thinkest: for as concerning **this sect (i.e. Natsarim)**, we know that every where it is spoken against."

The word "**Nazarene**" comes from the town Nazareth inside Galilee (Northern Israel) where Christ grew up at. It is based off the Hebrew Root word, "**Natsar**". The town was perched on or near the brow of a hill so many say it is derived from the Hebrew word Natsar which means "**to watch**". The Hebrew word "**Netser**" means "**a branch or a shoot**", which many say lines up with the Messianic prophecy in **Isaiah 11:1** when it says:

"Then a **shoot** will spring up from the stem of Jesse, and a **BRANCH** from his roots will bear fruit."

Note: *King David was not born in Nazareth, but was born in Bethlehem.*

Now take this into consideration.

The Most High showed Zechariah a vision of Joshua the High Priest of Israel, in regards to the state of the Israelites after their Babylonian captivity and the promise of the Messiah through Christ of the Seed of David-Jesse, not King David himself.

Zechariah 3:8 "Hear now, O **Joshua the high priest**, thou, and thy fellows that sit before thee: for they are men wondered at: for, behold, I will bring forth my servant the **BRANCH**."

יהושע

(**Above**) The Hebrew spelling of Joshua in the Old Testament......and the Hebrew spelling of "**Jesus**" in the New Testament. When pronounced "letter-for-letter" you get (**Yah-oo-sha**) or "**Yahusha**". In the Old Testament, these Hebrew letters that make up the 5-letter word for Joshua appear **216 times**. *Note: In the Old Testament, the 4-letter word for "Y'shua/Yeshua" appears only once.* The Greek transliteration of this word "**Yahusha**" is "**Ihsous**". In **Hebrews 4** and **Acts 7** the same Greek lettering is used for "**Joshua**" and "**Jesus**" is "**IHSOUS**". This confirms that in the Old Testament "Joshua's" name was pronounced the same as "Jesus's" name in the New Testament!

Now below is **Zechariah 3:8** in Hebrew. Notice the name of Joshua (**in bold**) is the same lettering as the Hebrew name for "**Jesus**".

שְׁמַע-נָא **יְהוֹשֻׁעַ** הַכֹּהֵן הַגָּדוֹל, אַתָּה וְרֵעֶיךָ הַיֹּשְׁבִים

לְפָנֶיךָ--כִּי-אַנְשֵׁי מוֹפֵת, הֵמָּה: כִּי-הִנְנִי מֵבִיא אֶת-

עַבְדִּי, צֶמַח.

So, as we can see the "**BRANCH**" is Christ. This can be seen in Isaiah 11:1 and Romans 1:3. Christ the Messiah is the branch from the almost extinct line of King David and Jesse (*see Zechariah 6:12, Isaiah 4:2, Jeremiah 23:5, Jeremiah 33:15, Luke 1:78*).

Fact: Even in the Catholic Apocrypha the word "**Joshua**" appears simply as "**Jesus**". Coincidence?

*Fact: Despite, what the Bible says, there are many beliefs that "**Only the 12 Tribes of Israel**" will be saved, leaving the rest of the world "pre-destined" to eternal damnation in the Lake of Fire after the "Great Tribulation". If this was the case why would there be a need for "**Judgement Day**" and the **Book of Life**?*

RAPTURE DOCTRINE CONTINUED:

Revelation 20:12-15

"And I saw the dead, small and great, stand before God; and the books were opened: and other book was opened, which is the **BOOK OF LIFE**: and the dead were judged out of those things which were written in the books, according to their works. And the sea gave up the dead which were in it; and death and hell delivered up the dead which were in them: and they were judged every man according to their works. And death and hell were cast into the lake of fire. This is the second death. And whosoever was not found written in the **BOOK OF LIFE** was cast into the lake of fire."

The Bible verifies in the Book of Revelation that living Israelites and Gentiles will experience the "**Great Tribulation**" if we look closely at the scriptures. The Bible shows us this chronologically if we go by the scriptures and it also gives us a "**sneak peek**" into the Book of Life. Let's start out in the 6th Chapter of the Book of Revelation before the 144,000 are sealed. You will see no evidence of a "**Rapture**" happening and you will in fact see that there will be many "**Blood DNA Israelites**" and "**Gentile (Spiritual Israelites) – Strangers amongst the Real Israelites**" who will die in the beginning of the "**Tribulations**" first "**6 SEALS**".

Revelation 6:9-13 "And when he had opened the **FIFTH SEAL (TRIBULATION)**, I saw **UNDER THE ALTAR** the **SOULS** of them that were **SLAIN (KILLED IN THE TRIBULATION)** for the word of God, and for the testimony which they held: And they cried with a loud voice, saying, How long, O Lord, holy and true, dost thou not judge and avenge our blood on them that dwell on the earth? And white robes were given unto every one of them; and it was said unto them, **that they should rest yet for a little season, until their fellow servants also and their brethren, THAT SHOULD BE KILLED as they were**, should be fulfilled. And I beheld when he had opened **THE SIXTH SEAL**, and, lo, there was a **great earthquake**; and the sun became black as sackcloth of hair, and the moon became as blood; And the stars of heaven fell unto the earth, **even as a fig tree casteth her untimely figs**, when she is shaken of a mighty wind."

Fun Fact: *The Fig Tree grows wild in the Middle East, especially Israel. The Bible says when things were well in Israel, every man was able to sit under his own fig tree (**1 Kings 4:25**). Christ also gives many parables about the fig tree. Well, the Bantus Kikuyu Tribe in Kenya are said to have been founded by a man named, "**Gikuyu**". He had a wife called "**Mumbi**" and prior to the Kikuyu's place of residence today Gikuyu and Mumbi lived in a land where the **Fig Tree grew wild and free.** This is not in Africa. The most varieties of the Fig Tree grow in **ISRAEL**. Many **Ki-kuyu, Ki-kisii and Ki-kamba** people in Kenya and even the Sukuma peope in Tanzania all say their ancestors came from "**The North**". I asked a Kenyan and Tanzanian Bantus man do they mean "**Ethiopia or Sudan**" and they all said, "**No, way north than that.**". I said to them, "well, way north than Sudan is Egypt and Israel. The land of Israel was famous for its Fig Trees as excavations from the City of Gezer, given to King Solomon as a dowry gift from his Egyptian father-in-law uncovered many old fig tree remnants. The Bantus Kenyans also say they* *migrated from West-Central Africa (Congo) region to modern day Kenya and they talk about King Solomon and their people as if they are kinfolk.*

So who are these "**slain people**" whose souls are "**under the altar**" that are seen after the **Fifth seal** is opened? Are these Israelites or Gentiles? Why are they called Saints? These are different "**White Robe**" Saints that were seen by John "**UNDER THE ALTAR**" and not "**IN FRONT OF THE THRONES**". This was during the "**Fifth Seal**".

So what happens before the "**Sixth Seal**" is let loose on the Earth? Read further in Revelation, Chapter 7!

Revelation 7:8 "Of the tribe of **Zebulon** were sealed **twelve thousand**. Of the tribe of **Joseph** were sealed **twelve thousand**. Of the tribe of **Benjamin** were sealed **twelve thousand**."

So here we see the 144,000 Israelites from all the Tribes (except Dan) are sealed. The Tribe of Benjamin is the last Tribe of Israel that is sealed. Now let see what happens after the last of the 144,000 Israelites are sealed!

Revelation 7:9-16 "After this I beheld, and, lo, **A GREAT MULTITUDE**, which no man could number, **OF ALL NATIONS, AND KINDREDS, AND PEOPLE, AND TONGUES**, stood before the throne (not under the altar) and, and before the Lamb, clothed with **WHITE ROBES**, and palms in their hands;"

Note: *There is some false doctrines being taught that **ONLY ISRAEL** shall be saved......meaning that everyone else on the planet is condemned automatically to the Lake of fire and eternal damnation. What about the "Gentile nations" that bear the testimony of Christ, have been baptized by water and baptized by fire (Holy Spirit), with evidence of speaking in tongues? When Romans 11:26 says "ALL ISRAEL WILL BE SAVED", is it talking about "ethnic" Bloodline "**Physical Israelites**" or does it also include "Gentiles" who believe in Christ, whom some may call "**Spiritual Israelites**"? Does it mean "Israel" now has a chance to be saved from sin?*

Nevertheless, why would Christ need the Book of Life, the throne and Judgement Day if "only Israel is to make it into the Kingdom"? We also have to remember that the Apostle Paul was not prophesying as Paul was not an Israelite Prophet. Paul also was not one of the 12 Disciples. Also, Remember, when Nicodemus asked Christ some questions about the Kingdom in John 3, Christ didn't say, "Only Israel will make it into the Kingdom". He said, "For God sent not His Son into the world to condemn the world, but that the world through Him might be saved." He also said, "He that believeth in the Son hath everlasting life; and he that believeth not the Son shall not see life, but the wrath of God abideth on him." Who words will you ultimately follow? Christ the Messiah or the Apostle Paul?

So, is Revelation chapter 9 revealing a "**sneak peek**" that John saw of the final conclusion of the "Tribulation" even though the "**Sixth Seal**" had not been unleashed on the earth?

The Book of Revelation 7:9 says **ALL NATIONS** stood before the Lamb in **white robes**. However, 4 scriptures later in the same chapter it gives hint that this is a vision of the "**end**" when the Christ dwells with man on a "**New Earth**" in the "**New City of Jerusalem**" where there is **no Sun, no tears** and **no real need to hunger or thirst**.

Revelation 7:13-17 "And one of the elders answered, saying unto me, What are these which are arrayed in white robes? And whence came they? And I said unto him, Sir, thou knowest. And he said to me, **THESE ARE THEY WHICH CAME OUT OF GREAT TRIBULATION**, and have washed their robes, and made them white in the blood of the Lamb. Therefore are they before the throne of God, and serve him day and night in his temple: and he that sitteth on the throne shall dwell among them. **They shall hunger no more, neither thirst anymore; neither shall the sun light on them, nor any heat**. For the Lamb which is in the midst of the throne shall feed them, and shall lead them unto living fountains of waters: and God shall wipe away all tears from their eyes."

So again, why are many "Israelites" saying that **only Israel can be saved with eternal life in the kingdom**. According to this doctrine, this means that the rest of the world is destined to the Lake of Fire. But what does the Bible say?

Let's break down this statement with Scripture using the Hebrew word for "**World**".

In **John 3:18-17** it in the King James Bible reads

"**For God so loved the world**, that he gave his only begotten Son, that whosoever believeth in him should not perish, but have everlasting life. **For God sent not his Son into the world to condemn the world; but that the world through him might be saved.**"

In the Aramaic-Hebrew New Testament the Hebrew Strong's word #5769 "**Olam**" is the word used for "**world**". What does "**Olam**" mean in Hebrew? It means "**Forever**", "**the ages**", "**Antiquity**", "**Futurity**", "**Eternal**" and "**Everlasting**".

Note: "**Futurity**" means "**a time to come**". "**Antiquity**" means "**Ancient times**". Together these two words represent the **past, present and future**. Christ in Revelation describes himself as "**which is, which was, and which is to come**". Many Christian scholars believe the Father-Christ appeared throughout time in our bible as different people (*i.e. Adonizedek-Shem, Melchizedek, Commander of Lord's hosts that Joshua worships, Joshua himself, Joshua/Yeshua the 1st High Priest selected during the rebuilding of the 2nd Temple and Yeshua (Jesus Christ)*".

John 14:9 "Yeshua (Jesus) saith unto him, Have I been so long time with you, and yet hast thou not known me, Philip? **he that hath seen me hath seen the Father**; and how sayest thou then, Shew us the Father."

John 10:30 "I and the Father are **one**."

Revelation 1:8 "I am Alpha and Omega, the beginning and the ending, saith the Lord, **which is, and which was, and which is to come**, the Almighty."

John 3:17-18 in itself encompasses **"Antiquity and Futurity"** or the Hebrew meaning of **"Olam-world"** which is also attributed to meaning **"Forever and Everlasting"**. The Hebrew word **"Tebel"** for the literal word **"World"** is used in Revelation 12:9.

So basically, Christ is saying in **John 3:18-19** that his **"Love is Forever and Everlasting"** for mankind. This is why **the Father (Yahuah Elohim) sent not his Son (himself) into the world to condemn the world; but that the world through him might be saved."**

Revelation 12:9 "And the great dragon was cast out, that old serpent, called the Devil, and Satan, **which deceiveth the whole world (Hebrew word "Tebel")**: he was cast out into the earth, and his angels were cast out with him."

olam: long duration, antiquity, futurity	tebel: world
Original Word: עוֹלָם	Original Word: תֵּבֵל
Part of Speech: Noun Masculine	Part of Speech: Noun Feminine
Transliteration: olam	Transliteration: tebel
Phonetic Spelling: (o-lawm')	Phonetic Spelling: (tay-bale')
Short Definition: forever	Short Definition: world

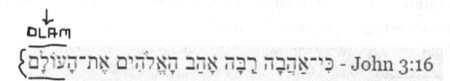

OLAM

{עֹלָם‎} כִּי־אָהֲבָה רַבָּה אָהַב הָאֱלֹהִים אֶת־הָעוֹלָם - John 3:16

So let's stop here and recap for a second. This multitude of "people" who seek to **"endure"** during the "Great Tribulation" can only consist of **"Physical Blood DNA Israelites"** and also **"Gentile Spiritual Israelites United in Christ"**. Why? Because the ethnic **"Physical Nation of Israel"** does not consist of **ALL NATIONS**. Revelation 7:9

wouldn't need to include the word "**ALL NATIONS**" to stand before the Lamb to be judged if everyone other than "**Israel**" was **pre-destined** to eternal damnation in the Lake of Fire. Also, if this were the case, **everyone** in the world would be a descendant of the 12 sons of Jacob. Also the people seen here are "**physical living people**".....at least it doesn't say in this scripture that these people are all dead or that some of them are dead souls in comparison to the "**Slain souls**" in white robes who were seen by John in his vision under the "**Altar**" in Revelation 6:9.

So, let's recap again what happens next with the 144,000 sealed "Israelites" and the rest of the people in the "Great Tribulation". What the "**Elders**" in Revelation ask John will give more insight to why we will experience the "Tribulation" period on earth.

Revelation 7:10-16 "And cried with a loud voice, saying, Salvation to our God which sitteth upon the throne, and unto the Lamb. And all the **ANGELS** stood round about the throne, and about the **ELDERS AND THE FOUR BEASTS** and the four beasts, and fell before the throne on their faces, and worshipped God, Saying, Amen: Blessing, and glory, and wisdom, and thanksgiving, and honor, and power, and might, be unto our God for ever and ever. Amen. **AND ONE OF THE ELDERS ANSWERED, SAYING UNTO ME (JOHN)**, What are these which are arrayed in white robes? and whence came they? And I said unto him, Sir, thou knowest. And he (**THE ELDER**) said to me, **THESE ARE THEY WHICH CAME OUT OF THE GREAT TRIBULATION**, and have washed their robes, and made them white in the **blood of the Lamb (Christ)**. Therefore are they before the throne of God, and serve him day and night in his temple: and he that sitteth on the throne shall dwell among them. They shall hunger no more, neither thirst any more; neither shall the sun light on them (**Revelations 21:23**), nor any heat."

So here we see this "**Great Multitude**" of Saints (Physical and Spiritual Israelites united in Christ) made it through (or came out) the "**Great**

Tribulation". Whether they made it "**Dead or Alive**" to the "**Great Throne**" the important thing here is that they made it.

Note: *The 144,000 Sealed Israelites had their own "**Special Mission/Task**". Many however believe that **only 144,000** Israelites will make it into the Kingdom. The 144,000 are "sealed" after the "Sixth Seal" is let loose on the Earth. These 144,000 sealed Israelites are mentioned before the last seven plagues are unleashed on the earth and before the "**Great Wrath**" of the Lamb on the Earth...but don't worry, there are still plenty of other Israelites during this time that will see eternal life.*

Revelation 14: 1-5 "And I looked, and, lo, a Lamb stood on the mount Sion, and with him **a hundred forty and four thousand, having his Father's name written in their foreheads**. And I heard a voice from heaven, as the voice of many waters, and as the voice of a great thunder: and I heard the voice of harpers harping with their harps: **And they sung as it were a new song before the throne, and before the four beasts, and the elders: and no man could learn that song but the hundred and forty and four thousand, which were redeemed from the earth.** These are they which were not defiled with women; for they are **virgins**. These are they which follow the Lamb whithersoever he goeth. These were redeemed from among men, being the **firstfruits** unto God and to the Lamb. And in their mouth was found no guile: for they are without fault before the throne of God."

CHAPTER 6

NEITHER JEW NOR GREEK? BARBARIAN OR SCYTHIAN? PROVING THAT THE EUROPEAN JEWS ARE THE "PROSELTYE JEWS", BARBARIANS, SCYTHIANS AND GREEKS THE NEW TESTAMENT SPEAKS OF IN THE EPISTLES OF PAUL

So here is the "Big Question". During the time of Christ, the "**Book of Acts**" and the "**Pauline Gospels (Books written by the Apostle Paul)**" what does the statement, "*Neither Jew, nor Greek*" mean? What kind of people were in Judea at the time? What does a so called "**Gentile**" Jew living in this time period of the 1st Century A.D. have to say about this? Read further:

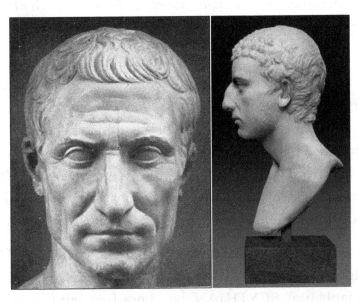

(Above) Gentile "Greek" Jewish Historian "Flavius Josephus" (Born 37 A.D. and died 100 A.D.)

"That country is also called **Judea**, and the people **Jews**; and this name is given also to **as many** as embrace *THEIR RELIGION* (the Israelites religion), **THOUGH OF OTHER NATIONS.**

(Note: The above statement by Flavius Josephus is proof that the Jews in that time were simply Judaism converts from other nations like Greece, Rome or Edom).

"But then upon what foundation so good a governor as Hyrcanus took upon himself to compel these **Idumeans (Edomites)** either to **become Jews** (BY RELIGION) or to leave their country, deserves great consideration. I suppose it was because they had long ago been driven out of the land of Edom, and had seized on and possessed the **Tribe of Simeon** (the land not the people), and all the **southern part of the land of the Tribe of Judah**, which was the peculiar inheritance of the worshippers of the **True God** without idolatry...."

Flavius Josephus, 1st century A.D. Roman-Judean historian.

Note: *John Hyrcanus I was a Greek Hasmonean Jew and **grandson of Matthias patriarch of the Maccabees, a family of Gentile Judean patriots of 2nd and 1st centuries B.C**).*

This adds up to how Paul described the people of the land in Judea. Some practiced the Greek Religion (*i.e. Zeus*) and some practiced the religion of Judaism. Europeans Greeks were not required to circumcise as this was specifically an "Israelite" custom. Many Gentiles had moved into Judea from Asia Minor and Europe after the Black Israelites were expelled from their land in the 8th-7th centuries B.C. They were "immigrants" back then to a new land...just as many Syrian or Iraqi Muslims are "immigrants" in Europe (*i.e. Greece, Spain, Germany*).

Colossians 3:11 "Whether there is neither **GREEK NOR JEW**, circumcision nor uncircumcision, **BARBARIAN** (Non-Roman/Greek European Japhetite), **SCYTHIAN**, bond nor free: but Christ is all, and in all."

This was penned by Paul, the Apostle to the Gentiles (*i.e. nations that were not Israel*).

So the question is who were the **Greeks, Barbarians, Scythians, Huns** and **Goths** during the Apostle Paul's time? Surely these were not his "**blood brethren**", the "Real Hebrew Israelites". Paul proves these Gentiles were not his "Israelite" brethren in the Book of Romans.

Romans 11:11-14

"Again I ask: Did they (*i.e. Blood Israelites*) stumble so as to fall beyond recovery? Not at all! Rather, because of their transgression (i.e. sin, broken covenant), **salvation has come to the Gentiles to make Israel envious**. But if their transgression (i.e. act that goes against a law) means riches for the world, and their loss means riches for the Gentiles, how much greater riches will their fullness bring! **I am talking to you Gentiles.** Inasmuch as I am the Apostle to the Gentiles, I make much of my ministry in the hope that I may somehow arouse **my own people (Israelites)** to envy and save some of them.

So, let's look at these **Scythians** and **Barbarians** the Apostle Paul talks about.

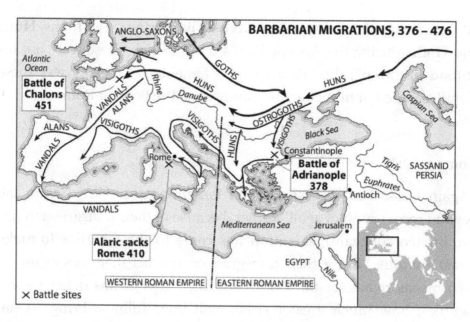

Barbarian = a member of a community or tribe not belonging to one of the great civilizations (Greek, Roman, Christian).

The Collapse of the Roman Empire with the Barbarians.

Let's recap again who the Barbarians were:

The Barbarians were people from Central and Northern Europe. In the 5th century A.D. they invaded the declining Roman Empire and they gradually carved it up the between them. The **Barbarians** never intended to destroy the Roman Empire, they wanted to share in its wealth but it was declining anyway and soon broke down altogether.

In December 406 A.D., a group of Germanic "Barbarian" tribes entered **Gaul** (*i.e. western Slavic territory-France*) and settled there. The Romans were unable to stop them. Nevertheless, at first the Germanic settlers accepted Roman rule. However, as the Roman Empire broke down they gradually formed **independent kingdoms** (*i.e. Spain, France, Germany, Portugal, Greece, Italy, England... including other parts of Europe*). **Again, these nations are not by coincidence the same people who persecuted the Israelites!**

Ok, so what about the "Scythians".

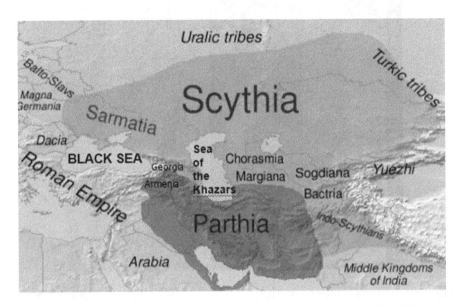

Scythia in Biblical times would be the same area the Khazarian Empire would founded at during the 8th to 11th Century A.D. What is interesting is that when genetic studies were done on ancient bones dug up in Scythian cities dating back to their time period the Y-DNA showed "R1a1a1 (R-M17", which the Ashkenazi Jews carry and claim is connected to the Tribe of Levi. But who traveled these lands first? Many believe it was the Sons of Shem who now reside in India, Afghanistan, Pakistan and other "Asian lands" who carry the older Y-DNA "R1a1" Haplogroup.

(**Left**) "**Red Jews**" wearing their "**cone hats**" depicted on an ancient church in Germany. (**Right**) Part of the "**Behistun Inscription**" relief carved on Mount Behistun in Iran (**Persia**).

The area of the Eastern Iranic people (Persia) used to be **Scythian-Sarmatian** territory in ancient times. The Behistun Inscription relief depicts the conquests of Persian King Darius over the **Scythian people** who lived beyond **the Caucasus Mountains/Sea of the Khazars** (Caspian Sea). Scythian King "**Skunkha**" is seen here captured with his hand behind his back by **Persian King Darius I** and his forces. During this time King Darius I led an attack on the **Eastern Saka (Scythian) people**. Is it a coincidence that these **Scythians** and the so-called "**Red Jews**" wear the same type of "**pointed**" hats? Both were also known to be **white-skinned** with **blue eyes** and **red hair** as well.

Now considered this amazing fact. In the Chinese "**Book of Han (200 B.C.)**", the valleys of the Ili River (**Kazakhstan-China**) and the Chu River (Kazahkstan) are where the people known as the "**Sai/Saka**" live. The people of **Kazahkstan** say their oral history points them to being descendants of the Japhetic **Khazar people**. Well, the Khazar people have been connected by DNA (*i.e. Y-DNA & mtDNA*) to the Ashkenazi Jews. DNA studies by scientists like Michael Hammer (University of Arizona) also prove that the Ashkenazi Jews, the Sephardic Jews and the Eurasian Arabs are all related to a single ancestor from Europe/Asia Minor. For example, the **Tarim Mummies** found in the **Tarim Basin in Xijiang, China** were found to be "Europoid" with mostly European DNA. These "Tarim mummies" were **white-skinned** with **blonde, brown** and **reddish hair**. Archaeologists also noted that they had **tattoos** on their bodies with the **crescent moon and the sun** done in the manner of the **Scythians**.

Note: *The Hebrews Israelites were forbidden by "Levitical Law" to tattoo themselves so these Tarim Mummies with the same DNA as the Ashkenazi Jews could not have been Israelites. In **Leviticus 19:28** it states, "**Ye shall not make any cutting in your flesh for the dead, nor print any marks upon you. I am the LORD.**" So, who were these "Scythian" people with the same DNA as Ashkenazi Jews that were tattooing their bodies, living in*

259

*the ancient land of the Jewish-converted Khazar Kingdom? They were descendants of Japheth, aka the "**Gentiles**" that the Bible speaks of.*

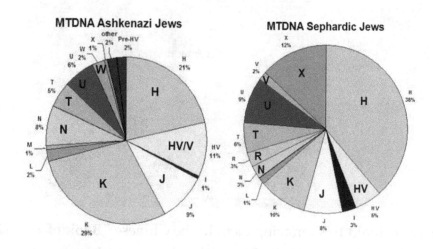

Maternal mtDNA analysis was done on these Tarim (Scythian/Khazar) mummies in the Xiaohe Tombs (Xijiang, China) which showed "**European**" mtDNA Haplogroups **H, HV, K, U, T and J.** **These are the same (maternal) mtDNA Haplogroups seen in Ashkenazi-Sephardic women and men passed down from their mothers.** The Paternal Y-DNA of these "Caucasoid Tarim Mummies" was found to be "**R1a1a/R1a1a1**" which is also found mostly in Eastern Europeans (Germanic/Slavic Ashkenazi Jews) and some Central Asians. This proves that Ashkenazi and Sephardic Jews genetic heritage is that of "**Europoid-Caucasoid**" Japhetic **Scythian-Khazarian** descent…instead of Biblical Hebrew Israelite descent. This proves the "**Chosen People of God**" claim by todays European Jews is a big fat lie. Shall we dig deeper? Yes we shall!

Scythians and the "Red Haired Jew" connection

In ancient literary works the Scythians were known and reported to have **red hair** and **blue eyes**. But so were the Khazarian Jews. In the Book, "**The Jews of Khazaria**" by Kevin Alan Brook, it explains how the Khazarian Jews were known by their neighbors (Arabs, Huns, Chinese) to have Red Hair. The Yiddish term "**Die Roten Juden/Di Royte Yidn**" means "**The Red Jews**"....obviously because of their "Red Hair" and not because they wore Red garments or were physically "**Red**" like the "**Kool Aid man**". How do we know this? It is a known fact that in various art, the Scythians are shown with various traits such as "**Red Hair**" and different **light-colored eyes**.

(**Above**) **Slavic territory**. The Slavic speaking countries in Europe are the **Czech Republic, Bosnia, Serbia, Bulgaria, Romania, Slovakia, Belarus, Macedonia, Croatia, Montenegro, Ukraine, Russia, Prussia and Poland**. Ask any Ashkenazi Jew today where their grandparents were born and they will likely name one of these countries. The Jews speak a mutt language called "**Yiddish**" which is Slavic, Turkish and Germanic (Germany/France) because their ancestors come from

Japheth. Hebrew Israelites speak Hebrew, not the Slavic, Turkish and Germanic languages.

In the Greek Historian Herodotus's literary work "**The Histories (4:108)**" dated to 400 B.C., he describes the **Budini Tribe of Scythia** as having "**deep blue eyes and bright red hair**". The Budini Tribe was believed to be a **Slavic Tribe** (*one of the component languages of the Ashkenazi "Yiddish Language"*). Mysteriously, the "Caucasian" **Kalash Tribe** in Pakistan and many other European nations have evidence of "**Red-Haired people**". Scientists and anthropologists claim they are of "**Bulgarian**" origin....which according to **King Joseph of Khazaria** in "**The Khazar Correspondence**" was one of the sons of **Togarmah**, son of **Gomer**, son of **Japheth**. According to King Joseph their Khazarian Kingdom was of the lineage of Japheth's grandson, Togarmah (*the father of all Turks and Armenians*) who had 10 sons: **Ujur**, Tauris, **Avar**, Uauz, Bizal, Tarna, **Khazar**, Janur, **Bulgar,** and Sawir. The **Kalash Tribe** as well as the **Burushaski Tribe** (*living in Afghanistan/Pakistan*) also claim to have part heritage from the descendants of Greek settlers during Alexander the Great's conquest of Egypt, Judea, Mesopotamia, India and Asia. The 1st century Roman author Pliny the Elder described the "**Seres/Scythians**" or **Tocharians (East Turkestan)** as having "**Red-Hair**" and "**Blue-Eyes**".

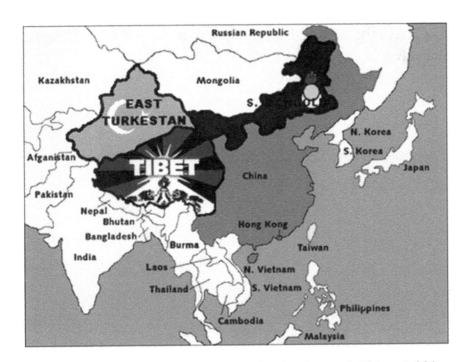

Fact: The **Western Xingjiang (Xijiang)** Province of China 1,000 years ago was inhabited by European people who controlled the "**Silk Trade Roads**" into China. In the 1930's, sections of the Xingjiang Province became independent, calling themselves the "**Islamic Republic of East Turkestan**". The "**East Turkestani**" people prior to this were called the "**Tocharians**" and were believed to be descendants of the **Scythians**. The major ethnic groups in Turkestan are the "**Uyghur/Ughar/Ughur**" and the "**Kazakh**" people who speak a **Turkish language (***which is one component language that makes up the Jewish "Yiddish Language"***).** They are also predominately Muslim. What is interesting is that in the 8th Century A.D. "**Khazar Correspondence**", King Joseph of Khazaria claims that "**Togarmah**" is the father of all **Turkish People**. Togarmah per King Joseph had sons. One was name "**Ujur**" similar to "**Uyghur**", one was named "**Avar**" similar to the **Avars** in Europe, one was named "**Bulgar**" similar to the Bulgarians in Russia/the "Balkans" and one was name "**Khazar**" of who the "**Kazakh**" people claim their heritage from. They **ALL** speak a "**Turkish Dialect**". What's even more crazy is that these Turkish

263

Tribes all have the same Y-DNA/mtDNA as the Ashkenazi/Sephardic Jews worldwide.

CHAPTER 7

ARE THE SONS OF CAIN, THE "RED HAIRED JEWS" AND ESAU "THE CONFEDERATE" THAT IS DESTROYING THE WORLD?

(**Above**) In the National Archaeological Museum in Madrid, Spain, there is a life-sized sculpture of a Neanderthal female with **red hair**, **blue eyes** and **white skin**.....a typical "**Caucasoid**", but also similar in appearance to the Khazarian "Ashkenazi-Edomite" Jews and the Scythians. Archaeologists determined based on **Neanderthal DNA** and hair samples that Neanderthals were white-skinned, reddish/blonde-haired, blue-eyed people. This "**European Trait**" exists in Scotland, Spain, Germany, the European Jews and other places. Remember, the most common trait of **ALL HUMANS** is black hair, brown-eyes and some shade of brown skin.

Genesis 3:15 "And I will put enmity (hostility) between thee (Seed of Satan-Cain) and the Woman (Seed of Seth-Israel), and between thy seed (Cain) and her seed (Israel); it shall bruise thy head, and thou shalt bruise his heel."

There are TWO SEEDS at war here:

1. **The Seed of Cain**
2. **The Seed of Israel**

This prophecy was before Egypt had a name or was even a civilization. This scripture already foretold the "**Messianic Prophecy**"....including the final battle between Satan and God (Christ).

In the Bible, the Seed of the "**Wicked One**" is the Children of Cain. In the Bible, it is a known fact that in the Book of Genesis it states that the Nephilim seed existed on the earth before and after the "Great Flood". The Nephilim were the offspring in the Bible of the "**Watchers**"....aka "**Disobedient Angels**" and womankind. So the offspring of these heavenly beings/angels were obviously different than the offspring of Seth. We know that Noah was "**perfect**" and "**pure**" in his bloodline according to the Bible. We also know that Cain mixed with the Nephilim as well because it doesn't say that Cain was "perfect" or "pure" and it does state that after Cain was banished to the "**Land of Nod**" to the East he found a woman and had children with her. Who was this woman and who were these people that he encountered? This is a big mystery as there are many theories of there being two women created (*i.e. Lilith and Eve*) in the Bible and perhaps two sets of humans living on the Earth in the beginning when the "Fallen Angels" were present on Earth. Some West African Tribes today have folklore stories about God creating "two women" and one man prior to the "Great Flood." Nevertheless, we know that there was a "**cleansing**" of the earth by God in the form of a "**Great Flood**" or "**Deluge**". But did any of the Sons of Cain survive? Is it possible that the Sons of Cain survived with help from the Nephilim and the Fallen Angels/Watchers?

Fact: The Sumerians documented in the "**Lost 14 tablets of Enki**" that the Annunaki (Nephilim) and some of the Sons of Cain survived the flood. Why would the Ancient Sumerians tell this story of the Sons of Cain surviving the Deluge? If this is the case, where are the Sons of Cain today? Are they amongst the Edomite people? Are they amongst the Gentile people of the world? In my first book "**Hebrews to Negroes:**

Wake Up Black America" I show strong similarities between the "**Curse of Cain**", the "**biblical characteristics of Cain**" and the "**Rechabite/Nethinim**" people that are known to always "mysteriously" place themselves in close vicinity to the Israelite people throughout the Old Testament. So with that being said, consider these amazing facts:

Supposedly in Genesis 4:1 in the Dead Sea Scrolls - (**Hebrew version**) it has been reported to read:

"**And Adam knew his wife Eve, who was pregnant by Samael, (Satan), and she conceived and bare Cain, and he was like the heavenly beings, and not like the earthly beings, and she said, I have gotten a man from the angel of the Lord.**"

If Cain was the offspring of Satan or a Fallen angel/Evil angel then that would make Cain and his offspring the seed of the serpent, their father being Satan as Yahusha (Jesus) told the Jewish Pharisees in John 8:44 and Matthew 23:33. Now keep in mind that "**Pharisee-ism**" today is the religion of the Ashkenazi and Sephardic Jews who practice "**Talmudic Judaism**".

Christ (Yahusha HaMashiach/Jesus) knew about the **Seed of Cain** and the **Seed of Edom** in his day although others didn't know.

John 8:44 "**Ye are of your father the devil,** and the lusts of your father ye will do. He was a murderer from the beginning, and abode not in the truth, because there is no truth in him. When he speaketh a lie, he speaketh of his own: for he is a liar, and the father of it."

Matthew 23:33 "Ye serpents, ye generations of vipers, how can ye escape the damnation of hell?"

Even John the Baptist called these certain Pharisees and Sadducees **generations of vipers**. But why would Yahusha (Jesus) and John the Baptist call the Pharisees **serpents**?

Matthew 3:6-7 "And were baptized of him in Jordan, confessing their sins. But when he saw many of the Pharisees and Sadducees come to his baptism, he said unto them, **O generation of vipers**, who hath warned you to flee from the wrath to come?"

The Sumerians claim that prior to the "**Great Flood**" the Annunaki beings came from the "sky/heavens" as their name means "**those who from the heavens came**". They claimed like the Egyptians that they had come from another Planet (*i.e. Nibiru*) and set up their bases in the "**Orion Constellation**" and the Star "**Sirius**". The Egyptians claim that their God Osiris and Horus came from the Orion Constellation and that Isis came from the Star "Sirius" aka the "Dogstarr" to many occultists. The irony behind all of this is that the Sumerian "Annunaki" beings were worshipped as "gods" just as Osiris, Isis, Horus and Set were worshipped as "gods" in ancient Egypt. These so-called "gods" of ancient Egypt-Sumeria also taught mankind magic-sorcery, the constellations-zodiac, science, astronomy, the zodiac, mathematics, building temples (pyramids-ziggurats), pagan worship of God's "creations", weapon making and other tools man used to advance just as the "Fallen Angels" taught mankind these things in the Book of Enoch.

(**Above**) Chinese **12 Statue Zodiac** Bronze Statues at the Wong Tai Sin Temple, Kowloon, Hong Kong. Where did they get this from? Could modern day Asians be a branch of the ancient Shemites….. Or are they descendants of Ham or Japheth? The Chinese Zodiac has been said to have proof of existence since 400 B.C. Did the Israelite Ancestors of the Native Americans pick up the "Zodiac" while traveling though Assyria, Medes and Asia?

Book of Jasher 9:7 "And the king (Nimrod) and all his servants, and Terah with all his household were then the first of those that served gods of wood and stone. And Terah (*i.e. father of Abraham*) had **TWELVE GODS OF LARGE SIZE (STATUES)**, made of wood and stone, after the twelve months of the year and he served each one monthly, and every month Terah would bring his meat offering and drink offering to his gods; thus did Terah all the days. And all that generation were wicked in the sight of the Lord, and they thus made every man his god, but the forsook the Lord (Yahuah) Who had created them."

Keep this in mind when you research the origin of "**pagan gods**" and "**idols**".

"Isis was aided in her search [for the slain body of Osiris] by Anubis, in the shape of a dog. He was Sirius (Satan), or the Dog-Star, THE FRIEND AND COUNSELOR OF OSIRIS, and the inventor of language, grammar, astronomy, surveying, arithmetic, music, and medical science; the first maker of laws; and WHO TAUGHT THE WORSHIP OF THE GODS, AND THE BUILDING OF TEMPLES."
Albert Pike, Morals and Dogma, p. 376, Teachings of the 24th Degree, Prince of the Tabernacle

So, Albert Pike is admitting here in his statement that Osiris's friend was Satan masquerading as Sirius. But what is also interesting is the fact that the same locations in the heavens that the Sumerians said the Annunaki resided was the same location according to occultists/Satanists that Lucifer and his fallen angels dwelt. Wow!

"Throughout the centuries, SIRIUS (the brightest star in the sky) has been recognized by most occultists and esoteric teachers as the LOCATION WHERE LUCIFER AND HIS HIERARCHY DWELL. In Christian terminology, Sirius is simply a secretive code word for 'hell'.
Christian Author Texe Marrs, Book of New Age Cults and Religions, 1990, p. 299

So, if the late Freemason Albert Pike had such respect for Osiris, Isis and Sirius (Satan), what else does Albert Pike have to say about Lucifer or Sirius? It seems that Lucifer, Satan, Sirius, Osiris, Horus/Heru and Isis are all connected? Maybe this is why the Egyptian sorcerers were able to perform their own "**magic**" in a desperate attempt to show the Pharaoh of Egypt that Moses's God "**Yahuah**" was not more powerful than the God of Egypt (**Ra**). The Egyptian supreme god "**Ra**" was the god of the Sun....however, the God of Israel proved to be in control of the Sun, and not "**Ra**". Yahuah made darkness come over Egypt for three days despite them calling on "**Ra**" for sunlight! That should've been enough for any smart Egyptian to figure out their god was a sham.

Exodus 10:21-23
"And the LORD said unto Moses, "Stretch out thine hand toward heaven, that there may be darkness over the land of Egypt, even darkness which may be felt." **And Moses stretched forth his hand toward heaven, and there was a thick darkness in all the land of Egypt three days**. They saw not one another, neither rose any from his place for three days; but all the children of Israel had light in their dwellings."

Despite all of this, Freemasons like Albert Pike, the Moors and other secret societies like the **Hermetic Order of the Golden Dawn** love to honor Egyptian false gods. But as many Freemasons admit, Lucifer/Satan is the god of the Egyptians and the one who taught the Egyptians to worship their multiple gods. Freemasons demand an oath to "a god" and they demand "worship" or "submission" to a god. Atheists cannot be Freemasons because the "G" stands for "Geometry, God or the Grand Architect of the Universe". At the highest levels of Freemasonry, this "god" is "**Allah-Lucifer**". Don't believe, read the Books of Moslem Shriner Freemasons and Freemasons such as **Albert Pike or Manly P. Hall**.

Let's connect the dots one more time....

- "Isis was aided in her search [for the slain body of Osiris] by Anubis, in the shape of a dog. He was **Sirius (Satan)**, or the Dog-Star, **THE FRIEND AND COUNSELOR OF OSIRIS**, and the inventor of language, grammar, astronomy, surveying, arithmetic, music, and medical science; the first maker of laws; and **WHO TAUGHT THE WORSHIP OF THE GODS, AND THE BUILDING OF TEMPLES**." - *Albert Pike, Morals and Dogma, p. 376, Teachings of the 24th Degree, Prince of the Tabernacle*

271

- "**Lucifer, the Light-Bearer**! Strange and mysterious name to give the Spirit of Darkness! **Lucifer, the Son of the Morning!** It is he who bears the light, and with its splendors intolerable blinds feeble, sensual or selfish Souls? Doubt it not!" – *Albert Pike, Morals and Dogma.*

- "That which we must say to a crowd is...**We worship a God**, but it is the God that one adores without superstition. To you, Sovereign Grand Inspectors General, we say this, that you may repeat it to the Brethren of the 32nd, 31st, and 30th degrees...**The Masonic Religion should be, by all of us initiates of the high degrees, maintained in the purity of the Luciferian Doctrine.** If Lucifer were not God, would Adonay whose deeds prove his cruelty, perdify and hatred of man, barbarism and repulsion for science, would Adonay and his priests, calumniate (*i.e. make malicious, false statements about someone*) him? Yes, **Lucifer is God**, and unfortunately Adonay is also god. For the eternal law is that there is no light without shade, no beauty without ugliness, no white without black, for the absolute can only exist as two gods: darkness being necessary to the statue, and the brake to the locomotive. Thus, the doctrine of Satanism is a heresy; and **the true and pure philosophical religion is the belief in Lucifer**, the equal of Adonay; but Lucifer, God of Light and God of Good, is struggling for humanity against Adonay, the God of Darkness and Evil." – *Albert Pike, Morals and Dogma.*

According to the Occultists and Secret Societies Lucifer is God. Yahuah which they call "Adonay" which means "Lord" is also a lesser important god to them. Luciferianists ascribe the God of Israel to being the God of Evil. This is how Satan deceives and how his followers deceive mankind. The "occult societies" also know that the **Sons of**

Cain exist.....which they sometimes refer to as **"Sons of the Fallen"**. So, knowing all of this information....one probably wants to know where did the **"Seed of Cain"** or the **"Nephilim"** go? If they survived the **"Great Flood"** where are they today? Are there any clues?

Consider another amazing fact:

The **Guanche people who were found centuries ago in the Canary Islands off the coast of Morocco and Southwest of Spain** claimed to be survivors of a **"Great Flood"** which destroyed their former homeland.   Could they be descendants of the Nephilim and sons of Cain? The Guanche people were found by the Spaniards in Medieval times and were nicknamed the **"White Indians"**. The Guanche's were a race of **pale white-skinned people with blonde or reddish hair that looked Nordic in appearance (***i.e. like people in Norway, Sweden, Finland***)**. These people were very primitive before being invaded by the Spanish in the 1400's. They lived in Stone Age conditions, living in caves and using sharpened rocks for cutting tools. They also practiced mummification of the dead, just like the Egyptians. Many of the Guanche's were massacred by the Spanish in fierce battles and others were sold into slavery...of course in Europe and not Africa. What is fascinating is that archaeologists have found pyramids in the city of **Guimar** and **Tenerife** on the Canary Islands that are aligned for the Summer Solstice solar cycles **(like the Egyptian Pyramids and Pyramids in Central/South America)**. The Guanche people also used stamps called a **"Pintadera"** that were in Pyramid Triangle shapes. Europeans called these people the **"White Indians of Nivaria"** and even wrote books about them.

Note: *Remember, according to the Bible, the "Children of Cain" always found their way to cause "hostility" to the "Children of Seth-Israel" from whom Christ came. Wherever on the planet the Israelites were scattered to, the Sons of Cain, Edom and Japheth were soon to follow.*

Genesis 3:15 "And I will put enmity (hostility) between thee (Seed of Satan-Cain) and the Woman (Seed of Seth-Israel), and between thy seed (Cain) and her seed (Israel); it shall bruise thy head, and thou shalt bruise his heel."

In order for them to do this they would have to "oppress" or "deceive" the "Authentic" Israelites in whatever land they would set up shop in. These people with the "bloodline of Cain" would also have to make sure they left no traces of their true identity in archaeological records.

"In the "**Temple of the Warriors in Chichen Itza, Mexico**" there are paintings of golden haired White men. In "**Matto Grosso, Brazil**", famous British Explorer **Colonel. P. H. Fawcett** disappeared while looking for the legend of "**white tribes**". He had gone there on expeditions in the early 1900's trying to find any sightings of blue-eyed, red-haired, white-skinned Indians. **Harold T. Wilkins** was also another European who was told by an old Spanish historian that there were **tall, red-haired, bearded** Amazon people called the "**Mayorumas**". He admitted their skin was pale white like Europeans. Harold T. Wilkins stated that in 1929, an American Traveler **Lawrence Griswold** was captured by **Shuar Indians** and taken deep into the Amazon (**Peru-Ecuador**). During his captivity by the natives he saw the ruins of an ancient city with pyramids. The Natives supposedly stated that the **tall, pale white, red-haired builders** of these pyramids were changed "**White**" because of their wicked behavior before the flood. (**Could this white skin be the "Mark of Cain"?**)

Note: The Shuar People are not pale white Indians; they are brown-skinned Indians. Mr. Griswold was tall, white and **red-headed** so the Indians thought that he was of the "**Lost Race**". Was this "**Lost Race**" the seed of Cain, who survived the flood?

Now it is a known fact that the "**MC1R gene**" is what gives Europeans **Red Hair**. The frequency of "**Red Hair**" is connected to the Ancient

"Celts" (**i.e. Scotland, Ireland, Wales, Britain**) by way of the Basque county people in Spain, which is in close vicinity to the Canary Islands (**where the white-skinned, red-haired Guanche people lived**). This MC1R gene was also found in the remains of red-haired, white-skinned Neanderthals.

Fact: *In Julius Caesar's literary work "**Gallic Wars**", he notes that all men of any high rank and dignity in **Gaul (Western Europe)** were either Druids or Nobles. Gaul was a territory in Western Europe consisting of **France, Luxemburg, Belgium, Switzerland (Gotthard base tunnel), North Italy, Central Italy, the Netherlands and Germany**. The Druids practiced medicine, magic, sorcery, human sacrifice, animal sacrifice and the practice of grove worship (i.e. oak tree groves). **Britain** was the main headquarters of the Druids who were a strong presence in Western Europe from 40 B.C. to 400 A.D., when the Romans were able to conquer that area of Europe. Many men of high rank in Europe in ancient times had red hair. Coincidence?*

According to the Ancient Chinese, the European nomads (i.e. Tarim mummies) had red hair, bluish-green eyes and long noses. But it gets deeper.....very deep! In 1992, the World's first DNA PCR investigation was done on supposed "biological evidence" from an Alien abductee. Bill Chalker, who was part of the "Anomaly Physical Evidence Group (APEG) believed that what most "alien abductee's" lacked was "biological evidence" of the alien perpetrator.

In 1992, a Lebanese man named **Peter Khoury**, had an "**alien abduction**" encounter with a tall white "Nordic" looking female and a light-brown skinned "Mongoloid-Asian" looking female. Somehow during this encounter, he was able to recover a piece of hair from the "alien perpetrator" that was unlike any human's hair. The analysis of the hair was from someone who was genetically close to humans, but of a different race. The DNA of the hair showed two types of lineages in one strand which can only be produced with "**Cloning**" and "**Genetic manipulation**". One was of a rare Chinese Mongoloid-type. Now this baffled researchers as the hair was not black like most Asians, but blonde. The other DNA type found on the hair sample was a rare **Basque/Gaelic type DNA**. The Basque people in **Spain** and the **Gaelic-Celtic** people in **Ireland-Scotland-United Kingdom** are known to have **Red Hair** and "**Rh-negative**" blood types. The Gaelic people were originally pagans who worshipped the "**Tuatha De Danann**" and they also believed in the "**Otherworld**". The "Tuatha" white-skinned, Red-haired/Blond-haired, blue eyed people were known to invade Western Europe where some of the Canaanites previously lived in Ancient times. In Basque folklore, the female God "**Mari**" is a powerful god with blue eyes and reddish-orange or blond hair. In Old Gaelic Irish folklore, "**the Tuatha tales**" also describe powerful, tall white "**Nordic-looking**" gods with blue eyes and reddish-orange or blond hair. Many researchers believe that these "white, red-haired" humanoids interbred with other humans in Europe and Asia, perhaps spreading their trait of "Red Hair" or "White Skin". This has also been said of the "Red haired Neanderthal woman" as well. Could this be the reason why some Asians are "white-skinned" and some are "dark-skinned"? The blond-red haired, blue-eyed Tarim mummies (*see "The Lady of Tarim"*) in China have brought attention to this matter as they are displayed in a museum in Beijing, China. In China, they also found a **Tocharian** (*i.e. Scythian*) female mummy with white skin and blonde hair wrapped in Celtic Cloth. Recovered from these Tocharian mummies were also "**swastika**" decorations on pottery which has been linked to the White "Nordic" alien race living inside the "**inner-earth/Shamballa**"......as witnessed by Admiral Richard Byrd in the 1940's (see Operation "Highjump"). Note: The Y-DNA "**R1a**" of the Tarim-Tocharian (*i.e. Scythian*) red-haired white mummies in China are also seen in the Ashkenazi "Khazar" European Jews and Germans.....who currently rule Europe (*aka the "shadow Holy Roman Empire"*) today.

It is a known fact that the Celtic-Gaelic Basque people in **Spain/France** have the highest percentage of the **Rh-negative Blood type** which is not seen in animals and the rest of the human race. Some people have reported that the **mule is a Rh-negative animal, which is a mix between a horse and a donkey,** but there have not been any major studies to prove this. Mules are often sterile animals because of their abnormal genetic make-up from the abnormal cross-mixing of animal species (*i.e. just as incest often leads to birth deformities*). The **mule** is also **unlawful to eat** according to the God of Israel. Now consider this amazing fact.

The **hare** or **rabbit** is also **unlawful/unclean to eat** according to the God of Israel. Medical hematologic studies were done in the 1940's by two men named **Landsteiner** and **Weiner** in regards to Rh-negative humans. What they found is that **Human RH-negative serum** behaves the same way as **Rabbit serum**. Why is this?

In these studies, those humans whose red blood cells did not clump together (*indicating a biologic rejection like receiving a blood transfusion from the wrong blood type*) when coming in contact with **Rabbit Serum** were considered to be "**Rh (Rhesus) Negative**". This "theoretically" means the RH-negative humans can have Rabbit serum infused into their bloodstream without the body rejecting it. Doesn't seem like a big deal, right? Well consider this. The majority of mankind and animals have the "**antigen D**" on their Red Blood Cells which makes them "**Rh-Positive**". Rh-negative individuals do not carry the "antigen-D". For this reason, if a "Rh-woman" is pregnant with a "Rh-positive" fetus (from a Rh-positive father) the fetus will unfortunately be attacked by the mother's immune system and die. This is considered "abnormal" in the medical world and is called "**The Hemolytic disease of the Newborn**". The Rh-negative blood type is primarily seen in the "**White Race**".

So, what this all means is that Rabbit Serum (Blood) is **COMPATIBLE** with Rh-negative humans and not that of Rh-positive humans which make up the majority of the world. When Rabbit Serum (blood) is infused into Pure Blooded Asians, Native Americans, East Indians, the Black race (Africans from Ham or Shem) and even Rhesus monkeys there is a "**rejection process**" that goes on in the body letting the body know that this serum (blood) is **FOREIGN**.

So the highest concentration of people with the Rh-negative Blood type are seen in Spain, in the Basque people…who are the forefathers of the Celtic-Gaelic (*i.e. Ireland, Scotland, Wales*) people who like the "**Basque people**" also are known to have the highest concentration of "**Red Hair**" in the world. The Basque people of Spain are known to eat Rabbit as a delicacy dish and the origin of the word "**Spain**" comes from a Basque language background (Basque-Euskara) which is a language not related to any Japhetic language family in Europe.

Many linguistic experts believe the Basque language reveals that the Basque people are "**foreigners**" to Europe. Here is why. All of the language families of Europe fall into broad categories. For example, there are the Indo-European languages, which include Romance, Germanic, Slavic and Celtic subgroups, along with Greek and Albanian. **The Iranian languages are closely related to the languages of India**. The languages of Finland and Hungary are **Finno-Ugric**. The Turkish languages and the Indus Valley languages are in their own group. Semitic languages also make up another group (*i.e. Amhara, Tigray, Ge'ez, Sabaean, Hebrew, Aramaic, Arabic, Sanskrit/Tamil, Malayalam*). The Basque language however is not related to any language and is thus considered a "**linguistic isolate**", or an "**orphan language**". Others believe it is somewhat "**Semitic**". For this reason, some believe the Basque people are the first modern humans to arrive to the European continent, heirs or a "**mixture**" of the **Neanderthal** and **Cro-Magnon people**. The Neanderthal and Cro-Magnon man would've been on the earth "hiding out" in Europe before Japheth and his family could populate the "**Isles of the Gentiles**". The only people this could be is the **Sons of Cain**, because the **Sons of Seth** (*i.e. Enoch, Methuselah, Lamech, Noah*) were not known to bear "**White-skinned**" children without "**extreme panic**" from their parents. This example is proven in **1 Enoch 106** when Lamech bore an albino child (Noah) which he thought was of the seed of the Sons of God. Keep in mind that back 2,000 years ago, the original "**Germans-Goth-Barbarian**" people were known to have "White-skin" and "Red-Blonde hair". Are we seeing a connection between the "Sons of Cain", "the Neanderthal people" and the ruling people of the world today?

Consider this:

Daniel 2:40-41 "And the **fourth kingdom** shall be as strong as iron: forasmuch as iron breaks in pieces and subdues **ALL THINGS**: and as iron that breaks all these, shall it break in pieces and bruise. And whereas thou saw the feet and toes, part of the potter's clay, and part of iron, the kingdom shall be **DIVIDED**; but there shall be in it of the strength of iron, forasmuch as thou saw iron mixed with clay."

Many Bible scholars believe the Kingdoms talked about in Daniel are as follows:

1. **Babylon**

2. **Persia**

3. **Greece**

4. **Holy Roman Empire 1.0 (Fallen)**

5. **Holy Roman Empire 2.0**-Today **(Risen)** *DIVIDED WITH* **(Germans & Islamic Muslims)**.

By the 6th Century A.D., the "**Germanic**" tribes replaced the former "**Roman Empire**" with their "independent kingdoms-countries" which still exist today. Britain was the head of the "European Union", but now it is "Germany". Is "Germany" moving into position for the arrival of the "Antichrist"? The Romans over time mixed with "**the seed of men**"......like iron mixed with clay. How so, the Romans back in ancient times mixed with the **Edomites, the Greeks, the German Barbarians, and the Islamic Muslims**. But guess what! The Rothschild family financially controls Europe, America and the World (*i.e. IMF, World Bank, IRS, Federal Reserve, Bank of London, United Nations, UNICEF*). They also finance the "**Vatican**" which is the "seat" of the Holy Roman Empire. The Rothschild family also "purchased" British Mandatory Palestine for the Germanic "Khazar" Gentile Jews. Where do the Rothschild family originate from? The Rothschild family is of **GERMAN** Jewish origin. Mayer Amschel Rothschild (1744 A.D.-1812 A.D.), the son of Amschel Moses Rothschild and Schoenche Rothschild, was born in **FRANKFURT, GERMANY**. Its original classification is "Frankfurter Judengasse", Free Imperial City of Frankfurt am Main, **HOLY ROMAN EMPIRE!**

Keep your eyes open for the moves that "Germany", "the Jews", "the Catholic Church-Pope" and the "Muslims" make.

CHAPTER 8

CLUES TO WHO THE CANAANITES ARE TODAY?

(Left) **Twa-Batwa Pygmy** Medicine man in the Congo/Zambia. (Middle) 1st Dynasty Egyptian-Canaanite Pygmy god "**Bes**". (Right) 1st Dynasty Egyptian-Canaanite god in pygmy form "**Ptah**". The Twa pygmies were found to have the same Egyptian-Canaanite "**Bes**" god in their pantheon of pagan gods. Coincidence? The Bantus Yoruba Nigerian pagan dwarf god" Son of **Obatala**" also bears striking similarities to the Canaanite pagan god "**Bes**". But the Bantus Yoruba people have a totally different DNA than the Pygmy people of Africa, meaning the Bantus people and the Pygmy people in Africa come from two different nations. If the Bantus Yoruba people are descendants of the Israelites, then it is possible that the Pygmy tribes are descendants of the Biblical Canaanites.

Fact: The Canaanite-Phoenicians of biblical times were known to have carved the pygmy god "Bes" on their boats for protection in travel. The ancient Egyptians had special hieroglyphs for dwarfs and loved dwarf-pygmy deities so much that in the 1st Dynasty (3150 B.C.), pygmies served and worked directly for the Pharaoh...including the royal household. Many pygmies were found buried in subsidiary tombs (lesser tombs) around that of the Pharaoh. In fact, the proportion of dwarfs in the Egyptian Royal Cemetery of the 1st Dynasty Kings (*Djer, Aha, Narmer*) were so numerous that many believed the pygmies were brought into Egypt from another land (i.e. Canaan) for some purpose. This purpose in the Old Kingdom and Middle Kingdom would be seen as form of "**servitude**" to the Egyptian Kings….just like the "**Curse of Canaan**". The pygmies were brought into Egypt as jewelers, tailors, cup-bearers, zookeepers, and entertainers. The pygmies were often used to **dance** for special occasions and religious festivals. By the New Kingdom period (1550-1070 B.C.) they would appear in Egyptian writings (**Papyrus-The wise doctrine of Amenemope, son of Kanakht**) as a people of "**ridicule**" or "**abuse**".

Genesis 9:24-26 "And Noah awoke from his wine, and knew what his younger son (Ham) had done to him. And he said, **Cursed be Canaan; a servant of servants shall he be unto his brethren** (i.e. *sons of Ham: Egyptians, Cushites, Phuttites*). And he said, Blessed be the LORD God of Shem; and Canaan shall be his servant."

So here we see in Genesis 9, that the Canaanites were cursed by Noah to be "**servants**" to the other sons of Ham, aka their "**blood brothers**".

Many Spanish historians say the word "**Espana**" meaning "**Spain**" in Spanish comes directly from the hidden word "**I-shepan-im/Isephanim/Sphania/Saphania**" which is a Phoenician-Canaanite word which means "**Land of Rabbits**". They state that the Black pygmy Twa-Batwa people named the land of Spain, "**Isephanim/Saphania**". Here is where it gets **DEEP**!

Leviticus 11:4-6 "Nevertheless these shall ye not eat of them that chew the cud, or of them that divide the hoof: as the camel, because he cheweth the cud, but divideth not the hoof; he is **UNCLEAN** unto you. And the **CONEY** (Hyrax-Shaphan), because he cheweth the cud, but divideth not the hoof; he is unclean to you. And the **HARE** (rabbit), because he cheweth the cud, but divideth not the hoof; he is unclean unto you."

(**Left**) Hyrax/Coney (Hebrew "**Shaphan**")..aka "**Rock Rabbit**". The Hyrax-Coney rodent-like animal called "**Shaphan/Shapanim**" in Hebrew is only seen in Africa and Israel/Syria (Middle East). (**Right**) More than half of the world's Rabbits-Hares are seen in Southwestern Europe (i.e. Spain) and North America. Rabbits are different than the Hyrax seen in Ancient Canaan (Israel). **One can see the obvious "differences by looking at the ears.** Now if the Twa Pygmies named Spain "**Isephanim/Saphania**" or "**Sphania**", the only way they could've known to call Spain this term would be by associating it with the Hebrew word for a "**rabbit-like**" animal familiar to their ancestors and ancient language....**Paleo-Hebrew/Phoenician**!

Phoenician	Paleo-Hebrew	Hebrew letter (Dfus)	English name		Proto-Canaanite	Early Phoenician	Greek
𐤀	𐤀	א	Aleph	'	𓃾	𐤀	A
𐤁	𐤁	ב	Bet	b	𓉐	𐤁	B
𐤂	𐤂	ג.	Gimel	g	⌐	∧	Γ
𐤃	𐤃	ד	Dalet	d	⋈	△	Δ
𐤄	𐤄	ה	He	h	𓀠	𐤄	E

(**Above**) Paleo-Hebrew and Proto-Canaanite/Phoenician script is so similar that many scholars today wonder whose language influenced who. Did the Canaanite language influence, shape and mold today's Hebrew language because of the constant mixing with the Canaanites in biblical times or is it the other way around?

So why did the Black "**Twa Pygmies**" call the land known today as Spain, "**I-shepan-im/Isephanim/Sphania**" or "**The Land of the Hyrax/Coney**" which the Spanish corrupted into "**The Land of the Rabbits**". The root word of "**Isephanim-Sphania**" is the Hebrew Strong's word #8227a "**Shaphanim/Shephanim**". Were the Twa Pygmies living in Southwestern Europe speaking "**Hebrew**" when they called "**Spain**" the "**Land of Rabbits/Hyraxes**"? No, the Black Twa pygmies were speaking Canaanite/Phoenician, which is identical to Paleo-Hebrew/Hebrew! Therefore, the Twa pygmies as well as other "pygmy tribes" must be the Biblical Canaanites! Need more proof! Don't worry, its coming!

Fact: *Hebrew Strong's #8227 word "Shaphan" in the King James Bible is used synonymously with the word "Coney" or "Hyrax". In Israel, the rabbit is normally not seen but instead it is the "hyrax" which is sometimes called the "Rock Rabbit". The "hyrax" is a small rodent looking animal that is only* *seen in Africa and the Middle East. Rabbits are seen in Spain. It is believed that the Canaanite (Hamitic) Phoenician tribes that inhabited the Iberian Peninsula 3,000 years ago and founded certain cities were the ones that nicknamed the land the "Land or Coast of Rabbits".*

In one of the oldest texts in Ireland dating back to the 11th Century A.D., called **"The Leabhar Gabhla"** or **"The Book of Invasions"** states that the first settlers of Ireland/Scotland were small dark-skinned people (i.e. **Twa Pygmies**-hence the **"leprechaun myth"**) called **"Fir Bolg or Firbolgs"**. Afterwards it is said a **"magical" WHITE SUPER RACE** (i.e. *red-haired, blond-haired, blue-eyed*) called the **"Tuatha de Danaan"** (*people of the Irish-Celtic Goddess Dana*) came to Ireland/Scotland...of course invading the land formerly occupied by the Black Twa pygmy people. Seems just about right seeing that the White Race throughout history has conquered and enslaved the people of many **"Black Lands"**. **The Irish-Celtic Goddess Danu/Dana is of course depicted with pale white skin and Red hair.** Were the **"Tuatha de Danaan"** people descendants of the Sons of Cain or the Fallen Angels? Why would they have "Red Hair" like many "Neanderthal mummies"?

(**Above**) **British Egyptologist Gerald Massey**. Mr. Massey, Albert Churchward, Scottish historian David Mac Ritchie and British antiquarian Godfrey Higgins all believed that the first people encountered by whites in the "**British Isles**" were pygmies who were described as being "**Black as Ethiopian**". This was also a common belief among ancient historians **Tacitus, Pliny** and **Claudian**.

Fact: In Pygmy mythology, there is an account of the "**Garden of Eden**" or a story similar to it, as well as a **Creator** and a **mortal savior** (*i.e. like Christ*). There is also a "**Flood**" Story amongst the pygmy tribes. So, if the pygmies are in fact descendants of the Biblical Canaanites, the pygmy people would've been around the earliest "**Hebrew**" man recorded in the bible (i.e. Abraham) and they would've been around the 12 Sons of Jacob when they were born in the Syria-Canaan area. With that being said....did the Hebrew Israelite Tradition/customs rub off on their Canaanite "pygmy" neighbors in the Land of Canaan (Israel)? Did they learn about the "**Messianic Prophecy of Christ**" from the Hebrew Israelites living in Canaan? Did they know about Joshua and Moses? Consider this amazing fact!

The Canaanites would also learn and practice circumcision on their babies and men as noted in the biblical story *"The Slaughter of the men of Shechem"* in Genesis Chapter 34. Many African countries like Nigeria, Cameroon and Ghana circumcise their babies on the 8th day as instructed by God to Abraham in Genesis 17:12. But do the "**pygmy tribes**" circumcise too? Let's look at the Slaughter of Shechem story with **Shechem, the son of Hamor the Hivite (Son of Canaan)**. Shechem was a **Canaanite Prince** who had sex with Jacob's only daughter Dinah.

Genesis 34: 13-24 "And the sons of Jacob answered Shechem and Hamor his father deceitfully, and said, because he had defiled Dinah their sister: And they said unto them, **We cannot do this thing, to give our sister to one that is uncircumcised; for that were a reproach unto us: But in this will we consent unto you: If ye will be as we be, that every male of you be circumcised; Then will we give our daughters unto you, and we will take your daughters to us, and we will dwell with you, and we will become <u>one people</u>**. But if ye will not hearken unto us, to be circumcised; then will we take our daughter, and we will be gone. And their words pleased Hamor, and Shechem Hamor's son. And the young man deferred not to do the thing, because he had delight in Jacob's daughter: and he was more honorable than all the house of his father. And Hamor and Shechem his son came unto the gate of their city, and communed with the men of their city, saying, These men are peaceable with us; therefore let them dwell in the land, and trade therein; for the land, behold, it is large enough for them; let us take their daughters to us for wives, and let us give them our daughters. Only herein will the men consent unto us for to dwell with us, to be one people, if every male among us be circumcised, as they are circumcised. Shall not their cattle and their substance and every beast of their's be our's? only let us consent unto them, and they will dwell with us. **And unto Hamor and unto Shechem his son hearkened all that went out of the gate of his city; and every male was circumcised, all that went out of the gate of his city.**"

Genesis 17:12 **"And he that is eight days old shall be circumcised among you."**

Fact: In the Book **"Totemism and Exogamy"** by James George Frazer, he states that in Sir Harry Johnston's (*pictured above*) venture into the Congo and Uganda he documented that **"all of the Congo pygmies were circumcised**, and both male/female sexes had their teeth filed or sharpened to a point." Mr. Johnston was a British explorer, botanist, linguist and colonial administrator during the 1800's. The **Congo** till this day holds some Bantus people with the oldest (Basal) forms of the Y-DNA "E1b1a" Haplogroup called **E(xE1b1a)**. Other countries with this ancient Haplogroup are Ethiopia, Nigeria, Malawi, Sudan, Kenya, Guinea and Columbia (South America). The majority of the "pygmy tribes" seen in Africa are located in the **Congo-Zaire** area. Coincidence? Seems as though the Canaanites still dwell among Israelites, not in Israel anymore, but Africa.

With all of this information it is not surprising that some pygmies in Africa today carry the Bantus Israelite "**E1b1a**" Y-DNA Haplogroup and the "**L2**" mtDNA Haplogroup seen mostly in African-American Negroes today. This proves that the Pygmy tribes have a long history of mixing with their Israelite neighbors.....just as the Bible tells us.

So, from the beginning of the Bible in **Genesis 24:3** to the 2nd Temple period in the **Book of Ezra/Nehemiah** we see the Canaanites co-habiting with the Hebrew Israelites. This is almost 2,000 years of co-mingling and intermarriage. It is definitely possible during this time that the Canaanites learned and adopted the Creation story (**in addition to the "Messiah prophecy"**) from the Israelite prophets. After all, Paleo-Hebrew and Canaanite Phoenician script is basically identical.

In the Pygmy "**Creation story**" God makes man modeled from the dirt of the earth (see Genesis 2:7). God breathes life into man, he becomes alive and is called "**Efe**" (*i.e. the same name as the Efe Pygmy tribe in the Congo*). God told Efe to have children and he gave Efe's seed dominion over everything on earth. Mankind did not have to work at this time and was immortal. The only thing God forbade them to do was to stay away and not eat from the "**Tahu Tree**". This was the first law that God told mankind not to do. Efe, his wife and children obeyed this law. After some time, Efe had ancestors who populated the earth. One day a pregnant woman convinced her husband to eat of the fruit of the Tahu tree. He didn't want to eat from the tree but the woman said it was a silly old law. The two argued about it and eventually the man gave in. Soon the man and the pregnant women gave all the pygmy people in the forest some fruit from the Tahu tree. They all thought God would never find out what they had done....but he did. After God found out what they had done, man lost his immortality and was able to get sick and die. The woman was punished with pain in childbirth and mankind was made to work the earth until death from that day on. **The Pygmy tribes were also aware of the giving of "commandments" by God and the second coming of what they called a "Pygmy Messiah".** The Pygmy people knew this ancient story thousands of years before any European Catholic influence or before Arabs would enter into Africa. The only people that the Pygmy-Canaanites spent the most time with and mixing was that of the Hebrew Israelites. The Egyptians did not have a "**Adam & Eve**" Creation story. The Egyptians did not have "**Garden of Eden**" story" nor did they believe in any "**Second coming of the Messiah**" story and if they did they got it from their father Ham who lived prior to the "**Great Flood**".

So, there was so much mixing of the two nations in the Bible that it would be somewhat hard to tell the difference between a full-blooded Israelite and a full-blooded Canaanite. This is similar to West Africans who are half-Ashanti/half-Ewe or half Yoruba/half-Igbo. How can anyone physically distinguish who is of what tribal stock just by looking? This is perhaps the way the Israelite "**Creation**" and "**Messiah prophecy**" story merged into Canaanite-pygmy culture. Still don't believe? The first book of the Bible, **Genesis** is the first book of the Torah written by Moses around what many believe is around 1400 B.C. Moses knew about his past ancestors and wrote the Torah with the "**Mosaic Law**" for the generations of Israelites that would follow well after his death. The last book of the Bible is Malachi, but chronologically it is the two Books of Chronicles, Ezra/Nehemiah, Esther and the Book of Malachi. These Books are dated to 400 B.C. Consider this, Terah and Abraham lived well before 2,000 B.C. and Ezra lived around 500-400 B.C. The Canaanites are mentioned living with the Hebrews in the Book of Genesis and the Book of Ezra.

Genesis 24:3 "And I (Abraham) will make thee swear by the Lord, the God of heaven, and the God of the earth, that thou shalt not take a wife unto my son of the daughters of the **CANAANITES (i.e. pygmies)**, among whom I dwell."

Ezra 9:1-2 "Now when these things were done, the princes came to me, saying, The people of Israel, and the priests, and the Levites, have not separated themselves from the people of the lands, doing according to their abominations, even of the **CANAANITES (i.e. pygmies)**, the

Hittites, the Perizzites, the Jebusites, the Ammonites, the Moabites, the Egyptians, and the Amorites. For they have taken of their daughters for themselves, and for their sons: so that the holy seed have mingled themselves with the people of those lands: yea, the hand of the princes and rulers hath been chief in this trespass."

From Abraham to Ezra, the Canaanites were around the Hebrews for about 2,000 years. A whole lot of mixing in marriage went on during this time. Wake Up!

CHAPTER 9

THE CHILDREN OF CAIN, THE WATCHERS, AND THE WHITE RACE?

In the Beginning of Creation, the fallen angels mated with the women of the earth, having children that would become giants. The big question is if these fallen angels would contaminate Noah and his sons. There are some Christians that believe that in order for "Giants" to exist after the flood that one of Noah's sons (or daughters) had to have carried the "Nephilim" gene. Or did the "giants" retreat into the "inner earth" with some of the Sons of Cain to escape the flood? To examine this, we must explore the **Book of Genesis** and the "**Fragments of the Book of Noah**" listed in the Book of Enoch Chapter 106.

Note: *The Book of Enoch (Fragment of the Book of Noah) is referenced in the Ethiopic Book of Jubilees written in Ge'ez and the Paleo-Hebrew Book of Jubilees found in the Dead Sea Scrolls dating back to 400 B.C. The Book of Enoch (Fragment of the Book of Noah) was also found written in Paleo-Hebrew in the famous Dead Sea Scrolls as well.*

Genesis 6:1-9 "And it came to pass, when men began to multiply on the face of the earth, and daughters were born unto them, That the sons of God (**fallen angels**) saw the daughters of men that they were fair; and they took them wives of all which they chose. And the LORD said, My spirit shall not always strive with man, for that he also is flesh: yet his days shall be a hundred and twenty years. **There were giants in the earth in those days (pre-flood); AND ALSO AFTER THAT, when the sons of God came in unto the daughters of men, and they bare children to them,** the same became mighty men which were of old, men of renown. And God saw that the wickedness of man was great in the earth, and that every imagination of the thoughts of his heart was only evil continually. And it repented the LORD that he had made man on the earth, and it grieved him at his heart. And the LORD said, I will destroy man whom I have created from the face of the earth; both man, and beast, and the creeping thing, and the fowls of the air; for it repenteth me that I have made them. But Noah found grace in the eyes of the LORD. These are the generations of Noah: **Noah was a just man and perfect in his generations**, and Noah walked with God.

Book of Enoch (fragment of the Book of Noah) Chapter 106:1-7

"And after some days my son **Methuselah** took a wife for his son **Lamech**, and she became pregnant by him and bore a son. **And his body was white as snow** and red as the blooming of a rose, and the hair of his head and his long locks were white as wool, and his eyes beautiful. And when he opened his eyes, he lighted up the whole house like the sun, and the whole house was very bright. And thereupon he arose in the hands of the midwife, opened his mouth, and conversed with the Lord of righteousness. And his father **Lamech** was afraid of him and fled, and came to his father Methuselah. And he said unto him: **I have begotten a strange son, diverse from and unlike man, and**

resembling the sons of the God of heaven (not in

heaven); and his nature is different and **he is not like us**, and his eyes are as the rays of the sun, and his countenance is glorious. **And it seems to me that he is not sprung from me but from the angels** (*i.e. Lamech had doubt his son was not his own but was a product of the fallen angels*), and I fear that in his days a wonder may be wrought on the earth. And now, my father, I am here to petition thee and implore thee that thou mayest go to Enoch, our father, and learn from him the truth, for his dwelling-place is amongst the angels."

So Lamech, was confused that Noah did not look like the Children of Seth. It made him question if perhaps his wife was impregnated by the **"Fallen Angels who fell from Heaven"** producing a child that was **"White as Snow"** just as the Fallen Angels were "White as Snow". So

Lamech, told his father Methuselah to go ask his father **"Enoch-who was in heaven"** for the answers to his dilemma. So, what did Enoch tell Methuselah? If the Bible says Noah was **"Pure"** in his generations….then Enoch should have told Methuselah that although Noah was "White as Snow" that he was indeed **"pure"** and not the seed of the Fallen Angels.

Book of Enoch (fragment of the Book of Noah) Chapter 106:18-19

"And now make known to thy son Lamech that he who has been born *is in truth his son*, and call his name **Noah**; for he shall be left to you, and he and his sons shall be saved from the destruction, which shall come upon the earth on account of all the sin and all the unrighteousness, which shall be consummated on the earth in his days. **And after that there shall be still more unrighteousness** than that which was first consummated on the earth; for I know the mysteries of the holy ones; for He, the Lord, has showed me and informed me, and I have read (them) in the heavenly tablets."

Book of Enoch (fragment of the Book of Noah) Chapter 107:1-2

"And I saw written on them that generation upon generation shall transgress, till a generation of righteousness arises, and transgression is destroyed and sin passes away from the earth, and all manner of good comes upon it. **And now, my son, go and make known to thy son Lamech that this son, which has been born, is in truth his son, and that (this) is no lie.** And when Methuselah had heard the words of his father Enoch--for he had shown to him everything in secret--he returned and showed (them) to him and called the name of that son Noah; for he will comfort the earth after all the destruction."

So according to the Scriptures, Noah was what one today would possibly call an Albino Black person but he was not "**white**" because of the Bloodline of the Nephilim/Fallen angels or Cain. But still....are there any clues that can help us figure out what exactly was this "**Tav**" or "**mark**" that was put on Cain? Was it "White Skin"? In Ancient Hebrew, the "**Tav**" letter which means "**Mark**" can be seen as a sort of "**X**" looking character. What is even more eerie is that Geneticists, when finding evidence of Neanderthal /Denisovan skeletal remains in Europe labeled this mtDNA as "**X**", the same appearance as the word "**Tav/Mark**" in Ancient Hebrew. Scientists all over the world have tried to recreate life-like clay models of the Neanderthal man and woman based on the skeletal remains...including the hair. What they always end up with is a pre-historic white man with red hair. This phenotype trait is mostly seen today in Europeans (*especially those with the Rh-negative blood type as in the Basque people of Spain*).

Ancient Hebrew

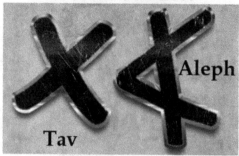

Aleph

Tav

Modern Hebrew
letter *tav*
(Hebrew square)

Hebrew letter
tav at the time
of Ezekiel
(Paleo-Hebrew)

In the Hebrew Bible, it says that God placed a "**Mark**" on Cain so that that no one would kill him. If the Sumerian Annunaki in the "**14 Lost Tablets of Enki**" claimed that when they got to earth, the "hominoids-humans" of the land were Black and they themselves were white, could the "**Mark**" that God placed on Cain was "**changing his skin from black to white**"? Could this had been a sort of deterrent for anyone that found Cain? Where the Fallen Angels "**changed to white**" when they fell from their original habitat? Is this what is meant by "**And he said unto them, I beheld Satan as lightning fall from heaven**" in Luke 10:18? When lightning strikes the Earth it is white. **Set, Baal, Zeus** where all chief gods of "**Thunder/Lightning**". They are also synonymous with Satan/Lucifer. Even today the "**Lightning bolt**" symbol is they Illuminati/Occult symbol for Satan among the "celebrity world". So, did the Fallen Angels or their seed "**The Nephilim/Annunaki**" insert their Genetic material into the "**Children of Cain**" creating a "**White Race**" while Noah and his son's lineage remained pure from the contamination of the "Fallen Angels abomination"? Did the people of earth at that time connect "**White beings**" to being "**divine beings**" from heaven?

(From Left to Right) The Symbol of the "**Mark of Cain**" in the Mind-Control Satanic **Oahspe Bible**, the Knights of Malta-Knights Templar symbol, the symbol for worldwide "**White Pride**" and the symbol of the White Supremacist Group "**the Klu Klux Klan**". The symbol of the "**mark of cain**" has also been said to be a "**Red Cross**" inside of a circle. Is this a coincidence?

Genesis 4:15 "And the LORD said unto him, Therefore whosoever slayeth Cain, vengeance shall be taken on him sevenfold. And the LORD set a **mark (Tav)** upon Cain, lest any finding him should kill him".

Was the "Mark of Cain" the changing of Cain's skin color from Black to White or was the seed of the Fallen Angels only the white people on earth before the flood? If the Book of Enoch (Chapter 107) states: "**And now, my son, go and make known to thy son Lamech that this son (Noah), which has been born, is in truth his son, and that (this) is no**

297

lie"....this implies that the Satanic Seed of the Fallen Angels must have been white in skin color for Lamech to get confirmation from his elders (Methuselah/Enoch) that his son (Noah) was indeed his son and not the seed of Fallen Angels. Either way it goes...we must consider that if two white parents cannot scientifically possibly have black babies that the "white race" had to have come after the original "black race". "When and how" was the white race created has been the mystery questions that have baffled mankind for generations.

226 [e]	7014 [e]	3068 [e]	7760 [e]
'ō·wṯ,	lə·qa·yin	Yah·weh	way·yā·śem
TAV → אֹ֤ות	לְקַ֖יִן	יְהוָ֨ה	וַיָּ֣שֶׂם
a mark	on Cain	the LORD	And put
Noun	Noun	Noun	Verb

The Lord put a "Tav" on Cain which in Paleo Hebrew looks like an "X". What would be the chance that the "Neanderthal gene" would be linked to the maternal (female) mtDNA "X". Could one of Noah's son's wives have been contaminated with the DNA of the Nephilim/Satan/Fallen Angels? If so, was it Japheth's wife? Or was the gene for "white skin" introduced to the Sons of Japheth from the surviving children of Cain or the Fallen Angels-Nephilim Giants. It is a known fact that the mtDNA "X" mostly seen in Europeans, Ashkenazi Jews, Sephardic Jews, Druze Middle Easterns, and White Arabs. It is not found in Sub-Saharan African populations.

Now consider this!

The **Druze people (Above)** are a monotheistic people who believe in the teachings of Plato (Greek), Alexander the Great (Greek), Aristotle (Greek), Socrates (Greek), and Akhenaten (Egypt). They believe that "no human" really knowns their "true religion". Their prophet and the person they say to descend from is **"Jethro" the Kenite**. The Druze people incorporate the religions of **Judaism, Islam, Gnostism, Christianity, Buddhism, Hinduism, Pythagoreanism** and **Neoplatonism**. They regard their religion as the "**Universal monotheistic religion**"......which is what the "**Antichrist**" will present to the world in the "**End of Days**". The Druze people have a very high percentage of the mtDNA "**X**" in their genetics which is also seen in the Neanderthal people. Druze men and women **ONLY** marry within their sect.....and they have been doing this for over 1,000 years. They live mostly in Syria, Lebanon and Israel.

JETHRO, THE KENITES, THE MIDIANITES, THE RECHABITES, THE SONS OF CAIN AND THE DRUZE PEOPLE

Jethro, according to the Bible was a **Kenite**, but was also known as "**Reuel**" in the Bible. He was Moses' father-in-law and the Priest of Midian (*Judges 1:16*). Jethro lived south of Canaan near Mount Sinai (*Exodus 3:1*). Now some say the **Land of Nod** (*Genesis 4:17*) that Cain was abolished to was the Sinai Peninsula (Egypt), Northwest Arabia,

South Canaan, Iran or the Tarim Basin (China). No matter what place was the "**Land of Nod**" it is verified in the Bible that Moses found his Midianite wife outside of Egypt. His Midianite wife, **Zipporah** was a Kenite/Midianite and also a Cushite (*see Numbers 12:1*). The Kenites were an ancient people who lived near the Land of Canaan around the time of Abraham (*Genesis 15:18-21*). But the question is, "Were the Kenites a people that lived amongst the Sons of Abraham and the Sons of Cush."? Did they "**graft**" themselves into "**people groups**" in Africa and Mesopotamia? This can be very confusing determining who is what in regards to a Kenite, a Midianite, a Cushite, and a Rechabite.

Genesis 15:18-19 "In the same day the Lord made a covenant with Abram, saying, Unto thy seed have I given this land, from the river of Egypt (**Nile River**) unto the great river, the **river Euphrates**: The **KENITES**, and the Kenizzites, and the Kadmonites."

So here we see that the Kenite/Midianite Tribes were known to dwell in the continent of Africa (*Egypt, Nubia/Cush/Sinai Peninsula*) and as far east as Mesopotamia-Levant.

But we know that some of the Kenites were living in the territory of Egypt (*including the Sinai Peninsula*) because **Jethro** tagged along with Moses and the Israelites when they were going through the Exodus into the land of Canaan. It wouldn't make sense if these Kenites were living in Iran, China of Northwest Saudi Arabia. This can be verified in Exodus Chapter 18.

Exodus 18:5 "And **Jethro**, Moses' father-in-law, came with his sons and his wife unto Moses **into the wilderness**, where he encamped at the **mount of God (Mount Sinai)**:"

In the Bible, in **Numbers 10:29**, Moses father-in-law is called "**Reuel the Midianite**" instead of Jethro......but in **1 Chronicles 2:55** it links the Kenites-Midianites to the **Tribe of the Rechabites**.

1 Chronicles 2:55 "And the families of the **SCRIBES** which dwelt at Jabez; the Tirathites, the Shimeathites, and Suchathites. These are the **KENITES** that came of Hemath, the father of the house of **RECHAB**."

How did the Kenites get the job of being "**scribes**" in the Israelite camp? How did the Kenites get into Israel? Did they get in when Jethro/Reuel were with Moses and the Israelites or did they get into Israel another way? After all, the **Druze people** in Israel that carry the mtDNA "**X**", which is identical to the "**Neanderthal mtDNA X**". They also claim to have been in Israel for a long, long time.........courtesy of their forefather/prophet......"**JETHRO THE PRIEST**". In addition, Neanderthal maternal DNA "**X**" has been found in Israel, hidden in skeletal fossil remains in Israeli caves.

(**Above**) In the 1930's, British Archaeologists Dorothy Garrod and Francis Turville-Petre excavated "**Neanderthal skeletal fossils**" in the Kebara Cave in Northern Israel. The skeleton was nicknamed "Moshe".

So how did the remains of the "Neanderthals" get into Israel? Were they living in or around the land of Canaan when Abraham and Terah lived? Remember Genesis 15:18-19 details this out…..even though the Bible doesn't cover the whole "genealogy" of the Kenites as it pertains to who their father is going back to the three sons of Noah. So why the mystery?

(**Above**) According to **British Assyriologist Archibald Henry Sayce**, it was believed that the word **"Smith"** comes from the Aramaic name **"Qeni"**, which comes from the Hebrew word **"Qayin"**. After the flood, we saw the Sons of Cain no more.....but the Kenites somehow emerged in the land of Abraham. Like the Nephilim Giants, did the Sons of Cain also survive the flood? The Nephilim Giants children are seen in the Levant with the Sons of Anak and the Philistine giant "Goliath". So what about the Kenites? When and how did the Kenites show up in the land of Abraham/Israel?

If you follow the scriptures closely you will see how the Assyrians in 700 B.C. helped place the Kenites into Israel.....along with the Kenite Scribes that made their way into the Southern Kingdom of Judah in 1 Chronicles 2:55.

1. **Numbers 24:21** "And he (*Balaam the diviner*) looked on the **Kenites**, and took up this parable, and said, Strong is thy dwellingplace, and thou puttest thy nest in a rock. Nevertheless the Kenite shall be wasted, until **Asshur shall carry thee away captive.**"

2. **1 Samuel 15:6** "And Saul said unto the **Kenites**, Go, depart, get you down from among the **Amalekites (*Edomites*)**, lest I destroy you with them: for ye shewed kindness to all the children of Israel, when they came up out of Egypt. So the Kenites departed from the Amalekites (*Edomites*)."

3. **II Kings 17:23-24** "And the **King of Assyria** brought men from Babylon, and from Cuthah, and from Ava, and from **HAMATH/HEMATH (Syria)**, and from Sepharvaim (Iraq), and placed them in the cities of Samaria (*Northern Israel*), **instead of the children of Israel**: and they possessed Samaria, and dwelt in the cities thereof."

Fact: The Druze people's oral history states they, like the Jews (*and Kenites*) fled from Egypt and "**wandered**" into Mesopotamia through the desert until they landed in Syria (*i.e. Hamath/Hemath*). The oldest Druze families today live North of Jordan in the Haran (Syria/Turkey), Northern Israel and Lebanon.

Here is how the **mtDNA "X"** of the Neanderthal man could've possibly been passed down to the **Druze People in Israel**. If the Neanderthal man is a distant descendant of the Sons of Cain.....and if this seed somehow "found a way" into the Kenite clan, then a subsect of the Kenite people (*whom Jethro supposedly belonged to*) could've brought their mtDNA "X" into Israel through "**planned entry with the Israelites**" or "**forced entry with the Assyrians**".

So, in 1 Chronicles, the Kenites, despite not being Israelites, somehow found their way into the Territory of Judah and his families. The Kenites seemed to get around from one place to another like a wanderer. Nomadic wanderers live in tents, never having an actual true place to call home. In Jeremiah 35:1-19, the scriptures explain how the Kenites (of the House of Rechab) bear a striking resemblance to the descendants of Cain (Seed of the Serpent). Remember in Genesis 4:11-

12, **Cain's seed was not supposed to be able to sow any seed or yield any harvest per God's curse for killing Abel**. Cain's seed was also cursed to be a wanderer (**vagabond**) on earth as a stranger in every land that they would encounter. Read closely:

Jeremiah 35:1-11 "The word which came unto Jeremiah from the LORD in the days of Jehoiakim the son of Josiah king of Judah, saying, Go unto the **house of the Rechabites**, and speak unto them, and bring them into the house of the LORD, into one of the chambers, and give them wine to drink. Then I took Jaazaniah the son of Jeremiah (not the prophet), the son of Habaziniah, and his brethren, and all his sons, and the whole house of the Rechabites; And I brought them into the house of the LORD, into the chamber of the sons of Hanan, the son of Igdaliah, a man of God, which was by the chamber of Maaseiah the son of Shallum, the keeper of the door: And I set before the sons of the house of the Rechabites pots full of wine, and cups, and I said unto them, Drink ye wine. But they said, **We will drink no wine**: for Jonadab the son of Rechab our father commanded us, saying, **YE SHALL DRINK NO WINE, NEITHER YE, NOR YOUR SONS FOR EVER: NEITHER SHALL YE BUILD A HOUSE, NOR SOW SEED, NOR PLANT VINEYARD, NOR HAVE ANY: BUT ALL OF YOUR DAYS YE SHALL DWELL IN TENTS; THAT YE MAY LIVE MANY DAYS IN THE LAND WHERE YE BE STRANGERS.** Thus we have obeyed the voice of Jehonadab the son of Rechab our father in all that he hath charged us, to drink no wine all our days, we, our wives, our sons, nor our daughters; Nor to build houses for us to dwell in: neither have we vineyard, nor field, nor seed: **But we have dwelt in tents, and have obeyed**, and done according to all that Jonadab our father commanded us. But it came to pass, when **Nebuchadnezzar king of Babylon came up into the land**, that we said, Come, and let us go to Jerusalem for **fear of the army of the Chaldeans**, and for **fear of the army of the Syrians: SO WE DWELL AT JERUSALEM.**"

Fact: At the age of 15, a teenager born to a Druze family can choose to follow the Druze faith or do his/her own thing. Members of the Druze who are ready are "initiated" like Freemasons into the religious sect. During this "initiation" it is said that some of the requirements is to not *drink alcohol/wine, do not eat pork and do not smoke.*

So, in Jeremiah 35, the Kenites were telling the truth because during the siege of Jerusalem by the Babylon King Nebuchadnezzar, the Chaldeans did help capture the **Zedekiah**, the King of Jerusalem, even slaying his sons in the process.

2 Kings 25:5-7 "And the army of the Chaldeans pursued after the king (Zedekiah), and overtook him in the plains of Jericho: and all his army were scattered from him. So they took the king and brought him up to the king of Babylon to Riblah; and they gave judgment upon them. And they slew the sons of Zedekiah before his eyes, and put out the eyes of Zedekiah, and bound him with fetter of brass and carried him to Babylon."

Fact: The Druze people are scattered in the U.S.A., Israel, Lebanon, Syria, Jordan, Columbia, Canada, Australia, West Africa and even China. Most sources on the Druze state that wherever they live, "**they do not have their own land**". They survive in different communities in different countries by remaining "**isolated**" and "**secretive**".

So, the Kenites were told by Jonadab that they would never build a house (*on their own land*), but live in tents (*houses*) as strangers in many lands (*like the Druze people today*). They were also told not to plant any seed. If a person doesn't plant any seed then they surely cannot till the earth. This all sounds familiar to the curse that God put on Cain. In Genesis 4, Cain is **cursed from the earth, never to sow seed**, and to be a **stranger/wanderer of the earth**.

In the dictionary, the word **"Sow"** means to plant seeds. **"Vagabond"** means a person who wanders from place to place without a home. A "**Fugitive**" is someone who moves from place to place. A person that is a "Vagabond" or a "Fugitive" doesn't have a home; therefore they live in tents like nomads. The **Kenites** lived in tents their whole lives just like vagabonds and strangers in the many lands that they dwelled in. This in a sense tells the story of the "**Druze people**".

Genesis 4:11-12 "And now art thou cursed from the earth, which hath opened her mouth to receive thy brother's blood from thy hand: When thou tillest the ground, it shall not henceford yield unto thee her strength; **a fugitive** and a **vagabond** shalt thou be in the earth."

So what is the coincidence that the "**Cainites**", or should we say "**Kenites**" both share the same instructions as to what they can or cannot do? Some of the Druze men share the same Y-DNA "**L**" that has been connected to the **Ancient Minni (Armenia) Empire** which was under the rulership of the **Ancient Assyrians** and later **Medes-Persians (Iran)**. How do we know this? The people of "Minni" in Jeremiah 51:27-29 were called the "**Mannai/Mannean**" people. Minni today is modern day "**Armenia**". According to ancient Assyrian cuneiform inscriptions, "Minni" was under control first by the Assyrians and then the Median Empire (Persia-Iran). According to a Babylonian Chronicle, in his tenth year of reign (636 B.C.), **Babylonian King Nabopolassar** (*i.e. father of Nebuchadnezzer II*) "captured the Manneans who had come to the Assyrians aid". When Babylon fell in in the 6th Century B.C., "Minni" and its people were ruled by the Medo-Persian Iranian Empire. (*See "Assyrian and Babylonian Chronicles by A.k. Grayson, 1975, p. 91*)

The Druze men who claim "**Jethro**" as their forefather-prophet have the Y-DNA "**L**", "**E1b1b**" and "**J**". Today, India, Pakistan and Afghanistan have the highest percentages of the Y-DNA "**L**" which has been connected to Ancient Assyria territory per genetic studies in the

Levant. The Y-DNA "**E1b1b**" has been linked to Edom's influence in the Middle East/Mediterranean/North Africa while the Y-DNA "**J1/J2**" has been linked to the Ottoman Turks (Togarmah) and the Black Shemitic Arabs of old. Both the Y-DNA "**J1**", "**J2**" and "**E1b1b**" has been linked also to the Samaritans in Israel who claim to be descendants of the Samaritans (*from Assyria*) that Christ told the disciples to avoid initially when ministering the Gospels (**see Matthew 10:5**). These Samaritans still speak and write a script similar to Ancient Paleo-Hebrew/Phoenician.

So, if you have been following all of this information.....you might be wondering why the Druze men can carry the paternal Y-DNA "**L**", "**J**" and "**E1b1b**" but still carry the mtDNA (maternal) "**X**" marker which the "**Neanderthal man and women**" were found to have. Remember, mtDNA is passed down from the mother to both sexes (male & female). Y-DNA is only passed down via the Father. So far, scientists have not been able to locate or "track" the Y-DNA classification of the Neanderthal Man. But hold up! Even though Cain, Abel and Seth had the same mother (Eve), some stories say that Cain's father was the "Wicked One" himself......or Lucifer/Satan/Helel. If scientists ever did happen to find out the Y-DNA of the "Neanderthal Man" do we really think they would make this "common knowledge"?

THE DRUZE PEOPLE MTDNA "X" AND THE NEANDERTHAL MTDNA "X". WHAT IS GOING ON HERE!

In the Oxford Journal Scientific study called "**An X-Linked Haplotype of Neanderthal Origin Is Present Among All Non-African Populations**" (Molecular Biology and Evolution, Volume 28, Issue 11, year 2011, pages 1957-1962) it reveals the that the "**White Red-Haired Neanderthal man and woman**" mixed his DNA with normal Homo Sapiens (Humans today) living in Europe. The Neanderthal is credited to have lived thousands of years ago...most likely before the flood when all types of pre-historic animals walked the earth. At least this is what modern TV and movies show us. But how could this type of "**Neanderthal Man**" survive the "**Great Flood**" or any other Earth "catastrophe" that would make the dinosaurs extinct? Was the Neanderthal man around during the existence of Atlantis and Lemuria? Could this have been Satan's or the Fallen Angels surviving seed (**Cain**) that was bent on mixing his bloodline with those in the continent of Europe and the Levant/Middle East? Could this mixing with the Children of Japheth in the North be the way that Satan would use his seed (or the Fallen Angel seed) to destroy the Children of Israel from who Christ came? Like the Rh-Negative Blood type, the maternal DNA (mtDNA) "**X**" is primarily not found in pure blooded Africans, Asians, East Indians and Native Americans. But why? All of these populations typically carry the Blood Group "O" (Universal Donor) while Europeans/Eurasians carry the Blood group "A".

So, you may be wondering what this means and what I am getting at. Again, in Genesis 3:15 it says:

Genesis 3:15 "And I will put enmity (hostility) between thee (Seed of Satan-Cain) and the Woman (Seed of Seth-Israel), and between thy seed (Cain) and her seed (Israel-Christ); it shall bruise thy head (Psalms 110:6, Habakkuk 3:13), and thou shalt bruise his heel."

So, who is the woman?

In **Revelation 12:4-5** it reads:

"…and the **Dragon** (Satan) stood before the **Woman** (Israel) which was ready to be delivered, for to devour her **Child** (Yahusha HaMashiach/Jesus Christ) as soon as it was born. And she brought forth a man child (Christ), who was to rule all nations (which Satan influences) with a rod of iron: and her child was caught up unto God (resurrection), and to his throne."

So here we see that in Genesis 3:15, the prophecy of the Messiah is laid out before Seth is born (Genesis 4:25) and before Noah even existed. So, in order for the "Seed of Satan (Cain)" to exhibit "hostility-enmity" towards the "Seed of Israel" through which "Christ the Messiah" came and in order for the Seed of Satan (Cain) to bruise the heel of (Israel/Messiah-Christ), **the Children of Cain had to somehow survive the "Great Flood" as the Nephilim did.**

The "Messiah" aka "Christ" according to Biblical prophecy was to bruise Satan's head...that is destroy Satan and all his works, including his "Mystery Babylon" Empire that is controlling the world today. If you look at all the "World Wars" you will see a common theme of a select group of people who are responsible for these wars: "Europeans and the Jews". What about the financing of these Wars? The Europeans and the Jews financed all of these wars.

(**Left**) Jewish Banker Paul Warburg (1868-1932) at the 1st Pan-American Financial Conference, Washington D.C., May, 1915. Warburg was one of the fathers of the Federal Reserve creation in America and was behind Wells Fargo Banking Firm and Kuhn Loeb Banking Firm. (**Middle**) Jewish Banker John D. Rockefeller. (**Right**) JP Morgan (founder of Chase Bank).

Note: Henry Ford stated in 1925 that Paul Warburg and the "**Money Master**" Jews were spearheading the movement in which the

Federal Reserve System was being used as an instrument **to bring about German control of America**, just like they had done in Rome with the Byzantine Roman Empire which later war partly conquered by the Ottoman Empire.

Both the Germans and the Ottoman Arabs are the Biblical "**Gog**" or **Gomer**...by way of **Ashkenaz, Togarmah and Riphath.** So if "**GOMER**" is the Germans (*including some of the Jews*) who control Europe (Roman Empire/America) and the Ottoman Arabs who control the Arab countries....then who is **MAGOG**? Remember, in the "**End of Days**" there will be a great battle which shall include "**Gog and Magog**" against **ISRAEL**.

Note: *English is a Western **Germanic** language like Dutch, German and Afrikaans (spoken in South Africa).*

Most people today would consider "**Russia**" and "**China**" to be **Magog**. But what does the research of past historians say?

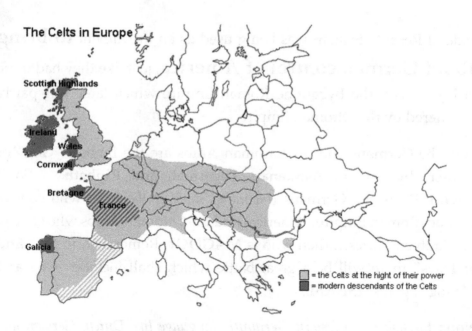

The Celts in Europe

Scottish Highlands

Ireland
Wales
Cornwall

Bretagne
France

Galicia

= the Celts at the hight of their power
= modern descendants of the Celts

(**Above**) The "**Celtic**" people were known to inhabit the **Scotland, Ireland, England-Britain, Wales, Spain, Portugal, France, Germany** and a good portion of **Western Europe**. These countries were involved in the Transatlantic Slave Trade of "**Negroes**" and the enslavement-oppression of the "**Native Americans**". Coincidence?

Throughout time the sons of Japheth have mixed together with one another...even mixing with some of the sons of Shem (*i.e. Assyrians, Black Arab Ishmaelites, Ludites*). By now, many of the sons of Gomer are still in Europe, **mixed with Magogites**, Edomites and possibly the surviving sons of Cain (*i.e. Children of the Wicked One*). Some say the whole **Celtic race** are the descendants of **Gomer**, where some sources say they are descendants of **BOTH** Gomer and Magog. The Irish Celts claim to be descendants of **Magog**, while the Welsh Celts claim to be descendants of **Gomer**. The Irish-Scotland area is a hot-spot for red-haired Europeans....and because of this they have been linked to the ancient Scythians, who some say were also known as "**Magogians**". The Germans, Scythians and Jews of "old" were documented by historians to also have "**red hair**". These Scythians however moved from Eastern Europe and "Turkishland" to Western Europe. The Ancient Greeks called them the "**Scythae**" or "**Celto-Scythae**". The

Latin called them "**Galli**" and the Romans referred to them as "**Gauls**". The Greeks would later use the words "**Galatai**", "**Galatae**", or "**Celtae**". Before the time of Christ, **the Gauls** (*aka/ Scythian-German-Barbarian people in Western Europe*) invaded Rome but were eventually pushed to the north-central part of Asia Minor (Anatolia-Turkey) from which the Biblical Gentile city "**Galatia**" is named after in the **Book of Galatians** (Apostle Paul). During the 1ˢᵗ Century A.D. time period, Roman-Gentile Jewish Historian **Flavius Josephus** also wrote that the Galatians or Gauls of his time was previously called "**Gomerites**" (*Antiquities of the Jews, Book 1, Section 122*).

What is also interesting is that Flavius Josephus links the "**Magogites**" to the **Scythians** who have been linked to the **Germans**, the **Barbarians** and the **European Jews**. So, from all of this info, is the "**Gog and Magog**" war in the Book of Revelation going to be consisting of "select" European countries (*including European Jews and Turkish Arabs*) against the "Real Hebrew Israelites"?

Here is another fun fact to ponder on. The Basque people of Spain/France have the highest frequency of "**Rh negative**" Blood type individuals. They also have high frequencies of "**Red hair, blue eyed**" babies....similar to the skulls of the Cro-Magnon/Neanderthal "**Pre-historic man**" and the Nephilim "**elongated**" giant skulls. Some believe the "**Basque**" people are a "**surviving**" white race from before the "**Great Flood**" and modern day "**Homo Sapiens**". In terms of "**genetics**", when the Basque people had their "**genetic samples**" compared to other races, they linked most closely to "**Germans**" and the indigenous "**white indian**" inhabitants of the **Canary Islands**. Here is the question again. Did the "**Sons of Cain-Sons of the Wicked One (Satan)**" survive the flood? Is their DNA somehow mixed in with the "**Germans**"? Did the "**Germans**" mix themselves with many nations in Europe including Rome, Italy? Could this be what Genesis 3:15 was referring to in regards to "**thy seed-Seed of Satan-Cain**" and "**her seed-Israel**"?

313

Are we seeing "**Bible Prophecy**" unfolding here?

But let's go back and take a look at **Cain's seed** and his connection with Edom to the "hostility" we see against the world and God's "**Chosen Seed**". We know that Cain/Edom's seed will be the end of this world and "The Children of Israel" or the "Children of the Kingdom" will be the beginning of the "New World". But if 2nd Century A.D. Greeks, or Christians wrote the Book of **2 Esdras**.....does this mean the Greeks or Christians during the times of the Maccabees...knew that the Edomites living amongst them would be the "**destruction of the world**"? **2 Esdras** (*i.e. IV Esdras in English and Latin Bibles*) **is only found written in Latin (Rome) as it was written too late to be included in the Greek Koine Septuagint.** 2 Esdras is accepted of course as "scripture" by the Roman Catholic Church, but was rejected by Protestants and Protestant Reformation leader **Martin Luther**. The Book of 2 Esdras was not written in Paleo-Hebrew or Aramaic. Nor was it found in the Hebrew Dead Sea Scrolls found in Qumran, Israel in the 1940's.

2 Esdras 6:9 "For **Esau** is the end of the age (world), and **Jacob** is the beginning of the one that follows."

Ask yourself, "who is controlling the world in these last days of wickedness and sexual immorality? Edom? Or is it Rome, the Vatican, ISRAEL and the United States?"

So, before the start of World War I in 1914, the European "**German**" Jewish Rothschild's loaned money to the **Germans**. The Rothschild's in Britain loaned money to the **British**, and the Rothschild's in France loaned money to the **French**. The Jewish Rothschild's also had control at this time over three European news agencies, **Wolff** (*est. 1849 in Germany*), **Reuters** (*est. 1851 in England*) and **Havas** (*est. 1835 in France*). The German born Rothschild's used the Wolff news agency to manipulate the German people into excitement for war. Because of this clever tactic, the Rothschild's throughout history have not been reported to be behind any of the "major" world wars, **back then and**

now because they have always controlled the Media/Press (*i.e. CNN, Fox, CBS, NBC, ABC, Newsweek, Time*).

CAIN/EDOM'S SEED IN EUROPE "PREDICTED" AND "INSTIGATED" ALL THREE WORLD WARS WITH STUNNING "BIBLICAL" ACCURACY? HOW COULD THEY DO THIS WITHOUT GUIDANCE FROM SATAN-LUCIFER HIMSELF?

Albert Pike (Left), a Grandmaster Scottish Rite Freemason and Luciferian was introduced into the "**German Bavarian Illuminati**" by Italian politician Giuseppe Mazzini (**Right**) in the 1800's. Albert Pike outlined the details for all Three World Wars in his literary works. He outlined:

1. **The First World War** was to be fought for the purpose of the Jewish Bolsheviks destroying the Tsars in Russia...as promised by Nathan Mayer Rothschild in 1815. Once taken out, the Tsar in Russia was to be replaced with Communist leaders used to attack religions, predominantly "**Christianity**". Millions of Christians were brutally killed in "**Gulag Prison camps**" by the Bolshevik Jews. The differences between the British and German Empires were to be used to stir up the war.

2. **The Second World War** was to be used to stir up the fight/controversy between the "totalitarianism-dictatorship-communist" Jewish governments and political Zionism. The "secret weapon" would be to create "**worldwide empathy**" with the "**planned**" oppression of the "**Fake Gentile Jews**" in Europe with the Holocaust which would eventually destroy "Communism (*which the Rothschild's created with communist-Jewish blooded leaders Stalin, Lenin and Trotsky*) and increase the Political Zionism (*i.e. Ashkenazi Theodore Herzl*) needed for the Jews to mastermind the purchase deal of the "**State of Israel**" by way of the Balfour Declaration in 1948. **Note: See "The Transfer Agreement" and Hitler.** This would set the stage for the "**Synagogue of Satan**" aka the seed of **Cain-Edom-Japheth (Gog & Magog)** to be in position to eventually build the Third Temple in Jerusalem for the **Biblical Antichrist** and **Islamic Mahdi (i.e. Anti-Christ)**.

3. **The Third World War**, Pike predicted the "**Hidden Jewish Masters**" plan was to "stir up" hatred for the Gentile Japhetic Muslim world (*using Jewish control Media and Secret Agencies*) for the purpose of playing the Islamic world, the Talmudic Jewish world and America against one another. While this was going, per Pike, the remaining nations would be forced to fight themselves into a state of mental, physical, sexual, spiritual and economic destruction. Albert Pike, agreed that these "Three World Wars" would bring "**Luciferianism**" to the forefront....just as the Elite wanted. This would pave the way for the "**Son of Perdition**"....or "**the Lawless One**" to appear on the scene....ushering in a "**New World Order**", a "**New World Religion**" and a "**New Economic System**". Part of the plan to do this also was to increase Terrorist Attacks in Europe and then in the United States of America......the "money powerhouses" of the world.

Fact: *In the White skinned Arabs, Europeans, the Druze, the Sephardic Jews and the Ashkenazi Jews, there is strong evidence of the **maternal DNA Haplogroup "X"** which has been labeled the "**Neanderthal**" gene or the "**Atlantean gene**" representing a certain race of people that lived before the Great Flood (i.e. Emerald Tablets of Thoth). Could this maternal DNA marker be the marker for "**Cain**" as it is the same character/picture that is used in the Hebrew Bible to describe the "mark" God placed on Cain. It is a known fact that the Nephilim somehow survived the flood and the Sumerians "Semitic" texts (**i.e. Lost 14 stone cuneiform tablet of Enki of the Annunaki/Sons of Anak**) describe that the Annunaki and some of the sons of Cain survived the flood.*

So, in my Books I prove with DNA and other sources that the bloodline of Edom and Cain (*i.e. Rechabite Scribes, Nethinims*) are in the genome of select Europeans, Ashkenazi Jews, Sephardic Jews and Arabs. This is why we have seen so much warring, colonization, pillaging, rape, murder, population control (sterilization/birth control) and slavery from these groups of people historically on the True "Children of Israel"......i.e. the so called Negro blacks scattered in the slave trades, Native Americans and their descendants, select groups in India and other Israelites scattered into Asia.

CHAPTER 10

EVERYONE KNEW THERE WAS A SINGLE "CREATOR" PRIOR TO THE FLOOD.

So many different doctrines and "**Creation stories**" are easily found on the internet, but we must have "**spiritual discernment**" and "**wisdom**" to decipher the "**Truth**" from the "**Lies**".

Many Blacks and Latinos today are torn between different theories presented from different sources such as the **Piso Family creation** of the New Testament, the **Oahspe "Mind Control" Bible (*with the Book of Thor and Apollo*)**, the **Islamic doctrine**, the **Egyptian Kemetic** African Spirituality doctrine, **Moorish Science**, **Gnostism**, the "**Annunaki** Creators of man" theory and the "**Curse of Canaan**" theory. What are the facts? How do we know who we are? How does the Bible and "**extra-biblical**" proof using archaeology prove who we are and who is the Creator?

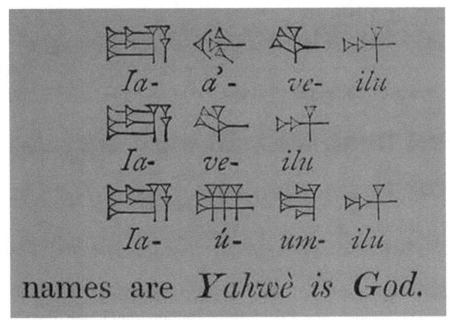

names are *Yahwè is God.*

(*Above*) **Neo-Sumerian-Akkadian Elba tablets** with the top depiction "Yahwe is God/**Ia a ve ilu**" and the bottom depiction "Yahuah the God/**Ia u um ilu**" read as "Yah(**Ia**)"-"U(**u**)"-"ah" (*note: "ah" is like a silent breath sound*) "the (**um**)" "God (**ilu**)".   Either way it goes we see the beginning word is "**Yah**".... Not Allah, Osiris, Horus, or Enki.

Fact: *Use of the **Akkadian script** in Assyria/Syria-Aram eventually gave rise to the **Eastern and Western Aramaic script**. The Aramaic script eventually gave rise to the **Arabic script**. Although the Akkadian/Babylonian Cuneiform script looks very much different than Paleo-Hebrew, the pronunciation is similar. "Ilu" in Akkadian is the word for "**God**". In Phoenician/Paleo-Hebrew it is "**El**", "**Eloah**" or "**Elohim (Plural)**". In Arabic, it is "**La**" or "**lat**" as "**Al-(i)lat/Al-lat**" means "**the Goddess**" and "**Al-(i)lah/Al-lah**" means "**the God**". In the Arabic Bible, the word "**Yahwah**" in Arabic is pronounced by Chaldeans as "**Yah-u-wah**" even though the "**u**" is not in the word.   Similar to "**Abdullah**" is based off the Arabic word "**Abd**" and "**Allah**" combined together with the "**u**" makes "**Abdullah**" which means "**Servant/Slave of Allah**".   "**Abd**" in Arabic means "**servant/slave**" and "**Allah**" means "**the god**".......thus making the phrase "**servant of the god Allah**" in all actuality.*

THE ELBA TABLETS

The Elba tablets written in the Akkadian-Babylonian script were discovered by Italian archaeologist **Paolo Matthiae** in 1974 during excavations in Ancient Assyria (Tell Mardikh, Syria). It dates back to 2500 B.C.

Example:
1. This man is a thief = Awil (man) um (the/this) su (he 3rd masculine pronoun) sarraq (thief).
2. The King cannot be rivaled = Sarr (King) um (the) la (not) sanan (opposed/rivaled).
3. The King's son = Sarr (King) im (the) mar (son).
4. The Master's dog = Bel (Master) im/um (the) Kalab (dog).

   Note: Dog in Hebrew is "Keleb", in Aramaic it is "Kalba" and in Arabic it is "Kalb". Master/owner in Hebrew is "Baal". In Akkadian/Assyrian/Babylonian it is "Bel".

(Above) In Indian mythology "**Matsya**" is the avatar of the Hindu god **Vishnu** in the form of a fish. Matsya forewarns a man named "**Manu**" about an impending "**Great Flood**". Matsya tells "**Manu**" to preserve all the seeds and animals along with Manu's family on a boat/ark to survive the flood. In earlier Pre-Puranic Indian literature, the Indian Creator-God "**Brahma**" is the one that warns Manu of the flood. This is before Vishnu and Shiva were even a household name as gods in India.

In 1872, Assyriologist **George Smith** at the age of 32 found a "**flood tablet**" from the 11th tablet of the "**Epic of Gilgamesh**" while studying tablets that were sent from Nineveh (North Iraq) that had been shipped to a British Museum where he was working at. Smith deciphered the text which talked about a "**Great Flood**", a ship full of animals, and a bird that was sent out to find land. This 3200 B.C. Semitic Sumerian-Akkadian story was exactly like the Semitic Biblical "**Noah's flood**" story. Flood stories are common in the Sumerian tablets, the **Deucalion** in **Greek mythology**, the **Native American Indians (Ojibwa Tribe)**, the **Mayan people** of Central America, the **Muisca people of Columbia**, the **Chinese (Gun-Yu story)**, the **Pygmy Tribes in Africa**, the **Bantus people in Africa** and the **people in India**. How is this possible? Ancient Egyptian scholars like to hide "**Egyptians Flood Story**" but it is there as well...proving the Bible is True.

Fact: There exists a "**Great Flood Myth**" in **Dwarka, India** where the "**Vedas Satapatha Brahmana/Matsya Purana**" Hindu text (pre-dating Christianity) tells of an epic flood that submerged the city of Dwarka and former civilizations. There were some survivors of the flood but the **Krishna Temple** established by the Hindu God **Krishna** was destroyed by the flood. A Hindu "**Noah-like character**" named "**Madel/Manu Vaivasvati**" prior to the flood built a ship in which he gathered various plants/seeds and animals to be used to restart civilization. The ship eventually landed on the top of a mountain when the waters receded. **After the flood, Manu and his three sons: Charma (Ham), Sharma (Shem) and Yapeti (Japheth) populated the earth.** Manu was guided by God during the "**Great Flood**" by a magical fish which the Hindu "Ark" in this story follows. This mirrors the "Great Flood" story of the Bible with Noah and his Three Sons: Ham, Shem and Japheth. Even the Indian names of Manu/Madel's three sons mimic the Hebrew names of Noah's three sons (*i.e. Hebrew Strong's Yepheth, Cham, Shem*). Here is an excerpt.

"O king-hearted man, you have care in your heart, listen now. Soon **the world will be submerged by a great flood**, and everything will perish. You must build a **strong ark**, and take along rope on board. You must also take with you the Seven Sages, who have existed since the beginning of time, and **seeds of all things and a pair of each animal**. When you are ready, I will come to you as a fish and I will have horns on my head. Do not forget my words, without me you cannot escape the flood."*-Hindu Vedic texts*

Fact: The Miao people of South China-Legend states there was a man name **NuWah** (Nuah/Noah) with his wife Gawboluen, three sons (Lo **Han**, Lo **Shen**, and **Jah-Hu**) and three daughters who escaped the flood in a ship. After the flood, it is said that **a tower was built** (*i.e. Tower of Babel*) and their speech was broken up into **six "parent" language families**. The names of son of the sons of Lo-Shen were **Elan** (Elam) and **Ngashur** (Asshur). The sons of Lo-Han were **Cu-Sah** (Cush) and **Mesay** (Mizraim). The sons of Jah-Hu were **Gomen** (Gomer). Fascinating, isn't it? The Bible is **TRUE!**

Fact: Many civilizations have a *"**Flood story**"* and a man who resembles "**Noah**" as the person who is told to build a boat, ark or raft before the coming Flood. Here are different civilizations and their "Noah" character.

- **Sumeria**-Utnapishtim
- **Babylon**-Atrahasis
- **Chaldean**-Xisuthrus
- **Persian/Iran** (Zoroastrinism)-Yima
- **Norse/Scandanavian**-Bergeimer
- **Greco/Roman**-Deaucalion
- **Hindu/India**-Manu
- **China**-Mahel/Maniu
- **Burma**-Lip Long
- **Hawaii**-Nuu
- **Masai (Africa)**-Tumbainot
- **Algonquian Indians**-Michabo
- **Aztec (Mexico)**-Tapi.
- **Australian Aborigines**-Pund-Jil or Gajara

In the Australian flood story, the survivors of the flood, Gajara (*i.e. Noah*) and his wife kill a kangaroo after landing on earth. They cook the kangaroo and eventually the smoke reaches the sky. Ngadja, the Creator, smells the savory smell of the kangaroo and is pleased. Ngadja (Creator) then puts a rainbow in the sky as a reminder that he would never let the rainfall rise too high where it would flood the earth. Sounds familiar to the Genesis Flood story, doesn't it?

This "flood story" was in the Australian Aborigines "oral history" before any European missionaries had arrived to the distant Island. If this is so, they obviously are the descendants of one of Noah's three sons: Ham, Shem or Japheth. How else could they know this story which lines up with the Bible. Perhaps they are Shemites because the Shemite Israelites were the ones who wrote the Hebrew Torah.

Genesis 8:20-21 "And Noah builded an altar unto the LORD; and took of every clean beast, and of every clean fowl, and offered burnt offerings on the altar. And the **LORD SMELLED A SWEET SAVOUR;** and the LORD said in his heart, **I will not again curse the ground any more for man's sake; for the imagination of man's heart is evil from his youth; neither will I again smite any more every thing living, as I have done.**"

Genesis 9:13-15 "I do set my bow (i.e. rainbow) in the cloud, and it shall be for a token of a covenant between me and the earth. And it shall come to pass, when I bring a cloud over the earth, that the bow shall be seen in the cloud: And I will remember my covenant, which is between me and you and every living creature of all flesh; and **the waters shall no more become a flood to destroy all flesh.**"

So, what about the Ancient Egyptians?

Even the Egyptians have a flood story and in the very earliest of their civilization they knew about "**one Creator**" and a "**Messianic Prophecy**". Of course, the "Fallen Angels" would corrupt this "truth" using "lies" to deceive their civilization and others. Here are two versions of the Egyptians Flood Story......which obviously would mean that the Egyptians were a "post-flood" Civilization like the rest of the ancient civilizations of the world. This would indicate that the

Egyptian Texts were **NOT** the originators of the creation story, the flood story or anything else they claim is the foundation for the Bible.

Egyptian "Flood" story – Version 1

"The god **Tem (i.e. Atum)** hath decreed that I shall see thy face, and that I shall not suffer from the things which pained thee. May every god transmit his throne to thee for millions of years. Thy throne hath descended to thy son **Horus**, and Tem (i.e. Atum) hath decreed that his course shall be among the holy princes. Verily he shall rule from thy throne, and he (**Horus**) shall be the heir of the Dweller in the **Lake of Fire.** Verily it hath been decreed that in me he shall see his counterpart, and that my face shall look upon the face of the Lord Tem."

Further it reads,
"Then **Thoth**, being the tongue of the Great God declares that, acting for the **Lord Tem**, he is going to make a **FLOOD**. He says: I am going to blot out everything which I have made. This earth shall enter into the watery abyss of **Nu** (i.e. Nunu) by means of a raging **FLOOD**, and will become even as it was in primeval time (*see Genesis 1:1-2*). I myself shall remain together with Osiris, but I shall **transform myself into a small serpent** which can neither be apprehended or seen." – "*From Fetish to God in Ancient Egypt*", *by E. A. Wallis Budge.*

Egyptian "Flood" story – Version 2

"The gods assembled as **Ra (*i.e. Egyptian solar god and creator synonymous with Atum/Tem*)** desired, and they made obeisance before him. Then they said: "Speak what thou desireth to say and we will hear." He addressed the gods, saying: "O Nu, thou the eldest god, from whom I had my being, and ye ancestral gods, hear and know now, that rebellious words are spoken against me by mankind, whom I did create. Lo! They seek even to slay me. It is my desire that ye should instruct me what ye would do in this matter. Consider well among yourselves and guide me with wisdom. I have hesitated to punish mankind until I have heard from Your lips what should now be done regarding them. "For lo! **I desire in my heart to destroy utterly that which I did create. All the world will become a waste of water through a great flood as it was in the beginning** (*see Genesis 1:1-2*), and I alone shall be left remaining, with no one else beside me save Osiris and his son Horus. **I shall become a serpent invisible to the gods**. To Osiris will be given power to reign over the dead, and Horus will be exalted on the throne which is set upon the island (*some sources say "lake"*) of fiery flames." – *"Egyptian Myth and Legend"*, by Donald Mackenzie (1907).

As we can see here there, the stories of a **"Great Flood"** by **"other nations"** is real and factual. There has to be some truth behind a "Great Flood" happening if different civilizations from the lineage of Noah (Ham, Shem, Japheth) all talk about it. The Egyptians, are the only major civilization that today do not openly "profess" to have a record of a **"Great Flood"** Story. Seems odd, doesn't it? But maybe, the Egyptians or the **"powers to be"** hid this story for a reason. People use the **Osiris, Isis and Horus story** to claim that the Bible is plagiarized from Ancient Egypt. For an Ancient Egyptian Civilization to acknowledge and document a past **"Great Flood"** that would mean that the Bible is **"credible"** and historically true according to Egyptian history. This would lay to rest that the belief that the Egyptians existed before the flood and were a separate people from Noah's sons. However, acknowledging that the "Great Flood" did exist in the past would mean that the Egyptians were a "post-flood" civilization like the ancient "Sumerians" and thus would line up with Biblical history that Mizraim (Egypt) was the grandson of Noah. It would end the belief that Egypt was the first civilization on earth and that all religions (including Christianity) came from it. However, there another problem with this **"Egyptian First Civilization"** belief. For many scientists and archaeologists, the cradle of Civilization started in Ethiopia or Mesopotamia. So, does Ancient Ethiopia or Ancient Mesopotamia give any proof as to the validity of the Bible? Well, the first mention of any Ethiopian converted to Christianity happens to be the "Ethiopian Eunuch" that was witnessed to by Philip the Evangelist. Philip was told by an angel to go to the road from Jerusalem to Gaza (*i.e. now Palestine area*), where he met the Ethiopian eunuch. The Ethiopian Eunuch was in Jerusalem worshipping (Acts 8:27) and was returning home to Ethiopia via way of Gaza leading into Egypt/Sinai Peninsula in Africa. The Eunuch according to the Bible (New Testament) was reading the Book of Isaiah (**53:7-8**) in the Old Testament. Was the Ethiopian reading the Book of Isaiah in **Greek, Hebrew** or "**Ge'ez**", the language of the Ethiopian Jews and the Ethiopian Tewahedo Orthodox Church? Many historians say that the Semitic Ge'ez language dates back to 500 or 400 B.C., while some say it goes back even earlier. So, let's dig deep into this using Ancient Mesopotamia and Ancient Cush/Ethiopia.

(**Above**) Cylinder seal of **Khashkhamer**, a governor of North Babylon (Iraq) 2400 B.C. The Ancient Semitic Sumerians worshipped a male moon god by name of **Nanna, Asimbabbar and Su'en (i.e. Sin)**. Later this "**moon god**" was given the title of the "**main god**" by the Arabs and eventually earned the title "**The god**" which in Arabic is "**al-ilah**" or "**Al-lah**". This name "**Al-lah/Al-ilah**" basically is the masculinized version of the "**Crescent Moon Goddess**" called "**Al-lat**" or "**Al-ilat**" as the "**t**" gives this word a "feminine" position. "**Ilu**" in the Akkadian language means "**God**". "**Al**" means "**the**" in Arabic. To further prove this, the three daughters of Allah in the Quran (*see Sura 53:19-22*) are "**Al-Lat**" which means "**the Goddess**", "**Al-Uzza**" which means "**the mighty one**" and '**Al-Manat** (*from the Arabic word "maniya"*)' which means "**the fate**".

Al-lat is associated again with the **Crescent Moon, Al-Uzza** is associated with the "**Full Moon**" and **Al-Manat** (or Manat) is associated with the "**Waning moon**". Al-Manat is the wise goddess of fate, destiny, prophecy, divination, death, doom, or destruction.

Su'en or Sin's Moon god symbol was a "**crescent moon**", the same symbol for **Islam**. The Assyrians (**Asshur**), Babylonians (**Arphaxad**) and the Akkadians (**Aram/Arphaxad**) took the word "**Su'en**" and transformed it into **"Sin"**. Therefore **"Sin"** was a word with Sumerian Origin which was borrowed by other Semite nations in Mesopotamia.

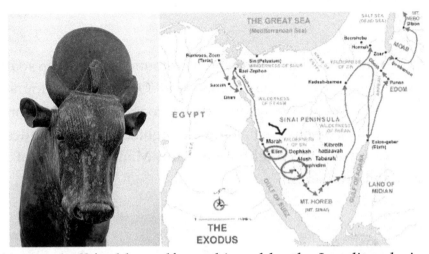

(**Left**) **Apis bull**/golden calf worshipped by the Israelites during the Exodus. (**Right**) The "**Wilderness of Sin**" was North of **Mt Horeb/Mount Sinai**, where Moses received the stone tablets of the Ten Commandments from God, later coming down the mount to find the Israelites worshipping the golden calf/bull. Abraham's grandchildren, the Keturahites and the Ishmaelites dwelt in the **SIN-ai Peninsula** and were known as the "**Arabs**". In the Sinai Peninsula, they dwelt in the **Wilderness of Sin**, the Wilderness of Paran and in the land to the east near Iraq.

Book of Jubilees (Ethiopic-Hebrew Version) 20:11-13 "And he gave to Ishmael and to his sons, and to the sons of Keturah, gifts, and sent them away from Isaac his son, and he gave everything to Isaac his son. And Ishmael and his sons, and the sons of Keturah and their sons, went together and dwelt from Paran (Sinai Peninsula) to the entering in of Babylon in all the land which is towards the East facing the desert. **And these mingled with each other, and their name was called Arabs, and Ishmaelites.**"

Fact: The Mesopotamian pagan god "Sin" was supposedly the father of Ishtar/Asheroth. In Tell-el-Obeid (Tell-al-Ubaid) in Southern Iraq, a copper calf with a crescent moon on its forehead was found. This is the same idol worshipped by the Children of Israel in the Wilderness of Sin (Sinai Peninsula).

Evidence of the "**Moon god**" worship was found also as deep south as North Arabia, South Arabia, Yemen and Qatar. Also, found by archeologists G. Caton Thompson and Carleton S. Coon were "**worship bowls**" used to worship Allah's three daughters, **Al-lat (goddess of fertility), Al-Uzza ("the mighty one") and Manat (goddess of fate, prophecy and divination)**.

(**Left**) Pre-Islamic worship of the "**crescent moon**" and modern day used of the same pagan crescent moon on "Islamic" mosques in the Middle East. (**Right**) Sun goddess "**Dhat Hamym**". Before Islam, the Arabians worshipped different moon gods such as **Hubal, Sin, al-lah, and Ilumquh. Ilumqu** was a male moon god who was married to the Sun goddess "**Dhat Hamymand (Dhat Hamym or Dhat Himyam)**". Supposedly the Moon god classified by the Arabs as "**Al-ilah**" or "**Al-lah**" or "**The (main) God**" had 3 daughters with the Sun goddess **Dhat Hamym**". These three daughters would be known as **Al-lat, Al-Uzza and Manat**......"Allah's three goddess daughters" which are listed in the Quran.

Allah's Three Daughters : Al-lat, Al-Uzza and Manat Quran Sura 53:19-22

(**Above**) Allah's three daughters (*numbered 1, 2, 3*) can be verified in the Quran in **Sura 53:19-22**. This is "pagan" worship being promoted by Allah in the Quran. All pagan and idolatry worship is forbidden in the Bible because it comes from Satan and the Fallen Angels.

Sura 53:19-20 "Have ye though upon **al-Lat**, and **al-Uzza**, and **Manat**, the third, the other?

Removed "satanic verses":
"These are the exalted cranes (**intermediaries-lesser gods**), whose intercession (**prayers**) is to be hoped for."

However, in the Quran it also states that Allah does not have a son/daughter or a wife (partner). So how can Allah have three daughters in the Quran if he had no wife? If Allah cannot have any sons according to the Quran.....then how can he have daughters? This proves the Quran is a false book.

Sura 17:111 (Yusuf Ali) "Say: Praise be to Allah, **who begets no son, and has no partner (wife) in his dominion**: Nor needs he any to protect him from humiliation: yea, magnify him for his greatness and glory!"

To apologize for asking Muslims to worship and pray to his three daughters in Sura 59:19-22 (**which contradicts Sura 17:111**),

Muhammad blamed this scripture/Quranic verse on **Satan** deceiving him. But true prophets of the Creator when **"The Spirit of the Lord"** is upon them cannot be deceived by Satan....and especially allow **"satanic verses"** to be included in a so-called **"Holy Book"** inspired by God.

Sura 22:52 "And we did not send before you any messenger or prophet except that when he spoke (or recited), **SATAN** threw into it some misunderstanding. **But Allah abolishes (gets rid of) that which SATAN throws in (i.e. satanic verse)**; then Allah makes precise his verses. And Allah is Knowing and Wise."

How can Allah, the **"Creator"** allow Satan....a "creation" to distort his "Holy Word"? This question needs to be answered. Since it cannot be answered me must assume the Quran was not inspired by God or any benevolent **(i.e. good)** angels.

*Fact: Many believe the "wilderness of Sin" (Sinai Peninsula) was an area where the Arabs (Sons of Ishmael/Sons of Keturah) worshipped the moon good "Sin". The word "Sinai" is believed to have stemmed from the word "Sin". According to numerus inscriptions, per the Book **"The Tombs and Moon Temple of Hureidha by G. Caton Thompson"** the moon god was named "Sin", but his title was "Al-ilah"....meaning **"the deity"** or **"the god"**. The Moon God in Arabia was called "Al-ilah" from the Arabic/Akkadian words "Al" which means **"the"** (ex. **al-kitaab means "the book"**, **al-jazirah means "the island"**). The Arabic word "al" prefixes Arabic nouns. The Akkadian word "ilu" means **"god/deity"**, similar to "El" meaning "god" in Ancient Hebrew/Phoenician and "Elah/ilah" meaning "god" in Aramaic (the precursor language for Arabic).*

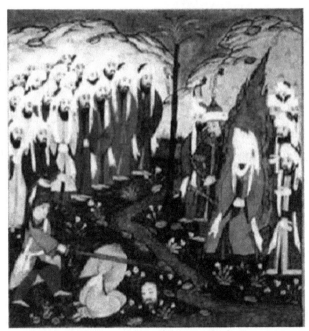

(**Above**) An "**unbeliever**" beheaded in front of Muslims while **Muhammad** (man with face blurred out) watches from his throne.

Sura 47:4 (Sahih International) "So when you meet those who disbelieve in battle, **strike (cut) their necks** until, when you have inflicted slaughter upon them, then secure their bonds, and either confer favor afterwards or ransom them until the war lays down its burdens. That is the command. And if Allah had willed, **He would have taken vengeance upon them himself,** but he ordered armed struggle to test some of you by means of others. And those who are killed in the cause of Allah – never will he waste their deeds."

Note: *Allah never takes vengeance upon man himself like "The Most High" or "Yahuah" does in the Old Testament with "The Great Flood" or with "Fire and Brimstone" in Sodom and Gomorrah. Even in the Quran it is Christ (Yahusha) and **NOT ALLAH** or the prophet Muhammad that defeats the Antichrist (Dajjal) for mankind and lays down "Judgement".*

The ancient Semitic peoples in Mesopotamia-Arabia believed strongly that "**sin**" or "**al-ilah**", or "**allah**" was the greatest of all gods and was

333

the supreme deity. When Muhammad stepped on the scene he decided that (*Sin the Moon god*) was not only the greatest supreme deity of the Arabic pantheon of gods (*like his forefathers*) but was "**the only god**". The use of the word "Sin" would then change to "The god" or "Allah", which is used by Muslims worldwide as the name of the God of Abraham, Isaac and Jacob. But Abraham never worshipped "**Sin**" the moon god and Abraham (*a Hebrew speaker*) did not worship an "**Oak Tree**" (*Hebrew Strong's #427 Allah=Oak Tree*). This is "**deceptive**" and is the reason why the god of Islam has "**no name**" but just a "**title**", unlike the God of Israel whose name according to the Semitic people of Mesopotamia was "**Yah, Yahuah, Yahuwa or Yahawah**".

Note: Muslims don't say "**Allah is great**"....they say "**Allah is the greatest**". Why would Muhammad say that Allah is "**the greatest**" or "**the best of creators** (Sura 23:14)" or "**the best of deceivers** (Sura 3:54, 7:99, 8:30)" except if it wasn't in a "**polytheistic context**"? The plural aspect of these sayings implies that there are other gods and goddesses that were present in Islamic belief. All the Semitic and Hamitic religions/civilizations worshipped multiple pagan gods except the Hebrew Israelites.

Deuteronomy 6:4 (Shema Prayer) "Hear, O Israel! The LORD (Yahuah) is our God (Elohim), the LORD (Yahuah) is **ONE**!

(**Above**) In North Ethiopia/Eritrea lies the "**Hawulti Obelisk**". It bears the same "**crescent moon**" and "**sun disk**" symbol seen in the Ethiopian **Yeha Temple** in North Ethiopia (Aksumite Kingdom). Here the crescent moon represents the lunar god "**Ilumquh/Almaqah**" which was worshipped in Arabia and **Da'amat/D'mt**. The Obelisk predates to 400 B.C. around the time that the Da'amat Ethiopian Kingdom was coming to an end preparing the way for the "**Aksumite Kingdom**". The language written on the obelisk is an ancient form of **Ge'ez** which is used by the Ethiopian Jews and Ethiopian Orthodox church.

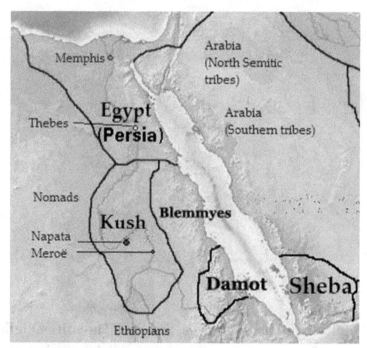

(**Above**) The Kingdom of Cush (**Nubia-Sudan**) was in close vicinity to the Kingdom of Aksum, D'mt/Damot (Da'amat), Sheba and Sabaea/Seba. Today the Kingdom of Cush can be seen in its purest form in the **Dinka, Nuer, Nuba** and **Shillik Nilotic people of Sudan**. Some tribes like the **Anuak Tribe** in Sudan/Ethiopia have a mixture of Nilotic Cushite stock and Israelite stock from their mixing centuries prior. Today many of the descendants of the Black Arabs are in Sudan...the same Ishmaelites/Hagarenes who take "crafty counsel" against Israel's seen in Psalms 83.

The Y-DNA associated with the Nilotic people of Sudan and South Ethiopia is "**A**". The DNA of the Black Arab Ishmaelite people in North Sudan is "**J1**".

Fact: *The **Wolayta** Omotic speaking people of Southern/Central Ethiopia claim their ancestry from the **Damot/D'mt Kingdom** before it was conquered by the Azumite Kingdom and Emperor Menelik (Hebrew Israelite). Their Y-DNA is partially Cushitic "A" with an influence from Shemitic blood (**E1b1b**) from Edom's mixture with the Shemitic Arabs and Hamitic North Africans.*

There are also very small traces of "**E1b1a**" from those Bantus Israelite males that had children with Wolayta women within the tribe.

The Cush people also mixed with the Canaanites creating a mixed race of "Cush (**Haplogroup A**)-Canaan (**Haplogroup B**)" in the Khoi-San people (**Y-DNA "A" and "B"**). The Khoisan people also had some dealings with the Bantus Hebrew Israelite people in Africa as well. This could stem from ancient times (900 B.C.) when the Israelite kingdom in Cush was established (Moses, King Solomon-Sheba) creating the "**Ethiopian Jews**". The Y-DNA genetic breakdown of the Ethiopian Jews is Y-DNA "**A**" and an ancient pre-form of the Y-DNA "E1b1a (Negro)" Haplogroup listed as "**E(xE1b1a)**" or "**E1b1c (E-M329)**". Because of the close proximity of Cush to Arabia....we see the "**Negroid-looking**" Arabs in Yemen, Oman, Qatar, and the United Arab Emirates. Countries like **Socotra** and **India** also bear "Semitic" influence (**Y-DNA J, Q, R, H, L**) because they are in close proximity to Arab lands via the Arabian Sea/Indian Ocean. Matter of fact, the area of **Hadhramaut, Yemen** is named after "**Hadoram**", one of the sons of **Joktan** in Genesis 10:27. In Hadhramaut, geneticists have discovered a nice amount of the people there who carry the Y-DNA "**E1b1a**" Haplogroup and who confess to be descendants of the "**Black Jews**".

(**Above**) The Eritrean-Ethiopian "**Hawulti**" Obelisk shows how the ancient Ethiopian "**Ge'ez**" language (**on bottom**) is similar to the "**Sabaean**" South Arabian Shemitic script from South Arabia (**on top**). The example above shows the evolution of the word "**hawulti**" from the Sabaean characters (**on top**) reading from right to left (**like Hebrew**). Except in those days there wasn't vowels so it is just spelled "HWLT". The Ge'ez letters are switched around "**Left to Right**" but still spell "**HWLT**" or **Ha Wu L Ti**.

Translit.	h	l	ḥ	m	ś (SA s²)	r	s (SA s¹)	ḳ	b	t	ḫ	n
Ge'ez	ሀ	ለ	ሐ	መ	ሠ	ረ	ሰ	ቀ	በ	ተ	ኀ	ነ
South Arabian	𐩠	𐩡	𐩢	𐩣	𐩦	𐩧	𐩬	𐩤	𐩨	𐩩	𐩭	𐩬

Translit.	'	k	w	'	z (SA ḏ)	y	d	g	ṭ	ṣ	ḍ	f
Ge'ez	አ	ከ	ወ	ዐ	ዘ	የ	ደ	ገ	ጠ	ጸ	θ	ፈ
South Arabian	𐩱	𐩫	𐩥	𐩲	𐩹	𐩺	𐩵	𐩴	𐩷	𐩮	𐩳	𐩰

(**Above**) Comparison of Ge'ez and Sabaean (South Arabian Semitic language).

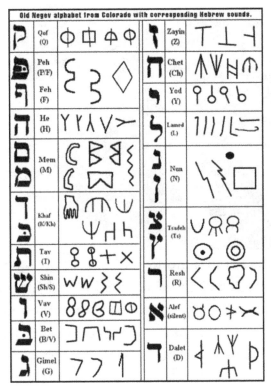

ק	Qof (Q)	Φ Φ Δ Φ	ז	Zayin (Z)	T ⊥ ⊣
פ	Peh (P/F)	ϵ ϱ ◇	ח	Chet (Ch)	Λ V ꓕ ꟼ
ף	Feh (F)		י	Yod (Y)	၄ ၄ ၄ b
ה	He (H)	Y Υ Λ V ⟩	ל	Lamed (L)	�𝖨⏐⏐⎰
מ	Mem (M)	Ϲ Ɓ Ȝ Ϲ ᗯ ⤳	נ	Nun (N)	⟍ ⟍ □
כ	Khaf (K/Kh)	ꟺ ⋔ Ψ Ψ ꓒ h	צ	Tsadeh (Ts)	∪ ꝶ ꝶ ⊙ ◎
ת	Tav (T)	�8 �8 + X	ר	Resh (R)	⟨ ⟨ ⟨⟩ ⟩
ש	Shin (Sh/S)	W W Ȝ Ȝ	א	Alef (silent)	ꝏ O ⊹ ꭗ
ו	Vav (V)	၄၄Ϭ⬜◐	ד	Dalet (D)	ꓔ Λ ꝡ Þ ⍕
ב	Bet (B/V)	Ɔ ꓵ ʮ Ɔ			
ג	Gimel (G)	7) ⌐			

Old Negev alphabet from Colorado with corresponding Hebrew sounds.

(**Above**) Modern Hebrew and "**Negev Hebrew**". "Negev" is synonymous with "**Dry**" and "**South**" in Hebrew. What is interesting is that in **Brazil** (*South America*) and **Colorado** (*North America*) there has been findings of Paleo/Negev Hebrew that are identical to "**Negev Hebrew**". According to Biblical Archaeologist Professor Pettinato, the "**Gillespie Stone**" shows the archaic reference to the name of God or "**El**" in Negev-Paleo Hebrew. Some call it "**Paleo-Canaanite**" but the Native Americas or Taino Indians were never depicted to be a "**Pygmy**" or "**Negrito**" race of people like the ancient Canaanite peoples that existed in Africa, Asia and the South Pacific Islands.

339

(**Above**) This is the **Paraiba Stone** in Brazil. Many scholars find it hard to believe that ancient civilizations could navigate the oceans from continent to continent. But the Paraiba stone shows proof of a people that left the Land of Canaan and made their way around Africa to the Americas. Read below what the inscription says:

"We are the Children of Canaan (**Israel**) from Sidon (**Tribe of Asher Territory**) of the Eastern Kingdom of Merchants and are cast, I pray, here beside a central land of mountains with this offered choice gift to the Most High Gods and Goddesses in year **19 of King Hiram (of Tyre/Sidon in I Kings 5)**, I pray still strong, from the **valley of Ezion-geber of the Red Sea**. Thereby **we journeyed with 10 ships** and we were at sea together assuredly two years **around** the Land of Ham (Africa). **We were separated by the hand of Baal** and no longer remained among our companions, I pray, we have come here, 12 men and 3 women at this new land. Devoted, I make, even whom men of wealth bow the knee, a pledge to the **Most High Gods** and Goddesses with sure hope."

These voyagers comment on two things that hint that these people were possibly Israelites that were a part of King Solomon's fleet of ships. They mention **King Hiram of Tyre** (*who often did business with King*

Solomon's fleet of ships) and **the Ezion-geber Israelite** ship port of the
Red Sea. Here is the proof.

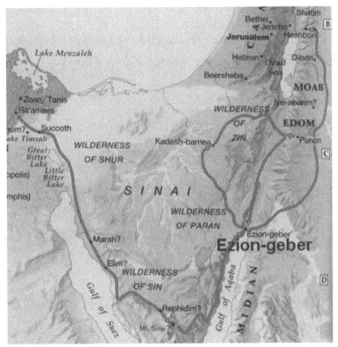

It is unlikely that Pygmy Canaanites had a fleet of ships docked at the
Ezion-Geber seaport especially if the Israelites were the ruling nation
at the time in Israel. Also, to have a fleet of ships required that a nation
has "**wealth**". It is a known fact that during the reign of Hiram King of
Tyre, that King Solomon had vessels to sail the seas to Ophir for spices,
exotic animals and precious metals like gold. During this time King
Solomon had **ALL** the wealth…..not the Canaanite Kings. King Hiram
of Tyre sent his servants to King Solomon, not vice-versa. King
Solomon had the "**navy of ships**" according to the scriptures…not King
Hiram of Tyre. This proof is also recorded in the bible.

1 Kings 5:1 "Now Hiram King of Tyre **sent his servants to Solomon,**
when he heard that they had appointed him king in place of his father,
for Hiram had always been a friend of David."

1 Kings 9:26 "And **King Solomon made a navy of ships in Ezion-geber**, which is besides Eloth (Elath), on the shore of the Red Sea, in the land of Edom."

Note: *The Red Sea body of water splits into the Gulf of Suez along Egypt's border and the Gulf of Aqaba along Arabia-Edom's border.*

"Belonging to Jotham"

A seal with the name of Jotham was discovered at Elath (Ezion-Geber, on the Gulf of Aqaba).

(**Above**) A seal was found at **Elath-Ezion-Geber** on the Gulf of Aqaba with the name of the **King of Judah** "**Jotham**" who reigned during the 8th Century B.C. prior to the Assyrian invasion of Israel in 701 B.C. This proves the Israelites were still in North Israel at the time and did frequent King Solomon's seaport of Ezion-geber. Jotham was the King of Judah during the life of the prophet Isaiah. King Uzziah (his father), King Hezekiah, King Ahaz and King Manasseh also ruled as Kings during this time frame.

2 Chronicles 27:1-2 "**Jotham** was twenty-five years old when he became king; and he reigned in Jerusalem sixteen years. His mother was Jerusha, the daughter of Zadok. Jotham did what was pleasing in the Lord's sight. He did everything his father, Uzziah, had done, except that Jotham did not sin by entering the Temple of the Lord. But the people continued in their corrupt ways.

Is there any other proof the Paraiba stone in Brazil was not written by Canaanites? **YES THERE IS!**

CHAPTER 11

FINDING THE CANAANITES IN AFRICA AMONGST THE BANTUS PEOPLE (ISRAELITES) TODAY

In the Bible, the Israelites do a lot of mixing with the **Canaanites**. This can be seen from the time period of Judges Chapter 3 (1300 B.C.) until Ezra Chapter 9 (500 B.C.). This is a very long time….twice as long as Black people have been in America. So, with that being said, shouldn't this "**Canaanite DNA**" be evident in the DNA of people claiming to be Israelites? Shouldn't there be some kind of "**marker**" or similar finding that is seen in any African Tribe claiming to be "Israelites" or a past history of "**Hebrew Traditions and Customs**"?

It is a known fact that the Bantus African people are very numerous in Africa. Prior to the "**Bantus Expansion**", the pygmy tribes were also numerous in Africa. But the Bantus people share "**one**" particular thing in common with the Black Lemba Jews of South Africa. **Something that people have overlooked.** The Lemba women all carry mtDNA Haplogroups that are only seen in Africa…in particular "**Bantus women/Negro women**" and "**Pygmy women**". How can this be if the Lemba Jews claim to be "**Set Apart**" from other African Tribes in regards to "**intermixing**" after settling into Southeastern Africa by way of Israel, Arabia and Yemen? Something about this "Set Apart" claim is not adding up according to genetics. But this is a "major" discovery in that it shows a common ancestry of the Lemba Jews and Bantus Africans (i.e. Ashanti/Akan, Bambara, Bini, Chewa, Temne, Kikongo, Buganda, Igbo, Yoruba, Mandingo, Bassa, Bamileke, Kikuyu, Sukuma, Zulu, Tutsi).

In 1993, South African - Indian descent geneticist **Himla Soodyall** when analyzing the Lemba Tribes maternal mtDNA, found **NO EVIDENCE** of Semitic (**Arab**) admixture or European "**Jewish**" admixture in the Lemba woman's mtDNA. This was quite "odd" because most of the Arab world carries the Y-DNA "**J1**" Haplogroup in some form or fashion. This is passed down paternally from one male father to his son and so on. Likewise, the majority of all Arab women or European Jewish women carry the mtDNA "**H, HV, U, J, K, and T**". The Lemba Jews are unique in that some of the Lemba men carry the Y-DNA "**J1**" which the Gentile European Ashkenazi-Sephardic Jewish community associates with the bloodline of "**Aaron**" the brother of Moses (Tribe of Levi). However, the Y-DNA "**J1**" Haplogroup is actually a Shemitic "Arab" marker with the "**purest**" of J1-Arab carriers seen in **Khaurton, Sudan, the Black Bedouins (Negev, Israel/Jordan), Yemen, Qatar, Oman, Socotra Island** and **India**. In the Arab world, the (paternal) Y-DNA "**J1**" goes hand in hand with the (maternal) mtDNA "**H, HV, U, J, K, and T**" in regards to modern day genetic testing. But the Lemba Jewish women did not have any trace of the mtDNA's seen in the daughters of Y-DNA "**J1**" Arab men carriers. **The Lemba women had evidence of the same mtDNA seen in Bantus West African and Bantus East African women**, which is only seen in the so-called "**Negro**".....with small amounts also seen in African Pygmy women.

They Lemba Jewish women who claim to descend from Israel even had evidence of the mtDNA Haplogroup "**L1 & L2**", which is seen in Pygmy (**Canaanite**) tribal women.....even though Pygmy tribes are not known to inhabit Israel...at least we didn't think they did until now. They also had evidence of the mtDNA Haplogroup "**L3**" which is most commonly seen in African-Americans and Bantus West/East Africans. Basically, who the world calls "**Negroes**".

Fact: *The Lemba* people (aka. Bantus for "Non-African or Respected Foreigner") are *also known as* **VaRemba** may be translated as "**the people who refuse**" – probably in the context of "**not eating with others**". This means the Lemba Jews are known to **NOT** associate themselves or mingle with other nations in Africa (i.e. Bantus, Nilotic Cushites, Black Arabs, Pygmy tribes). In Zimbabwe and South Africa, the people prefer the name *Mwenye*.

Keep in mind the Lemba Jews history states they left Israel around 600 B.C. and ventured south into Arabia....eventually settling in **Sanaa, Yemen**. But the DNA of the Lemba people suggest that **Canaanite-Pygmy DNA** and **Sub-Saharan "Negro" Bantus Israelite DNA** were once found in Israel thousands of years ago. How is this possible? Well, DNA is hard to make up and DNA studies show the Jewish Lemba women had "**Bantus**" Israelite blood and "**Pygmy**" Canaanite blood. If the Lemba Jews "**Israel migration story**" is correct, it means that Negroes and Pygmy Tribes lived in Israel many centuries ago.

Fact: *It is a fact that Lemba Jewish women by Hebrew Tradition are not allowed to marry non-Lemba men. If Lemba women violate this traditional law, they are disowned from the clan/tribe.* Lemba Men however are allowed to marry non-Lemba women as long as these women agree to convert to "Judaism". So, if the Lemba men spent most of their time in Israel and Arabia/Yemen, how is it that the Lemba women have evidence of Hebrew Israelite Bantus DNA and also Canaanite DNA? The only logical explanation for this is that the Canaanite Pygmies and Bantus "Negro" were found in Israel and Arabia during ancient times.

(**Above**) Baka Tribe Pygmies. Central African Republic (**CAR**). The Central African Republic is East of Cameroon and North of the Congo.

Consider this: If today's Lemba women living in South Africa are the descendants of the old Lemba Jewish women that gave birth to today's Lemba Jews where did the maternal mtDNA of the "Bantus" people and "Pygmy" people come from? The Lemba Jewish men do not profess to be "**Bantus**" and neither do their women. Modern Scientists and Archaeologists doing work in Israel have not released records or studies proving the evidence of "Bantus" or "Pygmy" Tribe DNA in Israel. This is the "**Big Cover-up**". But the "**Truth**" is coming out in this book as you will see further.

So again, how is this possible? Were their Pygmy tribes in **Arabia** and **Yemen...where the Lemba Jews spent most of their time at**? The answer in your "**google or yahoo search engine**" is "**No**". So where did the Lemba Jews pick up the genetic markers for **Pygmy Tribe women**? They got it in Israel, where the Canaanites (Pygmies) way back in the day were living in the midst of sub-sect "**Bantus**" Negro

Israelites. What was even more interestingly was that more than one-quarter **(>25%)** of the **Lemba** women sampled by **Soodyall et al. (1996)** had the African intergenic **COII/tRNA**Lys **9-bp deletion** liked to the **Pygmy Tribes**!

(**Above**) South African Bantu-speaker **Nelson Mandela** and a **Chinese Elderly man**. Both have the "**9-bp deletion**" in their human mtDNA. Amazing isn't it! Now we can start connecting dots. Both have the single epicanthal upper eyelid fold similar to the **Khoi-San** people who also have traces of the Y-DNA "B" seen in the Pygmy tribes. **Have we found one particular "Canaanite" tribe marker using DNA?** Nelson Mandela is from the **Bantus Israelite Xhosa Tribe** which is mainly found in the eastern part of South Africa. The Bantus people on the Eastern Cape part of South Africa are Xhosa in addition to **Nguni, Sotho-Tswana, Shangaan-Tsonga**, and the **Venda/Lemba Jews**. The **Bantus Israelite Zulu Tribe** live on the Western Cape of South Africa. After Zulu, the Xhosa language is the most spoken language for native South Africans.

Here is where it gets deep!

The "**9-bp deletion**" in human mtDNA, which is found at varying frequencies in **Asia, Southeast Asia, Polynesia**, and the **New World (Native Americans)**, was also found in **81** of **919** sub-Saharan Africans.

Here is where it gets even deeper. The Khoi-San people in Africa are known to have "**Asian-looking**" eyes. However, within Africa, the deletion was **not found** among Khoisan peoples (*Half Cush/quarter Israelite/less quarter Egyptian/less than half a quarter Canaanite*) and was **rare** in African countries to the West of Nigeria, but it did occur in Pygmy-Negroid (mixed) populations from Central Africa, in Malawi and **South African Bantu-speakers (i.e. Zulu, Xhosa, Nguni, Sotho)**. The distribution of the "**9-bp deletion**" in Africa suggests that the deletion could have arisen in Central Africa (**Congo**) with the pygmies and was then introduced to Southern Africa via the dispersion of "Pygmies" from their habitat after the "**Bantu Expansion**." So did this certain "marker" originate with the **Canaanites** who after being overtaken by the **Hebrew Israelites** in Africa migrated to South Africa spreading it there and then eventually into Asia? Or did it originate somewhere else?

Fact: The Bantus language had its early beginnings with the **Ba-Kongo** (Congo), **Ba-Mileke** (Cameroon), **Ba-mbara** (Mali), **Ba-ganda** (Uganda), **Ba-tswana** (Tswana people, South Africa, Lesotho), **Ba-sutu** (Sotho people-South Africa, Lesotho), and the **Ba-Tongo** (Xhosa people-Eastern South Africa). It is said that the Bantus people were heavily densely populated in the territory extending north into Mali to modern day Nigeria, Niger, Cameroon, the Congo and Gabon. During the "**Bantus Expansion**" they spread into South Africa. It was here that many Bantus Tribes were united under **Shaka Zulu**, the 17th-18th A.D. Century King of the Zulu people. The Nguni peoples and others spread across a large part of South Africa, absorbing and displacing other peoples. Many of these South African Bantus Tribes believed in "**One Creator**", the practiced "**circumcision**", they used a "**diviner/priest**" to connect to God or the spirit of their ancestors for answers and each tribe was led by a "**Chieftain**". Some have called the "**Zulu people**", the "**Wandering Jews of Africa**". The Y-DNA of the Zulu and Xhosa people of South Africa show mostly Bantus

"Negro" "E1b1a", followed by evidence of **Canaanite and Egyptian DNA**.

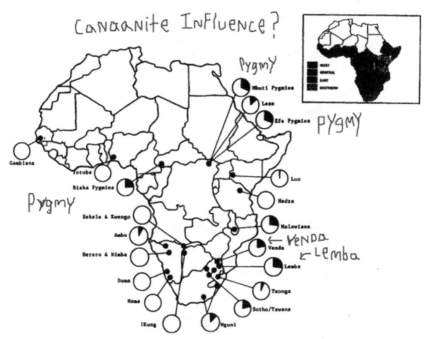

(**Above**) A map of the frequency of the "**9-bp deletion**" in Africa. As you can see the **highest** notable frequencies is seen in the Eastern Cape of South Africa where the Xhosa people live. It is also seen in a good amount of **Venda** and **Lemba Jewish people**. It is also seen in the different pygmy tribes such as the **Mbuti, Biaka**, and **Efe** tribes. Other people groups in Africa include the **Yorubas, Gambians** and **Malawians**.

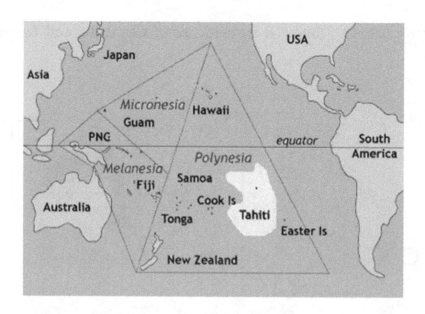

Fact: The **mtDNA 9-bp deletion marker** seen in Bantus East/South African women and the Lemba Jewish women is also seen in **very high frequencies** in the indigenous people of the Philippines (Negritos), Fiji Island, Hawaii, Samoa, Tonga, Cook Island, and Niue Island. It is also seen in very small frequencies in China, Japan, Taiwan, Vietnam and Korea. If the Lemba Jews claim they came from Israel eventually migrating into Arabia/Yemen (Shemitic territory) could this marker indicate that there are many Shemitic nations in South Asia who likewise mixed with different Canaanite tribes? If so, are the people living in Micronesia and Polynesia Israelites or are they Shemites (*i.e. Ammon, Moab, Asshur, Arphaxad, Elam, Aram, Lud, Ishmael, Edom*)? Either way we look at it Ezra 9:1-2 states the Children of Israel mixed with Canaanites, Ammonites and Moabites. So, it is safe to say that "Israelites" also scattered into the Pacific Islands and Asia.

Ezra 9:1-2 "Now when these things were done, the princes came to me, saying, **The people of Israel, and the priests, and the Levites,** have not separated themselves from the people of the lands, doing according to their abominations, even of the **Canaanites**, the Hittites, the Perizzites, the Jebusites, the **Ammonites**, the **Moabites**, the Egyptians, and the Amorites.

For they have taken of their daughters for themselves, and for their sons: **so that the holy seed have mingled themselves with the people of those lands:** yea, the hand of the princes and rulers hath been chief in this trespass."

Note: The Genetic DNA research by **Himla Soodyall** in 1996 proves there is no "**Semitic ancestry**" in the Lemba women's DNA (*per modern day genetic standards*)....even though Jewish Geneticists claim the Male Lemba Jewish Haplogroup "**J1c**" is Semitic. In the scientific/genetic world the mtDNA of Middle Eastern people-Arabs and the Ashkenazi Jews-Sephardic Jews are considered "**Semitic**". The "maternal" mtDNA of Bantus Sub-Saharan Africans, Hamitic Africans and the Lemba Jews is different than those of modern day Arabs-Jews. The paternal Y-DNA of the original Black Arab Semitic people has been diluted and "**watered down**" into today's white-skinned Arabs-Jews from centuries of intermixing. Therefore, Jewish scientists and of course the Ashkenazi-Sephardic Jewish population use the Y-DNA "**J1c**" Haplogroup to connect themselves to "**Semitic**" Ancestry. What they don't reveal is that the individuals with the highest composition of the Haplogroup "**J1**"in their genes happen to be "**Black Negroid-looking**" people (**i.e. those living in Yemen, Oman, Qatar, Sudan, Socotra, the Lemba Jews**). This poses a "**BIG PROBLEM**" in the Semitic Haplogroup "**J1c Cohenite theory**", but it also proves that in Ancient times, the descendants of the Black "Bantus" people and Pygmy people lived in what is now **Israel**....or the **Land of Canaan.** But don't take my word for it.....research it for yourself.

Source: *Soodyall, H., L. Vigilant, A.V. Hill et al. 1996. mtDNA control-region sequence variation suggests multiple independent origins of an "Asian-specific" 9-bp deletion in sub-Saharan Africans.* **The American Journal of Human Genetics.** *58(3): pg. 595–608.*

The American Journal of Human Genetics. 44: pg. 504-510, 1989 An Asian-specific 9-bp Deletion of Mitochondrial DNA Is Frequently Found in Polynesians M. Hertzberg, K. N. P. Mickleson,t S. W. Serjeantson,t J. F. Prior,§ and R. J. Trent

CHAPTER 12

"CURSE OF CANAAN" OR "CURSE OF THE PYGMIES"

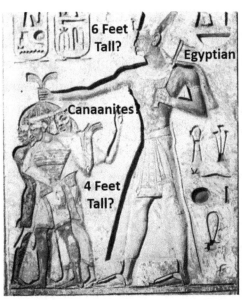

(**Above**) Pharaoh of Egypt with his Canaanite slaves caught by the hair (dreadlocks). The Canaanite/Levantine people in archaeological finds are most often shown to be wearing headbands-headscarf's. But in this picture, these grown Canaanite men caught by the hair seem to be very "**small**" in comparison to the Pharaoh of Egypt. Could it be that these Canaanites back then were the "**Pygmy**" Africans of today? In Ancient times, the Egyptians were not known to be short, and neither were the Cushites. In fact, many East Africans (*i.e. Dinka, Maasai*) are tall people (*i.e. taller than the average man or African*) and many East African Hamites or Hamitic-Shemitic mixes (*i.e. Nuba, Nuer, Dinka, Somalians, Beja, Afar*) all share evidence of the Y-DNA "**B**" in their people. They are also taller than most West Africans.

CANAAN SHALL SERVE HIS BROTHERS (BRETHREN). WHAT DOES THIS MEAN?

We know that the Sons of Ham dwelt in and around Africa. This is why Africa is called the "Land of Cham" and Egypt is referred to in many texts as "**Cham**". So who were the sons of Ham.....**Mizraim (Egypt)**, **Cush** (Nubia/Sudan, Ethiopia), **Canaan** and **Phut** (Libyan, Northwest Africans). So let's look at this, Canaan's brothers or brethren were **Cush (Sudan/Ethiopia), Mizraim (Egypt)** and **Phut** (Northwest Africa). The Bible says in Genesis 9:24-26:

"And Noah awoke from his wine, and knew what his younger son had done unto him. **And he said, cursed be Canaan; a servant of servants shall unto his brethren.** Blessed be the LORD God of Shem; **and Canaan shall be his servant.**"

So, who are the sons of Shem? The **Israelites**, Moabites, Ammonites, the Black Arabs and the Edomites? What about the descendants of Asshur, Elam, Aram, Lud and Arphaxad? They are Shemites too. In history has the "**Pygmy Tribes**" ever ruled over any nation of people in Africa? **No!** Has the "**Pygmy Tribes**" or the Asian "**Negrito Races**" ever ruled over any Semitic nation in Mesopotamia, Arabia or Asia? No! In fact, the Pygmies have been subjugated to "**oppression**" from the nations of Ham, the nations of Japheth, the nations of Shem including the nation of Israel in the land of Africa. Let's look at the scripture of the "**Curse of Canaan**".

Now consider this amazing fact,

The Republic of the **Congo** is a deeply stratified society of two major ethnic groups: **the Pygmies and the Bantus people**. The majority of Africans tested in the Congo and neighboring Cameroon are >95% **E1b1a Israelites**. However, the Pygmies are an "**older**" nation of people (**Y-DNA Haplogroup "B"**) who live in "**servitude**" to the Bantus people as well as other African Tribes. It is a known fact that the Bantus people make up the majority in the **Congo** and other countries in Africa where the pygmies are scattered. Prior to the Bantus expansion, the invasion of Egypt by foreign nations and the invasion of the "**Land of Canaan**", the pygmy tribes were numerous living all over Africa. However, in many African countries, **Pygmies belong from birth to the Bantus people in a relationship that some Bantus Israelite families call a "time-honored tradition"….however the pygmies call it "slavery".** Slavery is a form of "**SERVITUDE**". Interviews with dozens of Pygmies and Bantus over the years reveal an "**frenemy (friend + enemy)**" type of relationship that has recently in the 20th/21st Century attracted the attention of human-rights groups like **UNICEF**.

Fact: *The Pygmy tribe "**Twa people**" are stereotyped by others as backward, beggars, thieves, dirty, and stupid. The Twa are denied rights to land, they are denied the right to represent or speak for themselves, they are not permitted to eat or drink with other African nations or sit on the same bench or draw water from the same well.*

(**Above**) **Hazda** (Hadzabe) woman, Tanzania.

Fact: The **Hadza (Hadzabe)** people of Tanzania are a people who carry the same Y-DNA Haplogroup "**B**" as pygmies and to a lesser degree Y-DNA "**E1b1a**" (like the pygmies), which is seen in the Bantus "**Negro**" people. They are of short statue (*average height is 5 feet '3 inches for a man and less than 5 feet for a woman*) just like the pygmy people. Some also have an "**Asian-look**" to their outer facial appearance. They live in Northern Tanzania in the "**Great Rift Valley**". The Hadza are a nomadic people that grow no food, raise no livestock and live by no rules or calendars. They live close to the Bantus tribes in Tanzania called the "**Insanzu**" people and the "**Sukuma**" people. The Hazda people number less than 2,000 people in Tanzania. They often are forced to leave their encampment due to conflict with neighboring Bantus tribes, disease, death, droughts or to find a better land to hunt. The Hazda people say their ancestors lived during a time when there were "**giants**" called "**Akakaanebe**" or "**Gelanebe**". The also tell of **a single "Creator"** being named "**Ishoye**" who created animals, humans and giants (**Genesis 6:4**). Their oral history state the Giants turned out to be a disaster for everyone on earth as they ate the flesh of other humans (cannibalism) and even animals. **Note: This is in the Book of Enoch (Book of the Watchers).**

1 Enoch 7:9-15 "These are the names of their chiefs: **Samyaza**, who was their leader, Urakabarameel, Akibeel, Tamiel, Ramuel, Danel, Azkeel, Saraknyal, Asael, Armers, Batraal, Anane, Zavebe, Samsaveel, Ertael, Turel, Yomyael, Arazyal. There were the prefects of the **two hundred angels**, and the remainder were all with them. Then they took wives, each choosing for himself; whom they began to approach, and with whom they cohabited; **teaching them sorcery, incantations (***charms, spells like the Egyptian Book of the Dead, Coffin Texts & Pyramid Texts***), and the dividing of roots and trees (***medicine men***). And the women conceiving brought forth giants**. Whose stature was each three hundred cubits (?400+ feet tall). These devoured all which the labor of man produced; until it became impossible to feed them; **When they turned themselves against men, in order to devour them**. And began to injure birds, beasts, reptiles, and fishes, **to eat their flesh one after another, and to drink their blood**. Then the earth reproved the unrighteous."

According to the **Hazda people**, when Ishoye the "**Creator**" saw this, many of the giants were killed. This resembles the Biblical account of the Giants and the "**Great Flood**" that was sent to kill the evil wicked people of the earth, including the Giants. The Hazda people also claim in their mythology that there was a Bantus "**Isanzu**" man **(? Joshua the Israelite**) who defeated the Giants in the land of their people. This falls in line with the Hebrew Israelites coming into the Land of Canaan and being told by God to wipe out the Giants....including the Canaanites (**Exodus 33:2**). This is also written in the Book of Amos, Numbers and Joshua.

Exodus 33:2 "I will send an angel before you and I will drive out the **Canaanite**, the **Amorite**, the **Hittite**, the **Perizzite**, the **Hivite** and the **Jebusite**."

Amos 2:9-10 "Yet it was I who destroyed the Amorite before them, whose height was like the height of the cedars (100+ feet), and he was a strong as the oaks; yet I destroyed his fruit above and his roots beneath. Also it was I who brought you up from the land of Egypt, and led you forty years through the wilderness, to possess the land of the Amorite."

Numbers 13:32-33 "The land though which we have gone, **in spying out, is a land that devours (eats) its inhabitants; and all the people whom we saw in it are men of great size (giants).** There also we saw the Nephilim; and we became like grasshoppers in our own sight, and so we were in their sight."

In **Joshua 15:13** we are told that **Anak** was the son of **Arba**. We are also told in the Bible that the "**Anakim**" were giants. In Joshua 14:15 we are told that Arba was the greatest man among the Anakim. "**Kirjath Arba**" was the name of the old Canaanite city before it was renamed "**Hebron**" by the Israelites. This Canaanite city was also called "**Mamre-town**" in Genesis 35:27 in honor of the Amorite "**Mamre**" who owned the land there. In Genesis 14:13 "Mamre" was an Amorite and an ally of Abraham. **The Hazda people also claim that the Bantus "Israelite" people were allies of their ancestors and helped them defeat the Giants**....which Abraham's descendants (the Israelites) did with Joshua. And many Bantus Tribes in West Africa like the Igbo Tribe (Nigeria), the Yoruba Tribe (Nigeria), the Ewe Tribe (Ghana/Togo), the Ga-Dangme (Ghana), the Bamileke Tribe (Cameroon) and the Tutsi Tribe (Rwanda) all say that they are Israelites. Coincidence? I think not.

Today the Hadza (Hadzabe) people's existence is being threatened by the larger more numerous Tanzanian Bantus people taking over the land that the Hadza have been living on for thousands of years. **Note:** *This can be seen in the Documentary film "Hazda: Last of the First".* Before the "Bantus" Israelites migrated into Africa, the Land of Ham (Africa) was full of Hamitic tribes....including the Hazda people. Likewise, the pygmy people have also been losing their land to the more numerous Bantus people…thanks to the **"Bantus Expansion"**. But the struggle doesn't end there. The Pygmy people in Africa complain of not being paid fairly for often exhausting, back-breaking work. They also complain of discrimination that limits their access to health centers, schools, voting, owning land and traveling. Many Pygmies say the Bantus people consider them less than human. When interviewed about this, some Bantus people say, for their part, that Pygmies are an uneducated, less advanced people who cannot be trusted with money and still rely on the guidance of masters to survive.

Pygmies, who make up between 5 to 10 percent of Congo's population, are responsible for much of the hunting, fishing and manual labor in jungle villages. Pygmies are often paid at their master's discretion: in cigarettes, used clothing, or even nothing at all. They have no power over the other Tribes in Africa with Hamitic roots (*i.e. Dogon, Alur, Dinka, Nuba, Nuer, Hammer*).

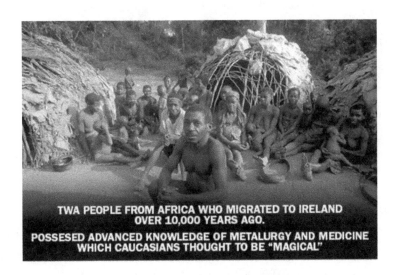

TWA PEOPLE FROM AFRICA WHO MIGRATED TO IRELAND OVER 10,000 YEARS AGO.
POSSESED ADVANCED KNOWLEDGE OF METALURGY AND MEDICINE WHICH CAUCASIANS THOUGHT TO BE "MAGICAL"

Does this sound like a people who are in a sort of **"servitude"** status to everyone around them? But it gets more interesting when we look at the Pygmy people and their similarities to the Biblical **"Canaanites"**. The Pygmy people still hold onto an old Egyptian-Canaanite god called

359

"**Bes**", who brought good luck to the people of Canaan. "**Bes**" was a dwarf god and was known for "**Good things**" like fighting off **evil spirits** or fertility so he was also associated with music, dancing and sexual pleasure. By 500 B.C., statues-images of "**Bes**" could be found as far North as Turkey and as far East as Iran or Central Asia. In Scotland/Ireland, the "Negroid" **Twa Pygmies** (pictured above) who were found to be living there were believed by other nations to have magical powers (*i.e. Metallurgy, Alchemy and the ability to cure disease with different remedies*). This is because the Canaanite-Egyptian god "**Bes**" was associated with good "**white magic**". The dwarf god "**Bes**" also loved gold and people believed he would bring wealth or good fortune to people's home. This is where the notion of the "**Leprechaun**" and "**Good luck wishes**" comes from.

(**Above**) Canaanite-Egyptian god "**Bes**" and a modern day "Leprechaun". British Egyptologists Gerald Massey, Albert Churchward, Scottish historian David Mac Ritchie, Sir Godfrey Higgins, Tacitus, Pliny, Claudian and other writers have described the people living in the British Isles, Spain, Portugal, Morocco and other parts of the world as "**Black as Ethiopians**". Other names were "**Cum Nigris Gentibus**", "nimble-footed", "**black dwarfs**" and so on. The noted that these "**Black pygmies**" buried their dead in **caves**....similar to how the Israelite patriarchs buried their dead in caves (*see Genesis*

23:9, Genesis 49:29-33) and how the Dzopa "**yellow pygmy**" big-headed alien race that landed their ship in the mountains of Tibet-China buried their dead in caves.

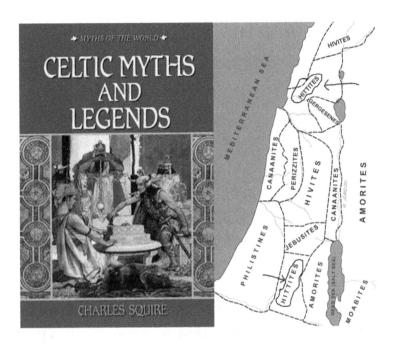

(**Above**) In the Book "**Celtic Myths and Legends**", author Charles Squire uses a quote from British Professor Thomas Henry Huxley from the 19th Century. He connects the "**Black Pygmy**" race seen in Europe, and Africa as being related to the **Canaanite "Sons of Heth"**....aka "**The Hittites**" from whom Abraham dwelt among in the Bible. The land of Canaan before the Israelites possessed it was inhabited by the Sons of Canaan. This included the **Hittites**, Amorites, Hivites, Jebusites, Perizzites, and so on. How did Professor Huxley in the 1800's come to this conclusion about the "**Pygmy Tribes**" being Canaanites?

Genesis 23:2-7 "Sarah died in Kiriath-arb (that is, **HEBRON**) in the land of **CANAAN**; and Abraham went in to mourn for Sarah (his wife) and to weep for her. Then Abraham rose from before his dead, and spoke to the **SONS OF HETH**, saying "I am a **stranger** and a **sojourner** among you; give me a burial site among you that I may bury my dead out of my sight." The sons of Heth answered Abraham, saying to him, "Hear us, my lord, you are a mighty prince among us; bury your dead in the choices of our graves; none of us will refuse you his grave for burying your dead."....So Abraham rose and bowed to the people of the land, the **SONS OF HETH**."

(**Above**) Map of Israel, with the Hittite city "**Hebron**" located below Jerusalem and Bethlehem. This is how we know that it is possible that in ancient times the "Pygmy Tribes" were the Canaanites of the Bible.

Genesis 10:15 "And Canaan begat Sidon his first born, and **HETH**".

(**Above**) British Professor and Biologist **Thomas Henry Huxley** 1825-1895 A.D.

But don't take my word for it...read **Professor Thomas Henry Huxley's** statement in the 1800's.

"In physique, it (**pygmies**) was short, **swarthy (dark-skinned)**, dark-haired, dark-eyed, and long-skulled; its language belonged to the class called "**HAMITIC**", the **SURVIVING** types of which are found among the **Gallas** (East Africa Hamites), Abyssinians (**Cushites**), Berbers (**Phuttites**), and other North African tribes; and it seems to have come originally from some part either of Eastern, Northern or Central Africa. Spreading thence, it was probably the first people to inhabit the Valley of the Nile, and it sent offshoots into Syria and Asia Minor (**Hittite territory**). The earliest Hellenes (**i.e. Ancient Greeks**) found it in Greece under the name of "**Pelasgoi**"; the earliest Latins in Italy, as the "**Estruscans**"' and the **Hebrews in Palestine**, as the "**HITTITES**".

One thing is for sure is that the **Estruscans** and **Pelasgoi** people were always depicted as being a "**melaninated**" people and not "**white**".

But something is "odd" about the Pygmy people's short stature in comparison to the other Hamitic people in Africa. Did God create a "**dwarf race**" of people or did the Fallen Angels and the Nephilim manipulate the genes of the Hamitic Canaanites when they mixed with them? Or did the Fallen Angels do a **"genetic experiment"** with some of the Canaanite people, thus prompting Abraham and Isaac to warn Jacob's seed to not to mix with the daughters of the Canaanites?

Genesis 24:2-3 "Abraham said to his servant, the oldest of his household, who had charge of all that he owned, "Please place your hand under my thigh, and I will make you swear by the LORD, the God of heaven and the God of earth, that you **shall not take a wife for my son from the daughters of the Canaanites, among whom I live.**"

Genesis 28:1 "And Isaac called Jacob, and blessed him, and charged him, and said unto him, **Thou shalt not take a wife of the daughters of the Canaanites.**"

Let's investigate this.

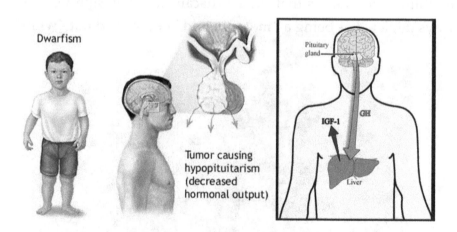

Dwarfism

Tumor causing hypopituitarism (decreased hormonal output)

Pituitary gland

IGF-1

GH

Liver

Fact: Pygmies do not exhibit the medical traits of **"dwarfism"** but they are still smaller than the average human. **"Dwarfs"** are short because of a tumor causing decreased function of the pituitary gland (i.e. hypopituitarism). **Pygmies** do not grow because they lack (IGF-1) or **"Insulin Growth Factor-1"**. The Pituitary gland secretes the **"Growth Hormone (GH)"** into the bloodstream stimulating a feedback mechanism that tells the **liver** to produce **"IGF-1"**. Children that

364

secrete too much "**Growth Hormone**" are diagnosed with "**Gigantism**". Adults that have too much "**Growth Hormone**" and thus elevated **IGF-1 levels** have an enlargement of bone, tissue and muscle which is called "**Acromegaly**". The Pygmy people have a problem with their "**GH-Growth Hormone receptor gene**". Therefore, giving pygmies the "**Growth Hormone**" will not cause any response in the liver to produce IGF-1 which is responsible for muscle, tissue and skeletal growth. Did the "Fallen Angels" do some type of manipulation of the human genome to cause these "**defects**" in the pituitary gland or the "GH receptors" creating a race of "**giants**" and a race of "**pygmies**"?

CHAPTER 13

SIMILARITIES BETWEEN THE PYGMY TRIBE ANCIENT ALPHABET AND THE PALEO-HEBREW/PHOENICIAN ALPHABET

Phoenician	Paleo-Hebrew	Hebrew letter (Dfus)	English name
𐤀	𐤀	א	Aleph
𐤁	𐤁	ב	Bet
𐤂	𐤂	ג	Gimel
𐤃	𐤃	ד	Dalet
𐤄	𐤄	ה	He
𐤅	𐤅	ו	Waw

(Above) Paleo Hebrew and the Canaanite-Phoenician writing script is basically identical. This is partly because of the constant mixing of the Israelites and Canaanites that started perhaps with the Ancient Hebrews (*i.e. Abraham, Nahor, Haran, Lot, Joktan*). We know that in the Bible (*i.e. Judges 3*), the Israelites started having children with the Canaanites before they even had their first King (Saul) in 1300 B.C. We also know Abraham (*i.e. the first Hebrew*), lived amongst the Hamitic Canaanite people. Could Ancient Paleo-Hebrew have sprung from the Phoenician script? **Could Abra-HAM have gotten his name from association with the Hamitic Pygmies? Did he teach the Canaanite people the Ancient Hebrew alphabet script?**

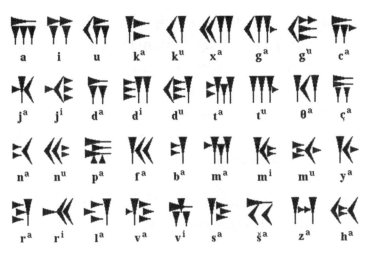

a i u kᵃ kᵘ xᵃ gᵃ gᵘ cᵃ

jᵃ jⁱ dᵃ dⁱ dᵘ tᵃ tᵘ θᵃ çᵃ

nᵃ nᵘ pᵃ fᵃ bᵃ mᵃ mⁱ mᵘ yᵃ

rᵃ rⁱ lᵃ vᵃ vⁱ sᵃ šᵃ zᵃ hᵃ

(**Above**) Shemitic Akkadian/Babylonian/Assyrian script. This is similar to the writing style of the Sumerians. The sons of Shem (**Asshur, Arphaxad, Aram, Lud, Elam**) wrote in a cuneiform script that was slightly different than Paleo-Hebrew, however the pronunciation of this language compared to Hebrew is very similar for certain words. The Akkadian/Babylonian/Assyrian language pronunciations also can be seen in India. To view this, simply compare the writing styles of the Sumerians, Akkadians, Babylonians and Assyrians. Also, compare these writing styles to the Indus Valley "**Harappan**" and the "**Brahma Tamil**" Cuneiform script.

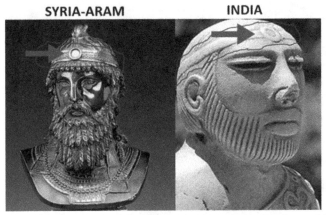

(**Left**) Syrian (Aram) Nobleman.   (**Right**) Indus Valley man (India/Pakistan).

From the Harappan and Brahma Script came the Indian languages **Malayalam, Telugu, Tamil, Bengali, Punjabi, Oriya, Gujrati, Sinhala** and the **Kannada** alphabet. Since we know these are not European **"Japhetic"** or African **"Hamitic"** languages....these have to be in the **"Shemitic"** parent language family. It is a known fact that the Malayalam language of Kerala has some Hebrew and Assyrian influences. How is this possible? Easy!

It shows in the Malayalam language of Kerala, Southwest India where they were often called "Untouchables" or "Dalits".

Kerala - Holy Spirit-Rooha
Hebrew-Ruach

Kerala - Angel-Malakha
Hebrew-Malak or Malakim

Kerala – Passover-Pesaha
Hebrew Pesach.

Kerala-Anointed-Mishiha
Hebrew-Mashiach.

Kerala-Mother-Amma
Hebrew-Ema/Ima/Eima.

Kerala-Moses-Moshe
Hebrew-Mosheh.

Kerala-Jehovah-Yehowah
Hebrew-Yahuah-Yahuwa

Kerala-Jesus-Yesu/Yeshu

Hebrew/Aramaic-Yahusha/Yeshua.

Kerala-Jew-Yehudim
Hebrew Yehudi.

So how can this be? Maybe these Indians are the Israelites scattered amongst the ELAMITES in ISAIAH 11:11 or Acts 2:9. Maybe these people in South India are descendants of the Hebrew Israelites that left Northern Israel around 700 B.C. and eventually settled in India for a home.

TECHNICAL DEVELOPMENTS OF THE ALPHABETIC SIGNS WHICH MAY BE TERMED AS "LINEAR SMALL HAND"	BRAHMI	SEMITIC AND CLASSICAL	TRADITIONAL INDIAN	PHONETIC VALUE
	૬		ई	F
				DH
♪ ♪ 370 PICXVII-13	ત	૬૨૬		SĀ S'
402 PIC XVII 414	ƷƑ Ƭ, ƲƑ	Ƴ	♉✕	ʒ A

(**Above**) Here you can see the transition from the Early "**Harappan**" script (left) to Brahmi to Semitic Paleo-Hebrew and Traditional "Indian" script (right). Can you can see the obvious similarities? The Semitic Harappan script eventually "evolved" in India/South India to Brahmi/Tamil Brahmi. **Tamil Brahmi is only seen in South India/Sri Lanka**. Again, notice the similarities between Traditional Indian script, Brahmi, Harappan and the Semitic Hebrew letter "**Alef**". Coincidence? How is the Indus Valley script similar to the Hebrew Semitic script? If you compare the Shemitic **Sabaean script** (*i.e. Joktanite script*) used in South Arabia you will see that it also has some similarities to the ancient "**Harappan**" Indus Valley Script.

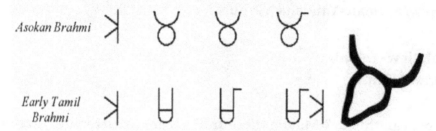

Asokan Brahmi

Early Tamil Brahmi

(Left) The **Harappan script** (2600 B.C. to 1900 B.C.), **Asokan Brahmi Script** (280 B.C.), and **Tamil Brahmi Script** (200 B.C. to 200 A.D.) are all B.C. scripts/alphabets that were used in the territory of **India**. Above is the first letter which would be considered "A" in the early Indus Valley script. (**Right**) The first letter "**Alef**" in the Paleo-Hebrew script. The Paleo-Hebrew **Ox-head** "Alef" symbol bears "striking" similarities to the **Asokan Brahmi script** of Ancient India.

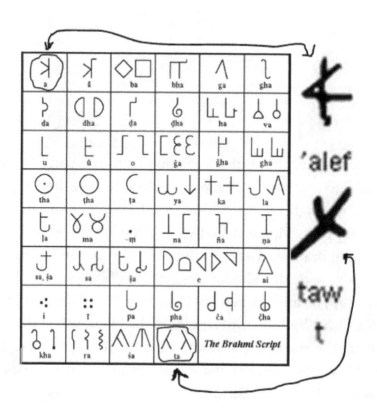

'alef

taw
t

The Brahmi Script

(**Above**) The 1st letter/symbol of the Indus Valley (India) Brahmi Script starts with an "**A**" letter-symbol that seems to mimic the 1st letter/symbol of the Paleo-Hebrew script "**Alef**". The last letter/symbol of the Brahmi Script is "Ta" which also resembles the last letter in the Paleo-Hebrew Alphabet "**Tav**". Coincidence? This is similar to the Ethiopian Jewish language of "**Ge'ez**".

From the Harappan and Brahma Script came the Indian Telugu, Tamil, Bengali, Punjabi, Gujrati, Sinhala, Malayalam and Kannada alphabet. Again, since we know these are not Japhetic European "**Germanic/Slavic/Turkish**" languages or African Hamitic languages....these have to be in the **Semitic language family**. This would make a lot of people in India the descendants of Shem. Now comes the big question. Which lineage of Shem do they belong to and are there more Shemites further east in Asia?

(**Above**) The **Gezer Calendar Stone** written in **Canaanite-Phoenician** script dates back to 925 B.C. during the era of **King Solomon** and **King David**. The Canaanite land of Gezer was one of many pieces of land given to King Solomon by other nations. Prior to "**Gezer's**" defeat by the Egyptians, the Israelites were not able to drive out all of the Canaanites in the city of Gezer. After taking over Gezer, King Solomon was given the Canaanite city "**Gezer**" by the Pharaoh of Egypt as a "**dowry gift**" for marrying his daughter.

1 Kings 9:16
"Pharaoh king of Egypt had gone up, and taken **Gezer**, and burnt it with fire, and slain the **Canaanites** that dwelt in the city, and given it for a portion unto his daughter, Solomon's wife."

- **Joshua 16:10 "And they drove not out the Canaanites that dwelt in Gezer**; but the Canaanites dwelt in the midst of Ephraim, unto this day, and became servants to do taskwork."
- **Judges 1:29** "And **Ephraim** drove not out the Canaanites that dwelt in **Gezer**; but the **Canaanites dwelt in Gezer among them.**"

The "**Gezer Calendar stone**" is considered Canaanite-Phoenician, or basically Old Paleo-Hebrew. But the scribe of the Gezer Calendar was written as "**Abiyah**" which means "**Yah is my Father**". This obviously was a Hebrew Israelite name as were many name of Hebrew Israelite slaves taken from West Africa. But if this stone was dated to 925 B.C. during King Solomon's timeline, was the writing influenced by the **Canaanites** or the **Hebrews**? After all, 400 years prior to this date in 1300 B.C. the Israelites and Canaanites were already mixing with the people of the lands (Canaanites/Philistines). This was during the time of the "**Judges**" like "**Deborah the Israelite Prophetess**" when Israel had no King and they were tested by God in battle or to see if they would not marry "foreign peoples" who would "sway" them to worship their pagan gods.

Judges 3:1-6 "Now these are the nations which the LORD left, to prove Israel by them, even as many of Israel as had not known all the wars of Canaan; Only that the generations of the children of Israel might know, to teach them war, at the least such as before knew nothing thereof; Namely, five lords of the **Philistines**, and all the **Canaanites**, and the Sidonians, and the Hivites that dwelt in mount Lebanon, from mount Baal Hermon unto the entering in of Hamath. And they were to prove Israel by them, to know whether they would hearken unto the commandments of the LORD, which he commanded their fathers by the hand of Moses. And the children of Israel dwelt among the **Canaanites**, **Hittites**, and **Amorites**, and **Perizzites**, and **Hivites**, and **Jebusites**: **And they took their daughters to be their wives, and gave their daughters to their sons, and served their gods.**"

So, by reading this, it would be hard to tell if the writing style of the "**Gezer Calendar**" by the scribe "**Abiyah**" was basically a "fused" writing style from the intermarriages of the Israelites and Canaanite tribes. Even today many Pygmy Tribes speak languages that favor the Bantu languages of the Bantu Tribes they live amongst (i.e. Congo, Cameroon).

Note: *Prior to King Saul, King David and King Solomon....the Israelites spoke (and wrote) Hebrew mixed with Egyptian influences. Other variations were Egyptian mixed with Hebrew influences. This was called "**Egyptian Hieratic**" script mixed with Hebrew. Many archaeological finds with this type of writing were found in Israel dating back to 1300 B.C. Because the Israelites mixed with the Egyptians for over 400 years and because they also left a "mixed multitude" with Moses (i.e. Joseph, his Egyptian wife, sons Ephraim/Manasseh) the Israelites were fluent in both languages (**Egyptian-Hebrew**). It was also reported that this Egyptian-Hebrew archaic type of writing found in Ancient Israel (i.e. dating back to 1300 B.C.) was also found to be similar to the writing of some Native America tribes by Mormon archaeologists.*

But this is just the "**Tip of the Iceberg**" as certain "Pygmy Tribes" were found to have a writing style similar to **Phoenician/Canaanite-Paleo-Hebrew** script in addition to knowledge of Canaanite gods (**i.e. "Bes"**) and Egyptian Gods (**i.e. Ptah, Horus**). How can this be possible? Well, perhaps the descendants of the "Canaanites of old" are today's pygmy tribes scattered all throughout the world. Now consider this "**stunning fact**".

Egyptian texts from around 2300 B.C. refer to the Pygmies as little men from the "**land of trees and spirits**" at the foot of the "**Mountains of the Moon**". In Ancient Biblical times, Egyptian **King Pepi II** Neferkare (2200 B.C.) sent an expedition into Central Africa (i.e. Congo, Central African Republic, Zaire) and returned with a dancing dwarf known as "**Akka**". In the "**Pyramid Texts**" of the sixth Egyptian dynasty ruler "**Pepi I**" it was declared that, "**He who is between the thighs of Nut is the Pygmy who danceth like the god and who pleaseth the heart of the god before his great throne.**" In ancient Egyptian mythology, "**Nut**" was the goddess of heaven-sky and the **mother of Osiris**. The small "pygmy" that was dancing between the thighs of Nut was the "**extremely short**" Canaanite god called "**Bes**".....the same god the Pygmies are familiar with. The "Canaanites" in ancient times were used in Egyptian palaces/temples to dance around and make people laugh. Today, the "Pygmies" are known for their dancing and "cheerful spirits". So, if the god between Nut's thigh is a short pygmy Canaanite god then this could be even more proof that the Canaanites of "old" were a race of short "pygmy people" in Africa.

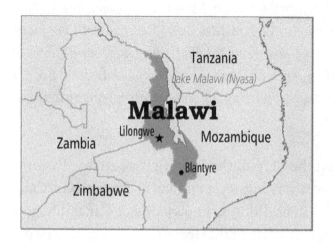

(**Above**) Malawi is an English-speaking country in which Bantus people like the **Chewa and Ngoni (Angoni) tribe** live. It was subjugated to slavery during the Arab Slave Trade and was invaded/colonized (i.e. *like Nigeria and other Bantus Israelite lands*) by the British (i.e. *like the British-Zulu Wars*). But in Malawi also live the "**Abatwa Pygmy**" people. Malawi Bantus people (*i.e. Chewa, Lomwe*) also carry the same Y-DNA "**E1b1a**" as other African-Americans and Bantus West Africans (*i.e. Igbo, Yoruba, Akan/Ashanti, Mandingo, Mande, Bambara*). DNA markers specific for the Chewa Tribe can be found in the Congo as well as in South America (Brazil, Columbia). It is a known fact that many slavetraders took Malawi/Mozambique Bantus around Africa west to the Americas and the Caribbean.

Well, moving right along.....the "**AbaTWA**" Pygmy people in Malawi claim to be the inhabitants of the ancient mountains of the "**San (*aka. Khoisan Bushmen*)**" people and the "**Twa**" people. They say that they lived amongst the "**Langwani Giants**" (*as many Canaanite tribes like the Amorites lived amongst the Giants after the flood in the Book of Joshua*). Even till this day, many Abatwa "**Sapitwa**" healers known as the "**Nganga**" or "**asing'anga amizimu**" still use an alphabet/writing script that is similar to **Ancient Phoenician-Canaanite** script despite their claims in history books as being "**illiterate**". Their name "**Nganga**" means "**healers dealing with the spirit**".

Ka	Ya	Ta	Chaa	ZA	Wa	Ha	Da	Ga	Ba	Ah
כ ך	י	ט	ח	ז	ו	ה	ד	ג	ב	א

Tha	Sha	Ra	Qa	Taza	Pa	I	Sa	Na	Ma	La
ת	ש	ר	ק	צ ץ	פ ף	ע	ס	נ ן	מ ם	ל

(Above) Modern Hebrew Alphabet with their "**suggested**" Paleo-Hebrew pronunciations (i.e. Ya, Ha, Wa, Sha, I).

It is "**suggested**" because there is not one group/race of people living today on the planet that still retain the knowledge of how to completely "speak" and "write" in Ancient Paleo-Hebrew (*without vowels/vowel points*).

Some people claim there are few "**Malawi Pygmies**" left in the Mulanje village that still know how to write the ancient "**Abatwa**" alphabet which many say is eerily similar to the Paleo-Hebrew/Phoenician alphabet. The Abatwa priests' language pronunciation "**Ah**" corresponds to the Modern-Paleo Hebrew letter "**A**" or "**Aleph/Alef**" but it matches with the Paleo-Hebrew pronunciation of "**Alef**". Their pronunciation "**Ba**" corresponds to the Modern-Paleo Hebrew letter "**B**" or "**Bet**". Their pronunciation "**Ca**" corresponds to the Modern-Paleo Hebrew letter "**C/Ch**" or "**H**" or "**Chet/Het**". This is similar to how some Paleo-Hebrew researchers/scholars pronounce the name of God as "**Ya-Ha-Wa-Ah (i.e. ah is silent)**" which is similar to what the Native Indians pronounced the Creators name as "**Ya-ho-wa**". This is also where they get the name "**Ya-Wa-Ha-Sh-I**" as the "**suggested**" Paleo-Hebrew name of Jesus Christ.

Fact: *In the Old Swahili Bible, the name of God is listed as "Yahuwa". It is a known fact that Swahili is composed of about **fifty-percent** "Bantus language" and about **twenty-five percent** "Arabic". If this is the case.....and "Old Swahili" evolved from Tanzania, Africa, where would the word "Yahuwa" come from to make its way into the early 1800's A.D. "Swahili Bible"? Did it come from the "**Arabic culture**" or the "**Bantus Hebrew Israelite culture**"?*

H#3068 + H#3467 = H#3091

𐤉𐤄𐤅𐤄 + 𐤏𐤔𐤉 = 𐤏𐤔𐤅𐤄𐤉

יהוה‎   ישע‎   יהושע‎

Yahuah + *yasha* = *Yahusha*

(Father)   (Saves)   (Messiah)

Yahuah Saves

Today, many use "**Yahuah**" or "**Yahawah**" or "**Yah**" + "**Hawah/Hayah**" which is the name of God in the Bible. Note: **Yah** + **Hayah/Hawah**" means "**God Exists/God will be**". Some Israelites choose to use the word "**Yahuah, Yahawah or Ahayah**" as the name of God. From the word "**Yah**" comes the word for Christ (Jesus) which many choose to write as "**Yahusha, Yahshua, Yeshua, Yehoshua**, and **Yahushua** which basically means in Hebrew "**God is my Salvation/Savior**". However, some state that Christ's name in Hebrew is the Hebrew word "**My Savior/deliverer**" which is pronounced "**Yashiya/Yashaya**" (from #3467 Yasha (Savior/Salvation) + Yod-Ya (Personal Pronoun like "**My, your, his/her, their**").

ישוע‎ = YESHUA USED 28 TIMES IN TANAK

יהושע‎ = YAHUSHA USED 216 TIMES IN TANAK

יהושוע‎ = YAHUSHUA USED 2 TIMES IN TANAK

ע ו ש ו ה י‎ YOD-HAY-UAU-SHIN-UAU-AYIN: "YAHUSHUA"

The two uses of this 6-lettered spelling are found at Deut. 3:21 and Judg. 2:7

Note: Depending on how one interprets the Hebrew pronunciation for what is in the Torah listed for the name "**Joshua**" one can come up with different variations of Christ's name....also depending if one uses the "**a**" vs the "**e**" after the letter "**Yod**". For some the "**Shin**" and "**Ayin**" represents the pronunciation "**sha**" in the word "**Yahusha**". For some, the "**Shin**", "**Vav/Waw/Uau**" and "**Ayin**" represents the pronunciation "**Shua**" in the words "**Yahshua/Yeshua**" or "**Yahushua/Yehoshua**".

DON'T FALL FOR ANY OF THESE TRICKS THAT SAY "YAH" OR "YAHUAH" IS PAGAN IN ORIGIN

Many Hebrew Israelites today simply reject "**Yah**" or "**Yahuah/Yahuwa**" as the name of the Creator because of the "**Asherah and Yahweh**" Inscriptions. This often leads to the "**Egyptian Moon god Iah**" DECEPTION. Therefore, many Israelites simply use "**Ahayah**" for the name of God based of the Hebrew letter "**Aleph**" + "**Hayah**" which can be similar to saying "**GOD EXISTS**" or "**THE CREATOR EXISTS**". Hebrew Strong's #1961 "**Hayah**" means "**To Become**", "**To be**", or "**To come to past**". In our King James Bible in Exodus 3:14 it is listed as "**I AM THAT I AM**" or "**I AM WHICH I AM**" or "**I WILL BE WHAT I WILL BE**". This comes from the verb "**Hayah**" plus the Hebrew Strong's #834 conjunction/adverb "**Asher**" which means "**Who, which or that**". But here is where it gets interesting. The word "**Ahayah**" has "**Yah**" in it and it also has the "**Aleph**" letter in it. So, when people think "Yah" is referring to a pagan god they need to ask why do they use it in "Aha**YAH**" or "Hallelu-**YAH**". All the Hebrew words have an intricate meaning behind it when you find out what the "Paleo-Hebrew" pictograph meaning is of the Modern Hebrew letter.

The "**Aleph**" symbolizes the "**Ox**", the "**Master**", "**Leader**", "**Lord**" and "**Strength**". But it also symbolizes the God-Man "Yahusha (Yahshua/Yeshua) HaMashiach"....aka Jesus Christ in our King James Bible. The Aleph symbolizes "**God the father**" as it is the beginning letter in the words "**Elohim**", "**Eloah**", "**El-Shaddai**", "**El Elyon**", and "**Abba**".

In **Philippians 2:6-11** it states, "Who (Christ), being in the form of God.....took upon himself the form of a servant...**as a man**". In **Revelation 22:13**, Christ refers to himself as the "**Aleph**" and "**Tav**", the First and the Last. Christ also reveals that the pictograph Paleo-Hebrew Alphabet would provide revelation about himself being God. This can be seen in **Isaiah 41:4, Isaiah 44:6** and **Isaiah 48:12** where "Yahuah (listed as The LORD)" refers to himself as the "**Aleph and Tav**", the "First and the Last".......and that there is no other "**god**" beside Him.

(**Left**) Modern Hebrew word for "Yahuah". (**Right**) Paleo-Hebrew word for "Yahuah".

In Paleo Hebrew, the "Tetragrammaton" (**Above**) or "**Yod-Hey-Vav-Hey**" four Hebrew letters that make up God's name can be deciphered as "**Behold the hand, Behold the Nail**"....giving reference to Christ the "**God-man**" being Crucified with nails in his hands.

Here is where the deception comes in. It was common for all ancient civilizations to attach a "**consort-wife**" to a male god. For the Hebrew Israelites, this was "**Asherah**". Asherah poles and idols were found in Israel in Samaria as it was used by the Israelites (*see 2 Kings 23*). But Asherah was also worshipped by King Solomon and was also synonymous with the pagan female goddess "**The Queen of Heaven**"....in Jeremiah 44/Jeremiah 7. In Babylon, she was linked to "**Astarte**" and "**Ishtar**". All throughout the Bible, the Israelites were told to cut down or break the "Asherah" poles.....because the God of Israel did not have a wife. This angered Yahuah so much that he told Jeremiah that they were to not to worship "Asherah" as the "Queen of Heaven". This practice of "Queen of Heaven" worship still continues today in the form of "Mami Wata" in West Africa, America and the Caribbean.

However, what people do not realize is that before Egypt existed, before Sumeria existed and before Canaan existed....the Children of Seth already knew of the name "**Yahuah**"

Genesis 4:26 "And to Seth, to him also there was born a son; and he called his name Enos: then began men to **call upon** the name of the **LORD (Yahuah)**."

But here is something to consider, since we do not have access to the Torah Dead Sea Scrolls written in Paleo-Hebrew dating back to 400 B.C., how do we know if there wasn't a "**word change**" by man in this English authorized Bible scripture?

"Then began men to **forget** the name of the LORD (Yahuah)."
"Then began men to **profane** the name of the LORD (Yahuah)."

Changing the word "call upon" to "**forget**" or "**profane**" creates a whole different meaning to the scripture.

In **Exodus 6:3** it reads "And I appeared unto Abraham, unto Isaac, and unto Jacob, by the name of God Almighty (El Shaddai), but by my name **YAHUAH** was I not known to them.

In this scripture, a simple change from an ending "**period**" to an ending "**question mark**" also changes the whole meaning of the scripture. See for yourself.

Exodus 6:3 "And I appeared unto Abraham, unto Isaac, and unto Jacob, by the name of **God Almighty (El Shaddai)**, but by my name **YAHUAH** was I not known to them?

Remember, in **Genesis 22:14** in our English King James Bible it reads: "And Abraham called the name of that place **Jehovah-Jireh (i.e. Yahuah provides)**: as it is said to this day, In the mount of the LORD it shall be seen."

In some translations, it reads "And Abraham called the name of that place **The LORD will provide**: as it is said to this day, In the mount of the **LORD** it shall be seen."

In the **Mechon-Mamre Hebrew Bible** it reads:

Genesis 22:14 "And Abraham called the name of that place **Adonai-Jireh**; as it is said to this day: 'In the mount where the **LORD** is seen."

This Jews replace the word "**Yahuah**" with the word "**Adonai**" because they do not want to acknowledge or reveal the True name of the Creator. But in the Hebrew script it reads:

וַיִּקְרָא אַבְרָהָם שֵׁם-הַמָּקוֹם הַהוּא, יְהוָה יִרְאֶה, אֲשֶׁר יֵאָמֵר הַיּוֹם, בְּהַר יְהוָה יֵרָאֶה.

Notice that there are two instances where the Tetragrammaton word for "**YAHUAH**" is seen as what the Jews replace with "**LORD**" or "**ADONAI**".

Notice that in the first book of the Bible (Genesis)…Abraham has to know the name of the Creator as YAHUAH in order to name the place were Isaac's sacrifice was stopped as "**Jehovah-Jireh**" or "**Yahuah-Jireh**". In the Second book of the Torah (Exodus) God reveals that Abraham, Isaac and Jacob knew of him as "El Shaddai/God Almighty" but didn't they also know his true name as **Yahuah**? This scenario could be possibly seen as so if the ending character was a "?" instead of a "." as such is below.

Exodus 6:3 "And I appeared unto Abraham, unto Isaac, and unto Jacob, by the name of **God Almighty (El Shaddai)**, but by my name **YAHUAH** was I not known to them?

Consider this extra-biblical archaeological fact. In the Elba Tablets from Syria/North Israel.....it was found that many names that used to be MichaEL changed to MikaYAH (i.e. Micah). The Ishmaelite Arabs knew the name of the Israelites creator as "**Yahuwa, Yah-Huwa, and Yahuah**" before Muhammad was born. Even many West African names for God such as OluWA (Yoruba), OsanobUWA (Benin-Edo), OsebrUWA (Western Igbos), ChukWU (Eastern Igbos), MaWU (Fon-Benin/Dahomey), NyaWE/NyaME (Akan-Ashanti) show proof that the Bantus West Africans still have evidence of their knowledge of the Creators original name. It is a known fact that the name Yahuah is listed in the Book of Psalms some 700 times and is in the Hebrew Tanakh over 5,000 times. The name Yahuah has been found written etched in stone and on papyrus leaves. Nowhere has "**Ahayah**" been found in the magnitude that "Yahuah-Yod/Hey/Vav/Hey" has been found. But consider this important fact!

Singular					
Person	Gender	Subject	Object	Prenominal Possessive	Possessive Pronoun
1st		I	Me	my	Mine
2nd		You	You	Your	Yours
3rd	M	He	Him	his	His
	F	She	Her	Her	Hers
	N	It	its	Its	Its

When God spoke to Moses he said "**I AM THAT I AM**".....which basically can be like saying "**I EXIST**". God was talking to Moses in "**1st Person**" with the verb "**to be, to become, or to exist**". Of course, God would not answer Moses with the 2nd person response "**YOU AM**

382

THAT YOU AM" or the 3rd person response "HE IS THAT HE IS". We also know that God would not answer Moses by saying "YOU AM" or "HE IS" when he is talking about himself....that wouldn't make sense. So, when Moses came back down off the mountain (Mt. Sinai), the Israelites probably were anxious to ask Moses the question, "**What did God say his name was while you were up there on the mountain?**" Moses, if using "3rd Person" as he should have been, would've said "**HE EXISTS**" or "**HE WILL BE WHAT HE WILL BE**". This was an easy way for God to tell Moses "**I am omnipotent**" and "**Existing**" without giving him a name. But in Exodus 3:15 God says:

"**MOREOVER (i.e. to top that)**, Thus shalt thou say unto the Children of Israel, **YAHUAH ELOHIM** (The LORD God) of your fathers, the God of Abraham, the God of Isaac, and the God of Jacob, hath sent me unto you: This is my **SHEM** (name) **FOREVER**, and this is my memorial unto **ALL GENERATIONS**.

So, let's consider what Moses would've said God's name was to the Children of Israel in **THIRD PERSON!**

(Left) Hebrew word "**Hayah**" or "to become, to be, or exist". (**Right**) Hebrew word "**Yahuah**" which means "**Behold the hand, Behold the nail**" or "**He Exists**". So who is "**He**"? The "**Creator**" of course! **Note:** The only different between "**Hayah**" and "**YAHUAH**" is the Hebrew "**Yod**" prefix letter at the beginning. Remember "**Hayah**" means "**To exist, to become or to be**".

AHAYAH OR YAHUAH?

It is a known fact in Hebrew grammar, there are several "**prefixes**" which are added to regular words to introduce a new meaning. These Hebrew letters that form "**prefixes**" are called "**formative letters**". These "formative" letters in the Hebrew script are known as **Aleph** (א), **Bet** (ב), **Hey** (ה), **Vav** (ו), **Yod** (י), **Kaf**(כ), **Lamed** (ל), **Mem** (מ) , **Nun** (נ), **Shin** (ש), and **Tav** (ת).

When the "**Yod**" letter is "prefixed" to the beginning of a verb stem (*i.e. in this case "hayah"*), it indicates **THIRD PERSON**! This is essentially **FUTURE TENSE** such as "**HE EXISTS**"

So, if Moses would've talked to the Israelites telling them the name of the Creator in 3rd person he would've pronounced the Hebrew letters "**Yod-Hey-Vav-Hey**" pronounced "**Y-ah-oo-ah**" or **Yahuah**! Not **Ahayah**. Moses had no reason to talk to the Israelites in 1st person the same way God spoke to Moses. Moses was not telling the Israelites his own name (*i.e. Moshe*), he was telling the Israelites what God said his name was. If the Israelites in the camp asked the question, "**Moses, what did God say his name is?**" Using "3rd Person" proper grammar....Moses would've said using the "**Yod**" + "**Hayah**"....HE EXISTS....or YAHUAH as it is pronounced. Not "**Aleph (I)**" + "**Hayah (Exist)**".

IAH THE EGYPTIAN MOON GOD THEORY IS A SATANIC DECEPTION.

In Egyptian funery beliefs, the Lunar Cycle was often used. However, lunar worship or "**lunar associations**" were not common in Ancient Egypt as most of the worship was to Sun Gods (Ra, Aten/Atum/Tem, Amun-Ra and Horus). When the moon was attributed to Egyptian gods it was usually linked to **Osiris, Thoth, Ra (i.e. crescent moon/sun disc) and Khonsu**. During the Egyptian New Kingdom (*i.e. when Joshua and the Israelites were already in the Land of Canaan*), the role of the moon

384

in afterlife was rare. But around 1250 B.C., 200 years **after the Biblical Exodus of Moses and the Israelites**.....the word "Iah" appeared **ONCE** in the **Papyri of Ani** (Chapter 2). "Iah"...whom many **FALSELY** translate to being "Yah" was linked to a moon god. The writing style of the Papyri of Ani was in Cursive Egyptian Hieroglyphics, which was primarily seen in the Egyptian Book of the Dead (*i.e. which was finished to its completion near time of the 1st Century B.C.*) and not the Old Kingdom/Middle Kingdom Egyptian texts. Most Biblical Scholars agree that the Hebrew Israelites spent their time in Egypt as slaves during the **Old and Middle Kingdom periods**. The Egyptian Book of the Dead, like the Jewish Talmud and Islamic Hadith, is a compilation of writings of multiple authors over a vast time period (i.e. hundreds of years). The Papyri of Ani was compiled into the Egyptian Book of the Dead 200 years well after Yahuah loosed the 10 Plagues on Egypt after Moses's warnings to "**Let my people go**"! The Egyptian Book of the Dead has "**necromancy**"...aka spells/magic which is of Satan. The Papyri of Ani was mainly linked to the Theban scribe named "Ani"....which was later added to the Egyptian Book of the Dead.

In the **Hebrew Torah** and in the **Hebrew Book of Jasher**, it states that the Pharaoh of Egypt during Moses time had no knowledge of any god name "**Iah**", "**Yah**" or "**Yahuah**".

Book of Jasher 79:41-44
"And Aaron hastened and stretched forth his hand and caught hold of the serpent's tail and it became a rod in his hand, and the sorcerers did the like with their rods, and they got hold, each man of the tail of his serpent, and they became rods as at first. And when they were restored to rods, the rod of Aaron swallowed up their rods. **And when the king saw this thing, he ordered the book of records that related to the kings of Egypt, to be brought, and they brought the book of records, the chronicles of the kings of Egypt, in which all the idols of Egypt were inscribed, for they thought of finding therein the name of**

YAHUAH, BUT THEY FOUND IT NOT. And Pharaoh said to Moses and Aaron, <u>**Behold I have not found the name of your God (Yahuah) written in this book, and his name I know not."**</u>

Exodus 5:1-3

"And afterward Moses and Aaron came and said to Pharaoh, "thus says **YAHUAH (THE LORD)**, the God of Israel, 'Let My people go that they may celebrate a feast to Me in the wilderness." But Pharaoh said, **"Who is YAHUAH (THE LORD) that I should obey His voice to let Israel go?" I do not know YAHUAH (THE LORD),** and besides, I will not let Israel go.".

Surely if **"Iah"** or **"Yah"** was a well-known Egyptian-Canaanite Moon deity the Book of Jasher or the Book of Exodus in the Hebrew Torah wouldn't have listed the Pharaoh as not having any knowledge whatsoever of the name **Yahuah**.

But wait, the plot thickens for those non-believers in calling on the name "**Yahuah**". Many will say, "The word "**Yeriho (Jericho) or "Yareach"** make reference to the moon. As the Canaanite city "**Jericho"** or "**Yeriho**" was nicknamed "**the city of the Moon**" by the Canaanites. Also, the word "**Yareach**" in Hebrew Strong's H3394 means "**Crescent Moon**". Well, Egyptologists, Kemetic Science believers and Nuwaubians say that the Egyptian hieroglyphs "**aah**" is mysteriously translated into "**Iah**" and then "**Yah**" to trick Hebrew Israelites into believing "**Yah**" or "**Yahuah**" is a false Moon god. They also try to link **Osiris (Asur/Asar)** to the word "aah" and then mysteriously link it to "Yah". This is very deceptive and cunning on their part to go through so much trouble to deceive God's Chosen People out of the Creator's True Name. But here are the facts:

The Hebrew-Canaanite (Phoenician) words "Yericho/Yeriho" and "Yereach" both start off with a "**Yod**" and a "**Resh**" Hebrew Letter.....not "**Yod**" and "**Hey**".....for the word "Yah". So, this is not where "Yah" and its false association with the moon comes from. The Canaanite deity "**Yarikh**" written as Jerah, Jarah, or Jorah was a city used by the Canaanites for moon worship. This city of "**Yarikh**" or even "**Yericho**" was already in existence way before the Israelites got into Canaan with Joshua. By the time Joshua and the Israelites got into the Land of Canaan they already knew the name of God from what Moses told them after coming down from Mt. Sinai in Egypt (i.e. Sinai Peninsula). If you research closely the Hebrew word "Yareach-(Hebrew Strong's #3394)" and "Yericho-(Hebrew Strong's #3405)" both have a "**Yod-Resh**" in the beginning but with two different vowels used ("a" and "e"). The Hebrew letter "Yod" and "Resh" are also the beginning 2 letters for the word "**Yarikh**". All of these words still do not have the pronunciation of "**Yah**" or "**Yahuah**"…being that they are supposed to link "Yah" with the moon. In **2 Kings 15:33** the name "**Yerusha or Yerushah**" appears, which means in Hebrew, "**Taken possession of**"….in this case "the mother of King Jotham". As you can see the Hebrew word "**Yer**" does not have anything to do with the moon. As a matter of fact, if you remove the "Resh" Hebrew letter from "Yerusha" and replace it with a "Hey" letter you get the beginning 4 letters of the name of the Messiah whose name does not mean "Moon" in no shape, form or fashion. Nobody on the Planet Earth can show the word "**Iah**" used 10 times in Egyptian literary works dating to the time period (2,000-1500 B.C.) when the Hebrew Israelites were in Egypt as slaves to even learn-adopt "Yah" or "Yahuah" as a Moon god. Case closed on this "**Deception**".

Alef	Beyt	Gimel	Dalet	Hey	Vav
Ox	House	Foot	Tent floor	To'	Nail
Strength	In	Camel	Pathway	Behold!	Peg
Leader		Pride		The	And

= Y PH

Zayin	Chet	Tet	Yod	Kaf	Lamed
Plow	Tent Wall	Basket	Arm and Hand	Palm of Hand	Staff
Weapon	Fence	Snake	Work	To Open	Contact
Cut Off	Separation	Surround	Deed		'to / from'

= ⊗ P (Tet)   = ∫ PH (Lamed)

Mem	Nun	Samekh	Ayin	Pey	Tsade
Water	Seed	Hand on Staff	Eye	Mouth	Man on Side
Chaos	Fish	Support	To See	Word	Desire
	Life	Prop	Experience	Speak	Need

= ∿∿ (P)★ H *Tadhe* = ≼ P

Qof	Resh	Shin	Tav
Sun on Horizon	Head	Eat	Mark
Behind	Person	Consume	Sign
	First	Destroy	Consonant

(P)★   † P★H

(**Above**) Pictograph Paleo-Hebrew/Phoenician script. Notice the "Kaf" Paleo-Hebrew letter looks like a bowl or the appearance of a palm of the hand open with 4 fingers (instead of five). Well, the **Malawi "Abatwa" Pygmy** writing was found to be similar to the Ancient Proto-Canaanite/Phoenician alphabet.

Cupped Hand   Kaph = Palm of the hand   kaf

The Malawi "Abatwa" Pygmy writing for the pronunciation "**Ka**" which is the letter "**K**" or "**Kaf**" in Modern Hebrew resembled the picture of a bowl (see below) with the meaning "**cupped hand**" for making "**nsembe**" offerings. Back then in Ancient times, the Abatwa Pygmies offered up their offerings using their hands open.....facing up, just like the Paleo-Hebrew/Phoenician pictograph.

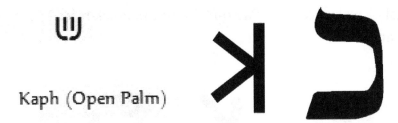

Kaph (Open Palm)

(**Left**) Early period Ancient pictograph Paleo-Hebrew for the letter "**K**" or "**Ka**" like what the Abatwa pygmy priest used when writing their letter "**K/Ka**". (**Middle**) Middle period Phoenician/Proto Canaanite/Paleo-Hebrew "**K**" (1400 B.C). It resembles a backwards English "**K**". (**Right**) Late period Modern Hebrew "**K**" or "**Kaf/Kaph**", which looks like a backwards "**C**". *Note: From the Paleo-Hebrew Kaf (K) is how the Greeks got their "K (Kappa)" letter from which evolved into our Latin/Old English "K".*

How could a Hamitic tribe in Africa have an alphabet like the Ancient Canaanites? It's because the Pygmies are the descendants of the Canaanites of Bible! Let's look at another example.

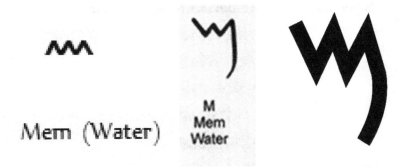

Mem (Water)

The Abatwa pygmies also drew their letter "**M**" or the letter for the "**M**" pronunciation" like a "**wave of water**". It symbolized "**water**" for them because in ancient times they had a Shrine to the **Rain gods** on the **Mulanje Mountain**. Is it a coincidence that this Pygmy "Abatwa"

389

wave symbol resembles the Paleo-Hebrew Phoenician letter for "**M**" which means "**water**"?

tav

(**Above**) The evolution from Proto-Canaanite/Phoenician, Paleo-Hebrew and Modern Hebrew for the letter "**Tav**" which sounds/looks like a "**T**". The letter "**T**" or the character associated with the "**T**" sound was drawn by the "**Abatwa Pygmies**" as a sort of "**X**" which was the language of the Twa/Abatwa "**Sapitwa Priesthood**". It is not a coincidence that the way the "**Abatwa pygmy priests**" wrote their letter "**T**" was the same way the ancient Canaanites wrote their letter "**T**".

Note: *Usually, the priests-diviners of many Bantus tribes are the ones who have knowledge of their people's past history and past language. If one researches the "old language" of the **Yoruba Ifa Priests** or the **Igbo Afa Dibia Priests** you will see strong similarities to "**Hebrew**".*

(**Above**) In Malawi, the "**Mulanje Mountain**" is over 3,000 feet old and is home to the "**Abatwa Pygmies**". Like the **Ethiopian** Orthodox Tewahedo priests, the **Igbo** Afa Dibia priests, the *Yoruba* Ifa Priests, and the **Sapitwa** "Abatwa priests"....they are all familiar with the ancient writing script of their forefathers. The Abatwa pygmies call very tall people "**ngwazi**" or "**langwani**". In their ancient Malawian tales, the Abatwa pygmies speak of a time when their people were "**numerous**" throughout the "**Land of Ham-Africa**" and how "**Giants**" who were the offspring of "**winged spirits**" had sexual relations with the people living in Africa (*see Genesis 6:1-8*). The Abatwa pygmies are believed by some to be children of the "**Mountain Spirit**". Other pygmies have heard that the "**Mulanje Mountains**" and its forest reserve are believed to be the "**first home**" of the **Amwandionerapati or Abatwa people**. Ironically, Egyptian texts from around 2300 B.C. refer to the Pygmies as little men from the "**land of trees and spirits**" at the foot of the "**Mountains of the Moon**" and it just so happens that most "Pygmy" tribes across the world live near the mountains and dense forests.

Ituri
Forest,
Zaire

(**Above**) In the "**Ituri**" forest area in the **Congo-Zaire region**, the "**Efe-Mbuti**" pygmies are supposedly the most loving, peaceful and caring people on the planet. They are said to have no crime, murder or assault within their tribe. Pygmy expert, **Dr. Jean-Pierre Hallet**, stated that the pygmies are forbidden to show physical violence. They discourage hatred, greed and competitive feelings. Dancing and singing is common among the Efe pygmies. The Efe pygmies have no chiefs, no courts or prisons. They believe in **shared** "communal" decision-making and believe in **one Creator**. Can this trait be seen in the Canaanites of the Bible? Remember, the Canaanites usually had things taken from them, like their land (cities), their livestock and their women/children.....just as what has been done to the pygmy tribes living in Africa by other Africans. See for yourself in the "**Slaughter of Shechem**" story.

Genesis 34:20-29
"And Hamor (Canaanite) and Shechem (Canaanite) his son came unto the gate of their city (Canaan/Israel), and communed with the men of their city, saying, **These men (*i.e. Israelites*) are peaceable with us; therefore let them dwell in the land, and trade therein; for the land, behold, it is large enough for them; let us take their daughters to us for wives, and let us give them our daughters. Only herein will the**

men consent unto us for to dwell with us, to be one people, if every male among us be circumcised, as they are circumcised. **Shall not their cattle and their substance and every beast of their's be our's? only let us consent unto them, and they will dwell with us.** And unto Hamor and unto Shechem his son hearkened all that went out of the gate of his city; and every male was circumcised, all that went out of the gate of his city. And it came to pass on the third day, when they were sore, that two of the sons of Jacob, **Simeon** and **Levi**, Dinah's brethren, took each man his sword, and came upon the city **boldly**, and **slew all the (Canaanite) males**. And they slew Hamor and Shechem his son with the edge of the sword, and took Dinah out of Shechem's house, and went out. The sons of Jacob came upon the slain, and spoiled the city, because they had defiled their sister. **They took their sheep, and their oxen, and their asses, and that which was in the city, and that which was in the field, and all their wealth, and all their little ones, and their wives took they captive, and spoiled even all that was in the house."**

All throughout history, from Biblical times to the "**Bantus Expansion**" in Africa, the Pygmy Canaanite tribes have been overtaken by others (*i.e. Sons of Shem-Israel and Sons of Ham*). This seems to fall right in line with the "**Curse of Canaan**". If the "pygmy" tribes still found in Africa and South Asia are the Biblical Canaanites, we would expect to see some "DNA" proof that would show their connection to those people groups that claim to be Jews/Israelites. The European Ashkenazi-Sephardic Jews Paternal Y-DNA or Maternal mtDNA cannot be found in Africa or even amongst the pygmy people. It has been genetically proven that there are some Pygmy Africans that share the same mtDNA "**L1, L2, L3**" or Y-DNA "**E1b1a**" as "Bantus Negro" Africans because of their past history of intermarriage/mixing. The scriptures in the Bible tell us this as proof. See for yourself.

Genesis 34 - These men (*i.e. Israelites*) are peaceable with us; therefore let them dwell in the land, and trade therein; for the land, behold, it is large enough for them; **let us (i.e. Canaanites) take their daughters to us for wives, and let us (i.e. Canaanites) give them (i.e. Israelites) our daughters.**

This falls in line with the Israelite-Canaanite mixing in the Bible. Pygmy tribes mixing with other **"nations of color"** instead of the Bantus people in Africa can also be proven in **Asia, South Asia** and **New World-Americas. This essentially proves that the European Ashkenazi-Sephardic Jews are NOT the Blood descendants of the Israelites of the Bible.**

CHAPTER 14

CHRIST THE MESSIAH REVEALED IN GENESIS 1:1 IN PALEO-HEBREW!

Note: Many Hebrew Israelites are embarking on the "mission" to reading or "**cross-referencing**" the English King James Bible in its most original language, **Paleo-Hebrew**. Many say that when reading the Old Testament (Tanakh) and the Torah in pictograph **Paleo-Hebrew**, all new magnificent breakdowns can be seen in the scriptures....like the Messianic prophecy of Christ in the "**End of Days**" being declared from **the beginning** in the Bible in the Book of Genesis. The Creator mapped out the plan of Christ and Salvation from the very beginning.

Isaiah 46:9-10 "Remember the former things of old: for I am God, and there is none else; I am God, and there is none like me, **declaring the end from the beginning, and from ancient times the things that are not yet done**, saying, My counsel shall stand, and I will do all my pleasure:"

400	10	300	1	200	2
ת	י	שׁ	א	ר	ב
TAV	YUD	SHIN	ALEPH	RESH	BETH
MARK	HAND	TOOTH	OX	FIRST	HOUSE
4	1	3	1	2	2

(Above) The word "Bereshith" is the first word in the Bible. It has a "hidden meaning" inside of it that no one can see when they read their English Bible where it says "In the beginning".

The Ancient Paleo-Hebrew alphabet Moses used has pictograph/hieroglyphic symbols similar to the Egyptian Hieroglyphic script. Each Paleo-Hebrew pictograph has a meaning. For instance, the Hebrew Letter **"Shin"** can represent **"Change"**. Like change from the Ancient past into the future. It also can mean a **"flame"** as it looks like a "Flame" or "Teeth". **A flame/fire consumes and transforms (i.e. changes) "matter" from one state into another.** When we eat, **we consume** food with our "teeth" which starts the process of transforming food into another state which our body can use for "energy" or "nutrition".

There are many ways we can look at the 6 letters in the Bible's **FIRST** Hebrew word **"Bereshith"** which is spelled **"Beth, Resh, Aleph, Shin, Yod, Tav"** from left-to-right. The Hebrew word for **"to create"** is Hebrew Strong's #1254 **"Bara"** which is the Hebrew letters **"Bet/Beth"**, **"Resh"** and **"Aleph"**. So if the first 3 letters of Bereshith mean **"God Creates"**. Well, the last three letters **"Shin"**, **"Yod"** and **"Tav"** could very well mean "**Christ consumes with fire or his mouth/teeth**" or "**Christ brings change?**"

After all it should not be a hard to see that the word "**Hand**" and "**Mark**" are synonymous with Christ's crucifixion just as in the Paleo-Hebrew meaning of the "**Tetragrammaton**". Thus, the first Hebrew word of the Bible could mean "**God Creates, Christ Consumes/Transforms or brings change**". After all Christ says in **Revelation 22:13**

> "**I am the Alpha and the Omega, the First and the Last, the Beginning and the End.**"

This scripture is pretty much summed up in the first Hebrew word "**Bereshith**" of the Bible in Genesis. Amazing!

If you are skeptical about this consider these scriptures.

The Hebrew word for "**Fire**" is Hebrew Strong's word #784 "**Esh**" which is the Hebrew "**Aleph**" + "**Shin**" (*just as the order of aleph-shin is in the Hebrew word Bereshith*). It can mean "fire, burning coals, burning, flame and even a **MAN**"!

Deuteronomy 9:3 "Understand therefore this day, that the **LORD THY GOD** is he which goeth over before thee; as a **CONSUMING FIRE** he shall destroy them, and he shall bring them down before thy face: so shalt thou drive them out, and destroy them quickly, as the LORD hath said unto thee."

Still not convinced that the God (Christ) and the Bible story is not summed up in the word "**Bereshith**"? Read further.

2 Peter 3:5-7 "But they deliberately overlook the fact that long ago by **GOD'S WORD (Christ)** the heavens existed and the earth was formed out of water and by water, **though which the world of that time perished in the flood (water).** And by that same **WORD (Christ), the present heavens and earth are RESERVED FOR FIRE, kept for the day of judgement and destruction of ungodly men.**"

In the bible, this "**WORD**" is God and this same "**WORD**" which is God became **FLESH** (*i.e. Christ as God manifested in flesh*). So, it is not surprising that at the time of the Second Coming of Christ, by the opening of his mouth on his command will all the evildoers and the "unrighteous" be consumed by fire. Death, Hades, the Devil and all those whose names are not written in the Book of Life will also be consumed by fire in the "**Lake of Fire**".

John 1:1 "In the beginning was the **WORD (Christ)**, and the **WORD WAS WITH GOD (meaning Christ)**, and the **WORD WAS GOD (Christ is God)**. The same was in the beginning with God. All things were made by him; and without him was not anything made that was made.

John 1:14 "And the **WORD BECAME FLESH (Christ)** and dwelt among us, (and we beheld his glory, the glory as of the only begotten of the Father,) full of grace and truth. John bare witness of him, and cried, saying, This was he of whom I spake, He that cometh after me is preferred before me: for he was before me."

But just as God (Christ) created the heaven and the earth, in the Book of Revelation 21:2 God (Christ) creates a New Heaven and a New Earth. This can all be seen in the first word of the Book of Genesis "Bereshith".

Revelation 19:14-16 "The armies of heaven, dressed in fine linen, white and pure, follow Him (Christ) on white horses. And from **HIS MOUTH** proceeds a sharp sword with which to strike down the nations, and He will rule them with an iron scepter. He treads the winepress of the fury of the **WRATH OF GOD, THE ALMIGHTY.** And He has a name written on His robe and on His thigh: King of kings and Lord of lords."

How will Christ strike down the nations? If you read further in the next chapter it tells you.

Revelation 20:8-10 "And will go out to deceive the nations in the four corners of the earth, **Gog and Magog,** to assemble them for battle. Their number is like the sand of the seashore. And they marched across the broad expanse of the earth and surrounded the camp of the saints (*i.e. holy ones*) and the beloved city. **BUT FIRE CAME DOWN FROM HEAVEN AND CONSUMED THEM.** And the devil who had deceived them was thrown into the **LAKE OF FIRE AND SULFUR,** into which the beast and the false prophet had already been thrown. There they will be tormented day and night forever and ever."

"Bar" = Son

"Abba" = Father

Alef = God-Lord

In the first **"Two"** letters of the word **"Bereshith"** we can see the letters that make up the Hebrew word **"Bar"** or **"Son"**. Adding **"Alef/Aleph"** to it turns it into **"Son of God"** or **"Son of the Father"** as the **"Aleph"** can be symbolized as the **God the Creator**. The "Hebrew" letter "Aleph" is linked to "Elohim", "Eloah", "El", "El Shaddai", "El Elyon" and "Abba".......which all represent God the Creator. The Hebrew word **"Abba"** or **"Father"** in Paleo-Hebrew also means **"Strong House"** or **"Leader/Master of the House"**. But the <u>first two letters</u> in **the beginning of the Bible** gives reference to **"the Son"**....meaning Yahusha (Yeshua) HaMashiach (i.e. Jesus Christ). **The <u>first three letters</u> in the beginning of the Bible** gives reference to the **"Son of God"**. In Paleo Hebrew, the word **"Bar"** or **"Son"** means **"Head of the House"**, **"Authority of the House"**, **"First of the House"** or **"Beginning of the House"**.

Since Christ is considered the **Son of God**, and he is the **"Beginning"** of the house.....what is considered the **"house"** of the Creator/Father?

Isaiah 66:1 "Thus says the LORD, **Heaven is my throne, and the Earth is my footstool**. Where then is a house you could build for Me? And where is a place that I may rest?

Isaiah 66:1 and the Paleo-Hebrew meaning of "**Bar**" basically reveals to us that Christ was the "**beginning**" of Heaven and Earth. Man can only build a house with 4 walls and a roof. The house of the Creator is different.

The word "**Abba**" means "**Leader of the House**" or "**Strength of the House**". In Paleo-Hebrew the two-letter word "Bar" or "Son" consists of the Hebrew meaning "**Head-Resh**" and "**House-Bet**". So, the Son (Christ) is the "**Head of the <u>House of God</u>**"....aka Heaven and Earth. But didn't Christ say that "**All Authority**" was given to him over Heaven and Earth? Didn't Christ say "All Authority" was given to him by the Father?

- **Matthew 28:18** "And Yahusha (Jesus) came up and spoke to them, saying, "All **AUTHORITY** has been given to Me in **heaven and on earth**."

- **Matthew 11:27** "**All things have been handed over to Me by My Father**; and no one knows the Son except the Father; nor does anyone know the Father except the Son, and anyone to whom the Son wills to reveal Him."

- **Colossians 2:10** "And in Him you have been made complete, and He is the head over all rule and **AUTHORITY**."

- **John 3:35** "The Father loves the Son and **has given all things into His hand**."

God's Son or Son of God = "Bar (Son)" + "Aleph (God)"

The first three letters of the Book of Genesis also gives reference to Christ being the "**Creator**" in the beginning and also "**The Son of God**". Why? The First two letters of the first word in the Bible "**Bereshith**" make the Hebrew word "**Bar**" or "**Son**". Why would the Bible start off with "**Son**" and not "**Aleph**" or "**Elohim**"?

But there is more!

LETTER	PICTOGRAPH	MEANINGS
Beyt	House/Tent	Family/House/Inside
Resh	Man's Head	First/Top/Beginning
Aleph	Ox's Head	Strong/Power/Leader
Shin	Two Teeth	Sharp/Press/Eat/Two
Yud	Arm and Hand	Work/Throw/Worship
Tav	Cross Sticks	Mark/Sign/Monument

(**Above**) In Paleo-Hebrew the Hebrew word "**Bereshith**" for the English word "**In the Beginning**" also has another hidden meaning if you can understand that the first three letters give reference to the **Son of God**:

"The Son of God will be pressed (i.e. consumed) by his own hand (i.e. work) on a cross (i.e or tree) as a sign/mark/monument for the world."

The word "**Monument**" is defined as "a lasting evidence, sign or mark", "a reminder" or "example of someone or something done that is notable or great".

Depending on how you interpret the Paleo Hebrew Pictograph meaning of the letters inside the letters that make up "**Bereshith**" you can also see the plan for Christ's death on the cross/tree.

Many religions claim Christ was just a prophet, a special man or some sort of Guru or Yogi. But in Flavius Josephus's literary work "**Antiquities of the Jews**" in Book 18 and 20 it gives a testimony about the existence of Christ (Yahusha-Jesus). It is usually referred to as the "**Testimonium Flavianum**" meaning "**The Testimony of Flavius Josephus**". Here is an excerpt from it revealing that Jesus Christ (Yahusha HaMashiach) according to Flavius was believed by Christians to be the Messiah, he was crucified and he appeared **three days later** to his followers.

"About this time there lived Jesus, a wise man, if indeed one ought to call him a man. For he was one who performed surprising deeds and was a teacher of such people as accept the truth gladly. He won over many Jews and many of the Greeks. He was the Christ. And when, upon the accusation of the principal men among us, Pilate had condemned him to a cross, those who had first come to love him did not cease. He appeared to them spending a third day restored to life (*other sources say "On the third day he appeared to them restored to life*), for the prophets of God had foretold (*prophesied*) these things and thousands of other marvels about him. And the tribe of the Christians, so called after him, has still to this day not disappeared. *-Flavius Josephus: Antiquities of the Jews, Book 18, Chapter 3, 3*

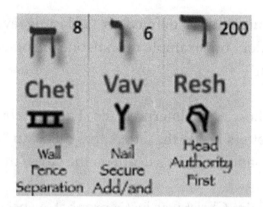

(Above) The **Ruach HaKodesh** aka **"The Holy Spirit"** can be interpreted as the **"Sacred Breath"** or **"Sacred Wind"**. But the Hebrew Strong's word #7307/7308 **"Ruach"** also has another **"hidden meaning"**. In Modern Hebrew **"Ruach"** means **"Breath, Wind and Spirit"**. Christ told us that his death, resurrection and ascension into heaven was necessary for the **"Comforter"** aka **"The Holy Spirit"** to come to men. After which **"POWER"** would come to those who received it.

John 16:7 "Nevertheless I tell you the truth; It is expedient for you that I go away: for if I go not away, the Comforter (i.e. Holy Spirit) will not come unto you; but if I depart, I will send him unto you."

Christ clearly stated in scripture that it was necessary for him to ascend to heaven so that the Holy Spirit could come and stay with man.

John 14:16 "And I will ask the Father, and He will give you another Advocate **(i.e. Holy Spirit)** to be with you forever."

So what does the Paleo-Meaning" of the "Sacred" Ruach (Breath-Spirit) reveal to us? Let's break down the three letters that make up the word "Ruach".

1. Resh-**HEAD, AUTHORITY**, Beginning, First
2. Vav-**SECURE**, Bind, Nail, Add
3. Chet-**SEPARATION**, Wall, Fence.

It seems as though it is saying the "**(God)-Head Authority**" **Secures our Separation**" with the Holy Spirit. As Israelites or followers of Christ we are to be "**Set Apart**" from the "Nations"......like separating the wheat from the tares. Is this "separation" lacking today in Christ's church? The Bible says to worship God in "**Spirit**" and "**Truth**". So how can we effectively worship God with "**Truth**" but no "**Spirit**" or vice-versa? This I believe is the "**missing link**" to unlocking the true "Power" of the "Israelite awakening/movement".

Acts 1:8 "But ye shall receive **POWER**, after that the **Holy Ghost** is come upon you: and ye shall be witnesses unto me both in Jerusalem, and in Judea, and in Samaria, and unto the uttermost part of the earth."

Leviticus 20:26 "Thus you are to be Holy to Me, for I the LORD am Holy; and I have **SET YOU APART** from the peoples to be Mine."

John 14:26 "But the **Comforter**, which is the **Holy Ghost**, whom the Father will send in my name, he shall teach you all things, and bring all things to your remembrance, whatsoever I have said unto you."

In the Old Testament, the Spirit of the Lord came upon the Israelite Kings and also the Israelite prophets when they were about to prophesy. But this Old Testament "**Spirit of Lord**" often came, sat upon the "**human vessels**" God was using at the time, and sometimes even left.

1 Samuel 16:14-15 "Then Samuel took the horn of oil and anointed him in the midst of his brothers; and the Spirit of the LORD came mightily upon David from that day from that day forward. And Samuel arose and went to Ramah. Now **the Spirit of the LORD departed from Saul**, and an evil spirit from the LORD terrorized him. Saul's servants then said to him, "Behold now, an evil spirit from God is terrorizing you."

Fact: *It is a known fact that in the Old Testament there was also no real mention of demonic possession or "**demons/evil spirits**" being cast out of people.*

So, is it possible that if Christ didn't come and go back to Heaven the "**Holy Spirit**" would not have come for man to receive permanently?

Acts 2:2 "And suddenly there came a sound from heaven as a rushing **MIGHTY WIND**, and it filled all the house where they were sitting.

If the "Ruach HaKodesh" secures us to be "Separated" we should strive on Earth to be led by the Spirit.   God wants us to be "**Set Apart**" to worship him in **Spirit** and **Truth**.   Christ told the Edomite Pharisee Nicodemus during the late hours of the night to have "**Eternal Life**" he would have to be "**born again**" by **Water and Spirit**. This "**Spirit**" is waking up God's Chosen People in these wicked days as a "**Final Call/Warning**" to clean up, turn from our wicked ways and turn back to the Creator through Christ. This Holy Spirit will lead and protect the Israelites like it was back then........including even till this day. It will also "**Set's us apart**" from other nations. The Apostle Paul said this "awakening" would be like "Life for the Dead" for his Israelite brethren.

Romans 11:15 "For if the casting away of them (Israel) be the reconciling of the world, **what shall the receiving of them (Israel) be, but life from the dead**?"

So let's get back to the "Validity" of Christ.

In regards to the Testimonium Flavianum written by 1st Century Gentile Jewish historian Flavius Josephus, some say there was an Arabic version from 900 A.D. that was translated from Greek. However, there was slight differences in the Arabic version. So, the question is....was this Arabic version really a translation of Flavius Josephus's work or was it a translation from someone else at the time who witnessed the "events" of Jesus's life, crucifixion and resurrection?   Remember the New Testament, contrary to other people's belief was written in Aramaic first and then was translated

to Greek (which make up most of the 3rd and 4th Century NT manuscripts which are safeguarded today). Keeping this in mind, it is very well possible that someone else (Aramaic, Greek or Latin speaking), also recorded the events that transpired with Jesus's life in the 1st century A.D. Here is what it said in Arabic about the Life of Christ:

"At this time there was a wise man who was called Jesus (Yeshua). And his conduct was good, and he was known to be virtuous. And many people from among the Jews and the other nations became his disciples. Pilate condemned him to be crucified and to die. And those who had become his disciples did not abandon his discipleship. They reported that he had appeared to them after his crucifixion and that he was alive; accordingly, he was perhaps the Messiah concerning whom the prophets have recounted wonders." *-Mahbub ibn Qustantin (Agapius), "Kitab al-Unwan" 10th century*.

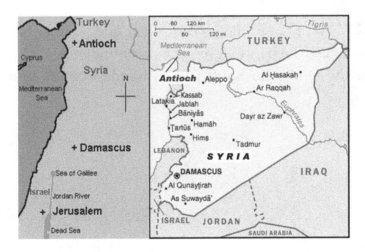

Mahbub ibn Qustantin, also known as "**Agapius**" was a 10th Century Arabic Christian writer and historian who is best known for his book "**Kitab al-Unwan**"....which means "**Book of the Title/Headings of History**". He was a Melkite Bishop of **Manbij, Syria**. The Melkite

Catholic Church is now a part of the Catholic Church. The Melkites are of mixed Levantine and Greek origin, tracing their history to the early Christians in **Antioch, Syria/Turkey**. This is where Christianity was introduced by Saint Peter and Saint Paul in the 1st Century A.D. (*See Galatians 2, Acts 13-15*). The headquarters is the Cathedral of the Dormition of Our Lady, Damascus, Syria. The territory the church covers is Egypt, Israel, Palestine, Jordan, Lebanon, Sudan and Syria.

The importance of this is that in Greek, Arabic and Aramaic it was known that a man whom the people called **Christ/Yeshua** existed. This man was followed by many, he was crucified during the times of Pontius Pilate and he appeared to his followers "**three days**" later restored to life (resurrection). Only God has the power to take life, bringing it to the grave and then to raise it back up (bring to life again).

1 Samuel 2:6 "The LORD killeth, and maketh alive: **he bringeth down to grave, and bringeth up.**"

Daniel the prophet told the Babylonian King Belshazzar that God controls "**Life and Breath**".

Daniel 5:23 "You praised the gods of silver and gold, of bronze, iron, wood and stone, which cannot see or hear or understand. **But you did not honor the God who holds in His hand your life and all your ways.**"

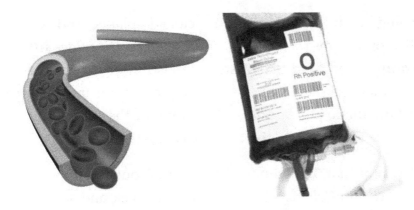

(Left) Endothelial Blood Vessel (i.e. veins, arteries). **(Right)** Pint of Blood, "**O positive**".

Leviticus 17:11 "The **life (Soul)** of all flesh is in the **BLOOD**".

Hebrew Strong's #5315 word "**Nephesh**", meaning "**Soul**" is what the Hebrew Bible says while our King James Bible says "**Life**".

No matter how much Scientists and Geneticists try, even with "Fallen Angel Hidden Knowledge"....no one can create "**Life**" but the **Creator**.

Leviticus 17:11 goes on to say further, "For the life (soul) of the flesh is in the blood: and **I (Christ)** have given it to you upon the **altar (crucifixion)** to make an atonement for your souls: for it is the **blood (i.e. from slain Christ the lamb of God)** that makes an atonement for the soul."

This was a "**Messianic Prophecy**" about Christ in the Torah. Here is where it gets fun. Satan wants to be like the Most High. He wants to teach mankind to be "God-like". He teaches mankind "**Gnostism**" or the concept of "self-salvation" with ultimate knowledge which is called reaching the level of an "**Ascended Master**". Some teach that this is called "**Christ-Consciousness**".

No matter how much knowledge one obtains, it will never come close to being able to "**self-save**". Before the flood, the Fallen Angels and Giants "sinned" against God's creation. Today the same thing is happening with cloned animals, cloned plants and Genetically modified organisms (*i.e. Salmon, cows, goats with spider silk protein, soy, corn*). The "**Mad Scientists**" are also inserting Synthetic (non-biologic) material (i.e. DNA) into "**biologic**" organisms. This is called "**Transhumanism**". We call it "The wave of the future".....the Bible calls it "**The emerging Anti-Christ Beast System**".

Christ taught that "redemption" came from outside of a person, and not from within (*John 6:44*). Christ came to seek and save those who were lost (*Luke 19:10*). Christ saves sinners who are helpless and cannot save themselves (*Romans 5:6-8*). The "**Illuminated Ones**" or the "Occult" simply teaches that "illumination-supreme knowledge" saves humans. Then the "**uninitiated one**" becomes the "**initiated one**". This is the kind of trickery that is going on in the world today.

So, in the search for "supreme" or "divine" knowledge, mankind destroys and corrups God's creation. Mankind (*being tricked by Satan*) makes everything worse. Satan promises "**Life**" but in reality is giving "**Death**" and "**Destruction**". Man in his quest to be "God" or to solve all the "Mysteries of the Universe" will never be satisfied until he can prove God doesn't exist and that humans can be like "**Gods**". But here is an example of how they can never be like the "**Most High**".

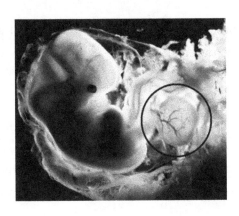

(**Above**) Human embyro yolk sac around 6-8 weeks gestation.

The artificial blood cell that man called himself making with "technological advances" is about 1/50th the size of a normal Red Blood Cell, and is **made from** purified human hemoglobin proteins that have been coated with a **synthetic polymer**. Notice the word "**made from**" and not "**created**". While a normal Red Blood Cell circulates in the body for about 3 months, this biologic/synthetic Red Blood Cell can only survive in circulation for 8-12 hours. The artifical cell was "designed" to hopefully deliver oxygen to tissues, but it doesn't do all the other number of functions that Red Blood Cells do on a daily basis. These other functions are "antioxidant protection" of tissues, regulation of blood flow, assistance in the immune response and aiding in forming blood clots or scabs. Red Blood Cells can also re-form in the body's circulation system, but scientists are still baffled as to what actually starts "blood formation" in the human embyro. Many scientists have speculated that "blood" is formed or told to "turn on" from the **Human Embryo Yolk Sac**, but they know that this is not entirely the case. Scientists have narrowed it down to something inside the endothelial lining of the blood vessel itself that causes "blood" to form, but they still don't fully understand how this would be. This in the scientific world is a continued source of debate and geneticists still cannot figure out, at the molecular level, how the transition of blood cell production from inside a blood vessel really happens. It is a mystery because it is something they **cannot see** happening with their mind. **They also cannot explain why, the moment a person dies, the blood is no good for use in a blood bank.**

With that being said, here is more!

Christ came on earth doing exactly **ONLY WHAT GOD (THE CREATOR)** can do, exerting his power over **Life and Death**. Muhammad or no other religious person in any other religion has not raised themselves from the dead or raised other humans from the dead.

John 10:17-18 "The reason my Father loves me is that I lay down my life in order to take it up again. **No one takes it from Me, but I lay it down of My own accord. I have authority to lay it down and authority to take it up again**. This charge I have received from My Father."

Christ is able to lay down his life and take it up again because from the beginning of time he was set to be the Saviour of the world being sent down to earth **BY HIMSELF** to take on the form of a man, **as God manifested in the flesh!**

Revelation 13:8 "And all that dwell upon the earth adored him, whose names are not written in the **Book of Life of the Lamb, which was slain from the beginning of the world.**"

This scripture means **God's/Christ's sacrifice** was recorded from the creation of the **WORD**......and by the very first word in the Hebrew bible "**Bereshith**".

Remember, Lazarus was dead for "**days**", well after many of the "**stages of death**" were past. However, nothing is "**impossible**" with God (Creator).

Stages of Death:

1. **Pallor Mortis** – first stage of death that causes "**paleness**" in those with light/white skin. When black people die, they tend to get darker. It is from the cessation of blood circulation.

2. **Algor Mortis** – this second stage of death is derived from the Latin word "**algor**" for "**coldness**" and "mortis-death", is when the body becomes cold.

3. **Rigor Mortis** – this third stage of death is heralded by chemical changes in the muscles that causes the body to stiffen. It can happen as early as **4 hours after death**.

4. **Livor Mortis** – this fourth stage of death is when there is settling/pooling of the blood into the dependent portions of the body. This is most often the back side of the person's body from the torso to the legs. It causes a purplish-red discoloration of the skin. Liver Mortis starts in 20-30 min but cannot be seen until 2-12 hours after death.

5. **Putrefaction** – this fifth stage of death is most commonly known as "**pre-decomposition**". It is caused by the breakdown of organic material by bacterial or fungal digestion which causes the release of gas inside the tissues.

6. **Decomposition** – this sixth stage of death is further breakdown of the body's tissues by bacteria and fungus causing a putrid odor. Often this is heralded by bloating of the abdomen and in the case of exposure to the outside environment, maggot feeding usually occurs at this time. The end of "**active decay**" is when the maggots leave.

7. **Skeletonization** – this final stage of death is where the tissues have decomposed leaving a skeleton. In warm climates or tropical climates, this can occur in just weeks. In arid or colder climates, this process takes longer.

John 11:38-44

"Jesus (Yahusha) therefore again, groaning in Himself, came to the grave. It was a cave, and a stone lay against it. Jesus (Yahusha) said, "Take ye away the stone." Martha, the sister of him that was dead, said unto Him, **"Lord, by this time there is a stench, for he hath been dead four days** (5th *stage of death already present*)**."** Jesus (Yahusha) said unto her, **"Said I not unto thee that if thou would believe, thou should see the glory of God? (message)"** Then they took away the stone from the place where the dead was laid. And Jesus (Yahusha) lifted up His eyes and said, "Father, I thank Thee that Thou hast heard Me. And I knew that Thou hearest Me always, but because of the people who stand by I said it, that they may believe that Thou hast sent Me." And when He thus had spoken, He cried with a loud voice, **"Lazarus, come forth!" And he that was dead came forth, bound hand and foot with graveclothes, and his face was bound about with a napkin.** Jesus (Yahusha) said unto them, "Loose him, and let him go."

Muhammad, Buddha or any other religious figure in history has not raised any person from the dead, let alone resurrect themselves from the grave. Likewise, there is no historical **"literary"** accounts of the life of Osiris, Isis, or Horus on earth. Despite the **Book of the Dead**, the **Pyramid Texts**, the **Coffin Texts**, the **Contending's of Horus and Seth**, the **42 Laws of Maat**, the **Emerald Tablets** and the **Metu Neter**.....Egyptian history shows **"unsatisfactory"** gaps and **"mystery"** authors that let down people searching for any knowledge about the Ancient Egyptians. It is not until around 200 B.C. during the Greek Ptolemaic ruling Empire in Egypt (*i.e. under Selucus, Alexander the Great, Cleopatra*) that writings about Egyptian history came forth. The Ancient writings of **Herodotus, Manetho, Flavius Josephus, Publius Scipio Africanus,** and **Eusebius of Caesarea** are the only detailed sources on Egyptian history......told by **European "Gentile" historians**. Egypt's **"validity"** is only supported by cross referencing Egyptian accounts with other **"accurate"** historical sources....such as the Hebrew Bible and the Assyrian/Babylonian Annals (*i.e. The Annals of Sennacherib*). The historical records of the Assyrians and Babylonians line up perfectly with the historical record of the "**Hebrew Israelites**" in the Old Testament.

Despite all of this "**Truth**" about Christ and the Bible, mankind still tries to convince himself that "**pagan false religions**" is the way.

CHAPTER 15

CLUES ABOUT THE SCATTERED "LOST TRIBES OF ISREAL" ARE HIDDEN IN THE BIBLE WRITTEN IN PALEO-HEBREW!

The changing of the Paleo-Hebrew to Modern Aramaic (Block) Hebrew that is used today changed the meanings of the words in the Bible...or if anything they made the meanings less clear. Once the "Real Hebrew Israelites" start to read the Bible in the language that it was first written in (Paleo-Hebrew), then some of the **"Hidden Mysteries"** can be revealed to us in regards to why it is important that God's True Chosen People understand their role in the "Last Days" prior to Christ's return and why the "Real Blood Israelites" of the Bible must come to Christ for Salvation. But what it also does is shed some "light" as to where the scattered "Lost Tribes of Israel" are today. The early Greek and Latin translators of the Hebrew Bible knew this. This is what led the **"converted"** Gentile European Spanish, Portuguese and Dutch Jews to look for the authentic **"Lost Tribes of Israel"** in lands only accessible by traveling the oceans by way of ships.

Here is a perfect example of this in the Bible in Paleo-Hebrew.

(**Above**) Reading and writing Hebrew is from Right-to-Left. The Hebrew Letters **Samekh-Yod-Nun-Yod-Mem** make up the word "**Sinim/Synym**". The word "**Sinim**" or "**SYNYM**" is used in the Book of Isaiah (49:12) to describe a location that some of the Children of Israel would be gathered from back to the Holy Land in Jerusalem, Israel. Some say it is the South, some say it is the East, and some say it is the Southeast. The Latin Vulgate describes it as "**Australi**" which denotes/means "**South**". The Greek Septuagint lists it as the "**Land of the Persians**". So, what could "**Sinim**" mean?

Greek (Koine) Septuagint Version
Isaiah 49:12 "Behold, these shall come from **FAR**: and these from the North and the West, and others from the **Land of the Persians**".

Latin Vulgate Version
Isaiah 49:12 "ecce isti de longe venient et ecce illi ab aquilone et mari et isti de **terra australi**."

Translation: Behold these shall come from afar, and behold these from the North and from the sea, and these from the **South country**.

Hebrew Version

הִנֵּה-אֵלֶּה, מֵרָחוֹק יָבֹאוּ; וְהִנֵּה-אֵלֶּה מִצָּפוֹן וּמִיָּם, וְאֵלֶּה " מֵאֶרֶץ סִינִים."

Translation: "Behold, these shall come from far; and lo, these from the North and from the West, and these from the land of **Sinim.**"

So here is the dilemma. Is "**Australia**" or "**South Asia**" the other part of the world that the Hebrew Israelites were scattered to?

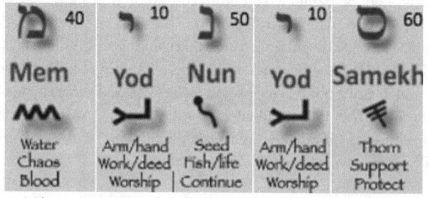

(**Above**) If we apply the Paleo-Hebrew meaning to the word "**Synym**" or "**Sinim**" we could possibly get the following meaning: **To Protect Worship (of Yahuah), to Continue (the Seed/Life) to Worship (Yahuah).....via Water**.

Could this mean that some of the Israelites would "**protect**" and "**support**" their worship of the Creator by traveling to distant Islands via the **waterways**? After all, using boats to cross massive bodies of water was the only way the Israelites could get to **Indonesia, Australia** and the many islands in **Micronesia-Polynesia-Melanesia.**

Consider this amazing fact.

(**Above**) Australian aborigines undergoing the religious ritual of "**circumcision**". Australian Aboriginal tribes like the **Warramunga Tribe** and the **Mardudjara Tribe** practice circumcision as a rite of "**manhood**"....just like many Bantus African boys undergo this "**religious rite of passage**" by the Elders of their tribe. In Ancient times, only Hebrew Israelites circumcised their boys. Those Egyptians who were influenced by this "**Hebrew practice**" also circumcised as well. This is in part because of the 430 years that the Israel lived amongst the Egyptians. 400 years is also just about the same number of years that African-Americans (i.e. Negroes) have been living in America. This is a long time. 400 years is long enough for anything...like Christianity to be widespread practiced and used by the "majority". However Ancient Egyptian oral history doesn't "openly" discuss a "**Great Flood**" story. But the Australian Aborigines oral history talk about a "**Great Flood**"....similar to what is written in the Hebrew Torah. So, are the Australian Aborigines **Hamitic Egyptians** or **Hebrew Israelites?**

Fact: The **Canaanite** "Pygmy" tribes in Africa.....who are known "**Hamites**" like the **Egyptians** know about the "**Great Flood**". They also know about God creating man and woman, with the women being deceived by an "**evil entity (*i.e. Satan*)**" which brings "**punishment**" to mankind. They also know about a "**Messianic Prophecy**". They also know about the Giants that lived on the earth and devoured human flesh. How did they know all of this? Did they learn it from their forefather "Ham" or "Noah"? Or did they learn it from the "Hebrew Israelites" they were living amongst. These "**similar bible-like**" stories are also recorded in other civilizations across the world. But keep this in mind, from the moment Satan deceived "Eve".....he and his band of fallen angels knew about the "**Messiah-Christ**" coming from the seed of a woman. This birthed the "**beginning**" of all the "**Virgin birth-Child Redeemer**" copy-cat stories that would be promoted in many different civilizations....of course with the doctrine of "**Polytheism (*worship of multiple pagan gods*)**". The Egyptians did it, the Babylonians did it and the Hindoos did it. Satan used this knowledge of the "**Messianic Prophecy**" during the Garden of Eden on Earth to trick all the civilizations that would exist up until this day.

Genesis 3:15 "And I (**Yahuah**) will put enmity (**hostility**) between thee (**Satan**) and the woman (**Israel**), and between thy seed (**Satan's Seed-Children**) and her seed (**Israelites**); it (**Christ**) shall bruise thy (**Satan's**) head, and thou (**Satan**) shalt bruise his (**Male Christ child**) heel."

This was the "**1st Messianic Prophecy**" that would spark the Fallen Angels "idea" to give mankind a pagan "**Trinity**" as a form of "**deception**", which would consist of a **Man, Woman and Child**. The woman would be regarded as the "**Queen of Heaven**" and the concept of a male deity having a **cosort (wife)** would be "**bootlegged**" from the Messianic Prophecy.......**first declared by the Creator in Genesis 3:15. This is how the worship of false gods and false idols got started in Ancient Sumeria/Ancient Egypt.**

The Fallen Angels all throughout history would promote "polytheism" where different gods had different names....until the last deceptive Anti-Christ Religion "Islam" would emerge. It is the job of the "occult" and religions like Babylonian Talmudic Judaism, Islam, Jehovah's Witness, Kemetic Science-

*Metu-Neter, Moorish Science, Buddhism and Hindooism to "**undermine**" the deity of Christ. But Yahuah says:*

Jeremiah 10:11 "Thus shall ye say unto them, **The gods that have not made the heavens and the earth, even thy shall perish from the earth,** even they shall perish from the earth, and from under these heavens."

One has to wonder, why does Ancient Egypt promote a "**Trinity**" story in **Osiris, Isis and Horus**......but has no "**Great Flood**" story? If Ancient Egyptian records were to acknowledge a "Great Flood" event, this would make the Bible even more "**credible**" in the eyes of the occult and rejecters of "**Christ**".

(**Left**) Biblical Noah's Ark during the flood. (**Right**) Australian Aboriginal man. Are there Israelites in Australia and the Pacific Islands?

Dr. Nick Reid, a linguistic expert at the University of New England found the ancient stories of the Australian Aborigines to be similar to stories told from people with "**Semitic**" **ancestry**. Most Semitic civilizations (*i.e. Hebrew Israelites, Sumerians*), including the Hindoo East Indians tell of a "**Great Flood**". In 18 traditional Aboriginal stories, they found that all 18 stories talked about "**the gods**" causing the **seas to rise causing a great flood** that changed the way landscapes looked before that time. *Note: None of Aboriginal stories told of the seas shrinking to expose new land after the flood was over. The concept of a heavy "outpouring" of water from the heavens above and a "quick" rise in the sea level globally has been attributed to the "Great Flood". This is not a coincidence.*

Fact: Archaeological fossil evidence from a rock shelter-cave in the Northern part of Australia proved that the first Australians landed in Northern Australia and Papua New Guinea. Eventually they moved inland to Queensland and Southern Australia. But where did they come from? Well in 2011, the DNA from the lock of hair from a 90+ year old "Negroid" Australian Aborigine was tested by British Anthropologists at the University of Cambridge in partner with Duckworth Laboratory. The DNA of the hair was compared with Asians, Africans and Europeans. It was found that the hair was most closely related to African hair than Asian and European hair. But here is where it gets even deeper. If this is the case, this means that Australian Aborigines migrated from an area were people with "**wooly**" hair lived. This could be Israel, the Middle East, Arabia or Africa as the Hebrews, the Israelites, including the Ishmaelite's were mixed with DNA from the **Sons of Ham**.

Paleo-Hebrew (Before 585 B.C.)

49:12

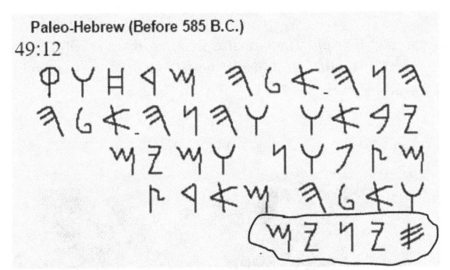

(**Above**) Paleo-Hebrew "**Isaiah**" Dead Sea Scrolls rendition of Isaiah 49:12. The Hebrew word "**Synym**" or "**Sinim**" is at the bottom left (circled).

Hebrew Transliterated

49:12 HNH-'aLH MUrChVQ YB'aV VHNH-'aLH MTShPhVN VMYM V'aLH M'aUrTSh SYNYM.

Latin Vulgate

49:12 ecce isti de longe venient et ecce illi ab aquilone et mari et isti de **terra australi (i.e. land of Australia)**

King James Version

49:12 Behold, these shall come from far: and, lo, these from the north and from the west; and these from the land of Sinim.

Note: *Did the Romans and Greeks know something we don't know? Why would they translate Isaiah 49:12 as "terra Australia" vs "Sinim? The word "Terra" in Latin means "Land" or "Earth". So, were they trying to reveal that some of "Israel" will be regathered from the Land of Australia? The word "Australis" in Latin means "southern" or as some would say back in the time of Latin 2nd Century legends, "unknown southern lands".*

423

Fact: *In Israel, Orthodox Jewish author Yair Davidi/Davidy published two literary works, "Joseph: The Israelite Destiny of America" (2001) and "Ephraim: The Gentile Children of Israel" (2001).* Was he trying to relay a "**hidden message**"?

(**Above**) Australian Aboriginal boys are not considered men until they undergo circumcision, similar to many Bantus Tribes in Africa. Sometimes after "Australian" circumcision, small marks are placed on the chest as well. The Australian Aborigines claim this practice was not introduced to them by the British or any Europeans. "**Circumcision**" is a Hebrew Israelite Tradition and Custom, but it has also been said to be custom of the Ancient Egyptians, perhaps from a "Hebrew" influence while they were in Egypt for over 400 years. The Australian Aborigines however do not resemble the Ancient Egyptians, nor do they practice the religious traditions-customs fashioned after the Egyptians like African tribes in the Horn of Africa (*i.e. Somalia*), Central Africa (*i.e. Alur Tribe*) and the African Great Lakes region do. Could we be on to something?

(**Above**) Australian Aboriginal men. Notice their wooly hair and somewhat Semitic features. While investigating Aboriginal cultures in Australia in the 20th century A.D., **Professor A.P. Elkin of Sydney University** came upon Aboriginal tribes in Australia displaying "**Semitic Mediterranean facial features**" with Egyptian words in their language. The Hebrew Israelites were "Semitic" and they knew the language of the Egyptians. Hebrew-Egyptian influences can also be seen in the **Bantus Ghanaian Ewe Tribe, the Bantus Ghanaian Ga-Dangbe Tribe** and the **Bantus Nigerian Igbo Tribe.**

Here is the proof, some…if not all of the Israelites knew how to speak and understand Egyptian.

Acts 7:22 "And Moses was learned in all the wisdom of the Egyptians, and was mighty in <u>words</u> and in deeds."

Need more proof? Abraham, the Israelites, the Edomites and Jesus (Yahusha) were all familiar with venturing into Egypt for refuge or for goods.

Genesis 42:1-8
"Now **when Jacob saw that there was corn in Egypt,** Jacob said unto his sons, Why do ye look one upon another? And he said, Behold, I have heard that there is corn in Egypt: get you down thither, and buy for us from thence; that we may live, and not die. And Joseph's ten brethren went down to buy corn in Egypt. But Benjamin, Joseph's brother, Jacob sent not with his brethren; for he said, Lest peradventure mischief befall him. And the sons of Israel came to buy corn among those that came: for the famine was in the land of Canaan. **And Joseph was the governor over the land, and he it was that sold to all the people of the land:** and Joseph's brethren came, and bowed down themselves before him with their faces to the earth. **And Joseph saw his brethren, and he knew them, but made himself strange unto them, and spake roughly unto them; and he said unto them, Whence come ye? And they said, From the land of Canaan to buy food.** And Joseph knew his brethren, but they knew not him.

Here in this passage there is some things that give clues to the Israelites "Egyptian-speaking" ability.   First, it says Joseph was governor over the land of Egypt. He was in charge of selling to all the people of the land and outside the land. The Egyptian people could not be governed by a "governor" who only spoke Hebrew. A "**governor**" or a "**president**" has to be able to speak the language of the people of the land. The scripture also says that Joseph saw his Israelite brothers and "**spoke to them roughly**", asking them the place from which they came from.   Did he speak to them in the "**Egyptian Language**"? Did he speak to them in the "**Hebrew Language**" or did he use an "**interpreter**" to speak to them in Hebrew.

Note: Joseph married an Egyptian woman and had two sons: **Ephraim** and **Manasseh**. King Solomon married an Egyptian princess and was given the **Canaanite city of Gezer** as a "**dowry**" gift by the Pharaoh of Egypt. Many of the Hebrew Israelites had Egyptian wives (Ezra 9:1-2). Many of the Israelite children of foreign women (Semitic or Hamitic) knew more how to speak the language of their mother's tongue than Hebrew. Is this where the African saying "**mother tongue**" comes from? This can be seen in the Book of Nehemiah. It is a known fact that the Nigerian "**Igbo**" language and the Ghanaian "**Ewe**" language have "**Hebrew/Egyptian**" influences in their language as well. The "Ewe" people of Ghana also claim to have settled in Egypt, the Land of Canaan (*i.e. Israel*), Sudan and Abyssinia (*i.e. Ethiopia*). The "Ewe" people....like other Bantus Negro Tribes, were afflicted by slavery by the Arabs, the Germans (Ghana), the British (Ghana), other Bantus Israelite Kings (Dahomey/Benin) and the French (Togoland). Coincidence?

Nehemiah 13:24 "And their children spoke half in the speech of **Ashdod** (Philistine territory, cousin of Mizraim (Egypt), and could not speak in the **Jews language**, but according to the language of each people."

If Joseph spoke Hebrew to them would it be a "**dead giveaway**" that he was an Israelite? Consider this, further in Genesis 42 we see that Joseph's Israelite brethren "**switch up**" their language to "**Hebrew**" in front of Joseph who is using an interpreter to talk to them. Joseph imprisoned his brothers for a couple days while in Egypt and allowed them to leave with corn to take it back to their land, however Joseph wanted his Israelite brothers to bring back the "**youngest Israelite**" son....which happened to be his "**full brother**" Benjamin by their same mother "**Rachel**". Reuben, the oldest son of Jacob was talking in Hebrew in front of his other brothers and Joseph, but of course Joseph heard it, being that he knew the Hebrew language.

The 12 Sons/Tribes	Name Means	Mother
1. Reuben	"behold a son"	Leah
2. Simeon	"God hears"	Leah
3. Levi	"joined"	Leah
4. Judah	"let him [God] be praised"	Leah
5. Dan	"judge"	Bilhah
6. Naphtali	"my wrestling"	Bilhah
7. Gad	"good fortune"	Zilpah
8. Asher	"happy"	Zilpah
9. Issachar	"man of hire"	Leah
10. Zebulun	"dwelling"	Leah
11. Joseph	"may God add"	Rachel
12. Benjamin	"son of the right hand"	Rachel

(**Above**) Sons of Jacob from Oldest (**Reuben**) to youngest (**Benjamin**).

During the whole time as Governor of Egypt, it is possible that Joseph talked his brethren in the "**Egyptian language**". If needed, as you will see, Joseph was able to speak to an Egyptian interpreter in the Egyptian language…who would then speak to the Sons of Jacob in **Hebrew** or interpret what they were saying in the Hebrew language converted to Egyptian. If this is not the case, it is definitely very likely that once the 12 sons of Jacob (*with their wives*) settled into Egypt and lived there for 400 years that many of them would become fluent in the Egyptian language. After all, how else would they understand and love the Egyptian gods, if not they were able to study the Egyptian religion in the language/script of the Ancient Egyptians. This is how many people in Afghanistan, Pakistan, and even Africa have a "**mother tongue**" but they also know how to speak "**Arabic**" because of of their "**Islamic**" faith.

Genesis 42:21-24

"If ye be true men, let one of your brethren be bound in the house of your prison: go ye, carry corn for the famine of your houses: But bring your youngest brother (*i.e. Benjamin*) unto me; so shall your words be verified, and ye shall not die. And they did so. And they said one to another, We are verily guilty concerning our brother, in that we saw the anguish of his soul, when he besought us, and we would not hear; therefore is this distress come upon us. **And Reuben answered them, saying, Spake I not unto you, saying, Do not sin against the child; and ye would not hear? therefore, behold, also his blood is required. And they knew not that Joseph understood them; for he spake unto them by an interpreter.** And he turned himself about from them, and wept; and returned to them again, and communed with them, and took from them Simeon, and bound him before their eyes."

This proves that either part, if not all of the time when Joseph interacted with his Israelite brethren, he spoke in the "**Egyptian language**" to an Egyptian interpreter who would then relay what Joseph said to his brethren in the "**Hebrew language**". So, if Joseph knew how to speak Egyptian in just the short period of time that he was governer in Egypt, wouldn't it be logical to say that some of the Israelites in the "Exodus" knew how to speak "Egyptian"?

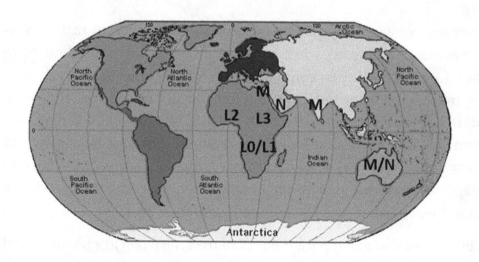

(**Above**) The Maternal "mtDNA's" found in Africa, Arabia, South Asia and Australia. The Australian Aborigines mtDNA have been recorded to be "**M42**" and "**Q2**"…which are the subgroups of the **mtDNA macrohaplogroup** "**M**". The Maternal mtDNA "**M**" is seen in **India, Yemen, Qatar, Socotra, Oman, Arabia and even the "Ethiopian Jews"**. Another subsect of the Australian Aboriginal people has been recorded to fall into the mtDNA "**S**", "**P**" and "**N12**"….which are the subgroups of the **mtDNA macrohaplogroup** "**N**". Maternal mtDNA "**N**" is seen in the **Middle East, the Jews of India, the Ethiopians Jews and it is also seen in residents of the Island of Socotra**. Socotra is home to the **Mehri (Meheri) Arabs** who speak the **Mehri language** and the **Soqotri language**. Both languages are Semitic South Arabia languages which had their origins from the languages spoken by the Semitic sons of Shem (*i.e. Joktan, Ishmael*).

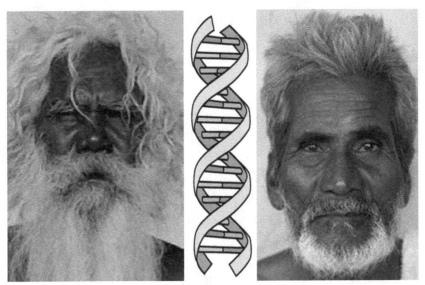

Fact: *Scientists found genetic mutations that are shared by* **South Indian** *"Dark-skinned"* **Dravidians** *and* **Australian Aborigines**. *It is a known fact that the languages of South India (***Malayalam, Tamil***) are of Semitic ancestry, and in certain words, the "***Hebrew language***" influence can be seen.*

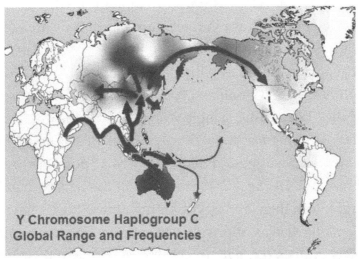

**Y Chromosome Haplogroup C
Global Range and Frequencies**

(**Above**) The "predicted" route of migration for those people groups carrying the Y-DNA "**C**" which is predominately seen in Australian Aborigines and Native Americans. In 2016, the work of Harvard Geneticist **Iosif Lazardis** was shown in the **BioRXIV** magazine with the title, "***The genetic structure of the world's first farmers.***" What this study would reveal is that the Y-DNA of Australian Aborigines, Native

431

Americans, South "Dravidian" Indians and Bantus "Negroes" were found in the Ancient Skeletal remains dug up from inside "Caves" in Israel!

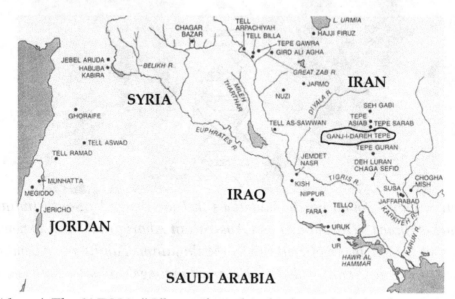

(**Above**) The **Y-DNA "C"** was found in biological skeletal samples in **Ancient Medes-Persia (Iran)** in the **Ganj-Dareh Tepe** area (**circled**) of Western Iran. The **Y-DNA "C"** was also found in the **Natufian, Israeli** Ancient "**Levantine**" samples dating back to Neolithic Pre-Pottery B.C. Era (*i.e. PPNB, PPNC some 3,000 years ago*). Some scientists researched the "**Levantine**" people who practiced the domestication of livestock (*i.e. sheperds like King David*) in the PPNB and PPNC time periods. One theory suggested that there was a "**possible time**" where people whose Y-DNA (*i.e. "C"*) was found in the Levant, had in earlier times brought with them an "**Egyptian influence**" to the Levant (*Israel, Palestine, Jordan*). It was afterwards that these "Egyptian influenced" Nomadic Pastoralists (*i.e. with livestock*) would make their way to the Levant. They would mix-intermarry with the "hunter-gatherer" populations in the area (i.e. Canaanite Pygmy tribes?) and then would be removed to Syria (Northern Assyria) after which they would make their way down to Southern Iraq (Southern Assyria). This seems to sound very similar to the exile of Samaria and the Northern 10 Tribes of Israel. If this is so, meaning the **Y-DNA "C"** was found in skeletal samples in **Israel (Natufian)** and in **Ancient Assyria (Iraq, Iran-Medes/Persia)**......this would mean that the "Australian Aborigines-Native Amerindians" bearing the Y-DNA "C" could be the descendants of the "**Exiled Northern Tribes of Israel**"!

2 Kings 17:6 "In the ninth year of Hoshea the King of Assyria took **Samaria (i.e. Northern Israel)**, and carried away Israel into Assyria, and placed them in Halah and in Habor by the river Gozan, and in the **cities of the Medes (i.e Iran-Persia).**"

Scientists believe the Australian Aborigines were an early "**Out of Africa**" Civilization. Some believe they were the Original inhabitants of Arabia before the Caucasoid-Japhetic **Turkmen (Togarmah)** Muslims from Asia Minor invaded Arabia. But no one in the biblical world or anthropology world suggest that the Australian Aboriginal people are descendants of the Hebrew Israelites or even a race of Ancient Semitic peoples. However, the Australians have practiced **circumcision**, they tell of a "**Great Flood**" story, they have been killed off by disease by the Europeans (British), they have been enslaved like other Hebrew Israelites in Africa by the British, their land has been completely "**colonized**" by the British (*i.e. like Africa, the Caribbean, South Africa, India, the Americas*), they have experienced drought/famine in their land, and they still are an "**oppressed**" people in their own land (*i.e. poverty, drugs, alcoholism, unemployment*). Doesn't this constitute the "**Curses of Israel**"? Are we overlooking the possibility that the **Lost Tribes of Israel** were scattered to the South/Southeast lands as the Bible states in **Isaiah 49:12**?

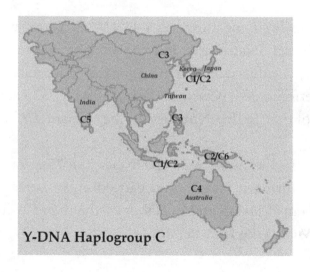

Y-DNA Haplogroup C

The Australian Aboriginal **Y-DNA Haplogroup "C"** is unique in that it is not seen in Africa (*which we would expect if they were descendants of the Ancient Egyptians*). In fact, the Y-DNA Haplogroup "**C**" is seen in its most "**Basal (oldest)**" form in **Australia, Indonesia, Papua New Guinea** and **Japan** (*home of the Ainu/Jomon Black Japanese people*). The Y-DNA Haplogroup "C" is also seen in **Afghanistan, Pakistan, Nepal, Central Asia, Arabia, Iraq, the Americas** (*i.e. Na-Dene Indian family like the Apache, Dogrib, Cheyenne*) and of course in East Asia/Southeast Asia. In addition to this the maternal mtDNA of the Australian aboriginal women and men (**mtDNA M/N**) point to a Semitic ancestry. How so? Because it is seen in the women in Indonesia, India, Yemen, Socotra, Oman, Arabia, and even the Ethiopian Jews/Northern Semitic Ethiopians. What is also interesting is that (Canaanite) Pygmy tribes are also found in Papua New Guinea which is right above Australia. That being said it is possible that the Canaanites and Israelites made their way Southeast as far as the Pacific Islands.

Fact: In 2016, Harvard's Medical School Genetics department, Dr. **Iosif Lazardis**, published the article, "**The genetic structure of the World's first farmers**" (BioRxiv). One of the Y-Haplogroups seen in Ancient Israel was the Y-DNA Haplogroup "**E1b1a**", which scientists say formed in Northeast Africa (Egypt/Nubia-Cush) and later migrated into the Levant (Israel). The other "E" Haplogroup seen in the Levant was "**E1b1b**". This goes along with **Edom's influence** in Northeast Africa (**E1b1b**) with all the mixing he did with the Egyptians, Canaanites, Ishmaelites and the Mediterranean Children of Japheth. But get this, the "E" Y-DNA Haplogroup was not the only Haplogroup found in Israel. Y-DNA "**C-Australian Aborigines/Native Indians**", Y-DNA "**H-South Indian**", Y-DNA "**G-Greece**", "**L-Assyrio-Babylonians/Samaritans**", "**R-Native Americans, East Indians, Pakistanis, Black Moors group,**", "**Q-Native American**" and "**T-Somalia**" were found too! But to better understand all of this we must understand how Genetic Haplogroups mostly "reveal" migration patterns of a people over time (i.e. centuries).

The genetic articles going over the archaeological remains from "Ancient Israel" state that the remains found in Israel dating back to B.C. times suggest that these people migrated from North or Sub-Saharan Africa into Israel (i.e. Moses and the Exodus of Israelites/Egyptians). They also state in the article that "**Craniometric analysis**" of "Ancient Israel skeletal-cranio remains" suggested a North/Northeastern/Sub-Saharan ancestry which is not seen in other ancient males from West Eurasia.

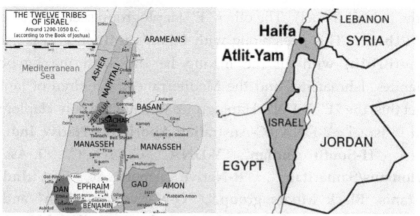

(Above) The Pre-Pottery Neolithic Period "C" skeletal remains found in **Atlit-Yam, Israel** matched up with the Australian Aboriginal Y-DNA "C" Haplogroup. The city of Atlit-Yam falls into the ancient territory of the **Tribe of Manasseh** and the **Tribe of Asher**. Remember, Manasseh was the offspring of Joseph (Israelite) and an **Egyptian woman**. While investigating Aboriginal cultures in Australia in the 20th century A.D., **Professor A.P. Elkin of Sydney University** came upon Aboriginal tribes in Australia displaying "**Semitic Mediterranean features**" with **Egyptian words in their language**.

Note: *Eucalyptus oil/leaves which are seen in Australia have been found in West Africa used among the Bantus people and they have also been found in Egypt.*

Fact: The maternal **mtDNA "N"** was also found in the Natufian skeletal remains in Israel. The Maternal mtDNA "N" is seen in select groups in Yemen, Socotra, and the Ethiopian Jews…but it is also part of the larger mtDNA "**Macrohaplogroup**" that gave rise to the mtDNA "A" and "B" which is primarily seen in Native Amerindians or Mexicans (**Aztec empire**).

(**Above**) The **Rarámuri** or **Tarahumara** are a Native American people of Northwestern Mexico who are renowned for their long-distance running ability. The Tarahumara language belongs to the Uto-**Aztecan** family, hence these indigenous natives are descendants of the Aztec people. Although it is in decline under pressure from Spanish, it is still widely spoken. But guess what, the Tarahumara (Ramaruri) women often carry the MtDNA "**A**" or "**B**" which is seen in many Mexicans. The mtDNA "**A**" and "**B**" is a smaller subgroup of the mtDNA macrohaplogroup "**N**" which is seen in Northeast Africa (North "Amhara" Ethiopians, Ethiopian Jews), Arabia, Arabia Felix (Yemen, Socotra, Oman, Qatar) and **Israel (Natufian study)**. This proves that the indigenous Indians are of Semitic ancestry and have migrated from the Middle East (Israel-Levant) to where they are now (Americas).

(**Above**) **Hopi Indians**, Arizona. The Hopi Indians also carry the mtDNA "**A**" and "**B**"....which is a smaller "**subgroup**" of the mtDNA Macrohaplogroup "**N**", which is mostly seen in the Middle East/Northeast Africa. **But how did the Hopi "Pueblo" people get from the Middle East to Arizona?** How come they do not have "white skin" like modern-day Arabs that are in the Middle East today"? Surely we cannot blame the sun for everything because there are many Arabs living in the Deserts of Egypt and Arabia who have been "**white-skinned**" for generations.

(**Above**) Hopi Indian runners in Arizona, (19th Century). The Hopi people are known to have higher-than-normal rates of "**albinism**" which is seen in the Bantus "Israelite" people of Africa (*i.e. Tanzania, Nigeria, Ghana, Kenya, Congo*) and also the people of South India. Remember, in the Hebrew Torah Book of **Leviticus** (Chapter 13-14), it deals with "**hypopigmented skin disorders**" such as "**albinism**" and "**vitiligo**". Therefore, we know that "**Albinism**" or "**diseases that caused whitening of the skin**" was prevalent enough in the Israelite camp to cause God to give the Israelites 2 Chapters in the Torah discussing how to deal with it.

(**Above**) Hopi Indians, with an Albino Hopi Indian boy (**arrow**) sitting amongst the group.

In a 2010 article published in the "**Journal of Human Genetics**", Geneticist Helene C. Johanson discusses how there are very high numbers of albino people found in the South Pacific. For instance, in the "**Polynesian**" Islands, halfway between Australia and Hawaii there is "**Tuvalu Island**". The Tuvalu people have the mtDNA "**B**" which is a sub-group of the "**Middle Eastern**" mtDNA macrohaplogroup "**N**". The Tuvalu people, like the **Hopi Indians, Nigerian Igbos, Bantus Tanzanians** and **Bantus Congolese** people have "high frequencies" of **albinism (Oculocutaneus albinism type 2-OCA2).** Some of the Tuvalu people also have evidence of "**Negroid**" characteristics such as "**brown skin**" and "**curly wooly-afro**" hair. The Hopi Indians were also found to have moderate rates of the "**9-bp mtDNA deletion**", which is seen in many Bantus South Africans, including the Lemba Jews!

Helene C. Johanson, "Inheritance of a novel mutated allele of the OCA2 gene associated with high incidence of oculocutaneous albinism in a Polynesian community," Journal of Human Genetics, Vol. 55, 2010, pp. 103-111, _www.nature.com/jhg/journal/v55/n2/abs/jhg2009130a.html_.

*Helene C. Johanson, **Pacific Islands Stories: Pacific Albinism Project**, February 26, 2012, http://blog.spevi.net/2012/02/pacific-islands-stories-pacific.html.*

(**Above**) The people of the Lesser Sunda Islands, Indonesia with such Islands as **East Timor** and **Lembata** also carry the same **Y-DNA "C" or the mtDNA "M/N"** as the Australian Aboriginal people/Native American people. As you can see they are brown-skinned. Some look "**Negroid**" and some look "**East Indian**".

(**Above**) **Trireme shipping vessel** used by the Phoenicians/Israelites and other nations in the Middle East. **King Solomon and King Hiram of Tyre** went on sailing expeditions all over the world according to the Bible. Is it possible that the Hebrew Israelites or the Canaanites made their way on ships all the way to Australia? The Australian Aboriginal people of Australia are not a "**pygmy race**", nor do they have any evidence of "**significant**" genetic markers (*i.e. 9 bp-deletion on mtDNA*) seen in the pygmy tribes of Africa or South Asia. Could the Australian Aboriginal people be a group of Israelites that have less "**Canaanite**" ancestral mixing and more "**Egyptian**" ancestral mixing. Or perhaps they are descendants of the ancient Hebrew Israelite families that over the last 2,000 years did not mix with the Sons of Ham.

The Phoenician Alphabet ~ 1250 BC

(**Above**) As many can see, the **Phoenician (Canaanite) alphabet** is identical to the Paleo-Hebrew alphabet. If the Phoenician Alphabet is identical to Paleo-Hebrew how can archaeologists decipher who once visited "**far lands (*i.e. America, Australia, Pacific Islands*)**" when finding so-called "**Phoenician writings**" on rocks? They can't, but if you take into account the **religious traditions/customs of the people,** including **Bible History, DNA** (*i.e. when compared to other nations*) and "**Critical Thinking**" you can narrow down "**who is who**". Mainstream "Jewry" loves attributing everything in far lands that looks "**Hebrew**", to be so-called "**Phoenician-Canaanite**" script. This way they can attribute the people in far-away lands to being descendants of the **Hamitic Canaanites,** since Phoenician/Canaanite writing is similar to "**Paleo-Hebrew**". This is how they easily "**dismiss**" any of the 12

Tribes of Israel as being "**ancestors**" of the Native Americans, Bantus Sub-Saharan Africans, Australian Aborigines, Asians, South Asians or even the Taino Indians of the Caribbean.

(**Above**) Assyrian siege of the Israelite city of Lachish, Israel with **Israelite prisoners** and **King Jehu**, the 10th Israelite King of the Northern Kingdom kneeling before the Assyrian King. In 701 A.D., the Assyrians invaded the Northern Kingdom of Israel. As you can see here the Israelites are sporting **caps-hats**, **fringed garments** and **beards**. Well, At the mouth of the **Glenelg River, South Australia**, was found aboriginal art of human figures resembling **Phoenician seafarers** dressed in "**Semitic clothing**" and what the described as "**peculiar caps**". Not "**Hamitic**" clothing, but "**Semitic**" clothing...as many Ancient Hamitic nations (*i.e. Egyptians, Cushites, Canaanites*) because of the hot climate in Africa didn't wear much clothing or "**peculiar hats**". The big question is.....were the Coastal Israelites (**i.e. Manasseh, Asher**) known to the Greeks as "**Phoenicians**" or were these "Phoenicians" true **Canaanite seamen?** Canaanite men typically did not wear garments and caps. So, has the European world "**tricked**" Biblical historians and Church Christians again? **Remember for centuries, "White" Christian lies have taught that the "Negro" in America is simply a descendant of Canaan, the son of Ham....therefore our "people" are subject to the "Curse of Ham-Canaan".** So why wouldn't they also lie about who the other "**Melaninated**" nations are in the distant lands to the "**East**". We need to cover "all" the possibilities that some of the Israelites traveled further

443

"**East**" after leaving Israel over 2,000 years ago. The Bible says the Israelites would be scattered to the "Four Corners". This is not only the Western Hemisphere of the World (*i.e. Americas, Caribbean, Africa*).

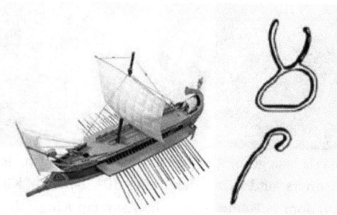

(Left) Trireme Levantine shipping vessel. (Right) Paleo Hebrew "**Aleph**" and "**Lamed**" making up the word "**EL**" or God in Hebrew. If a Jewish archaeologist was to find these symbols written in **Australia** or **South America** would they call it "**Phoenician-Canaanite**" or would they call it "**Paleo-Hebrew**"? To preserve the 2,000-year old lie that the Jews are "**white**", coming from Europe to Israel in 1948, any Jewish archaeologist would likely label it as "**Phoenician**" so that they can link it to the Biblical Black Hamitic Canaanites and not the Israelites of the Bible. Clever, isn't it? But a lie cannot live forever and what is hidden in the dark....will always come to the light.

Fact: Egyptian-type hieroglyphs were found on rocks off the **Hawkesbury River**, north of **Sydney, Australia**. Could this suggest that visitors from Africa or the Middle East visited Australia a long time ago? Aboriginal carvings of a ship were also found in Australia. But what was "**amazing**" was that the ship resembled a Middle Eastern/Levantine "**Trireme**" shipping vessel. In 1978, a black stone with Phoenician/Paleo-Hebrew letters was found in **Katoomba, Southeast Australia**. In addition, at certain Western Australian coastal sites the remains of ancient Levantine (*i.e. Land of Canaan/Israel*) and Middle Eastern pottery have been found. Numerous Middle Eastern symbols have also been found in Aboriginal cave art in the areas of **north-west Kimberley, Arnhem Land** and **Cape York, Australia**. Among the symbols was the Ancient Paleo-Hebrew symbol **"Nechash/Nechosheth"** for **"Copper/Bronze"** (*which is abundant in South Australia as there are many Copper and Tin mines there*). **Note: Bronze is mostly Copper mixed with a little Tin.** Now why would there be Hebrew letters that describe "Copper/Bronze" in Australia? **Maybe it is because some Hebrew Israelites made it all the way to Australia just as Isaiah 49:12 describes!** But were these Israelites seamen from King Solomon's fleet of ships looking for copper or tin that ended up landing in Australia? Or did they leave Israel and the Middle East landing in Australia fleeing persecution?

Fact: Tin was found in **Haifa, Israel** which is near the Territory of the **Tribe of Manasseh** and the **Tribe of Asher**. How did it get there? Did the Israelites get the Tin from Iberia (Spain/Portugal-Tarshish)? Did they get it from Africa or did they get it via ships from Australia? If the Tin was from Australia from King Solomon's shipping voyages....did the **"exiled"** Northern Kingdom Israelites travel **"East"** to lands that they were once familiar with during King Solomon's shipping voyages? This could be a possibility.

Ezekiel 22:20 "As they gather silver and bronze and iron and lead **and tin** into the furnace to blow fire on it in order to melt it, so I will gather you in My anger and in My wrath and I will lay you there and melt you."

Numbers 31:21-23 "Then Eleazar the priest said to the men of war who had gone to battle, "This is the statute of the law which the LORD has commanded Moses: **only the gold and the silver, the bronze, the iron, the tin** and the lead, everything that can stand the fire, you shall

pass through the fire, and it shall be clean, but it shall be purified with water for impurity. But whatever cannot stand the fire you shall pass through the water."

1 Kings 9:26-27 "**And King Solomon made a navy of ships** in Ezion-geber, which is beside Elath/Eloth, on the shore of the Red Sea, in the land of Edom. **And Hiram sent in the navy his servants, shipmen that had knowledge of the sea, with the servants of Solomon.**"

CHAPTER 16

IS THERE ANY ARCHEOLOGICAL DNA PROOF CONNECTING THE BLACK HEBREW ISRAELITES AND THE BLACK CANAANITES DIRECTLY TO THE LAND OF ISRAEL?

(**Left**) British Archaeologist **Dorothy Annie Elizabeth Garrod** (1892-1968 A.D.) worked on excavations at Mount Carmel in Palestine (*before the State of Israel was purchased by the German Rothschild family*), demonstrating "ancient" skeletal fossil remains in the caves of Tabun, El Wad, Shuqba and the Kebara. (**Right**) Near the town of **Shuqba**, Dorothy Garrod found an interesting set of skeletal remains in a cave, dubbed now the "**Shuqba cave**". The Shuqba cave is located on the northern bank of **Wadi en-Natuf** which is located in modern day Palestinian "West Bank" territory in Israel. There was no name for the people these skeletal remains belonged to so they named these people the "**Natufians**", named after "Wadi en-**Natuf**". Using techniques such as harvesting "petrous bone" from the inner ear/skull, scientists have been able to use these ancient skeletons for "DNA testing". The results, have shown a "scientific" connection between the Sub-Saharan

447

"Negro" and the Ancient Israelites from 3,000 years ago. How bout that!

Fact: Scholars point to the Natufian remains as being "**Sub-Saharan**" African after analyzing the skulls (*i.e. craniometry*) of the Natufian people. They state that the Natufian people in Northeast Africa (*i.e. Egypt/Nubia-Sudan*) migrated into the Levant (*i.e. Israel, Palestine, Jordan, Lebanon*) some thousands of years ago. This was their scientific conclusion of the "origin" of the Natufian people based on craniometry, anthropology, DNA and archaeological evidence. But according to the Bible and the Lost Books of the Bible (**i.e. Book of Jasher, Book of Jubilees**), we know that the Hebrew Israelites left **Egypt/Nubia-Cush** (Northeast Africa) during the "**Exodus**" to find a home in the Land of Canaan (*Israel*). We also know that along the way the Israelites mixed their seed with the daughters of Cush, Mizraim (Egypt) and Canaan. We can prove this in the scriptures and also based off the simple fact the "early" Israelites married Hamitic women (*i.e. Joseph-Egyptian woman, Moses-Cushite woman, Judah-Canaanite woman*). Therefore, from this we would expect the Israelites to also gain some "**Hamitic**" physical features (*i.e. from Hamitic DNA*) and customs during their early centuries of becoming an "**Israelite Nation**". According to Israeli Archaeologist, **Dr. Ofer bar-Yosef** the original settlers of "**Canaan**" were hunter-gatherers and secondary foragers which was later followed by the appearance of the earliest farmers-pastoralists (*i.e.* **Hebrew Israelites**).

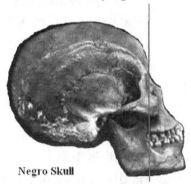

Mandible protrusion of the Jaw past the line is called **prognathism**.

Negro Skull

(**Above**) Caucasian or "**Caucasoid**" European people do not have "**Prognathic**" Jaws......**Negroid** people do.

According to Israeli Archaeologist **Dr. Ofer bar-Yosef**, British-American Biological-Forensic Anthropologist **Dr. John Lawrence Angel** and others, the Natufian skeletal finds exhibited "**Negroid Traits (*i.e. Ethiopic, Bushmanoid*)**". How so? The skull shape, the nose, the teeth, the "**prognathism**" of the jaw and DNA markers excluded people with "**White skin**", proving the Natufians in Israel were not a race of "White people (*i.e. Ashkenazi Jews, Sephardic Jews or modern-day Arabs*)". Therefore, these "**Natufian people**" in Ancient Israel (B.C. times) were "**Negroid-looking**" people. Who were these Natufian people? Well, scientists mentioned the word "**Sub-Saharan**" and "**Niger-Congo**" in their studies. This basically mean "**Bantus Negroes**"....aka the same "**stock**" of people that were captured as slaves and sold from Africa.

Note: First century A.D. Gentile Jewish writer Flavius Josephus (37-100 A.D.) wrote the oldest non-biblical witness of Jesus from Roman official records to which he had access to. He passed this information taken from Roman official records to his "**Halosis of Jerusalem**" work or "**Capture of (Jerusalem)**", written around 72 A.D. Josephus discussed "the human form of Jesus and his wonderful works." A biblical scholar

Robert Eisler, in a classic study in 1931, rebuilt the testimony of Josephus based on an old translation of the newly discovered Russian translation which preserved the original Greek text, adopted from the "original" Aramaic texts of "**The Jewish Wars**" by Josephus. According to the reconstruction of Eisler, the oldest non-biblical description of Jesus reads as follows:

"**At that time, also appeared a man of magical power ... if it is worth calling him a man [whose name is Jesus], whom [certain] Greeks called the son of God, but his disciples call him "the true prophet" ... he was a simple - looking man, middle age, black-skinned (melagchrous), short stature, three cubits high, hump, prognathous, a long nose, eyebrows that met above the nose ... with little [curly] hair, but with a line down the middle of the head the fashion of Nazarenes and an underdeveloped beard.**"

This description of Christ does not match up with todays Arab man or today's Caucasoid European Jew. But wasn't Christ descendant from the Tribe of Judah? Here we see 2,000-year-old literary proof that lines up perfectly with modern archaeological scientific proof. Caucasians **DO NOT** have prognathous Jaws, like Christ (an Israelite) was depicted to have. Note: European Jews are genetically European Caucasians that "converted" to the religion called "Judaism". The have no blood-ties to the *Ancient Hebrew Israelites/12 Tribes of Israel* of the Bible.

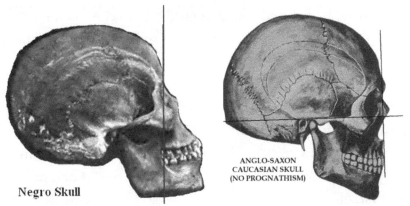

Negro Skull

ANGLO-SAXON
CAUCASIAN SKULL
(NO PROGNATHISM)

Notice how we see the word "**prognathous**" and "**melogchrous**" in the depiction of **Christ.** The word "**prognathism**" means "**protruding**" as in "**protruding jaws**" seen in Negroid races. The word "**melanin**" comes from the Greek word "**melas**" which means "**black/dark**". Archaeological and craniometry studies of the Natufian skulls found in Israel prove that the people living in Ancient Israel during Biblical Times were not "**Europoid**"......they were more "**Negroid**". Is this a coincidence?

French Bioanthropologist-archaeologist **Dr. Fanny Bocquentin** and British-American Bioanthropologist **Dr. John Lawrence Angel** in their Natufian research pointed that the northward migration of Northeastern African populations carrying sub-Saharan biological elements is concordant with the **morphological homogeneity** of the **Natufian populations**, which present **morphological affinity** with **sub-Saharan populations (Negroid people)**. What this means is that the sub-Saharan African population in Northeast Africa had the same physical attributes and traits as the ancient Natufian people found in the caves of Israel!

1. **Morphology** is defined as: relating to the **form or structure of things**.
2. **Homogeneity** is defined as: the quality or state of **being all the same** or all of the same kind.

3. **Affinity** is defined as: a relation between biological groups involving **resemblance** in structural plan and **indicating a common origin**.

Even American Bio-Paleoanthropologist **Dr. Charles Loring Brace** in the Journal, *"Proceedings of the National Academy of Sciences of the United States of America"* acknowledges that **Sub-Saharan (Niger-Congo)** African populations have a clear link to the "**Ancient**" Natufian people of Israel.

Haplogroup E-V38/ E3a/ E1b1a	
Possible time of origin	approx 25,000-30,000 years BP[1]
Possible place of origin	Horn of Africa [2]
Ancestor	E-P2
Descendants	E-M2, E-M329
Defining mutations	L222.1, V38, V100

(**Above**) According to geneticists, **Y-DNA E-P2** arose in the Horn of Africa or what some would consider Northeast Africa. Y-DNA **E-P2** would give rise to **E-M2 (E1b1a-Negroes)** and **E-M329 (E1b1c-Semitic Ethiopians-Amhara, Eritrea, Tigrayan)**. E-M329 (E1b1c) is linked to the descendants of the Ethiopian Hebrew Israelite Solomonic/Aksumite Dynasty.....however this Ancient Haplogroup sub-group has been "**cleverly**" erased by the European Genetic world.

(**Left**) Beja man from Northeast Sudan (Ancient Upper Egypt). The Beja Tribe are known to live in the **Hala'ib Triangle** which is the **Egyptian-Sudanese** border. (**Right**) Sub-Saharan Bantus slave. During the invasion of Northeast Africa by the Black Arabs many Beja tribesmen were "**Islamized**". Both the Black Arabs and other tribes were partakers in driving out many Bantus Israelites from Egypt-Sudan further south into Ethiopia, Kenya, Uganda, Tanzania, Mozambique, Malawi or west into West Africa. If the Bantus Israelites stayed in Egypt-Sudan, they were subjugated to slavery and possibly death. This is why the Y-DNA "E1b1a" is not seen in high frequencies in Egypt or North Sudan. The Y-DNA "**J1-M267**" of the Black Arabs is seen in North Sudan like the city of Khartoum. The Beja Tribe would over time mix with the Black Arabs and even the seed of Edom in Egypt, Africa (*i.e. Edomite Hadad-son Genubath*). For this reason, their Y-DNA shows the "**E1b1b**" and "**J1-M267**" Haplogroup. The Beja people also show some "**genetic closeness**" to the North African **Black Tuareg Berbers** whom 5th Century A.D. Greek Historian Herodotus linked to the Ancient Phuttite Libyans (*i.e. Fezzan-Garamantes*). Remember Phut and Mizraim (Egypt) in the Bible were Hamitic brothers and neighbors geographically in North Africa.

According to Abbasid 9th Century Muslim Geographer "**Ahmad al-Ya'qubi**" the Beja people in Ancient times had kingdoms stretching from **Aswan** (South Egypt) to **Massawa** (Eritrea). Some Egyptologists say linguistically, the Beja Tribe has similarities to the language of the Ancient Egyptians, just like certain tribes in Somalia. Their language also falls into the **"Cush family"** of languages as Sudan-Nubia....aka Upper Egypt was apart of Ancient Egypt in B.C. times. To top this off, German born 19th century Egyptologist **Emile Brugsch** traced a certain clan of the Beja people to the Egyptian people of the 20th Dynasty!

But, something occurred in Northeast Africa, that would create different "branches" in the Y-DNA E Haplogroup. The **"Exodus"** of the Israelites from Egypt into the land of Canaan would happen followed by the scattering of certain Israelites back into Africa. This would be followed by the influx of **"Edomites"** into North Africa. The Shemitic Ishmaelites, Edomites and Hebrew Israelites would mix with **ALL** the Sons of Ham creating a massive "E" Haplogroup that would make up most of the Y-DNA Haplogroups seen in Africa. These "E" branches would be formerly known as **E1a, E3a, E3b** and **E2**. Today they are known as **"E-M33/E-M132"**, **"E1b1a"**, **"E1b1b"** and **"E-M75"** respectively and a hidden **"E1b1c"** that no longer exists in the "Genetic world".

Geneticist, **Dr. Peter A. Underhill** from Stanford University admitted in his research that sub-Saharan genetic lineages affiliated with the Y-DNA **E-P2** migrated through Egypt into Israel, the Middle East and as far north as Turkey. In genetics, it is a known fact that the ancestral Y-DNA E-P2 underwent a mutation called **V38** and **V100** that created two new groups of people. These groups were labeled Y-DNA **"E-M2"** and **"E-M329"**. **E-M2** would be later called **"E1b1a"** and **"E-M329"** would be called **"E1b1c"**. E1b1c would be only confined to Cush-Sudan (Upper Egypt)/Ethiopia, while E1b1a would be mainly confined to Sub-Saharan Africa until the slave trades began (Arab Slave Trade, Transatlantic Slave Trade). These two Y-DNA "E" groups would exist and dominate in B.C. times........that is until the influence of Edom's seed mixing with the Hamites in North Africa/Northeast Africa would cause the mutation **"M215"** which would give rise to the Y-DNA

"E1b1b". Y-DNA **"E1b1b"** can be seen in modern day North African Arabs, Northeast Africans, and European people living off the coast of the Mediterranean Sea (Spain, Portugal, Italy-Rome, Greece, Turkey).

Don't Believe? Here are some scientific articles to cross-reference.

"The questionable contribution of the Neolithic and the Bronze Age to European craniofacial form", PNAS, (2006), Volume 103. Pg. 242-247. C. Loring Brace.

"The Natufian Culture in the Levant, Threshold to the Origins of Agriculture." Evolutionary Anthropology, (1998), 6 (5), pg 159-177. Bar-Yosef, Ofer (1998).

"Biological relations of Egyptian and Eastern Mediterranean populations during Pre-dynastic and Dynastic times." Journal of Human Evolution, (1972), 1(3), pg 307-313. Angel, J. L.

"The phylogeography of Y chromosome binary haplotypes and the origins of modern human populations." Annals of Human Genetics, (2001), Jan; 65 (1), pg43-62. PA Underhill.

(**Above**) Born in the late 1800's, **Sir Arthur Keith** was a Scottish anatomist and anthropologist. He documented that the **Natufian people of Israel** had obvious "**Negroid**" traits when observing their skeletal remains. How much "proof" from Eurasian Anthropologists, Geneticists, Archaeologists, and Scientists do we need to accept the Truth? How much proof do the Ashkenazi, Sephardic and Mizrahi Jews need to accept that they are simply "religious converts" to Judaism (**i.e. proselytes**)? Even Christ in his time knew what was going on in Judea with "**everyone**" converting to "**Pharisee-ism**" calling themselves "**Jews**". This is called a "**Proselyte**".

Matthew 23:15 "Woe to you, scribes (*i.e. Nethinim/Rechabites/Kenites*) and Pharisees, hypocrites, because you travel around on sea and land **to make one proselyte;** and when he becomes one (*i.e. a Jew*), you make him twice as much a son of hell as yourselves."

Fact: Starting from the early 1900's many studies have been done on the Natufian remains found in the caves of Israel. This information was not readily accessible to White or Black people in America. Around **Shukbah** and **Mount Carmel** in Israel, multiple caves were excavated. The dental, cranial and limb remains of the Natufian people in Israel showed a strong affinity to **Sub-Saharan "Negroid" people**. Scientific

456

literary works and Magazines like "**The New York Times**" noted the "**Negroid**" features of the Natufian people of Israel. They noted these features:

- Long-headed people with cap shaped occiputs (*i.e. seen in Bantus West and East Africans*).
- The dimensions of their heads were greater than Egyptian heads/skulls.
- Short and wide faces.
- Prognathous jaws (*i.e. Negroid*).
- Nasal bones were wide with a low arch.
- Non-prominent chins, masked by the fullness of their jaws/teeth.
- Some were short stature (*5 feet 3 or 5 inches tall compared to Cushite Nilotic East Africans like the Dinka and Maasai Tribe who on average are 6 feet tall*).
- Teeth extraction of the upper canine incisors. This is common in Cushitic Tribes and Bantus East Africans (*Somalians, Ethiopians, Sudanese, Kenyans and Tanzanians*). It was practiced in the old generation as form of beauty, healing disease, tradition and rite of passage. Many white Transatlantic Slave traders noticed this in their Negro slaves. Filing of all the teeth or the two front teeth were also done by some Hamitic and Bantus tribes. Tooth extraction and infant tooth mutilation began as an ancient practice by traditional healers in Sub-Saharan Bantus Africa. It was done for superstitious, aesthetic or other reasons depending on the Tribe and its traditions. During the 1700's in West Africa many slaves were noticed to have evidence of dental mutilation by their slave masters. (*i.e. see **Journal of Ethnobiology and Ethnomedicine, "The Role of Traditional Healers in Tooth Extractions in Lekie Division, Cameroon**. Ashu M. Agbor, Sudeshni Naidooo, and Awono M Mbia. DOI: 10.1186/1746-4269-7-15*).

Need more proof?

Dr. Iosif Lazaridis, Department of Genetics at Harvard Medical School in his study/article "**The genetic structure of the world's first farmers**" in *BioRxiv, the preprint server for Biology,* proves with Y-DNA research that the skeletal remains found in Israel matched that of **Y-DNA E1b1a, E1b1b, C, Q, H, T, P and R.** His research proves genetically that the people that lived in the time period **AFTER THE NATUFIANS,** consisted of Bantus Sub-Saharan Negroes bearing the Y-DNA "**E1b1a**" and other race groups today that are **Majority-Melanated** (*i.e. having Brown skin with the ability to tan*). This time period is known as the **Pre-Pottery Neolithic B (PPNB)** time period (*i.e. B.C. time era*) in the Levant (Israel/Assyria) where the domestication of plants and livestock was in its early beginnings in Israel/Canaan.

Remember the Hebrew Israelites were primarily pastoralists (i.e. *herding cattle, growing vegetables, raising livestock*). While the Israelites were in Egypt during 400 years of captivity we would assume that the Israelites did very little raising livestock.....that is until they got their own land where their livestock could flourish. Prior to the Israelites entering into the Land of Milk and Honey (Canaan), the Hamitic Canaanites were Hunter-gatherers and foragers, something the Israelites probably also learned how to do as well from co-mingling with the Canaanites. Just as the Natufian research claims, the Israelites did bring with them out of Egypt **flocks and herds of livestock** into the Land of Canaan during the **Natufian-PPNB** "B.C." period. Do we have any more proof to back this up? The proof is in the Bible!

During the Exodus of the Hebrew Israelites with Moses, the Children of Israel brought "**livestock**" with them out of Egypt into the Land of Canaan. The Egyptians also gave the Israelites precious metals as well before they made the "Exodus" to the Land of Canaan. The proof is in our Bibles!

Exodus 12:31-32 "And he called for Moses and Aaron by night, and said, Rise up, and get you forth from among my people, both ye and the children of Israel; and go, serve the LORD, as ye have said. **Also take your flocks and your herds, as ye have said, and be gone (*i.e. to the Land of Canaan*); and bless me also.**"

Exodus 12:35-38 "Now the **sons of Israel** had done according to the word of Moses, for they had requested from the Egyptians articles of **SILVER** and articles of **GOLD**, and **CLOTHING**; and the LORD had given the people favor in the sight of the Egyptians, so that they let them have their request. Thus they plundered the Egyptians. Now the sons of Israel journeyed from Rameses to Succoth, about six hundred thousand men on foot, aside from children.....A mixed multitude also went up with them, along with flocks and herds, a very **LARGE NUMBER OF LIVESTOCK.**"

Note: The Pre-Pottery Neolithic period (PPNA/PPNB) represents early B.C. times in the Levant (Israel/Canaan) and Assyria. The Pre-Pottery Neolithic period succeeded the Natufian period as many scientist's state that the domestication of **plants** and **livestock SKYROCKETED** during this time. How could the Bible verify this as being from the "Israelites" presence in the Land of Canaan/Levant? Simple.

Exodus 12:38 "A mixed multitude went up with them also, and **flocks and herds, a great deal of livestock**."

Could the Pre-Pottery Neolithic period be when the Israelites started widespread livestock and agricultural practices under the Kingdom of Israel with King Saul? Nevertheless, geneticists and scientists using "DNA" technology were able to record the "**nations of people**" according to "**Haplogroups**" who were living in Israel during these time periods. The "**breakdown**" of the results may just shock you.

Here is the brief breakdown of these Y-DNA Haplogroups that were found in the skeletal remains in the Natufian cave area and other locations in Israel.

- **Y-DNA E1b1a**-Negroes/Sub-Saharan Bantus people. This includes African-Americans, Caribbean Blacks, Afro-Latinos and those Bantus Africans scattered into India. Also includes Semitic Ethiopians (Amhara), Eritreans and Tigrayans by way of our ancestor older **"father"** Haplogroup **"E-P2"**.
- **Y-DNA E1b1b**-Edomite influence. Remember, prior to Moses and the Israelites venturing into the Land of Canaan, the Edomites and the Canaanites were living in the Land of Canaan. Edom's first wives in Genesis 36:2 were Canaanite women. These Canaanite women if they managed to run back to Canaan would have "let loose" mixed-breed sons in Israel/Canaan bearing their "Edomite" passed-down Y-DNA "E1b1b". The Edomites also did some mixing with the Hamitic Egyptians (*see "1 Kings 11:19-20"*). During 600 B.C., 200 B.C. and leading up to the time of Christ the **Edomites** also lived in Israel/Land of Canaan (*i.e. hence the Book of Obadiah*). Here they mixed with the Greeks, Romans, Syrians, North African Hamites and other Semitic peoples.
- **Y-DNA C**-most commonly seen in Australian Aborigines and Native Americans (*i.e. Na-Dene groups*). Also seen in select groups in Indonesia, Polynesia, Micronesia and Melanesia. It is also seen in Asia.
-
- **Y-DNA P**-most commonly seen in the **"Negritos"** population in the Pacific Islands (*i.e. Aeta or Agta people in Luzon, Philippines*) and also Papua New Guineans. This could very well be the ancestral Haplogroup of those Canaanites that traveled **"East"** with or without the Israelites into the far islands off the Pacific.

Note: Remember, the "Negritos" in the Philippines have the same mtDNA (maternal) 9-bp deletion marker that is seen in the Lemba Jews, South African Bantus Israelites, Native Americans and the Black Ainu/Jomon Japanese people.

- **Y-DNA Q-**most commonly seen in Native Americans and indigenous people of the Americas/Caribbean. It is also seen in select groups in Asia.

- **Y-DNA R-**most commonly seen in the descendants of the Black Moors/Black Jews who lived in Iberia. It is also seen in its earliest "basal" form in people in India, Pakistan, Afghanistan and Native Americans. The Y-DNA "R" was originally created from the mixing of "Shemitic" people with other "Shemitic" people and to a lesser extent "Hamitic" and "Japhetic" people. **Remember, the Shemitic Children of Asshur and Lud were known to have had territories extending into modern day "Turkey".**

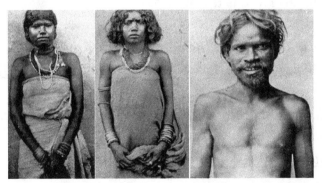

(**Above**) Irula men and women, **Tamil Nadu/Kerala**, South India. They have the same mtDNA **9-bp deletion marker** as African pygmies, Negrito pygmies and other short races found throughout the world.

- **Y-DNA H**-most commonly seen in the **Dravidian** "South" Dark-skinned Indian (*i.e. Kerala, Tamil Nadu*). Some sources may label them as the "**Dalits**" or the "**Untouchables**".
  Note: The mtDNA (maternal) DNA 9-bp deletion marker found in the Lemba Jews including other South African Bantus Israelite Tribes was also found in four South Indians populations: the **Irula (Dravidian)**, the **Yanadi (Dravidian)**, the **Black Negro-looking Siddi's, Maria Gond-Bastar (Dravidian)**, and the **Mongoloid-looking Nicobarese people**.

- **Y-DNA T**-seen mostly in Somalians and Djiboutians like the **Dir Clan/Issa Clan**. **Note:** *Somalians also have strong Egyptian ancestry and Semitic Ancestry*. The Egyptians were well familiar with the Land of Punt (Somalia). Egyptian men and women often strove in the camp of the Israelites (*see Leviticus 21:10*). It is also seen in traces in the **Afar Tribe** and the **Anteony/Antemoro** people in Madagascar.

Don't believe? Here is the article.

"The genetic structure of the world's first farmers". *BioRxiv, the preprint server for Biology (2016). Lazaridis, I.* https://doi.org/10.1101/059311.

"Genomic insights into the origin of farming in the ancient Near East". *Nature. (2016).*
http://dx.doi.org/10.1038/nature19310.

Fact: Scottish anatomist and anthropologist, Sir Arthur Keith believed the Ancient "**Natufian people**" in Israel were "Negroid" people. This stirred up a lot of controversy in the late 1800's to early 1900's but not without some people claiming the "**Negroid Bones**" found in Natufian Caves near Wadi an-Natuf in Israel were of "**Cannibals**".
Fact: *In Israel in the Qafzeh, Es Skhul, Amud, Kebara, and Tabun caves, numerous skeletal remains of "Neanderthals" were recovered. Neanderthals,*

*Cro-Magnon men or "**Cave men**" as people like to call it today were considered the "ancient man" that walked the earth prior to modern day humans....aka "**homo sapiens**" by the scientific world. These "Neanderthal people" according to some, were what some of the people that lived prior to "Noah's Flood" looked like. The Neanderthal bones found in Israel were tested using genetics and it was found that the Neanderthals living in Israel did not have brown skin like that of Negroes. They had white skin with reddish, brown or blonde hair. They also didn't exhibit African-like body proportions. **Could these "Neanderthal" bones found in Israel have been the remains of the descendants of Cain (sons of the Wicked One) or were they the offspring of the Fallen Angels in Noah's time before the flood?***

CHAPTER 17

DID THE FALLEN ANGELS AND THEIR SEED BRING A "PYGMY" TRAIT TO THE BIBLICAL "CANAANITES" IN THE LEVANT? IF SO, WHAT ELSE DID THEY BRING TO THE OTHER SONS OF NOAH?

Fact: Neolithic **pygmy skeletons** have been found in Spain, Indonesia, Greece, Northwest Russia (Near Finland) and even China. A mass grave of "**dwarf-like**" people was found in the "**Bayan (Baian)-Kara-Ula area**, which is a mountainous area that sits on the **China** and **Tibet border**. An Archaeological expedition, led by **Chi Pu Tei**, a professor of archaeology at Beijing University, China, discovered a number of unique burial sites located in caves in the Baian-Kara-Ula area. In 1937-1938, in these caves what Chi Pu Tei found was a complex system of tunnels and underground storerooms. The walls were square and glazed, as if the mountain rock was cut with extreme heat. Now this kind of stone masonry work is also seen in **Ancient Egypt** but inside these caves there were the skeletal remains of "**yellow-white**" pygmies with "**disproportionately large skulls**". At first the site workers thought it was the skeletal remains of apes or monkeys but they realized that the "**ape world**" is not known for "**burying the**

dead"…especially in tombs or caves. The size of the skeletons ranged from 3 feet to 4 feet….just like the **pygmy tribes** or the "**Negrito**" people seen all across the world. The only thing these skeletons had in common with the pygmy people is their small stature. African Pygmy skulls **ARE NOT** disproportionately large compared to their body.

(**Above**) This picture is of a "**Dropas**" couple. 10 years after discovering the caves of the Bayan **(Baian)-Kara-Ula area on the China/Tibet border,** the "Dropas/Dzopa" people and the "**Hans (sometimes named Ham/Cham)**" people were still found living in the caves/mountains. The couple, **Hueypah-La** (4 feet tall) and **Veez-La** (3 ft. 4-inch-tall) were believed to be descendants of the "**yellow-white**" pygmy people whose skeletons were found in that region. Unlike Chinese, Tibetan or Mongolians, the Dropos people were very small in height, had larger than normal heads and large sometimes wide-spaced eyes. They had very little hair on their bodies as well…which is common in Asians.

(Above) Modern day Alien and an **Alien-human hybrid** being.

Supposedly, according to the local past oral history in **Central Asia**, centuries ago the Dropas pygmy people were considered so ugly that they were hunted down and killed by the so-called "**Mongols**" riding on horseback in that region. According to many, Tibet wasn't ruled by China during this time.   It wasn't until the early 1900's that the "Dropos" pygmy people caught the attention of an English scientist named **Dr. Kayrl Robin-Evans**.   Dr. Evans carried out his own expedition to Asia, eventually making his way into Tibet near the Bayan **(Baian)-Kara-Ula area,** only to be abandoned by many of his Tibetan guides who were terrified of the "**Bayan area**". On the way there they visited the Buddhist **Dalai Lama** who gave them some insight into the area and what lied there. Once in the village area of Bayan Kara Ula, Dr. Evans was introduced to the language of the Dropa people and their history from a man named "**Lurgan-La**" the religious guardian/priest of the area. Lurgan-La revealed that the Dropas people came from the **Sirius Star System** thousands of years ago only to be trapped on earth during the crash of their spaceship in the 11th Century A.D.

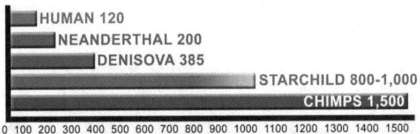

HUMAN 120	
NEANDERTHAL 200	
DENISOVA 385	
STARCHILD 800-1,000	
CHIMPS 1,500	

0 100 200 300 400 500 600 700 800 900 1000 1100 1200 1300 1400 1500
NUMBER OF MUTATIONS IN MITOCHONDRIAL DNA

Facts: This "**Dropas**" story prompted the writings of the books "**Sungod" in exile**" by **David Gamon** and "**The Chinese Roswell**" by **Hartwig Housdorf**. In 2003, the "**Starchild**" project head by Geneticists **Dr. Ripan Malhi** and **Dr. Jason Eshleman** found proof that the a "**Starchild**" skull consisted of more "**foreign-alien DNA**" than human DNA. Dr. Ripan Malhi and Dr. Jason Eshleman also worked on testing the genetics of the ancient **Kennewick man** found in Washington State, America in 1996. But what is also interesting is that the Starchild's Skull DNA proved to have a **high number of mutations** compared to humans, **Neanderthals** and the **Denisovan** (Cro-magnon) man.

Fact: *The Nilotic "**Cushite**" people of Sudan (i.e. Dinka Tribe, Nuer, Nuba, Shillik), including the **Khoi-San** people of South Africa have the oldest DNA on the planet with little to no mutations (according to man's genetic classification).*

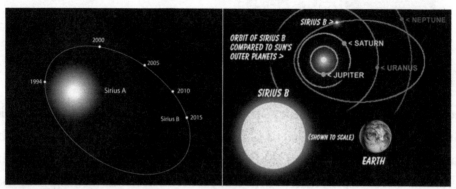

(Above) The **Sirius Star system** is a binary star system. The orbit of Sirius A & B (*where the Egyptians say Isis/Osiris is from*) takes about twice as long as to come into Earth's vicinity to be seen in detail by astrologers with telescopes. Sirius B is smaller and fainter than Sirius A (*i.e. the Doggstar*). The Egyptians worshipped this binary-star system as the **Star of the Nile** or the **Star of Isis**. In Arabic, it means "**the sparkling one**". Sirius is known the brightest "star" in the night sky.

(Above) Ancient hieroglyphs representing "**Sirius**" contains **three** elements/parts. A "**phallic-penis**" obelisk-steeple (*representing Osiris' magical re-assembled penis cut off by his brother Set*), a "**womb-like**" dome (*representing Isis' womb*) and a Star (*representing the son – Horus/Heru*). Notice how "steeple-looking obelisks" are seen on most old Catholic Churches and the "dome" is seen on most Islamic Mosques. Coincidence? **Nope! But wait till we see how it all connects to Satan-Lucifer.**

Consider this as well. In the Quran in Chapter 53 (An-Najm or "The Star") it reads:

Sahih International, Quran 53:42-52 "And that to your **Lord (Allah)** is the finality. And that it is He who makes one laugh and weep. **And that it is He who causes death and gives life (*i.e. only God gives life*).** And that He creates the two mates – the male and female. From a sperm-drop when it is emitted and that incumbent upon Him is the next creation. And that it is He that enriches and suffices. **And that it is He (Allah) WHO IS LORD OF SIRIUS.** And that he destroyed the first people of Aad and Thamud (*i.e. Arabia/Arabia Felix*) – and He did not spare them. And the people of Noah before. Indeed, it was they who were even more unjust and oppressing."

So, in this scripture in the Quran, it would seem that Allah is the **LORD of SIRIUS**. In Satanism or the "Occult" who is Sirius? In Egyptian mythology who is "Sirius"? The Sirius star is part of the Canis Major constellation system. Remember, the Bible tells us not look up to the heavens at the Sun, Moon and Stars to worship them. This is God of Abraham (**Ishmael's father**), Isaac and Jacob. This is the God who created the Archangel Gabriel whom the Muslims call "**Jibril**". How can the God of Abraham, Ishmael, Isaac, Jacob, and Moses in the older "Paleo-Hebrew Torah" forbid man to "**venerate**" the constellations but the "newer" Arabic Quran disregards this commandment?

Deuteronomy 4:19 "And beware not to lift up your eyes to heaven and see the sun and the moon **and the stars**, and all the hosts of heaven, and **be drawn away and worship them and serve them**, those which the LORD your God has allotted to all the peoples under the whole heaven."

Note: *Whenever the Quran mentions the word "**He**" or "**Us**" with the first letter in "**capitals**" it is usually referring to **Allah** himself or Allah and his* *angels. It is **NOT** referring to Muhammad himself…..instead it is referring to Allah, the God of the Muslims.*

So if the Quran mentions that Allah is Lord of Sirius, does this mean that Islam and the Quran was also inspired by "**Fallen Angels**"? The Egyptians, the Romans, the Greeks all seem to have been "**fans**" of worshipping multiple pagan gods, the sun, moon, planets and the constellations. Why else would the Quran mention Allah as Lord of the Star Sirius and for Muslims to worship Allah's 3 daughter goddesses (Al-Uzza, Al-lat, Al-Manat) in Sura 53:19-52 (*excluding the "Satanic Verses" removed centuries ago*). This doesn't seem right at all.

Now here is something interesting to think about. The **Sirius Star system** is the same place the pagan Egyptian and Sumerian "gods (*i.e. Annunaki*)" were said to have lived-visited before coming to earth. Isis, Anubis, Thoth and basically all of Egypt's religion stems from the **Sirius Star System** (Sirius A-**Isis**, Sirius B-**Osiris**).

This "**Sirius**" star story is also told by the **Dogon tribe** in Mali, Africa in regards to the "**Nommos**" people that came from the heavens. The Egyptians knew that once a year the Sun would align with the Sirius star system (*aka the Dog-Starr*) and the Orion Belt during the solstices (*winter/summer*). The Pyramids (*including the Pyramid of Giza*), like many other megalithic rock structures all across the world were also built to be in alignment with the Sirius star system. What many people don't know is that these pyramids scattered all over the world are also "**gateways**" to the "**inner earth**"….aka the "**Halls of Amenti**" where the Seed of Satan and the Giants dwell. If you don't believe it read what the Egyptian "**Emerald Tablets**" say written supposedly by the Egyptian pagan god of wisdom, **Thoth** (Tehuti).

EMERALD TABLETS OF THOTH

"I lie in the **sarcophagus of stone (Pyramid) in my chamber**. Then reveal I to him the great mysteries. Soon shall he follow to where I shall meet him, <u>**even in the darkness of Earth shall I meet him**</u>, I, **Thoth, Lord of Wisdom**, meet him and hold him and dwell with him always. **Builded I the Great Pyramid**, patterned after the pyramid of Earth force, burning eternally so that it, too, might remain through the ages (*i.e. after the flood*). In it, I builded my knowledge of "**Magic-Science**" so that I might be here <u>**when again I return from Amenti (Hell/underworld)**</u>, Aye, while I sleep in the Halls of Amenti, my Soul (*i.e. spirit*) roaming free will incarnate (*i.e. spirit entering a flesh body*), **dwell among men in this form or another**. (Hermes, thrice-born.) Emissary (*i.e. representative*) on Earth am **I of the Dweller (Satan)**, fulfilling his commands so many might be lifted (*i.e. initiated/deceived*). Now return I to the halls of Amenti, **leaving behind me some of my wisdom**. Preserve ye and keep ye the command of the Dweller (**Satan**): Lift ever upwards your eyes toward the light. Surely in time, ye are one with the Master, surely by right ye are one with the Master, surely by right yet are one with the ALL. Now, I depart from ye. Know my commandments, keep them and be them, and I will be with you, helping and guiding you into the Light. **Now before me opens the portal**. Go I down in the **darkness of night**."

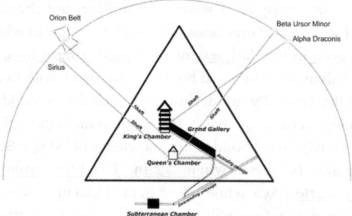

Sky over Giza 2500 BC

(Above) **Star alignment with the Great Pyramid of Giza. Orion (associated with the god Osiris) is aligned with the King's Chamber while Sirius (associated with the goddess Isis) is aligned with the Queen's Chamber.**

This may seem all interesting, fine and dandy for some but the Bible tells of Fallen Angels teaching mankind all of these things in regards to the **Zodiac and the Star Constellations**. How else would ancient man (*without a modern-day telescope or Observatory/Planetarium*) in Biblical times know about the star systems (*i.e. constellations*) and planets? How else could the Egyptians line up their Pyramids with the stars in the heavens? Why else would they worship the stars, the planetary bodies and the constellations and not the God (Yahuah) who created the "**hosts of heaven**"? The Fallen Angels taught them! Read Below!

Deuteronomy 4:16-20

"**16Lest ye corrupt yourselves, and make you a graven image, the similitude of any figure, the likeness of male (*Zeus, Apollo*) or female (*Isis, Ishtar, Asherah, Asheroth*),**

17 The likeness of any beast (Anubis, Thoth, Seth, Apis bull, Ptah) that is on the earth, **the likeness of any winged fowl (*Horus, Ra, Nisroch*)** that flieth in the air,

18 The likeness of any thing that creepeth on the ground, **the likeness of any fish (*Dagon, Nommo, Mami Wata*)** that is in the waters beneath the earth:

19 And lest thou lift up thine eyes unto heaven, and **when thou seest the sun, and the moon, and the stars, even all the host of heaven, shouldest be driven to worship them (*Islam, Catholic Church, Talmudic Judaism*), and serve them**, which the LORD thy God hath divided unto all nations under the whole heaven.

20 But the LORD hath taken you, and brought you forth out of the iron furnace, **even out of Egypt**, to be unto him a people of inheritance, as ye are this day."

From Enoch 6

"And they (Fallen Angels) were in all two hundred; who descended in the days of Jared on the summit of Mount Hermon…"

…And all the others together with them took unto themselves wives, and each chose for himself one, and they began to go in unto them and to defile themselves with them, and **they taught them charms and enchantments (magic), and the cutting of roots, and made them acquainted with plants**. And they became pregnant, and they bare great giants, whose height was three thousand ells: Who consumed all the acquisitions of men. And when men could no longer sustain them, the giants turned against them and devoured mankind…

And **Azazel taught men to make swords, and knives, and shields, and breastplates, and made known to them the metals of the earth and the art of working them, and bracelets, and ornaments, and the use of antimony, and the beautifying of the eyelids,** and all kinds of costly stones, and all coloring tinctures. And there arose much godlessness, and they committed fornication, and they were led astray, and became corrupt in all their ways. **Semjaza (Semyaza) taught enchantments (magic/sorcery), and root-cuttings,** 'Armaros the resolving of enchantments, **Baraqijal (taught) ASTROLOGY, Kokabel the CONSTELLATIONS (STARS), Ezeqeel the knowledge of the clouds,**

Araqiel the signs of the earth, Shamsiel the signs of the sun, and Sariel the course of the moon. And as men perished, they cried, and their cry went up to heaven . . ."

(**Above**) Dogon Elder, Mali.

The **Dogon people** without Telescopes understood the binary nature of Sirius, which is, in fact, composed of two stars named **Sirius A** and **Sirius B**. They also claimed to have information on **Sirius C**. The Sirius star was an important marker in the Egyptian Calendar. Ancient Egyptian mythology states the pagan god **Isis** came from **Sirius A** and the pagan god **Osiris** came from **Sirius B**. How the Dogon Tribe knew this nobody knows. Many scholars believed the Dogon tribe to be a descendant of the ancient Egyptians due to their knowledge of the constellations which the ancient Egyptians knew. What is also striking is that the Y-DNA of the Dogon Tribe, called "**E-M132/E-M33**" is most likely that of the Ancient Libyans who bordered Egypt to the West and also ruled over the Egyptian Dynasties. The **Fulani people** (*i.e. in Cameroon, North Africa*) are another African tribe who have similarities that link them to the **Ancient Libyan (Phuttite) people** who once ruled as Pharaoh's of Egypt during the 22nd and 23rd Dynasties. Some

Fulani's in West Africa were also found to have small amounts of this **E-M132/E-M33 Y-DNA Haplogroup**.

Note: *Not all of the Fulani people have the same Y-DNA. Some have the same "E1b1a" DNA as Bantus people (i.e. Fulani people in Guinea-Bissau). This is from intermixing.*

Other people of course have come up with different "theories" as to how the Dogon Tribe had the knowledge of the stars and planetary bodies. In 1976, a man named Robert K. G. Temple, author of the book **"The Sirius Mystery"** believed that the Dogon people had "**direct**" connections with "**Star Beings**" from Sirius. The Dogon did say the "**Nommos**" people who lived in world circling the Sirius Star system came to earth in Ancient times in a vessel accompanied with fire and thunder. They claimed the Nommos beings were amphibious, hermaphroditic (*having both-sexes like the Satanic Baphomet figure*) and were fish-like reptilian creatures. In **Freemasonry** and the **Occult** world of Evil, **Sirius** aka the "**Blazing Star**" is the final destination that one tries to reach as their body dies and soul passes to another realm. This is utterly Satanic as Freemasonry and the Occult is connected to "**Luciferianism**".

Here are the facts to support this.....of course straight from the horse's mouth, the Grandmaster Freemasons themselves.

"Isis was aided in her search [for the slain body of Osiris] by Anubis, in the shape of a dog. He was Sirius (Satan), or the Dog-Star, THE FRIEND AND COUNSELOR OF OSIRIS, and the inventor of language, grammar, astronomy, surveying, arithmetic, music, and medical science; the first maker of laws; and WHO TAUGHT THE WORSHIP OF THE GODS, AND THE BUILDING OF TEMPLES."
Albert Pike, Morals and Dogma, p. 376, Teachings of the 24th Degree, Prince of the Tabernacle

So, Albert Pike is admitting here in his statement that Osiris's friend was Satan masquerading a Sirius.

"Throughout the centuries, SIRIUS (the brightest star in the sky) has been recognized by most occultists and esoteric teachers as the LOCATION WHERE LUCIFER AND HIS HIERARCHY DWELL. In Christian terminology, Sirius is simply a secretive code word for 'HELL'.
Christian Author Texel Mars, Book of New Age Cults and Religions, 1990, p. 299

Albert Pike (1809-1891) 33 Degree Grandmaster Freemason

Famous Freemason Albert Pike, also revealed in his book, *Morals and Dogma*, that the "**Pentagram**" Masons call the "**Blazing Star**" of their Lodges represents Sirius, the Dog Star! Pike even referred to Sirius as the "**Guardian and Guide of our Souls ... which to the Ancients was the Sun.**" [Morals and Dogma, Page 15-16]. Pike also would be considered a Freemason Moslem Shriner. Moslem Shriners worship and call God "**Allah**". They also follow the Quran in secret.....but secretly all of it is tied to Satan worship using code names like "**Sirius**". Why else would Islam mention "Lord of Sirius"? Why else would Freemasons and Satanists mention Sirius? The Bible doesn't focus on constellations, the sun, or the planetary hosts of heaven. The Bible teaches against this. The Moors also use the "**Pentagram**" with the Red flag, the **Egyptian "winged-disc" symbol** and the "**pyramid**" as their symbols. This falls in line with their belief in "**Allah**" and the Egyptian "**Horus/Heru**". This is purely Satanic.

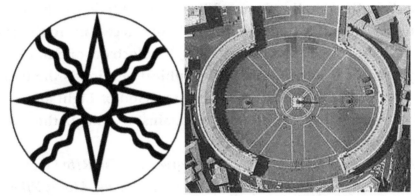

(Left) Symbol for the Babylonian Sun God "Shamash". (Right) Aerial view of St. Peter's Square, Vatican (Rome, Italy). Egyptian worship of Ra, Amun-Ra and Aten/Atum/Tem were all centered around "**Sun worship**". The Solar (Sun) Deity "**Shamash**" was a Semitic pagan god fashioned after the Sumerian sun god "**Utu**". In the Book of Enoch, the Fallen Angel named "**Shamsiel**" teaches mankind "**sun worship**". This comes from the Hebrew Strong's word "Shemesh" + "El". **Shemesh** means "**Sun**" in Hebrew (**Strong's #8121**). "El" is a different way to say "God" in Hebrew. The 8 rays of the pagan Sun god also mimic the 8 straight lines (rays) coming from the center of the Vatican's (St. Peter's square) Egyptian obelisk used in ancient times to worship the **Sun god Ra/Horus**. Coincidence?

How do we know Egyptology is Satanic or "Luciferian"? Let's read what Albert Pike said again.

"That which we say to a crowd is…We worship a God, but it is the God that one adores without superstition. To you, Sovereign Grand Inspectors General, we say this, that you may repeat it to the Brethren of the 32nd, 31st, and 30th degrees…The Masonic Religion should be, by all of us initiates of the high degrees, maintained in the purity of the LUCIFERIAN DOCTRINE. If Lucifer were not God, Would Adonay whose deeds prove his cruelty, perdify and hatred of man, barbarism, and repulsion for science, would Adonay and his priest, calumniate him? YES, LUCIFER IS GOD, and unfortunately Adonay is also god. For the eternal law is that there is no light without shade, no beauty without ugliness, no white without black, for the absolute can only exist as two gods: darkness being necessary to the statue, and the brake to the locomotive. Thus, the doctrine of Satanism is a heresy; and the true and pure philosophical religion is the belief in Lucifer, the equal of Adonay; but Lucifer, God of Light and God of Good, is struggling for humanity against Adonay, the God of Darkness and Evil."

Sovereign Grand Commander, 33rd Degree Scottish Rite Freemason, Satanist, and founder of the KKK in Arkansas, Albert Pike

Manly P. Hall (1901-1990) Scottish Rite 33 Degree Freemason

"When the Mason learns that the key to the warrior on the block is the proper application of the dynamo of living power, he has learned the mystery of his Craft. The seeing energies of Lucifer are in his hands and before he may step onward and upward, he must prove his ability to properly apply energy."
Master Mason and author of the "The Lost Keys of Freemasonry"
Manly Palmer Hall

(Left) The Star Sirius and its system. (Right) Masonic Art displaying the "**Blazing Star**" Sirius that Masons strive to achieve on their journey of degrees of "**secret knowledge**" up the ladder leading to Satan/Lucifer. Hebrew Strong's #1966 word "**Hellel**" means "**the shining one**" in connection to **Lucifer** since the modern name **Lucifer** wasn't used to describe "Satan" in ancient times. In Freemasonry, it is taught that the **Blazing-Shining Star** is a symbol of a deity, of omnipresence (*i.e. the Creator is present everywhere*) and of omniscience (*i.e. the Creator knows all*). Satan/Lucifer is not present everywhere and does not see or know everything. Sirius is therefore the "**sacred place**" all Masons must **ascend to**: It is the source of divine power and the destination of divine individuals who want to be linked to Lucifer.

2 Corinthians 11:14 "And no marvel; for Satan himself is transformed into an angel of light."

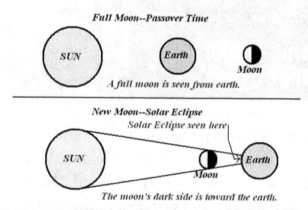

Full Moon--Passover Time

SUN   Earth   Moon

A full moon is seen from earth.

New Moon--Solar Eclipse

Solar Eclipse seen here

SUN   Moon   Earth

The moon's dark side is toward the earth.

Note: Satan has no control over the **Sun, Moon, Stars and the planets**. Neither does Ra, Horus, Osiris, Thoth, of Amen-Ra. Only God the Father has that control as he is the Creator. During the Crucifixion and death of Christ there was **"Three hours"** of darkness recorded by many historians living during the 1st century A.D. (**See "Hebrews to Negroes" Book**). This was recorded in the Bible in **Luke 23:44** using the Hebrew word **"Erets"** which means **"Land"** or **"Earth"**. However, this is not scientifically possible being that the Crucifixion took place on a Full Moon during the Passover. During a **Full Moon phase**, the moon is not between the Sun and the Earth, it is on the opposite side (see diagram). Only during a "**New Moon Phase**" is the Moon in a position directly between the Sun and the Earth. Even more, a Solar Eclipse can only last for a maximum of **7 minutes**, not 3 hours. So, what caused the Earth to have "darkness" for 3 hours? The hand of the Creator! The Egyptians worship the stars, the sun, moon, the constellations and their many pagan gods but the very gods they worship have no control over universe. It is obvious that the universe responded to the Creator's (*God manifested in Flesh as the Christ*) suffering in the body of a man and the eventual death of the fleshly body of Christ. **This was a supernatural event that occurred which testifies to "Christ's" Divinity**.

(**Left**) **Ubaidian** (proto-Sumerian) **Reptilian goddess** breastfeeding her reptilian-looking baby (6800 B.C.-3500 B.C.). Many believe these were the Fallen Angels or their "**Abominations/Mess ups**" (*thanks to genetic manipulation*) that existed before the Flood that Noah and the Sons of Shem (i.e. Sumerians) had knowledge of. In the Lost Tablets of Enki, you can find verses that depict the Sumerian pagan god **Enki** attempting to manipulate what God already created (*man & animals*)

creating **"mistakes"** or **"abominable"** creatures which some may read and liken to today's modern day big-headed grey alien. **(Right) Mami Wata** is usually depicted as a half woman-half amphibious/fish being. The spirit of **"Mami Wata"** is conjured up in many African-Caribbean divination practices as well as in the Americas (*i.e. Santeria-Brazil/Argentina voodoo, Haitian Voodoo*). This spirit can also be conjured up by worshipping the ancient Egyptian gods (**i.e. Sekhmet**). Again, in Dogon mythology, humanity was said to be created by the **Nommo**, a race of **amphibians (perhaps reptilian-like) beings** who were inhabitants of a planet circling the Sirius star. The Nommo people were said to have descended from the heavens to the earth, accompanied with **fire** and **thunder**, at which they gave their knowledge to humans. Doesn't this sort of line up with what the Sumerians and Hebrews might have known as well? After all, the Bible makes many references to Satan as the **Serpent, Dragon, Viper, Snake** and so on. All which are **"reptilian"** beasts.

Luke 10:17-19 "The seventy-two returned with joy and said, "Lord, even the demons submit to us in Your name. So he (Christ) said to them, "**I saw Satan fall like lightning (? *accompanied with thunder*) from heaven.** See, I have given you authority to tread on snakes and scorpions, and over all the power of the enemy. Nothing will harm you..."

Note: *Christ is saying that he was there when Lucifer (Satan) was kicked/thrown out of heaven. Did the Fallen Angels whom the Dogon people called the "**Nommo**" people tell the "**pre-flood**" inhabitants of Earth the story of how they came to earth.... including the fall of their leader "Satan/Lucifer"? Was this passed along as "knowledge" to the Sons of Seth...including Noah and his three sons (Ham, Shem, Japheth)...who then passed it to the Hamitic races in Africa? Possibly so.*

Interesting enough is that the Lucifer/Satan/Devil in the Book of Genesis is described as a "**Fiery Serpent**". Amphibians can appear serpent or lizard like....which is also a feature when people describe the female pagan deity of the Bantus Israelites, "**Mami Wata**" aka "**Queen of Heaven/Ishtar/Asheroth**". In the Hebrew Strong's Lexicon #5175 "**Nachash**" means "**Serpent**" (i.e. Genesis 3:14). In the Bible, the angels are sometimes classified under **Cherubim** (Strong's #3742) and **Seraphim** (Strong's #8314). It is the word "**Seraphim**" that represents a "**Fiery Serpent**". So, could the Dogon Tribe's creation story of humans be referring to a "**corrupted version**" of Genesis that involves the "**Fallen Angels**" coming to earth and having children with the daughters of men? It is something we should certainly consider.

Job 2:2 "And the LORD said unto Satan, From whence comest thou? And Satan answered the LORD, and said, From going **to and fro IN THE EARTH**, and from **walking up and down IN IT**."

Note: We live **ON EARTH**, not **IN EARTH**. But know our King James Bibles says "**In Earth, as it is in heaven**" instead of "On Earth, as it is in heaven".

Matthew 6:9-11 "After this manner therefore pray ye: Our Father which art in heaven, Hallowed be thy name. Thy kingdom come. Thy will be done **IN EARTH**, as it is in heaven. Give us this day our daily bread."

Note: *Could this be Satan, CERN, D-Quantum Wave Artificial Intelligence computers manipulating our bibles?*

So how did the teachings of the Fallen Angels make its way to the Sons of Noah (*i.e. Sumerians, Egyptians, Hindoos, Buddhists, Babylonians, Akkadians, Assyrians, Cushites, Persians, Hebrews, Israelites, Ishmaelites*) after the flood? Here is how, but you won't find it in the King James Bible.

Jubilees 8:1-7 "In the twenty-ninth jubilee, in the first week, in the beginning thereof **Arpachshad (Son of Shem)** took to himself a wife and her name was Rasu'eja, the daughter of Susan, the daughter of **Elam** (Shem), and she bare him a son in the third year in this week, and he called his name **Kainam. And the son grew, and his father taught him writing, and he went to seek for himself a place where he might seize for himself a city. And he found a writing which former (generations) had carved on the rock, and he read what was thereon, and he transcribed it and sinned owing to it;** <u>for it contained the teaching of the Watchers (fallen angels) in accordance with which they used to observe the omens of the sun and moon and stars in all the signs of heaven</u>. And he wrote it down and said nothing regarding it; for he was afraid to speak to Noah about it lest he should be angry with him on account of it. "

CHAPTER 18

FALLEN ANGELS, NORDIC-LOOKING "TALL WHITE" ALIENS, SHORT "PYGMY" PEOPLE AND ASIANS?

(**Above**) Also linked to the **Dzopa (Dropa) pygmies** of Tibet/China was the "**Lolladoff plate**". This was described by Professor Karyl Robinson-Evans in the 1970's in his book "**Sungods in exile: secrets of the Dzopa of Tibet**". The plate displays what seems to be a sort of UFO disc-like spaceship, a grey-alien looking figure, two octopus like figures, some reptile beings and the sun in the middle. Some say that all the talk on the "**Dzopa**" people and the "**Lolladoff Plates**" are just a product of a "fictional story", thereby erasing its credibility as fact.

(Above) Dzopa plates

If this isn't enough, more discoveries were made in the caves in **(Baian)-Kara-Ula**, Tibet-China. On the walls, there were carved hieroglyphs/pictograms of the heavens including the Solar system as we know it in a "**circle**", the Earth, the Sun, the Moon, the planets and the Stars. The Sun was in the middle and the heavenly bodies on the walls were connected by pea-sized dots...which sort of revealed their trajectory in orbit in space. Archaeologists found 716 stone discs with a hole in the middle. On these discs found written in a circular fashion was a message that only a few ancient linguistic experts were able to decipher. This is what it supposedly said:

"**The Dzopa** came down from the clouds with their air gliders (*i.e. spacecraft*). Ten times the men, women and children of the Kham (*i.e. the people living in Ancient Egypt/Africa at the time*) hid in the caves until the sunrise. Then they (*i.e. the people in Egypt/Africa*) understood the signs and saw that the **Dzopa** came in peace **this time**."

Does the above statement mean the Dzopa people came twice to Earth, one during the 11th Century A.D. and another previously in Ancient past, perhaps shortly after the flood?

(**Above**) The **Khoi-San** people in South Africa have one of the oldest DNA Haplogroups in all of Africa. They also have "**Asian**" features which nobody in Africa, except perhaps a select few "Bantus" tribes in South Africa. This "**Asian eye Trait**" then picks up in Asia? What happened? Why isn't this trait seen in more than one tribe in Africa? Why isn't it seen in Europe? Why isn't it seen in India, the Middle East or Asia Minor? Is this a coincidence?

But a bigger question was unanswered.

"**Did the Dzopa people come to earth shortly after the Great Flood happened, mixing with some of the Children of Cham or Ham/Hans (Africa)**"? If this is case, was the Khoi-San people one of the first "people" that the Dzope people made contact with in Africa? According to Twa pygmies past oral history, the **Khoi-San people** were in Africa before the Aba**TWA**/Sapi**TWA** pygmies were in Africa. The Khoi-San people also have evidence of the two oldest Y-DNA Haplogroups in the world: Haplogroup "**A**" and Haplogroup "**B**".

(**Left**) Khoi-San woman in Botswana. (**Right**) Dinka Tribe boy in Sudan. The Khoi-San people have the same Y-DNA "**A**" as the Cushite Dinka Tribe people and to a lesser extent the Negro Israelite Y-DNA "**E1b1a**" and the Pygmy Tribe Y-DNA "**B**".

In the **Mulanje Mountain of Malawi** there lives Pygmies and Bushmen people. This mountain is called by the local people "**Sapitwa**". Sapitwa means, the ancient mountain of the ones nicknamed "**San**". Legend there has it that it is the mountain of (spirits) called "**mizimu**" who are different than regular ancestral spirits called "**mizimu yamakolo**" which are commonly prayed to by many tribes in Africa for protection or guidance. It is believed to be by the locals the dwelling place of the gods and goddesses who "**ran away**" when they arrived to earth. Could this have been the "Dzopa" people or "Fallen Angels" as described in the Egyptian Emerald Tablets? The Mulanje mountain is also said to be inhabited by a "**Serpent-like**" mystical character named "**Napolo**". The appearance of the "**Sirius Star**" system is also regarded as their "**New Year**". He we see "common themes" which point to Lucifer and his Fallen Angels.

1. Extraterrestrial beings come to earth then run away, hiding in the mountains/caves.
2. A Serpent mystical beast lives in these mountains, that is linked to the Sirius Star.
3. The Sirius Star in the occult and Freemasonry is linked to Lucifer/Satan.

Here is a valid question. Did the fallen angels or their seed on earth "introduce" something "genetically" into some of the Canaanite Tribes causing "Asian" eye traits or "anomalies" in the height of some of the Sons of Ham. Did Terah, Abraham and their family know about the "tainted" Canaanites? Did they know that the Fallen Angels had contact with some of the Sons of Ham? Is this why they were so against intermarrying with the daughters of Canaan?

Could the statement, "**Then they understood the signs and saw that the Dzopa people came in peace this time**" be referring to the fact that the people living in the Land of Ham (**Africa**) hid in caves when the Dzopa people came during a "**post-flood**" era because when they came prior to the flood, they wreaked havoc on the earth? Also, did the Dzopa people mix their genes with the people living in Africa, Mesopotamia and Asia? If the Dzopa people came from "the clouds/heavens" to earth during biblical times, perhaps this knowledge of the "**Fallen Angels**", "**strange-looking pygmy people**" and the "**Giants**" were passed on from Noah to all his sons, including their generations. This would explain why the Israelite men were told to stay away from the Canaanite women and why people with "**white skin**" were considered "**unclean**". Obviously, white skin, giants and pygmies were synonymous with a "**tainted seed**".

Note: *In the Egyptian Emerald Tablets written by Thoth….it states that land of Cham is associated with Egypt or in a broad sense Africa. Startling evidence can also found in North Africa that hints on an advanced race of beings who lived in Ancient Egypt in Biblical times. Even down to "spaceships" and "masonry" stone work in building the pyramids.*

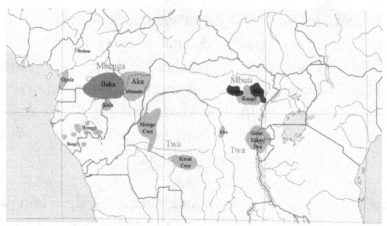

(**Above**) Map of the pygmy tribes in Africa.   In China-Tibet today, there can be seen the so-called Pygmy "**Drozpa people**", the "**Taron Pygmy tribe**" and the "**Derung Pygmy tribe**". All throughout South Asia there are "**Negrito Tribes**"....aka "**Little Negroes**".   In Africa, there are the **Baka, Aka, Twa**, the **Mbuti** and **Efe pygmies**.

	Test	L1-L3			
	#	%			
East Africa:					
Ethiopians[c]	74	55	3	10	8
Ethiopian Jews[c]	46	52	0	15	15
Somalians[d]	27	70	0	11	11
Nubians[e]	80	58	0	10	9
Southern Sudanese[e]	76	92	0	4	0
Kenyans[d]	63	95	3	2	0
West Africa:					
Overall[d,f,g,h]	447	89	3	0	0
Central Africa:					
Mbuti and Biaka[f]	37	100	0	0	0
Equatorial Guineans[i]	95	99	1	0	0
Southern Africa:					
Kung and Khwe[f,j]	98	100	0	0	0
Mozambicans[k,l]	416	100	0	0	0

(**Above**) The percentage of mtDNA L1, L2, and L3 in different African nations. The mtDNA "**L1a, L1c and L2a**" is common in the "**pygmy**" tribes such as the Mbuti pygmies but it is also common in African-

Americans (*i.e. people of Sub-Saharan Bantus African descent from West/East/South Africa*).

The most common mtDNA in African-Americans and Bantus Africans is "**L2**" **and** "**L3**". Many African-Americans also carry the maternal **L0** and **L1** mtDNA. **L0** is mostly seen in the Khoi-San people of South Africa, some pygmy tribes (*i.e. Mbuti/Baka*), some Ethiopians and the Black Hadhrami Arabs of East Yemen. **L1a** is seen most frequently in West Africa (*i.e. Gambia, Senegal, Nigeria-Igbo, Ghana-Akans, Ivory Coast-Akans, Lemba Jews, and Egyptians*). **L1b** is seen in 17% of the Senegal population and has also been found in Nigerian Igbos, Mauritanians, Akan-Ashanti people, Algerians, the Lemba Jews and select Egyptians. **L1c** however is seen primarily in the Mbenga pygmies (Ba-kola, Ba-benzele, Baka/Biaka), the Tikar pygmy people (*even children from Bantus men and pygmy women*), the Bakoya pygmies, the Ba-bongo pygmies and the Sao Tome-Principe-Gabon-Angola-Equatorial Guinea Bantus people who were the "**Black Jews**" banished from Iberia (Spain/Portugal) in 1492.

Note: Because there are many **African-Americans** and "**Bantus**" people that carry the same mtDNA "**L1/L2**" shared also by the "**Pygmy people**" this can only mean one thing. The Bantus "Israelite" people in Africa mixed heavily with the "pygmy" people....who most likely are the descendants of the biblical "**Canaanites**". In the chart above you can see that the **L1-L3 mtDNA,** which shows a common "**maternal ancestry**" is seen in roughly **89%** of Bantus West Africans, and **100%** of the Pygmy/Bushmen Tribes (Mbuti/Biaka, Khoi-San). The Kung and Khwe South African (San) Tribes are known to also carry the same maternal DNA/mtDNA markers seen in African-Americans-West Africans. Remember, maternal "**mtDNA**" is passed down from the mother to both **son** and **daughter**. In the Bible, the Canaanite men took Israelite women to be their wives and Israelite men took Canaanite women to be their wives. Of course, children were born to both people groups. This is why we see an overlap of the same maternal (mtDNA) shared by the Bantus people and the Pygmy people.

Ezra 9:1-2 King James Version (KJV)
"Now when these things were done, the princes came to me, saying, The people of Israel, and the priests, and the Levites, have not separated themselves from the people of the lands, doing according to their abominations, even of the **Canaanites, the Hittites, the Perizzites, the Jebusites,** the Ammonites, the Moabites, the Egyptians, and the Amorites.

For they have taken of their daughters for themselves, and for their sons: so that the people hath mingled themselves with the holy seed have of those lands: yea, the hand of the princes and rulers hath been chief in this trespass."

(Above) Bantus Yoruba man, 1800's. Like African-Americans and Caribbean blacks....his Y-DNA (paternal) is **"E1b1a"**. Likewise, his mtDNA (maternal) is **"L2-L3"**.

Here is something else to ponder on. If the Lemba men supposedly carry the **"J1"** Haplogroup passed down from their father and non-

Lemba men are not allowed in their village how come in genetic studies half of the DNA of the "Lemba Jews" is **E1b1a** (Negro Bantus Y-DNA)? Could it be that some **"other"** Black Semitic nations way back took Lemba Jewish women as wives thus creating a mixture of Y-DNA Haplogroups "J1" and "**E1b1a**" among the Lemba Jewish community? How did the Lemba Jews get the same "E1ba" as the so-called Negro. Remember, some Egyptian men with their Israelite wives were with Moses during the Exodus when the Israelite spent 40 years in the Wilderness. So this theory is not impossible.

Leviticus 24:10 "And the son of an **Israelitish** woman, **whose father was an Egyptian,** went out among the children of Israel: and this son of the Israelitish woman and a man of Israel strove together in the camp;"

Leviticus 18:26 "But as for you, you are to keep My statutes and My judgments and shall not do any of these abominations, neither the native, **nor the alien** who sojourns (*i.e. temporarily stays*) among you."

2 Chronicles 2:17-18 "Solomon numbered all the **aliens** who were in the land of Israel, following the census which his father David had taken; and 153,600 were found. He appointed 70,000 of them to carry loads and 80,000 to quarry stones in the mountains and 3,600 supervisors to make the people work."

As we can see here, the so-called "**Stranger/Alien**" lived amongst the full-blooded Israelites during the days of Moses and King Solomon. In Leviticus 24, "**Son**" of the **Israelitish woman** and **Egyptian man** had blasphemed-cursed the name of the LORD (Yahuah). Because the half Egyptian/half Israelite son was under the same "**Law**" while residing with the Israelites, he was subject to the same punishment any other Israelite would get for cursing the name of their God according to the Mosaic Law...which was death by stoning.

Leviticus 24:22 "Ye shall have one manner of law, as well for the "stranger", as for one of your own country: for I am the LORD your God. And Moses spake to the children of Israel, that they should bring forth him that had cursed out of the camp, and stone him with stones. And the children of Israel did as the LORD commanded Moses."

(Left) Bes was a dwarf pagan god who protected individuals from evil. (Right) Canaanite-Egyptian pagan god "Ptah". The pagan god "Bes" was adopted into the **Egyptian, Cushite** and **Canaanite-Phoenician** pantheon. Bes statues have been found in Egypt, Sudan, Tunisia and other places in Africa. He assumed a prominent role by the ninth century B.C., possibly the time when **King Hezekiah and Isaiah** lived before the Assyrian invasion of Samaria (**10 Northern Tribes of Israel**). It was especially thought that Bes was the protector of pregnant women. Many sources state **"Bes"** was a household Egyptian-Canaanite deity responsible for the welfare of pregnant women, happiness in the home, warding off evil spirits and the prevention of disease. Ptah was a dwarf-pygmy pagan god fashioned after the pygmy Canaanites that was associated with regeneration and rejuvenation. The Canaanites pygmy tribes like the red-skinned **"Tellem pygmies"** of Mali and the **"Twa pygmies"** in the Congo/Scotland/Ireland were believed to have **"magical powers"**. **Like many other Canaanite gods such as "El", Ptah and Bes was**

adopted into the religion of Levantine/Mesopotamian/Northeast African civilizations.

It is a known fact that many Asians are small (**i.e. 5'0 feet size**) like the Baka pygmies (**Above**). Could Asians be small because of some Pygmy "**Canaanite**" blood in them?

The Native Amerindians usually were taller than Europeans when you look at pictures from the 18th, 19th and early 20th Century. This excludes them from being Canaanites or having moderate amounts of Pygmy-Canaanite "**autosomal**" DNA contribution to their phenotype (*i.e.*

observable outer appearance). Even Mexicans that have seen "Native Americans" on reservations in Latin America know that the indigenous "Indians" are typically "**darker**" and "**taller**" than the average Mexican.

The Ancient name of China, "**Sina**" is also believed by some to be from the Canaanite Tribe...the "**Sinites**" listed in **Genesis 10:17**.   **The Bantus men that mixed with Pygmy women for hundreds of years could've resulted in the average size of the Bantus people (i.e. Igbo's, Congolese) to be less than 6 feet**.

On the opposite side of the spectrum, many Nilotic East Africans (*i.e. Dinka, Maasai*) are taller than West Africans with some women and men in these tribes reaching 7 feet tall. Many years ago the East African Nilotic "Cushite" and "Egyptian" tribes intermixed with the Bantus people as their Y-DNA is evident in the **Luo Tribe (Kenya, Tanzania, South Sudan, Uganda)**, the **Maasai Tribe (Kenya)** and many Somalian Tribes.

Note: *Former President Barack Obama's father was a Luo man. The Luo people have a history that has their origins in Egypt. They state that when Islam emerged in the 7th Century A.D., bringing forth Arab invaders to the Northeast Africa they moved further south into South Sudan along the Nile River. When the Arabs also encroached into Sudan with "**Mohammedanism**" the Luo people migrated further south into Kenya and Tanzania. During British colonialism in East Africa the Luo people did not have their land taken from them like the Bantus "Israelite" people. The Luo people also do not circumcise like the Bantus people but they did observe the "**Levirate**" Hebrew Tradition. The **Dhuluo language** of the Luo people has a strong similarity to the Alur language which has strong "**Egyptian influences**". The Luo Tribe is a very large tribe in Kenya and some of their people can be found to have the **E1b1a Y-DNA** or the **E1b1b Y-DNA**, probably from mixing with their Bantus neighbors. They also have small traces of the Y-DNA "A" of the Cushites (i.e. Dinka, Nuer, Nuba).*

(Left) Egyptian-Canaanite God "**Bes**". **(Middle)** Sculpture of a Yoruba figure called a Child of Obatala. **(Right)** Kongo (Congo God). All of them have skull necklaces and all are short stature pot-belly gods....like the Canaanite pygmy god "**Bes**". Now why would the "Bantus People" in Africa have pagan "**Canaanite**" Bes statues in their culture if they did not live amongst the Canaanites. The only people that lived and mixed with the **Canaanite people** in the Bible were the **Hebrew Israelites**.

PYGMIES ALL OVER THE WORLD

Fact: If you look closely you can see the Pygmy characteristics for "**short stature**" in other "**Negrito**" blacks all over the world. The **Twa** pygmy people were said to live from the Nile Valley to Mali (where they were called "**Tellem**" people). **The Tellem people according to the Dogon Tribe were short reddish-people who lived in the mountains and possessed the power of "flight".** They vanished without a trace. Dutch Geneticist John Huizinga, founder of the Utrecht Institute of Human Biology, devoted a good part of his life researching the origin and genetics of the Tellem pygmy people.

Pygmy tribes were also said to live in Portugal, Scotland, Wales, Ireland, Germany and England (**called Picts and Lapps**). They lived in Scandinavia where they are called **Finns** (Finland name after them). The Twa pygmies lived in Groeland, Canada (called **Skraelings**), and North America (called **Mound Builders**). Today they also live in the tip of South America where they are called the "**Fuegians**". Moving West to Hawaii the Twa were called "**Menehune**". In the Philippine Islands, they were called "**Negritos**" by the Spanish. In Indonesia on the Island of Flores skeletons of Twa were called "**Hobbits**". In India, we find a mixture of "**Twa blood**" in Island in the "Bay of Bengal" where they are called "**Andaman Islanders**". In every "**Pygmy**" or "**Negrito**" population across the world there is two common factors.

1. The pygmy races are "**short**".
2. The pygmy races are a "**Hunter-gatherer**" people.

While traveling "East" into different climates and mixing with different nations, the Y-DNA of the people they mixed with experienced mutations to what it is today. Unlike the Canaanite-Pygmy tribes, **the Bantus people**, like in accordance to their Israelite forefathers are **Farmers and Pastoralists** (herders of cattle/sheep).

So, if we can establish that the Pygmy Tribes are the Biblical Canaanites.... and that they did somehow come into contact with the Fallen Angels "**i.e. Watchers**" after the flood we can possibly come to the conclusion as to why they have been a "**mystery**" to many civilizations throughout time. We can also conclude that the Hebrew Israelites in Africa that mixed with the Biblical Canaanites throughout time are the "**Bantus People**". The pygmy people have "**mythological**" stories and oral histories that mimic the Bible. Likewise, the Pygmy people and San Bushmen (*with the Asian Single Epicanthal fold*) have one of the oldest DNA's on the planet (*besides the Nilotic Africans from Cush*). But the Pygmy people are also not as dark as the Cushite Nilotic people of East Africa. Could there have been a race of "**multicolored** pygmies" and "**red-haired giants**" in the days before the flood? What caused this?

Pygmies do not exhibit the same "**anatomy**" as those with "**dwarfism**". And the mechanism that makes them small is a "*defective*" receptor that does not respond to the **Growth Hormone/Insulin Growth Factor-1** from the Anterior Pituitary Gland. Remember, God did not create a "**defective**" man, beast, fowl or fish during his "**creation**" of the world in six days. Could the same "**Fallen Angels**" that sinned against God's creation creating "Giants" and "Pygmies" have been responsible for transforming the Children of Japheth from "**Black**" to "**White**"?

CHAPTER 19

CONNECTING THE DOTS: FALLEN ANGELS (WATCHERS), PYGMIES, GIANTS, THE WHITE RACE AND PAGAN WORSHIP

ቃለ፡ በረከት፡ ዘሄኖክ፡ ዘከመ፡ ባረከ፡ ኅሩያነ፡ ወጻድቃነ፡ እለ፡ ሀለዉ፡ ይኩኑ፡
በዕለተ፡ ምንዳቤ፡ ለአሰስሎ፡ ኵሉ፡ እኩያን፡ ወረሲዓን፡፡

(Above) Book of Enoch 1:1 in the Ethiopian Jews (Beta Israel) language "Ge'ez"

Translated in English, it reads: *"Word of blessing of Henok, wherewith he blessed the chosen and righteous who would be alive in the day of tribulation for the removal of all wrongdoers and backsliders."*

Note: This is an accurate "direct" translation of the Book of Enoch that most people read today in English.

The Book of Enoch prior to the finding of the Dead Sea Scrolls in 1947-48 in Qumran, Israel were only known to be in its complete form as a manuscript among the **Ethiopian Orthodox Tewahedo Church**. The Book of Enoch was believed to be written first in Hebrew or Aramaic or perhaps both. Before the 1800's A.D., only small scattered fragments were found translated in Greek and Latin. During this time, the Book of Enoch was essentially regarded as **"Lost"** to the world, except to the Ethiopian Christians and Ethiopian Jews. The language of the Ethiopic Book of Enoch was written in **Ge'ez**, a B.C. language whose beginnings (*see Yeha Temple*) predates the Arabic language by almost 1,000 years. Without "Catholic Church" influence, the Ethiopian Coptic Church preserved the name of Christ as **"Eyesus Kirestos"**. The **Zadokite "Essene"** group of priestly Israelites were believed to have kept the important Hebrew manuscripts safeguarded throughout time. The Dead Sea Scroll "Book of Enoch", believed to have been written by the

Essenes, were found in Israel but were kept by the Israeli government who just so happened to be the new inhabitants of the land around that time (*after kicking out the Arab Palestinians*). Prior to this, Europeans had to get their hands on the Ethiopian Book of Enoch to study it and compare it with their supposed research. Between 1769 and 1772 Scottish explorer and known Freemason James Bruce Kinnaird, was able to get his hands on the Ethiopic Book of Enoch during his travels to Abyssinia. The Ethiopic "Book of Enoch" (*in addition to Book of Jubilees*) confirmed the authenticity of the Ethiopians book in comparison to the 5th Century B.C. Israeli Paleo-Hebrew Dead Sea Scroll manuscripts. But there was more to the Book of Enoch. Today there is **1 Enoch, 2 Enoch** and **3 Enoch**. The Book of Enoch, which was found in the Dead Sea Scrolls is known as "**1 Enoch**". But a Slavonic-Greek inspired 1 Century A.D. work called "**The Secrets of Enoch**" emerged and was renamed "**2 Enoch**". In this work, the Fallen Angels....listed as "**Watchers**" are described as being "**White**", similar to what Lamech described as the color of the offspring of the Fallen Angels (**Sons of God**) in 1 Enoch Chapter 105.

Book of Enoch 105:1-3 (Fragment of Book of Noah)
"After a time, my son Mathusala (Methuselah) took a wife for his son Lamech. She became pregnant by him, and brought forth a child, **THE FLESH OF WHICH WAS WHITE AS SNOW**, and red as a rose; the hair of whose head was white like wool, and long; and whose eyes were beautiful. When he opened them, he illuminated all the house, like the sun; the whole house abounded with light. And when he was taken from the hand of the midwife, opening also his mouth, he spoke to the Lord of righteousness. Then Lamech his father was afraid of him; and flying away came to his own father Mathusala (Methuselah), and said, I have begotten a son, **UNLIKE OTHER CHILDREN. HE IS NOT HUMAN; BUT RESEMBLING THE OFFSPRING OF THE ANGELS OF HEAVEN**, is of a different nature from ours, being altogether unlike to us."

So here is the interesting part....where you will see a trend in the description of the "**Fallen Angels**" and their "**Seed/Children**" with being "**white-skinned**" in appearance. Could this be the "smoking gun" as to how the "white race" evolved? Is white skin a "**genetic mutation**" of black skin.....a Fallen Angel science experiment gone wrong? **Albinism,** a hypopigmentation disorder seen heavily in "Brown-skinned" races is a **genetic mutation** which causes the skin to be white. However, Caucasian-Europoid races do not have "Albinism" at astounding rates. So where do "Caucasians" get their white skin from? Did the Fallen Angels manipulate the DNA of the Black man, thus creating the beginnings of the "white race". Was this Fallen Angel genetic experiment done before or after the "**Great Flood**"? Could a Pre-Flood white man survive the flood? If so, was he able to find a way to survive living his life in a part of the world where his skin could most handle the weather (*i.e. without extreme heat/UV rays*)? Did this Pre-Flood white man migrate from the "Levant" into Europe? Did this Pre-flood race of "**white people**" also mix with the **Sons of Cain**, creating a bloodline that was "**tainted**" compared to Noah and his family from the lineage of Seth? After all the Bible says Genesis 6:9 that Noah was "**perfect**" in all his generations.

This is an excerpt of **2 Enoch 1:4-5** (Secrets of the Book of Enoch)

"And there appeared to me (Enoch) **two men very tall (*i.e. like giants*),** such as I have never seen on earth. And their faces shone like the sun, and their eyes were like burning lamps (*? Red-eyes*); and fire came forth from their lips. Their dress had the appearance of feathers...., their **wings** were brighter than gold; **THEIR HANDS WHITER THAN SNOW**. They stood at the head of my bed and called me by my name."

So, whether this **2 Enoch Book** was written by **Gentile Jews, Edomites, Greeks** or **Slavs (Scythians)** during the 1st Century A.D., the fact that cannot be denied is the repeated reference to the "**Watchers-Fallen Angels**" as white-skinned individuals. Likewise, their seed-offspring is also described as being "**white-skinned**" as mentioned by Lamech in **1 Enoch Chapter 105**.

So, what does all of this mean?

(**Left**) **Vusamazulu Credo Mutwa**, Zulu Shaman. (**Middle**) German Dictator/Nazi Leader **Adolf Hitler**. (**Right**) Nazi portrayal of the Master Nordic "**Aryan Race**" with Blond hair and blue eyes.

Vusamazulu Credo Mutwa, is a Zulu Shaman and an author of many books mixing Zulu folklore with his knowledge of extraterrestrial encounters. In his works, he describes an extraterrestrial "**Nordic**" white race of beings called the "**Mzungu**" who visited Earth before Africa was densely populated with the Black race. He described them as a race of "**White, blond-haired, blue-eyed**" people who came to earth in the beginning of time (pre-flood), eventually vowing later (post-flood?) to return to take over the entire continent of Africa. Today, Nordic looking Caucasians can be found in **Denmark, Finland, Iceland, Norway, Sweden, the Faroe Islands, and Greenland**.

Supposedly, deep underneath the ice in Antarctica (South Pole) there was found the remains of **giant humanoid alien beings**, some with **elongated skulls** and some with "**Asian features**". They were described as being "**white-skinned**" with **blond hair** as well. Many conspiracy theorists state that during the years 2015-2016, U.S.

Secretary of State John Kerry, Buzz Aldrin (Astronaut), Patriarch of the Russian Orthodox Church "**Kirill**" all visited the cold continent of Antarctica (South Pole). Why? Were they summoned there by "**someone**" or "**something**"? Some people believe a snow-covered pyramid-mountain in Antarctica was found that housed something of "**pure evil**". So evil that some ritual had to performed there under the orders of Pope Francis (Roman Catholic Church)…but not without the mysterious "**Ark of Gabriel**" that was entrusted to the Islamic prophet Muhammad by a "**Watcher-Fallen Angel**" (*i.e. Muslims claim "Gabriel" or "Jibril/Jibreel"*). This "**Ark of Gabriel**" was to remain buried underneath the "**Grand Mosque**" **Shrine** of worship in Mecca, Saudi Arabia until the "**Day of Resurrection (Yahm al-Qiyamah**". Is this a "Day of Resurrection" for the Giants, the Fallen Angels or the Antichrist? Pagan Shrines in the Bible (Deuteronomy Chapter 12) are forbidden by the **Most High** (Creator) himself so I doubt the Archangel "Gabriel" has higher authority over the one who created him.

Fact: *The German flying saucer **Haunebu I, II** and **III** in the 1940's was believed to be able to reach speeds of 40,000 km/hr (25,000 miles/hour) without any sound, vibration or exhaust. It was never verified to have been flown but it could easily seat a crew of 8-9 men. Some eyewitnesses to this German flying saucer said "**It glided through the air**". Note: it takes speeds of 40,000 km/hr to project a craft (i.e. Space Shuttle) into space. This is called "**Escape velocity**".*

Adolf Hitler researched the Occult, advanced technology like "**Space flight**", "**Time travel** (*i.e. The Bell*)", Ancient civilizations and Ancient Religions. Many historians believe the Germans were in contact with "**Aliens-Fallen Angels**", who shared their knowledge to advance the Germans Military. He believed that the Earth should only be filled with a "**master superior race**" which he called the "**Aryan Race**". The characteristics of Hitler's "Aryan Race" was "**White skin, Blond hair and Blue eyes**"....similar to the seed of the Fallen Angels in the Book of Enoch. Some people claimed that the German Nazi's had secret military bases in the tip of South America and Antarctica (South Pole). It was here that the German Nazi Occult (*i.e. Vrill*) would find access into the "**inner earth**" where so-called "**Aliens**" or "**Ancient people**" lived. These people supposedly had survived the "**Great Flood**" using a network of tunnels, caves, Pyramid shafts and possibly portals. In 1946-1947, **Admiral Richard Byrd** went investigating these "**Secret Nazi Bases**" in Antarctica under "**The United States Navy Antarctic Developments Program**", nicknamed "**Operation High Jump**". Hitler, Admiral Richard Byrd and others from exploring the "**inner earth**" were able to connect "**flying saucers**", the "**white Nordic race**", the "**Swastika Symbol**" and the "**Maltese Cross**" symbol all together. The place where all of this was found was called "**Shamballa**", by the ancients. This place called "Shamballa" however was also known to other groups of people like Buddhist Tibetan Monks and Freemasons. Freemason author **Lynn Perkins** in the book "**Masonry in the New Age**" states:

"**Shamballla** has a bearing on the ancient origins of Freemasonry and upon its future in the coming Aquarian Age."

Note: *Some people claim we entered the "Age of Aquarius" in the year 2012.*

In the same book, **Lynn Perkins** says in a subliminal way that Freemasonry comes from Satanism. Luciferian **Alice Bailey**, founder of the **Lucifer Publishing Company** in 1920 (*re-named Lucis Trust in*

1922) stated while influenced by her demonic master "**Master Djwhal Khul the Tibetan**" wrote:

"**Shamballa is the mythological place where the Lord of the World (Satan), "Sanat Kumara" or Shiva is supposed to be.**"

Note: *In Hinduism, the god "Shiva" is the equivalent of Satan in Christianity.*

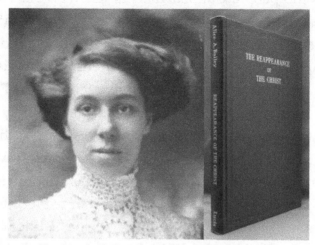

(**Above**) **Alice Bailey** in her book, "**The Reappearance of the Christ**", states that her "**Christ**"....aka the "**Antichrist**" doesn't care what religion you follow as long as you worship him (Satan). Most Christians pray using the phrase "**God Willing**"? Under the Luciferian Doctrine and "Theosophical Society New Age Religious Movement" it is "**Do What Thou Wilt**". The Anti-Christ is "**against**" Christ and wants to "**remove**" Christ/Messiah out of mankind's thoughts or actions.

This will be how the Antichrist ushers in a "**One World Religion**" using the "**Ecumenical**" and "**Interfaith**" movement spearheaded by the Roman Catholic Church. The New World Order "Beast System" hopes to bring all the religions together as "**One**", also bringing all the nations together under a "**Digital ID**" (*i.e. where cash is eliminated and all monetary transactions are electronic*). The plan is to have everyone "**share**" the resources of the world (*i.e. Roman Catholic Church "Global Citizen Agenda" and "2030 Agenda for Sustainable Development"*).

So, as Satan prepares to lead the world astray (including "Israelites" and "Saints"), the Most High-Messiah is waking his "Lost Sheep" out of their sleep to prepare themselves for his return. Is it a coincidence that all of this is happening now in the 21st Century? Not at all!

WHO ARE THE "TALL WHITES" OR THE SO-CALLED "NORDIC HUMANOID ALIEN PEOPLE"?

The Native American people in the "New World" had an old prophecy about "**tall white men**" invading their land. Their prophecy said that in the future a race of **tall bearded white-skinned men** would come to their land bringing "**destruction**". This ultimately would happen in 1519 A.D. when the **Spanish Conquistadors** under **Hernan Cortes** would lead an attack on the **Aztec Empire in Mexico**. The Aztecs believed Hernan Cortes was the returning god "Quetzalcoatl", who in Aztec culture was portrayed as "**tall**", "**white**" with **reptilian symbolism**.

Fact 1: There have been reports by American Military men stationed at a Turkish Base in the 1970's making contact with a "**tall, white, blond-haired**" race of people who lived inside the earth/mountains around the North Pole during flight expeditions. Like the "**Extraterrestrial Contact**" report of **Admiral Richard Byrd** (1888-1957) who flew over the Earth's Poles only to be "sucked into" a hole by some sort of "electromagnetic gravitational force", both stories report meeting a "tall white humanoid Alien race" who had symbols of the "**Maltese Cross**" and the modern day "**Nazi Swastika**". Admiral Richard Byrd in his lifetime had made many expeditions to the North Pole and to the South Pole.

Fact 2: In the book **"Our Haunted Planet"** by John A. Keel, it quotes, "According to the traditions of many isolated peoples, the first great emperors in Asia were god-kings who came down from the sky, displayed amazing superhuman abilities, and took over. There was a veritable worldwide epidemic of these god-kings between 5,000 and 1,000 B.C....The myths and legends of Greece, India, and South America describe their rule. They were **taller** and more imposing than the men of the time, with **long blond hair, marble-like white skin, and remarkable powers which enabled them to perform miracles.**" Where these the offspring of the Fallen Angels?

THE MALTESE CROSS

(Left) Maltese Cross with a Swastika inside used by the Nazis and Adolf Hitler. **(Right)** The Maltese Cross (Traditional). The symbol worn by Freemasons, the Priests of Horus (Egypt), Jesuits and the Knights of Malta is the "**Maltese Cross**. It is also the symbol of British royalty as Queen Elizabeth of England and the Royal family wear it. This Cross has also been associated with "**Lemuria**", the no-longer seen continent which once sat between Australia and the Americas in the Pacific Ocean. The continent of **Lemuria, Atlantis and Pan** are all said to have existed before the "**Great Flood**". The Maltese Cross was also connected to the "**Knights Templar**" Secret Society which was in its later years linked to the **Baphomet**-devil figure.

Ancient legends talk about "**Lost Continents**" that sank after natural disasters such as a "**Great Flood**", "**Earthquakes**", "**Volcanoes**" or "**Asteroid/Meteors**" destroying much of the earth. In the Indus Valley Sanskrit legends of **India**, there was large continent called "**Rutas**" which sank under the Indian Ocean. The Arabian Sea leads to the Indian Ocean which leads to the Pacific Ocean. **Old Tamil** (Dravidian Indian) writings recorded on palm tree bark also tell of a giant land mass that connected Southern India to Australia. Tamil is mostly spoken in South India (*i.e. Tamil Nadu*) and Northern Sri Lanka. The "**Tamils**" of old say 5,000-year-old records claim their land was once part of "**Le-MU-ria**" and that they shared this land with the "**Dravida/Dravidian**" people of South India (*i.e. Kerala*). According to some, this massive continent known as "**Mu**" or "**Lemuria**" was the birthplace of man.

509

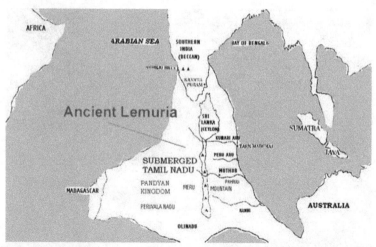

(**Above**) One version of ancient Lemuria on the map. Today the remnant of the "sunken" Lemuria land mass are believed to be **Sri Lanka, Madagascar, Indonesia, Papua New Guinea, "Mu" are Samoa, Fiji, Hawaii**. It is believed that a piece of the western part of the continent of "**Mu/Lemuria**" broke off becoming "**Madagascar**" where most "**Lemur**" monkeys live today. **Note:** Lemur means "**Ghosts/Spirits**" in Latin.

So, the question is, could the "**Pygmies**" and "**Giants**" back in ancient times been a result of the Fallen Angels tampering with the "natural man" in his "natural state" which was pure from the Creator? It is a known fact that the Average Life Expectancy of Pygmies is between **16-24 years of age**. The Average Life Expectancy of Giants (*i.e. Andre "the Giant" Rene Roussimoff-7 foot, 4inches, Manute Bol-7 foot, 7 inches*) is considered to be **10 years less than that of the Average Life Expectancy of the Average man**. Anything "foreign" that is introduced to God's creation (man) or anything that goes against "God's Laws of nature" seems to "**negatively**" affect the human race. For example, incest produces children with "**birth defects**", bestiality causes "**cancer**" in humans, and genetically modified foods has caused the increase in health conditions/diseases (*i.e. allergies, autoimmune disorders, cancer, inflammatory disorders, infertility*).

THE FALLEN ANGELS FIRST STOP: CUSH, CANAAN, EGYPT AND THE SEMITIC RACES.

It is a known fact that the Cushites worshipped the Sun, Moon, Stars and the same pagan gods which overlapped with the Ancient Egyptians. Both Nubia (Cush) and Egypt are filled with Pyramids or Obelisks. Likewise, the Egyptian pantheon of gods also overlapped into the Canaanite pantheon of gods. Some of the oldest civilizations are centered in Nubia, Egypt, Canaan/Israel, and Mesopotamia but one thing is common amongst all these Ancient Civilizations. They all worshipped multiple gods. Some kept their bloodline "pure" and some mixed with the "nations". This can be proven by the simple fact that the earliest Y-DNA Haplogroups: **A, B, C, D,** and **E** are all seen in "**brown races of people**". The oldest people genetically on the planet are seen in the people carrying the Y-DNA "**A**" and "**B**". These people groups have little to no "**genetic mutation**" compared to other races.

MUTATIONS: DETECTING WHO IS WHO?

Mutations are basically "**genetic alterations**". Genetic alterations or mutations that occur in more than 1% of the population in the scientific world are called "**Polymorphisms**". These mutations are responsible for the differences in people's eye color, hair color, facial bone structures, hair texture, height, weight, and blood type. Some mutations predispose certain race groups to certain diseases and some are protective of certain diseases (*i.e. Sickle Cell protects against Malaria in West Africa*). Y-DNA (SNP) tests, are designed to determine a male's branch on the big "ancestral tree" of mankind. **Family Tree DNA, 23 and Me** and **Ancestry DNA** are companies founded by Ashkenazi Jews. They have a database of millions of SNP's, Y-DNA, mtDNA all over the world. By having these DNA testing companies the European Jews are able to track data on certain Y-DNA types. For instance, like where are all the "**E1b1a**" Negro Israelite carriers in the world. Geneticists, also have found that by using "SNP's (*i.e. Single Nucleotide Polymorphisms*)", they can predict an individual's (*or certain racial groups*) response to certain drugs, toxins or changes in the environment. They can predict if a certain race will be "**resistant**" or "**susceptible**" to a certain disease or pathogen. In regards to the Negro Y-DNA "E1b1a" Haplogroup we must understand that every letter or number seen after the letter "**E**" is defined by a series of SNP (Single Nucleotide Polymorphisms). Each additional letter or number makes the Haplogroup-Subgroup more "**specific**" and "**unique**". For example:

- Haplogroup E, by itself, is defined by L339 and 10 more equivalent SNP's.
- "E1" is defined by the SNP mutation **P147**
- "E1b" is defined by the SNP mutation **P177**
- "E1b1" is defined by the SNP mutation **P179** and 4 more equivalent SNP's
- "E1b1a" is defined by the SNP mutation **M2** and 9 more equivalent SNP's.
- "E1b1b" is defined by the SNP mutation **M215** and **M35**, and less common **M282**.
- "E1b1a" is Sub-Saharan and "E1b1b" is North Africa/Mediterranean.

(**Left**) Khoi-San Bushmen Child. In the Khoi-San people geneticists have found the Y-DNA "**A**", "**E1b1a**" and "**B**". (**Right**) Nilotic Dinka Child with Y-DNA "**A**". One has "Asian-like eyes (single upper eye-lid) with light brown skin. One has a double upper eye-lid with very dark brown skin. Most Africans with "**Cushitic-Sudanic**" Nilotic Ancestry carry the Y-DNA "**A**".

Note: *Half of the Ethiopian Jews blood DNA is of **Cushitic "Nilotic"** Y-DNA "**A**" ancestry and the other half is an "old" form of the Bantus Y-DNA "**E1b1a**" bloodline. But didn't King Solomon have a child, "**Menelik I**" with Queen Makeda (Sheba) of the Cush Empire? Wouldn't it make sense that half of the Ethiopians Jews bloodline is from Cush (**Y-DNA "A"**)?*

This means that "**Cush** (Sudan, Ethiopia, Arabia/Yemen) could be the cradle of civilization as most people already speculate from reading the "**Book of Genesis**" and seeing that one (if not two) of the 4 rivers that sprang from the **Garden of Eden** which was believed to be located in East Africa (i.e. Nile) during "**Pangea**". Also, by reading the bible we know that the **Canaanites** were the Grandsons of Noah....which makes them a "**very old**" people. We also know that the Bible talks about the Fallen Angels-Giant seed coming through different Canaanite tribes.

The Fallen Angels according to the Bible (Genesis) and the Book of Enoch mated with the women of the earth. In the Sumerian Tablets of the "**Lost Books of Enki**" it describes these fallen angels (i.e. Annunaki) trying to create a "**slave race**" to do their bidding. Many Bible readers want to know if the Fallen Angels literally had sex with mortal women producing children or did they insert a "**foreign material**" during an "**in-vitro fertilization**" type of procedure done to the women of the earth? Or did they simply manipulate the human genome thus "**altering**" and causing the first "**mutation**" of God's perfect creation? Because they were not the Creator, they could not "**create**" a human being or humanoid out of "**nothing**". Instead many believe they genetically manipulated God's creations, creating monstrosities, "**mess ups**" and abominations that would give rise to other so-called Alien beings, the "tall whites", beasts, giants and the dinosaurs. These fallen angels were "**Divine Beings**" with "**Divine superpowers**" and "**Vast Knowledge**". The ancient Egyptians were able to align the Pyramids with the stars because the **Fallen Angels** taught and helped them do it. Without a telescope, this would be an impossible feat. The Fallen Angels (Watchers) manipulated DNA and sinned with man…including the animal kingdom (*i.e. mammals, fish, birds*). They lived when the Sons of Cain existed and they existed before the Flood when "**Pangea**" existed. They existed when other lands/continents existed like **Lemuria/Mu**, **Atlantis** and **Pan**. Much research has also been done to prove these "pre-flood" beings had dwelling places that were accessible via the North Pole, South Pole (Antarctica), pyramid structures across the world and caves. The Fallen Angels and their "**biological experiments** (*i.e. like Frankenstein*) even existed after the flood possibly by hiding in the "**Hollow Inner Earth**" which the Buddhists Monks called "**Shambhala/Shamballa**".

NEANDERTHALS, SONS OF CAIN, GERMANS AND THE EUROPEAN JEWS

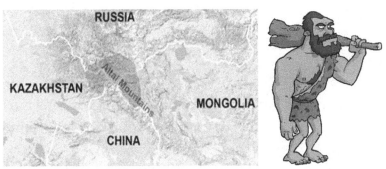

(**Above**) Altai Mountains and a Caveman (Neanderthal). The Gentile Jewish nation called "Khazaria" lived in the "Pale of Settlements" in South Russia, parts of Kazakhstan and the Caucasus Mountains. The Y-DNA (R1a) and the oral history of the Kazakhs all line up with the "**Khazars**".....who are the ancestors of a large majority of Ashkenazi Jews today. In this area, "**Neanderthal fossil remains**" also have been found.

It has been proven through archaeological studies that fossil remains of the Neanderthal man/woman have been found all over Europe, in Israel and in the **Altai Mountains** in Central Asia. Many mummies found in these areas (*i.e. Tarim Mummies*) have white skin and reddish hair.....like the Neanderthal people and the Red-haired Giants with elongated skulls found in Peru, South America (*i.e. Paracas skulls*). But back in Ancient times the Jews were often referred to the Greeks as "**Red Jews**".....because of their "**Red Hair**", which happen to resemble "**Neanderthal traits**". Can we prove this? 1st Century A.D. Roman Senator and Historian, **Publius Cornelius Tacitus** proved it in his literary work called "**Germania**".

(**Left**) 2nd Century A.D. map of **Germania Magna** which was a Roman term for North-Central Europe....or the **Germanic/Slavic lands**. This is also where most of today's Ashkenazi Jews come from. Hispania is "**Spain**" and Gallia is "**France**" aka "**Western Slavic**" territory. (**Right**) Modern day Europe which shows Poland, Germany, Hungary, Austria, France and many other European countries from which the Ashkenazi Jews "**stock**" comes from. Don't believe? Let a Roman historian from 2,000 years ago tell you the facts!

"For my own part, I agree with those who think that the **tribes of Germany** are free from all taint of intermarriages with foreign nations, and that they appear as a **distinct, unmixed race**, like none but themselves. Hence, too, the same physical peculiarities throughout so vast a population. **All have fierce blue eyes, red hair, huge frames**, fit only for a sudden exertion. They are less able to bear laborious work. **Heat** and **thirst** they cannot in the least endure; to cold and hunger their climate and their soil inure them.
1st century A.D. Roman Senator and Historian, Cornelius Tacitus, Germany (Germania) Book 1

Fact: *The same Y-DNA "R1a" seen in the white-skinned, Red-haired Tarim mummies found in Central Asia can also be found in Germanic/Slavic/Turkish "***Ashkenazi Jews***" today. Is this a coincidence?* ***It is a known fact that gene code "MC1R" for "Red Hair" has been found in numerous Neanderthal fossil remains.*** *The "MC1R" protein also gives rise to light colored eyes (i.e. blue, green, gray) and skin that does not have the ability to tan (i.e. white skin).*

516

There have been scientific studies that show that the "**Neanderthal gene**" is mainly found in Caucasian "**White Races**"…..such as that in Europe, Asia Minor and the White Arabs/Jews in the Middle East. Scientists have proven over and over again that the Neanderthal man/woman were blue-eyed, white people with blond, reddish and even brown hair. **Their mtDNA "X" can be seen in Sephardic Jews, Ashkenazi Jews and the Druze people in Israel.** So, where did the "Neanderthal Man" come from? Is the Neanderthal man a "pre-flood" race of humans that somehow survived the flood? Is the Neanderthal man a descendant of the "Sons of Cain" or is he a product of the Fallen Angels "unholy" and "un-natural" union with the "daughters of men"? Some say the Neanderthal is the reason why the "**Sons of Japheth**" turned "**White**". Some also say the Neanderthal man is the reason why some Europeans carry the **RH Negative Blood Type**. Nevertheless, Neanderthal Bones and DNA (**mtDNA "X"**) have been extracted from archaeological sites stretching from Spain/Portugal and East to the **Altai Mountains**. The Altai mountain range is in Central-East Asia, where Russia, China, Mongolia and Kazakhstan (*home of the Khazarian Empire Jewish converts*) come together. The Altai Mountains mean "**Gold Mountain**" in the Mongolian and the Turkish language. It is a known fact that the Altai Mountains are also home to the **Denisovan (Cro-Magnon Neanderthal) people**.

In 2008, in the mountains of southern Siberia, in a cave, the pieces of "**Neanderthal/Denisovan**" bones and tools were found. Scientists found skeletal remains of a beefy, thick-browed, white "**Neanderthal woman**" in these caves dating back thousands of years ago. What they also found was within this Neanderthal woman's DNA were traces of Human (Homo Sapien) DNA, which suggested that the Neanderthal people mated with "post-flood" humans many, many years ago. This finding would make sense of why one of Noah's sons (Japheth) would eventually have his seed turn "white".

Scientists were able to prove that the "**Neanderthal DNA**" found in the "**white races**" caused decreased effectiveness in the human immune system, increased depression and an increased tendency to become addicted to nicotine. One can argue that when Noah's three sons "**spread out**" into the nations, the sons of Japheth encountered the "**Neanderthals**" who were already living in cold environments, in caves with little UV sun-rays to cause skin cancer, heat strokes or sunburns. In essence, they could not survive in hot tropical/arid climates like that of Mesopotamia and Africa. For this reason, it is possible that a **mutation** caused the introduction of RH negative blood type humans found in Caucasoid "White-skinned" races (i.e. Europeans, Jews, Arabs) and not pure blood natives of Africa, Asia or America (Native Indians).

Fact: "**Neanderthal**" archaeological evidence has also been found in Israel as well in the cities of Kebara (**Kebara cave**), Tabun (**Tabun cave**) and Amud (**Amud cave**). Again, their **mtDNA** "**X**" can be seen in Sephardic Jews, Ashkenazi Jews, the Levantine Druze people and Arabs.

Fact 2: In Mesopotamian culture and Indus Valley Civilizations there is a "**Noah**" figure who saves his family during the flood. In Mesopotamia "**Ziusudra**" (Eridu Genesis), "**Utnapishtim**" (Epic of Gilgamesh) and "**Atrahasis**" (Epic of Atrahasis) are the Noah-like flood hero figures. In each storyline, the ark/boat rests on a mountain (*i.e. Mount Ararat*) when the flood subsides. According to the story, when the waters subside, those on the boat survive....as well as the **giants** and "**others**" who lived prior to the flood. Coincidence?

Knowing all of this, is it possible that the Neanderthal Cro-Magnon people (i.e. possible sons of Cain), the Giants and Pygmy people all lived in the "**Land of Canaan**" prior to the "Exodus"? If so, did the

Israelites drive out these "**peoples**" from the land or did they leave on their own? According to the Bible, the Giants that existed before the flood, existed after the flood also and they were not fully exterminated by the Israelites. Also, according to **Tablet 10 of the Sumerian Tablets of Enki** some of the **Sons of Cain** survived the "**Great Flood**".

So far we can see that the Pygmy "Canaanite" tribes, the Giants and the Neanderthal people (? Sons of Cain) all traveled different directions across the earth. They did not all stay close to Africa and the Middle East. This is proven with genetic and archaeological proof.

But how else do we know this to be true? In the Bible, Joshua and the Israelites were not able to kill off all the Giants according to the Bible.

Joshua 11:22 "**There was none of the Anakims left in the land of the children of Israel: <u>ONLY in Gaza, in Gath, and in Ashdod, there remained.</u>**"

Note: As we see in the bible, it never speaks of the Nephilim or "**Sons of Anak**" bloodline ever ending.

Book of Enoch 15:8-12
"And now, the giants, who are produced from the **SPIRITS AND FLESH**, shall be called **EVIL SPIRITS (DEMONS) UPON THE EARTH**, and on the earth shall be their dwelling. **EVIL SPIRITS (DEMONS)** have proceeded from their **BODIES**; because they are born from men and from the holy Watchers is their beginning and primal origin; they shall be evil spirits on earth, and evil spirits shall they be called. As for the **SPIRITS OF HEAVEN (GOOD ANGELS)**, in heaven shall be their dwelling, but as for the spirits of the earth which were born upon the earth, on the earth shall be their dwelling. And the spirits of the giants afflict, oppress, destroy, attack, do battle, and work destruction on the earth, and cause trouble: they take no food, but nevertheless hunger and thirst, and cause offences. And these

spirits shall rise up against the children of men and against the women, because they have proceeded from them."

(**Above**) Big-headed, Big-eye, blink-less, and sexless (*no penis or vagina*) Grey Alien. In the 14 Stone Sumerian Tablets of Enki, it seems to describe the Annunaki trying to create their own "**humanoids**", which every time ended up in a "**defective humanoid creature**". This is not surprising as most genetically modified organisms and clones do not live long. Most have health problems and diseases that make these "abominations" more prone to death. According to Sumerian mythology the "Annunaki" people on the Planet Nibiru had **elongated skulls**, they were **giants** (8 to 9 feet tall), they possessed nuclear weapons and they needed gold for their atmosphere. They were all united under a "**King Anu**" who was the predecessor of many Nibiru Kings, including **Enki**.

Sumerian (Lost Tablets of Enki) Tablet 6
Verses 2-82
"**Enki and Ninmah** drank beer, their hearts became elated, and then Ninmah said to Enki: "Man's body can either be good or bad and whether I make a fate good or bad depends on my will. Enki answered Ninmah: "I will counterbalance whatever fate—good or

bad — you happen to decide. **Ninmah took clay from the top of the abzu in her hand and she fashioned from it first a man** who could not bend his outstretched weak hands. **Enki looked at the man who could not bend his outstretched weak hands,** and decreed his fate: he appointed him a servant of the king. Second, she (Ninmah) **fashioned one who turned back the light (white skin and scaly fish-like skin like some alien renditions...reflect light), a man with constantly opened eyes (alien eyes don't seem to blink).** Enki looked at the one who turned back the light, the man with constantly open eyes, and decreed his fate allotting to it the musical arts, making him as the chief....in the king's presence. **Third, she fashioned one with both feet broken, one with paralyzed feet.** Enki looked at the one with both feet broken, the one with paralyzed feet and...him for the work of...and the silversmith and ...she fashioned one, a third one, **born as an idiot**. Enki looked at this one, the one born as an idiot, and decreed his fate: he appointed him as servant of the king. **Fourth, she fashioned one who could not hold back his urine.** Enki looked at the one who could not hold back his urine and bathed him in enchanted water and drove out the "**namtar demon (Mesopotamian god of disease and death)**" from his body. **Fifth, she fashioned a woman would could not give birth.** Enki looked at the woman (*i.e. Rh-Negative women with a RH positive fetus cannot have a normal birth*) who could not give birth. Enki looked at the woman who would not give birth, and decreed her fate: he made her belong to the queen's household. **Sixth, she fashioned one with neither penis nor vagina on its body (i.e. modern day Grey aliens are "sexless").** Enki looked at the one with neither nor vagina on its body and gave it the name "**Nibru eunuch**"), and decreed as its fate to stand before the king. Ninmah threw the pinched-off clay from her hand on the ground and a great silence fell. The great lord Enki said to Ninmah, "I have decreed the fate **OF YOUR CREATURES** and given them their daily bread. Come now I will fashion somebody for you, and you must decree the fate of the **newborn one!**"

The Ancient Egyptian

Winged Sun Disk Symbol

(**Left**) Ancient Aztec/Mayan civilization disc found in a pyramid in Mexican depicting of Black Triangle on the Sun with the appearance of UFO's/Flying saucers. On March 12, 2012 a Black Triangle was seen on the Sun appearing as a "**Black coronal hole**" in the shape of a triangle appearing on NASA's SDO website using the SOHO satellite (Solar & Heliospheric Observatory). (**Right**) Planet "X" or the Annunaki planet Nibiru is seen in space as a disc planet with wings.....just like the **ancient "winged sun disk" symbol** of the **Ancient Egyptians (pictured)**, Assyrians, Babylonians and Persians. Back then, 4,000 years ago, this image was worshipped. Perhaps they were worshipping the "**Fallen Angels**" as "Gods" who came from the "**Winged Planet**"....called **Planet X**.

Now consider this information about the Sumerians who lived in the land of Shem (Arphaxad) and knew about the "Great Flood" from their ancestors. The Sumerians wrote that when the Annunaki planet "**Nibiru**" made its elliptical orbit close to earth, signs started appearing on the earth such as black spots appearing on the Sun's Surface (*i.e. like 2012 triangle coronal hole on sun*), weakening of earth's magnetic field, melting of the polar ice caps (*which some people attribute to the Great Flood in the Bible*), and increasing weather events (*i.e. volcanoes, tsunamis, earthquakes, strange weather*).

Isn't this what is happening right now? Research "**HAARP**", the movie "**Geostorm 2017**" and the movie "**Aloha**".

In the First Sumerian Tablet of the Lost Books of Enki it says:

"The words of the lord Enki, firstborn son of Anu, who reigns on Nibiru."

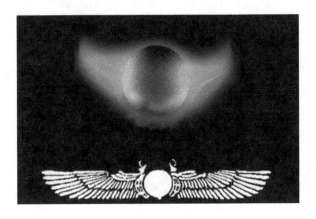

(Above) Picture of the planet **Nibiru**…the winged planet. It has many names such as **"Planet X"**, **"Wormwood"**, **"The Great Destroyer"**, **"The Red Star"**, **"Ison"**, or the **"T Tauri Star"**. The Sumerians documented that when this planet came close to earth inside the solar system, **"the gods"** or **"Annunaki"** came with it giving mankind knowledge.

Fact: *Facebook is working on a Mind-reading interface that will allow people to connect to their computer, TV or Smartphone with the thoughts from their brains. They have tested it with success on deaf, mute and patients with Lou Gehrig's disease (i.e. ALS-Amyotrophic Lateral Sclerosis). They plan on using the Optic Nerve and Retina (**i.e. only body part externally attached directly to the brain**) to make it work. We will simply be able to think our thoughts to be typed into a "**Word Document**" or think to move the mouse to wherever we want it on the screen. Totally "seamless", which is what the world will see as another "**cool convenience**". They are also working on augmenting our **reality** with **fiction** with more TV propaganda so that "**Virtual Reality**" will take the place of physical interaction with humans. Silicon Valley techs are also working on using this "fallen angel" technology* *to be able to have the people of the world communicate with anyone across the world without the barrier of different languages or even speech! This goes back the days when Noah and Nimrod lived on the Earth and there was "one speech" throughout the world as in the "Tower of Babel" story.*

Matthew 24:37 "But as in the days of Noah were, so shall also the coming of the Son of man be."

Genesis 11:1 "And the whole earth was of one language, and of one speech.

Genesis 11:6 "And the LORD said, Behold, the people is one, and they have **one language**; and this they begin to do: and now nothing will be restrained from them, which they have imagined to do."

THE FALLEN ANGELS ARE THE ANNUNAKI

In the first few Tablets of Enki, the Sumerians tells of their Annunaki story similar to the Genesis story but with a more "**fictional story line**" where the Annunaki seemed to be "**long-living mortals**" capable of reproducing and dying. The Sumerians were taught by the Annunaki that the planet **Jupiter** was the **5th celestial planet** from their home planet "**Nibiru**". They also detailed that the Biblical "**Firmament**" was called the "**Hammered Bracelet**" from the root verb "**raqa-Hebrew Strong's #7554** which means "**hammered**", which gave rise to the Hebrew word "**raqia-Hebrew Strong's #7549**". The Sumerians wrote that they hammered the "**Firmament-Rock Bracelet**" with lasers weapons as they crossed through the "**heavens above**" headed for "**heavens below**" and planet Earth. The remains of the "**Hammered Rock Bracelet**" or "**Firmament**" is what Astrologers would call today the "**Asteroid Belt**" which sits between **Mars** and **Jupiter**.....the same place the Sumerians wrote that the "firmament" used to be. The waters (Hebrew-mayim) **below/under** the old "rock firmament" were set apart from the waters **above** the "rock firmament". Water today can

524

exist in **three states**: solid (ice), liquid (water), and gas (vapor). The planets under today's asteroid belt are **solid planets**, with some having evidence of water (Earth, Mars?). The planets above the asteroid belt are all "**gaseous planets**", meaning they are like a big ball of vapor. God called it "**heaven**" or "**Shamayim**" in Hebrew'. Interesting isn't it.

Genesis 1:7 "And God made the firmament, and divided the waters which were <u>under</u> the firmament from the waters which were <u>above</u> the firmament: and it was so."

The Sumerians knew from the "Annunaki beings" that **Mars** was reddish-brown in color and that it was the **6th planet** from **Nibiru** (*i.e. how else would anybody know this without a telescope*). They also knew that **Earth** was the **7th planet** from **Nibiru**. How could the Sumerians know this? Who were the Annunaki beings that came from the Heavens to tell the Sumerians this information? Many believe they were the Fallen Angels that were kicked out of Heaven or their "**First Estate**" as in **Jude 1:6**.

Jude 1:6 "And the angels which kept not their first estate (home/habitat), but left their own habitation, he hath reserved in everlasting chains under darkness (**Abyss, Tartarus, Sheol**) unto the judgement of the great day (Day of the Lord-Revelation)."

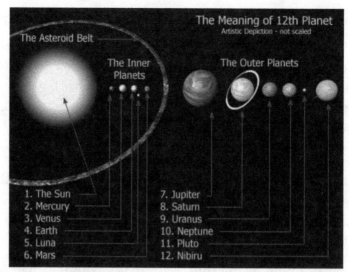

The Meaning of 12th Planet
Artistic Depiction - not scaled

The Asteroid Belt

The Inner Planets

The Outer Planets

1. The Sun	7. Jupiter
2. Mercury	8. Saturn
3. Venus	9. Uranus
4. Earth	10. Neptune
5. Luna	11. Pluto
6. Mars	12. Nibiru

(**Above**) Solar system with 12 planetary bodies which matches up with what the Ancient Sumerians knew 5,000 years ago. As you can see, **Jupiter** is the **5th planet** from **Nibiru (Planet X)**, **Mars** is the **6th planet** from Nibiru and **Earth** is the **7th planet** from Nibiru. The Asteroid belt orbits the Sun and separates the Gaseous "**Outer Planets**" without form from the Terrestrial "**Inner Planets**" with form (including water). The Sumerians knew this from the information given to them from the Annunaki. The Annunaki knew that "**water**" was abundant below the "firmament" which the Sumerians supposedly "hammered-through" to get from Nibiru to Earth, thus creating our "**asteroid belt**". Was some of this knowledge from the Semitic Mesopotamian Sumerians passed down to the Biblical forefathers of **Terah, Abraham and Moses**?

It is a known fact that "**before**" and "**after**" the Great Flood Satan was busy at work tricking mankind into worshipping the "Fallen Angels (Watchers)" as "gods", including the host of heaven. This "demonic" deception was carried out and passed down the generations of Noah's sons: Ham (Egypt), Shem (Terah) and Japheth (i.e. Rome/Greece). The teaching of the constellations of the stars and planets were given by the "Fallen Angels" whom the Sumerians called "Annunaki". This pagan knowledge would give rise to the **Zodiac** and the Babylonian-inspired Kabballah **"Tree of Life"**.

1 Enoch 19:1 "Here shall stand in many different appearances the spirits of the angels which have united themselves with women. **They have defiled the people and will lead them into error <u>so that they will offer sacrifices to the demons as unto *gods*</u>**, until the great day of judgment in which they shall be judged till they are finished."

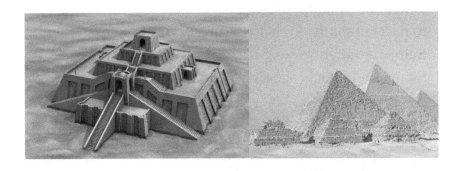

(Left) Ziggurat of Ur, Iraq (Mesopotamia). This Temple was built in honor of the Sumerian god **Nanna/Sin**. **"Nanna"** or **"Sin"** was the god of the **moon** in Mesopotamia....which later gave rise to **"Sin"** becoming the **"main god"** of the Arabs known under a new name as **"Al-ilah"** or **"Al-lah"**, which means **"The god"**. How so? Because the Islamic goddess **"Al-lat"** means **"The goddess"** and **"Al-Uzza"** means **"The Mighty One"**. (*see the Quran Sura 53:19-23*). **Nanna/Sin** was the son of the Sumerian gods **"Enlil"** and **"Ninlil"**. **(Right)** The Great Pyramids in Egypt are Temples for the Egyptian gods like **Osiris, Isis, Set and Horus**. There have also been pyramids found buried underneath grass mountains in China and ice-covered mountains in Antarctica.

In the Book of Enoch, it describes which **"Fallen Angel"** taught mankind different types of sorcery, astrology and the worship of the planets/constellations. These fallen angels would influence the Sons of Shem.....including Abraham's father "**Terah**".

1. **Araqiel**: taught the signs of the earth.
2. **Armaros**: taught the resolving of enchantments (**Magic spells & sorcery**).
3. **Azazel**: taught the making of weapons of war.
4. **Barqel**: taught **astrology**.
5. **Ezequeel**: taught the knowledge of the clouds.
6. **Gadreel**: taught the art of cosmetics.
7. **Kokabeel**: taught the mystery of the **Stars**.
8. **Penemue**: taught writing.
9. **Sariel**: taught the knowledge of the **Moon**.
10. **Semjaza**: taught Herbal enchantments.
11. **Shamshiel**: taught the signs of the **Sun**.

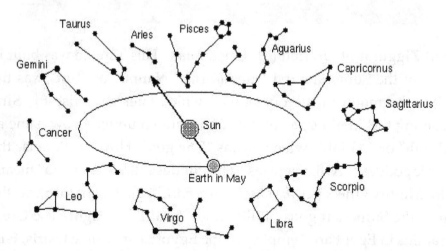

(Above) **12 constellations of the Zodiac signs which dates back to ancient Sumeria (Iraq/Iran/Assyria). The Fallen Angels deceived the Sons of Shem.....including Abraham's father Terah to worship the hosts of heaven (i.e. planets, stars, moon, sun)....giving us the "Zodiac".**

Book of Jasher 9:6-9

And **Abram** was in Noah's house thirty-nine years, and Abram knew the Lord from three years old, and he went in the ways of the Lord until the day of his death, as Noah and his son Shem had taught him; and **all the sons of the earth in those days greatly transgressed against the Lord, and they rebelled against him and they served other gods, and they forgot the Lord who had created them in the earth;** and the inhabitants of the earth made unto themselves, at that time, every man his god; gods of wood and stone which could neither speak, hear, nor deliver, and the sons of men served them and they became their gods. And the king and all his servants, and Terah with all his household were then **the first of those that served gods of wood and stone.**

And Terah had **twelve gods** of large size, made of wood and stone, after the twelve months of the year (Zodiac), and he served each one monthly, and every month Terah would bring his meat offering and drink offering to his gods; thus did Terah all the days.

And all that generation were wicked in the sight of the Lord, and they thus made every man his god, but they forsook the Lord who had created them.

(**Above**) Even the Ancient Chinese worshipped 12 pagan statues for their Zodiac as depicted at **Sik Sik Yuen Wong Tai Sin Temple** in Hong Kong, **China**. Where did they get it from? Who told them about it? It came from the Fallen Angels!

Later in the Book of Jasher 9:10-19, it shows how "**Noah**" and "**Abraham**" were special individuals unto God as they knew **YAHUAH** as the "**Creator**" of all things. They would not be deceived by the "Fallen Angels" tricks. Abraham would find this out by using "**Critical Thinking**".

Book of Jasher 9:10-19
"And **there was not a man found in those days in the whole earth, who knew the Lord** (for each man served his own God) **except Noah and his household,** and all those who were under his counsel knew the Lord in those days. And Abram the son of Terah was waxing great in those days in the house of Noah, and no man knew it, and the Lord was with him. And the Lord gave Abram an understanding heart, and he knew all the works of that generation were vain, and that all their gods were vain and were of no avail. **And Abram saw the sun shining upon the earth, and Abram said unto himself Surely now this sun that shines upon the earth is God, and him will I serve.** And

Abram served the sun in that day and he prayed to him, and when evening came the sun set as usual, and Abram said within himself, Surely this cannot be God? And Abram still continued to speak within himself, **Who is he who made the heavens and the earth? who created upon earth? where is he?** And night darkened over him, and he lifted up his eyes toward the west, north, south, and east, and he saw that the sun had vanished from the earth, and the day became dark. **And Abram saw the stars and moon before him, and he said, Surely this is the God who created the whole earth as well as man, and behold these his servants are gods around him: and Abram served the moon and prayed to it all that night**. And in the morning when it was light and the sun shone upon the earth as usual, Abram saw all the things that the Lord God had made upon earth. And **Abram said unto himself Surely these are not gods that made the earth and all mankind, but these are the servants of God, and Abram remained in the house of Noah and there knew the Lord and his ways' and he served the Lord all the days of his life**, and all that generation forgot the Lord, and served other gods of wood and stone, and rebelled all their days."

Based on this!

So, during the times of Abraham, even when he had **Isaac** and **Ishmael**........in "**Abraham's house**" there was **NO WORSHIP** of multiple Pagan gods, nor was there any worship of the Moon or the Sun. It would be later after Abraham was long gone that his descendants would stray away from the Creator.

CHAPTER 20

LINKING THE SONS OF SHEM TO INDIA USING THE SUMERIAN LANGUAGE/TEXTS AND THE BIBLE

Elohim called the firmament "**Heaven**". Hebrew Strong's #7549 lists the "**Raqia**" as the "**firmament**". The Hebrew word for waters is "**Mayim**" listed in Hebrew Strong's #4325. The Hebrew word for "heavens" is "**Shamayim**", listed in Hebrew Strong's #8064. It stems from the "prefix" use of the Hebrew letter "**Shin**" which means "**that, which, who or whom**". So the Hebrew word "**Heavens**" means "**where the waters were**" or "**whom the waters were**". It is a known fact that the "**inner planets**" inside (or below) the asteroid belt (*i.e. Mercury, Venus, Earth, Mars*) are terrestrial planets (*some with liquid water, ice water, vapor evidence*) while the "**outer planets**" outside of the asteroid belt (*i.e. Jupiter, Saturn, Uranus, Neptune, Pluto*) are just gaseous planets. The Hebrew word "**Raqia**" comes from the Hebrew Strong's #7554 verb "**Raqa**" which means "**beaten**" "**stamped**" or "**hammered out**".

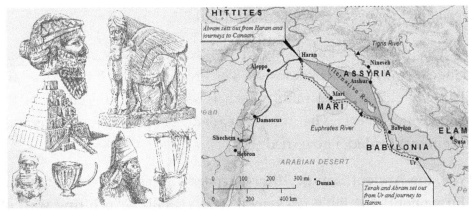

(**Left**) Sargon of Akkad (**i.e. Sargon the Great**) reigned from 2334 B.C. to 2279 B.C. in the **Land of Ur** in modern day **Iraq**. He was the founder of the Neo-Akkadian Empire that came into power after his conquering of the Sumerian Empire. (**Right**) The Land of Ur was the homeland of the Ancient Sumerians and the territory ruled by Sargon the Great around the time Terah or Abraham possibly lived. Today, the city of "Ur" sits in South Iraq near the Persian Gulf. This same city of "Ur" is where Abraham's family had their beginnings. In the "Legend of Sargon the Great" it depicts the Akkadian ruler as the King of the "black-headed" people.

Genesis 11:26-31

"And **Terah** lived seventy years and begot **Abram, Nahor, and Haran**. Now these are the generations of Terah: Terah begot Abram, Nahor, and Haran; and Haran begot Lot. And Haran died before his father Terah in the land of his nativity, in **Ur of the Chaldeans**. And Abram and Nahor took for themselves wives: the name of **Abram's wife was Sarai**, and the name of Nahor's wife, Milcah, the daughter of Haran, the father of Milcah, and the father of Iscah. But Sarai was barren; she had no child. **And Terah took Abram his son, and Lot the son of Haran his son's son, and Sarai his daughter-in-law, his son Abram's wife; and they went forth with them from Ur of the Chaldeans to go into the land of Canaan;** and they came unto Haran and dwelt there.

Legend of Sargon the Great (Translation)

"Sargon, the might king, king of Agade, am I. My mother was a changeling, my father I knew not. The brothers of my father loved the hills. My city is Azupiranu, which is situated on the banks of the **Euphrates** (River)...**The black-headed people (*i.e. Sumerians-Akkadians*) I rule**d, I governed.

Well, the Ancient Semitic **"*Black-headed*"** Sumerians wrote that the **"Firmament"** the Bible talks about was actually a **"orbiting wall of continuous rock"** which was as thick as the diameter of the moon. According to the Sumerian 14 Tablets of Enki, when the Sumerians used their Nuclear-powered weapons in their spaceship they were able to **"Hammer through"** the **"so-called Rock Firmament"** which was positioned beyond the "fifth planet-**Jupiter**" from their planet **"Nibiru"**. They noted that the sixth planet from their planet was a **"Red Planet (Mars)"** and the seventh planet which they called **"the planet with gold and waters"** was **Earth**. At first according to the Sumerians, the planet Mars had water and then it dried up....leaving Earth as their new target planet for water. In the Sumerian 14 Lost Tablets of Enki it talks about Earth being a part of a place called "Tiamat" and that the Earth's satellite was the moon.

Fact: Hebrew Strong's # 3220 "**Yam**" corresponds to the word "Sea". Hebrew Strong's #8415 "**Tehom**" also corresponds to the word "Sea", "Abyss" or "Depths/Deep". The Sumerian word for Sea (Celestial or Earthly) is "**Tiam**" or "**Tiamat**". Is it a coincidence that the Sumerian word "**Tiam**" and the Hebrew word "**Tehom**" have similar pronunciations/meanings? The Sumerians were descendants of the Sons of Shem and their language is the "**Parent Language**" of the South Dravidian Indian language of "**Tamil**". Many Language Scholars like **Dr. K. Loganatha Muttarayan** (Malaysia) have proven that the South Indian Language of Tamil is related to the Iraqi/Pre-Babylonian language of Sumerian Sanskrit. Archaeologists have even found evidence of Dravidian Indian pottery with Sanskrit writings in

Ancient **Sumer** (Babylon, Iraq), **Arabia**, and **Northeast Africa** (Egypt, Ethiopia).

(**Above**) The **Kesh Temple** in Ancient Sumeria (Iraq) was located near the city of **Kish**. The Kesh Temple Hymn was a place of worship to the Sumerian goddess **Nintud/Ninmah**. This Sumerian Hymn along with the "**Instructions of Shuruppak**" were composed and written on clay tablets as early as 3000 B.C. They are considered to be one of the oldest surviving literary works in the world.

(**Left**) Tamil Girl from South India 19th-20th Century A.D. (**Right**) Iraqi girl 19th-20th Century A.D. Who is the original Shemitic "**Mesopotamian**" from Sumer/Iraq? Whose people invaded Sumer/Iraq and whose people migrated out of Sumer/Iraq? If you go by the eye-witness description of many Arab historians in the 8th or 9th Century they will say that the "original" Shemitic-Arab peoples of the "**Middle East**" were Brown-skinned people....akin to the "**people of color" today in Africa, India, South Asia and the Pacific Islands**. **Note:** *I prove this in Book 2 and Book 3.*

There has been very strong research done by **Dravidian Indian-Tamil** language speakers who have proven that the Tamil language descends from Ancient Sumeria and Mesopotamia.....the land that Abraham (Grandfather of the Israelites) came from. The late **Professor A. Catacivam (Sathasivam)** from Sri Lanka and **Dr. Ulakanatan Muttarajan (Loganathan Muttarayan)** from Malaysia are pioneers in this research connecting the Semitic Sumerians to the South Dravidian Indians/Tamil Speakers. The Sumerians lived in the modern day country of Iraq, which in Biblical times was the territory of Shem's son "**Arphaxad**"....the ancestor of Eber, Peleg, Terah and Abraham.....grandfather of the Hebrew Israelites. This can be verified in the *Hebrew Book of Jubilees* in Chapter 8 and the *Hebrew Book of Jasher* in Chapter 10.

Genesis 10:21 "Unto Shem also, the father of all the children of Eber (i.e. Hebrew), the brother of Japheth the elder, even to him were children born. The Children of Shem; Elam, and Asshur, and **Arphaxad**, and Lud, and Aram."

(**Above**) **Singapore Malay** family 1800's. Notice some of the men and children look "**Black**" or "**Asian**". In Ancient times, the people in **Singapore** and **Malaysia** spoke "**Tamil**" whose "**Parent language**" family comes from the "**Middle East**" in Mesopotamia (Iraq, Syria, Iran). The White Arabs we see today are Japhetic "**Invaders**" from the North who have settled in the land of the "Brown-skinned" **Shemitic** peoples......forcing the real Shemites to flee South and East into Asia.

Note: Malay-Tamil-primary language schools started declining when the British and the Chinese colonized Singapore. Coincidence?

Today the Dravidian people in India are located in **Kerala, Tamil Nadu, Karnataka and Andhra Pradesh**. Tamil speakers are also native to **India, Sri Lanka, Singapore and Malaysia**.

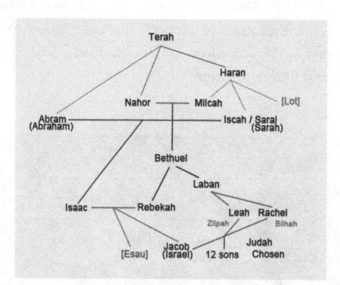

(**Above**) Genealogy of the first Hebrew mentioned in the Bible, **Abraham** and his descendants which include the 12 Tribes of Israel. If it can be shown that the people in South India (Dravidians), Sri Lanka and other South Asian countries are descendants of Shemitic Mesopotamians (**Arphaxad, Elam, Asshur, Aram, Lud**) then it can be proven that the Jews during biblical times could not have been a people with "**white skin**". It also proves that not everyone in the Middle East are really "**Shemitic people**".

Below are two lines from the Babylonian Sumerian "**Instructions of Shuruppak (Suruppak)**" from 2600 B.C. which were found in modern day "Tell Fara" in **Iraq (*i.e. Ancient Babylon or "Land of Ur" of the Chaldees and Sumerians*)**. There are strong similarities between the Sumerian dialect and the South Indian Dravidian dialect called "Tamil". This very well proves that the Dark skinned Dravidian Indian people are the long-lost descendants of the Ancient Semitic Sons of Shem (**Arphaxad, Asshur, Aram, Elam, or Lud**). After all, Assyria in ancient times consisted of the territory of Arphaxad,

Asshur, Aram and Elam. Proving that the original Shemites were a people of "**brown skin color**" like the Dravidian Indian also proves that Eber, Peleg, Terah, Abraham, Nahor, Haran, Isaac, Jacob and the Hebrew Israelites of the Bible could not have been **WHITE ARABS OR WHITE JEWS. What else does it prove?** That the original Hebrews (*i.e. sons of Ebers*) were not all "**Negroid**" looking people with tight-curled wooly hair, prognathous jaws, and full lips. Why? Because not everyone in South Asia looks identical to "**Negroes**" in America.

Sumerian script for "**Instructions of Shuruppak**" 3,000-2,600 B.C from "**Tell Abu Salabikh**" Manuscripts (**Iraq**)

Sumerian Line 61. uru.tus lu-ka na-ab-ta-bal-e-de (translation: *Do not transgress people's dwelling places*).

Sumerian Line 62. si-du-un si-me-si-ib-be-e-ne (translation: *Go away! Go away! -- they will say to you*).

Below is the Indian *Tamil script* (using English Letters for pronunciation). Note: if you look closely comparing the two languages of Sumerian and Tamil you can see the similarities. Often the only difference in the "scripts" is a letter switch from "p-b" or "s-c" or "e-i" or "b-p" This is not a coincidence.

Tamil Line 61. uurutunjcu ulu-aka naa aabta paalyidee

Tamil Line 62. celiduun celiuduu siimmee ceppiyinee

Tamil writing (Below) of Line 61-62

ஊருதுஞ்சு உளு.அக நா ஆப்த பால்யிடே
செலிடுஎன் செலிடுஎன் சீம்மே செப்பினே

Sumerian "**uru**" (Tamil = **uuru**: town, city).

Sumerian "**tus**" (Tamil = **tunjcu**: to sleep).

Sumerian "**bal**" (Tamil = **paal** ; to cross over).

Sumerian "**e-de**" (Tamil = **idu**: todo, an auxiliary verb).

Sumerian "**si**" (Tamil = **cel**: to go away).

Sumerian "**si-ib-be**" (Tamil = **ceppu** : to tell).

Sumerian "**ene**" (Tamil = **inam**: a collectivity, here plural marker).

Note: *According to the Hebrew and Ethiopic Book of Jubilees, "**Ur Kasdim**" and "**Chaldea**" took their names from **Ura** and **Kesed**, descendants of **Arphaxad**, son of Shem. In Hebrew, the term "**Chaldean**" came to mean "Astrologer" as well as the inhabitant of the land of Chaldees (Iraq). The term "**Magi**", which is used in the New Testament, refers to possible Babylonian astrologers from the "**East**". The Bible often calls these men the "**Three Wise Men**". Some say these Magi Astrologer-Priests were the old astrologer-priests of **Zoroastrianism**. Today, most Zoroastrianism followers are in **India** and not Persia. Back in the day when the Hindu Vedas exisited, India and Central Asia (i.e. Tibet/Nepal) had tons of Guru's and Wise Men. The people in India/Tibet, are taught in school about the birth and travels of a "**young Jesus**" whom they call "**St. Issa**". Could the 3 Magi from the "East" have been modern day "East Indians" or "Central Asians"? The Buddhist monks in Tibet/Nepal also claim Jesus/St. Issa was "**Afro-Asiatic**" in appearance. The term "Afro-Asiatic" refers to someone of **Hamitic-Shemitic** stock.*

Matthew 2:1-3 "Now when Jesus was born in Bethlehem of Judaea in the days of Herod the king, behold, **there came wise men from the EAST to Jerusalem**, Saying, Where is he that is born **King of the Jews**? For we have seen his star in the east, and are come to worship him. When Herod the king had heard these things, he was troubled, and all Jerusalem with him."

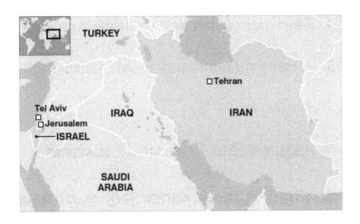

(**Above**) The land "**East**" of Jerusalem (Israel) is Jordan (*Moabite territory*), **Iraq** (*ancient Sumer*), **Iran** (*ancient Medes-Persia*) and **Old India** (*ancient Mauryan Empire*). The people living in the territory of Arphaxad back then are most likely the Ancient Dravidian people we now see today in South India and South Asia.

With that being covered, let's see another example of the Tamil "**East Indian**" language in comparison to the Babylonian Shemitic Sumerian language.

Here is another sample from the Sumerian (Babylonian) **Kes Temple Hymns** from around 2200 B.C. The Hymns are attributed to "**Enheduanna**", the daughter of the Sumero-Akkadian King **Sargon the Great**.

Kes Temple Hymns (2,200 B.C, Iraq)

Sumerian Line 14. e-kes mus-kalam-ma gu-hus-aratta (translation: *Kes temple, foundation of the country, fierce ox of Aratta*).

Sumerian Line 15. hur-sag-da-mu-a an-da gu-la-a (translation: *Growing up like a mountain, embracing the sky*).

Below is the *Tamil script* (using English Letters for pronunciation). *Compare both Lines 14 & 15 in the Sumerian and Tamil script.*

Tamil Line 14. il-kes mutu-kalamma koo ushna Arattaa

Tamil Line 15. kursen-odu muuu-a vaan-odu kulaa-a

Tamil writing (Below) of Line 14-15

இல்கேசி முதுகளம்ம கோ உஷ்ண அரத்தா

குற்/.உசென்னிஒடு மூஉ-அ வான்.ஒடு குலாவ்-அ

Sumerian "**e**" (Tamil = **il**: house, koo-il: temple).

Sumerian "**kes**" (Tamil = **keeci**: a name for Siva like the Siva Temples the Tamil Saiva saints worshiped at).

Sumerian "**mus**" (Tamil = **mutal** : the foundation).

Sumerian "**kalam**" (Tamil = **kaLam**: country, land).

Sumerian "**gu**" (Tamil = **koo**: bull, cow, ox).

Sumerian "**hus**" (Tamil = **ushNa**, ukkira: intense heat, fierce).

Sumerian "**hur-sag**" (Tamil = **kunRu-senni**: the peak).

Sumerian "**mu**" (Tamil = **muuu. muuL, muLai**: to sprout, move forward).

Sumerian "**an**" (Tamil = **vaan**: sky).

Sumerian "**du**" (Tamil = **odu**: comitative case marker that denotes "in company with" or "together with").

Sumerian "**gu-la**" (Tamil = **kulaa** (vu): to jostle, push, bump or elbow against someone, get close to or "interact with" like embracing someone).

All of this information may leave you with one question......."Were the early Hebrews (*including Israelites*) a mixture of Brown-skinned Hamites (*Cush, Mizraim-Egypt*) and Brown-skinned Shemites (*i.e. Dravidian people*)? Yes!!

Consider this before we move on. Nimrod was the son of Cush (Ethiopia-Nubia) in Africa. This is verified in **Genesis 10:8.** Now read this.

Book of Jubilees 8:7-8 "And she bare him a son in the fifth year thereof, and he called his name **Eber**: and he took unto himself a wife, and her name was '**Azurad'**, the **daughter of Nimrod (***i.e. "Nebrod" in the Greek translation***),** in the thirty-second Jubilee, in the seventh week, in the third year thereof. And in the sixth year thereof, she (**Azurad**) bare him son, and he called his name **Peleg**; for in the days when he was born the children of Noah began to divide the earth amongst themselves: for this reason he called his name Peleg."

Note: Peleg was Abraham's **Great-Great-Great Grandfather.** **Terah** is the father of Abraham, the grandfather of Jacob, the father of the Children of Israel.

Book of Jasher 7:49-51 "And **Terah** the son of Nahor, **prince of Nimrod's host**, was in those days very great in the sight of the king and his subjects, and the (Cushite) king and (Cushite) princes loved him, and they elevated him very high. And Terah took a wife and her name was **Amthelo** the daughter of **Cornebo (Cushite Priest)**; and the wife of Terah conceived and bare him a son in those days. Terah was seventy years old when he begat him, and **Terah called the name of his son that was born to him Abram**, because the king had raised him in those days, and dignified him above all his princes that were with him.

If Terah held a "**high position**" in the Cushite Royal family with **Nimrod** we should assume that his wife "**Amthelo**", the daughter of

Priest Cornebo....was most likely of Cushite stock. This **"Cushite"** woman **"Amthelo"** and the **"Hebrew"** man **"Terah"** would give birth to Abraham. This would make Abraham an **"Afro-Asiatic"** brown-skinned man.

CHAPTER 21

ANCIENT SUMERIA PROVES THE BIBLE IS VALID AND WHY GOD GAVE THE CHILDREN OF ISRAEL "SPECIFIC" COMMANDMENTS.

Many people today are abandoning the Bible because of their beliefs that the "**literary works**" of Ancient Egypt and Ancient Sumeria are "**untampered**" by the "white man". They claim the Bible is a plagiarism of ancient religious texts and therefore cannot be trusted. Even, Muslims believe the Quran is the "**untampered**" word of God when Muhammad somehow studied the Bible (Old Testament/New Testament) enough to include in his religion (Islam) the lives of **Noah, Abraham, Isaac, Jacob and Jesus Christ**. What many Bible readers fail to realize is that the Bible is a "**historical**" book written from the viewpoint of a certain group of Shemitic people called the "**Hebrew Israelites**" who existed generations after "Great Flood". What makes the Bible more than just a "book" is that it covers history more accurately than any religious book on the planet in addition to covering "**morality-laws**", "**spirituality**", "**prophecy**", and "**salvation**".

(**Above**) The **Annunaki** were depicted as giants compared to the people on earth. This is because their history states the Annunaki people living on Nibiru were around **9 feet tall**. They also wore tall hats, some of them fashioned after the head of an eagle. They were also noted to sometimes have wings. This account is also similar to the rulers of the Ancient Land of Atlantis.

In the Sumerian 14 Lost Tablets of Enki, one of the Kings of the Annunaki (*before Anu or his father was king*) is called "**Alalu**". In the Sumerian Tablets, a "**Celestial Emissary (Ambassador)**" named "**Little Gaga**" shows the King of the Annunaki and his fleet of nuclear packed space ships the way past the "**Firmament**" stone hammered bracelet wall. In some sources "**Gaga**" or "**Kaka**" is a name given to Pluto....which corresponds to an old Babylonian (Sumer) hermaphroditic deity. According to the Sumerians, "**Gaga**" was a messenger of "**Anshar (Saturn)**". In the occult and Satanic world, "**Saturn**" or the "**Black Cube**" is associated with **Satan**. This can be researched further in "*The Religion of Babylonia and Assyria*" by Morris Jastrow and "*The Enuma Elish: The Seven Tablets of Creation*" by Leonard William King.

Fact: "*Gaga*" *in the Sumerian texts was a messenger of Saturn (Satan). It is a known fact that during singer "Lady Gaga's" shows (Super Bowl, live performances, videos) one can see all the occultism, Satanic symbolism. Lady Gaga also promotes sexual ambiguity "sexual/gender confusion" similar to what a hermaphrodite is. In 2012 on the "Jimmy Kimmel Live" Show,* **Lady Gaga** *talks about song-making and her team not having the right "frequency" to move forward. She responded to Jimmy by saying that she handles her team by sometimes blurting out,* **"If you don't get this right now I swear to LUCIFER I'm gonna...".** *Most people swear to* **God** *and not* **Lucifer.** *This quick saying by Lady Gaga was a true "sign" that she walks with Satan, however most of the "sleeping" deceived world did not pick this up. Christ told his disciples to not swear at all in* **Matthew 5:34-37.**

Note: *Occultists believe that before the "Great Flood", Saturn...or should I say "Satan/Lucifer" was regarded by all mankind as the supreme god and ruler of the kings on earth. The occultic world also believe that Satan with his followers ruled the Kingdom of Atlantis.*

Could this "**Little Gaga**" person in the Sumerian tablets of Enki have been **Satan/Lucifer** himself showing his band of fallen angels the way to Earth? Or was this "Little Gaga" person a high ranking Fallen Angel like **Azazel**?

Sumerian "Lost 14 Tablets of Enki"
Second Tablet
"To snow-hued Earth Alalu set his course, but secret from the Beginning he chose his destination. **TO REGIONS FORBIDDEN** (*Note: who declared the regions "forbidden"*) Alalu made his way; **NO ONE HAS GONE THERE BEFORE** (*fallen angels had not been to earth until they were banished there*), No one at the **HAMMERED BRACELET** (*i.e. Rock Firmament*) a crossing had attempted. A secret from the beginning Alalu's course determined, the fate of Nibiru (*Jude 1:6*) in his hands it placed, by a scheme his kingship to make universal! On Nibiru exile was certain, there death itself he was chancing (*Annunaki people could die?*). In his scheme, risk was in the journey; eternal glory of success was the reward! Beyond the Fifth planet (Jupiter) the utmost danger was lurking, so indeed he knew. The **HAMMERED BRACELET** (*i.e. the biblical "firmament"-Hebrew Strong's word "Raqa #7554/Raqia #7549"*) ahead was reigning, to **DEMOLISH IT** was awaiting! **Of ROCKS and BOULDERS** (*i.e. before it became the asteroid belt*) was it together hammered, like orphans with no mother they banded together. Surging back and forth, a bygone destine they, followed; Their doings were loathsome; troubling were their ways. Nibiru's probing chariots (*i.e. spaceships*) like preying lions they devoured; the precious gold (*Annunaki used gold on their planet*), needed for surviving, they refused to dislodge. The chariot (*spaceship*) of Alalu toward the Hammered Bracelet (*firmament*) was headlong moving, the ferocious boulders in close combat to boldly face. Alalu the Fire Stones (*lasers/nuclear weapons*) in his chariot more strongly stirred up, That Which Shows the Way with steady hands he directed. The ominous

boulders (*rock meteors/asteroids*) against the chariot charged forward, like an enemy in battle **ATTACKING**. Toward them Alalu a death-dealing **missile** (?) from the chariot (*i.e. spaceship*) let loose; Then another and another against the enemy the terror **weapons** he thrust. As frightened warriors, the boulders turned back, a path for Alalu granting. Like by a spell the Hammered Bracelet a **DOORWAY** to the king it opened (*i.e. the Annunaki fallen angels made it through the firmament towards Earth*). In the dark deepness Alalu the heavens could clearly see (**see Genesis 1:6-9**); by the Bracelet's (*now Asteroid belt between Mars and Jupiter*) ferocity he was not defeated, his mission was not ended! In the distance, the Sun's fiery ball its brilliance (light-rays) was sending forth; Welcoming rays toward Alahu it was emitting. Before it, a Red-brown planet (**Mars**) on its circuit was coursing; the sixth (planet) in the count of celestial gods it was. Alalu could but glimpse it: on its destined course from Alalu's path it was quickly moving. Then snow-hued Earth appeared, the seventh (planet from Nibiru) in the celestial count."

Note: The Creation Story by the Sumerians seems to be more of a tampering with man's DNA with the Annunaki DNA (*i.e. like in-vitro fertilization of a human male sperm, a human female egg and DNA material from the Annunaki into the womb of either a mortal woman or Annunaki woman*) than an actual "creation" of a lifeform out of nothing. In the Sumerian myth, Enki...one of the Annunaki Kings is challenged by his half-sister/wife, "**Ninmah/Ninhursag**" in regards as who can "create" the best lifeforms. Before coming to Earth, the Annunaki said there was a class system of "**Higher gods**" and "**Lesser gods**". The "Lesser gods" actually had to do work but soon got tired of working so they asked the Mother goddess **Nammu** of the Sea (Deep/Abyss), **Enki** and **Ninmah** to create a race of beings even though the Sumerian Tablets acknowledge that there were already "**black headed humanoids**" on the Earth when they arrived. In Sumerian texts, before the "**gods**" were created a "**void**" existed in the form of 2 words: "**Apsu/Abzu**", which the Sumerians called "sweet/fresh water" and "Tiamat" which the Sumerians called "salt water-Earth". The Sumerians gave both of these words the position of gods, then made them a man-wife married couple. Then like many ancient civilizations in religious mythology, these two gods (male and female) had children. This mimics the "Creation" story of Genesis 1 where the earth was void, while the "Spirit of God" moved upon the face of the waters.

Genesis 1:1-2 "In the beginning God created the heavens and the earth. And the earth was without form and void; and darkness was upon the face of the deep (waters). And the Spirit of God moved upon the face of the waters."

In the beginning tablets, we find out that the Annunaki King "Enki" is the god of the "sweet waters of the deep" in addition to the god of "wisdom" and "magic". This is similar to the Egyptian pagan deity "Thoth" who is accredited as being "The Atlantean" and builder of the "Great Pyramid" prior to the Great Flood. This would mean that Thoth would use man (*with the Fallen Angels and their humanoid science experiments "gone wrong"*) to build pyramids before Noah's time and during the time of "Ham". Ham would give birth to his son "Mizraim", who would help build further Pyramids....or at least do "upgrades" to the pyramids already in place. Remember...Mizraim, Cush, Canaan and Phut are all the Sons of Ham, but Mizraim is accredited to being the father of the Ancient Egyptians and the Ancient Philistines (*i.e. modern day Palestine*).

THE EMERALD TABLETS OF THOTH, TABLET 5: THE DWELLER OF UNDAL

The "**Dweller**" aka "**Satan**" gives the order to Thoth a "Demonic Fallen Angel" to:

Take all your records, **Take all your magic**. Go thou forth as a teacher of men. Go thou forth reserving the records until in time LIGHT (**Illuminated ones**) grows among men. LIGHT (**Illuminati**) shalt thou be all through the ages, hidden yet found by enlightened men. Over all Earth, give **WE** ye power, free thou to give or take it away. Gather thou now the sons (**fallen angels**) of Atlantis. Take them and flee to the people of the **rock caves**. Fly to the land of the **Children of KHEM (CHAM-HAM-EGYPT)**. Then gathered I the sons of Atlantis. **Into the spaceship, I brought all my records**, brought the records of sunken Atlantis. Gathered I all of my powers, instruments many of **mighty magic**.

The account above seems to be of an "alien" force that is ordered to enter a ship and go to the land of a people who lived in caves, and to begin to colonize, and civilize life. Was this shortly after the "Great Flood". Did Atlantis exist before the "Great Flood"?

The account never uses the word "earth", but when one looks at the time of the writings dating back thousands of years, and considers the appearances of prehistoric people who lived on the earth at that time....it is easy to see we are reading the accounts of an exploration on planet earth made by advanced beings (i.e. Fallen Angels) from the heavens.

Keep in mind this thought.

What were known as "**gods**" to ancient civilizations 5,000 years ago by many are today considered "**fallen angels**", "**Aliens**" or the genetic experiments of the Fallen Angels today. So, it could be that what we refer to as aliens today, were regarded as angels, or gods, a few thousand years ago.

Enoch 15:1-8.

"And He answered and said to me, and I heard His voice: 'Fear not, Enoch, thou righteous man and scribe of righteousness: approach hither and hear my voice. And go, say to the **Watchers of Heaven** (angels), who have sent thee to intercede for them: "You should intercede" for men, and not men for you: **Wherefore have ye left the high, holy, and eternal heaven, and lain with women, and defiled yourselves with the daughters of men and taken to yourselves wives, and done like the children of earth, and begotten giants (as your) sons.** And though ye were holy, spiritual, living the eternal life, you have **defiled yourselves** with the blood of women, and have begotten (**children**) with the blood of flesh, and, as the **Children of Men**, have lusted after flesh and blood as those also do who die and perish. Therefore have I given them wives also that they might **impregnate them**, and **beget children** by them, that thus nothing might be wanting to them on earth. **But you were formerly spiritual, living the eternal life, and immortal for all generations of the world.** And therefore I have not appointed wives for you; for as for the spiritual ones of the heaven, in heaven is their dwelling. **And now, the giants, who are produced from the spirits and flesh, shall be called Evil Spirits (demons) upon the earth, and on the earth shall be their dwelling.**

In the great city of **KEOR** on the island of **UNDAL (Atlantis)**, in a time far past, I began this incarnation (**i.e life**). Not as the little men of the present age did the **mighty ones of Atlantis live and die (Nephilim)**, but rather from aeon to aeon did they renew their life (**demonic spirits**) in the Halls of Amenti (**Hell**) where the river of life flows eternally onward.

In the **Sumerian Tablets**, "Sumerian Annunaki gods" manipulate the "created creatures/humans of God" which end up being "**Giants**", "**creatures**", "**monsters**" and "**abominations**". Such as combining the hind legs of one creature to the front legs of another creature.

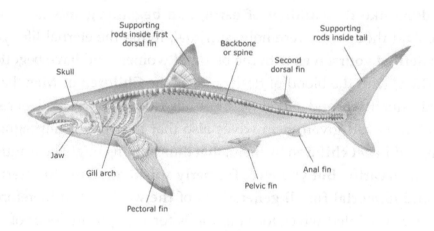

(**Above**) Depiction of **Shark** and its skeletal make up.

Sharks have fins, not appendages that look like fingers hidden under their skin. Dolphins have bony "appendages" inside of their fins that look like a human hand with fingers. Sharks also have a "**type of scale**" that overlays their skin, not like dolphins or whales. Sharks as well as other fish in the Sea/Ocean are **"cold-blooded animals"** compared to **"warm-blooded dolphins & whales"**. Why is there a difference between Sharks, other fish and dolphins/whales? Could it be hidden in the Book of Enoch and God's **"Dietary Law"** given to the Israelites in the Torah?

Leviticus 11:9-12
"These shall ye eat of all that are in the waters: **whatsoever hath <u>fins</u> and <u>scales</u> in the waters, in the seas, and in the rivers, them shall ye eat**. And all that have **not fins and scales** in the seas, and in the rivers, of all that move in the waters, and of any living thing which is in the waters, **they shall be an abomination unto you**: They shall be even an abomination unto you; ye shall not eat of their flesh, but ye shall have their carcasses in abomination. **Whatsoever hath no fins nor scales in the waters, that shall be an abomination unto you**.

(**Above**) It is a known fact that Dolphins and Whales **DO NOT** have fins or scales. This is a Dolphin Skeleton with what seems to be **5 bony appendages for fingers, like a human hand**. Over these 5 bony fingers, dolphins have flippers (fins) but they cannot stretch out their fingers or grasp things because of the fact that they have flippers (fins) and not hands despite their skeleton having 4-5 bony fingers. Sharks have fins and no bony fingers like whales and dolphins. Whales and Dolphins do not have scales. One is a mammal, one is considered a fish. One is highly intelligent, one is not. **The Bible forbade the Israelites from eating fish without scales**. Are these intelligent "marine" mammals the product of "DNA manipulation" with the Fallen Angels? **Could this be why God gave the Israelites a dietary law?** Perhaps the dietary law was to prevent the Israelites from eating any unclean "animal, fish, or bird" that had been "genetically tampered with" by the fallen angels.

Enoch 7:2-7:5 "And they became pregnant and brought forth great giants whose stature was three thousand ells. These devoured all acquisitions of mankind till men were unable to sustain themselves. And the giants turned themselves against mankind in order to devour them. **And they began to sin against the birds and the beast, and against the creeping things, and the fish**, and devoured their flesh among themselves, and drank the blood thereof. Then the earth complained of the unjust ones."

Note: In the Sumerian Tablets, there seems to be a correlation of these so called "Annunaki-Fallen Angel" gods creating modern day "Grey Aliens". Could these different types of "Aliens" and "Monsters (**i.e.**

Lochness Monster, Yeti, Bigfoot, Mermaids) simply be "created creatures" done with "DNA manipulation" by the Fallen Angels.

The Book of Enoch admits that the "Fallen Angels" were at one point "Spiritual beings, **IMMORTAL**"....not needing a wife because God didn't appoint wives to the Angels in Heaven. Once Lucifer and his band of Angels fell from heaven they were no longer immortal and God allowed them to participate in what mankind was able to do....that is somehow "mate" their seed with mankind and maybe even each other. Let's look at the Book of Enoch again. Was this hinted on in the ancient "Sumerian tablets"?

ENOCH 15

"Therefore have I given them (Fallen Angels) wives also that they might **impregnate them**, and **beget children** by them, that thus nothing might be wanting to them on earth. **But you were formerly spiritual, living the eternal life, and immortal for all generations of the world.** And therefore I have not appointed wives for you; for as for the spiritual ones of the heaven, in heaven is their dwelling. **And now, the giants, who are produced from the spirits and flesh, shall be called Evil Spirits (demons) upon the earth, and on the earth shall be their dwelling.**

Sumerian (Lost Tablets of Enki) Tablet 6
Verses 2-82 Continued:

"Fifth, she fashioned a woman would could not give birth. Enki looked at the woman (*i.e. RH-Negative women and RH positive man with RH positive fetus*) who could not give birth. Enki looked at the woman who would not give birth, and decreed her fate: he made her belong to the queen's household. **Sixth, she fashioned one with neither penis nor vagina on its body (i.e. modern day Grey aliens are**

"sexless"). Enki looked at the one with neither nor vagina on its body and gave it the name **"Nibru enuch"** (like planet Nibiru), and decreed as its fate to stand before the king. Ninmah threw the pinched-off clay from her hand on the ground and a great silence fell. The great lord Enki said to Ninmah, "I have decreed the fate **OF YOUR CREATURES** and given them their daily bread. Come now I will fashion somebody for you, and you must decree the fate of the newborn one!"

Did the **"Fallen Angels"** try to figure out how to **"sin"** with mankind once they were kicked out of heaven? Did they experience some difficulties and **"abominable"** creatures until they finally got it right? Even though the Fallen Angels "succeeded" in the Bible, they ended up creating Giants and other monstrosities that have been sighted throughout the history of earth.

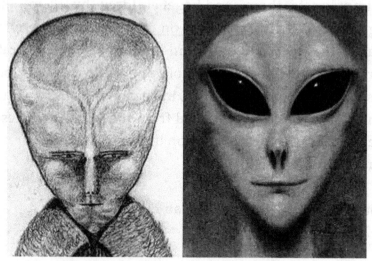

(Left) Drawing depicting "LAM", a demonic **"dark entity"** conjured up by Satanist **Aleister Crowley** when he spent the night in the Egyptian Pyramid of Giza in the early 1900's. **(Right)** Modern picture depicting a Grey Alien.

Aleister Crowley was guided to travel to pyramids in Egypt where he was visited by an entity called **"Aiwass"** who was the messenger of

Horus according to his revelation while at visiting the Egyptian "**Boulaq (Bulaq)**" Museum in Cairo, Egypt. It is not a coincidence that this "**LAM**" figure looks like a typical "**Grey Big-headed Alien**". Many people today who pray, worship and channel different Egyptian Gods (*i.e. Sekhmet, Thoth, Anubis, Hathor, Isis, Horus*) attract dark demonic, satanic entities. Any type of magical power not of God is "**Sorcery, witchcraft and voodoo**". This is part of the reason why the Bantus people in West Africa, East Africa, Negroes scattered into the Caribbean (Jamaica, Haiti, Cuba) and Negroes scattered into the Americas still experienced the "**Curses of Israel**" for their continuation of these forbidden practices (**i.e. Santeria, Voodoo, Candomble, Afa, Ifa, Sande society, fetishism, Opon Ifa divination tray**).

Deuteronomy 18:9-14
"When thou art come into the land which the LORD thy God giveth thee, **thou shalt not learn to do after the abominations of those nations**. There shall not be found among you any one that maketh his son or his daughter to pass through the fire, or that useth **divination**, or an **observer of times**, or an **enchanter**, or a **witch**. Or a **charmer**, or a consulter with **familiar spirits**, or a **wizard**, or a **necromancer (i.e. communicating with the dead to predict the future). For all that do these things are an abomination unto the LORD**: and because of these abominations the LORD thy God doth drive them out from before thee. **Thou shalt be perfect with the LORD thy God.** For these nations, which thou shalt possess, hearkened unto observers of times, and unto diviners: but as for thee, the LORD thy God hath not suffered thee so to do."

No matter what country or civilization, Satan always has a way to keep his "**worship**" going. When people channel "**spirits**" for health and other things it is always tied into Satan. The Israelite pagan goddess **Queen of Heaven**, the African goddess **Mami Wata** (Yemajo/Yemaya-Yoruba), the Egyptian goddess **Sekhmet**, the Judaism/Kabbalism goddess **Shekinah**, the Roman goddess **Venus**, the Greek goddess

Aphrodite, the Babylonian goddess **Ishtar**, the Canaanite goddess **Asheroth/Astarte**, or the Sumerian goddess **Inaana** are all tied into the Luciferian doctrine. In the occult these goddesses are considered **witches**.

CHAPTER 22

FALLEN ANGELS, CANAAN AND ASIA

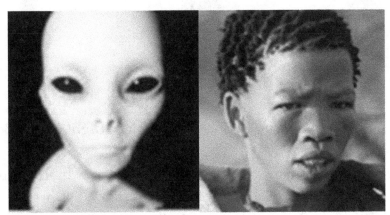

(**Left**) Rendition of a Hybrid Alien-Humanoid. (**Right**) San (Khoi) Bushmen from South Africa (Namibia).

The appearance of "**wide-set eyes**", no "**eyelids** (i.e. single epicanthal eyefold/eyelid)" and "**short stature**" of modern grey aliens seems to be a possible "**Fallen Angel**" trait that was passed down from the "**Watchers/Fallen Angels**" in the Book of Genesis/Book of Enoch. The story of "**Star Beings**" or "**Fallen Angels**" coming from the heavens tampering with mankind and his DNA is also seen in the Lost Sumerian Tablets of Enki. In the Bible, the **Canaanites** seemed to be one of the main sons of Ham that mixed with the Fallen Angels.

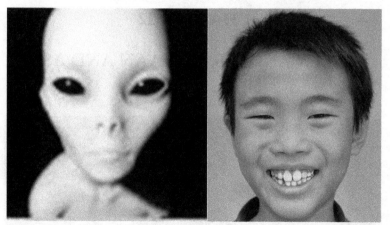

(**Left**) Rendition of a Hybrid Alien-Humanoid. (**Right**) Asian Boy.

Like the San "Bushman" African people, Asians exhibit "**wide-set**" eyes and the absence of a "**double-eyelid**" like most people on the planet. This "**single-eyelid**" is typically called "**Asian-eyes**" or its medical teminology, "**Single Epicanthal Fold**". Most Grey Alien sightings report them to be small in height, which is also exhibited by most Asians and also the San Bushmen pygmy people of South Africa. Is this a coincidence? The San Bushmen pgymy people have evidence of the Y-DNA Haplogroup "**B**" which is "older" than the typical Asian Y-Haplogroup "**O**". So the "Asian-Eye" feature could have been passed down from the "**Original Brown-skinned "Canaanites**" in the Land of Ham (Africa) from the Fallen Angels and then "**deposited**" in Asia as some Canaanite tribes (*i.e. Sinites/Shina/China*) ventured into Asia.

Genesis 10:15-17 "And **Canaan** begat Sidon his firstborn, and Heth, and the Jebusite, and the Amorite, and the Girgasite, and the Hivite, and the Arkite, and the **Sinite**."

Fact: The Chinese people have been sometimes linked to the Sinites as the prefix "**Sino**" has some connection to Ancient China. For example, the "**Sino-Japanese War**" from 1894-1895 and the "**Second Sino-Japanese War**" from 1937-1945 refers to China as "**Sina/Sino**". Also the study of Chinese History and Language is called "**SIN-ology**". In Isaiah 49:12, the word "**SIN-IM**" is used to describe the countries/land "**East**" of Israel (**Canaan**). If the Sinite Canaanites aquired the "**Asian-Eye**" trait from their interaction/mixing with the Fallen Angels or even if they had this trait "**naturally**" it would make sense that it would be carried to the "**East**" if the Canaanites left their land while Joshua and the Israelites were taking over their land killing Canaanite Kings.

In that scenario it would appear that the "**Asian-eye**" trait came from the "San Bushmen (Khoisan) people in Africa and then it was spread into Asia. There is also reason to believe that this "Asian-eye trait" was passed down as a "**recessive**" gene from the "Pygmy" Canaanite tribes who may have had some contact in Ancient times with the Fallen Angels. Or did the "Asian-eye" trait start in Asia with "visitors" from outer space (*i.e. the heavens*) which was passed from Asia into Africa? The "earlier" scenerio with an "**Out of Africa into Asia**" spread of this "eye-trait" seems to make the most "logical sense" if you read the Bible. We know that the Canaanites had to have been a "Brown skinned" people if their father Ham had other sons (Cush, Egypt (Mizraim), Phut) who were also Brown-skinned melaninated people. Also, it has been genetically proven that Asians descend from people from Africa.

DOES GENETICS SHOW SOME PROOF THAT THE FALLEN ANGELS OR THE NEANDERTHAL SONS OF CAIN PASSED AN "FOREIGN TRAIT" TO THE PEOPLE IN AFRICA/ASIA?

South African Geneticist Himla Soodyall in the article "**mtDNA Contro-Region Sequence Variation Suggests Multiple Independent Origins of an "Asian-Specific" 9-bp Deletion in Sub-Saharan Africans (***American Journal of Human Genetics.* **58 (1996): *pg 595-608)***", shows the correlation between certain Africans (i.e. pygmies) and Asians. But what is also interesting is that there is some link to the

Neanderthal maternal **mtDNA "X"** and this two races from different areas of the planet.

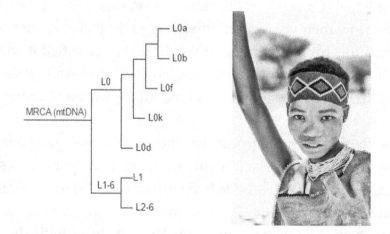

(**Above**) The maternal mtDNA "**L0d**" is seen mostly in the **Khoi-San Bushmen people of South Africa**. In 2014, ancient DNA analysis of a 2,330 year-old male skeleton in South Africa was found to belong to the mtDNA "**L0d2c1c**" subclade which is most commonly seen in the Khoi-San "Bushmen" people. Many geneticists call the mtDNA "L0" the "**mitochondrial Eve**". From the mtDNA "L0" came "**L0a**" which is most common in **Mbuti** and **Biaka Pygmies** in Africa. Maternal mtDNA "L0a" is also seen in 1/4th of the "**Hadramaut**" people in Yemen. It is a known fact that the Y-DNA "E1b1a" is seen in mild-moderate frequencies in the Hadramaut people in Yemen (Arabia Felix), especially the Hadramaut Jews that reside there.

Here is where it gets deep!

In the genetic world there is a **T-to-C transition mutation** that occurs on position "**16189**" in the human genome. Thymine (T) and Cytosine (C) are both nitrogenous bases seen in DNA. This "**16189 mutation**" is only seen in certain populations across the world. According to geneticists, this "mutation" is fixed on both "**Asian**" and "**African**" sequences. This mutation also defines the mtDNA "**B**" seen in Asia (*i.e. China/Mongolia/Siberia*) and the Americas (*i.e. North American Native*

Americans-Aztecs-Mexicans) where both races are often referred to as "**Mongols**". But there is something interesting about this. Geneticists have found out that the "**mtDNA 9-bp deletion mutation**" and the "**16189-Cytosine mutation**" are both seen in select **Asian** populations, **Native Americans**, **Pacific Islanders**, select **Sub-Saharan Bantus Africans**, **African pygmy tribes**, and the **Black Lemba Jews** of South Africa. Coincidence? What does all these groups have in common? For one, the majority of these groups claim to have Ancestry from Israel (Land of Canaan). If the Pygmy Tribes are the Biblical Canaanites, then whoever they mixed with (*i.e. Israelites in the Bible*) would also have this "16189-Cytosine mutation". With that being said, have we found out an "**Canaanite**" marker or an "**Israelite**" marker? Let's dig deeper because the answer is coming soon. Remember, the Canaanites were "**a people**" that Abraham and Isaac didn't want their seed to mix with. Why? Were some of the Canaanite Tribes "**infected**" with the DNA of the Sons of Cain or the Fallen Angels-Nephilim? Despite all of this, the Israelites didn't follow the advice of their Grandfather (Isaac) or Great-Granfather (Abraham).

Judges 3:5-6 "*And the children of Israel dwelt among the Canaanites*, Hittites, and Amorites, and Perizzites, and Hivites, and Jebusites. *And they took their daughters to be their wives*, and gave their daughters to their sons, and served their gods."

(**Above**) Khoi-San Bushmen woman from Botswana, South Africa. They have what some say is the oldest DNA on the planet and they have the "**Asian-Eye**" trait. Their hair is also very tight-curled and their skin complexion ranges from light brown skinned to dark-brown skinned. They carry the mtDNA **L0, L0d, L0k** from which the "**Pygmy mtDNA L0a**" stems from.

Geneticists say that the African mtDNA "**L0a2**" linked to the Pygmy tribes (Biaka, Mbuti, Twa) is basically the sister mtDNA of the Asian/American mtDNA "**B**". But in these Genetic studies they have found that the "**np 16189 mutation**" shows "**variability**" in select humans (*i.e. some Asians, Native Americans, Bantus Africans, Pacific Islanders, Pgymy Tribes, Arabs*) but it is "**fixed**" in the *Neanderthal mtDNA "X" (see Hagelberg, E. "Recombination or Mutation Rate Heterogeneity: Implications for Mitochondrial Eve," Trends in Genetics. (2003), 19 (2): pg 84-90.*

Note: *Neanderthal mtDNA "X" is also seen in the 16189 T-to-C mutation. Does this verify that the Canaanites also mixed with the "Neanderthal people"? How else could this "16189 mutation" be seen in the mtDNA of Native Americans, Bantus Africans, Pacific Islanders, select Asians, and the Lemba Jews of South Africa?*

With that being said, did the Sons of Cain/Fallen Angels/Nephilim somehow mix with the Canaanites (Pygmies) while they were in Afria and Asia? Why else would we see "**Asian-Eye like**" traits in the San

Bushmen, Asians, Pacific Islanders, Coloured South Africans and certain Bantus Tribes in South Africa (i.e. Zulu, Xhosa). If we know that the Bantus people across the world or the Lemba People are **NOT** "**Canaanites**", then this would mean "**ONE THING**"! It would mean that the bloodline of the Canaanites was spread thoughout the nations in certain regions.....thus proving that these other race groups were actually Israelites that had some "run-ins" with the Canaanite tribes.

Let's prove the Fallen Angels mixed their seed with the different Canaanite tribes using the Bible since there may be some skeptics to this theory. But for many Bible readers and Christians, the saying, "**If it is not in the Bible, then it is not right**" will be used to show that this theory is perhaps right.

- **Jude 1:6-7 "And the (fallen) angels which kept not their first estate, but left their own habitation, he hath reserved in everlasting chains under darkness unto the judgment of the great day.** Even as Sodom and Gomorrah, and the cities about them in like manner, giving themselves over to fornication, and going after strange flesh, are set forth for an example, **suffering the vengeance of eternal fire.**"

- **Genesis 6:1-4** "And it came to pass, when men began to multiply on the face of the earth, and daughters were born unto them, That the **sons of God** saw the daughters of men that they were fair; and they took them wives of all which they chose. And the Lord said, My spirit shall not always strive with man, for that he also is flesh: yet his days shall be an hundred and twenty years. **THERE WERE GIANTS IN THE EARTH IN THOSE DAYS; AND ALSO AFTER THAT (after the flood),** when the sons of God came in unto the daughters of men, and they bare children to them, the same became might men which were of old, men of renown."

- These Fallen angels called *"Sons of God"* or *"Watchers"* in our KJV bible came down and mated with human women. For doing this deed they were cast out of heaven, never to return and some of them were cast into **"Tartarus"** which is another word for **"Abyss"** or **"Hell"**. Daniel quoted about these "Watchers" in his book and the story of the angels being cast from heaven can be seen in **2 Peter 2:4**.

- **Daniel 4:13** "I saw in the visions of my head upon my bed, and, **behold, a Watcher and a holy one came down from heaven;"**

- **Daniel 4:17 "This matter is by the decree of the Watchers,** and the demand by the word of the holy ones: to the intent that the living may know that the Most High ruleth in the kingdom of men, and giveth it to whomsoever he will, and setteth up over it the basest of men."

- **Daniel 4:23 "And whereas the king saw a Watcher** and a holy one coming down from heaven."

- **2 Peter 2:4 "For if God spared not the angels that sinned,** but cast them down into hell, and delivered them into chains of darkness, to be reserved unto judgment;"

Ok, so what about the connection to the Fallen Angels, the Nephilim and the Sons of Ham (*Canaan, Mizraim-Egypt, Philistines, Cush, Phut*)? We know that the Fallen Angels mixed with the Canaanites possibly causing Canaanite Giants and Canaanite pygmies. Is it referenced in the Bible? Sure it is!

- **Genesis 10:15-16 "And Canaan begat Sidon** his firstborn, **and Heth**, and **the Jebusite**, and **the AMORITE**, and the **Girgashite**."

- **Amos 2:9** "Yet destroyed I the **Amorite** before them, **whose height was like the height of the cedars**, and he was strong as the oaks; yet I destroyed his fruit from above, and his roots beneath."
- Amalekites
- Amorites (Canaanite-Genesis 10:15-18)
- Anakims,
- Ashdothites
- Canaanites (Numbers 11, Deuteronomy 2:10-11)
- Girgashites (Canaanite-Genesis 10:15-18)
- Hittites (Canaanite-Genesis 10:15-18)
- Hivites (Canaanite-Genesis 10:15-18)
- Jebusites (Canaanite-Genesis 10:15-18)
- Sidonians/Zidonians (Canaanite-Genesis 10:15-18)

The Anakim or Rephaim were known in the bible as descendants of the Nephilim Giants. Here is their connection to the Canaanites, which would also connect them to the Children of Israel…..especially the Israelites that have mixed the most with the descendants of certain Canaanite tribes from 1400 B.C. until now (*See Judges 3, Ezra 9:1-3*).

For example, some of the Bantus **Zulu** and **Xhosa people** (*i.e. Nelson Mandela*) sometimes can be seen with an "**Asian-eye**" look in their appearance. They share the same specific "**9-bp deletion**" genetic marker that is also seen Asia, Southeast Asia, Polynesia, the Americas and Pygmy populations. **The "9-bp deletion" genetic marker has been seen mostly in South African "Bantus" populations as well as the Lemba Jews of South Africa.**

- Anak ("long-necked; giant")
- Anak was the son of Arba (in Hebrew, it means "**Strength of Baal**")
- Joshua 15:13 "**And unto Caleb the son of Jephunneh he gave a part among the children of Judah, according to the commandment of the LORD to Joshua, even the city of Arba the father of Anak, which city is Hebron (Palestine). And Caleb drove thence the three sons of Anak, Sheshai, and Ahiman, and Talmai, the children of Anak.**"
- Arba was one of the "**sons of Heth**" who built the city of Hebron (called Kirjath-Arba, meaning the city of Arba-Genesis 23).
- Heth was the **second** son of **Canaan**-Genesis 10:15 "**And Canaan begat Sidon his firstborn, and HETH.**"
- Canaan was the son of **Ham**, and was **black** in appearance.
- Abraham and his wife Sarah were buried in the land of Heth in the city Hebron (**In the Cave of Patriarchs**)
- Genesis 25:10 "**The field which Abraham purchased of the sons of Heth: there was Abraham buried, and Sarah his wife.**"

- Anak, Arba's son had three descendants in the days of Moses and Joshua who were giants: **Ahiman, Sheshai** and **Talmai**. They dwelt in Hebron around 1490 B.C. (Joshua 15:14).
- **More notable mentioned scriptures**: Deuteronomy 1:28, Deuteronomy 2:10, Deuteronomy 2:11, Deuteronomy 2:21, Deuteronomy 9:2, Joshua 11:21-22, Joshua 14:12, Joshua 14:15, Joshua 15:14

Fact: Arba was the father of the Anakim. The Giant Arba had the city in Israel named "Hebron" named after him as it was called in ancient times "**Kirjath-Arba**" or "**The City of Arba**". The Anakim giants were also known by different names by other nations.

Deuteronomy 2:11 **"Like the Anakites, they too were considered Rephaites, but the Moabites called them Emites."**

CHILDREN OF MIZRAIM (EGYPT)

Note: *Mizraim* was the Biblical name of "*Kemet*" or "*Egypt*". The Philistines were cousins of the Egyptians. Philistine is now modern-day Palestine. The city of Ashdod was a Philistine city where many Israelite men took wives from…just as Samson was involved with a Philistine woman named **Delilah**. This can be proven in the scriptures. Did the Egyptians mix with the Canaanites? Where are the remnant of the Ancient Egyptians? Genetic Studies using "**Match Likelihood Index**" scores based on "**STR-short random repeat**" profiles show that the descendants of the Ancient Egyptians settled in the African Great Lakes region, the Horn of Africa and South Africa. Are there any Africans that live in these areas that don't carry the "**9-bp Deletion mutation**" or the "**16189-Cytosine mutation**". **Yes there is! As a matter of fact the Alur Tribe, the Luo Tribe and and many other African Tribes do not carry these mutations.** This would make sort of sense because the Israelites were known in the bible to intermarry with the different Canaanite Tribes. The Canaanites would mix mostly with the Israelites because the Israelites were the only ones that were living in the Land of Canaan in B.C. times. The Egyptians were still living in Egypt, where the Israelites left them after the Exodus. **The Bible clearly proves that the Israelites mainly mixed with those that lived amongst. This included the Philistines, the Ammonites, the Moabites and the Canaanites.**

- **Nehemiah 13:23-25** "In those days, I (**Ezra**) also saw that the Jews had married women from **Ashdod**, Ammon and Moab. **As for their children, half spoke in the language of Ashdod, and none of them was able to speak the language of Judah**, but the language of his own people. So I contended with them and cursed them and struck some of them and pulled out their hair, and made them swear by God, "**You shall not give your daughters to their sons, nor take of their daughters for your sons or for yourselves.**"

- **Genesis 10:13-14** "And **Mizraim** begat Ludim, and Anamim, and Lehabim, and Naphtuhim, and Pathrusim, **and Casluhim, (out of whom came <u>PHILISTIM,</u>)** <u>and Caphtorim</u>.

- **1 Chronicles 1:12** "And Pathrusim, **and Casluhim, (of whom came the PHILISTINE,)** <u>and Caphthorim</u>."

- **Jeremiah 47:4** "Because of the day that cometh to spoil all the Philistines and to cut off from Tyrus and Zidon every helper that remaineth: for the Lord will spoil the **PHILISTINES, <u>the remnant of the country of Caphtor.</u>**"

- **Amos 9:7** "Are ye not as children of the Ethiopians unto me, O children of Israel? saith the Lord. Have I not brought up Israel out of the land of Egypt? **and the PHILISTINES from Caphtor,** and the Syrians from Kir?"

- **II Samuel 21:19-20** "And there was again a battle in Gob with the Philistines, where Elhanan the son of Jaare-oregim, a Beth-lehemite, slew the brother of Goliath the Gittite, the staff of whose spear was like a weaver's beam. And there was yet a battle in Gath, where was **a man of great stature, that had on every hand six fingers, and on every foot six toes, four and twenty in number; and he also was born to the giant."**

- **1 Samuel 17:4** "And there went out a champion out of the camp of the Philistines, name **Goliath, of Gath**, whose height was **six cubits and a span** (i.e. 9 feet, 6 inches)."

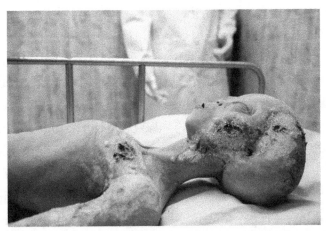

(**Above**) Model of Alien body during secret autopsy from the Roswell, New Mexico UFO ship crash in 1947. Supposedly the alien during the autopsy was noted to have **six-fingers and six-toes**.....just like the Giants in the bible who were the offspring of the Fallen Angels/Watchers. Coincidence?

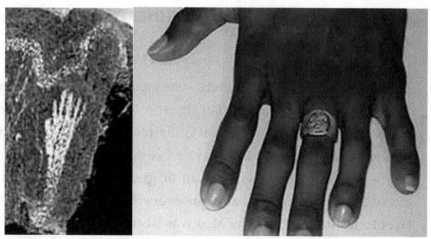

(**Above**) Rock imprints and drawings of giant people with six fingers and six toes can be seen from the Americas to the Solomon Islands in the Pacific Ocean to Australia. In the medical world, this is called "**polydactyly**".

Polydactyly is seen primarily in people of color (i.e. African-Americans, Bantus Africans, Native Indians, East Indians, Australian Aborigines). **It is also a known fact that 1:143 live births born to Africans/African-Americans have "polydactyl" compared to 1:1,339 births in Caucasians**. Polydactyl is usually passed down maternally from mother to daughter. If this is the case perhaps the Israelites past Canaanite wives (i.e. with mixed with trace Nephilim blood) is the reason why this "trait" is seen in these select "**nations of color**". In Kenya, Bantus children born with "six-fingers" are believed to be "**special people**"….representing "**royalty or kingship**". In America, it is not uncommon to see African-Americans or Caribbean blacks have babies born with six fingers.

In reading the Bible we see that the Israelites encountered these **six-fingered, six-toed**, Giant Nephilim while in the land of Canaan. **These Nephilim giants intermixed with Egyptians, the Philistines (Goliath), and the Canaanite tribes.**

Here are some testimonies of random people who were born with "**Polydactyl**".

EXAMPLE 1

"**I was born with six fingers** too on each hand. **I am an AFRICAN** and this phenomenon is quite **WIDESPREAD**. In ancient times a child who was born with such defects was raised to be a **King** from the early stages. Even today the theory is that those born with six fingers are bound to be successful in life and I bear testimony to that, I have also witnessed several folks who are also successful."

EXAMPLE 2

(**Above**) During the 1800's Europeans kidnapped Black people to work in the Pacific Islands for slave/indentured servitude work. These people's ancestry can be traced beginning in Bantus East Africa to eventually Australia where they were slaves on "**Cane/Fruit**" plantations in **North and South Queensland**, (Australia).

"Couple of years ago I was talking to an elderly lady who was taken to see some aboriginal rock art in **North Queensland, Australia** by a well-known explorer of such things. One painting she was shown in a hidden location was a **huge ancestral figure** painted on a cliff face. **It had six fingers on each hand**. When she returned to her home base at the time of Kuranda on the Atherton Tablelands, Australia she went to the local hotel and **an aboriginal (BLACK) man came up to her and insisted on shaking her hand. His hand had six fingers."**

(Above) Solomon Islander "Negroid" boy with "natural" blonde hair.

Fact: There are statues of Giants in the Solomon Islands (Melanesia) which have 6 fingers and 6 toes. The Solomon Islands are in the South Pacific Ocean northeast of Australia. Per local folklore, the giants live in an intricate network of caves on the island (**which some say lead to the "inner earth"**) and rarely venture out into the public. **Even the Natives of America knew about the Giants with red hair.**

(Above) Pawnee Indians

EXAMPLE 3

"These **statues** are made to symbolize these giants of old, sons of angels. As you have obviously shown they were known to every culture across the world. The term **Nephilim translated into Greek means Titan whom were also sons of the gods. These men were said to have six fingers**. There is even a story in William F. "**Buffalo Bill**" Cody's autobiography (1846-1917 A.D.) about an encounter with the **Pawnee Indians in Oklahoma-Nebraska-Wyoming-Kansas** that reads:

"While we were in the sand hills, scouting the Niobrara country **(Wyoming, USA)**, the **Pawnee Indians** brought into camp some very large bones, one of which the surgeon of the expedition pronounced to be the thigh bone of a human being. The Indians said the bones were those of a race of people who long ago had lived in that country. They said these people were three times the size of a man of the present day, and that they were so swift and strong that they could run by the side of a buffalo, and, taking the animal in one arm, could tear off a leg and eat it as they ran." **They too had six fingers on their hands,** which was why the Indians raised their hands when they greeted someone, so that they could count the fingers, **for they feared the six fingered men.**"

575

There are also accounts of "white" humanoid beings appearing out of nowhere helping the government throughout history **with also the traits of six-fingers**. These visitors always appear to be benevolent good beings from outside our planet here to help mankind. But who are these beings really? Are they good angels or are they evil fallen angels here again to deceive mankind? Here is one account:

PHILIP SCHNEIDER AND THOR: THE SIX FINGERED STRANGER FROM VENUS

This is the story of Philip Schneider (1947-1996), a geologist and engineer with "**Level-1 US government security clearance**" who worked for the U.S Government building underground military bases (**DUMB**) all around the country. In 1979, at Dulce, New Mexico (site of the Roswell Alien Crash in 1948) while working on adding additional bases to the already military underground base, Philip Schneider and his crew accidently uncovered an underground Grey Alien base. There was a fire fight, and 67 workers and military personnel were killed. Philip was one of only 3 people to survive. After surviving this fight, Philip would later go on to giving lectures all across the United States about Government cover-ups, Black Budgets and UFO's. Philip died in 1996, in which many people said was an execution. Philip was found in his apartment with a piano wire wrapped around his neck. Sources stated that Philip was brutally tortured for days before his death and his ex-wife, Cynthia Drayer believed Philip was murdered because he publicly revealed the truth about the U.S government's involvement with UFO's. He also talked about how during February 20-21, 1954, six years after the Roswell Alien Crash, President Eisenhower was allowed to meet some Aliens for the first time, in which he learned about their agenda. From this event, President Eisenhower came up with the 1954 "**Greada Treaty**" a.k.a "**The Men in Black Treaty**". In the treaty, the

Fallen Angels/Aliens were able to live on Earth as long as they agreed to let the Government know where they were located at, even if it happened to be underground. They also were allowed to do experiments (*i.e. abductions, genetic experiments with humans, animal mutilation etc.*) on earth as long as they kept the Government informed. No one was to harm them and they would not harm humans. In return, they would secretly give or teach the Government all the technological advances and secrets they knew (i.e. just like in the days of Noah before the flood). Here is an excerpt from one of Philip Schneider's lectures:

There was white-appearing man named "**Valiant Thor**" who worked for the U.S. Government in the 1950's before leaving Earth. Schneider met **Thor**, along with Dr. Frank Stranges, detailed in his book titled "**Stranger at the Pentagon (1997)**". Schneider shows a "1943" picture of "Thor" during his lecture at the **1995 Preparedness Expo**. Schneider explains in his lecture that "Thor" was a human-looking "**alien**" from the planet **Venus** who had been working for the U.S. Military since 1937. Thor had **SIX FINGERS ON EACH HAND**, an oversized heart, one giant lung, **copper oxide blood like an octopus**, and an IQ estimated at 1200 (**Highest IQ according to Guinness Book of World Records is 228**). Thor could speak 100 languages fluently, including alien languages. Thor had told the Government that his lifespan was 490 years, something not heard of in a human being. According to Philip Schneider and Dr. Stranges accounts, Thor was about 6 feet tall, 185 pounds with brown wavy hair and brown eyes. Dr. Stranges stated that both U.S President Dwight Eisenhower and Richard Nixon both met this alien humanoid man named "Thor". Another former U.S Government consultant and UFO researcher, Timothy Good also accounts that President Eisenhower met Aliens. According to Dr. Stranges, Thor left Earth on March 16, 1960 from Alexandria, Virginia. In ancient mythology, "**Thor**" is the most prominent "**Nordic god**", the same "**Nordic Aryan**" race of people that Hitler was convinced was the "**Master Race**". Thor like the Cartoon character "**He-Man**" was white with blond hair. Many believe the Germans had secret bases in

Argentina near the South Pole, which was how they were able to conduct missions into the **"inner earth"** or **"Shamballa"**....that the Buddhist Monks knew about. Inside the "inner earth" lived these **"Tall Nordic White"** humanoids.

(**Above**) The **Octopus** is a unique animal that many scientists believe is of **"Alien"** origin. Octopuses have **copper blood** which makes their blood **"blue"** rather than most of the animal kingdom which uses iron to carry oxygen...making their blood **red**. The Octopus can transport oxygen in very cold temperatures and in environments where there is very little oxygen because of the use of copper instead of iron. The Octopus has 33,000 genes compared to 25,000 for humans. The Octopus is very intelligent with the ability to open jars, solve puzzles, and use tools. **They also can edit their own DNA/RNA at an astounding rate which many say is the way they can camouflage in milliseconds by changing color**. Octopuses can also detach their own arms and regrow it back within weeks. Mr. Thor from above was said to have **"copper-oxide"** blood like an octopus and he was a so-called "Alien". In the movie **"The War of the Worlds (1953)"** and **"Arrival (2016)"** the aliens from outer space resemble an octopus with multiple appendages. In the movie "Arrival" the alien also has the ability to squirt **"black ink"** to communicate with humans. Coincidence?

CHAPTER 23

DO THE FALLEN ANGELS HAVE SOME KNOWLEDGE ABOUT THE PAST AND THE FUTURE?

(Above) Demonic possession is real. Christ sent demons into a herd of pigs in the **Book of Matthew**. But the demons said something very "**strange**" to Christ, revealing the possibility that demons/fallen angels have knowledge of what is to come in the future....especially in regards to their fate. **They also know their time is running out.**

So, did the "**Demons**" cast out by Christ have some "**insight**" into their future from their vast knowledge of time and space?
You be the judge.

Note: In the Netflix TV series "**Travelers**" the so-called Travelers are from the "**future**". Therefore, these "Travelers" know the fate of humanity and the exact date of death for people in the 21st century....the time period they are sent back in time to intervene on behalf of the planets survival.

The Demons in **Matthew 8** seem to know of their fate before the "**appointed time**". The so-called "Illuminated ones" or the "Illuminati" are in direct contact with Satan and his demons...receiving knowledge about certain things in the future as well as the "mysteries of the universe". This is how the "**Evil ones**" enslave mankind and use "**propaganda**" via the media (*TV, movies, music*) to steer us in whatever "Evil" direction they want.

Matthew 8:28-32

And when he was come to the other side into the country of the Gergesenes, there met him **two possessed with devils**, coming out of the tombs, exceeding fierce, so that no man might pass by that way. And, behold, they cried out, saying, **What have we to do with thee, Jesus (Yahusha), thou Son of God? art thou come hither to torment us** *before the time*? And there was a good way off from them a herd of many swine feeding. So the devils besought him, saying, If thou cast us out, suffer us to go away into the herd of swine. And he said unto them, Go. And when they were come out, they went into the herd of swine: and, behold, the whole herd of swine ran violently down a steep place into the sea, and perished in the waters."

So what "**time**" is this the demons were talking about when Christ is to torment them? Is it in the Book of Revelations in regards to the Lake of Fire?

Jude 6 "And the angels which kept not their first estate, but left their own habitation, he hath reserved in **everlasting chains under darkness** unto the **judgment** of the **GREAT DAY**"."

Revelation 20:1-3 "And I saw an angel come down from heaven, having the key of the bottomless pit and a **great chain** in his hand. **And he laid hold on the dragon, that old serpent, which is the Devil, and Satan, and bound him a thousand years**, And cast him into the bottomless pit (**Hell**), and shut him up, and set a seal upon him, that he should deceive the nations no more, till the thousand years should be fulfilled: and after that he must be loosed a little season."

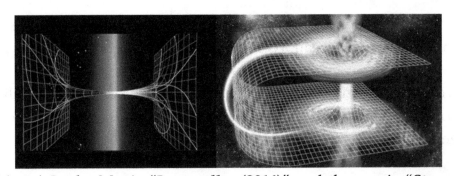

(**Above**) In the Movie "**Interstellar (2014)**" and the movie "**Stargate (1994)**" it talks about time travel. But in the movie **Stargate** it talks about time travel through an actual "Stargate" that is obtained from the ancient UFO/Fallen Angel technology given to the Ancient Egyptians. In the movie "Stargate" the film starts off with the unearthing of the "Stargate machine" in Giza, Egypt in 1928. The military brings the "Stargate machine" to a military base in Colorado, the same place where two Freemason "Grand "Lodges" are located in addition to the Freemason Denver, Colorado Airport (*i.e. Secret Doomsday Bunker*). A military team powers up the Stargate and walks through it into the time era of Ancient Egypt. While in the past time period of Ancient Egypt, the Egyptians are ruled over by an "**Alien-Fallen Angel**" posing as the Egyptian god "**Ra-Horus**", who happens to be linked to "**Enki**" in Sumerian Annunaki mythology in the "**Lost Tablets of Enki**". In the movie, "**Ra**" has a spaceship buried within the Pyramids of Giza and/or the Sphinx (*just as in the Emerald Tablets of Thoth*). The spaceship of "Ra" tries to leave Egypt but the Military team sent into the past somehow manage to blow it up using a bomb. In Ancient Egyptian mythology Ra's counselor, secretary and right hand "god" was **Thoth**. Thoth was believed however in Ancient Egyptian mythology to not have any parents and he was associated with the "**moon god**".....like Islam (*i.e. Sin, Hubal, Allah*). Thoth also reveals in the "**Emerald Tablets**" that his spaceship is buried in Egypt, possibly under the Sphinx in Giza.

Remember, it was in Egypt, that Bible readers are first introduced to unfamiliar spirits (demons), witchcraft and sorcery. This was common practice among the Priests of Horus. **"Divination-Voodoo"** is still common in the Caribbean, West Africa and the Americas.

Leviticus 20:27 "A man also or woman (witch) that hath a familiar spirit, or that is a wizard, shall surely be put to death: they shall stone them with stones: their blood shall be upon them."

EMERALD TABLETS OF THOTH

Yet ever to him who has knowing,
open shall be the path to AMENTI.
Fast fled we then on the wings of the morning,
fled to the land of the children of KHEM (Ham-Egypt).
There by my power,
I conquered and ruled them.

Raised I to LIGHT,
the children of KHEM.
Deep 'neath the rocks,
I buried my spaceship,
waiting the time when man might be free.

(Above) Great Sphinx in Giza, Egypt. Head of a man, body of a lion. Date built: unknown to man.

<u>Over the spaceship,</u>
<u>erected a marker in the form</u>
<u>of a lion yet like unto man.</u>
<u>There 'neath the image rests yet my spaceship,</u>
<u>forth to be brought when need shall arise</u>.

Know ye, O man, that far in the future,
invaders shall come from out of the deep (i.e. inner earth).
Then awake, ye who have wisdom.
Bring forth my ship and conquer with ease.
Deep 'neath the image lies my secret.
Search and find in the pyramid (GIZA) I built.

Each to the other is the Keystone;
each the gateway that leads into LIFE.
Follow the KEY I leave behind me.
Seek and the doorway to LIFE shall be thine.
Seek thou in my pyramid (Giza),
deep in the passage that ends in a wall.

Fact: The Masonic Keystone and the Islamic Kaaba Holy Shrine is a "Cube". The Moslem "Shriner" 33 Degree Grandmaster Freemasons "secretly" call god Allah. So does the faithful Muslim.

The Osiris Stargate Device

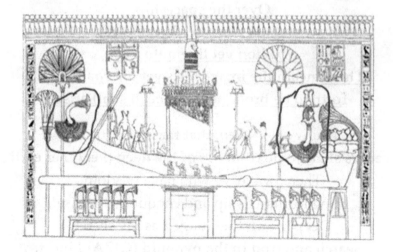

(Above) Osiris Chapel at Abydos is the **Osiris "Stargate" Device**. This ship resembles a modern drawing of a wormhole. Pay particular attention to Set (Satan) who appears to have transformed his body into the Osiris Device… or is coming out of it.

According to researcher William Henry, the ancient Egyptian object named **Ta-Wer** aka the **"Osiris"** device, was a **Stargate machine capable to open wormholes or dimensional openings used by Seth and Osiris to "travel across the underworld."** But many people do not realize that the so-called gods of Ancient Egypt were no more than "Fallen   Angels".

Fact: *Today, **CERN's "Large Hadron Collider"** in Switzerland is the new "**Osiris Ta-Wer**"? Many believe it is a modern Stargate machine based on Ancient Egyptian-Sumerian technology.   CERN's Large Hadron Collider was completed in 2015. By now the collider should have twice the power. Scientists believe CERN's "Large Hadron Collider" will help unlock more of the universe's mysteries and to explore an entirely new realm of physics.   Be aware, this technology was given to man by Fallen Angels.....which will ultimately help the rise of the Antichrist Beast System on Planet Earth. Another new technology that has arrived in the 21st century* is *"D-Wave Quantum Computer technology"..aka "Artificial Intelligence"*. *Many of today's top leading scientists claim the "D-Wave Computers" are the "future" of humanity but in* **Time Magazine** *(February 2014) the front cover read:*

"It promises to solve some of humanity's most complex problems. It's backed by Jeff Bezos, NASA, and the CIA. Each one costs $10 million dollars and nobody knows how it actually works."

So meanwhile as everyone is pre-occupied with Satan's distractions, the "Elite" was busy funding a computer so powerful that it is described as **"tapping into the fundamental fabric of reality"** and the man who owns the company says being near one is like **"standing at the altar of an alien God"**. For centuries people have believed that the wonders and miracles the Antichrist will perform would be strictly supernatural in origin, coming directly from the **SATAN** himself. These wonders, however, only might have appeared to be miracles to a first-century prophet (**John**) having visions of them, just as they might to anyone living before the age of advanced technology. But there are two questions we need to ask ourselves in light of these statements about "D-Wave Quantum Computers".

1. **If Quantum technology is not of this world, but was given to us by somebody or something beyond our "veiled" level of perception. Who gave it to us and for what purpose?**
2. **Are those who are behind this "new technology" with CERN or D-Wave Quantum computers benevolent (*i.e. with good intentions*) or malevolent (*i.e. with evil intentions*)?**

(**Above**) Are we moving into an age where we will be "**completely**" plugged into the "**Matrix**"? A world where Electronics, Robots and the internet rules over mankind? Like the TV series "**Humans**", the movie "**The Matrix**" or "**Terminator Genisys**"?

Right now, Mastercard and Hong Kong Standard Bank of China (HSBC) have developed a debit/credit card that will use Biometrics (**i.e. fingerprint, thumbprint, retinal scan**) for identification. By 2020, every person carrying a Passport will also have their biological information (i.e. biometrics) integrated into the RFID chip that is already in Passports now. Facebook also has developed a "**mind-reading**" interface system capable of using computers to tap into our brain so that we can interact and control electronics with just the "**thoughts**" from our Brains. Typing a book using just your thoughts or moving a mouse with just your thoughts is now a reality as it has been tested in labs already on patients with Neurological diseases/disabilities.

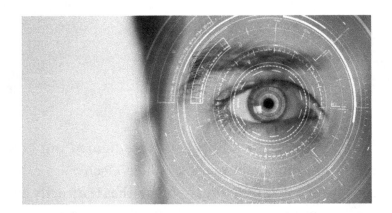

(**Above**) Facial recognition, retinal scans and fingerprint scans are already here. Satellites and "**Smart Devices**" with Bluetooth-NFC-RFID technology are already here monitoring our every move. With constant surveillance comes "**absolute control**". The "**All-Seeing Eye**" of Satan has wanted to be like the Most High since the beginning of time. But there is a reason why we have a **Creator**. There is no one higher than "**The Most High**".

These Technology guru's and Scientists have figured out how to use our "eyeballs" to connect humans to their electronics. **Note: the eye/retina is the only external human organ that is directly connected to the Brain**. Therefore, it can supply feedback/data to a computer about humans than can be used for a "**Sync feature**" of man and machine. Mankind synced with the powers of Satan. Remember the movie "Matrix"? The computer was connected to a port on the back of human's skulls. Wake up people!

These Fifth-Generation D-Wave Quantum Computers will be able to learn, associate, infer, and understand. With no keyboard, the machine will be able to understand spoken language and perform whatever function you ask of it, gleaning needed information from a '**knowledge bank**' or from other computers it may be in contact with. Soon talking to one will be indistinguishable from speaking with a live operator — the computer will "understand" your words and respond in a human-sounding voice with logical and typical statements. With our "**monetary**" and "**health system**" tied into the "**digital world**"....there will be no hiding or running from the Evil powers to be. If we are totally dependent on government entitlements-benefits, our jobs, our digital money, our digital bank accounts, the digital barcode labels on food, the digital barcode labels on products/goods, our digital ID's, and our digital electronic medical records we are essentially being led like sheep to the slaughter in the "**Antichrist Beast System**".

There is a saying:

"**Control oil**, you control nations; **control food** and you control the people".

Fact: A normal healthy person can go without food or water for 1-2 weeks but it takes a full season (4 months), for a seed to grow into edible food. Five corporations control global grain trade (Cargill, Bunge, Archer Daniels etc.). **Monsanto, Syngenta, Bayer, Dupont and Dow Chemical** control all genetically modified-engineered seeds. **Nestle** controls about 70% of the worlds bottled water market followed by **Pepsico** and **Coca-Cola**. **RWE/Thames, Suez/ONDEO, and Veolia** controls the majority of the water market in Europe. **American Water Works, ITT Corp, and GE Water** also have their hand in the majority of the water in the United States. So, the Jewish Rothschilds control all the money of the World, and therefore they also control the majority of "governments" across the world. They also control the United Nations. The Saudi Arabia and America have the "**Petro-Dollar**" system on lock across the globe which basically keeps the Stock Market from crashing. The "Elite" also control all of the food (seed) and water supply of the world which we spend billions of dollars for every year. The Elite have also placed "**patents**" on different "**life forms**". Everything on the Earth which was once "**free**", given to man by God (Creator), is now turned into a "**business**" and thus "**control**" by Satan.

Genesis 1:28-30 "God blessed them; and God said to them, "Be fruitful and multiply, and fill the earth, and subdue it; and rule over the fish of the sea and over the birds of the sky and over every living thing that moves on the earth. Then God said, "**Behold, I have given you every plant yielding seed that is on the surface of all the earth, and every tree which has fruit yielding seed; it shall be food for you**; and to every beast of the earth and to every bird of the sky and to every thing that moves on the earth and to every bird of the sky and to every living thing that moves on the earth which has life, I have given every green plant for food"; and it was so..."

Well folks, in the 21ˢᵗ Century, nothing is free, except air for those that are not dependent on home oxygen. This means the "**Anti-Christ**" Beast system is already "**emerging**". The sad thing is that many of us have no clue as to what is going on, nor the severe consequences it entails in the future for this generation or the next.

Is this what John was trying to warn us about on the Island of Patmos when he had a vision about the "**End of Days**" in the **Book of Revelation**?

Revelation Chapter 13

"**And he causeth all (*not forces all*)**, both small and great, rich and poor, free and enslaved, to receive a **mark in their right hand, or in their foreheads,**

"**And that no man might buy or sell, except he that had the mark, or the name of the beast, or the number of his name.**

"Here is wisdom. Let him that hath understanding count the number of the beast; for it is the number of a man; and his number is **six hundred threescore and six.**"

It is also said that these D-Wave Quantum computers which are 100 million times faster than an intel core i7 microprocessor PC computer will be able to have the ability to **"teleport"** matter.

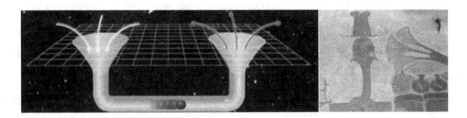

(Left) Wormhole that transports one through time and space. **(Right)** A depiction of the **"Osiris Stargate machine"** used by the Fallen Angels and possibly Ancient Egyptians.

Fact or Fiction: In 2004, Washington-based attorney Andrew D. Basiago told his story of a top-secret organization called **Project Pegasus**. Even though he was seven years old at the time, Basiago claims he had, from 1968 to 1972, participated in a number of bizarre experiments that took him on journeys through time, space, and potentially into parallel universes (i.e. *similar to the 1940's Philadelphia Experiment and Project Rainbow*). Supposedly Project Pegasus was tied to **DARPA** and the **Philadelphia Experiment** that many say Albert Einstein and Nikola Tesla were knowledgeable of. In the ABC TV series **"Lost (2004-2010)"** it gives hint into **"magnetic energy"** enabling Time Travel and the disappearance of objects or people. The "Lost" TV series also talks about **DARPA** (*i.e. Defense Advanced Research Projects Agency*), which is like the US Militarys **"Mad Scientist"** department. It is said that upon Nikola Tesla's death in a New York City Apartment in 1943, the government found the **"schematics"** for a **"Teleportation machine"** like Hitler's **"Bell machine"**. At CERN…by combining and separating matter with anti-matter…**radiant energy** is formed. Radiant energy is a form of energy that Tesla discovered that is latent and pervasive in the universe, having the capability to **bend time and space**.

But wait, there is more "**diabolical**" things the Elite have for us that is on its way here….including things that are already happening right now.

Fact: At the "**Rockefeller Institute**" a lot of "agendas" are made for the world. The **New Order of Barbarians** is the transcript of three tapes of reminiscences made by **Dr. Lawrence Dunegan**, of a speech given on March 20, 1969 by **Dr. Richard Day** (1905-89), an insider of "**The Order**," recorded by Randy Engel in 1988. Dr. Dunegan claims he attended a medical meeting on March 20, 1969 where **Dr. Richard Day** (*who died in 1989 but at the time was Professor of Pediatrics at Mount Sinai Medical School in New York and was previously the Medical Director of Planned Parenthood Federation of America*) gave "**off the record**" remarks during an address at the Pittsburgh Pediatric Society to a meeting of students and health professionals, who were destined to be leaders in medicine, health care and technology. Dr. Richard Day was an establishment insider who knew about the **Elite Group** that ruled the Western World for the creation of a **World Dictatorship**. This "World Dictatorship" would be a **Global Tyranny** which is usually called today "**The New World Order**". This New World Order would contain a secular and a spiritual component -the **One World Government** and the **One World Religion**: A future reality that those who understand such things call it "**Lucifer's Totalitarian World Empire**" aka "**Luciferianism**". Before Dr. Richard Day would begin his talk, he asked everyone to turn off all tape recorders and to stop taking notes. Dr. Dunegan was present during this talk and sensed Dr. Day's message was important….so he secretly recorded it using napkins for notes. The following topics was talked about by Dr. Richard Day….and recorded by Dr. Dunegan.

- Population Control (*Agenda 21, Mass "tainted" Vaccinations to reduce the population with Cancer, Autism, health diseases, random epidemics*). Bill Gates is on the forefront of this mission. – **ALREADY HERE**

- Permission to have babies.

- Redirect purpose of sex without reproduction (*i.e. Sexual fluidity promoting sexual perversion with the same sex, children or animals*). Today in the 21st century homosexuality, transgenderism, pedophilia and bestiality are seen by some as a "healthy sexual lifestyle choice". **– ALREADY HERE**

- Contraceptives available to all (*i.e. Birth Control for Men and women*). **– ALREADY HERE**

- Immoral Sex education as a tool (*i.e. Transgender, Homosexuality and removing gender classifications in public school*). **– ALREADY HERE**

- Tax funded abortion as a population control for blacks (*i.e. Planned Parenthood, abortion clinics readily available in Black cities*). **– ALREADY HERE**

- Encouraging homosexuality (*i.e. special attention to African-Americans*). This is being promoted on T.V., Movies, and music. **– ALREADY HERE**

- Diminish "Families" (*i.e. with special target being Black families*). Use the media to promote interracial relationships between Black men and White women and Black women with White men. This is called "Self-Racial Genocide". Use Welfare and the "Friends of the Court" to keep the Black Family "separated". **– ALREADY HERE**

- Euthanasia and the "Demise Pill". **– ALREADY HERE**

- Limit access to affordable Medical, thereby eliminated the elderly (*i.e. Obamacare, high deductibles, high premiums, hire only part-time employees to avoid paying for health insurance*). **– ALREADY HERE**

- Control Medicine/Eliminate Private Doctors (*i.e. Socialized Medicine incorporated creating a multitude of "Health Systems" with private doctors all falling succumb to being employed by these giant Hospital Systems*). – **ALREADY HERE**

- Untreatable and resistant diseases (*i.e. Superbugs, highly virulent strains of Ebola and E. Coli. Also, the increasing emergence of multi-drug resistant bacteria*). – **ALREADY HERE**

- Suppressing cancer cures to control population. – **ALREADY HERE**

- Inducing heart attacks as a form of 21st century "assassination" in combination with prescribed or illegal substance abuse claims. – **ALREADY HERE**

- Change the religious text of Christianity (*i.e. Mandela Effect and the Bible*) to fit the gradual movement of mankind into a "One World Religion" where all religions are considered "one" and all persons (*i.e. homosexual, bisexual, pedosexual, transgender, gender reassignment*) are heirs to the Kingdom of God. This will pave the way for the worship of Satan and the Antichrist. – **ALREADY HERE**

If you don't believe the "Elite" are making slow changes to our physical Bibles using "**CERN**" and the new "**D-Wave A.I. Quantum Computers**" please research "**The Mandela Effect**" in which "**memory anomalies**" is making people question if the "**physical**" world we know of today is actually "**changing**". Decide for yourself. But also listen to what Dr. Richard Day (*i.e. New Order of Barbarians-Germans*) and others had to say about this subject.

"Not everyone is accepting the updates. For some, "the veil" isn't working on some people. Currently it is spiraling out of control, and we anticipate a larger population that will experience memory

594

anomalies within the next few years. By 2020 everything will settle."-*anonymous scientist*

But the major religions of today have to be changed because they are not compatible with the changes to come. The old religions will have to go. **Especially Christianity**. Once the Roman Catholic Church is brought down, the rest of Christianity will follow easily. Then a **new religion** can be accepted for use all over the world. It will **incorporate** something from all of the old ones to make it more easy for people to accept it, and feel at home in it. Most people won't be too concerned with religion. They will realize that they don't need it. -*Dr. Richard Day*

Changing the Bible through Revisions of Key Words – Dr. Richard Day (cont.)

"In order to do this, **the *Bible*** will be changed. It will be rewritten to fit the new religion. Gradually, key words will be replaced with new words having various shades of meaning. Then, the meaning attached to the new word can be close to the old word. And as time goes on, other shades of meaning of that word can be emphasized, and then gradually that word replaced with another word. I don't know if I'm making that clear. **But the idea is that everything in "scripture" need not be rewritten, just key words replaced by other words.** And the variability in meaning attached to any word can be used as a tool to change the entire meaning of scripture, and therefore make it acceptable to this **new religion**. Most people won't know the difference; and this was another one of the times where he said: "**... the few who do notice the difference won't be enough to matter.**" – *Dr. Richard Day*

Here are some scriptures to read for yourself and cross reference with your Bible. There is plenty more but I cannot list them all because it is easily over 20 pages of "new changes" that many Bible readers do not recognize as being there before. Use your past memory and knowledge of Bible scripture to determine if this is what it has always been. **Note:** Although "**subtle**" changes have been happening throughout many bible versions, they are mostly happening in the King James Version of the Bible (*i.e. not the Queen James Version of the Bible made by the LGBTP community*).

Note: The words in the parentheses "( )" is what many bible readers remember the "**TRUE**" word to be.

- **Malachi 4:2** "But unto you that fear my name shall the **Sun** (Son) **of righteousness** arise with healing in his wings; and ye shall go forth, and grow up as calves of the stall."

- **Genesis 1:1** "In the beginning God created the **heaven** (heavens) and the earth.

- **Genesis 2:1** "Thus the **heavens** and the earth were finished, and all the host of them."

- **Revelation 3:20** "Behold, I stand at the door, and knock: if any man (anyone) hear my voice, and open the door, **I will come in to him** (I will come in), and will sup with him, and he with me."

- **Exodus 32:15-16** "And Moses turned, and went down from the mount, and the **two tables of the testimony** (tablets of the covenant law) *were* in his hand: the tables *were* written on both their sides; on the one side and on the other *were* they written. And the **tables** (tablets) *were* the work of God, and the writing *was* the writing of God, graven upon the **tables** (tablets)."

- **Job 21:24** "**His breasts are full of milk**, and his bones are moistened with marrow.

- **1 Timothy 2:5** "For *there is* one God, and one mediator between God and men, **the man Christ Jesus** (the Son of Man, Yeshua the Messiah);"

- **Acts 14:12-13** "And they called Barnabas, **Jupiter** (Zeus); and Paul, Mercurius (Hermes), because he was the chief speaker. Then the priest of **Jupiter**, which was before their city, brought oxen and garlands unto the gates, and would have done sacrifice with the people.

- **Sun and Moon removed from Genesis 1:14.**

- **Matthew 2:9-11** "When they had heard the king, they departed; and, lo, the star, which they saw in the east, went before them, till it came and stood over where the young child was. When they saw the star, they rejoiced with exceeding great joy. And when they were **come into the house (manger)**, they saw the young child with Mary his mother, and fell down, and worshipped him. **Joseph and Mary couldn't find room in an inn so they had to use a manger/hay, not a house**.

- **James 2:3** "And ye have respect to him that weareth the **gay** (fine) **clothing**, and say unto him, Sit thou here in a good place; and say to the poor, Stand thou there, or sit here under my footstool:"

- **2 Corinthians 11:3-4** "But I fear, lest by any means, as the serpent beguiled Eve through his subtilty, **so your minds should be corrupted from the simplicity that is in Christ**. For if he that cometh preacheth another Jesus, whom we have not preached, or *if* ye receive another spirit, which ye have not received, or another gospel, which ye have not accepted, **ye might well bear with** *him*. (Let him be accursed)."

- **Acts 12:4** "And when he had apprehended him, he put *him* in prison, and delivered *him* to four quaternions of soldiers to keep him; **intending after Easter** (Passover) to bring him forth to the people."

- **Leviticus 25:34** "But the field of the **suburbs** (Pasturelands) of their cities may not be sold; for it *is* their perpetual possession.

- **Acts 1:20** "For it is written in the book of Psalms, Let his habitation be desolate, and let no man dwell therein: and **his bishoprick** (someone else) let another take. **Bishoprick = Catholic Bishop**.

- **Luke 20:24** "Shew me a **penny** (Denarius). Whose image and superscription hath it? They answered and said, Caesar's.

- **Note: Romans didn't use pennies. This can be researched and verified.**

- **Exodus 22:7** "If a man shall deliver unto his neighbour money or **stuff** (goods) to keep, and it be stolen out of the man's house; if the thief be found, let him pay double.

- **Hebrews 1:1-2** "God, who at sundry times and in divers manners spake in time past unto the fathers by the prophets, Hath in these last days spoken unto us by his Son, whom he hath appointed heir of all things, by whom also he made the **WORLDS** (how many worlds are there?);

- **Hebrews 11:3** "Through faith we understand that the **WORLDS** were framed by the word of God, so that things which are seen were not made of things which do appear".

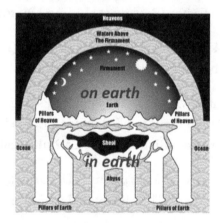

(**Above**) Do we remember saying "The Lord's Prayer" at night using "**in earth**"??? Or did we use "**On earth, as it is in heaven**"? After all, humans don't live "**inside the earth**", we live "**on earth**". In earth is "**Sheol-Hell-Hades**" or the "**Abyss**".

- **Matthew 6:19-12** "After this manner therefore pray ye: Our Father which art in heaven, Hallowed be thy name. Thy kingdom come. Thy will be done **in earth** (on earth), as *it is* in heaven. Give us this day our daily bread. And forgive us our debts, as we forgive our debtors."

(**Above**) A **Cockatrice**. How is this in the Bible now?

- **Isaiah 11:4-8** "But with righteousness shall he judge the poor, and reprove with equity for the meek of the earth: and he shall smite the earth: with the rod of his mouth, and with the breath of his lips shall he slay the wicked. And righteousness shall be the girdle of his loins, and faithfulness the girdle of his reins. **The wolf also shall dwell with the lamb** (? lion and the lamb), and the leopard shall lie down with the kid; and the calf and the young lion and the fatling together; and a little child shall lead them. And the cow and the bear shall feed; their young ones shall lie down together: and the lion shall eat straw like the ox. **And the sucking child shall play on the hole of the asp, and the weaned child shall put his hand on the <u>cockatrice' den</u>.**"

- **Acts 17:22** "Then Paul stood in the midst of **Mars' hill**, and said, *Ye* men of Athens, I perceive that in all things ye are too superstitious."

599

Since when is Mars and Jupiter in our Bibles? **Where is Plato, Saturn, Uranus, and Venus?**

- **Luke 19:23** "Wherefore then gavest not thou my **money into the bank**, that at my coming I might have required mine own with usury?"

  There were no banks like Bank of America or Chase during the time of Christ.

- **Proverbs 26:10 King James Version** "The great God (?) that formed all things both **rewardeth the fool, and rewardeth transgressors.**"

  Note: How does The Most High reward fools and people that sin? The Israelites **"transgressed"** the law and therefore were punished with the "Curses of Israel"….not rewarded.

- In the **Proverbs 26:10 Hebrew breakdown** of this scripture, the Hebrew concordance breaks this down as:
    1. **Rab**=Great, or Multitude, or many, or god,
    2. **Chuwl**=bear or brings forth,
    3. **mehowlel**=wounds,
    4. **Kol**=all or the whole,
    5. **Sakar**=hires or rewards,
    6. **Chesil/Kesil**=Orion or Giants,
    7. **Sakar**=hires or rewards,
    8. **Abar**=cross over or pass over or transgress/sin.

  Can someone explain why does the Hebrew version have a whole **"hidden"** meaning than what the English version of the scripture has?

- **Proverbs 26:10 NASB (New American Standard Bible)** "Like an archer who wounds everyone, So is he who hires a fool or who hires those who pass by."

Note: How is Proverbs 26:10 **TOTALLY** different in the Hebrew version, the King James Version and the New American Standard Bible Version? Need proof? This can be verified by going on www.biblehub.com or www.biblegateway.com

CHAPTER 24

DID THE DESCENDANTS OF EBER, TERAH AND ABRAHAM LIVE AMONGST THE SEMITIC PROTO-SUMERIAN PEOPLE?

While it is hard to decipher which "**Son of Shem**" the Sumerian people stemmed from we do know that based on the region that the Sumerian civilization existed that the Sumerians were **NOT** of the seed of Ham or Japheth. So, did the Sumerians and the Hebrews influence each other? Did Abraham, his forefathers and children live amongst the descendants of the Sumerians in addition to the Canaanites? After all Abraham and Terah lived in the "**Land of Ur**" which is Modern day **Iraq**. It is also believed that Abraham's wife and in-laws were from **Haran, Syria**. The ancient language of the Babylonians, Akkadians, Assyrians and Sumerians are all "**Cuneiform Script**". How convenient is this. The language of the Canaanites (Phoenician) and Hebrew Israelites/Hebrews (Paleo-Hebrew) are pretty much identical as well. Coincidence? Not at all.

Elba Tablets
The **Elba tablets** are a collection of clay tablets and fragments from the ancient Syrian city of Elba. The Tablets were found by Italian archaeologist **Paolo Matthiae** and his team in the 1970's. They date back to 2200-2500 B.C., right around the time that **Terah** and **Abraham** lived. The language written on the tablets were Sumerian but there were many "Hebrew" names found in it. How is this possible unless the "**Hebrews**" once dwelt in this area of Mesopotamia? The Elba tablets were found to have Hebrew names like "**Mi-ka-Ilu**" which is Akkadian/Assyrian/Babylonian for "**Who is like El (God)**" since "**Ilu/Ila/Ilah**" meant "**God**" in the **Sumer-Akkadian** Semitic language of Mesopotamia. The word used for "**King**" on the tablet was "**Malikum**"…similar to "**Melek**" for the Hebrew word "**King**". The

word "**man**" was pronounced "**adamu**" which in Hebrew is "**adam**". Over some time the appearance of the word "**Ya**" or "**Yah**" was amazingly found on the end of names such as "**Mi-ka-YAH**" which seemed to replace "**Mi-ka-ILU**". Professors like Professor Pettinato made the finding that from Eber's family tree and his descendants eventually the word "**Ilu** (Akkadian/Babylonian/Assyrian)" or "**El** (Egyptian-Canaanite)" for God was substituted in people's names for "**Yah**". This lines up with Biblical scripture as the Hebrews before Moses were familiar with using "**El-God**", "**El-Shaddai-God Almighty**" or "**El Elyon-The Most High God**" instead of "**Yah**" or "**YAHUAH**". Many biblical scholars today would place Terah, Abraham and Isaac as living before or around 2,000 B.C., before the Twelve Tribes of Israel were a nation.

Deuteronomy 6:3 "And I appeared unto Abraham, unto Isaac, and unto Jacob, by the name of God Almighty (**El Shaddai**), but by my name YHWH (**YAHUAH**) was I not know to them."

The **Elba tablets** from Syria (**Padad-Haran**)....aka the place where Abraham's wife "**Sarai**" was supposedly from, also contained references to Israelite-Canaanite biblical cities such as "**Salem/Salim**", "**Hazor**", "**Lachish**", "**Megiddo**", "**Sodom**", "**Gomorrah**", "**Gaza**", "**Dor**", "**Joppa**", "**Damascus**" and "**Urusalima/Jerusalem**". Amazing! This means there is "**archaeological proof**" that the "**Hebrews**" were in fact a people who lived in the Levant, Mesopotamia and Africa!

Paddan-Haran was where Rebekah wanted Isaac to fetch a wife for Jacob.

Genesis 27:46, 28:1-2 "And Rebekah said to Isaac, I am weary of my life because of the daughters of Heth (**Son of Canaan**): if Jacob take a wife of the daughters of Heth, such as these **WHICH ARE OF THE DAUGHTERS OF THIS LAND**, what good shall my life do me? And Isaac called Jacob, and blessed him, and charged him, and said unto him, Thou shalt not take a wife of the daughters of Canaan. Arise, go to **"Paddan-Aram"**, to the house of Bethuel thy mother's father: and take thee a wife from thence of the daughters of **Laban thy mother's brother."**

In **Genesis Chapter 24**, we even see how Abraham's servant was to get a wife (i.e. Rebekah) for Isaac from outside of the **"Land of Canaan"** in the old territory of Assyria/Syria in Mesopotamia which sometimes is referred to as **"Paddan-Haran"**, the same area where the **"Elba Tablets"** were found!

CHAPTER 25

THE CREATOR AND CHRIST THE MESSIAH ARE THE SAME! THE PROOF IS IN THE BIBLE WRITTEN IN PALEO-HEBREW!

"**Be-reshith**" is the first word of the Hebrew bible. **It means "In the beginning"** in our English Bibles and it also means **"Genesis". Written in Paleo Hebrew the "word" בְּרֵאשִׁית (Bereshith) letter by letter would be:**

- *Beth – <u>HOUSE</u>,* family, floor plan, "in".
- *Resh – <u>FIRST</u>,* top, head of a man, <u>*AUTHORITY*</u>, <u>*BEGINNING*</u>.
- *Aleph – <u>GOD</u>,* strong, power, leader.
- *Shin- <u>DESTROY</u>,* separate, teeth, consume.
- *Yod-* Worship, work, throw, <u>*HAND*</u>.
- *Tav- <u>CROSS</u>,* covenant, mark, sign.

Could this mean:

The House of First Authority (i.e. Christ) in the beginning who is "God (the Creator)" shall be destroyed by his own hand on the Cross?

Or

The "Head" of God's Household (Christ) who is also the Creator, shall be destroyed by his own hand as a sign, covenant or a mark.

Christ told his disciples that he could lay his life down and resurrect it again. He told them he had the "**authority**" to do so. In the Bible only "**God**" giveth life as he blew life into man and made him a living being.

In the scripture of John 10:16-17, Christ is proclaiming his "**God status**" while in the flesh as Yahusha/Yeshua.

Deuteronomy 32:39 "See now that I, I am He, And there is no god beside Me; **It is I who put to death and give life**. I have wounded and it is I who heal, And there is no one who can deliver from My hand."

1 Samuel 2:6 "The LORD **killeth**, and **maketh alive**: he bringeth **down to the grave**, and **bringeth up**."

John 10:16-17 "Therefore doth my Father love me, **because I lay down my life, that I might take it again. No man taketh it from me, but I lay it down of myself. I have power to lay it down, and I have power to take it again**. This commandment have I received of my Father."

Christ here obviously is talking from his "**God-incarnate**" self while in a human body. But the Pharisees of course get mad, claiming this statement to be of the Devil. The Pharisees didn't know that they were in the presence of the "**Messiah**" and the man whose name meant "**God with us (Emmanuel)**, "**God is salvation**" or "**Yah is Salvation (Yahusha/Yeshua)**".

Yahuah (YHUH/YHWH), aka the "**Creator**" established a "**Covenant**" with the Israelites in the Old Testament, but the Bible tells of how **Christ** will restore a "**New Covenant**" with his people (**Jeremiah 31, Revelation 21 & 22**). The Biblical Feast Days give reference to Christ and so much more. See for yourself.

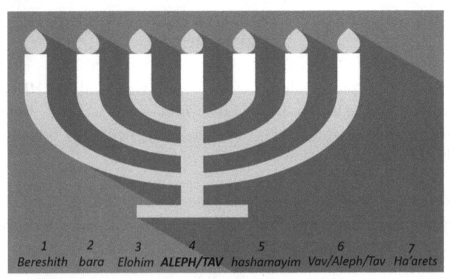

1	2	3	4	5	6	7
Bereshith	bara	Elohim	**ALEPH/TAV**	hashamayim	Vav/Aleph/Tav	Ha'arets

(**Above**) **Genesis 1:1** has **7 words** in the Hebrew Bible. 7 is the number of "**completion**" in the Bible and the number "**7**" is used all throughout the Bible. The **4th** Hebrew word in Genesis 1:1 is an "**untranslatable mark**" called the "**Aleph/Tav**" which is the Hebrew "**Aleph**" and Hebrew "**Tav**" together. In the Syriac Aramaic New Testament, it is "**Aleph and Tav**". In the Greek translation of the New Testament it is "**Alpha and Omega**". They both stand for "**The beginning and the end**". Christ is the **only one** in the bible who says "**I am the beginning and the end**". Remarkably, the **4th position** on the Menorah lines up with the "**Aleph-Tav**" mark **4th word** in Genesis 1:1. Interestingly the **4th commandment** in the Torah is:

"**Remember the Sabbath Day, to keep it holy**. Six days shalt thou labor, and do all thy work: But the seventh day is the **Sabbath of the LORD THY GOD**."-Exodus 20

So the Torah says the 7th day is the **Sabbath** of the **Creator** (**The LORD**). Interesting, **Christ**…aka the "**Son of Man**" says in the New Testament the same thing but in a different way:

"**For the Son of Man IS LORD (Yahuah) even of the Sabbath day**" - Matthew 12:8

THE SON OF MAN IS YAHUAH (LORD) = CHRIST IS THE CREATOR

These two scriptures alone reveal Christ was God (YAHUAH) manifested in flesh....the lamb of the world. But it gets even deeper! How does this "untranslatable mark" listed as Aleph/Tav connect to **Yahusha Hamashiach** (Jesus Christ)?

Revelation 1:8 "I am the Alpha **(Aleph)** and Omega **(Tav)**, **the beginning and the ending**, saith the Lord, **which is**, and **which was**, and **which is to come**, the Almighty.

Revelation 22:13 "I am Alpha **(Aleph)** and Omega **(Tav)**, **the beginning and the end**, the first and the last."

Here is an interesting fact to note again:
- The first verse of the Bible in Genesis 1:1 is made up **of 7 words**.
- The correct spelling of the Messiah's name **(Yahusha)** from Hebrew to English (*used 216 times in the Bible*) **is 7 English letters.** **OWYƎZ-YAHUSHA**. Even if you use the word "Yahshua" you get "7" English letters.
- God created the Heavens and the Earth in **7 days**.
- God rested on the **7th day** and declared it a "**Day of Rest**" and "**The Lord's day**". Noah's Hebrew name is "**Noach**" from the Hebrew word "Nuach" means "**Rest**". Noah was told to take **7 pairs** of all "clean" animals male and female into the ark.
- Our weeks are fashioned after **7 days**.
- There are **7 feasts** the Israelites were to keep which are all listed in **Leviticus 23**. **Note:** *Purim and Hanukkah are not Feast Days ordained by any Israelite prophet or the Most High himself.*
- The "**Day of Atonement**" feast or "**Yom Kippur**" is celebrated on the 10th day of the **7th month**. This was the only time the

608

Cohenite High Priest of Israel was allowed to go into the "**Holy of Holies**" room where the Ark of the Covenant was and the "**Spirit of God**" dwelled. The "**Veil**" separated man from the holiness of God during this time.

- On the 7 "**Menorah**" candle piece the central candle position is the "**fourth**" candle position. The "**Aleph/Tav**" or "**Alpha and Omega**" or "**The Beginning and the End**".
- In the Book of Revelation during the "Great Tribulation" **7 bowls, 7 trumpets** and **7 vials** signal the "**woes**" of the earth.
- **Naaman** the Syrian Leper had to bathe **7 times** in the Jordan river before he his skin complexion was restored (2 Kings 5:10).
- Joshua was commanded to march around Jericho **7 times** and 7 **priests** were to blow **7 trumpets** (Joshua 6:3-4).
- The phrase "**After the order of Melchizedek**" occurs **7 times** in the Bible.
- Jesus performed **7 miracles** on the Sabbath in Matthew 12:9, Mark 1:21, Mark 1:29, Luke 13:11, Luke 14:2, John 5:8-9, and John 9:14. The Pharisees were upset that Jesus performed "**miracles**" on the Sabbath which they believe was considered "**work**". But Christ said, he is "**Lord of the Sabbath**"....therefore he can do as he pleases on the Sabbath as he ordained it for the Israelites.
- And the list goes on!

Here are some more breakdowns of **Genesis 1:1**, the Hebrew word "**Bereshith**" and **Christ**. Christ was revealed to us in the very beginning of time, in the very "**first**" word of the Bible!

† ⅃ ⊔⊔ 𐤀 ⊓

*(Above) Hebrew word "**Reshith**" in Paleo-Hebrew, the writing style the Torah was written in. The Paleo-Hebrew Letter "**Resh**" looks like a man's Head. **Resh** in Paleo-Hebrew correlates with "**Head**", "**First**", "**Top**", "**Beginning**". Christ is the HEAD of the Creator's household (Beit).*

Hebrew Strong's "Reshith" means "Firstfruits" in addition to "the beginning".

Firstfruits is the 3rd day after the Passover. Christ resurrected on the "Third Day" after his Crucifixion....just as he said.

Creator (bara')

ﬦ   Hebrew name: BEYT. Picture: Tent. Meaning: Family. Tent provides cover for family

ᖴ   Hebrew name: RESH. Picture: Head of a man. Meaning: Top, first in rank.

ᗞ   Hebrew name: AL. Picture: Head of an ox. Meaning: Strong.

ᗞ   (God)   ᖴﬦ   (Son)

Son of God

The first two letters in this word "Bereshith" is "Bar" which means "Son". The first three letters in the same word is "Bara" which means "Create". If you separate the two as in "Bar Aleph" you get "Son of the Father", "Son of the Creator" or "Son of God". Bereshith can also mean "Son of Firstfruits".

Firstfruits is defined as **"The first agricultural produce of a season, especially when given as an offering to God."**

1 Corinthians 15:22-23 "For as in Adam all die, so in Christ all will be made alive. But each in his own turn: **Christ the FIRSTFRUITS;** then at His coming, those who belong to Him.."

Colossians 1:16 "For by him (Christ/Father/Holy Spirit) were all things created, that are in heaven, and that are in earth, visible, and invisible, whether they be thrones, or dominions, or principalities, or powers: all things were created by him, and for him."

In Genesis 1:1 (**the beginning**), the "**Torah Code**" which can be understood only by reading the Torah in **Paleo-Hebrew** proclaims who will be the "**Messiah**" and bring "**Judgement**" to the Earth during the "**End days**"….aka "**The Day of the Lord**". In the beginning "**Christ**" is proclaimed as the one who will bring us to the "**End**". This is supported by the Prophet Isaiah.

Isaiah 46:9-10

Remember the former things of old: **for I am God**, and there is none else; **I am God**, and there is none like me, <u>**Declaring the end from the beginning**</u>, and from ancient times the things that are not yet done, saying, My counsel shall stand, and I will do all my pleasure:

Consider this:

In **John 14:8** "Philip saith unto him, Lord shew us the Father, and it sufficeth us. Yahusha (Jesus) saith unto him, Have I been so long time with you, and yet hast thou not known me, Philip? **He that has seen me hath seen the Father; and how sayest thou then, Shew us the Father?**"

1	2	3	4	5	6	7
Bereshith	bara	Elohim	**ALEPH/TAV**	hashamayim	Vav/Aleph/Tav	Ha'arets

The first words of Genesis 1 are "**Bereshith** (In the beginning), **Bara** (created) **Elohim** (God), **Aleph/Tav** (Christ), **Ha-Shamayim** (the heavens), Vav/Aleph/Tav (and) **Erets** (Earth).

Note: *There are a total of 2,251 "**Vav/Aleph/Tav**" symbols in the entire Old Testament and over 1/3 of these appear in the Torah. When the "**Vav**" character is in front of a Hebrew word like "**Yahuah-Tetragrammaton/YHWH**" it denotes the word "**and**". When the "**Bet**"*

611

character is in front of "YHWH-Yahuah" it denotes the word "*in*". When the "*Lamed*" character is in front of "YHWH-Yahuah" it denotes the word "*to*". When the "*Mem*" character is in front of "YHWH-Yahuah" it denotes the word "*from*". Likewise, the "*Shin*" character in front of the Tetragrammaton denotes the word "*who*" and the "*Hey*" Hebrew word in front of the Tetragrammaton denotes the word "*The*".

IN THE BEGINNING GOD-CHRIST (*ALEPH-TAV*) CREATED THE HEAVENS AND CHRIST (*VAV/ALEPH-TAV*) CREATED THE EARTH.

Because the "**Vav**" letter which supposedly means by many as "**and**" is not standing alone by itself....but is in fact "**together**" with the "Aleph/Tav (Christ)" mark, this implies that the Biblical "Father" and "Son (Christ)" were working together as **ONE** creating the **UNIVERSE** (Heavens & Earth).   The "Aleph/Tav (Christ)" appears **before** the word "**Heaven**" appears and the "Aleph/Tav (Christ)" also appears **before** the word "**Earth**" appears.

The first letter of the bible is "**Bet**". Christ according to many was the "**Living Word of God**". In **John 1:1** it says that in the beginning "**The Word**" or **Christ** "**was God**". God's spoken word is "**The Law**" or "**Christ**".   Christ came not to abolish the Law but to fulfill the Law....why...because "**He was the Law** (*Torah... spoken word of the Creator/God*) and **God** embodied in the flesh".

Note: **Fulfill** means "to bring to **COMPLETION** or bring to **REALITY!**" Christ came to bring "**God's spoken word**" to reality (**flesh**). Everything Christ taught was straight out of the Torah and his body was considered "**Bet-El**" or the "**house/habitation of God Almighty (father)**".   The Creator (father) had a plan for the world....and that was to send Christ as the sacrificial lamb of the world. Christ's life on earth embodied the **7 major/minor Israelite holidays written in the Tanakh/Torah.**

612

Consider this: Christ was the Lamb of God. Christ was without sin or blemish…just like a **Passover Lamb**. Pontius Pilate could not find any fault with him. Christ was the sacrifice/atonement for our sins which in the Old Testament was done with a Lamb. In the Old Testament, in Exodus 12:3 the Israelites were required to select a Lamb without blemish on the **10th day of Nisan (March-April)**. In Exodus 12:6 on the **14th day of Nisan** the Israelites were to kill the Lamb at twilight and use the blood on the doorposts to protect them from the **10th plague** that was going to come upon Egypt. This was the Lord's first Feast Holiday, **"The Passover"** or the **"Pesach"**. The Blood of the Lamb was the **"mark of protection"** for the Israelites back during the Exodus around 1450 B.C.

Fact: *The "Ga-dangme" tribe in Accra, Ghana confess to be Israelites….like the* **Ewe Tribe** *(Ghana/Togo) and the* **Igbo Tribe**. *The "Ga-dangme" people celebrate* **3 main feast holidays** *which line up with the Bible. Coincidence? I think not.*

1. Homowo-(Passover-Pesach)
2. Nmaayeli-(Pentecost-Shavuot)
3. Nmaatoo-(Feast of Tabernacles-Sukkot)

Exodus 12:1-11
"And the LORD spake unto Moses and Aaron in the land of Egypt saying,

This month shall be unto you the beginning of months: it shall be the first month of the year to you.

Speak ye unto all the congregation of Israel, saying, In the **TENTH DAY of this month (Nisan) they shall take to them every man a lamb,** according to the house of their fathers, a lamb for a house:

And if the household be too little for the lamb, let him and his neighbor next unto his house take it according to the number of the souls; every man according to his eating shall make your count for the lamb.

Your lamb shall be without blemish, **a male of the first year**: ye shall take it out from the sheep, or from the goats:

And ye shall keep it up until the fourteenth day of the same month: and the whole assembly of the congregation of Israel shall kill it in the evening.

And they shall take of the blood, and strike it on the two side posts and on the upper door post of the houses, wherein they shall eat it.

And they shall eat the flesh (i.e. meat) in that night, roast with fire, **and unleavened bread**; and with bitter herbs they shall eat it.

Eat not of it raw, nor sodden at all with water, but roast with fire; his head with his legs, and with the purtenance (i.e. *internal organs*) thereof.

And ye shall let nothing of it remain until the morning; and that which remaineth of it until the morning ye shall burn with fire.

And thus shall ye eat it; with your loins girded, your shoes on your feet, and your staff in your hand; and ye shall eat it in haste: it is the **LORD'S PASSOVER (PESACH).**

Now consider this:
Christ appeared during what is now called **"Palm Sunday"** (*which Christians celebrate before Easter Sunday usually in March*) riding on a **colt/ass riding into Jerusalem on the 10th day of Nisan. Christ was crucified on the 14th day of Nisan (some say 15th day of Nisan)**, during the Passover holiday. The Blood of Christ protects us today, **especially**

those Israelites today who trust and believe in Christ, following the commandments of the Father. The Lamb was eaten after it was sacrificed to the Lord. Today, during communion in Church, eating bread and drinking wine signifies the body of Christ that was sacrificed with bloodshed.

Luke 22:14-20
"And when the hour was come, he sat down, and the twelve apostles with him. And he said unto them, **With desire I have desired to eat this Passover with you before I suffer**: For I say unto you, **I will not any more eat thereof, until it be fulfilled in the kingdom of God**. And he took the cup, and gave thanks, and said, Take this, and divide it among yourselves. For I say unto you, **I will not drink of the fruit of the vine, until the kingdom of God shall come**. And he took bread, and gave thanks, and brake it, and gave unto them, saying, **This is my body which is given for you: this do in remembrance of me**. Likewise also the **cup** after supper, saying, **This cup is the new testament in my blood, which is shed for you**.

Keep in mind that Christ was sacrificed/crucified on the 14th day of Nisan or the **"Passover"** which at that time appeared a **Full Moon**. During Christ's death, there was **six hours of darkness in the land** which was scientifically impossible as a Solar Eclipse cannot happen during a Full Moon. Also, Solar Eclipses only last a maximum of 7 ½ minutes.....not 6 hours.

The Old Testament book of Zechariah as well as other Books of the Prophets list **"Messianic Prophecies"** which came true with the birth of Christ.

(**Left**) French Ethnographer Maurice Delafosse. (**Right**) Fang Tribe men from **Gabon**. Maurice wrote books with artwork of these Gabonese people who were followers of Christ. Is it a coincidence that "Whitenized" **Christianity** and **Islam** (*pagan false religion of the Arabs*) found its way to the Bantus "Israelites" of Africa?

The Fang people's oral history states they came from Israel (Land of Canaan). They state in their "ancient land" they battled "**Red Giants**". The Fang people today inhabit **Equatorial Guinea, Cameroon and Gabon**. They state they were once in the territory now known as Nigeria during the "**Bantus Expansion**" but later had to leave when the Islamized "**Hausas**" moved into North Nigeria. The Fang people believe in the existence of **ONE GOD (Creator)**. Some call him "**Mebe'e or Anzam**". The Fang now are guided by the "**spirits of their ancestors**" and meditate in hopes they will guide their lives. When the Fang were interviewed by Europeans they admitted to **NOT** obeying their "**Creators**" commandments. They state the Creator abandoned them and doesn't care for them.....the reason why they fear and worship the "spirits of their ancestors". **This was referred to as "Fetichism" by European Travelers to Africa.** In the 1904 Book, "*Fetichism in West Africa*" by Robert Hamill Nassau it reads the following about the "**Bantus people**" in general:

In their migrations the tribes (*i.e Bantus Tribes*) have been like a river, with its windings, currents swift or slow; there have been even, in places, back currents; and elsewhere quiet, almost stagnant pools. But they all—from the Divala at Kamerun (*i.e. Cameroon*) on the West Coast across to the Kiswahile (*i.e. Kenya-Tanzania*) at Zanzibar on the East, and from Buganda (*i.e. Uganda*) by the Victoria Nyanza at the north down to Zulu (*i.e. Zulu nation-Shaka Zulu*) in the south at the Cape—**have a uniformity in language, tribal organization, family customs, judicial rules and regulations, marriage ceremonies, funeral rites, and religious beliefs and practice**. Dissimilarities (*i.e. differences in traditions/customs*) have crept in with mixture among themselves by intermarriage, the example of foreigners (*i.e. Hamites*), with some forms of foreign civilization and education, degradation by foreign vice, elevation by Christianity, and compulsion by foreign governments."

It also stated in the book "*Fetichism in West Africa*":
"**Circumcision is practiced universally by all these tribes**. An uncircumcised native is not considered to be a man in the full sense of the word,—fit for fighting, working, marrying, and inheriting. He is regarded as nothing by both men and women, is slandered, abused, insulted, ostracized, and not allowed to marry."

Note: The Bantus Fang Tribe in Gabon, like the Australian Aborigines, were "Circumcising" their boys before any European Christian missionary or European Gentile Jewish Slave trader stepped foot in Africa. The Hebrew Israelites were the only people throughout history that "**circumcised**" their male boys and worshipped "**ONE GOD**".

What is even more fascinating is that he Fang Tribe circumcise and they have a legend that a "**Son of God-Messiah**", by name **Ilongo ja Anyambe**, was to come and deliver mankind from trouble and give them happiness (**i.e. Tanakh messianic prophecy in Isaiah 7:14, 9,6-7, Daniel 3:25**); but as he had not as yet come according to their knowledge, they were no longer expecting him. The Fang people also had their division of time, six months, making an "**upuma**," or **year**, **and a rest day (i.e. Sabbath)**, which came **two days after the new**

617

moon, and was called **Buhwa bwa Mandanda,**—it was a day for dancing and feasting. Is this a coincidence that the Bantus Fang Tribe have all these "**Hebrewisms**"? Is it a coincidence that they also have knowledge of a "**Messianic Son of God**" prophecy passed down to them from their elders? No, it is not a coincidence. These Fang Tribesmen were descendants of the Hebrew Israelites from B.C. times who also had knowledge in the Books of Israelite Prophets (i.e. Isaiah, Jeremiah) of the coming "**Messiah**".

This proves that the White European Ashkenazi-Sephardic Jews are "**imposters**" and are therefore **NOT** the true blood descendants of the Biblical Hebrew Israelites. Genetically the Black Fang Bantus people have no connection to the European White Jews. **Therefore, the Black Jews are not related to the White Jews**. The Black Israelites did not "**mysteriously**" turn white, nor did they intermarry with "White Europeans" diluting the skin color and changing the original Black Bantus African people "phenotype (*i.e. appearance*)".

If the Fang "Bantus" people in Gabon were simply Hamites (*i.e. Canaanites, Egyptians, Cushites or Phuttites*) why would they still retain in their oral history the prophecy of a "**Son of God-Messiah**" figure, by name **Ilongo ja Anyambe**? Also, why would they "circumcise" their males? Obviously, the kept this oral history because their ancestors were the Hebrew Israelite prophets of the Old Testament.....like Jeremiah, Zechariah and Isaiah. The Hebrew Torah, is also a book that commanded the Israelites to circumcise their boys.

Zechariah 9:9 "Rejoice greatly, O daughter of Zion; shout, O daughter of Jerusalem: behold, they King cometh unto thee: he is just, and having salvation; lowly, **and riding upon an ass**, and upon a colt the foal of an ass."

Matthew 21:5-13

"Tell ye the daughter of Sion, Behold, **thy King cometh unto thee, meek, and sitting upon an ass, and a colt the foal of an ass**. And the disciples went, and did as Jesus commanded them. And brought the ass, and the colt, and put on them their clothes, and they set him thereon. And a very great multitude spread their garments in the way; others cut down branches from the trees, and strawed them in the way. And the multitudes that went before, and that followed, cried, saying, **Hosanna (*i.e. Hebrew word for "save us"*)** to the son of David: Blessed is he that cometh in the name of the Lord; Hosanna in the highest. And when he was come into Jerusalem, all the city was moved, saying, Who is this? **And the multitude said, This is Yahusha (Jesus) the prophet of Nazareth of Galilee**. And Yahusha (Jesus) went into the temple of God, and cast out all them that sold and bought in the temple, and overthrew the tables of the moneychangers, and the seats of them that sold doves. And said unto them, It is written, **My house** shall be called the house of prayer; but ye have made it a den of thieves."

(Above) New Moon

Note: The Jewish-**Old Israelite calendar** is based on a lunar-solar cycle. Towards the beginning of the moon's cycle, it appears as a thin crescent. This is the signal for a new Jewish month. The moon grows (*i.e. waxing*) until it is full, which is in the middle of the month (Full moon). Then it begins to wane (*i.e. fade out*) until it cannot be seen. It remains invisible for 2 days and then a thin crescent appears, and the cycle of another month begins again. The entire cycle takes 29.5 days. The first month of the Jewish Calendar is called "**Nisan**" which is around March/April. Modern European Jews celebrate "**Rosh Hashanah**" on the 1st and 2nd days of the month of Tishri. In **Leviticus 23:23-25 and Numbers 29:1-2** it states in the Torah that the first day of the 7th month (Tishri) is to be a day of "**Rest**". After the Israelites did their period of "captivity" in Evil Babylon, many believe this is when the notion of the month of Tishri being the Jewish New Year called in the Pharisee "**Mishnah**"…."**Rosh Hashanah**" or the "**Anniversary of the Creation of Adam**" came into being. Some say this date is influenced from the Babylonian "**Day of Judgement**" as there is no mention of "**Rosh Hashanah**" as being the Israelite "*New Year*" in the Torah. As a matter of fact, the start of the year using the month of Nisan was used in Ancient times to keep track of the number of years an Israelite King ruled. From this, one would think that the correct

"**Jewish New Year**" would be in "**Nisan**". But it is not according to European Babylonian "Evil" Talmudic Modern Jewry and their beliefs.

Note: Before the Israelites left Egypt, God told Moses and Aaron this "**Chodesh**" (new moon or months) shall be to you the head of months, the first months of the year (Exodus 12:2). During this time, the month was called "**Abib**" and not "**Nisan**".

Exodus 12:1-3 (First Passover) "Now the LORD said to Moses and Aaron in the land of Egypt, **This month (Abib/Nisan) shall be the beginning of months for you**; it is to be the first month of the year to you. Speak to all the congregation of Israel, saying, On the **tenth** (day) of this month they are each one to take a lamb for themselves, according to their fathers; households, a lamb for each household."

Calendar for March 2017 (Israel)

Sun	Mon	Tue	March Wed	Thu	Fri	Sat
			1	2	3	4
			Adar 3	Adar 4	Adar 5	Adar 6
5	6	7	8	9	10	11
Adar 7	Adar 8	Adar 9	Adar 10	Adar 11	Adar 12	Adar 13
12	13	14	15	16	17	18
Adar 14	Adar 15	Adar 16	Adar 17	Adar 18	Adar 19	Adar 20
19	20	21	22	23	24	25
Adar 21	Adar 22	Adar 23	Adar 24	Adar 25	Adar 26	Adar 27
26	27	28	29	30	31	
Adar 28	Adar 29	Nisan 1	Nisan 2	Nisan 3	Nisan 4	

Phases of the Moon: 5 ◐ 12 ○ 20 ◑ 28 ●
Holidays and Observances: 12: Purim (Tel Aviv), 13: Shushan Purim (Jerusalem)

Fact: March 28, 2017 (**New Moon**) is Nisan 1....the Real Israelite New Year according to the Bible.

CHAPTER 26

FEAST HOLIDAYS ALIGNED WITH CHRIST AND THE SEVEN CANDLE MENORAH

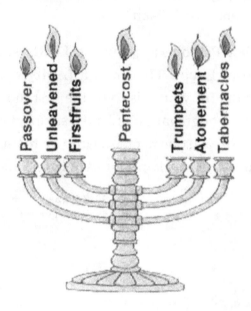

1. **Passover Feast (March/April)**-signifies the Feast of Salvation. In the Old Testament, a lamb without blemish is sacrificed. In the New Testament (**B'rit Chadashah**), Christ is the Sacrificial Lamb. **This holiday represents the death or crucifixion of Christ.** On the **10th day** a "choice" lamb is selected for each Israelite household and on the 14th day (evening) it is killed. In ancient times, the blood of the lamb was put on both doorposts of the Israelites homes and the doors were shut closed for the night. During the night, the lamb was eaten with unleavened bread, bitter herbs and possibly wine to drink. **Note: When Christ was being crucified he was offered wine and myrrh which was a "bitter drink".** He refused it. Coincidence?

2. **Feast of Unleavened Bread (March/April)-**In the Old Testament on the **15th day** of Nisan is the Feast of Unleavened Bread. So let's take it back and show this step-by-step. At twilight, as the 14th day of Nisan was ending, the Passover Lambs in all the Israelite households were killed. Sunset the next day began the 15th day of Nisan and the 1st day of the "Feast of Unleavened Bread". Christ was buried just in time for the "**Feast of Unleavened Bread**".

Numbers 28:16-17 "Then on the **fourteenth day** of the first month (Nisan) shall be the LORD'S Passover. On the **fifteenth day** of this month shall be a feast, unleavened bread shall be eaten for seven days."

Leviticus 23:6 "Then on the **fifteenth day** of the same month there is the **Feast of Unleavened Bread** to the LORD; for seven days you shall eat unleavened bread."

3. Seven days the Israelites were to eat unleavened bread (*bread made from 5 grains without yeast*). These seven days eating unleavened bread symbolized a Holy walk with God. Christ was born in **Bethlehem** (Bet Lechem) which means "**House of Bread**". Christ said in John 6:35 "**I am the Bread of Life: he that cometh to me shall never hunger; and he that believeth on me shall never thirst.**" When Christians take communion, eating the bread signifies the "**Body of Christ**". In **Luke 22:19** during the "Last Supper" Christ says to his disciples, "**This is my body which is given for you: this do in remembrance of me.**" **This holiday represents the burial of the body of Christ.**

Fact: Many former followers of Christ are being deceived to abandon the New Testament because of the **Piso Family** hoax and other tricks. But when they find out who is holding and **"hiding"** the **"African Papyrus New Testament writings"** they start to stretch their heads. The Vatican (Rome) and the Jews hide the truth for a reason. When people research Ancient **"New Testament"** manuscripts how is it that the Ethiopians have written documents about Christ in the Semitic Ge'ez language (*which some say predate Latin, Aramaic and Arabic*)? The Biblical canonical books held by the Ethiopian Orthodox church also line up perfectly with the 5th Century Paleo-Hebrew Dead Sea Scrolls. Paleo-Hebrew and Ethiopian Semitic "Ge'ez" is **NOT** influenced Greek, Aramaic, Latin, or Arabic. Also, there is **NO** standard way of transliterating the Ge'ez script into the Latin Script. The Ethiopian Orthodox Church claims to have its origins from the Ethiopian Eunuch who was witnessed by Philip the evangelist in **Acts 8:27**. It is a known fact that the Freemasons (**Roman Catholics**) hate the **Ethiopian, Egyptian and Syriac-Aramaic Coptic Bibles** for a reason. In 2015, on CNN and other media outlets….it was reported that an ancient New Testament manuscript was found….this one was found hidden in the mask of a body buried in **Egypt**. This ancient **"Aramaic"** piece of "New Testament" material was from the "**Book of "Mark"**, the Israelite "Saint" to the Israelites in Egypt and founder of the Coptic Orthodox Church of Alexandria Egypt around **42 A.D.** **Note: Josephus Flavius was born in 37 A.D., died in 100 A.D., but is claimed to be the Roman "Arrius Piso", the author of the New Testament**. So, if Josephus Flavius was the author of the New Testament how did he write the New Testament when he was born in 37 A.D. and St. Mark (*an Israelite*) had already established a Christian Church in 42 A.D.? St. Mark wrote his Hebrew-Aramaic New Testament Gospel of Christ before Josephus Flavius would be old enough to write. **Did Josephus Flavius begin writing the New Testament in Greek when he was 5 years old?** Of course not! The Egyptian manuscript written on papyrus leaves of the Gospel of Mark was reported by **Joel Baden**, professor of Hebrew Bible at Yale University and **Candida Moss**, professor of the

New Testament and early Christianity at the University of Notre Dame. The announcement of the discovery was made by **Craig Evans**, professor of New Testament at Acadia Divinity College in Wolfville, Nova Scotia. A team of researchers using carbon dating and handwriting analysis (Paleography) determined the fragment of the Gospel of Mark to be written before 90 A.D.....**and it was not written in Greek or Latin**! Doubters to the validity of the New Testament also ignore the Eastern Syriac-Aramaic New Testament manuscript that were found to date earlier than 70 A.D., the time of the "**Roman-Jewish Wars (War of the Jews)**" Flavius Josephus also penned. Proved to be accurate by the world's leading paleographer, **Dr. Dan B. Wallace**, an American professor of New Testament Studies and the founder of the Center for the Study of New Testament Manuscripts brought this remarkable evidence to light in 2012. The 1st Century New Testament fragment was from the Book of Mark...like the one found in Egypt. So how could one man, "Flavius Josephus" write all his literary works (**i.e. "War of the Jews", "Antiquities of the Jews"**) and the **New Testament** during such upheaval in Judea? How is it that the reference of "Christ the Messiah" seen in Paleo-Hebrew in the Old Testament Torah and the Book of Revelation seems to prophecy celestial events....including the advent of Biometrics/RFID implantable chips for a future world without "cash"? What about all the other many historians from that time era in the 1st century A.D. that were writing about the "**Natsarim**" (*followers of Christ, the Nazarene*) being killed for not worshipping Roman or Greek pagan gods? Why would people die for an imaginary religion and an imaginary man called "Christ" the Messiah? Why would 1st Century A.D. historians write about the phenomena of "**Glossalia**", calling the Holy Spirit and "**speaking in foreign tongues**" a "**Strange Phenomenon**" which still happens today in Churches internationally (*especially the Black Church*). What about the people in India who have documented proof of "**Jesus (St. Issa)**" travels to India/Tibet before his re-appearance in Israel as a young man shortly after it was known that **Herod the Great** died. Or what about Christian Indians in **Kerala, India** who attest the **Biblical Saint Thomas** witnessed to them in South India (*along with the Hebrew Israelites in India seen by Sephardic Jew Benjamin Tudela*) the Gospel of Christ?

If this isn't enough proof Christ and the New Testament is valid, let's go to the Torah with some more of the 7 major Israelite Feast Days to see what we can find hidden in it!

PASSOVER

(Above) Passover "Matzah" bread which is unleavened.

During the Passover holiday **"matzah"** or **unleavened bread** is supposed to be eaten for the whole seven to eight days of the festival. **Matzah** is also crushed for baking as well. God commanded the Israelites not to eat anything with leaven during this time. **(See Exodus 12, 23, Leviticus 23:5-6, Numbers 28:16-17, Deuteronomy 16:1-8).** When leaven is put into dough it causes the dough to rise…as in when people cook biscuits, cornbread and other types of breads. The bread becomes **"puffed up"**. Leaven was considered a **symbol of sin.** In Rabbinic tradition, every part of the house is inspected and not one bit of leaven is allowed to be in the house. It is also Jewish tradition that the Matzah be "**pierced**" by creating holes. The holes create a dimpling effect, thus ensuring the Matzah bread **remains flat** (*due to the air pockets from the holes*). This "**piercing**" also gives the matzah a "**striped**" appearance as well. Well this connects to the prophecy of Christ the Messiah in the prophetical Book of Isaiah.

Isaiah 53:3-11

"He is despised and rejected of men; a man of sorrows, and acquainted with grief: and we hid as it were our faces from him; he was despised, and we esteemed him not. Surely he hath borne our griefs, and carried our sorrows: yet we did esteem him stricken, smitten of God, and afflicted. **But he was wounded (pierced in his side) for our transgressions (sins)**, he was bruised for our iniquities: the chastisement of our peace was upon him; and **with his stripes we are healed. All we like sheep have gone astray**; we have turned every one to his own way; and the Lord hath laid on him the iniquity of us all. **He was oppressed, and he was afflicted, yet he opened not his mouth: he is brought as a lamb to the slaughter**, and as a sheep before her shearers is dumb, so he openeth not his mouth. **He was taken from prison and from judgment**: and who shall declare his generation? for he was cut off out of the land of the living: <u>**for the transgression of my people was he stricken**</u>. And he made his grave with the wicked, and with the rich in his death; because **he had done no violence, neither was any deceit in his mouth**. Yet it pleased the Lord to bruise him; he hath put him to grief: **when thou shalt make his soul an offering for sin, he shall see his seed, he shall prolong his days, and the pleasure of the Lord shall prosper in his hand**. He shall see of the travail of his soul, and shall be satisfied: by his knowledge shall my righteous servant justify many; for he shall bear their iniquities (sins).

Also, in the Tanakh (Old Testament) in the Book of Zechariah:

Zechariah 12:10 "And I will pour upon the **HOUSE OF DAVID**, and upon the inhabitants of Jerusalem, the spirit of grace and of supplications: and they shall **LOOK** upon me whom **THEY HAVE PIERCED**, and they shall mourn for him, as one mourneth for **HIS ONLY SON**, and shall be in bitterness for him, as one that is in bitterness for his **FIRSTBORN**."

If this doesn't blow your minds away consider this:

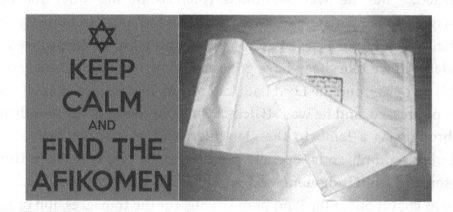

(Above) The last part of the **Seder Meal (Passover Meal)** is when the Matzah unleavened bread is broken into three pieces. The first half goes into a **Matzah tash** (*i.e. a special ceremonial bag with three compartments*), but the second "**middle**" half becomes the "**Afikomen**". In Greek, this means "**That which comes last**". In **Genesis 1:1**, hidden in Paleo-Hebrew you can decipher that "God creates the Heavens and the Earth in the beginning and **Christ in the end brings judgement with a New beginning**".

(Above) On Mount Calvary, Christ was Crucified in the "middle" of two other criminals condemned to death. This falls in line with the Passover.

Luke 23:33-35 "When they came to the place called "The Skull", **they crucified Him there, along with the criminals, one on His right and the other on His left**. Then Yahusha (Jesus) said, "Father, forgive them, for they do not know what they are doing." And they divided up His garments by casting lots. The people stood watching, and the rulers sneered at Him saying, "He saved others; let Him save Himself if He is the **Christ of God**, the **Chosen One**."

So one of the traditions of the Passover/Feast of Unleavened Bread is the **three layers/pieces** of the "matzah". At one point during the holiday service, the "**middle piece**" of the matzah is broken, wrapped in fine linen and is hidden (**i.e. buried**). The children are to hunt for this hidden-buried piece of matzah. During the crucifixion at a place called "**Golgotha**" or "**Place of the Skull**" which we call "**Mount Calvary**", Christ was in the **middle**, surrounded to the left and right by two other men that were convicted to death by crucifixion. Even in the Trinity-Godhead (Father-**SON**-Holy Spirit), Christ is the "**middle**". The hidden "**middle**" piece of matzah bread (*which is broken into three pieces*) is called "**afikomen/afikoman**". When the child finds this piece of bread wrapped in fine linen, this is the last thing that everyone eats that night. Christ states in **Luke 22:16-18** that he would not eat or drink wine until the Kingdom of God was established. This obviously in an "amazing way" screams the **Last "Passover Seder" meal** Christ had with his disciples when he said in Luke 22:19 "**This is my body, which is broken for you. Do this in remembrance of me.**" This shows the obvious connection between the Creators "**Holy Feast Holidays**" for the Israelites and **Christ the Messiah**.

FEAST OF FIRSTFRUITS

Feast of Firstfruits (March/April) - the morning after the Sabbath following the "Unleavened bread", Leviticus 23 starts off with the Firstfruits which in ancient times a **sheaf (omer)** of barley was waved before the Lord to start the counting of the 49 days to the harvest festival of the Pentecost (Shavuot). When Christ was **resurrected**, he was the "**firstfruits**" offering "ripened" like barley. Christ's resurrection was like a "**wave offering**" presented before the **Father (Creator)** as the firstfruits of the harvest to come in the future. Christ's death and resurrection brought forth the rebirth/resurrection of saints who had fallen asleep/died. Christ was the firstfruits or first-begotten of the Father (Creator) and firstfruits of Creation. This is hidden inside Genesis 1:1 (*in the Paleo-Hebrew hidden meaning*).

Matthew 27:52-23 "The tombs were opened, and many bodies of the saints who had fallen asleep were raised, and coming out of the tombs after his resurrection they went into the holy city and appeared to many."

FEAST OF PENTECOST

Feast of Pentecost (May/June) - After 7 weeks or **49-50 days** (Leviticus 23:16) there was a "offering" required of the Israelites. The summer harvest time and the "**Pentecost (Shavu'ot)**" feast holiday required an offering with two loaves of bread…..both of which is baked **WITH LEAVEN**. Many believe these loaves of **LEAVENED BREAD** represents the "**Gentiles**" that were offered "**Salvation**" being that Israelites were supposed to eat **unleavened bread** as a sign of obedience and holiness. Many of the Israelites that were still around in Israel at the time rejected the Messiah or were to "stubborn" to accept him. Therefore, salvation was offered unto the "**Gentiles**" or the "**Wild Olive branch**" as described by the Apostle Paul in Romans 11.

Leviticus 23:16-17 "Even unto the morrow after the seventh week shall ye number **fifty days**; and ye shall present a new meal-offering unto the LORD. Ye shall bring out of your dwelling two wave-loaves of two tenth parts of an ephah; they shall be of fine flour, they shall be **baked with leaven**, for first-fruits unto the LORD."

Keep in mind though, that as the "**Time of the Gentiles**" comes to a close (*see Luke 21:24-29*), the "*natural branch*" or the physical authentic "blood-line" descendants of the Children of Israel will be re-grafted in to the root from which they naturally came. This "awakening" of the authentic Twelve Tribes of Israel to Christ the "**right way**" without a spot or blemish was likened unto Paul as quote: "**An awakening from the dead**".

Romans 11:11-15 "I say then, Have they (*Israelites*) stumbled that they should fall? God forbid: but rather through their fall salvation is come unto the Gentiles (*non-Israelite nations*), for to provoke them to jealousy. Now if the fall of them be the riches of the world, and the diminishing of them (*Israelites*) the riches of the Gentiles; how much more their fulness? For I speak to you Gentiles, inasmuch as I am the apostle of the Gentiles, I magnify mine office (*of Israel*): If by any means I may provoke to emulation (*ambitious or envious rivalry*) them which are my flesh (*i.e. Israelites*), and might save **some of them**. For if the casting away of them (*Israelites*) be the reconciling (*bringing together*) of the world (*i.e. in Christ*), what shall the receiving of them (*Israelites*) be (*i.e. that accept the Gospel of Christ*), but life from the dead?"

Feast	Date	Meaning	Status
Passover (Pesach)	March/April	Redemption Sacrifice/Death of Messiah	Fulfilled
Unleavened Bread	March/April	Sanctification Burial of Messiah/No Decay	Fulfilled
Firstfruits Grain harvest	March/April	Resurrection Resurrection of Messiah	Fulfilled
Weeks (Shavuot)	May/June	Pentecost Holy Spirit Sent by Messiah	Fulfilled
Trumpets (Rosh Hashanah)	Sept/Oct	Jewish New Year Messiah returns to Israel	FUTURE
Day of Atonement (Yom Kippur)	Sept/Oct	Day of Atonement Messiah saves Israel	FUTURE
Tabernacles/Booths (Sukkot)	Sept/Oct	Wedding Feast/Golden Age Messiah starts Millennium	FUTURE

FEAST OF TRUMPETS

Feast of Trumpets (September/October) – The Feast of Trumpets (**Yom Teruah/Rosh haShanah**) signifies the "**Second Coming of Christ**" and the "**Call of the trumpet**". In the Old Testament, the High Priest blew the trumpet so that people would stop harvesting and come to worship in the Temple. In **Revelation 11:15** the last of the 7 trumpets of Judgement is sounded. "**Yom Teruah**" means "**Day of the Awakening Blast**". At "**Judgement time**" in the Book of Revelation when the "**Trumpets**" are sounded time the world will receive "**The Wrath of Judgement**" for treating the Children of Israel the way it has done for thousands of years. The nations will also receive the **"Wrath of God"** for all their sins. This would be a glorious day for **"The Saints (Holy Ones)"** but a dreadful day for everyone else. This was prophesied in the Old Testament.

- **Obadiah 15 "The Day of the Lord is near for all nations**. As you have done, it will be done to you; your deeds will return upon your own head."

- **Joel 1:15** "Alas for the day! For the day of the Lord is at hand, and as a destruction from the Almighty shall it come."

- **Joel 2:1** "Blow the **trumpet** in Zion; sound the alarm on my holy mountain: let all the inhabitants of the land tremble: for the day of the LORD cometh, for it is nigh at hand."

- **Revelation 11:15** "And the seventh angel sounded; and there were great voices in heaven, saying, The kingdoms of this world are become the Kingdoms of our Lord, and of his Christ, and he shall reign for ever and ever."

  Once this **"Final Trumpet"** in Revelation (Future) is blown it will signify our **"Redemption"**.

DAY OF ATONEMENT

Day of Atonement (Sept/October) – The Day of Atonement or **"Yom Kippur"**. This was the only time when the High Priest could enter the **"Holy of Holies"** room and call upon the name of the LORD (**Yahuah**) to offer a blood sacrifice for the atonement of the Sins of Israel. It occurred once a year on the tenth day of **Tishri, the seventh month** of the Hebrew Calendar. This sacrifice practice was abolished when Christ died and the Temple Veil torn was torn in two. Again, in the Old Testament, this was a day of **"purification"** where the Israelites could be cleansed from their transgressions and sins. This however required an animal sacrifice by the High Priest. This will be completely fulfilled in the future with Christ as he is our "**High Priest**" forever after the order of **Melchizedek** (Hebrews 5:10, 6:20).

(**Above**) It was custom during the Sukkot to arrange a bouquet while standing in each individual "**Booth**". The Israelites would have to arrange this leafy bouquet of four items which was sometimes called the "**lulav**". When Christ rode into Jerusalem on a donkey (ass) people waved the arrangement of "**four species**" and sung "**Hosanna**" which means "**Save us**" in Hebrew. The Messiah's name in Hebrew "**Yahusha**" means "**Yah (God) is Salvation**". "**Emmanuel**" in Hebrew means "**God with us**" (*Isaiah 7:14, Matthew 1:23*).

FEAST OF TABERNACLES/INGATHERING

Feast of Tabernacles or Feast of Ingathering (Booths) (September/October) – The last feast day "**Sukkot**" in the Old Testament was a reminder to the Israelites of how God provided shelter to his people in the wilderness. The "**Booths**" in the Messianic age is represented by Christ reigning on earth with the New Temple and New Jerusalem. The Lord will establish his "**Tabernacle**" and "**Heaven**" on Earth with man (**Ezekiel 37:26**). The world will come every year to appear before Christ to worship him (**Zechariah 14:16-17**). Thus while some Jews observe the Sukkot for eight days (in Israel) and nine days (in the diaspora) it represents our dwelling in the Body/Tabernacle of God. It was custom during the Sukkot to arrange a bouquet while standing in each individual "**Booth**". The Israelites would have to arrange this leafy bouquet of four items which was sometimes called the "**lulav**". The Palm Branch occupied the central part of the bouquet of four species of plants (**Etrog, Lulav, Hadas, Aravah**). During the waving of the **lulav (or the bouquet of 4 species)** the people of Israel would sing out **Psalms 118:25-26**

"Save us (Hosanna), we pray, O LORD! O LORD, we pray, let us thrive! Blessed is he who comes in the name of the LORD! We bless you from the house of the LORD."

Psalms 118 was regarded as a **Messianic Psalm**. And When Christ appeared in Jerusalem before the Passover in Matthew 21:8-9; Luke 19:38, and John 12:13 he was greeted with shouts of "**Save us (Hosanna)**" and the people waved the lulav as the **MESSIAH (CHRIST) AS KING** came to deliver the people. When Christ returns bringing "**Heaven**" and the "**Tabernacle**" on earth he will reign as our **King forever**.

On that note, prior to the New Testament......in the Old Testament...prior to the flood mankind had **one creation story** and one

"**Supreme God**". It is a known fact that in the very beginnings of most major civilizations people believed in a single Creator. When Osiris was the god of "**Vegetational Decay**" and before the Egyptians knew about the pagan god called "**Ptah**" the Pre-dynastic Egyptians Sons of Mizraim knew there was one "**Creator**". Then Satan stepped in influencing the Egyptians to conjure pagan worship of gods fashioned after birds (*i.e. Ra, Horus, Thoth*) and animals (*i.e. Anubis*). The Sumerians called the "**God**" that brought the flood on earth "**Huwuwa (similar to Yahawah or Yahuah)**" as recorded in the Epic of Gilgamesh. The "**Wa**" or "**Wu**" or "**We**" is seen often at the end of words in Africa used to describe the "Creator".

Romans 1:21-24 describes:

"Because when they knew God, they glorified Him not as God, neither were thankful; but became vain in their imaginations and their foolish heart was darkened. Professing themselves to be wise, they became fools, **And changed the glory of the uncorruptible God into an image made like to corruptible man, and to birds, and four footed beasts, and creeping things**. Wherefore God also gave them up to uncleanness.

If one reads the Lost Tablets of Enki (Sumerian) closely you can see that the **Annunaki** or Enki's people, know that they have certain "**Universal**" laws/rules to abide by and that if they break them…punishment follows. They know that there is a "**Creator**" higher than them…that made them, causing them to be in the predicament that they are in. But through the Sumerians and the sons of Shem the Creator chose a single family to preserve his worship. When Abraham was in Canaan he met "**Melchizedek**" or "**Christ**" the Priest of the Most High God (Genesis 14:18-20).

Before Abraham's descendants could conquer the Land of Canaan, Balaam (Syrian-Iraqi) the "diviner" was asked to curse Abraham's descendants. But he could not curse what the Creator blessed.

Therefore, the Children of Israel were a "Blessed Seed" worshipping only the Creator before they even made it into the Land of Canaan with Joshua. Prior to Abraham, the early civilizations of Sumeria, Egypt, India, China and Mexico (Native Americans) all were once "monotheistic". Even the Canaanites (Pygmies) and the Ainu/Jomon Black Japanese people knew of "**One Creator**"…the same Creator that was responsible for their "**Great Flood**" Stories…which of course is seen in the Bible. But don't just take my word for it. See for yourself.

For example, Yoruba Nigerians use "Olu-**wa**" for the word God. Igbo Nigerians use "Chuk-**wu**. The people of Ghana call the Supreme Creator "**Nyame**" in which the "m' is often substituted for "w" giving the pronunciation "**Nya-we**". Nyame's wife is "**Asase-Ya**". In the Bini language (Benin/Edo) "Osanob-**Uwa**" is a name for God. In Igbo "**Osebru -Wa**" is also a name for God. Some Native American Indians call God "**Ya-Ho-Wa**". The name of the God of Israel is pronounced "**Yah-oo-ah**" or "Yah-oo-wa(h)". The ending of the Creator's name is a "breath sound" as the Hebrew letter "Hey" in the YHWH makes the "breath sound" "**ah**"…..just as when little kids are learning how to pronounce each letter of the alphabet using the "**A**(h)", "**B**(ah)", "**C**(ah)", "**D**(ah), "**F**(ah)", "**G**(ah)", "**H**(ah)" and so on. Like on the children's learning show "**Sesame Street**".

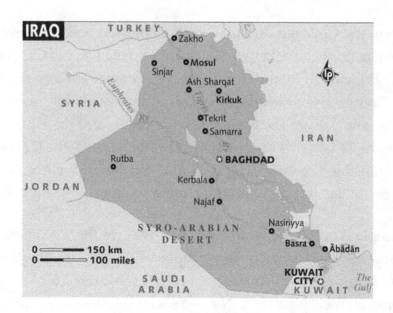

Fact: The Roman Catholic Dominican Order arrived in Iraq around 1200 A.D. Mosul, Iraq and Qaraqosh, Iraq is home to the Iraqi Christians....named today "**Chaldeans**", whose heritage comes by way of the **Ottoman Turks**. Back in the day however the Chaldees heritage was linked to Northern Iraq (Ancient Assyria) and the land of Ur in Southern Mesopotamia (Iraq). Today Iraqi's (Muslim or Christian) speak either **Syriac Aramaic** or **Arabic**. In the **Arabic Bible** of Yefet ben Eli (920-1010 A.D.), the Tetragrammaton (**YHWH-Creator's name**) was listed as "**Yahwah**" and "**Yahuwah**".

Fact: Chaldeans today read an Arabic Bible. I showed the Arabic scriptures with the word "**Yah**" and "**Huwa**" to a Chaldean woman and she acknowledged that the Arabic word "**Huwa**" means "**He is**" or "**O He**". She looked at the Bible I showed her written in Arabic and pronounced the Arabic word as "**Huwa**". Then I asked the Chaldean woman to read the other Arabic word preceding it and she pronounced it as "**Yah**" in Arabic. She said that "**Yah**" had no place or meaning in the Arabic Bible and she didn't understand why it was there. I told her it was from a "**very old**" Arabic Bible. If combined the word "**Yah**" and "**Huwa**" would mean "**Yah (Creator) HE IS**" or "**YAH EXISTS**". I showed the Chaldean woman the Arabic word for "**Yahwah**" and she pronounced not as "**Yahwah**" but as "**Yah-u-wah**". I asked her what it meant and she said that it meant what American Christians pronounce as the English word "**Jehovah**". The Hebrew word "**YAHUAH**" was **transliterated** by the Greeks/Romans from the Hebrew name of the Creator (**YAHUAH**)...into later "**Jehovah**"....which was later removed out of the King James Bible and replaced with "**THE LORD**".

Fact: Hebrew Strong's #1943 "**Hovah**" means "**disaster, ruin** or **mischief**". Therefore Ya-Hovah or Ja-Hovah or Je-Hovah means "**God of disaster**" or the "**God of mischief**". Jehovah is a false name.

In the Dominicans Fathers-Dominican Bible in **Iraq** dated to **1875** the name "**Yahuwah**" is listed as the Creators name and not **Adonai** or **Allah**. In fact, several Muslim Imams (*i.e. Sufi Imam Abu-l-Qasim-al-Junayd-835 A.D., Sunni Imam Fahr al-Din al-Razi-1149 A.D.*) that lived almost 1,000 years ago mentioned in their writings that the Supreme name of God was **Ya-Huwa (O He)** and **NOT** Allah.

٢٧ و كسر وتصاليب وياسمائك العالية الطاهرة

٢٨ المطهرة الممدوحة الرفيعة الجليلة الكريمة

٢٩ الجميلة ياه ياه ياه هو هو هو يالله

(**Above**) Muslim Sufi text from the 900 A.D. portraying the Supreme Name of God in Arabic as "**Yah-Huwa**". This is also seen in the 19th Century **Swahili bible**, which was influenced first by the "**Bantus Languages in Tanzania**" before the Roman Latin script language and the Arabic language could also influence Swahili. Tanzania has the oldest records of "**Old Swahili**" which is the country where "Swahili" had its first beginnings. **Tanzania** was also the main East African country targeted by the Arab Slave Trade for Israelite slaves.

٢٧ وكسر وتصاليب وياسمائك العالية الطاهرة

٢٨ المطهرة الممدوحة الرفيعة الجليلة الكريمة

٢٩ الجميلة ياه ياه ياه ياه هو هو هو هو يالله

On the last line of this Arabic text the words, "**Yah, Yah, Yah, Huwa, Huwa, Huwa**", meaning "**Oh, Oh, Oh, He, He, He**" was a way the Sufi Muslims pronounced the divine name of God. They would sing this out loud many times often using the words, "**Yah hu', Yah hu', Ya hu'"** in order to achieve an overwhelming feeling of great happiness or joyful excitement. The Sufi/Soufi Muslims were some of the first Muslims in the 7th century A.D. and many believe this "**mystic**" group of Abrahamic believers existed before the pagan pre-Islamic Arabians.

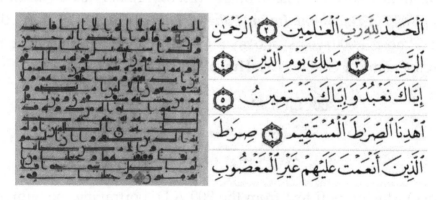

(**Left**) 8th Century Quranic Sura in the Kufic Script from 700 A.D., shortly after Islam was created. (**Right**) Arabic script from the Quran. Remember, the Quran was believed to have been completed when Muhammad died in 632. A.D. During that time, the common writing style of the Arabs were **Kufic** and **Hijazi** script.

Let me explain further,

Before Arabic was widely used to write the Quran, the "**Kufic Script**" and the "**Hijazi-Yemeni Script**" was what the early Quran was written in (*i.e. see the Sana'a palimpsest/manuscript*). Today's Quranic texts are written in Arabic. If you don't believe research the Samarkand

"Kufic" Quran, the **Topkapi manuscript** and the **Qur'an of Uthman** from Cairo, Egypt.

Note: The **Sana'a (Yemen) "Hijazi" manuscript** dating back to the 7th and 8th Century A.D. is a collection of fragments of what many say is the earliest Quranic texts known to Muslims. The Samarkand (Iraqi) "Kufic" manuscript dates back to the 8th and 9th Century A.D. But what Muslims like to keep "**hush-hush**" is that the Kufic (Iraqi) Quran, the Hijazi (Yemeni) Quran and the Topkapi Quran's **ALL** reveal "**deviations**" from the Modern standard Quranic text that Muslims read today. These "**deviations**" debunk the statement that in the Quran for the last 1,400 years "**not one dot or letter has been changed**". This proves that the Quran is **NOT** the perfect, timeless and unchanging word of the pagan God "Allah". Many scholars believe from these "**aberrations-deviations**", that the Quran is basically a **man-made "created religious text"**. Others say the Quran and Islam is a creation of the Roman Catholic Church (*i.e. see the book "**The Prophet**" and former Jesuit priest **Alberto Rivera**).

When Western Arabia (Hijaz) and Arabia Felix (i.e. Yemen) was inhabited by the pre-Islamic Arabs, the word "**Huwa**" meant "**HE**" or "**God**" or "**HE IS**". When Islam was created the early Quran still used this word for "**God or the Creator**". In the Quran, one might read, "**Allahu la ilaha ila Huwa**". This means "**God there is no god but HE (Huwa)**". The Sufi Mystic Muslims of Old would say, "O HE (who is), O HE (who is), O HE whom no one knows what He Himself is but Himself." What they were actually saying was "**Yah Huwa, Yah Huwa, Yah Huwa** whom no one knows that He Himself is but Himself". Which is basically like saying "**Yahuah/Yahuwa Exists**". Therefore, many Muslim Arabs who knew the truth understood "**Ya Huwa**" as the **CREATOR OF ALL THINGS** or in this case "**Oh He**" or "**He who is**". Mansur Al-Hallaj (858 A.D.-922 A.D.), a Persian Sufi wrote this and was labeled a madman and was crucified in Bagdad, Iraq for it.

Psalms 83:18 "That men may know that thou, whose **NAME ALONE IS YAHUWA/YAHUAH**, art the Most High over all the earth."

Isaiah 42:8 "I am the **LORD (YAHUWA/YAHUAH)**: that is my **NAME (Hebrew Strong's #8034 "Shem")**: and my glory will I not give to another, neither my praise to graven images."

In the Isaiah Dead Sea Scrolls of **Isaiah 42:8** the Hebrew Strong's word #8034 says "**SHEM**" which means "**NAME**". This is also seen in the Paleo-Hebrew version of **Psalms 83:18**.

God's Divine name is a **Noun (Yahuwa/Yahuah)**, not a **verb-adverb-verb** like "**Ahayah asher Ahayah**". The Masoretic Jewish scholars who lived during 500-900 A.D. could not have forged the **Tetragrammaton** (Divine Name) of God over 7,000 times on **rock** or **papyrus paper**. This is absurd.

Fact: The Catholic Church removed the "**True**" name of the "**Creator**" out of the Holy Bible and replaced it with "**Jehovah**" and "**The LORD**" to deceive people. Islam, denies the divinity of Christ, his title as "**The Son of God**", the Messiah and Saviour of mankind. The Jews and Muslims deny that Christ and the Father are **ONE**. They also don't believe Christ is the "**mediator**" between Man and the Creator (Father). But here is where it gets DEEP! The Catholic Church is regarded as "**Mystery Babylon, the mother of all harlots**". According to the Bible, judgment is coming to "**Babylon**" and the world. The Bible also says in **Revelation 18:4**:

"And I heard another voice from heaven, saying, **Come out of her, my people,** that ye be not partakers of her sins, and that ye receive not of her plagues."

Well, the Roman Catholic Church has to set up the "**Antichrist Beast System**" according to the Bible. Therefore, it has do everything to make sure that world will accept a "**One World Religion**". How does that happen? By force! Remember the majority of all Catholic Priests are "Freemasons" and the 33rd Degree Grandmaster Moslem Shriner Freemason worship "Lucifer" behind the religion of Islam with "Allah" being their secret "God" cover name. During the beginnings of the Roman Catholic Church, Satan had to create a "**Anti-Christ**" religion that would persecute the "**true believers**" of the Bible in its purity towards the "End Times". This would be "Islam". The Roman Catholic Church had to held "create" Islam to cause conflict, wars and to deceive "Bible" believers into a future "False Religion. The Roman Catholic Church needed to keep "control" of Jerusalem for the future "Anti-Christ" that would sit on the throne in the "Third Temple", built by the Gentile Jews. This is why the Gentile European Jews and the Gentile Arab nations respect the Roman Catholic Church Pope. The Pope (*a so-called Christian and therefore "infidel" or "enemy" to Islam*) can attend Islamic services in Mosques with top Muslim Imam's and he can meet with the top Jewish Rabbis in Israel......all with "Peace". This is a "**RED FLAG**".

Note: *Every Islamic Terrorist Group (Hamas, Hezbollah, ISIS) we see on T.V. "mysteriously" manages to avoid invading* **Jerusalem** *(Israel),* **Mecca** *(Arabia) and* **Medina** *(Arabia). Why?*

It is a known fact that the Romans invaded Arabia and Arabia Felix (Yemen) before Islam existed. It is believed that the Romans and the Edomites helped influence the creation of Islam....including the Kaaba

Stone in Mecca. The Romans goddess (**i.e. Cybele**) and the Edomites god (**Qos-Allah-Qaush**) helped influence the creation of Allah and his three goddess daughters (**Al-Uzza, Al-Manat, Al-Uzza**) as seen in the Quran in **Sura 53:19-22**. Before all of this the Nabataeans, the Edomites and the Sabaeans in Arabia were worshipping "**moon gods**" married to "**sun gods**". After Muhammad was used by the Romans/Edomites to rally the Arabs under **ONE** false god, "**Mystery Babylon**" had everything set up for the coming "**Antichrist**". How so?

2 Esdras 6:9 "**For Esau (Edom) is the end of the world**, and Jacob is the beginning of it that followeth."

Even the "Greeks" who wrote the book of 2 Esdras knew prior to Muhammad's birth knew that Edom's seed was "evil".

Even Christ warned us that "**Edomite**" Pharisees in Israel were evil.

John 8:44-45 "**Ye are of your father the devil**, and the lusts of your father ye will do. He was murderer from the beginning, and abode not in the truth, because there is no truth in him…"

Even Christ knew that the Pharisees were "**Edomites**". These Edomites were descendants of Abraham according to the Bible who lived with the Sons of Cain (*Kenites*) and the Canaanites (*see Genesis 15:18-21*) in the territory of Abraham (*Nile River to Euphrates*). The mistake the Edomite Pharisees did was acknowledging that they had no history of "**captivity-bondage**" like the Israelites….thus giving away who they really were.

John 8:33 "They answered him, **We be Abraham's seed, and were never in bondage to any man**: how sayest thou, Ye shall be made, fee?

The Israelites whole history was full of bondage to the Egyptians, the Assyrians, the Babylonians, and the Greeks. The Edomites had not history of bondage. But how did the Edomites infiltrate the **Roman Catholic Church, Modern Babylonian Talmudic Judaism** (aka "Pharisee-ism") and **Islam**? Here we go!

EDOM'S INFILTRATION OF ROME

In the Book of Jasher 61, it states that during the 12 Tribes stay in Egypt, that "**Zepho**" the grandson of Esau, fled Africa to later rule over **Chittim** (i.e. Rome).

Jasher 61:24-25 "And the children of Chittim saw the valor of Zepho, and the children of Chittim resolved **and they made Zepho king over them, and he became king over them, and whilst he reigned they went to subdue the children of Tubal** (*Turkey, home of the Ottoman Turkish Arabs*), and all the surrounding islands. And their king Zepho (grandson of Esau) went at their head and they made war with Tubal and the islands, and they subdued them, and when they returned from battle they renewed his government for him, and they built for him a very large palace for his royal habitation and seat, and they made a large throne for him, and Zepho reigned over the whole land of Chittim and over the land of Italia fifty years."

EDOM'S INFILTRATION OF JUDAISM/PHARISEE-ISM

1st Century A.D. Jewish Greco-Roman "**Gentile**" Historian **Flavius Josephus** writes in his book "*Antiquities of the Jews*", in Book 36, page 37:

"**That country is also called Judea, and the people Jews; and this name is given also to as many as embrace their religion (Judaism), though of other nations.** But then upon what foundation so good a governor as Hyrcanus (grandson of Mattathias patriarch of the Maccabees, a family of Judahite patriots of 2nd and 1st centuries B.C.) **Took upon himself to compel these Idumeans (Edomites) either to become Jews or to leave their country**, deserves great consideration. I suppose it was because they had long ago been driven out of the land of Edom, and had **SEIZED ON AND POSSESSED THE TRIBE OF SIMEON** (their land not the people), **AND ALL THE SOUTHERN**

PART OF THE TRIBE OF JUDAH, WHICH WAS THE PECULIAR INHERITANCE OF THE WORSHIPERS OF THE TRUE GOD WITHOUT IDOLATRY..."

Likewise, in Flavius Josephus's *"Antiquities of the Jews"* in Chapter 9, it states that the Greek Hasmonean "Maccabean" Hyrcanus subdued the Idumea/Edomite cities of Dora and Marissa, **converting the Edomites into Jews after forced "circumcision"**. Thereafter, they were known not as "**Edomites**" but "**Jews**".

EDOM'S INFILTRATION OF THE ISHMAELITE ARABS AND ISLAM

Genesis 28:9 "Then went Esau unto **Ishmael**, and took unto the wives which he had **Mahalath (i.e. Bashemath)** the daughter of Ishmael Abraham's son, the sister of Nebajoth, to be his wife."

Before the Greek ruler **Alexander the Great** conquered Egypt and the Middle East, the children of Edom had already mixed with Ishmael's seed through his daughter **Mahalath** whom he re-named "**Bashemath**". These children of this **Edomite-Ishmaelite** union would be called "**Nabataeans**". They would settle in **Petra, South Jordan** (Edomite Territory) and North Arabia. Over time, going into the 1st Century A.D. they would expand their territory to cover a good portion of Arabia, mixing in with the Arab Keturahites and Arab Ishmaelites before the birth of Muhammad.

Note: Although Edom mixed with the Sons of Shem, the Sons of Ham and the Sons of Japheth....Yahuah made sure that Edom as a "**nation**" or "**people**" would be "small" in the midst of the nations. This is how we know that Edom is not the whole "White race".

Obadiah 1:2 "Behold, I have made you (Edom) small among the heathen: you are greatly despised."

As you can see, "**Edom**" is very clever and Satan has a plan to use Edom's seed to create "**Chaos**" amongst the "**Nations**". Even though the Roman Catholic Church, Modern Jewry and Islam seem "**separate**", they are all **ONE**. They all have and still take "**Crafty Counsel**" amongst the "Real" **Chosen Seed of Israel**.

Many historians claim it was different Catholic Popes that issued "**papal bulls**" granting the Arabs (*i.e. Saracens*) permission to invade and conquer "**North Africa**", which at the time was under "soft" Roman rule. During this time, millions of Hebrew Israelites were already living in Egypt, Libya, Tunisia, Morocco and Algeria. Later the Roman Catholic Church would issue more "**papal bulls**" allowing European "Gentile" Jews and European countries to "**enslave**" Black Negro Israelites and Native Indian Israelites wherever they may be. This required paying close attention to Biblical clues to the whereabouts of the Lost Tribes in Zephaniah 3:10, Isaiah 49:12 and 2 Esdras 13:40-46.

By the 8th Century A.D. the "**Foreign**" Black Arab invasion of North Africa, along with the mixing of these Arabs with Israelites and Hamitic North African Berbers (*Libyan Phuttites/Egyptians*), would give rise to the "**Black Moors**".

(**Above**) Excerpt from the literary work "**Pugio Fidei**". **Raymond Martini** was a Northern Spain (Catalan) Dominican friar and theologian. He is famous for his literary work "**Pugio Fidei**" dated to the 13th Century A.D. when the **Black Moors** and **Black Jews** (*i.e. Mandingo/Yoruba/Congolese tribes*) were in Iberia (Spain/Portugal). He was one of **eight friars** appointed the task of carrying a missionary to the Black Jews and Black Moors. He wrote the name of the Creator in his Book as "**Yohoua**" and not the Latin version "**Yehouah**". He was a scholar in Hebrew and of course was familiar with Sephardic cursive Hebrew at the time, which was similar to the ancient writing style of the **Mandingo/Soninke people** living Senegal, Gambia, Guinea and Mali.

With that being said, is there any evidence of the Creator's name in other races or people across the earth?

(**Above**) Aboriginal "**Maori**" natives of **New Zealand** (1800's). As you can see some of them had sort of curly-wooly hair. They called their main God "**Mawe**" after which the North part of the Island was named after. New Zealand is East of the Island of Tasmania and Australia. The god "**Mawe**" was also used in Hawaii.

Note: In Gabon and in Zambia (Lozi-Barotse people) they call the Creator "**Niambe**" or "**Anyambe**". The Akans of "Asanteland/Ashanti land" in Ghana call the Creator "**Nyame**" or "**Onyame**".

Note: In Dahomey, (Benin, Africa) the god "**Mawu**" created the world, plants, animals and humans.

(**Above**) Hindu Trinity god "**Trimurti**".

The people in India called the creator "**Brahma (similar to Abraham)**" whose consort (wife) was **Sariswati** (similar to Sarah). They say that he was the "**Creator**" and part of a Trinity whom they called "**Trimurti**". The Trinity consisted of the Hindu gods **Brahma, Vishnu and Shiva**. But of course, the Fallen Angels knew about the existence of the "**Trinity**" in the beginning as Yahuah, Yahusha (Christ) and the Holy Spirit (Ruach HaKodesh). The name of the Creator was known by Adam's son "**Seth**" and his son "**Enos**" in **Genesis 4:26**. This was before the "**Great Flood**" and perhaps before the Fallen Angels (i.e. "**Thoth-Hermes Trismegistus**") could start building the "Great Pyramid of Giza" and the Great Sphinx in Egypt.

Fact: *Thoth aka in Greek "Hermes Trismegistus" has a quote in the Egyptian-Greek text "**The Hermetica**" which says:*

*"Hermes bowed his head in thankfulness to the **Great Dragon (Satan)** who had taught him so much, and begged to hear more concerning the ultimate of the human soul."*

It also says:

"If then you do not make yourself equal to God, you cannot apprehend God; for like is known by like".

The Egyptian pagan god **Tehuti** or Thoth or **Hermes** was known and worshipped as the god of **"wisdom/knowledge and magic" (power is either of the Devil or God).** Egyptologists don't understand that the very pyramids in Egypt and all over the world are inspired by fallen angels (like Azazel-Book of Enoch) who existed before the Great Flood. In the Sumerian Lost 14 Tablets of Enki it states that the Sumerian Annunaki beings that came from heavens were deified by man....especially **"Enki".** It states that in Egypt, the Annunaki **"Enki"** was known as **"Ra"** or **"Amon/Amun Ra".** Amon-Ra became the major pagan god of Egypt and Thebes (*Capital of Egypt*) by the 18th Century. Jeremiah the Israelite prophet recognized this in Jeremiah 46:25 in the Bible.

Jeremiah 46:25 "The Lord of hosts, the God of Israel, said: "Behold, I am bringing punishment upon **Amon (Ra) of Thebes, and Pharaoh and Egypt and her gods."**

These fallen angels taught man "**Magic/Sorcery**" and the secrets of the universe and stars....and with it they crafted the pagan religions of major civilizations from Atlantis to Egypt to the Sumerians and the Hindoos. Prior to the flood man knew there was **ONE GOD.** Even Hindu followers in India know this as **Brahma** in Hinduism is the Sole Creator and mysteriously his consort is named "**Sarah-swati**" which is similar to **A-BRAM** or **A-BRAHAM**" and his wife "**SARAH**". Satan and his fallen angels desire the worship of man...they are already powerful beings. Satan wanted Christ to worship him. But Christ says to worship the same Creator that Seth and Enos knew before Noah was born.

CHAPTER 27

TRACING THE USE OF "ORACLES" IN ANCIENT ISRAEL TO PINPOINT THE ISRAELITES TODAY

The Bible and the Hebrew Israelites story can be tracked in "Actual history" with archaeological proof from the Ancient walls of the Egyptian, Babylonians, Assyrians, Grecians, Persians and Romans. And it ALL lines up with the bible. Even the Sumerians and the Zhou-Shang Dynasty in China knew about the Great Flood but Egypt doesn't talk about it....however there exists archaeological proof of Semitic people in Egypt around the time of Joseph and the 12 Sons of Jacob. Even the "Urim and Thummim" Divination practices of the Israelite High Priests can be seen in the Native American Shaman Priests, Yoruba Ifa Priests, Igbo Afa Dibia Priests and the Bambara priests in Mali. But the key to who ruled Egypt as "Real Egyptians" can be seen in the Dogon, Masalit, Fur and Alur Tribes. Who taught the Egyptians about the Orion & Sirius constellations without a telescope? How did they know about the Planet Nibiru and from where did their pagan gods came from? The Egyptians say Osiris and Horus came from the Orion Belt and Isis came from the Dogstar Sirius. These are Fallen Angels/Watchers which taught the Egyptians this. WAKE UP!

Joseph Eidelberg, in his book "**Bambara: In the footsteps of the pillar of fire**", highlighted the presence of Israelite descendants migrating into West Africa during the Exodus. The Book is a hidden treasure as he only wrote the book in Hebrew. He records the Israelite influence he noticed amongst various African cultures; particularly focusing on the people of **Bambara**....who happen to have "**Divination**" traditions/customs that are similar to the **Yoruba Nigerians** and **Native Americans**.

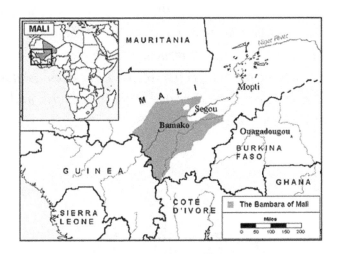

The **Ghana Empire** was one of the first Israelite Kingdoms in Mali, Africa during the 11th Century A.D. The Ghana Israelite Kingdom encompassed **Mauritania, Guinea, Mali, Gambia and Senegal**. All year round the average temperature in this region was **90-100 degrees Fahrenheit**...obviously an area where "White European Jews" would not fare well. The capital city of Mali was "**Bamako**" named after the Bambara word "**Crocodile Tail**". The ancient people of this city traded Gold, Ivory, Salt and **Kola Nuts**....which the Yoruba's use on their **Opon Ifa Divination Board**. The **Bambara people** are a Bantus people who live amongst the Soninke (Mandingo) people of Mali. They are also known to live amongst the Wolof, Mande and Jolof Bantus tribes in Africa. Their Y-DNA is "**E1b1a**"....just like that of African-Americans, Caribbean Blacks, Yoruba Nigerians, Igbo Nigerians, Ashanti Ghanaians and Kikuyu Kenyans. The Bambara, Yoruba and Igbo people all have many stories which connects their forefathers to

Egypt/Canaan.....but their traditions-customs point to a Hebrew origin. Could this reference to **Egypt** and **Canaan** be a hint of the Bantus Bambara/Yoruba/Igbo/Kenyan people's origin? Yes it is!

Fact: *Dierk Lange, the author of "**Origin of the Yoruba and The Lost Tribes of Israel**" quoted: "On the basis of comparative studies between the dynastic tradition of the **Oyo-Yoruba** and ancient Near Eastern history, the present article argues that Yoruba traditions of provenance (i.e. place of origin), claiming immigration from the Near East are basically correct. According to Oyo-Yoruba tradition, the ancestral Yoruba saw the **Assyrian conquests** of the Israelite kingdom from the ninth and eight centuries B.C. (i.e. 800-700 B.C.) from the perspective of the **Israelites**. After the fall of Samaria in 722 B.C., they were deported to Eastern Syria and adopted the ruling Assyrian Kings as their own."*

(Above) Bambara people (1800's). The Bambara people say they are a branch of the larger **Mande** tribe and the smaller **Mandingo branch** of Tribes.

(Left) "Opon Ifá" is a Yoruba Divination board. The **Ifa** is the most prestigious form of divination among the **Yoruba**. It is a type of geomancy (*i.e. earth divination; the oduns of Ifa are marked on a tray which represent the Earth*) that depends on the generation of certain signs (**oduns**) and the interpretation of their meaning by means of a collection of stories. On the "**Opon Ifa Board**" the **Babalawo** (*i.e. Yoruba Diviner Priest*) throws sixteen palm or **kola nuts** onto the flat surface and determines which eight of the 256 possible sets of signs are displayed. **Some Bantus tribes use "Sticks" instead of stones or nuts.** This is similar to the **Umim and Thummim** divination practices of the **Ancient Israelites**.

Note: *The Ifa has 256 oduns (signs) and it is said that there are at least 16 stories attached to each." –Making the Gods in New York: The Yoruba Religion in the African American Community, By Mary Cuthrell Curry, PG 183.*

Some African Bantus Tribes in West Africa still to this day use a form of **geomantic divination. "Geomancy" is a method of divination that interprets markings on the ground or the patterns formed by tossing soil, sand, sticks or rocks.** Although the Bambara's form of geomancy is different from the Nigerian Yoruba Ifá system, it does have the Number 16 in common with the Ifá system. The **16 stories** attached to each of the Ifá oduns could possibly be related to the **16 divination symbols** of the Bamana system. Some say this was learned by the

Yoruba Israelites in Babylon or Assyrian captivity around 700 B.C. to 500 B.C.

Purine / Pyrimidine
Boy / Girl
King / Priest
1 / 0
On / Off
Yes / No
White / Black
Light / Dark
Right / Left
South / North
Innocent / Guilty
Truth / Lie
Good / Evil

URIM
אורים

THUMMIM
תמים

"An **ephod** was an artifact and an object to be revered in Ancient Israelite culture. The ephod was closely connected with oracular practices and priestly rituals… In the Book of **Exodus** and **Leviticus** the ephod is described as being created for the Jewish High Priest to wear as part of his official vestments (garments) in **Exodus 28:4, 29:5, 39:2** and **Leviticus 8:7.**"

(**Above**) The **Urim** and **Thummim** stones were kept inside the Cohenite (Aaronite) High Priests **Breastplate of Judgement.** They were used as a form of **"Geomancy"** and **"Divination"** to answer questions or to judge the Children of Israel. **Divination** is defined as **"the art or practice that seeks to foresee or foretell future events or discover hidden knowledge usually by the interpretation of omens or by the aid of supernatural powers."**

Tav   Alef

תמים   אורים

Tumim   Urim

The words "**Urim** and **Thummim**" are believed to be plural. But interesting enough, in Hebrew, the words "Urim and Thummim" start with the letters **"Aleph (Beginning)"** and **"Tav (Ending)"** respectively. Some scholars believe it is based off the singular word "Ur" and "Tumm" which many believe has its roots to the older Semitic Cuneiform (Sanskrit based) language of Mesopotamia (Ur-Babylon) from where Abraham descendants were from. In Babylonian-Sumerian terms **"urtu"** and **"tamitu"** means **"oracle"** and **"command"** respectively. Many Jewish scholars however believe that Urim means **"cursed/guilty"** while Thummim means **"innocent/faultless"**. Others however, believe **"Urim and Thummim"** means **"lights"** and **"perfection"** as Hebrew Strong's word #217 **"Ur"** means **"light or flame"**, hence the meaning of the archangel **"Uriel** (i.e. Flame of God)". The Hebrew Strong's word #8537 **"Tom"** and #8552 **"Tammam"** means **"completion/finished"**.

Many believe the Israelite priests used the Ephod **"Urim and Thummim"** to determine God's will in a particular situation. Only the Diviner (priest) in the Bantus villages was the one that dealt with situations that needed a **"divine answer"**. Some people believe that the Israelites carried two stones or two sticks that would somehow give a **"yes"** or **"no"** answer to a specific question. For example, should Israel be threatened by another nation or tribe, they would seek guidance from the High Priests whether or not to go to battle using the Urim and Thummim. The High Priest would shake or toss the stones/sticks (*i.e. just as the Bantus diviner would*) and if they turned up a certain way it would indicate the answer of whether it was God's will to go to battle or not. Some believe that the stones perhaps would glow, indicating the answer from God. This was considered one form of "divination" that God allowed in the Old Testament.

Here are some examples:

- **Exodus 28:30** "And thou shalt put in the breastplate of judgement the **Urim and the Thummim;** and they shall be upon Aaron's heart, when he goeth in before the Lord: and **Aaron shall bear the judgment of the Children of Israel upon his heart** before the Lord continually."

- **Numbers 27:21** "And he (Joshua) shall stand before Eleazar the priest, who shall ask counsel for him after the **judgement of Urim before the Lord:** at his word shall they go out, and at his word they shall come in, both he, and all the children of Israel with him, even all the congregation."

After the Israelites left Egypt and made it into the Land of Canaan, around the time when the prophet Samuel died, the Israelites did not have anyone to go to get an answer from the Lord, either by dream, **the Ephod (Urim and Thummim)** nor the prophets. Samuel was an ancestor of Levi (the Priesthood tribe) through Kothath and Elkanah (his father in 1 Samuel 1:1, 1 Chronicles 6:33-38). **Samuel was the Israelite prophet who anointed King Saul and King David as King of Israel.**

1 Samuel 28:2-15 details this all out.....and even given hints to Sheol, Tartarus and Abraham's bosom **"inside"** the earth.

1 Samuel 28:3-15

Now **Samuel was dead,** and all Israel had lamented him, and buried him in Ramah, even in his own city. **And Saul had put away those that had familiar spirits, and the wizards, out of the land.** And the Philistines gathered themselves together, and came and pitched in Shunem: and Saul gathered all Israel together, and they pitched in Gilboa. And when Saul saw the host of the Philistines, he was afraid, and his heart greatly trembled. **And when Saul enquired of the LORD, the LORD answered him not, neither by dreams, nor by Urim, nor by prophets.** Then said Saul unto his servants, **Seek me a woman that hath a familiar spirit** (i.e. diviner), that I may go to her, and enquire of her. And his servants said to him, Behold, there is a woman that hath a familiar spirit at Endor. And Saul disguised himself, and put on other raiment, and he went, and two men with him, and they came to the woman by night: and he said, **I pray thee, divine unto me by the familiar spirit, and bring me him (Samuel the Israelite Prophet) up, whom I shall name unto thee.** And the woman said unto him, Behold, thou knowest what Saul hath done, how he hath cut off those that have familiar spirits, and the wizards, out of the land: wherefore then layest thou a snare for my life, to cause me to die? And Saul sware to her by the LORD, saying, As the LORD liveth, there shall no punishment happen to thee for this thing. **Then said the woman, Whom shall I bring up unto thee? And he said, Bring me up Samuel.** And when the woman saw Samuel, she cried with a loud voice: and the woman spake to Saul, saying, Why hast thou deceived me? for thou art Saul. And the king said unto her, Be not afraid: for what sawest thou? And the woman said unto Saul, **I saw gods (*i.e. souls of deceased men or angels*) ascending out of the earth.** And he said unto her, What form is he of? And she said, **An old man cometh up; and he is covered with a mantle** (i.e. *cloak/shawl that High Priest usually wore, including Ezra in Book of Ezra 9:3*). And Saul **perceived** that it was Samuel, and he stooped with his face to the ground, and bowed himself. **And Samuel said to Saul, Why hast thou disquieted me, to bring me up?** And Saul answered, I am sore distressed; for the Philistines make war against me, and God is departed from me, and answereth me no more, neither by prophets, nor by dreams: therefore I have called thee, that thou mayest make known unto me what I shall do."

This passage proves that without a prophet and the "**Urim and Thummim**" divination stones the Israelites did not know how to receive instructions from God. This passage in 1 Samuel 28 also details out the summoning of "**ancestors**" which is still done by the Bantus people of Africa today. Some may call it "**Ancestor worship or prayers to the Ancestors/Elders**" while some may call it Voodoo. Likewise, in West Africa, there is a lot of "**Diviners**" who call upon "familiar spirits-demons" or pagan idols for answers to their questions. King Saul, used someone (**with a familiar spirit**) who might have been considered a "**diviner-priest-shaman-medicine man**" today to communicate or "summon" the spirit of Samuel.

(**Above**) "Sheol" was the place that all people descended to at mortal death. It represented a sort of "**holding place**" for the dead (*unrighteous and righteous*). It was further separated into a sort of Paradise or "**Abraham's bosom**" and "**Tartarus/Hell**". It was believed that the "**righteous dead**" went to Abraham's bosom to await the final

"**Judgement day**". In the Book of Revelation those sentenced to eternal damnation are cast into the "**Lake of Fire**", the final judgement.

Luke 16:19-25 "There was a certain rich man, which was clothed in purple and fine linen, and fared sumptuously every day: And there was **a certain beggar named Lazarus**, which was laid at his gate, full of sores, And desiring to be fed with the crumbs which fell from the rich man's table: moreover the dogs came and licked his sores. **And it came to pass, that the beggar died, and was carried by the angels into Abraham's bosom**: the rich man also died, and was buried; And in hell he lift up his eyes, being in torments, and seeth Abraham afar off, and Lazarus in his bosom. And he cried and said, Father Abraham, have mercy on me, and send Lazarus, that he may dip the tip of his finger in water, and cool my tongue; for I am tormented in this flame. But Abraham said, Son, remember that thou in thy lifetime receivedst thy good things, and likewise Lazarus evil things: but now he is comforted, and thou art tormented."

"Familiar Spirits", "Voodoo", ancestor worship and idolatry worship just as it was practiced in ancient Israel.....it carried on with the Israelites that left Israel into Africa during Biblical times. For this reason, the "Curses of Israel" still continued on the Bantus people in West Africa and East Africa.

(**Above**) **1762 Map of West Africa**. Notice the words "**Juda**", "**Dahome**", and "**Biafara**". These areas are in modern day Nigeria and Benin.

In the Book "**Fetichism in West Africa**" by Reverend Robert Hamil Nassau it reads:

"Rev. J. L. Wilson, D.D., says of the condition of **Dahomey** (*i.e. Benin, West Africa*) fifty years ago, that in Africa "there is no place where there is more intense heathenism; and to mention no other feature in their superstitious practices, **the worship of snakes** at this place **Whydah** (*i.e. "Kingdom of Juda in Ouidah, Benin*) fully illustrates this remark. A house in the middle of the town is provided for the exclusive use of these reptiles, and they may be seen here at any time in very great numbers. They are fed, and more care is taken of them than of the human inhabitants of the place. If they are seen straying away, they must be brought back; and at the sight of them the people prostrate (*i.e. lay face down*) themselves on the ground and do them all possible reverence. To kill or injure one of them is to incur the penalty of death. On certain occasions, they are taken out by the priests or doctors, and paraded about the streets, the bearers allowing them to coil themselves around their arms, necks, and bodies. They are also employed to detect persons who have been guilty of witchcraft. If, in the hands of the priest, they bite the suspected person, it is sure evidence of his guilt; and no doubt the serpent is trained to do the will of his keeper in all such cases. **Images (*i.e. graven images-idols*), usually called 'gregrees,'** of the most uncouth shape and form, may be seen in all parts of the town, and **are worshipped by all classes of persons. Perhaps there is no place in Africa where idolatry is more openly practiced, or where the people have sunk into deeper pagan darkness."**

(Above) 1747 Map of West Africa. One of the places known for export of "Negro Israelite Slaves" was the town of **"Whydah"**, sometimes spelled **"Whidah"**.....in the **Kingdom of Judah.** This was known by Europeans as the "Slave Coast". To the local Africans it was known as part of the **Kingdom of Dahomey** (*Bini/Edo people*) and the **Oyo "Yoruba" Empire.** In ancient maps, sometimes the people in this area was known as the **"Black Jews in Africa"** or the **"Dahomey Jews".**

In the Book, **"Fetichism in West Africa"** it also reads:

Also, of the people on the southwest coast at **Loango** (*i.e. Gabon, Congo and Angola coast*): **"The people of Loango are more addicted to <u>idol worship</u> than any other people on the whole coast.** They have a great many **carved images** (*i.e. graven images*) which they set up in their fetich houses and in their private dwellings, and **which they worship;** but whether these images represent their forefathers, as is the case among the Mpongwe (at Gabon), is not certainly known."

Idol worship, aka **"graven image"** worship was forbidden under the **"Covenant Law"** given to the Israelites by the Creator. Violation of the Covenant ensured the **"Curses of Israel"** to the Bantus people of West Africa....and their future seed.

Deuteronomy 5:8-10 "Thou shalt not make thee any graven image, or any likeness of any thing that is in heaven above, or that is in earth beneath, or that is in the waters beneath the earth: **Thou shalt not bow down thyself unto them, nor serve them:** for I the LORD thy God am a jealous God, visiting the iniquity (*i.e. sinfulness*) of the fathers upon the children unto the third and fourth generation of them that hate me, and shewing mercy unto thousands of them that love me and keep my commandments."

The remnant of those **10 Northern Israelite tribes** that traveled **"East"** into the Americas...aka what people call the **"Native Americans"** also worshipped graven **"totem pole"** images or relied on **"Diviners"** within their camps.

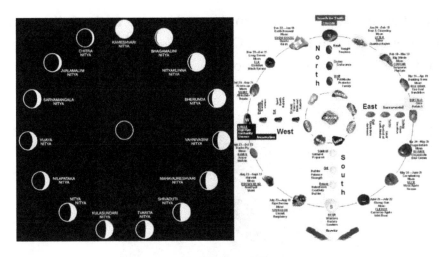

(Left) **16 Lunar phases of the Moon.** (Right) The **16 Lunar phases of the moon** were named after animals and other things by the **Native Americans**. Such as Otter, Cougar, Red Hawk, Buffalo, Beaver, Deer, Flicker, Bear, Sturge Oil, Brown Bear, Raven, Eagle, Snake, Elk, Snow Goose, Cougar.

The Hebrews were said to have **16 signs** in the **Urim and Thummim** oracle. The Native Americans and Sioux have a divination system using **16 stones** reflecting the **16 directions** on the medicine wheel. Adding again a single line and double line to the trigrams then produces the **16 tetragrams.** These 16 tetragrams represent the **16 fractals** or fractions of light reflected on the moon by the sun. This is also the universal application of the **Yoruba Nigerian Priestly Ifa's 16 signs.** What is interesting about all of this is that these same principles are reflected throughout indigenous world, but not as specific and identical to the way that the Bantus Africans/Native Americans practiced their divination rites.

Not only do the 16 mother odus show up in West African traditions including the Yoruba, Dahomey, Igbo, Fon, Ewe, etc, they also show up all over the world including the Americas and Indus Valley civilizations (India). So, the "16" is related to the full moon and or

the number of days it takes from the dark moon to the full moon. 15 are visible and the 16th is not. Other ways it has been presented is through the 16 phases of the moon.

(Above) Dibia Afa **Igbo Priests** are people who speak on behalf of God. Their divination practices are similar to the Yoruba Ifa priests, the Native American Indian Shamans and the Bambara Priests. They claim descent from Ancient Egypt......but their language has evidence of Hebrew with an Egyptian influence. Could this be another clue as to who are the Real Israelites?

Satan had to deceive mankind by using his own made up "Trinity" pagan gods to help usher in **"nature/creature"** worship and **"planetary/constellation"** worship. With this and the "Trinity" copycatting going on they could come up with their own elaborate **"False Christ"** story that would deceive man even up until the 21st century. More pagan gods would be added to Satan's Bootleg **"Trinity Pantheon"** thus forming hundreds of gods and with it plenty of temples. For example, the Osiris, Isis, Horus Trinity in Egypt. Anu, Ea (Enki) and Enlil Trinity in Sumeria. Zeus, Poseidon, and Adonis was the Greek Trinity. In Rome it was Jupiter, Neptune and Pluto. Trimurti was the trinity in India as Brahma, Vishnu, and Shiva.

Fact: "*Trimūrti is the Trinity of the supreme God in Hinduism in which the function of creation, maintenance/preservation, and destruction is seen in Brahma the creator, Vishnu the preserver, and Shiva the destroyer. When all three deities of the Trimurti incarnate into a single avatar, the avatar is known as "Dattatreya" similar to the so called "Satanic World teacher" Maitreya and his follower Benjamin Creme. Supposedly in the future, this "World Teacher" called "Maitreya" will appear on American Television and around the world speaking in everyone's language telepathically or using some sort of advanced technology. He will come calling for peace, justice and freedom for the whole world. Beware when this happens.*

Before I close, the time is upon us where "**God's Chosen People**", the Hebrew Israelites will have to make a choice as to what "**God**" they will choose to serve. If we choose to worship the "**God of Israel**" and accept **Christ as our Saviour** we must keep in mind that the world is going to get worse according to Bible prophecy. Worse especially for the Children of Israel who keep "**God's Commandments**" and bear witness to the Testimony/Gospel of Yahusha (Yahshua) HaMashiach. When the world moves more and more into a "**Satanic Beast-Antichrist System**" with "**Global Basic Income**" or the "**2030 Agenda for Sustainable Development**" we must decide on which two paths to take. The wide path that leads to destruction or the narrow path that leads to **LIFE**. If we choose "Life" and "Christ" we must become a "**Set Apart**" people. Set apart Israelites can be "alive" in this world but we are not to be apart of "**The World**". Why? Because the World is going to face "**Judgement**" and God's wrath in the end. We want to be as "far" from it as possible....physically, financially, mentally and spiritually.

Matthew 7:13-14 "Enter ye in at the strait gate: for wide is the gate, and broad is the way, that leadeth to **DESTRUCTION**, and **MANY** there be which go in thereat: Because straight is the gate, and narrow is the way, which leadeth unto **LIFE**, and few there be that find it."

Why is it important that we know who are the Israelites? The Book of Revelation is a book of prophecy about the Biblical **"End of Days"**. Those Israelites who are "alive" during these times will be under the **"Attack"** of Satan himself.....so we must get ready.

Revelation 12:17 "And the dragon (Satan) was wroth (i.e. intensely angry) with the woman (Israel), and went to **MAKE WAR WITH THE REMNANT OF HER SEED** (i.e. Israelites), which **KEEP THE COMMANDMENTS OF GOD,** and have the **TESTIMONY OF YAHUSHA (YAHSHUA) HAMASHIACH.**"

Revelation 18:4 "And I heard another voice from heaven, saying, **Come out of her, MY PEOPLE**, that ye be not partakers of her sins, and that ye receive not of her plagues."

CHAPTER 28

WILL ESAU AND HIS RELIGION BE THE END OF THE WORLD?

(**Above**) In order to understand what is at stake here and who will be the **ONE** who helps usher in the Antichrist....we have to understand what group of people did the **Edomites** mix themselves within? All we have to do is look at the three "**Abrahamic**" Religions that are always in the "**spotlight**" causing conflict and are the ones involved in "wars". These are none other than the **Roman Catholic Church, Babylonian Talmudic Judaism** and **Islam**. Throughout time, all of three of these religious groups have controlled **Jerusalem**. Throughout time Edom's seed has mixed with Mediterranean Europeans, African Hamites, and Arab Ishmaelites. This is in the scriptures.

(**Above**) "**The Kuzari**" by 12th Century (1080-1141 A.D.) Sephardic Jew Yehudah HaLevi and "**The Roman Empire, The Empire of the Edomite (1853)**" by William Beeston. Edom mixed with people of Rome (Italy) aka "**The Holy Roman Empire (Catholism)**" and he mixed with the **Arab Ishmaelites (Islam)**. Edomites (Haddad) also had children (i.e. Genubath) with Hamitic Egyptians and Canaanites. Edomite "converted" Jews also mixed with the Greeks and Syrians during the era of the Maccabees. They also were the ones who "introduced" **Babylonian Talmudic (Judaism)** to the Japhetic "**Khazar**" Kingdom during the 8th Century A.D. in Europe/South Russia. These are the major 3 religions influencing the world today and they all have pagan ties to Egypt...but also "**Satan/Lucifer**".

Once you dive deep into the history of the **Khazari** (Kuzari – Khazars-Ashkenazi Jews) and the Hebrew **Book of Jasher** you will see that **Esau's (Edom's) bloodline** has been oppressing Black "Bantus" African Israelites, the Native Indians of the New World-Caribbean and other Israelites scattered all across the globe. But it gets even deeper than that!

Here is an excerpt from this 11th Century Jewish convert name **Yehuda HaLevi:**

"The king and his vizier travelled to the deserted mountains on the seashore, and arrived one night at the cave in which some Jews used to celebrate the Sabbath. **They disclosed their identity to them, embraced their religion, were circumcised in the cave, and then returned to their country, eager to learn the Jewish law.** They kept their conversion secret, however until they found an opportunity of disclosing the fact gradually to a few of their special friends. When the number had increased, they made the affair public, **and induced the rest of the Khazars to embrace the Jewish faith.** They sent to various countries for scholars and books, and studied the Torah. Their chronicles also tell of their prosperity, how they beat their foes, conquered their lands, secured great treasures, how their army swelled to hundreds of thousands, how they loved their faith, and fostered such love for the Holy House that they erected a tabernacle in the shape of that built by Moses. They also honored and cherished the Israelites who lived among them." - *The Kuzari – Yehuda HaLevi*

So, I know you might be wondering, "Who were those people living in the cave that were practicing the Sabbath and why did the Khazars call them "Israelites?" Well from the time the Assyrian Kings took the Israelites out of Israel, replacing Israel with other people. Therefore, the land of the Israelites continued to be colonized by the "**Gentiles**". The Greeks and Edomites spent a lot of time colonizing Israel from 330 B.C. until the Roman "Byzantines" took over in 70 A.D. These Samaritans and Gentiles that Yahusha (Jesus) talked about in the New Testament fought hard during the "**Roman-Jewish Wars**" to save Jerusalem but eventually were finally driven out after the "**Battle of Masada**". Many of those Jews that fought during the Battle of Masada to save Judea were of **Edomite origin** but were sometimes regarded as "Israelites". Therefore, many Edomite Jews and perhaps Greek Jews converted the pagan Khazars to Judaism while in Europe.

671

Strabo, a Greek historian who died around 23 A.D., when Christ was alive wrote that the Idumeans (Edomites) **whom he identified as of Nabataean origin (Arab)**, constituted the majority of the population of Western Judea, where they commingled with the Judeans and adopted their customs. In Genesis 36, it lists the Kings of Edom each after their "**clan**", which is a common term used in the Arab world. The Hebrew word for "clan" is "**alluph**" from Hebrew Strong's word #441b. The word "**Clans**," or "**Dukes**" were used back then to describe the Edomites and Moabites. These titles of "**Dukes**" are used today in the **British Royal Family** (Duke) and the **Arabs (Clan)**. The Gentile Jews of mixed Edomite-Greek-Roman stock, whom the Book of Maccabees often calls "**Israelites**" eventually migrated back into Europe, from which they were from (**i.e. Romaniote Jews, Sephardic Jews, Turkish Jews**). These white Gentile "converted" Jews did not all venture into Africa; if that were so we would have seen thousands of White Jews returning back to Israel in 1948 from Africa. Below the Saharan Desert, the majority of people were black. The Khazarian King simply ran into Samaritans, mixed Edomites and Greek "converted" Jews living in these caves.

BUT WHAT ABOUT ESAU/EDOM? WHO WAS EDOM?

The country which was given originally to Esau and his seed was called the "**Country of Edom**" or the "**Land of Seir**" (Genesis 32:3). This is because this country/territory before had been called "Mount Seir". According to Flavius Josephus in his "**Antiquities**" the name "**Seir**" was due to the fact that Esau was hairy, but according to Genesis 14:6 this area was called "**Mount Seir**" prior to Esau's birth when the Horites lived there.

Genesis 14:6 "And the Horites in their Mount Seir, unto El-paran, which is by the wilderness. "

The boundaries of Edom stretched to the west along the route followed by the Israelites from the Sinai Peninsula (Plains of Paran) in the "wilderness" to Kadesh, southward as far as the city "Elath/Eliath" and "Ezion-geber", which was the seaport of Edom, northwards toward the territory of Moab (ex. the brook Zered was the boundary separating Edom and Moab) to the East where the "**Nabatu (Nabataean) Tribes**" were in Arabia. People like to say that the Hebrew Israelites were made up by the Greeks but little do they know that the Egyptians wrote about the "**Hebrews**" as well as "**Edom**".

Here are some examples:

- In **Thebes, Egypt** a Papyrus was found dating back to 1900 B.C. in regards to the Biography of Sinuhe in which he talks about Esau's son "**Jeush**" who was a "**Chief/Duke**". On lines 219-220 it reads:

  "Prince of Meki from the East (Qedem), Jeush the mountain chiefs from Edom (Kushu), Menus from the lands of Phoenicia (Fenkhu)."

  It is currently in the Berlin Museum.

  This correlates to the Bible: **Genesis 36:18** "And these are the sons of Aholibamah Esau's wife; **Duke Jeush**, duke Jaalam, duke Korah: these were the dukes that came of Aholibamah the daughter of Anah, Esau's wife."

- In Iraq (ancient day Assyria) a clay inscription was found dating back to 732 B.C. in which Assyrian King Tiglath-Pileser III received a tribute from King Ahaz of Judah, Ammon, Moab and **Edom**. On lines 56-63 it reads:

673

"I received the tribute of Sanipu of Ammon, Salamanu of Moab, Mitinti of Ashkelon, Ahaz of Judah, **Kaush-malaku of Edom**, Hanno of Gaza: gold, silver, tin, iron, multicolored linen, native costly objects of sea or land, the choice treasures of their kings, horses, mules trained for the yoke... from Metenna of Tyre 150 talents of gold."

This is supported in the Greek Septuagint version of **Kings IV 16:5-18**, King James **2 Kings 16:5-18**, and **2 Chronicles 28:19-22**.

- In El-Hiba, Egypt a Papyrus manuscript dating back to 1000 B.C. was found written in **Egyptian hieroglyphics** depicting what biblical archaeologists believe was **Hadad the Edomite** in 1 Kings 14-22. In it reads:

"If only I had sent him off to Nahrin (Syria) in order to fetch the hidden "tmrgn" (aka a gemstone/guide)" he would then have gone to the "people of Seir (Edomites) and he would have returned to us again. Would that he had reached my people "sbtyw" (i.e Edomites)".

This writing implies that perhaps "**Hadad**" the Edomite left some other "**Edomites**" in Egypt when he left. Perhaps these "left-over" Edomites in Egypt were hoping their "Edomite Prince" (Hadad) would return. **This Papyrus sits today in the Pushkin Museum in Moscow, Russia.** Below is a summary of why Haddad the Edomite came to Egypt and then why he left.

In **I Kings 11**, it describes how the Edomite males were being killed off by King David and Joab because the Edomites were causing problems for Israel. Hadad the Edomite fled into Egypt as a child with other Edomite servants to avoid the massacre by King David. During this time Hadad the Edomite grew up in Egypt to a man. The Pharaoh of

Egypt was so pleased with Hadad that he gave him land, money and the sister of his own wife to marry, thus Edomite-Egyptian children **(i.e. a son Genubath)** were born. But eventually Hadad the Edomite wanted to go back to his land when he found out that King David and Joab were dead. Hadad the Edomite went back to become an adversary again to Israel, this time with King Solomon. But at that time Rezin the King of Syria (Damascus) was also new adversary of Israel (King Solomon), who had control of part of the Edomite territory of Elath/Ezion-geber (the seaport of King Solomon).

- **1 Kings 11:14** "And the Lord stirred up an **adversary** unto Solomon, Hadad the Edomite: he was of the King's seed in Edom."

- **1 Kings 11:21** "And when Hadad heard in Egypt that David slept with his fathers (buried), and that Joab the captain of the host was dead, **Hadad said to Pharaoh, Let me depart, that I may go to mine own country** (also some texts reads "Send me away")."

- In Nineveh, Iraq (Capital of Ancient Assyria) the Palace of King Sennacherib's son "Esarhaddon", King of Assyria from 680 B.C.-669 B.C. the Manasseh King of Judah Prism depicts the King of Judah, **King of Edom** and other nations. It dates back to 673 B.C. and sits in the British Museum. It reads:

"I called up 22 Kings of the Hatti-land: Ba'lu, King of Tyre, Manasseh (Me-na-si-i) King of Judah (Ia-u-di), <u>**Quashgabri King of Edom**</u>, Musuri King of Moab, Sil-Bel King of Gaza, Mentinti King of Ashkelon, Ikausu King of Ammon, Ahimilki King of Ashdod...all these I made transport building material for my palace under terrible difficulties to my capital city of Nineveh."

So clearly, we can see extra-biblical archaeological proof that the **Kings of Judah** and **Kings of Edom existed**. We have hard tangible evidence of their existence on Manuscripts, Papyrus, and Hexagonal prisms from the Middle East/Egypt. But who is Edom today? Where did Edom go. What proof outside of the Hebrew Bible do we have to track Edom's whereabouts or what nation of people did they mix their bloodline with. It sure wasn't Sub-Saharan Africa, Asia or the New World (Americas), where the Real Hebrew Israelites were already scattered into. Let's look.

(**Above**) In Ancient Pagan Mythology, Nimrod was synonymous with the masculine "**Sun God**". The Catholic Church is linked to "**Sun Worship**" as Roman Emperor Constantine declared "**SUN**-day" as the day of worship for Christians and the aerial view of St. Peter's square in the Vatican is the symbol of **Shamash**, the Babylonian "**Sun God**". **Semiramis**, the wife of Nimrod was synonymous with the feminine "**Moon God**"…heralded by her symbol the "**crescent moon**". In Islam, "**Sin**" and "**Hubal**" were the major Moon Gods that rose to the title of "**The God**" by the Arabs which was pronounced "**Al-ilah**" or "**Al-lah**" or "**Allah**". The Roman Julian and Gregorian calendar which we use today is based on the **Sun**. The Islamic calendar Muslims use today is based on the **Moon (Lunar)**. The Hebrew Israelite calendar is "**Solar-Lunar**". The offspring "child" of the Catholic Church combined with Islam will be the Biblical "**Antichrist**". This is why Pope Francis is trying hard to form "**Chris-Lam**" in which Islam and Christianity are viewed as the same. The European Jews are simple a "**smokescreen**" for the world, as no group of people could carry the task of building the Third Temple for the Antichrist except a "**people**" who claim to be "**God's Chosen People**" and a "**people**" who worship in synagogues.

Revelation 2:9 "I know thy works, and tribulation, and poverty, (but thou are rich) and I know the blasphemy of them which **say they are Jews, and are not**, but are the **Synagogue of Satan.**"

2 Esdras 6:9 "For **Esau** is the end of the age (world), and **Jacob** is the beginning of the one that follows."

So, who is controlling the world in these last days of wickedness and sexual immorality? Is it **Edom**? Or is it **Rome**? Is it the **Vatican, ISRAEL** and the **United States**? Or is it **Moslem Freemasons** who worship "**Allah**".

The Book of **2 Esdras** is accepted as Scripture by the Roman Catholic and Orthodox Church, but is rejected by Protestants like Protestant Reformation founder "**Martin Luther**". 1st and 2 Esdras is traditionally referred to as the Book of Ezra and Nehemiah which whom "**Ezra**" from B.C. times is the author. 2 Esdras is believed to be the work of Greeks, Christians and multiple authors written perhaps as late as 100 A.D. to 200 A.D. 2 Esdras is not written in **Paleo-Hebrew** and it was written two late to be included in the **Greek Koine Septuagint Bible**. Therefore it is only seen in the **Latin Vulgate Bible**. Some believe 2 Esdras was written shortly after the destruction of the 2nd Temple in Jerusalem in 70 A.D. or during the reign of roman Emperor Domitian (81 A.D. to 96 A.D.).

So, 2 Esdras says "Edom" would be the end of the world. Did the Greeks, Romans and other nations living in the 1st-2nd Century A.D. foresee the "**destructive**" nature of the Edomites they were living amongst? Did they see "**Edomite dominance**" being spread throughout Europe, North Africa and Arabia? The **Book of Obadiah** gives some hints to who Edom is…then and now.

Obadiah 1:4-6 "Though thou exalt thyself **AS THE EAGLE**, and though thou set thy nest among the stars, thence will I bring thee down, saith the Lord. If thieves came to thee, if robbers by night, (how art thou cut off!) would they not have stolen till they had enough? If the grape gatherers came to thee, would they not leave some grapes? **HOW ARE THE THINGS OF ESAU** searched out! How are his hidden things sought up!

(**Above**) **North Arabia** was the territory of the Arab Ishmaelites and the Edomites that mixed with them in the **Nabataean Kingdom**. Rome also conquered the Nabataen Kingdom. South Arabia consisted of Arabs as well as the **Shemitic sons of Joktan (Yoqtan)** and the **Hamitic Cushite Empire**. Around 100 A.D. the Romans under **Emperor Trajan** took control of the Nabataen Kingdom and renamed it "**Arabia Petrea**".

In the bible Edom mixed with the daughter of Ishmael (Basemath)...who was the sister of **Nebaioth/Nabaioth** (Genesis 36:3). Therefore, Edom married the female lineage of the **Nabataean Arabs** in Arabia. From Arabia would come Islam....however Islam is a **"false"** religion that has deceived many "Hebrew Israelites" into "conversion" (i.e. Africa, America). But let's prove how this is really a "deception".

1. **Abraham** was the Grandfather of Israel (Jacob), and father of the **"Hebrews."**

2. Abraham had Isaac, who had Jacob. From Jacob and his descendants came the "Prophethood" lineage. If Muhammad was truly the last prophet sent by God to mankind, this would mean that Muhammad was an Israelite. We know that Muhammad was **NOT** an Israelite. The Israelites were the **ONLY** Prophets of the Bible. Ishmael and Keturah's sons were **NOT PROPHETS**. Even in the Quran Allah states that **"Prophethood"** was **NOT** given to Ishmael and his descendants.

   Quran 28:27 "And we gave to him Isaac and Jacob and placed in his descendants (The Israelites) PROPHETHOOD AND SCRIPTURE.

3. Allah was considered the **ONLY DEITY**, Creator of the Universe and omnipotent, however in the Quran in **Sura 23:14** it states that **"Allah is the BEST OF CREATORS."** The word **"Creators"** is plural which means that there is more than one god and one creator. In the Quran in Sura 3:54 and 8:30 it says that **"Allah is the best of deceivers"**. Some versions will say **"Allah is the best of planners"**. But in the Arabic version Allah refers to himself as **"Khayrul-Makereen"** which correctly translated means "Allah is the greatest of deceivers." This is verified by looking up the root letters **Meem, Kaaf, Makr and Rah** which point to the meaning **"deceive"**. Even in the work called **"Successors of**

the Messenger" by Khalid Muhammad Khalid, p. 70 he talks about this "deception" from his God weeping saying: **"By Allah! I would not feel safe from the DECEPTION (same Arabic word) of Allah, even if I had one foot in paradise."**

Even in **Sura 7:99** the Pickthall, Shakir, Asad, Yusuf Ali, Sahih International, and Dr. Ghali versions of this verse cannot choose between using the word scheming, devising, or planning.

Pickthall Version Sura 7:99 "Are they then secure from Allah's **SCHEME**? None deemeth himself secure from Allah's **SCHEME** save folk that perish."

Nevertheless, in the Quran if it says "**Planners**" or "**Deceivers**" this implies that there is more than one person operating as a God in heaven. The letter "**s**" added to deceive or planner makes it plural, meaning that there is more than one person. There is no "**Trinity**" or "**Godhead**" in Islam and the Quran states God cannot have children. So who is 2nd and 3rd place on the "**Creation Level-contest**"? Marvel Superheroes are put into classes based on their Superpowers but the Bible and the Quran are not Marvel Comic Books.

4. The **Quran** says God cannot have a **child** (son or daughter). But in Islam, Allah has three daughters whom are "**Goddesses**". They are **Al-Lat, Al-Uzza** and **Manat**. Muslims don't view them as pagan deities but Muhammad himself commanded his followers to offer prayers (**intercession**) to these Daughters of his in the "**Revealed Quran**". He later retracted this statement and blamed it on the Devil. (**Note: This was also done by Joseph Smith, founder of the Mormons in regards to polygamy.**) But here are the original verses including the verse that tells Muslims to worship these goddesses Muhammad said was incorrectly given to him by the Satan/Devil. This verse was

680

deleted from the Quran in later versions: See below the "**Satanic Verses**" and the Sura verse in the Quran in which this "**error**" was blamed on Satan.

Satanic Verses

Sura 53:15-22 "Near it is the Garden of Abode. Behold, the Lote-tree was shrouded (in mystery unspeakable!) (His) sight never swerved, nor did it go wrong! For truly did he see, of the Signs of his Lord, the Greatest! Have ye seen Lat, and Uzza, and another, the third goddess, Manat? **These are the exalted cranes (intermediaries) Whose intercession (prayers-worship) is to be hoped for (*Deleted Verse*).** What! For you the male sex, and for Him, the female? Behold, such would be indeed a division most unfair!"

Sura 22:52 "And we did not send before you any messenger or prophet except that when he spoke (or recited), Satan threw into it some misunderstanding. **But Allah abolishes (gets rid of) that which Satan throws in (i.e. satanic verse)**; then Allah makes precise his verses. And Allah is Knowing and Wise."

In the Quran it states that Allah does not have a son, daughters or a wife (partner). So how can Allah have three daughters in the Quran? This Sura is still in the Quran till this day with Allah's three goddess daughters "**Al-lat**", "**Al-Uzza**" and "**Al-manat**". This shows that "Allah" is **NOT ALL KNOWING** or that "Allah" is even a god.

Sura 17:111 (Yusuf Ali) "Say: Praise be to Allah, **who begets no son, and has no partner (wife) in his dominion**: Nor needs he any to protect him from humiliation: yea, magnify him for his greatness and glory!"

To apologize for asking Muslims to worship and pray to his three daughters in Sura 53:19-22 (which contradicts Sura 17:111), Muhammad blamed this scripture/Quranic verse on **Satan** deceiving him. True prophets of the creator cannot be deceived by Satan....and especially allow "**satanic verses**" to be included in a so-called "**Holy Book**" inspired by God.

WHAT ABOUT EDOM'S AND ISLAMS CONNECTION TO EUROPEN PANTHEONS?

(**Left**) **On the chariot is Cybele,** the "**Mother Goddess**" of the Anatolians, Greeks and Romans. Cybele predates **Islam** by 1,000 years. As you can see the **Crescent Moon and Star** is pagan.......also used by the Abyssinians in the Temple of Yeha dating back as far as 700 B.C. (1300 years prior to Muhammad's birth. (**Right**) **Artemis** was the Greek goddess of the **Moon** and her **Roman "Byzantine"** equivalent was "**Diana**" **the Moon goddess**, as depicted on the ancient coins of Rome (**Above**). So if the Romans were worshipping-using the "crescent moon" and "star" prior to Islam, where did the Arab Muslims get their "**Crescent Moon and Star**" symbol from? Could it be the Roman Catholic Church? This is what many people believe.

Allah's three daughter's **Al-Lat, Al-Uzza** and **Al-Manat** are all goddesses associated with the **phases of the moon**. This was before the religion of Islam even existed. Therefore, we see that the "crescent moon and star" has been pagan and Satanic for a very long time.

In the Bible, the goddess "**Ashtoreth**", seen in **1 Kings 11:5** was one of the main goddess the many nations built "**groves**" or "**obelisks**" for. Today these Obelisks can be seen in Rome, Washington D.C, London City and Egypt. The Babylonian goddess Ishtar, the Islamic goddess

Al-lah, and the American goddess "**Columbia** (*the name given to America by Freemasons worshipping the Illuminati goddess*) are all examples of pagan worship. The first national anthem of the United states was "Hail Columbia".

Crescent Moon and star flag of Islam

The "**Star**" seen in Islam refers to the star, "**Sirius**", which is the most significant star in **Satanism**! It is sacred to the Egyptian god, "**Set**" who was once co-ruler of Egypt and the God of the Tamahu (*i.e. "created white*) people. In the occult world "Set" is associated with Satan.

"Pre-Islamic worship of goddesses by the Sabaeans, the Nabataeans (capital is Petra), and the Edomites were primarily associated with Al'Lat, which simply means 'the goddess' as Al-Lah means "The God".

The Arabic word "**al**" prefixes Arabic nouns.   The Akkadian-Babylonian word "**ilu**" means "**god/deity**", similar to "**El**" meaning "god" in Ancient Hebrew/Phoenician and "**Elah/ilah**" meaning "god" in Aramaic (the precursor language for Arabic).

- *Al-lat = "the goddess"*

- *Al-lah = "the god"*
- *Al-uzza = "the mighty one"*
- *Al-manat = "the fate"*
- *Al-majisti = "the greatest"*
- *Al-akhdar = "the green one"*

As you can see from above, the name "Allah" means "the god". This is "**ambiguous**" and "**deceptive**". All gods have names.

The word "**ambiguous**" is defined as: *unclear or inexact because a choice between alternatives has not been made.*

Herodotus says of the Arabs: "**They deem no other to be gods save Dionysus and Heavenly Aphrodite ... they call Dionysus Orotalt and Aphrodite Alilat**" (Negev 101).

In Sumeria "**Allatu**" or "**the goddess**" is an epithet of Ereshkigal the goddess of the underworld. Like **El** and **al-lah** which simply means "**god**" and "**the god**" respectively, "al-Lat" (the goddess) is identified with many female deities, such as **Aphrodite, Venus, Isis and Ishtar**. It is believed that when Al-lat became the goddess of the Nabatean Arabs, she became "**Al-Uzza**", the "**mighty one**". During this time the Nabateans/Edomites conducted human sacrifices to "**Al-Uzza**". In Nabatean mythology, it is believed that she gave birth to **Dhu-shara** (Lord of Shara Mountain), in which she had a temple dedicated to him/her in Petra, Jordan (*Edom territory*). **Dhu-Shara** was the ancient aniconic deity worshipped by the **Edomites** (*along with Qos-Allah*), and by the Arabians of Nabatea (*thanks to co-mixing*) in just the way Jacob worshipped and erected a stone at Bethel. The Nabataeans were pagans and worshipped many deities depicted mostly as stone idols instead of human idols. The believed that their deities had "**special powers**" and created altars, steles (obelisks) and **stone cube monuments** as "houses" for their pagan gods. They also made stone "Pyramids" with steps at the base to worship their pagan gods. Uncut three cubic stones or "**Baityls**" signified **Dhu-Shara** on coinage from **Petraea-Bostra**. Now, follow this:

1. **Dhu-Shara** was frequently worshipped as an uncut stone cube or **Ka'aba...like the Muslim Arabs**.

2. **Dhu-Shara** supposedly was linked to "**Zeus/Dionysus**" and was worshipped by the **Nabataeans/Edomites** at the "**Qasr el-Bint Faroun**" temple (Petra, Jordan) with a gigantic altar where he was symbolized by a "**Black Stone**".....like the Black "**Kaaba**" cube Muslims worship today.

3. Herodotus says of the Arabs: "**They deem no other to be gods save Dionysus and Heavenly Aphrodite ... they call Dionysus Orotalt and Aphrodite Alilat**" (Negev 101). The **Crescent Moon** is and **Black Cube** was linked to these two pagan Greek-Roman deities before Muhammad was born.

(**Above**) Horned stele with **Qos-allah**, a seal attributed to the Edomite lunar deity "**Qos/Qaush**". The stele is dedicated to **Qos-allah**... '**Qos is Allah**' or '**Qos the god**', by Qosmilk (melech - king) is found at Petra (Jordan). Qos is identifiable with Kaush (**Qaush**) the pagan god of the older Edomites. The Edomite seal near Petra identified with Kaush/Qaush displays "**a star and a crescent moon (like Islam)**, both consistent with a **moon deity**. In the above picture (**bottom left**) is a "**djinn block**" which is believed to house Arabic pagan spirit-gods. Djinn Blocks, were dedicated to the Pre-Islamic Arabian pagan gods and were the locations of tombs for the Nabateans Arabs. Djinn blocks are different than "god blocks" (baetyls) being that baetyls were worship stones (Cubes) that represented pagan gods....like Al-Lat, Al-Uzza, Al-Manat, Dhu-Shara, Qos-Allah and later "**Allah**

Note: *The Ancient temple dedicated to the pagan god "Al-Uzza" had the sacred color "Green".....which is also the sacred color of Islam. This can be observed simply by looking at the Mecca Clock at night in Saudi Arabia.*

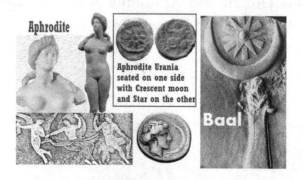

If the Greek goddess of Love "**Aphrodite**" and the Canaanite god "**Baal**" was associated with the Crescent Moon and Star centuries prior to Islam then who influenced "**Islam**"? Satan is very crafty. The names of pagan gods change all throughout history but the worship still goes to Satan.

Baal

(**Above**) The symbol for the pagan god "**Baal**" was a "**crescent moon and star**" and also a "**thunderbolt**". The symbol for Islam is a "**crescent moon and star**". This symbol is seen on every Islamic mosque from the Middle East, Asia Minor, North Africa to America. Coincidence?

Fact: A reconstructed "**Altar to Baal**" from Palmyra, Syria was unveiled in London, England, New York, NY and Dubai, United Arab Emirates. The "**Altar or Arch to Baal**" was used at the World Government Summit Meeting in Dubai to welcome participants who are interested in creating a "**One Antichrist World Government**". 4,000 world leaders from 130 different countries attended this even from February 12-14th, 2017. To understand how serious this is, consider this:

The original "**Arch of Baal**" or "**Roman Victory Arch**" stood for almost 2,000 years in Palmyra, Syria until it was destroyed by **ISIS** in 2015. A 28-foot replica was created by Oxford and Harvard Universities. Now when Jacob left for Padan-Aram (Syria), Esau realized his parents did not approve of his marriages to the Canaanite women. So Esau (Edom) found a wife from Ishmael's seed, forming an alliance with the **Arabs**. The Edomites, Ishmaelites/Hagarenes would form an "**alliance**" to come against Israel according to the Bible. Shortly after this, **Zepho**, the grandson of Edom (*by way of his son Eliphaz*) made an alliance with the **Romans**. Zepho was kin to Amalek.

Psalms 83:3-6 "They have taken crafty counsel against **THY PEOPLE (ISRAELITES)**, and consulted against thy hidden ones. They have said, Come, and let us cut them off from being a nation; that the name of Israel may be no more in remembrance. For they have consulted together with one consent: they are confederate against thee: The tabernacles of **Edom**, and the **Ishmaelites (Arabs)**; of Moab, and the Hagarenes (**Arabs**);"

Many of the "**Gentile European Judaism-convert Jews**" see this "**United Nations World Government**" honoring "**Baal**" with the Arabs in Dubai (United Arab Emirates) as "**Esau Rising**" and the emergence of the "**Antichrist Beast System**". But what is really going to come out of this? We know for centuries the European Jews (*including Catholic Europeans*) and the Arabs were the main ones that participated in the selling of "**Black Hebrew Israelite Slaves**". Today, even though slavery is "illegal" in America....the Jews and Arabs still have Blacks in America "enslaved" with their "economic position of power". We are still "enslaved" or in "bondage" to these nations in America as the ancient Israelites were in bondage to the Egyptians before the Biblical Exodus. That is.....until the Hebrew Israelites under the leadership of "Moses" started to WAKE UP! This is what is happening now..... and pretty soon, there will be another "**LET MY PEOPLE GO**" event where "**God's Chosen People**" or "**Elect**" will "**Come up out of her**" just before God's Wrath is poured upon the nations on earth.

CHAPTER 29

DOES THE BIBLE WARN US OF THE ISLAMIC ANTICHRIST BEAST SYSTEM?

Many African-Americans and Bantus Africans are "**blindly**" following Islam not knowing it's connection to Satan. Islam is the only major religion where "God" doesn't have a name. The Fallen Angels had names in the Book of Enoch. The Egyptian gods had names. The Roman, Greek, Assyrian, Babylonian, Cushite, Canaanite, Moabite, Ammonite, Edomite, Persian, and even Hindoo (Indian) people had names for their pagan gods. Muslims do not have a name for their "Creator". "Allah" simply means "the god". This is highly "suspicious" when you really think about it. Unlike the Paleo-Hebrew tetragrammaton name "Yahuah (Yahuwa)" which has a "**hidden messianic meaning**", the word "Allah" has no significant meaning. Muslims defend Islam by saying that the Quran is the "**word of god**" and that the bible cannot be trusted as they say that it has been tampered with. Islam right now is the most "newest" religion but yet it has attracted millions of followers. We know that Satan desires to be like the "Most High" as this is quoted in scripture (Isaiah 14:14). So, if you were Satan, what would you do as a "**final last attempt**" to confuse humanity into a false religion after Christianity was established? Simple, you use the very "Bible" that God "inspired" through the writings of Israelite prophets to come up with a "copy-cat" false religion. But think about it. If the Most High gave mankind the Old Testament and New Testament, why would there be a need for another book with "**contrary instructions**" to the one the Most High has given? Somebody who wants to "**copy**" something has to have the "**original**" in order to make that copy. This has always been the case for "pagan religions" all throughout history. For example, can a person counterfeit money without seeing or knowing about the original money to be counterfeited? Well, this applies to Islam whose Quran wasn't even in existence until 600 years after the completion of the New Testament and 1,000 years after the last book of the Old Testament was finished around 400 B.C.

Note: Saying the Quran is "True" and the Bible is "False" is impossible…..because like the Quran, a "counterfeit" book cannot exist without having first an "original book" that is "True". This "Book of Truth" is the Bible. The "Book of Lies" is the Quran. A counterfeit dollar bill should be almost "identical" to the "original" dollar bill. But this is not the case in the Quran. In the Quran, God tells Abraham to sacrifice Ishmael. In the Hebrew Torah written in Ancient Paleo-Hebrew *(which predates the Arabic language by over 2,000 years)* and the Ethiopic "Torah", God tells Abraham to sacrifice Isaac. In the Hebrew Torah, all of Noah's three sons survives the Great Flood. In the Islamic Quran, one of Noah's three sons dies in the flood *(see Sura 11:42-43)*.

Here is where it gets deep!

Muslims say Muhammed did in fact give "pin-point" prophecies which came to past. Well, there are certain individuals or things that have **"predicted"** certain things that come to past, like Nostradamus, the Illuminati or the Simpsons cartoons *(i.e. Prince's death, 9/11, Bruce Jenner becoming a Transgender, Trump becoming President, Economic Collapse of Greece, Ebola outbreak, Siegfried and Roy tiger attack, NSA scandal, Horse meat in food scandal, 2016 Nobel Prize winner)*. But is the Simpsons producer, Nostradamus or the Illuminati Card founder "**prophets of the Most High**"? Of course not. In the 2015 movie "Mission Impossible: Rogue Nation" the "Syndicate" is an international crime organization that causes "negative world events" to happen. But consider this. When a person or a group of evil people work with Satan and his fallen angels "directly" they can safely say that something is going to happen in the future if "Satan" or his henchmen influence this "future event" to happen. If this "**future event**" is not in "**God's Will**" it **WILL NOT** happen. Remember the story of Job in the Bible? The

Most High allowed Satan to do all the bad things to Job. So throughout the good and the bad….God's will is always done! Now this is the "Perfect Plan".

Job 1:8-12 "And the LORD said unto Satan, Hast thou considered my servant Job, that there is none like him in the earth, a perfect and an upright man, one that feareth God, and escheweth evil? Then Satan answered the LORD, and said, Doth Job fear God for nought? Hast not thou made an hedge about him, and about his house, and about all that he hath on every side? thou hast blessed the work of his hands, and his substance is increased in the land. **But put forth thine hand now, and touch all that he hath, and he will curse thee to thy face. And the LORD said unto Satan, Behold, all that he hath is in thy power; only upon himself put not forth thine hand**. So Satan went forth from the presence of the LORD."

Isaiah 45:5-7 "I am the LORD, and there is no other; Besides Me there is no God (i.e no Allah), I will gird (surround) you, though you have not known Me; That men may know from the rising to the setting of the sun that That there is no one besides Me. I am the LORD, and there is no other. **The One forming light and creating darkness, Causing well-being and creating calamity; I am the LORD who does all these."**

With all this **POWER** the Most High has, the Most High didn't tell the Israelite prophets to tell the rest of the Israelites to "**force**" all of the world to submit to "**Law of Moses-Torah**". Islam forces people to submit to "**Allah**" and "**Islam**". Forcing mankind to accept a false god or face "**decapitation**" is not of God. The Bible allows us to "freely" choose to worship Christ the Messiah….Islam doesn't. Islam is a religion of "**Force**" and it teaches "**forced**" submission to "**Allah-Sharia Law**". In the Book of Revelation, the people of the Earth are going to be slowly "**trained**" to accept the "Mark of the Beast" system so that choosing between the Antichrist "**Mark of the Beast**" or food will be an easy task. Most people love the things of this world and how their lives are. Because of this most people on earth are **"comfortable"**, **"lost"** and **"unprepared"**.

Matthew 10:39 "He that findeth his life shall lose it: and **he that loseth his life for my sake shall find it.**"

(Left) The **"Proto-Freemasons"** were called originally **"Knights Templar** (i.e. *Caucasians in white robes pictured looking up at the Satanic Baphomet figure in the air*). The Freemasons today at the "highest levels" practice Luciferianism-Islam. Their god is Lucifer-Allah. 33rd Degree Scottish Rite Grandmaster Freemason **"Albert Pike"** acknowledged this in his book "Morals and Dogma". So, if Islam is not Satanic, then why do we have satanic, evil people with "hidden practices" and "hidden symbols" all connected to calling on the name of god "Allah"?

Fact or Fiction? *In the 1861 Book, "**Life of Mahomet**" it describes followers of Islam as "**Mahometans**". Some believe the word "**Mahomet**" like the Satanic Goat Figure "**Baphomet**" is simply a "French" corruption of the word Muslims know today as "**Mohammed/Muhammed**". Because of this, some will link Muhammed to the Satanic Baphomet.*

Revelation 20:4

And I saw thrones, and they sat upon them, and judgment was given unto them: and I saw the souls of them that were beheaded for the witness of **Yahusha** (Jesus), and for the word of God, and **which had not worshipped the beast, neither his image, neither had received his mark upon their foreheads, or in their hands**; and they lived and reigned with Christ a thousand years."

Did John in his vision foresee the rising of the "**Islamic Antichrist**" in alliance with the **Holy Roman Empire**.....and with it the "**beheading**" of those "**Holy Ones/Saints**" who refused to worship "**Allah**"?

In the Quran in **Sura 8:39** (Sahih International) it reads "**And fight them until there is no fitnah (persecution) and until the religion, ALL OF IT, is for Allah, and if they cease – then indeed, Allah is Seeing of what they do.**"

Both the Roman (*Edom-mixed*) Catholic Church and Islamic (Edom) religions believe in using **FORCE** to "**convert**" or impose their will to the unbelievers (*i.e. Spanish Inquisition, The Crusades*). The "**Syllabus of Errors**" says that it is an error to say that the "Church" cannot use force. The Quran says to fight against and **SLAY OR KILL** those who refuse to convert to **ISLAM**.

Sura 2:191 (Sahih International) "And **KILL THEM** wherever you overtake them and expel them wherever they have expelled you, and fitnah (persecution) is worse than killing. And do not fight them at al-Masjid al-Haram (Inviolable Place of Worship) until they fight you there. **But if they fight you, then kill them. Such is the recompense of the disbelievers.**"

Sura 47:4 (Sahih International) "So when you meet those who **disbelieve** in battle, **strike (cut) their necks** until, when you have inflicted slaughter upon them, then secure their bonds, and either confer favor afterwards or ransom them until the war lays down its burdens. That is the command. **And if Allah had willed** (*the Most High "wills" and it is done, for Allah it is the exact opposite*), **He would have taken vengeance upon them himself,** but he ordered armed struggle to test some of you by means of others. And those who are killed in the cause of Allah – never will he waste their deeds."

Note: Allah never takes vengeance upon man himself like "**The Most High-Yahuah**" does in the Old Testament with "**The Great Flood**" or with "**Fire and Brimstone**" in Sodom and Gomorrah. Even in the Quran it is Christ (Yahusha) and **NOT ALLAH** or the prophet Muhammad that defeats the Antichrist (Dajjal) for mankind and lays down "**Judgement**". Also, it is important to understand why "Muhammad" was not a Prophet and why "Allah" is a pagan god rooted in Satanism.

The Quran that Muslims read acknowledges that only the Hebrew Israelites were to be the progenitors of the "Prophets" sent from God to mankind. Muhammad according to Islamic history was a descendant of "Ishmael".

Sura 29:27 (Noble Quran) Al-Ankabut

"And We gave to Him **ISAAC** and **JACOB (NOT ISHMAEL)** and placed in his descendants prophethood and scripture. And We gave

694

him his reward in this world, and indeed, he is in the Hereafter among the righteous."

Muhammad **did not**, receive any message from the mouth of God and therefore he **was not** a prophet of God. He was **NOT** the last prophet sent to the planet earth by the Most High (Yahuah/Yahuwa). Christ tells us to beware of those that say they are Prophets **AFTER HIM**. The Bible makes it clear that Christ **FORETOLD US EVERYTHING**.

For this reason, there was no need for Muhammad or Allah. The Bible already told us "**everything**" to look out for.

A prophet "foretells" the future from the words of God.

Mark 13:21-23 (Words of Christ) "And then if any say to you: Behold there is the Christ, or: Behold here, be not believing. But false Christs and **FALSE PROPHETS** will arise and will make signs and wonders in order to be deceiving if possible, the chosen. But you be looking; **I HAVE FORETOLD YOU EVERYTHING**".

This statement foretells that many deceptive false prophets will follow after Christ. In Mark 13, Christ does not foretell the coming of any later true prophets like Muhammad, **for there is nothing more for a prophet to foretell after the death, burial and resurrection of Yahusha HaMashiach (Jesus Christ).**

Hebrews 1:1-3 "Long ago, at many times and in many ways, God spoke to our fathers by the prophets, but in these last days he has spoken to us by his Son (Christ), whom he (the Creator/Father) appointed the **HEIR OF ALL THINGS**, through whom he (Christ) **CREATED THE WORLD**. He is the radiance of the glory of God and the exact imprint of his nature, and he upholds the universe by the word of his power.   After making **PURIFICATION OF SINS** (Atonement), he sat down at the right hand of the Majesty on High."

Hebrews 1:1-3 shows that Christ and the Creator (Father) are **ONE**, being that through Christ the world was created and he is the **HEIR OF ALL THINGS**. The Father came to Earth in the form of a man for the "atonement of sins" just as the High Priest did for the Israelites in ancient times. So in this scripture Christ can be seen as our **God (Elohim)**, our **Saviour**, our **High Priest** forever, our **King** forever, and the **Last Prophet** when he was on earth in the form of a man. Christ was the "atonement" Lamb and he was also the "Living Word" in the flesh! Note: In the Quran, Muhammad does not give one "**specific**" prophecy…instead he gives "**fail-safe**" prophecies which are not real prophecies.

Matthew 7:15 "Beware of **false prophets** who come to you in sheep's clothing but inwardly are ravenous wolves."

Deuteronomy 18:20-22
"But a prophet who presumes to speak in my name anything I have not commanded him to say, **or a prophet who speaks in the name of other gods, must be put to death**. You may say to yourselves, 'How can we know when a message has not been spoken by the LORD?' **If what a prophet proclaims in the name of the LORD does not take place or**

come true, that is a message the LORD has not spoken. That prophet has spoken presumptuously. Do not be afraid of him."

Islam teaches against the "divinity" of Christ. So does **Talmudic Judaism** and so does the **Non-Messianic Israelite** doctrine. This is "**Anti-Christ**" doctrine.

The Bible warns of this:

1 John 2:2-23 "Who is a liar but he who denies that Yahusha (Jesus) is the Christ? **He is the antichrist who denies the Father and the Son.** Whoever denies the Son does not have the Father either; he who acknowledges the Son has the Father also."

1 John 4:1-3
"Beloved, do not believe every spirit, but test the spirits, whether they are of God; because many false prophets have gone out into the world. By this you know the Spirit of God: Every spirit that confesses that Yahusha HaMashiach (Jesus Christ) has come in the flesh is of God, and every spirit that does not confess that Yahusha HaMashiach (Jesus Christ) has come in the flesh is not of God. **And this is the spirit of the Antichrist, which you have heard was coming, and is now already in the world.**"

The Bible says that the "**Spirit of the Antichrist**" rejects the divinity of Christ and that Christ came as God in the flesh. This proves that Islam is paving the way for the "**emerging**" Antichrist beast system. This is also happening today within the "**Hebrew Israelite**" movement as many former Christ believers are now rejecting the New Testament, Christ, the divinity of Christ, the virgin birth and the Holy Spirit (Comforter) that Christ promised would come after his ascension into heaven.

So was Muhammad a prophet?

Sura 7:184 "Then do they not give thought? There is in their companion (Muhammad) no madness. He is not but a clear "**warner**".

Sura 7:188 "Say, "I hold not for myself (the power of) benefit or harm, except what Allah has willed. **And if I knew the unseen**, I could have acquired much wealth, and no harm would have touched me. **I am not except a warner and a bringer of good tidings to a people who believe**."

Sura 11:2 "Through a messenger, saying, "Do not worship except Allah. Indeed, I am to you from Him a **warner and a bringer of good tidings**."

Sura 11:12 "Then would you possibly leave out some of what is revealed to you, or is your breast constrained by it because they say, "Why has there not been sent down to him a treasure or come with him an angel?" **But you are only a warner**. And Allah is Disposer of all things."

It is a known fact that Muhammad did not perform any miracles, nor did he give any "specific" pinpoint prophecies. He essentially regarded himself as a "**warner**". A "siren" can warn people. A regular person can warn people using the Bible. This does not line up with the title of a "**prophet**". In the Quran, many unbelievers challenged Muhammad to perform miracles, **which he refused to do**. In the Bible Moses and Elijah performed miracles to prove that they were "**True Prophets**" of God sent to deliver a message from the "Creator". Elijah made fire come down from heaven in 1 Kings 18, but when the Arab Ishmaelites asked their leader to do the same thing, Muhammad couldn't do it, because he wasn't a prophet and his god was not the Most High (Yahuah).

Read closely!

1 Kings 18:19-40

"Now therefore, send and gather to me all Israel unto Mount Carmel, and the prophets of Baal four hundred and fifty, and the prophets of the Asherah four hundred, who eat at Jezebel's table." So Ahab sent unto all the children of Israel, and gathered the prophets together unto Mount Carmel. **And Elijah came unto all the people and said, "How long halt ye between two opinions? If the LORD be God, follow Him; but if Baal, then follow him." And the people answered him not a word.** Then said Elijah unto the people, "I, even I only, remain a prophet of the LORD, but **Baal's prophets are four hundred and fifty men.** Let them therefore give us two bullocks. And let them choose one bullock for themselves and cut it in pieces, and lay it on wood and put no fire under it; and I will dress the other bullock, and lay it on wood, and put no fire under it. And call ye on the name of your gods, and I will call on the name of the LORD **(YAHUAH)**; and **the God that answereth by fire, let Him be God." And all the people answered and said, "It is well spoken."** And Elijah said unto the prophets of Baal, "Choose you one bullock for yourselves and dress it first, for ye are many; and call on the name of your gods, but put no fire under it." **And they took the bullock which was given them, and they dressed it, and called on the name of Baal from morning even until noon, saying, "O Baal, hear us!" But there was no voice, nor any that answered.** And they leaped upon the altar which was made. And it came to pass at noon that Elijah mocked them and said, "Cry aloud, for he is a god! Either he is talking, or he is pursuing, or he is on a journey, or perhaps he sleepeth and must be awakened." And they cried aloud, and cut themselves according to their manner with knives and lancets, till the blood gushed out upon them. And it came to pass, when midday was past, and they prophesied until the time of the offering of the evening sacrifice, that there was neither voice, nor any to answer, nor any that regarded. And Elijah said unto all the people, "Come near unto me." And all the people came near unto him. And he repaired the altar of the LORD that was broken down. And Elijah took twelve stones, according to the number of the tribes of the sons of Jacob, unto whom the word of the LORD came, saying, "Israel shall be thy name." And with the stones he built an altar in the name of the LORD, and he made a trench about the altar as great as would contain two measures of seed. And he put the wood in order, and cut the bullock in pieces, and laid him on the wood and said, "Fill four barrels with water, and pour it on the burnt sacrifice and on the wood." And he said, "Do it the second time." And they did it the second time. And he said, "Do it the third time." And they did it the third time. And the water ran round about the altar; and he filled the trench also with water. And it came to pass at the time of the offering of the evening sacrifice, that **Elijah the prophet came near and said, "LORD God of Abraham, Isaac, and of Israel, let it be known this day that Thou art God in Israel, and that I am Thy servant, and that I have done all these things at Thy word**. Hear me, O LORD! Hear me, that this people may know that Thou art the LORD God, and that Thou hast turned their heart back again." **Then the fire of the LORD fell and consumed the burnt sacrifice, and the wood and the stones and the dust, and licked up the water that was in the trench**. And when all the people saw it, they fell on their faces and they said, "**The LORD, He is the God! The LORD, He is the God!**" And Elijah said unto them, "Take the prophets of Baal. Let not one of them escape!" And they took them; and Elijah brought them down to the Brook Kishon and slew them there."

Now let's do a comparison with Muhammad in the Quran.

Sura 3:183-184

"They are those who said. "Indeed, **Allah has taken our promise not to believe any messenger until he brings us an offering which fire from heaven will consume**." Say, "There have already come to you messengers (i.e. Israelite prophets) before me with **clear proofs** and even that which you speak. So why did you kill them, if you should be truthful?" Then if they deny you, O Muhammad-so were messengers denies before you, who brought clear proofs and written ordinances and the enlightening Scripture (Bible)."

Sura 6:37 "And they say, "**Why has a sign not been sent down to him from his Lord (Muhammad's god Allah)?**" Say, "Indeed, Allah is Able to send down a sign, but most of them do not know."

In the Bible, the God of Israel sends a sign down for his prophets (*see Elijah and the Prophets of Baal in 1 Kings 18:20-40*). In the Quran, it says that Allah is able to send down a sign......however he doesn't do so for Muhammad, and when Muhammad's "Prophethood" is questioned he simply shows that he is not a prophet because he is unable to perform a miracle for the people. It isn't until 200 years later after Muhammad's death that his followers "invent" miracles and ascribe them to him. This shows the "**deception**" of Islam.

Do we need more facts to prove "**Islam**" is the final "Antichrist" pagan religion sent by Satan to deceive mankind....including the descendants of the 12 Tribes of Israel?

Well, did the early 7th Century A.D. converted Arab Muslims scholars know the **Truth** about the Creator? Did some of them know that Christ was the Son of God despite what Muhammad taught? Did they hide this information in fear for their lives......hoping that one day, some Muslims would wake up to the truth?

The Arabic letters "**Alif, Lam, Meem, Ya Seen, Ha Meen, Ra**" are known seen throughout the Quran with no explanation as to why they are there and to whom they were directed to....or who was the one that put them there.

About one-quarter of the Quranic suras (i.e. scriptures) are preceded by these "**mysterious Arabic letters**" called "**muqatta'at**" aka "**disjointed letters**" or "**fawatih**" aka "**openings**". These mysterious letters appear at the beginning of relevant suras in the Quran. Out of the 28 letters of the Arabic alphabet, 14 letters occur preceding many Arabic scriptures, either singly or in varying combinations of two, three, four or five Arabic letters. These letters always appear "singly" not combined to form a word. The significance of these Arabic letters has confused and perplexed Arabic scholars from way back. According to many Arabic Quranic scholars, there is no evidence of Muhammad referring to these "mysterious Arabic letters", nor any of his followers having ever asked him for an explanation of these "mysterious" letters.

Some Arabic scholars believe that these letters are the "**initials**" of the scribes or companions of Muhammad who wrote down the individual revelations of Muhammad as he spoke them. Other Arabic scholars believe these "mysterious Arabic letters" are the "abbreviations" of certain words or phrases relating to God (the Creator) and his qualities. It has been said that these "**mysterious letters**" or "**hidden arabic codes**" happened during the first three Islamic Caliphates (*i.e. Umayyad Caliphate, Abbasid Caliphate, Fatimid Caliphate*). But the big mystery is "what does it mean"?

The earliest Quran was written in the "**Kufic-Iraqi**" script which is based off the Nabataean script that was familiar to the Semitic peoples (*i.e. Edomites, Ishmaelites*) living in Iraq/Babylon and Arabia. From 600 A.D. to 1,000 A.D. the earliest Quran's were mostly written in this script and not "**Arabic**". It is during this time era that many Arabs knew of the Creator according to the Hebrew Israelites as "**Yahuwah**" or "**Yahuwa**".

THE HIDDEN MEANING OF THE "MYSTIC SYMBOLS"

The Arabic characters "**Alif**", "**Laam**", "**Meem**", "**Seen**", and "**Ra**" all have their origins in Ancient Hebrew as the Arabic language is derived from **Aramaic** which is derived from **Ancient Paleo-Hebrew**. These "**Mystery Arabic Letters**" called "**Al-Muqattaat- the abbreviated letters**" are in 29 Suras in the Quran. Muslims claim that only Allah knows the meaning of these "**mystic-mysterious letters**" while others claim they are the names of God or "Allah" to the Muslims.

So what could it mean? Some say in the Arabic language it means "**Yeshua (Isa) HaMashiach is the Son of God**" while some say it means "**Yeshua (Isa) HaMashiach is God**" flat out. If Muslims knew this as the hidden meaning of these Arabic Letters in their Quran....it might shatter their very foundation of belief in the Quran and turn them back towards the Bible (Scriptures). This would contradict the very Quran Muslims follow as it teaches that God (the Creator) cannot have a child.

Sura 6:101 "[He is] Originator of the Heavens and the Earth. **How could He have a son** when He does not have a companion and He created all things? And He is, of all things, Knowing."

So here in the Quran the question is asked, "How can someone have a son without a **spouse/cosort**....in this case in Sura 6:101 a "**wife**".

However, in the Quran, Mary (*the mother of Jesus*) asks the same question to the angel of Allah.

Sura 19:19-21 "He said: I am only a messenger of thy Lord, that I may bestow on thee a faultless son. She said: "**How can I have a son when no mortal hath touched me, neither have I been unchaste?**" He (Allah) said: **So it will be. Thy Lord saith: It is easy for Me (Allah).** And it will be that We may make of him a **revelation for mankind** and a **mercy from Us**, and it is **a thing ordained**."

Mary is basically asking in the Quran, "How can I have a son when I have not had sex with a man-husband? Allah responds with, "This is easy". So in the Quran, the "Virgin-birth" is accepted, but Christ being the Son of God is not accepted.

Allah states Mary will have an **"immaculate conception"** bringing forth a son without having sex when he says, **"so it will be"** and **"it is easy for me"**.

So isn't it ironic that when discussing the **"identity"** and **"prophecy"** of Yahusha HaMashiach (Jesus Christ), the Quran says that Allah cannot have a son without a woman, but Allah allows Mary to have a son without a man." This is very confusing and contradictory to Muslim leaders. If the Creator (*so called "allah"*) is powerful enough to cause a "Holy immaculate conception with Christ, he is powerful enough to send himself in the fleshy form of a Man to redeem the world.

Once again, the Quran fails to live up to its **"Perfect Book"** status. Muhammed knew about the Messiah, Mary, the Jews and the written law (Torah) given to the Israelites when they were out of the land of Egypt. He also knew about the "Whole" Bible.

For example, Muhammad knew about God's Covenant with Israel, the 10 Commandments being the **"written law-Torah"** given to the Israelite prophets straight from God in heaven, and the Laws of the Sabbath which Muslims do not keep.

Sura 4:153-155
"**The People of the Scripture (Israelites)** ask you to bring down to them a book from heaven (*i.e. Torah/Tanakh/Ten Commandments*). But they had asked of Moses even greater than that and said, "Show us Allah outright," so the thunderbolt struck them for their wrongdoing. Then they took the calf for worship after clear evidences had come to them, and We pardoned that. And We gave Moses a clear authority. And we raised over them the mount of refusal of their **COVENANT**;

and We said to them, "Enter the gate bowing humbly", and We said to them, "**DO NOT TRANSGRESS ON THE SABBATH**", and We took from them a solemn covenant. And We cursed them for their breaking of the covenant and their disbelief in the signs of Allah (**Note: *Allah in Hebrew Strong's #427 means "oak tree". Alah in Hebrew Strong's #422 means "to curse".***) and their killing of the prophets without right and their saying, "Our hearts are wrapped". Rather, Allah has sealed them because of their disbelief, so they believe not, except for a few."

So with that being said….with all this knowledge of the Old Testament and the New Testament (*which I will explain later*), did Muhammad or the Ishmaelite Arabs know that Yahusha (Jesus) was the "Son of God". Keep in mind, according to this scripture, Muhammed knew about the Sabbath and the Covenant given to the Israelites. Let's ask this question when thinking about the early Arabs who accepted Islam as their religion.

1. Did they know that Christ was "**One**" with the **Creator (Father)** and that the Creator's true name was "**Yahuah/Yahuwa**" and his son's name was "**Yahusha**" or "**Yeshua/Yahshua (Aramaic)**"?
2. Did they know that Christ was not some "**lesser prophet**" to Muhammad?
3. Did they know that "**Christ was the Messiah and Saviour of the world**" and did they know that "Christ" actually was crucified…only to resurrect "three days" later?
4. Did they know the covenant of God was given to Israel, and that the Sabbath was holy unto God?
5. If they knew this, why would they accept a whole new religion?

Let's exam these so called "**Mystic Symbols/Letters**" that are seen in the Quran. Maybe this will reveal some "hidden truths" the pre-Islamic and post-Islamic Arabs knew. Could this shake up the "**Islam**" world?

In **Sura 13:1** it reads: "**Alif (Alef), Lam (Lamed), Meem (Mem), Ra (Resh)**. These are the verses of the Book (i.e. Bible or the Quran?); and what has been revealed to you from your Lord is the truth, but most of the people do not believe."

What "**Book**" is this Sura referring to? Is it the Bible or the Quran? Let's see.

Many Muslims say these abbreviations or 4 letters are a "**secret message or meaning**" only Allah knows. Or where they secretly "**inserted**" in the Quran by someone to warn the Arabs of the **TRUTH** when many Muslims would figure out it's true meaning and turn back to the "**Biblical Christ**" before his Second coming? Hold on to your seats because the answer is coming! Stay with me.

ISLAMIC "JESUS (ISA)" VS BIBLICAL "JESUS (YAHUSHA)"

In the Quran-Hadith, the Muslims say they believe in Christ's Second Coming and his defeat of the Antichrist whom they call the "**dajjal**". But is the Biblical Christ the same as the Islamic Christ? Is the Biblical Antichrist the same as the Islamic Antichrist (dajjal)? Islam is very "deceptive" and what you will see is that their "End Times" prophecy has a twist to it. Beware!

The Islamic Hadith is collection of opinions and stories of Muslim scholars over a period of centuries. The Arabic meaning of "Hadith" means "**report, narrative, account**". These "Arabic Collections of Men" like the Jewish Talmud are a collection of traditions containing the supposed sayings of Muhammad. The Hadith is supposed to guide the lives of Muslims as the Jewish Talmud is supposed to guide the lives of the Gentile European Jews. Different branches of Islam (Sunni, Sufi,

706

Shia, Ibadi) refer to different collections of the Hadith. Only a few Muslims reject the Hadith.

In the Hadith it reads:
"All those who embraced the evil of **dajjal** (*i.e. Islamic Antichrist*) shall perish even as the breath of **Isa** (*i.e. Islamic Jesus*) touches them."

The **Hadith** also states:
"Then all battles shall cease and the world will know an age of peace. **Then truly the sheep will lie in the shadow of the wolf without fear**. The rule of Isa will be just and all shall flock to him to enter the folds of the one true religion, Islam."

Notice this Islamic Hadith verse is a "copy-cat" of the Bible. This is what Satan does best.

Isaiah 11:6 "The wolf also shall dwell with the lamb, and the leopard shall lie down with the kid; and the calf and the young lion and the fatling together; and a little child shall lead them."

Note: *The word "Islam" is based off the Arabic root word "Salema" or "Salam" which means "peace" like the Hebrew word "Shalom". The word "Islam" however is said to mean "surrender" or "submit" in Arabic.*

In Islam, the "dajjal" Antichrist figure is supposed to return and fight for Israel against the Muslims of the world. According to Islam, the dajjal will return to earth and claim to be Christ the Messiah. In the Bible, Christ the Messiah fights for Israel in the **Battle of Armageddon-Gog and Magog War** against the nations (*including Muslims*) that seek to destroy the Israelites in their land. In Islam, the 12th Mahdi is Islam's awaited "Messiah". Muslims believe he will come to help them defeat the followers of Christ who keep the Commandments of the Most High. In the Bible, the person who seeks to "defeat & destroy" the followers of Christ who keep the Commandments of the Most High is none other than "Satan". **The Islamic 12th Mahdi is the Biblical Antichrist-Satan!**

Revelation 12:17 "And the **dragon** (Satan) was wroth (i.e. angry) with the **woman** (Israel), and went to make war with the remnant of **her seed** (Israelites), which keep the commandments of God, and have the testimony of Jesus Christ."

In Quran-Hadith, "**Isa**" is Islam's Jesus figure. Muslims believe Jesus was a "**lesser prophet**" and they do not believe he was the Son of God or the Saviour of the world. They believe Jesus (Isa) will return and deny that he ever said he was God. In Islamic belief, he will join forces with the 12th Mahdi and direct the world to **WORSHIP** the 12th Mahdi and **SUBMIT** to Allah. Remember, in the Quran "**non-believers**" were to have their "**necks striked**".....aka "**decapitation-beheading**" for not submitting to Islam and Allah. This "**warning**" of the Islamic Antichrist is in the Bible.

Revelation 13:15-18 "The **second beast** was permitted to give breath to the image of the **first beast**, so that the image would also speak and cause all who **REFUSED TO WORSHIP IT TO BE KILLED**. And the second beast required all peoples small and great, rich and poor, free and slave, to receive a mark on their right hand or on their forehead, so that **no one could buy or sell unless he had the mark, the name of the beast (i.e. first beast) or the number of its name (*i.e. "In the name of Allah, Vicarius Filii Dei, Rome's number?*).** Here is a call for wisdom: Let the one who has insight calculate the number of the beast, for it is the number of a man, and that number is **six hundred, sixty-six (666)**."

In the Bible, the Second Beast is linked to the False Prophet, whose job is to point mankind to the Antichrist. In the Book of Revelation, they both receive the same fate.

Revelation 19:20 "**And the beast was taken, and with him the false prophet that wrought miracles before him**, with which he deceived them that had received the mark of the beast, and them that worshipped his image. **These both were cast alive into a lake of fire** burning with brimstone."

(**Left**) Sheep/Lamb. (**Right**) Goat. The bible says the **First Beast** arises out of the sea and the **Second Beast** arises out of the earth. The Second Beast has two horns like a lamb, but his speech is like a dragon. The Goat throughout history and the "occult" has been associated with "**Satan**". Is the First Beast an "Empire" and the Second Beast its leader? According to the Bible this "**Empire**", its "**Leader (religious or political)**", and the "**False Prophet**" will all be working with the "**Biblical Antichrist**". Who is the "Empire"? Is it Rome? Who is its leader? Will this leader have authority over the nations of Gog and Magog? Remember, the "white" **Gentile Ottoman Turkish Arabs** are of the seed of Japheth (*i.e. Gomer, Magog, Tubal*). Their seed dominate the affairs of the Muslim world today. The **Gentile Roman Empire** and the **Gentile Ashkenazi-Sephardic Jews** are also of the seed of Japheth (*i.e. Gomer, Magog, Tubal, Javan, Meshech, Tiras, Ashkenaz, Togarmah*). Their seed dominate the affairs of the Catholic Church and Modern Judaism respectively today. All together we have all the "Three Abrahamic" religions in one bunch.

No matter how we look at it, the "False Prophet" will be a religious leader that will be able to perform miracles (fire come down from the sky…lightning?). He will tell people what they want to hear and attract large masses of people.

So, if the **12th Mahdi** is the **Islamic Messiah** and the **Islamic Jesus** named "**Isa**" is the one who helps the the world worship the 12th Mahdi, who is the False Prophet? Even more, who is the Antichrist and who is Satan/Lucifer? The Islamic Jesus (Isa) is the Biblical False Prophet, the 12th Mahdi is the Biblical Antichrist and Allah is **SATAN-LUCIFER**!

The 12th Mahdi forces the world to follow Islam and thus their false god "**Allah**". The Freemasons call on their god or "**G**" symbol as "**Allah**". 33rd Degree Grandmaster Freemasons Albert Pike and Manly P. Hall state the Freemason's god is "**Lucifer**"…the "**light bearer**".

Consider this statement by Muhammad.

*"At the end of the time of my ummah (i.e. people), the Mahdi will appear. Allah will grant him rain, the earth will bring forth its fruits, he will give a lot of money, cattle will increase and the ummah will become great … his name will be my name, and his father's name my father's name … Even if the entire duration of the world's existence has already been exhausted and only one day is left before Doomsday, Allah will expand that day to such length of time as to accommodate the kingdom of a person from my Ahlul-Bayt [family of Muhammad] who will be called by my name. …"- **Hadith** (al-Haakim in his Mustadrak, 4/557-558).*

So, after reading all of this, it is evident that the "Biblical Antichrist" will be heralded by the arrival of the "Islamic 12th Mahdi". The Biblical Antichrist is going to promote the worship of Satan-Lucifer-Allah….who if you follow history back far enough you will see Luciferian-Satanic worship connected to all the 3 major "**Abrahamic Religions**" we see today (*i.e. Roman Catholic Church, Modern Judaism and Islam*).

Did any 7th century A.D. Muslim scholars know this when they penned the Quranic suras? If so, were they so "**scared**" of telling the truth to their people that they wrote a "**secret code**" in the false Quran detailing the "**Truth**"?

Consider this amazing find!

The **Arabic Alif**=Alef in Hebrew, the **Arabic Lam**=Lamed in Hebrew, the **Arabic Meem**=Mem in Hebrew and the **Arabic Ra**=Resh in Hebrew.

- Alef (Hebrew) became "Alif" in Arabic
- Lamed (Hebrew) became "Lam" in Arabic
- Mem (Hebrew) became "Meem" in Arabic
- Resh (Hebrew) became "Ra" in Arabic

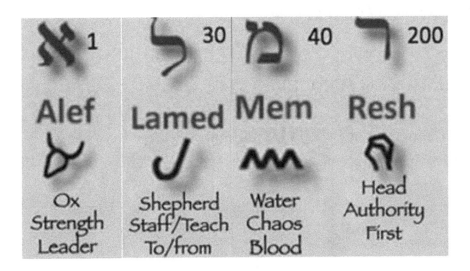

In Paleo-Hebrew this is what those letters mean:
- ALEF: **God**, Strong, Power, Leader/Picture-**Ox Head (God the Father-Creator).**

- LAMED: **Teach, Yoke,** To, Bind/Picture-**Shepherd staff (draws sheep-mankind) together.**
- MEM: **Blood,** Mighty, Chaos/Picture-**Water (i.e. Life).**
- RESH: **First,** Top, Beginning/Picture-**Head of a Man (Christ).**

The above Arabic letters **Alif, Lam, Meem, and Ra** in Paleo-Hebrew could be a secret meaning showing that whoever wrote the Quran (*i.e. Catholic Monk, Rabbi who believed in Christ or an Arab believer in Christ first before being deceived by Satan*) understood that Christ was the Son of God and was God in the flesh (incarnate).

So the meaning of these words in Paleo-Hebrew if you put them all together are:

ALEF **GOD (THE OX),** who draws LAMED **(BINDS)** mankind together (taking the **YOKE**), bearing the Burden (Sins) of all of us, through MEM **BLOOD/DEATH** (atonement of sins) which brings **LIFE,** starting a new RESH "BEGINNING" through God incarnate (**Son of MAN/CHRIST**).

If you simplify this by **ONLY** using the Hebrew words in the Paleo-Hebrew pictograph meaning what do you get?

Note: Remember the Hebrew letters "**Aleph**" and "**Lamed**" together mean "**El**" or "**God**".

El
God

1. God (Ox) = **ALEPH**
2. Binds (takes the Yoke) = **LAMED**
3. Blood = **MEM**
4. Beginning = **RESH**

If this doesn't spell "**Christ**" I don't know what is. Now take the meaning of "Alif, Lam, Meem, and Ra"....applying them to the Scriptures in the Bible whose history predates the Quran by over 2,000 years.

John 10:11 "I am the **good shepherd; the good shepherd (Christ) lays down His life for the sheep (Mankind)."**

John 7:38 "**He who believes in Me**, as the Scriptures said, 'From his innermost being will flow rivers of **living water**."

John 4:14 "But whoever drinks of the water that I will give him shall never thirst; **but the water that I will give him will become in him a well of water springing up to eternal life**."

Now consider this amazing fact. The Paleo-Hebrew "**Alef**" symbol is an "**Ox head**". An "**Ox**" is one who is willing to bear the **BURDEN**, to do the work, taking on the **YOKE** and to even **SACRIFICE** himself.

In the Old Testament, it reads:
Psalm 55:22 "Cast your **BURDEN** on the **Lord (YAHUAH)**, And He shall **SUSTAIN YOU**; He shall never permit the righteous to be moved."

In the New Testament Christ says:
Matthew 11:27-29 "All things have been entrusted to Me by My Father. No one knows the Son except the Father, and no one knows the Father

except the Son and those to who the Son chooses to reveal Him. **COME TO ME, ALL YOU WHO ARE WEARY AND BURDENED**, and I will give you rest. **TAKE MY YOKE** upon you and **LEARN FROM ME** (*I.E. CHRIST TEACHES US THE WAY TO ETERNAL LIFE*): for I am gentle and humble in heart, and you will find rest for your souls."

So here we see that the Quran was made by Satan to **"deceive"** the **"nations"** away from Christ. How do we know this? Simple.

Let's use the example of **the Crucifixion/Resurrection of Christ.**

In **Sura 4:157-158** it reads: "And for their saying, "Indeed, we have killed the Messiah, Jesus, the son of Mary, the messenger of Allah." **And they did not kill him, nor did they crucify him; but another was made to resemble him to them**. And indeed, those who differ over it are in doubt about it. They have **NO KNOWLEDGE OF IT** except the following of assumption. And they did not kill him, for certain. Rather, Allah raised him to Himself. And ever is Allah Exalted in Might and Wise."

Well Josephus Flavius, the Jewish convert Roman historian accounts of Christ and his death in his literary works, but what about other accounts of Christ's Crucifixion?

The 9th Century Roman Christian chronicler **George Syncellus** cites **Sextus Julius Africanus** as writing in reference to the darkness recorded in Matthew 27:45, Mark 15:33, and Luke 23:44. Here is what it said:

"On the whole world there pressed a most fearful **darkness**; and the **rocks were rent** by an earthquake, and many places in Judea and other districts were thrown down. This darkness **Thallus**, in the third book of his "**History**", calls, as appears to me without reason, an **eclipse of the sun**."

Thallus (*52 A.D.*) was a 1st Century A.D. Greek Historian. Thallus believed the "darkness of six hours" was from a "strange" Solar Eclipse. But 2nd Century Christian **Sextus Julius Africanus** (*i.e. linked to Libyan, Roman, Judean descent*) noted in his works that since Christ was crucified during the Passover, which occurs during a full moon, it was impossible for a solar eclipse to occur....thus making the "**darkness**" after Yahusha (Jesus) death a **supernatural event**.

Cornelius Tacitus (*56 A.D.-120 A.D.*) was a 1st Century A.D. Roman historian who stated that "**Christians**" were a "sect" that was formed from followers of "**Christus**" who "**suffered the extreme Roman penalty**" of death by Crucifixion during the reign of the 2nd Emperor of Rome, **Tiberias Claudius Nero**....aka **Tiberius Julius Caesar** (*who lived from 42 B.C.-37 A.D.*) at the hands of the Roman Governor at the time **Pontius Pilate**. Pontius Pilate existed and under his hand Christ was crucified.

Fact: Pontius Pilate was the fifth governor of Roman Judea, under whose governance Yahusha (Jesus) of Nazareth was crucified (Matt 27:2, plus 60 additional occurrences in the gospels, Acts, and 1 Timothy). The "**Pilate stone**" inscription was found in 1961 in the ruins of an amphitheater at **Caesarea Maritima, Northwestern Israel**. The inscription is on a limestone block which was a dedication to Roman Emperor Tiberius Julius Caesar.

This "**Pilate stone**" inscription is absolute proof that a man called Pontius Pilatus (Pilate) **LIVED** and was the fifth Governor of the Roman province of Judaea, from AD 24 A.D. to 37 A.D.

The existence of Pontius Pilate is also confirmed by canonical gospels, the works of Philo and Josephus, a brief mention by Tacitus, and **THE GOSPEL OF NICODEMUS OR ACTS OF PILATE**.

Lucian of Samosata (*125 A.D-180 A.D.*) was a 2nd Century A.D. Greek writer who called "Christians" poor wretches and foolish people who accept things on faith alone. He said the Christians in Judea were ones "who worshipped the man in Palestine who was crucified because he brought this new form of initiation into the world." He said that Christians all believed that they were considered "brothers" the moment they disobeyed the law of the land (Judea), denied the Greek gods and begin worshipping the crucified "teacher" by living by his laws.

So after all of this has been presented….. is there **more proof** that Satan will use "**Islam**" and it's possible "**merging**" with "**Christianity**" via the Vatican/Roman Catholic Church to usher in the "**Antichrist Beast System**"?

Keep this in mind….

Note: Muslims don't say "**Allah is great**"….they say "**Allah is the greatest**". Why would Muhammad say that Allah is "**the greatest**" or "**the best of creators** (Sura 23:14)" or "**the best of deceivers** (Sura 3:54, 7:99, 8:30)" except if it wasn't in a "**polytheistic context**"? The plural aspect of these sayings implies that there are other gods and goddesses. All the Shemitic, Japhetic and Hamitic religions/civilizations worshipped multiple pagan gods except the **Hebrew Israelites**.

Deuteronomy 6:4 (Shema Prayer) "Hear, O Israel! The LORD (Yahuah) is our God (Elohim), the LORD (Yahuah) is **ONE**!

Fact or Fiction?
There are some theorists that state the 3rd most Holiest site in Islam…."**The Dome of the Rock**"…including the Al-Aqsa Mosque is the former **Temple of Jupiter (Osiris, Dionysus) and Venus**

(Aphrodite). Some say it is the "**Rock**" where many souls left from the bodies of faithful martyrs slain for the "**Word of God**".

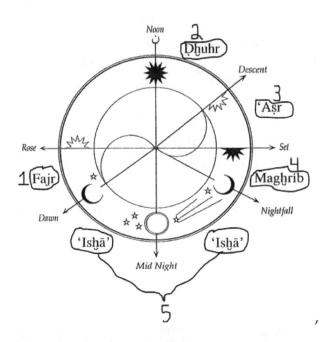

(**Above**) The **1ˢᵗ Islamic prayer** is "**FAJR**" or "*Adah*", which takes place right before the sun rises because the planet "**Venus**" is the Planet which appears as a "**star**" before Sunrise. The **2ⁿᵈ prayer** is "**DHUHR**" or "*Ruth*" which is right before the sun reaches its "peak position" in the sky. The **3ʳᵈ prayer** is "**ASR**" or "*Esther*", which is when the sun is setting (declining) from its "peak position". The **4th prayer** is "**MAGHRIB**" or "*Martha*", which is when the sun is setting in the evening. The **5th prayer** is "**ISHA**" or "*Ishtar/Electra*"…the Babylonian name of Venus, when it is "mid-night".

LANDMARKS.

1. A belief in the existence of a Supreme Being.

2. In the Order of the Eastern Star there are only five degrees, known as Adah, the daughter; Ruth, the widow; Esther, the wife; Martha, the sister; and Electa, the mother.

Note: The Planet Venus sometimes appears as a "star" again in the evening during certain times of the year at the same time there is an appearance of a "crescent moon" in the sky. This is also a "celestial" sign that perhaps influenced the "Crescent Moon" and "Star" symbol of Islam. The Planet Venus is also significant in the Female Masonic order of "**Eastern Stars**".

(**Left**) Symbol for Islam which is the Crescent Moon and Star. (**Middle**) Planet Venus (star) and the Crescent Moon like Islam. (**Right**) Baal worship with Crescent moon and Star (Venus).

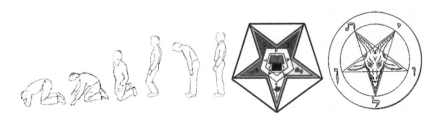

(**Left**) The ritual of prayer for Muslims. (**Middle**) The Masonic "pentagram" Eastern Star. (**Right**) The Satanic Baphomet Pentagram used to invoke "**demons**" or "**dark forces**"....often inside of a circle with the name of the Creator in Hebrew placed along the border of the circle used as a protective shield to keep the "Demons" from entering into the bodies of humans trying to summon "Lucifer/Satan and his demons".

Is the worship of Allah, the God of Freemasonry/Eastern Stars all giving praise to Lucifer? Many of the husbands of "**Eastern Stars**" are Master Masons or 33 Degree Grandmaster Masons. These Moslem Shriner "**Grandmaster**" Freemasons worship God as "**Allah**" and they also admit that their God is "**Lucifer**"....the "Light-bringer/Lightbearer". Even 33 Degree Grandmaster Mason Albert Pike admits to this. But the Founder of the Church of Satan..also admits to it as well.

"**By now, even the most hardened of skeptics should be convinced that European-Egyptian inspired Freemasonry is Lucifer/Satan worship.** However, for those who may still need more convincing, let us consider the **Infernal Names by which Masonry masks its many references to Satan**. In the Satanic Bible, we see **77 names** by which pagans have referred to Satan over the centuries. Let us quickly review some of the "Infernal Names" of Satanism found within Masonry." - *Satanic Bible, Anton LaVey (Founder of the Church of Satan), p. 144-46.*

But even Plato, the 4th Century B.C. Greek philosopher linked Venus to Lucifer. **Note:** Venus and Uranus are the only planets that spin

counter-clockwise compared to the other planets in the solar system. Muslims likewise circle the Kaaba pagan shrine "**counter-clockwise**" like the occult-Satanists do in their rituals. Coincidence?

"Time, then, and the heaven came into being at the same instant in order that, having been created together, if ever there was to be a dissolution of them, they might be dissolved together. It was framed after the pattern of the eternal nature, that it might resemble this as far as was possible; for the pattern exists from eternity, and the created heaven has been, and is, and will be, in all time. Such was the mind and thought of God in the creation of time. The sun and moon and five other stars, which are called the planets, were created by him in order to distinguish and preserve the numbers of time; and when he had made their several bodies, he placed them in the orbits in which the circle of the other was revolving — in seven orbits seven stars. First, there was the moon in the orbit nearest the earth, and next the sun, in the second orbit above the earth; then came the morning star (**Venus**) and the star sacred to Hermes (**Mercury**), moving in orbits which have an equal swiftness with the sun, but in an opposite direction; and this is the reason why the sun and Hermes and **Lucifer** overtake and are overtaken by each other. *-Plato (Greek Philosopher and Historian).*

(**Left**) Moslem Shriner Grandmaster Mason and American Botanist, Luther Burbank. (**Middle**) Adolf Hitler, brother of the Masonic Craft. (**Right**) Albert Pike, 33 Degree Grandmaster Freemason. Freemasons at the highest level call their God "**Allah**" and "**Lucifer**". Coincidence?

Albert Pike quoted:

1. To you, Sovereign Instructors of **Grade 33**, we tell you: you have to repeat to the brothers of inferior grades (i.e. 3ʳᵈ Degree Masons) that we worship only one God to whom we pray without superstition. It is we, initiated in the **SUPREME GRADE** (i.e. Degree), that are to keep the **REAL MASONIC RELIGION** preserving **PURE THE LUCIFER DOCTRINE.**"

2. "The Third World War must be fomented (*i.e. instigated or stirred up*) between the **Christians and the Islamic World** (*by design*). The War must be conducted in such a way that Islam and Christianity mutually destroy each other leaving the Political Zionists (*fake Jews*) in Control."

In closing I will leave with you with the words of Yahusha HaMashiach, the Alpha and the Omega, the Beginning and the End…he who is, and who was, and who is to come, the Almighty.

Matthew 24:3-4 "And as he (Christ) sat upon the mount of Olives, the disciples came unto him privately, saying, Tell us, when shall these things be? And what shall be the sign of thy coming, and the end of the world? And Yahusha (Jesus) answered and said unto them, **"TAKE HEED THAT NO MAN DECEIVE YOU."**

WAKE UP....a prudent person forsees danger and takes precautions, but the simple (foolish) keep going and are punished.

Which kind of person will you be?

Thank you for taking the time to read this book.

"A LIE CANNOT LIVE FOREVER".
Shalom

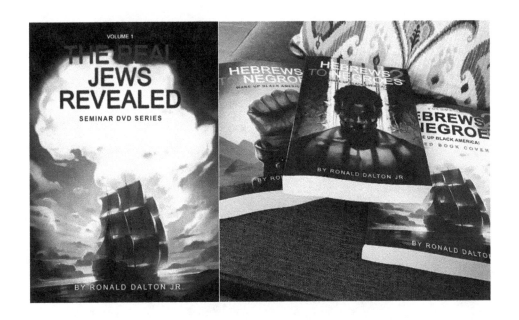

CHECK OUT "THE REAL JEWS REVEALED" 6-VOLUME

SEMINAR DVD'S AND MY OTHER THREE "HEBREWS TO

NEGROES" BOOKS AT WWW.THENEGRONETWORK.COM

STAY TUNED FOR THE "HEBREWS TO NEGROES" MOVIE

DOCUMENTARY! THE TRAILER CAN BE SEEN ON YOU

TUBE AS "HEBREWS TO NEGROES MOVIE TRAILER".

RBDFREESTYLE@YAHOO.COM

CREDITS FOR IMAGES

"Image(s) or Footage (as applicable), used under license from Shutterstock.com"

Ryan Rodrick Beiler / Shutterstock.com

CatherineL-Prod / Shutterstock.com

Mikadun / Shutterstock.com

Tristan tan / Shutterstock.com

Quick Shot / Shutterstock.com

Robertonencini / Shutterstock.com

David Bokuchava / Shutterstock.com

Dietmar Temps / Shutterstock.com

ChameleonsEye / Shutterstock.com

Arturo Las Pinas Jr / Shutterstock.com

Angela Ostafichuk / Shutterstock.com

Pio3 / Shutterstock.com

Quick Shot / Shutterstock.com

John Wollwerth / Shutterstock.com

Franco lucato / Shutterstock.com

Rickson Davi Liebano / Shutterstock.com

Sergey Uryadnikov / Shutterstock.com

John Wollwerth / Shutterstock.com

Anton_Ivanov / Shutterstock.com

Rickson Davi Liebano / Shutterstock.com

Sergey Uryadnikov / Shutterstock.com

ChameleonsEye / Shutterstock.com

Kobby Dagan/Shutterstock.com

Erichon / Shutterstock.com

Featureflash Photo Agency / Shutterstock.com

Arturo Las Pinas Jr / Shutterstock.com

Debby Wong / Shutterstock.com

Everett Historical / Shutterstock.com

Greg Ward NZ / Shutterstock.com

Istvan Csak / Shutterstock.com

Juan Aunion / Shutterstock.com

Nussar / Shutterstock.com

Pio3 / Shutterstock.com

Rose Carson / Shutterstock.com

Greg Ward NZ/Shutterstock.com

Nussar / Shutterstock.com

Jane Rix / Shutterstock.com

Franco lucato / Shutterstock.com

Oliver Foerstner / Shutterstock.com

Tristan tan / Shutterstock.com

Arturo Las Pinas Jr / Shutterstock.com

Rose Carson/Shutterstock.com

Gil C/Shutterstock.com

9 780997 157925